QUALITATIVE APPROACHES TO CRIMINAL JUSTICE

This book is dedicated to my loving wife,
Professor Lyn Taylor,
whose support throughout the production of this project
made its completion possible.
Thanks for your patience and confidence in me.

QUALITATIVE APPROACHES TO CRIMINAL JUSTICE

PERSPECTIVES FROM THE FIELD

EDITOR

MARK R. POGREBIN

University of Colorado at Denver

SAGE Publications
International Educational and Professional Publisher
Thousand Oaks ■ London ■ New Delhi

For information:

Sage Publications, Inc.
2455 Teller Road
Thousand Oaks, California 91320
E-mail: order@sagepub.com

Sage Publications Ltd.
6 Bonhill Street
London EC2A 4PU
United Kingdom

Sage Publications India Pvt. Ltd.
M-32 Market
Greater Kailash I
New Delhi 110 048 India

Printed in the United States of America

Library of Congress Cataloging-in-Publication Data

Qualitative approaches to criminal justice : perspectives from the
field / Mark Pogrebin, editor.
    p. cm.
Includes bibliographical references (p.   ) and index.
ISBN 0-7619-2602-X-ISBN 0-7619-2603-8 (pbk.)
   1. Criminology-Research-Methodology. 2. Criminal justice,
Administration of-Research-Methodology. I. Pogrebin, Mark.
HV6024.5.Q35 2003
364′.072—dc211

                2002008057

02   03   04   05   10   9   8   7   6   5   4   3   2   1

Acquiring Editor:	Jerry Westby
Editorial Assistant:	Vonessa Vondera
Production Editor:	Claudia A. Hoffman
Copy Editor:	Barbara Coster
Indexer:	Molly Hall
Cover Designer:	Janet Foulger

ACKNOWLEDGMENTS

I thank my colleague Eric Poole for 17 years of academic partnership and his support for this book. A very special thanks to Jerry Venor, friend and colleague, for his input throughout this project. I also thank John Klofas from the Rochester Institute of Technology and Stan Stojkovic from the University of Wisconsin in Milwaukee for their insightful suggestions on the structure of the book, along with Henry Pontel for his encouragement to produce this anthology. A very special thanks to Patricia Dahl, doctoral student and mother of two, without whose help this project would have proven to be much more difficult. I owe a debt of gratitude to my editor at Sage, Jerry Westby, for his belief in the need for a book like this to fill an important gap in the study of criminal justice, and to Vonessa Vondera, editorial assistant, for her help with all the necessary tasks that have to be completed before an anthology is ready to be published.

CONTENTS

PREFACE

Perhaps the best way to begin this introduction to researching the criminal justice system through the use of qualitative methods would be to share a research experience that a colleague and I had some years ago. In 1986, the Annual Conference of the International Association of Women Police met in Denver. Some female police graduate students of ours who were attending the meeting suggested we conduct a research project with the conference participants, because they could arrange the cooperation necessary to collect the data we would need. To be brief, we designed a survey instrument that we placed in each participant's registration package. It was a self-report type of questionnaire eliciting information on a variety of issues concerning women police. Out of a total conference population of 430 women police, 343 returned their questionnaires. Those who completed the instrument had no idea who designed it. In short, we remained anonymous.

We presented our findings on a panel with four female police officers who were analyzing the extensive gender problems among policewomen in law enforcement organizations. Approximately 200 policewomen attended this session. We announced that we were two local criminal justice professors from a state university who had developed the surveys and that, according to their self-report responses, only one variable was found to be significant out of sixteen that we had attempted to measure.[1] At that point, the entire audience began to address us in quite an emotional manner. What they were telling us, despite our survey findings, was that all was not well with their police career. After things quieted down, the audience participants related many tales of harassment, gender discrimination, and a host of unsolved problems they experienced on a daily basis as a result of being a female in a male-dominated occupation. Their frustrations with the treatment they received were universal, yet our self-report instrument failed to elicit the type of responses we heard from those policewomen on that day.

The lesson that we as researchers learned that day was something that has stayed with us ever since. We realized that even with a solid theoretical basis, a tested survey instrument, and an excellent response rate, we failed to capture the very problems the self-report survey attempted to elicit. However, the very issues that the questionnaire covered were verbally related to us by those audience participants attending the session. Rather than speculate on why our survey failed to measure the variables the women police discussed openly at the session where we presented our findings, I would like to concentrate on what other research methodology might have proved to be more fruitful in discovering those occupational problems that gender causes for females in law enforcement. It could be argued that we should have interviewed a number of the conference participants, or that our female police graduate students should have conducted the interviews, due to the sensitivity of gender-oriented subjects. In retrospect, we could have utilized multifaceted qualitative approaches. Suffice to say, through this illustrative tale I have attempted to point out that quantitative methods, at least in our case, did not elicit the information it should have for a large population study. In hindsight, we would have been more successful had we used a small purposeful sample of policewomen and conducted in-depth interviews (Miles & Huberman, 1994). However, I do not wish to spend time arguing the merits between positivism and interpretism, quantity and quality.[2] Rather, I wish to present a case for the reliance of qualitative methods, especially for research on the criminal justice system. Rather than provide an in-depth discussion on qualitative research techniques, as Shaffir and Stebbins do so comprehensively in the book's first article, "Introduction to Qualitative Methods," I prefer to offer some of my own and other qualitative researchers' points of view concerning its value as a method to collect data and interpret social phenomena.

QUALITATIVE METHODS

Qualitative research techniques have witnessed an increased popularity in the past 15 to 20 years throughout the social sciences (Bryman & Burgess, 1994; Denzin, 1994; Marshall & Rossman, 1999; Morse, 1994). Its use as an accepted methodology has been demonstrated in subject areas that traditionally used positivistic methods of the quantitative variety (Barnes et al., 1999; Black, 1996; Ritchie & Spencer, 1994). More recently, there has been an increase in the research literature encouraging and promoting the utilization of qualitative research methods in order to gain a more comprehensive understanding of the social phenomenon being studied (Attride-Stirling, 2001). Denzin and Lincoln (1998, vii) offer an insightful explanation for the method's increased popularity.

> In more than two decades a quiet methodological revolution has been taking place in the social sciences. A blurring of disciplinary boundaries has occurred. The social sciences and humanities have drawn closer together in a mutual focus on an interpretive, qualitative approach to research and theory. Although these trends are not new, the extent to which the qualitative revolution has overtaken the social sciences and related professional fields has been nothing short of amazing.

Interestingly, Spradley (1979) over two decades ago spoke of a "quiet revolution" that spread through the social sciences and other applied disciplines that had come of age. He was referring to the many uses of ethnography, which he defined as the study of culture. Spradley felt the qualitative-ethnographic approach was the best way to understand humankind and saw its techniques as emerging among the disciplines of education, urban planning, sociology, nursing, psychology, law, political science, and many others. Reasons for using qualitative methods, according to Truzzi (1974), are for purposes of presenting in-depth knowledge necessary to portray the perspectives of that population which is being researched through their social worlds as they experience them. Altheide and Johnson (1994) claim that one of the primary reasons for using qualitative methods is to better understand the meaning, depth, and scope of the subjective experience of social situations. This research approach is usually used for identification, description, and generating explanation (Crabtree & Miller, 1999). It emphasizes current personal experience rather than just theorizing about individual or group behavior (Schensul, 1980). The strengths of qualitative research, claims Maxwell (1996), stem from its inductive approach, its emphasis on specific situations and the people who experience them, and its utilization of language rather than numerical explanations. Maxwell (1996, 17) lists five purposes for which qualitative methods are best suited:

1. Understanding meaning based on interpretations of events and actions perceived by the study participants who are involved in them

2. Comprehending the context in which those being studied act, and the degree of influence and effects this context has on their behavior

3. Generating the continuing process of grounded theory[3] based on unanticipated new social phenomenon

4. Understanding the process through which events and activities occur and observing the processes that lead to particular outcomes

5. Developing explanations for these events and processes

According to Denzin and Lincoln (1998, 3), qualitative research methods reflect a multifaceted perspective, involving "an interpretive, naturalistic approach to its subject matter. This means that qualitative researchers study things in their natural settings, attempting to make sense of, or interpret phenomena in terms of the meanings people bring to them." It is up to the researchers to comprehend the shared meanings of the social world that is being observed. They should further gain an appreciation of the lives and concerns of that population being studied. An interpretive understanding of their environment, lives, behaviors, and thoughts is fundamental (Emerson, 1983).

ETHNOGRAPHY

The majority of the articles in this book could be defined as ethnographic. Spradley (1980, 5) points out that in every society, people consistently use complex systems of meaning to "understand themselves, and others, and to make sense out of the world in which they live. These systems of meaning constitute their culture. Ethnography always implies a theory of culture."Agar (1986) notes that ethnography focuses on making sense of alien worlds and that it is the job of ethnographers to describe how social action in one world makes sense to the point of view of another. Ethnography should discuss accounts and interpretations by group members of a particular culture by grasping the everyday routine events that occur in their lives (Van Maanen, 1988). However, Geertz (1974) argues that it is an absolute necessity for researchers to relate what those being studied think about their daily routines. In this way, we can better interpret the natives' point of view.

Qualitative fieldwork perspectives stress interpretive, ethnographic methods that provide for insightful knowledge at a close range (Daly & Chesney-Lind, 1988) and reveal parts of the social world that remain hidden by more traditional methodological techniques (Caufield & Wonders, 1994). According to Prus (1966), the study of ethnography refers to the way of life of a particular group of people. As a research method, its investigative techniques rely mainly on observations, participant observation, and open-ended interviews.

> Thus, ethnographers strive for intimate familiarity with the lived experiences of those they study, and they attempt to convey as fully as possible the viewpoints and practices of those people to others. (Prus, 1966, 103)

There are some who believe ethnography excludes qualitative research approaches where the researcher has not spent a long period of time observing the study participants in the field in order to become sufficiently knowledgeable of the setting being studied (Glaser & Strauss, 1967). Herein lies the methodological controversy. There are studies in this anthology that rely solely on interview data without the researchers' having spent a long time in the field observing those people who comprise the research population. There are others who take issue with the viewpoint that ethnography must be based on extensive time observing in the field.

Kleinman, Stenross, and McMahon (1994) argue that the capacity of the interview to elicit discussion of desired subjects, when rapport has been established, has advantages over participant observation for the exploration of study participants' feelings and perceptions. Lengthy interviews, suggests McCracken (1988), offer those being studied opportunities to discuss their ideas about subjects that often get neglected or suppressed in spontaneous conversations with researchers involved in participant observation. Finally, Hobbs and May (1993) suggest that in-depth interviews are the best way to gather data that could never be obtained by just observing the activities of people. They perceive the in-depth interview as an acceptable methodological technique by which to obtain grounded subjectivity in qualitative research.

Although qualitative scholars on both sides of this issue offer convincing arguments that are quite persuasive, readers have to seek answers for themselves for the methodological issues raised by interpreting the quality and reliability of the findings for these two ethnographic methods. I suggest that readers compare those studies that focused on participant observation with those that relied on in-depth interviews with participants in the field setting but did not involve any other unobtrusive data-gathering techniques. Perhaps such a comparison will provide you with some clarity; however, it may only confuse the issue even more. But it's worth a try.

As the editor of this book, it is my hope that those of you who are assigned it for class will enjoy the articles to the extent that you are inspired enough to go out and conduct your own qualitative research project.

The articles selected for this anthology explore the application of qualitative research to a wide range of criminal justice topics. This book is not intended to provide a systematic review of all the qualitative research methods that exist per se. Rather, its focus is upon those fieldwork practices that describe and analyze the points in the criminal justice system that directly affect the actors who are part of the occupational cultures that define our formal system of social control. Moreover, the article selections do not purport to encompass all aspects of the criminal justice system. Not surprisingly, the balance of the selections reflect a desire to provide an indication of the range of some qualitative techniques and perspectives used by various fieldwork researchers, as well as to offer students the real world experiences of those who are employed in the system. In this way, I have attempted to organize this book from two criminal justice perspectives: one being qualitatively oriented and the other system oriented. Sort of a two-for-one approach.

Last, some explanation for the span of years that the articles cover is required. The collection of readings does include published works written several years ago as well as some prepared more recently. The research and subject matter in the earlier pieces are recognized as authoritative findings and problem statements that focus on issues that continue to remain problematic even today. The more contemporary writings attempt to analyze the changing problems that criminal justice organizations have had to address in recent years.

The organization of this book is focused around five areas of qualitative research within the criminal justice system. The first section introduces fieldwork practices and addresses important methodological and experiential tales of past researchers that are important to understand. The next three sections—police, judicial, and corrections—provide good examples of problematic issues that currently exist in the agencies studied and, further, offer a firsthand look at the way actors in the system interpret their occupational environment. Various types of qualitative approaches to fieldwork methods are used as examples in order for students to comprehend how this research process is applied in the field. And in the final section of the book, three researchers discuss their experiences while in the field and offer reflective accounts of conflicting issues they encountered while conducting their studies.

Along with the articles, each of the five sections has an overview that discusses the actual qualitative method used by the different authors. These brief research descriptions are meant to assist students in understanding the how and why of each research approach to data collection. In addition to the research overview, I have provided brief commentaries before each article that highlight the study.

By providing the reader with varied examples of the applications of qualitative research methods for studying the criminal justice system, I have attempted to create an appreciation for this unique methodological approach to demonstrate its use in extending knowledge and providing social actors with their own voices. Such strategies provide a unique opportunity for those persons we do not often hear from firsthand to contribute their own experiential perspectives and interpretations within the social world of the criminal justice system.

NOTES

1. See Poole and Pogrebin (1988). "Factors Affecting the Decision to Remain in Policing,"*Journal of Police Science and Administration*, 16:49–55.

2. See Denzin and Lincoln's (1998) position on "Qualitative Versus Quantitative Research"in *Collecting and Interpreting Qualitative Materials*, pp. 8–11.

3. "Qualitative Research is open ended and emergent. We cannot predict where our inquiry will take us" (Charmaz, 2000, p. 538). Patton (2001) sees grounded theory as inductively generated from field research and that theory is developed from field observations and interviews conducted within the world of those being studied.

REFERENCES

Agar, M. (1986). *Speaking of Ethnography: Qualitative Research Methods. No 2*. London: Sage.

Altheide, D., & Johnson, J. (1994). Criteria for assessing interpretive validity in qualitative research. In N. Denzin and Y. Lincoln (Eds.), *Handbook of Qualitative Research* (pp. 485–499). Thousand Oaks, CA: Sage.

Attride-Stirling, J. (2001). Thematic networks: An analytic tool for qualitative research. *Qualitative Research*, 1, 385–405.

Black, N. (1996). Why we need observational studies to evaluate the effectiveness of health care. *British Medical Journal*, 312, 1215–1218.

Bryman, A., & Burgess, R. (1994). *Analyzing Qualitative Data*. London: Sage.

Byrnes, J., Stein, A., & Rosenberg, W. (1999). Evidence based medicine and evaluation of mental health services: Methodological issues and future directions. *Archives for Diseases of Childhood*, 80, 280–285.

Caufield, S., & Wonders, N. (1994). Varieties of Criminology. In G. Barak (Ed.), *Gender and Justice: Feminist Contributions to Criminology* (pp. 213–229). Westport, CT: Praeger.

Charmaz, K. (2000). Looking backward, moving forward: Expanding sociological horizons in the twenty-first century. *Sociological Perspectives*, 43, 529–547.

Crabtree, B., & Miller, W. (1999). *Doing Qualitative Research*. Thousand Oaks, CA: Sage.

Daly, K., & Chesney-Lind, M. (1988). Feminism and criminology. *Justice Quarterly*, 5, 497–535.

Denzin, N. (1994). The art and politics of interpretation. In N. Denzin and Y. Lincoln (Eds.), *Handbook of Qualitative Research* (pp. 500–515). Thousand Oaks, CA: Sage.

Denzin, N., & Lincoln, Y. (1998). *Collecting and Interpreting Qualitative Materials*. Thousand Oaks, CA: Sage.

Emerson, R. (1983). Introduction. In R. Emerson (Ed.) *Contemporary Field Research* (pp. 1–16). Boston: Little-Brown.

Geertz, C. (1974). From the native's point of view. *Bulletin of the American Academy of Arts and Sciences*, 28, 27–45.

Glaser, B., & Strauss, A. (1967). *The Discovery of Grounded Theory: Strategies for Qualitative Research*. Chicago: Aldine.

Hobbs, D., & May, T. (1993). Foreword. In D. Hobbs and T. May (Eds.), *Interpreting the Field: Accounts of Ethnography* (pp. vii–xviii). New York: Oxford University Press.

Kleinman, S., Stenross, B., & McMahon, M. (1994). Privileging fieldwork over interviews: Consequences for identity and practice. *Symbolic Interaction*, 17, 37–50.

Marshall, C., & Rossman, G. (1999). *Designing Qualitative Research*. Thousand Oaks, CA: Sage.

Maxwell, J. (1996). *Qualitative Research Design*. Thousand Oaks, CA: Sage.

McCracken, G. (1988). *The Long Interview*. Newbury Park, CA: Sage.

Miles, M. B., & Huberman, A. M. (1994). *Qualitative Data Analysis: A Sourcebook for New Methods*. Thousand Oaks, CA: Sage.

Morse, J. (1994). *Critical Issues in Qualitative Research Methods*. Thousand Oaks, CA: Sage.

Patton, M. (2001). *Qualitative Research and Evaluation*. Thousand Oaks, CA: Sage.

Poole, E., & Pogrebin, M. (1988). Factors affecting the decision to remain in policing: A study of women officers. *Journal of Police Science and Administration*, 16, 49–55.

Prus, R. (1996). *Symbolic Interaction and Ethnographic Research*. Albany: State University of New York Press.

Ritchie, J., & Spencer, J. (1994). Qualitative Data Analysis for Applied Policy Research. In A. Bryman & R. Burgess (Eds.), *Analyzing Qualitative Data* (pp. 173–194). London: Sage.

Schensul, S. (1980). Anthropological fieldwork and sociopolitical change. *Social Problems*, 27, 309–319.

Spradley, J. (1979). *The Ethnographic Interview*. New York: Holt, Rinehart, & Winston.

Spradley, J. (1980). *Participant Observation*. New York: Holt, Rinehart, & Winston.

Truzz, M. (1974). *Verstehen: Subjective Understanding in the Social Sciences*. Reading, MA: Addison-Wesley.

Weick, K. (1985). Systematic Observational Methods. In G. Lindzey & G. Aronson (Eds.), *The Handbook of Social Psychology* (pp. 256–634). New York: Random House.

Van Maanen, J. (1988). *Tales of the Field*. Chicago: University of Chicago Press.

1

INTRODUCTION TO QUALITATIVE METHODS

IN THE FIELD

In their comprehensive overview of fieldwork practices, Shaffer and Stebbins discuss the realities of conducting naturalistic inquiries and the difficulties that researchers encounter while in the field. After relating the historical experiences of various prominent qualitative researchers, the authors then provide an in-depth analysis of the following topics: the relationship of qualitative and quantitative methods, history of fieldwork, issues of validity and reliability, ethical concerns, studying unfamiliar social phenomenon, and the marginal status of field researchers with study participants as well as within their own profession.

INTRODUCTION TO FIELDWORK

WILLIAM B. SHAFFIR
ROBERT A. STEBBINS

Fieldwork must certainly rank with the more disagreeable activities that humanity has fashioned for itself. It is usually inconvenient, to say the least, sometimes physically uncomfortable, frequently embarrassing, and, to a degree, always tense. Although anthropology and sociology still appear to have the largest proportion of field researchers among the social sciences, their number is growing significantly in such diverse disciplines as nursing, education, management, medicine, and social work. Field researchers have in common the tendency to immerse themselves for the sake of science in situations that all but a tiny minority of humankind goes to great lengths to avoid. Consider some examples: Raymond A. Friedman (1989) said that the first contact with his research subjects in a study of labor negotiations was a disaster. The plant manager was opposed to his presence. He entered the field in the middle of a rancorous intraunion fight over seniority. And he initially chose an inopportune place (a bar) to interview workers. Carol S. Wharton (1987) managed over a ten-month period the delicate observer-as-participant role of researcher and counselor-advocate in a shelter for battered women. Peggy Golde (1986, pp. 67-96) struggled to learn about aesthetic values and practices in a Mexican village against the odds of physical isolation, a contaminated water supply, and a new language.

For most researchers the day-to-day demands of fieldwork are fraught regularly with feelings of uncertainty and anxiety. The process of leading a way of life over an extended period that is often both novel and strange exposes the researcher to situations and experiences that usually are accompanied by an intense concern with whether the research is conducted and managed properly. Researcher fieldwork accounts typically deal with such matters as how the hurdles blocking entry were overcome successfully and how the emergent relationships with subjects were cultivated and maintained during the course of the study; the emotional pains of this work rarely are mentioned. In discussing anthropologists' fieldwork accounts, Freilich (1970) writes:

> Rarely mentioned are anthropologists' anxious attempts to act appropriately when they knew little of the native culture, the emotional pressures

to act in terms of the culture of orientation, when reason and training dictated that they act in terms of the native culture, the depressing time when the project seemed destined to fail, the loneliness when communication with the natives was at a low point, and the craving for familiar sights, sounds, and faces. (p. 27)

Despite the paucity of accounts describing the less happy moments of fieldwork, such moments are likely to be present in most, if not all, field studies. This is suggested in the discussions of membership roles in field research (Adler & Adler, 1987) and field relations (Hammersley & Atkinson, 1983), and by the frequency with which they become topics of conversation among researchers. Perhaps most unhappy moments in the field are not as painful as that of Gini Graham Scott (1983) whose position as covert observer of a black magic group (Church of Hu) was discovered by other members:

At first, as I walked in, I was delighted to finally have the chance to talk to some higher-ups, but in moments the elaborate plotting that had taken place behind my back became painfully obvious.

As I sat down on the bed beside Huf, Lare looked at me icily. "What are your motives?" she hissed.

At once I became aware of the current of hostility in the room, and this sudden realization, so unexpected, left me almost speechless.

"To grow," I answered lamely. "Are you concerned about the tapes [containing research data]?"

"Well, what about them?" she snapped.

"It's so I can remember things," I said.

"And the questions? Why have you been asking everyone about their backgrounds? What does that have to do with growth?"

I tried to explain. "But I always ask people about themselves when I meet them. What's wrong with that?"

However, Lare disregarded my explanation. "We don't believe you," she said.

Then Firth butted in. "We have several people in intelligence in the group . . . we've read your diary . . ."

At this point the elaborate plotting going on behind my back became clear, and I couldn't think of anything to say. It was apparent now they considered me some kind of undercover enemy or sensationalist journalist out to harm or expose the Church, and they had gathered their evidence to prove this. Now they were trying the case, though it was obvious the decision had already been made. Later, Armat explained that they had fears about me or anyone else drawing attention to them because of the negative climate towards cults among "humans." So they were afraid that any outside attention might lead to the destruction of the Church before they could prepare for the coming annihilation. However, in the tense setting of a quickly convened trial, there was no way to explain my intentions or try to reconcile them with my expressed belief in learning magic. Once Firth said he read my diary, I realized there was nothing more to say.

"So now, get out," Lare snapped. "Take off your pentagram and get out."

As I removed it from my chain, I explained that I had driven up with several other people and had no way back.

"That's your problem," she said. "Just be gone by the time we get back." Then threateningly she added: "You should be glad that we aren't going to do anything else."

"There are buses," Huf remarked. (pp. 132-133)

Nonetheless, after hearing field researchers discuss their work, one has to conclude that there are exceptional payoffs that justify the accompanying hardships. And for these scientists, the payoffs go beyond the lengthy research reports that present sets of inductive generalizations based on direct contact with other ways of life. Fieldwork, its rigors notwithstanding, offers many rewarding personal experiences. Among them are the often warm relations to be had with subjects and the challenges of understanding a new culture and overcoming anxieties. In short, entering the research setting, learning the ropes once in, maintaining working relations with subjects, and making a smooth exit are difficult to achieve and sources of pride when done well.

From another perspective, the desire to do fieldwork is founded on motives that drive few other kinds of scientific investigation. To be sure, field researchers share with other scientists the goal of collecting valid, impartial data about some natural phenomenon. In addition, however, they gain satisfaction—perhaps better stated as a sense of accomplishment—from successfully managing the social side of their projects, which is more problematic than in any other form of inquiry. Though they raise questions of validity (Johnson, 1975, p. 161), gratifying relations between observers and subjects frequently emerge in the field. At the same time, being accepted by subjects as a group is crucial for conduct of the study (Cicourel, 1964, p. 42). Observers must be able to convince their subjects (and sometimes their professional colleagues) that they can satisfactorily do the research and that their interests are of enough importance to offset the frequent inconvenience, embarrassment, annoyance, and exposure that necessarily accompany unbiased scientific scrutiny of any group. It is in attempting to solve this basic problem, which recurs throughout every study, that many of the unforgettable experiences of fieldwork occur.

Completion of a fieldwork project is also an accomplishment because the "situation of social scientists" (Lofland, 1976, pp. 13-18) discourages it so. Lofland notes that many social scientists are unsuited temperamentally for the stressful activity of such an undertaking because they are rather asocial, reclusive, and sometimes even abrasive. Furthermore, all university-based research must be molded to the demands of the university as a large-scale organization. Getting acquainted with an essentially foreign way of life is complicated further when the research is pursued intermittently after classes, before committee meetings, between deadlines, and the like (e.g., Shaffir, Marshall, & Haas, 1980). To this is added the lack of procedural clarity that characterizes field research; there are few useful rules (unlike other forms of social research) available for transforming chaotic sets of observations into systematic generalizations about a way of life. Then there is the preference of funding agencies for quantitative investigations, which pushes the field-worker yet another step in the direction of marginality. Finally, the very style of reporting social scientific findings, abstruse and arcane as it tends to be, contrasts badly with the down-to-earth routines of the people under study. When they find it next to impossible to see themselves in the reports of the projects in which they have participated, they are rendered ineffective as critics of the accuracy of the research.

Fieldwork is carried out by immersing oneself in a collective way of life for the purpose of gaining firsthand knowledge about a major facet of it. As Blumer (1986) puts it, field research on another way of life consists of:

> getting closer to the people involved in it, seeing it in a variety of situations they meet, noting their problems and observing how they handle them, being party to their conversations and watching their way of life as it flows along. (p. 37)

Adopting mainly the methodology of participant observation—described as "research that involves social interaction between the researcher and informants in the milieu of the latter, during which data are systematically and unobtrusively collected" (Taylor & Bogdan, 1984, p. 15)—the researcher attempts to record the ongoing experiences of those observed in their symbolic world. This research strategy commits the observer to learning to define the world from the perspective of those studied and requires that he or she gain as intimate an understanding as possible of their way of perceiving life. To achieve this aim, the field researcher typically supplements participant observation with additional methodological techniques in field research, often including semistructured interviews, life histories, document analysis, and various nonreactive measures (Webb, Campbell, Schwartz, Sechrest, & Grove, 1981).

Most fieldwork projects are exploratory, this means that the researcher approaches the field with certain special orientations, among them *flexibility* in looking for data and *open-mindedness* about where to find them. These are needed to explore the phenomenon under study when relatively little is known about it. Following Max Weber's model, the first step to be taken in the scientific study of social life is to acquire an intimate, firsthand understanding (*Verstehen*) of the human acts being observed. It follows that the most efficient approach is to search for this understanding wherever it may be found by any method that appears to bear fruit. The main goal of exploratory research is the generation of inductively obtained generalizations about the field. These generalizations are eventually woven into a "grounded theory" of the phenomenon under consideration, the procedure for which is found in a series of publications by Glaser (1978), Glaser and Strauss (1967), and Strauss (1987).

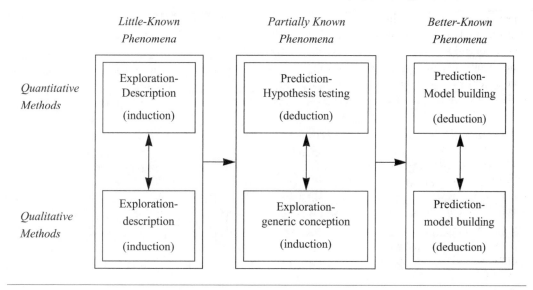

Figure A.1   The Relationship of Qualitative and Quantitative Methods

The left side of Figure A.1 indicates that both quantitative and qualitative data may be gathered during exploration. Most exploratory studies, however, are predominantly qualitative, possibly augmented in a minor quantitative way by such descriptive statistics as indexes, percentages, and enumerations. As we come to know better the phenomenon we have chosen for examination, we move to the right across Figure A.1. That is, we come to rely less and less on exploration and more and more on prediction along the lines of hypotheses obtained deductively from the grounded theory. This process typically unfolds over the course of several studies. It is paralleled by an expansion of the grounded theory through its application to an ever-wider range of phenomena and through its internal development of an ever-growing number of generic concepts (Purs, 1987).

On the far right side of Figure A.1, we find a well-developed grounded theory about a reasonably known, broad range of related phenomena. At this point concern is chiefly with enhancing the precision of the theory, a process that is pursued commonly through prediction and quantification including a heavy reliance on inferential statistics. Even here, however, qualitative data can sometimes play a role. Such data, for example, may help confirm certain hypotheses or bring to our attention through exploration important recent changes in social process and structure that the narrower focus of confirmation of hypotheses has led us to overlook.

Although descriptions and analyses of the various dimensions of the field research experience have become more plentiful recently, it is unfortunate that the social aspects both underlying and shaping this experience have received so little critical attention. These social aspects, which include feelings of self-doubt, uncertainty, and frustration, are both inherent in field research and the basic stuff of which this methodology consists.

Field research is accompanied by a set of experiences that are, for the most part, unavailable through other forms of social scientific research. These experiences are bound together with satisfactions, embarrassments, challenges, pains, triumphs, ambiguities, and agonies, all of which blend into what has been described as the field research adventure (Glazer, 1972). It is difficult to imagine a field project that does not include at least some of these features, however skilled and experienced the researcher. Anyone undertaking field study for the first time—usually an undergraduate or a graduate student—encounters a mix of these feelings but, unlike the seasoned investigator, blames him- or herself for the problem, seemingly a result solely of inadequate preparation and experience.

HISTORY OF FIELDWORK

The history of fieldwork as a set of research techniques, an approach to data collection, can be related, in good measure, to the issues of validity and reliability, ethics, and the study of the unfamiliar. In grappling with them, fieldwork procedure has gained in distinctiveness and respectability, and its place in the scientific process has been clarified.

Rosalie Wax (1971), who has written one of the most extensive histories of fieldwork, points out that descriptive reporting of the customs, inclinations, and accomplishments of other societies goes back almost to the origin of writing. From the Roman period on, travelers have been so fascinated with the cultural differences they experienced that they have recorded their observations as a matter of interest to themselves and their compatriots. And as world passage became easier in the late nineteenth century, so the accounts of "backward" peoples multiplied. Some of these "amateur" reports, as contemporary anthropologists refer to them, are accurate enough to be of scientific value.

While the travelers busied themselves writing biased accounts of foreigners, educated men and sometimes women (e.g., lawyers, physicians, physical scientists, administrative officials) were gathering firsthand information on certain sections of their own societies with which they were unacquainted initially. In the early twentieth century Charles Booth, for example, combined statistical data with extensive interviewing and participant observation to complete a vast study of the working people of London. In fact, several investigations were conducted in the late nineteenth and early twentieth centuries in England, France, and Germany that used participant observation and interviews (sometimes supplemented by questionnaires) to produce data.

Bronislaw Malinowski (1922) was perhaps the first social scientist to live in a preliterate community for an extended period and to record as objectively as possible what he saw. His intimate involvement in the daily lives of his subjects is regarded as a turning point in the history of fieldwork procedure. Malinowski also wrote detailed descriptions of how he gathered his data.

Several decades later, sociologist Robert Park (a former journalist) and anthropologist Robert Redfield turned the University of Chicago into a center for participant observer-based fieldwork that was without parallel anywhere in the world. During the 1920s, the first generation of sociologists here concentrated on subjects such as the hobo, the ghetto, the neighborhood, and the gang. Succeeding generations of students and faculty examined, among others, French Canada, an Italian slum, juvenile delinquents, and governmental agencies (Blau, 1955), a mental hospital (Goffman, 1961), and medical students (Becker, Geer, Hughes, & Strauss, 1961). Unlike Malinowski, however, those who came under the influence of Park and Redfield at Chicago were expected to integrate their field data with the ideas of Weber, Simmel, Dewey, and other prominent social theorists of the day. Furthermore, the fieldwork of this period maintained the stance of scientific objectivity, which started with the colonial period of world history and the dominance of natural science methods in world intellectual circles. As Barnes (1963) put it:

> The ethnographer took for granted that the observations and records he made did not significantly disturb the behavior of the people studied. In the classical mechanics of the nineteenth century it was assumed that physical observations could be made without affecting the objects observed and in much the same way ethnographers assumed that in their researches there was no direct feedback from them to their informants. (p. 120)

Barnes goes on to state that times have changed. Modern field research is apt to deal with literate people who can read the researcher's reports, write letters to influential authorities, and perhaps sue. In response to this threat and others, ethics committees have emerged in many universities, where they assess proposed social research for its possible unfavorable impact on subjects. And modern field research frequently centers on topics within the investigator's society. Thus the possibility must be faced that some subjects, when in the researcher's presence, will not be candid in their behavior and conversations for fear that their actions and statements, which may be unacceptable to certain people, will become available to those persons.

"There may still be an exotic focus of study, but the group or institution being studied is now seen to be embedded in a network of social relations of which the observer is an integral if reluctant part" (Barnes, 1963, p. 121).

Meanwhile, certain trends have forced field researchers to clarify their position in the scientific process. The use of questionnaires gained widespread acceptance through the rising popularity of public-opinion polling and its close association with the ideas of Paul Lazarsfeld and Robert Merton (R. Wax, 1971, p. 40). Rigorous research designs, quantitative data, statistical techniques, and at first mechanical and later electronic information processing became hallmarks of social scientific procedure, while fieldwork was regarded more and more as an old-fashioned and "softheaded" approach.

In other words, whereas one of the widely acknowledged strengths of fieldwork has been its potential for generating seminal ideas, its capacity for effectively testing these ideas has been increasingly questioned. Field researchers helped to confuse its role by claiming Znaniecki's (1934) method of "analytic induction" as a model of their procedure. In analytic induction, hypotheses are generated not only from raw data but also are tested by them. A lively debate sprang up some time later over the logical possibility of conducting both operations simultaneously (based on the same data) and over the general utility of analytic induction (see Robinson, 1951; Turner, 1953).

More than 30 years elapsed after the publication of Znaniecki's book before social scientists sorted out the place of inductive hypothesis-generating procedure in the broader scientific process. Glaser and Strauss (1967) firmly established that no procedure can concurrently generate and test propositions. The first requires flexibility, unstructured research techniques, intuition, and detailed description; the second uses control, structured techniques, precisions, and logical movement from premises to conclusions. The "constant comparative method," as Glaser and Strauss describe the approach, is an effective means for generating hypotheses and grounded theory.

We finally have learned that as our knowledge about an area grows—as hypotheses grounded in direct field study begin to coalesce

into a theory about it—fieldwork and its less structured techniques fade into the background. At the same time, more controlled techniques come into use (see Figure A.1). Today, some social science fields are largely or significantly exploratory in their procedural orientation, among them anthropology, community psychology, symbolic interactionism, and classroom studies.

Others, such as small group research and family sociology, generally appear to have passed beyond this stage.

Although initial exploration has been the chief role of qualitative research, we are not claiming that in its exploratory stage it is always "preliminary" in its import. Exploratory studies have been so effective as to have become classics—for example, Whyte's (1943/1981) *StreetCorner Society* or Goffman's (1959) *The Presentation of Self in Everyday Life*. In these instances and others, social science has subsequently learned through more controlled study that the initial observations were empirically sound and theoretically significant. Glaser and Strauss (1967, pp. 234-235) advance three reasons why exploratory investigations often turn out to be the final research on a particular topic. First, the qualitative findings are taken by social scientists to be definitive. Second, interest wanes in conducting further research on the phenomenon. Third, before researchers can mount more rigorous studies of it, the phenomenon has changed considerably.

A parallel history of growing self-consciousness about the special status of fieldwork is evident in two ways: in the organizational developments that have come to surround it, and in its literature. Every year since 1984, McMaster University, the University of Waterloo, and more recently York University have sponsored conferences on qualitative methods and research projects. Although more specialized, the annual University of Pennsylvania Ethnography in Education Research Forum has been around even longer (since 1980). The Qualitative Interest Group (QUIG) at the University of Georgia offered in early 1990 its third international conference on qualitative research in education. Educationists were also instrumental in starting in 1987 in Quebec the francophone *Association pour la recherche qualitative*;

however, it embraces qualitative research in all fields. It is possibly the first association devoted exclusively to qualitative research.

Concerning self-consciousness about the special status of fieldwork as seen in the progression of its literature, Junker (1960, p. 160) notes that in the first two decades of this century the publications of field researchers contained little about their problems and experiences. He traces the tendency to discuss these matters in the final report, however briefly, to Robert and Helen Lynd's study of Middletown. But it was not until after 1940 that theoretical treatments of fieldwork issues and experiences began to occur with regularity. Even in 1960, Junker could write that "full accounts are still rare, considering the large number of field studies published and still coming off the presses" (pp 160-161).

Since then, however, candid descriptions of fieldwork that frequently touch on the issues of validity and ethics have become routine in monographic reports. Several texts and readers devoted exclusively to this method also have been produced. Some of the most recent of these have been written or edited by Berg (1989), Emerson (1983), Hammersley and Atkinson (1983), Lofland and Lofland (1984), and Taylor and Bogdan (1984). Since 1986 Sage Publications has published the Qualitative Research Methods series of short introductions to the methodological tools of qualitative studies, and since 1977 the Sociological Observations series of monographs. Approximately two decades ago John Lofland (1971, p. 131) urged researchers to present detailed accounts of the social relations and private feelings experienced in the field. Also of note are the two main journals for qualitative research, the *Journal of Contemporary Ethnography* (formerly *Urban Life and Culture* and then *Urban Life*), founded in 1972, and *Qualitative Sociology*, founded in 1978. Nonetheless, in sociology and especially anthropology, articles on qualitative methods and research projects frequently appear in many of the general and specialty journals.

ISSUES IN FIELDWORK

Besides acquainting unseasoned field researchers with the nature of the experiences that await them, there are three reasons why a collection of accounts is valuable. They are seen in the three issues traditionally considered in methodological discussions of the field approach that are affected by the nature of the researcher's experiences in gathering data: validity and reliability, ethics, and the study of the unfamiliar. Because field researchers are virtually part of the data-collection process, rather than its external directors, their experiences there are critical.

Validity and Reliability

The problem of validity in field research concerns the difficulty of gaining an accurate or true impression of the phenomenon under study. The companion problem of reliability centers on the replicability of observations; it rests on the question of whether another researcher with similar methodological training, understanding of the field setting, and rapport with the subjects can make similar observations. In field research these two problems fall into the following categories:

(1) reactive effects of the observer's presence or activities on the phenomena being observed;

(2) distorting effects of selective perception and interpretation on the observer's part; and

(3) limitations on the observer's ability to witness all relevant aspects of the phenomena in question (McCall & Simmons, 1969, p. 78).

The experiences of the researcher bear on all three.

Reactive effects are the special behavioral responses subjects make because the observer is in the setting, responses that are atypical for the occasion. Webb and his colleagues (1981, pp. 49-58) treat four reactive effects that frequently invalidate social science data, two of which—the guinea pig effect and role selection—are germane here. In the first, subjects are aware of being observed and react by putting their best foot forward; they strive to make a good impression. In the second, which is closely related, they choose to emphasize one of several selves that they sense is most appropriate given the observers presence.

Special reactive effects may take place when a researcher's rational appearances fail (Johnson, 1975, pp. 155-160). Observers are human, too. At times they get angry, become sympathetic, grow despondent, and are unable to hide these sentiments. Jean Briggs's (1986, pp. 34-38) indignation at the Kapluna (white) fisherman who damaged a canoe owned by the Eskimos she was studying resulted in subtle ostracism that lasted three months. The validity of the data is certainly jeopardized, in some measure, by such outbursts. Perhaps, too, maintaining rationality when emotion is conventionally expected produces the image of a researcher who is callous or lifeless and should be treated accordingly.

Another condition under which reactive effects could blemish the quality of data is the disintegration of trust between the observer and one or more subjects. Once the researcher has found or been placed in a role in the group being studied, whether that of observer or something more familiar to its members, a certain degree of trust develops whereby he or she is allowed to participate in many of their affairs. Behavior of the observer that contradicts the belief that he or she belongs in that role may break the bond of trust. Still more unfortunate, it may suddenly come to light that the observer is just that, an observer, rather than a pure member—one of the chief hazards in operating as a concealed researcher. This possibility haunted Kathryn Fox (1987) in her study of punk rockers. She knew that if her identity as a researcher became generally known, she would effectively be denied access to the local punk scene. This situation severely limited her participation there.

Observers also selectively perceive and interpret data in different ways that ultimately and sometimes seriously bias their investigations. The most celebrated of these is "going native," or so thoroughly embracing the customs and beliefs of the focal group that one becomes incapable of objective work. Certain other problems bear mention as well. Johnson (1975, pp. 151-155) points out that the observer's apprehension that commonly attends entry to the field can slant the perception of events during his or her early days there. Moreover, our commonsense assumptions about life are disturbed during these initial weeks, causing us to see things that other people, with different presuppositions about everyday affairs, would miss.

Special orientations towards subjects, whether love, hate, friendship, admiration, respect, or dislike, also influence our views of these people and their behavior. One wonders what consequences the close bond between Doc and William F. Whyte (1943/1981) or Tally and Elliot Liebow (1967) had for the observers' perceptions of these informants and the informants' social involvements. Undoubtedly there were both advantages and disadvantages to these arrangements. Of equal importance are the desires felt by many field researchers to help their subjects in some way. They face a profound dilemma, however, when the need for help is so great that it threatens the study itself by monopolizing the time the researcher has to commit to the latter (Lofland & Lofland, 1984, p. 34).

The third category of validity and reliability problems deals with limitations on the observer's ability to witness all that is relevant to the study. For example, Richard V. Ericson (1981, pp. 25-26) found in his study of detective work that it appeared on certain occasions that cases were assigned intentionally to another team of detectives to which there was no field researcher attached. On other occasions the detective sergeant responsible for case assignments would give a case to a team with a researcher because he believed the case would be interesting to the researcher.

Taylor and Bogdan (1984, pp. 44-45) discuss a related fieldwork predicament that can cut off researchers from events of great importance to them. Observers, having become established as individuals who are knowledgeable about the local scene, may be called upon to mediate conflict or advise on how to solve a problem. Those who follow this lead and try to help may find themselves alienated from members of the group whose lives were affected unfavorably by or who were opposed to the suggested solution.

The status of the researcher may engender still another type of observational limitation. One thorny status problem, prevalent in anthropology and sociology, is the exclusiveness of sex. Being male, for instance, tends to bar one from direct observation of female activities, as Shaffir (1974, p. 43) discovered while studying the Lubavitcher Chassidim of Montreal. He was forced to accept different orders of data for males and females in that community. Rosalie Wax (1971, p. 46) describes the exclusiveness of certain age and sex categories she encountered as a woman scientist who has worked in several different groups.

All research is subject to the problem of reliability and validity. Although they are common to the experiment and the survey, they also are found in fieldwork. The critics of fieldwork lack confidence in the analysis of and conclusions drawn from field data. This sentiment hinges on their belief that the undisciplined procedures of fieldwork enable researchers, to a greater degree than practitioners of other methodologies, to influence the very situations they are studying, thereby flagrantly violating the canons of scientific objectivity.

A common feature of all social science research is the subjects' response to the "demand characteristics" of the investigation (Orne, 1962; Rosenthal, 1970; Sherman, 1967).

> Researchers in the social sciences are faced with a unique methodological problem: the very conditions of their research constitute an important complex variable for what passes as the findings of their investigations. . . . The activities of the investigator play a crucial role in the data obtained. (Cicourel, 1964, p. 39)

In fieldwork, researchers' very attempts to establish rapport with the people they are studying may be achieved at the expense of a degree of accuracy as to how they normally behave or present themselves in the situations being observed. Indeed, Jack Douglas (1976) argues, for these reasons and others, that traditional methods of field research must be discarded in favor of more penetrating or "investigative" procedures that permit access to these private spheres of life. As Becker (1970, pp. 39-62) so persuasively argues, however, in contrast to the more controlled methods of laboratory experiment and survey interviews, fieldwork is least likely to permit researchers to bias results to correspond with their expectations.

> First, the people the field worker observes are ordinarily constrained to act as they would have in his absence, by the very social constraints whose effects interest him; he therefore has little chance, compared to practitioners of other methods, to influence what they do, for more potent forces are operating. Second, the field worker inevitably, by his continuous presence, gathers much more data and . . . makes and can make many more tests of his hypotheses than researchers who use more formal methods. (pp. 43-44)

One way to attack the validity problem is to play back one's observations to one's subjects in either verbal or written form. From the perspective of the experience of fieldwork, this practice tends to enhance rapport with subjects (assuming the observations are of interest to them and of little threat) by casting them in the roles of local experts and helpful participants in the research project. "Member validation" is one of several contributions that informants can make.

Ethical Issues

Only part of the seemingly endless list of ethical issues that plague social scientists is germane to the social experience of fieldwork. These issues are of three kinds: ethics of concealment, changes in research interests, and violations of the researcher's moral code. The oft-discussed questions of what to write about the group under study, how to protect confidentiality against legal proceedings, and the like are of greatest concern after leaving the field. They appear to play no significant role in the actual collection of data.

Of the three kinds, the ethics of concealment has been examined most thoroughly in the professional literature. It has several facets, one being the issue of the covert observer, or social scientific investigator whose professional aims are unknown to the subjects. They take the individual for someone else, usually one of them. The majority of writers on this topic oppose concealment (e.g., Davis, 1961; Erikson, 1965; Gold, 1958, pp. 221-222), though some scholars argue the contrary (e.g., Douglas, 1976). One way in which this issue can affect the actual experience of fieldwork is recounted by Wallis (1977), who secretly observed a Scientology group:

At the Scientology lodging house the problem was equally difficult. The other residents with whom I dined and breakfasted were committed Scientologists and in a friendly way sought to draw me into their conversations. I found it difficult to participate without suggesting a commitment similar to their own, which I did not feel. Returning to the course material, I found as I progressed that I would shortly have to convey— either aloud or by my continued presence—assent to claims made by Ron Hubbard, the movement's founder, with which I could not agree and of which I could sometimes make little sense. (p. 155)

Even where the observer's true role is known, ethical considerations may arise when there is concealment of certain aspects of the project. Occasionally, the project's very aims are kept secret; Reece and Siegal (1986, pp. 104-108) present a fictive case along these lines and then explore its ethical implications. Or concealment may be more subtle, but no less questionable in the eyes of some scientists, when data are gathered by means of a hidden tape recorder, inadvertently overheard remarks, or intentional eavesdropping. These clandestine methods add tension to the conduct of fieldwork because there is always the risk that what is hidden will somehow be uncovered. Finally, individual researchers may question the propriety of concealing opinions that are diametrically opposed to those held by their subjects. Howard Newby (1977, p. 118), for example, suffered pangs of conscience of this sort when as a liberal university student he interviewed conservative farm workers about their political attitudes. On a related theme, Yablonsky (1965, p. 72) sees the researcher's failure to moralize, when accompanied by an intense interest in deviant life styles, as subtle encouragement of the subject's aberrant behavior.

Changes in research interests are inevitable in field study, where one of the central aims is to discover data capable of generating original theory. Johnson (1975, p. 58) notes how investigators may gain entry to a field setting by stating a particular set of interests, only to find themselves in a moral dilemma because their observations have spawned new interests, ones that the sponsors had no opportunity to consider. To make things worse, these new interests may touch on sensitive matters, where formal permission for observation or interviewing might never be granted.

Then there is the question of the ethical conflict suffered by field researchers who feel compelled to engage in, or at least witness, illegal activities. Should such activities be reported? The agency whose permission has made the research possible may expect this will be done. Should researchers try to maintain or strengthen rapport with their subjects by participating in unlawful events when invited to do so? Polsky (1967/1985, p. 127), who systematically observed criminals in their natural habitat, says that this is up to the individual investigator but that, in the study of criminals anyway, one should make clear what one is prepared to do and see and not to do and see. William Whyte (1943/1981, pp. 313-317) got caught in the ethical dilemma of whether to vote in place of another man in a mayoralty election.

Although all field researchers are faced with ethical decisions in the course of their work, a review of the fieldwork literature reveals that there is no consensus concerning the researcher's duties and responsibilities either to those studied or to the discipline itself. As Roth (1960) has so aptly argued, the controversy between "secret research" and "nonsecret research" is largely misguided, for all research is secret in some way. A more profitable line of investigation is to focus on "how much secrecy shall there be with which people in which circumstances" (p. 283). Most field researchers hold that some measure of responsibility is owed the people under study, though the extent of this conviction and its application are left to each researcher's conscience.

Studying the Unfamiliar

Dealing with the unfamiliar is bound to produce at least some formative experiences. In field investigations the use of unstructured procedures, the pursuit of new propositions, and the participation in strange (for the scientist) activities are the stuff of which memorable involvements are made.

Unlike controlled studies, such as surveys and experiments, field studies avoid prejudgment of the nature of the problem and hence the use of rigid data-gathering devices and hypotheses based on a priori beliefs or hunches concerning the research setting and its participants. Rather, their mission is typically the discovery of new propositions that must be tested more rigorously in subsequent research specially designed for this purpose. Hence field researchers always live, to some extent, with the disquieting notion that they are gathering the wrong data (e.g., Gans, 1968, p. 312), that they should be observing or asking questions about another event or practice instead of the present one. Or they are bewildered by the complexity of the field setting and therefore are unable to identify significant dimensions and categories that can serve to channel their observations and questions. These feelings of uncertainty that accompany open-ended investigation tend, however, to diminish as the investigator grows more familiar with the group under study and those of its activities that bear on the research focus.

Blanche Geer (1964) describes the confusion of her first days in the field as she set out to examine the different perspectives on academic work held by a sample of undergraduates:

> Our proposal seems forgotten. Of course, there were not enough premedical students at the pre-views (summer orientation for freshmen) for me to concentrate on them. To limit myself to our broader objective, the liberal-arts college student, was difficult. The previewers did not group themselves according to the school or college of the University they planned to enter. Out of ordinary politeness . . . I found myself talking to prefreshmen planning careers in engineering, pharmacy, business, and fine arts, as well as the liberal arts. Perhaps it is impossible to stick to a narrow objective in the field. If, as will always be the case, there are unanticipated data at hand, the field worker will broaden his operations to get them. Perhaps he includes such data because they will help him to understand his planned objectives, but he may very well go after them simply because, like the mountain, they are there. (p. 327)

The requirement that a researcher discover something only increases the anxiety of field-work. Nowhere does originality come easily. The field experience does offer a kaleidoscope of contrasts between the observer's routine world and that of the subjects. New patterns of thought and action flash before the observer's eyes. But the question is always: Are these of any importance for science? Researchers note these contrasts and often virtually everything else they perceive. Nevertheless, the ultimate goal is conceptual. One strives to organize these novel perceptions into a grounded or inductive theory, which is done to some extent while still in the field. Some of the generalizations that constitute the emerging theory are born from on-the-spot flashes of insight. Herein lies the art of science. And these insightful moments can be among the most exciting of the fieldwork experience, while their absence can be exasperating, if not discouraging.

As if unstructured research procedure and obligatory discovery were not enough, field investigators must also be ready to cope with unfamiliar events. Furthermore, they must learn new ways of behaving and possibly new skills, the mastery of which are crucial for success in their projects. Powdermaker (1968) describes this problem for the field anthropologist:

> During the first month or so the field worker proceeds very slowly, making use of all his sensory impressions and intuitions. He walks warily and attempts to learn as quickly as possible the most important forms of native etiquette and taboos. When in doubt he falls back on his own sense of politeness and sensitivity to the feelings of others. He likewise has to cope with his own emotional problems, for he often experiences anxieties in a strange situation. He may be overwhelmed by the difficulties of really getting "inside" an alien culture and of learning an unrecorded or other strange language. He may wonder whether he should intrude into the privacy of people's lives by asking them questions. Field workers vary in their degree of shyness, but most people of any sensitivity experience some feelings of this type when they first enter a new field situation. (p. 419)

MARGINALITY

If there is one especially well-suited adjective that describes the social experiences of field-work, it is *marginality*. Field researchers and their activities are marginal in several ways. For one, field research—because of its emphasis on direct human contact, subjective understanding of others' motives and wants, and broad participation in their daily affairs—is closer to the humanities than most forms of social scientific research. Although structured data collection is now the most traveled methodological route in many social sciences, field researchers are riding off in a different direction. For this they are scorned by many positivists, who see field research as a weak science. From the humanists' perspective, however, it is still too scientific, owing to its concern with validity, testable hypotheses, replicability, and the like. The public, who might be expected to take a neutral stand in this intellectual debate, sometimes appears to have embraced the stereotype that good social science is characterized only by quantitative rigor. Thus it occasionally happens that field researchers also have to convince even their subjects and sponsors that theirs is a legitimate approach for the problem at hand.

Yet the field researcher who is identified as an atypical social scientist has an advantage. For here is a scientist who is viewed by group members as interested enough in them and their activities to maintain extensive direct contact instead of relying solely or chiefly on such substitutes as questionnaires and measurement scales. Many subjects appreciate this special effort. They seem to know that their lives are too complicated to be studied accurately and adequately by structured means alone. By the same token, it is to be expected that field researchers will make some subjects uneasy by their tendency to plumb the group's dark secrets.

Field researchers are also marginal in their own professions (except in anthropology). Recall Lofland's (1976, p. 13) observation that many social scientists are unsuited for engaging in field study. Being rather asocial, reclusive, and occasionally abrasive, they would fail to gain entrance to the setting to be examined or, if they somehow succeeded, they would fail to maintain the level of rapport upon which good field research depends. Social scientists who have the requisite interpersonal skills to do fieldwork are a minority; providing they discover their talents, they find occupational fulfillment in ways most of their colleagues see as strange or exotic.

Once in the field, all participant observers, if they are known as such to their subjects, are more or less marginal to their subjects' world.

The former never quite belong, especially while the research is getting under way—a fact that is made amply clear time and again. As Hughes (1960) argues, even though the sociologist might report observations made as a member of the group under study, "the member becomes something of a stranger in the very act of objectifying and reporting his experiences" (p. ix). In a similar vein, Freilich (1970), writing about anthropologists, cautions against the common desire among researchers to become a native:

> Irrespective of what role he assumes, the anthropologist remains a *marginal man* in the community, an outsider. No matter how skilled he is in the native tongue, how nimble in handling strange social relationships, how artistic in performing social and religious rituals, and how attached he is to local beliefs, goals, and values, the anthropologist rarely deludes himself into thinking that many community members really regard him as one of them. (p. 2)

From the researcher's standpoint there are humbling experiences inherent in this kind of marginality. Lofland (1976, p. 14) points out that one must admit to laymen that one is ignorant, though willing to learn. Such an admission is incongruent with the self-image of savant, of dignified university professor, of learned Ph.D. As a field researcher, one is a mere student in need of particular instruction or general socialization.

What is worse, subjects have been known to take advantage of this situation and put on or mislead the observer about aspects of their lives of interest to the study (e.g., Visano, 1987, p. 67). Field researchers must be alert to such deception but be prepared to take it in good stride. Nonetheless, being the object of a put-on, while it adds zest to the subjects' routine, frequently is embarrassing to the "mark" (Stebbins, 1975).

And fieldwork, even when conducted in the researcher's own community, has been known to become all-absorbing, leaving time only for absolutely mandatory family and work activities. Marginality is the best characterization of the committed social scientist, who spends practically every waking minute riding with police or observing juvenile gangs. As with professionals in any occupation, the line between work and leisure is sometimes erased for field researchers, which casts them in a strange light when viewed from the perspective of a leisure-oriented society.

On balance, marginality, despite its drawbacks, seems to breed a peculiar strain of motivation among committed field researchers. Being atypical in one's profession, to the extent that such a condition is free of stigma, has the potential appeal of salutary visibility, of being commendably different. Field researchers have stories to tell about their data-collection exploits that enchant students and colleagues, most of whom have no such accounts to swap. Field researchers have "been around" in a way seldom matched by the run-of-the-mill social scientist. They have gained in personal sophistication through contact with other cultures and lifestyles and through solving thorny interpersonal problems in the course of completing their projects.

CONCLUSION

As most field researchers would admit, the so-called rules and canons of fieldwork frequently are bent and twisted to accommodate the particular demands and requirements of the fieldwork situation and the personal characteristics of the researcher. The following observations reflect this view clearly and accurately:

> As every researcher knows, there is more to doing research than is dreamt of in philosophies of science, and texts in methodology offer answers to only a fraction of the problems one encounters. The best laid research plans run up against unforeseen contingencies in the collection and analysis of data; the data one collects may prove to have little to do with the hypotheses one sets out to test; unexpected findings inspire new ideas. No matter how carefully one plans in advance, research is designed in the course of its execution. The finished monograph is the result of hundreds of decisions, large and small, made while the research is underway and our standard texts do not give us procedures and techniques for making these decisions. . . . I must take issue with one point . . . that social research being what it is, we can never escape the necessity to improvise, the surprise of

the unexpected, our dependence on inspiration. . . . It is possible, after all, to reflect on one's difficulties and inspirations and see how they could be handled more rationally the next time around. In short, one can be methodical about matters that earlier had been left to chance and improvisation and thus cut down the area of guess work. (Becker, 1965a, pp. 602-603)

The sociological enterprise of theory and research has been presented as an idealized process, immaculately conceived in design and elegantly executed in practice. My discussions of theory, measurement, instrumentation, sampling strategies, resolutions of issues of validity, and the generation of valid causal propositions by various methods proceeded on an assumption. This assumption was that once the proper rules were learned, adequate theory would be forthcoming. Unfortunately, of course, this is seldom the case. Each theorist or methodologist takes rules of method and inference and molds them to fit her particular problem—and personality. (Denzin, 1989, p. 249)

REFERENCES

Adler, P.A. (1985). Wheeling and Dealing. New York: Columbia University Press.

Adler, P.A., & Adler, P. (1987). Membership Roles in Field Research. Newbury Park, CA: Sage.

Barnes, J.A. (1963). Some Ethical Problems in Modern Fieldwork. *British Journal of Sociology*, 14, 118-134.

Becker, H.S. (1963). Outsiders: The Sociology of Deviance. New York: Free Press.

Becker, H.S. (1965a). Review of Sociologists at Work. *American Sociological Review*, 30, 602-603.

Becker, H.S. (1970). Sociological Work: Method and Substance. Chicago: Aldine.

Becker, H.S. & Geer, B., Hughes, E.C., Strauss, A.L. (1961). Boys in White. Chicago: University of Chicago Press.

Berg, B.L. (1989). Qualitative Research Methods. Boston: Allyn & Bacon.

Blau, P.M. (1955). The Dynamics of Bureaucracy. Chicago: University of Chicago Press.

Blumer, H. (1986). Symbolic Interactionism. Berkeley: University of California Press.

Briggs, J.L. (1986). Kapluna Daughter. In P. Golde (Ed.), *Women in the Field* (pp. 19-46, 2nd ed.). Berkeley: University of California Press.

Cicourel, A.V. (1964). Method and Measurement in Sociology. New York: Free Press.

Davis, F. (1961). Comment on "Initial Interaction of Newcomers in Alcoholics Anonymous." *Social Problems*, 8, 364-365.

Denzin, N.K. (1989). The Research Act (3rd ed.) Englewood Cliffs, NJ: Prentice-Hall.

Douglas, J.D. (1976). Investigating Social Research: Individual and Team Field Research. Beverly Hills, CA: Sage.

Emerson, R.M. (Ed.). (1983). Contemporary Field Research: A Collection of Readings. Boston: Little, Brown.

Ericson, R.V. (1981). Making Crime: A Study of Detective Work. Toronto, Ont: Butterworths.

Erikson, K.T. (1965). A Comment on Disguised Observation in Sociology. *Social Problems*, 14, 366-373.

Fox, K.J. (1987). Real Punks and Pretenders. *Journal of Contemporary Ethnography*, 16, 344-370.

Freilich, M. (1970). Toward a Formalization of Field-work. In M. Freilich (Ed.), *Marginal Natives*. New York: Harper & Row.

Friedman, R.A. (1989). Interaction Norms as Carriers of Organizational Culture: A Study of Labour Negotiations at International Harvester. *Journal of Contemporary Ethnography*, 18, 3-29.

Gans, H. (1968). The Participant Observer as a Human Being: Observations on the Personal Aspects of Fieldwork. In H.S. Becker, B. Greer, D. Reisman, & R. Weiss (Eds.), *Institutions and the Person* (pp. 300-317). Chicago: Aldine.

Geer, B. (1964). First Days in the Field. In P. Hammond (Ed.), *Sociologists at Work* (pp. 322-344). New York: Basic Books.

Glaser, B.G. & Strauss, A.L. (1967). The Discovery of Grounded Theory. Chicago: Aldine.

Glaser, B.G. & Strauss, A.L. (1968). Time for Dying. Chicago: Aldine.

Glazer, M. (1972). The Research Adventure: Promise and Problems of Fieldwork. New York: Random House.

Goffman, E. (1959). The Presentation of Self in Everyday Life. Garden City, NY: Doubleday.

Goffman, E. (1961). Asylums: Essays on the Social Situation of Mental Patients and Other Inmates. Garden City, NY: Doubleday.

Golde, P. (1986). Odyssey of Encounter. In P. Golde (Ed.), *Women in the Field: Anthropological Experiences* (pp. 67-96, 2nd ed.). Berkeley: University of California Press.

Gold, R.L. (1958). Roles in Sociological Observations. *Social Forces*, 36, 217-223.

Hammersley, M. & Atkinson, P. (1983). Ethnography: Principals in Practice. London, UK: Tavistock.

Hughes, E.C. (1960). Introduction: The Place of Fieldwork and Social Science. In B.H. Junker (Ed.), *Fieldwork: An Introduction to the Social Sciences* (pp. iii-xiii). Chicago: University of Chicago Press.

Johnson, J.M. (1975). Doing Field Research. New York: Free Press.

Junker, B.H. (1960). Fieldwork: An Introduction to the Social Sciences. Chicago: University of Chicago Press.

Liebow, E. (1967). Tally's Corner. Boston: Little, Brown.

Lofland, J.A. (1971). Analyzing Social Settings: A Guide to Qualitative Observation and Analysis. Belmont, CA: Wadsworth.

Lofland, J.A. (1976). Doing Social Life: The Qualitative Study of Human Interaction in Natural Settings. New York: John Wiley.

Lofland, J.A. & Lofland, L. (1984). Analyzing Social Settings: A Guide to Qualitative Observation and Analysis (2nd ed.). Belmont, CA: Wadsworth.

Malinowski, B. (1922). The Argonauts of the Western Pacific. London, UK: Routledge.

McCall, G.J. & Simmons, J.L. (Eds). (1969). Issues in Participant Observation. Reading, MA: Addison-Wesley.

Newby, H. (1977). In the Field: Reflection on the Study of Suffolk Farm Workers. In C. Bell & H. Newby (Eds.), *Doing Sociological Research* (pp. 108-129). London, UK: Allen & Unwin.

Orne, M.T. (1962). On the Social Psychology of the Psychological Experiment. *American Psychologist*, 17, 776-783.

Polsky, N. (1985). Hustlers, Beats, and Others. Chicago: University of Chicago Press. (Original work published 1967)

Powdermaker, H. (1968). Fieldwork. In D.L. Sills (Ed.), *International Encyclopedia of the Social Sciences* (Vol. 5, pp. 418-424). New York: Macmillan.

Prus, R. (1987). Generic Social Processes: Maximizing Conceptual Development in Ethnographic Research. *Journal of Contemporary Ethnography*, 16, 250-293.

Reece, R.D., & Siegal, H.A. (1986). Studying People: A Primer in the Ethics of Social Research. Macon, GA: Mercer University Press.

Robinson, W.S. (1951). A Logical Structure of Analytic Induction. *American Sociological Review*, 16, 812-818.

Rosenthal, R. (1970). Interpersonal Expectations. In R. Rosenthal & R. Rosnow (Eds.), *Sources of Artifact in Social Research* (pp. 181-277). New York: Academic Press.

Roth, J. (1960). Comments on Secret Observation. *Social Problems*, 9, 283-284.

Scott, G.G. (1983). The Magicians: A Study of the Use of Power in a Black Magic Group. New York: Irvington.

Shaffir, W.B. (1974). Life in a Religious Community. Toronto: Holt, Rinehart & Winston.

Shaffir, William, Marshall, Victor, & Haas, J. (1980). Competing Commitments: Unanticipated Problems of Field Research. *Qualitative Sociology*, 2, 56-71.

Sherman, S.R. (1967). Demand Curves in an Experiment on Attitude Change. *Sociometry*, 30, 246-261.

Stebbins, R.A. (1975). Putting People On: Deception of Our Fellow Man in Everyday Life. *Sociology and Social Research*, 59, 189-200.

Strauss, A.L. (1987). Qualitative Analysis for Social Scientists. New York: Cambridge University Press.

Taylor, S. J. & Bogdan, R. (1984). Introduction to Qualitative Research Methods: The Search for Meaning (2nd ed). New York: John Wiley.

Turner, R.H. (1953). The Quest for Universals in Sociological Research. *American Sociological Review*, 18, 604-611.

Visano, L.A. (1987). This Idle Trade: The Occupational Patterns of Male Prostitution. Concord, Ont: VitaSana.

Wallis, R. (1977). The Moral Career of a Research Project. In C. Bell & H. Newby (Eds.), *Doing Sociological Research* (pp. 149-167). London, UK: Allen & Unwin.

Wax, R.H. (1952). Field Methods and Techniques: Reciprocity as a Field Technique. *Human Organization*, 11, 34-37.

Wax, R. H. (1971). Doing Fieldwork: Warnings and Advice. Chicago: University of Chicago Press.

Webb, E.J., Campbell, D.T. Schwartz, R.D. Sechrest, Lee, & Grove, J.B. (1981). Nonreactive Measures in the Social Science (2nd ed.). Boston: Houghton Mifflin.

Wharton, C.S. (1987). Establishing Shelters for Battered Women. *Qualitative Sociology*, 10, 146-163.

Whyte, W.F. (1981). Street Corner Society. Chicago: University of Chicago Press. (Original work published 1943)

Yablonsky, L. (1965). Experiences with the Criminal Community. In A. Gouldner & S.M. Miller (Eds.), *Applied Sociology* (pp. 55-73). New York: Free Press.

Znaniecki, F. (1934). The Method of Sociology. New York: Farrar & Rinehart.

Jorgensen's contribution to this volume introduces and defines the qualitative methodology of participant observation. Direct involvement with the population that is being studied on a frequent basis provides access to peoples' lives and allows for a strategy of inquiry of social phenomena that would otherwise be obscured from an outsider. The author discusses and identifies the uses and limitations of this fieldwork method along with those distinguishing factors that characterize its approach. Throughout his discussion, Jorgensen compares and contrasts participant observation with that of other research methodologies, mainly survey research and experimental designs of data collection. Numerous examples of qualitative researchers' theoretical views about this observational technique are presented, along with a number of studies the researchers conducted that illustrate the historical roots of participant observation as a research tool.

THE METHODOLOGY
OF PARTICIPANT OBSERVATION

DANNY L. JORGENSEN

USES OF PARTICIPANT OBSERVATION

The methodology of participant observation is appropriate for studies of almost every aspect of human existence. Through participant observation, it is possible to describe what goes on, who or what is involved, when and where things happen, how they occur, and why—at least from the standpoint of participants—things happen as they do in particular situations. The methodology of participant observation is exceptional for studying processes, relationships among people and events, the organization of people and events, continuities over time, and patterns, as well as the immediate sociocultural contexts in which human existence unfolds.

Participant observation is especially appropriate for scholarly problems when

- little is known about the phenomenon (a newly formed group or movement, emotion work, fundamentalist Christian schools, improvised human conduct);

– there are important differences between the views of insiders as opposed to outsiders (ethnic groups, labor unions, management, subcultures such as occultists, poker players, or nude beachers, and even occupations like physicians, ministers, newscasters, or scientists);

– the phenomenon is somehow obscured from the view of outsiders (private, intimate interactions and groups, such as physical and mental illness, teenage sexuality, family life, or religious ritual); or

– the phenomenon is hidden from public view (crime and deviance, secretive groups and organizations, such as drug users and dealers, cultic and sectarian religions).

The methodology of participant observation is not appropriate, however, for every scholarly problem. Questions about fairly large populations, the precise causal relationships among limited sets of variables, and measurable amounts of something are better addressed by other methods, such as surveys or experiments. Participant observation is most appropriate when certain minimal conditions are present:

– the research problem is concerned with human meanings and interactions viewed from the insiders' perspective;

– the phenomenon of investigation is observable within an everyday life situation or setting;

– the researcher is able to gain access to an appropriate setting;

– the phenomenon is sufficiently limited in size and location to be studied as a case;

– study questions are appropriate for case study; and

– the research problem can be addressed by qualitative data gathered by direct observation and other means pertinent to the field setting.

Participant observation is especially appropriate for exploratory studies, descriptive studies, and studies aimed at generating theoretical interpretations. Though less useful for testing theories, findings of participant observational research certainly are appropriate for critically examining theories and other claims to knowledge.

FEATURES OF PARTICIPANT OBSERVATION

The methodology of participant observation consists of principles, strategies, procedures, methods, and techniques of research. Participant observation is defined here in terms of seven basic features:

(1) a special interest in human meaning and interaction as viewed from the perspective of people who are insiders or members of particular situations and settings;

(2) location in the here and now of everyday life situations and settings as the foundation of inquiry and method;

(3) a form of theory and theorizing stressing interpretation and understanding of human existence;

(4) a logic and process of inquiry that is open-ended, flexible, opportunistic, and requires constant redefinition of what is problematic, based on facts gathered in concrete settings of human existence;

(5) an in-depth, qualitative, case study approach and design;

(6) the performance of a participant role or roles that involves establishing and maintaining relationships with natives in the field; and

(7) the use of direct observation along with other methods of gathering information.

Ultimately, the methodology of participant observation aims to generate practical and theoretical truths about human life grounded in the realities of daily existence.

THE INSIDERS' VIEWPOINT

In the course of daily life, people make sense of the world around them; they give it meaning and they interact on the basis of these meanings (Schutz, 1967; Blumer, 1969; Denzin, 1978). If people define a situation as real, it is real in its consequences (Thomas and Thomas, 1928). People, of course, may be "mistaken" about what something means, yet even erroneous beliefs have real consequences. The world of everyday life constitutes *reality* for its inhabitants, natives, insiders, or members (Lyman and Scott, 1970, 1975; Berger and Luckmann, 1966). The insiders' conception of reality is not directly accessible to aliens, outsiders, or nonmembers, all of whom necessarily experience it initially as a stranger (Schutz, 1967; Simmel, 1950).

It is not possible to acquire more than a very crude notion of the insiders' world, for instance, until you comprehend the culture and language that is used to communicate its meanings (Hall, 1959, 1966). Greater comprehension requires that you understand the words of a language as they are used in particular situations (see Hall, 1976). Insiders manage, manipulate, and negotiate meanings in particular situations, intentionally and unintentionally obscuring, hiding, or concealing these meanings further from the viewpoint of outsiders (Goffman, 1959, 1974; Douglas, 1976).

The methodology of participant observation focuses on the meanings of human existence as seen from the standpoint of insiders (Znaniecki, 1934; Spradley, 1980). The world of everyday life as viewed from the standpoint of insiders is the fundamental reality to be described by participant observation. Put still differently, the methodology of participant observation seeks to uncover, make accessible, and reveal the meanings (realities) people use to make sense out of their daily lives. In placing the meaning of everyday life first, the methodology of participant observation differs from approaches that begin with concepts defined by way of existing theories and hypotheses.

Ellis (1986) became a participant observer in two Chesapeake communities for the purpose of describing everyday life activities within these fishing communities from the perspective of its members. Latour and Woolgar (1979) and Lynch (1985) described the insiders' conception of laboratory science using participant observational methods. Through participant observation, Mitchell (1983) described the experiences and meanings of mountaineering from the insiders' viewpoint. Kleinman (1984) used a participant observational methodology to reveal the meanings of seminary life from the standpoint of insiders. Chenitz and Swanson

(1986) advocated participant observation for developing theories grounded in practice that are useful for nursing. Gallimeier (1987, forthcoming) focused on meanings and experiences of professional hockey players on the basis of participant observation of this sport. In short, then, the methodology of participant observation provides direct experiential and observational access to the insiders' world of meaning.

THE WORLD OF EVERYDAY LIFE

The world of everyday life is for the methodology of participant observation the ordinary, usual, typical, routine, or natural environment of human existence. This world stands in contrast to environments created and manipulated by researchers, as illustrated by experiments and surveys. In comparison with their natural habitat, animals are known to behave and interact differently in environments (such as a zoo or a laboratory) constructed and manipulated by researchers. Human beings likewise behave differently when they know they are being studied, especially when the researcher is very obstrusively manipulating the environment (see Roethlisberger and Dickson, 1939; Douglas, 1976; Douglas et al., 1980).

The *here* and *now* of everyday life is important to the methodology of participant observation in at least two fundamental ways. One, that is where the researcher begins with the process of defining and refining issues and problems for study. Two, they are where the researcher participates. No matter the original source of the study problem (abstract theory, practical experience, coincidence, or whatever), precisely what will be studied and how it will be regarded as problematic must be clarified and refined by reference to human existence in everyday life situations. Similarly, the researcher participates and observes in everyday life situations. Every effort must be made to minimize the extent to which the researcher disrupts and otherwise intrudes as an alien, or nonparticipant, in the situations studied. Taking the role of a participant provides the researcher with a means of conducting fairly *unobtrusive* observations.

Sanders (1988), for instance, participated directly in four tattoo parlors as a "regular" while observing this everyday life environment. To study the social world of preschool children, Mandell (1988) participated with and observed children on playgrounds, in classrooms, hallways, bathrooms, and lunchrooms of two daycare centers. Hockey (1986) studied the culture of enlisted men in the British Army from the concrete situations and settings of initial recruitment and basic training, to daily life in an infantry battalion, patrol in Northern Ireland, and rambunctious off-duty social life. To study stress and mental health as well as design an appropriate intervention strategy in a southern Black community, Dressler (1987) participated in and observed this environment, gathered information from key informants, and recruited research assistants and consultants from the community being studied.

INTERPRETATIVE THEORY AND THEORIZING

The methodology of participant observation aims to provide practical and theoretical truths about human existence. From this standpoint, a "theory" may be defined as a set of concepts and generalizations. Theories provide a perspective, a way of seeing, or an interpretation aimed at understanding some phenomenon (see Blumer, 1969; Agar, 1986). The methodology of participant observation provokes concepts and generalizations formulated as interpretative theories. These concepts and generalizations may be used to examine critically existing hypotheses and theories. Concepts, generalizations, and interpretations inspired through participant observation are useful for making practical decisions (see Chenitz and Swanson, 1986; Williams, 1986).

Interpretative theory differs from conceptions of theory aimed at explanation, prediction, and control of human phenomena (see Douglas et al., 1980; Polkinghorne, 1983; Agar, 1986). Explanatory theories are composed of logically interrelated propositions. Ideally, they contain lawlike propositions providing causal explanations. Explanatory approaches to theorizing stress the testing of propositions (or hypotheses) anticipating relations among concepts (see Wallace, 1971; Gibbs, 1972; Blalock, 1971).

Explanatory theorizing, especially in the form of hypothesis testing, involves a "logic of verification" (Kaplan, 1964). This logic operates by (1) the definition of a problem for study in the form of a hypothesis or hypotheses derived from or otherwise related to an abstract body of theoretical knowledge, (2) the definition of concepts contained in these hypotheses by procedures for measuring them (called operationalization), and (3) the precise measurement of concepts, preferably *quantitatively* (by degrees or amounts). Experiments and many forms of survey research, for instance, are employed for the purpose of testing hypotheses and explanatory theories.

Altheide (1976), to illustrate, conducted a study of television news through participant observation. He was interested in bias or distortions in news making. Having reviewed relevant scholarly literature, Altheide was aware of several different perspectives on this issue, as well as specific contentions (hypotheses) explaining why or how news is biased. He suspected that bias was somehow related to how news workers put together television news programs. With this general idea, but without specific hypotheses (operational definitions or measures), Altheide set out to describe news workers' images of their jobs and how they actually did their work. His findings describe in qualitative detail how practical and organizational features of doing news work promote ways of looking at events that distort them. The emergent, interpretative theory of the news perspective as bias provided a solid, empirical basis for questioning the accuracy of some previous claims (if not the complete rejection of these hypotheses) and reinterpreting other theoretical claims. This study, furthermore, resulted in subsequent research and refinement of Altheide's interpretative theory of news making (see Altheide, 1985; Altheide and Snow, 1979).

The participant observational study of delinquents by Emerson (1969) resulted in the more general concept of "last resorts" (Emerson, 1981). Suttles's (1968) participant observational study of slums led to theorizing about communities (Suttles, 1972). Irwin's (1970) participant observational study of prisoners resulted in a typology of felons and a theoretical critique of contemporary prisons. Fox's (1987) participant observational study of "punks" resulted in a typology of punk status and a general conception of the informal stratification of this antiestablishment subculture. Goffman's (1961) highly influential theoretical concept of "total institutions" emerged from participant observation in a hospital (see also Richard, 1986).

AN OPEN-ENDED LOGIC AND PROCESS OF INQUIRY

Participant observational inquiry may proceed on the basis of some more or less abstract idea or it may derive from involvement with a field setting. Either way, what is problematic must be defined or redefined specifically by reference to the actual study setting. The methodology of participant observation stresses a "logic of discovery," a process aimed at instigating concepts, generalizations, and theories (Kaplan, 1964). It, in other words, aims to build theories grounded in concrete human realities (Glazer and Strauss, 1967; Agar, 1986). This requires a flexible, open-ended process for identifying and defining a problem or problems for study, concepts, and appropriate procedures for collecting and evaluating evidence.

The methodology of participant observation encourages the researcher to begin with the immediate experience of human life in concrete situations and settings, and make the most of whatever opportunities are presented (see Whyte, 1984). Scott (1968), for instance, took advantage of a longstanding interest in horse racing to conduct a participant observational study of the racing game. While the researcher may have a theoretical interest in being there, exactly what concepts are important, how they are or are not related, and what, therefore, is problematic should remain open and subject to refinement and definition based on what the researcher is able to uncover and observe. This process and logic of inquiry requires the researcher to define the problem of study and be constantly open to its redefinition based on information collected in the field. It further encourages the researcher to define concepts by providing elaborate *qualitative* descriptions of

them in terms of what people do and say in everyday life situations.

Wallis (1977), for instance, used participant observation to gather information on Scientology concerning a set of "broad themes" rather than hypotheses. Weppner (1983) participated in an addiction treatment program prior to defining problems precisely for further study. Much like Weppner, Sudnow (1978) studied and played jazz piano before making the organization of improvised conduct the subject of study. In other words, Sudnow's special interest in how improvised conduct is organized and accomplished partly derived from and was informed by his piano-playing experiences.

IN-DEPTH CASE STUDIES

Case studies take a variety of forms, most of which do not involve participant observations (see Yin, 1984). The methodology of participant observation, however, generally is practiced as a form of *case study*. This involves the detailed description and analysis of an individual case (Becker, 1968, pp. 232-38). Case studies stress the holistic examination of a phenomenon, and they seek to avoid the separation of components from the larger context to which these matters may be related. The case studied may be a culture, society, community, subculture, organization, group, or phenomenon such as beliefs, practices, or interactions, as well as almost any other aspect of human existence. Gans (1962), for instance, studied the case of urban villagers. Lofland (1966) studied the case of religious conversion. Becker et al. (1961) studied the case of student medical school culture.

Case studies conducted by way of participant observation attempt to describe comprehensively and exhaustively a phenomenon in terms of a research problem. Scholarly definition of the problem generally provides a logic justifying study of a single case. The phenomenon, for instance, may be sufficiently important or unique to justify intensive investigation. Whether or not, or to the extent to which, the case is representative of some larger population may be regarded as not especially relevant, or this matter simply may be left open to further study. Comparative case studies generally depend on previous studies of a single case. Ellis (1986), for instance, participated in two fishing communities. This enabled her to compare and contrast different cases. The logic of the case study clearly differs from the survey research emphasis on gathering data on a large cross section of some population, or the emphasis of experiments on demonstrating causation by control and comparison of variables.

For some participant observational studies, questions concerning representativeness or possible bias resulting from study of a single instance receive further attention (see Douglas, 1985). The research may have good reasons for focusing on a single case, such as argument that it is "typical," among other bases for sampling theoretically (Glazer and Strauss, 1967). The use of nonprobability (theoretical) sampling techniques also applies to selective observation conducted *within* a case. Although participant observational case studies generally do not employ conventional methods of probability sampling, such techniques certainly may be used. Participant observations in this way differs from most forms of survey research, as well as from experiments that use probability to select subjects.

Hochschild (1983), for instance, was interested in the private and public face of human emotions, or simply "emotion work." This study was exploratory and aimed to generate theory. Partly for this reason Hochschild conducted an in-depth case study—based on a participant observational methodology—of emotion work, rather than conducting an experiment or some form of survey research.

Theoretical logics were used to select phenomena for study. Initially a questionnaire was used like a fishing net to catch indications of how people manage emotions. Hochschild had a variety of good theoretical reasons for participating as a flight attendant while observing: emotion work is especially important in service occupations; flight attendants are neither high nor low prestige; and male flight attendants make possible gender comparisons. Interviews were conducted with people in the industry (union officials, pilots, bill collectors, a sex therapist, a receptionist, recruiters, managers, and other attendants) partly to gain different existential perspectives on emotion work. Even

the selection of Delta Airlines was justified theoretically; its standards were higher and its worker demands lower than other companies. Emotion work was more visible and sharper in this exaggerated instance. Hochschild does supplement the Delta data, however, with observations of several other airlines, thereby checking for too extraordinary results.

THE PARTICIPANT ROLE

The methodology of participant observation requires that the researcher become directly involved as a participant in peoples' daily lives. The participant role provides access to the world of everyday life from the standpoint of a member or insider. Human meaning and interaction is approached through sympathetic introspection (Cooley [1930] 1969), verstehen (Weber, 1949), a humanistic coefficient (Znaniecki, 1934), or sympathetic reconstruction (MacIver, 1942). Participant observation, in other words, is a very special strategy aspects of method for gaining access to the interior, seemingly subjective aspects of human existence (see Krieger, 1985). Through participation, the researcher is able to observe and experience the meanings and interactions of people from the role of an insider.

Participant involvements may range from the performance of nominal and marginal roles to the performance of native, insider, or membership roles (Junker, 1960; Gold, 1954, 1958, 1969). The researcher's involvement may be *overt* (with the knowledge of insiders), *covert* (without the knowledge of insiders), or—most likely—insiders selectively will be provided with knowledge of the researcher's interests and purposes (see Adler and Adler, 1987; Adler, Adler, and Rochford, 1986). It is highly desirable for the participant observer to perform multiple roles during the course of a project, and gain at least a comfortable degree of rapport, even intimacy, with the people, situations, and settings of research.

As a participant, the researcher must sustain access once it has been granted, and maintain relationships with people in the field (see Johnson, 1975). The relationship between the participant as observer, people in the field setting, and the larger context of human interaction is one of the key components of this methodology. The character of field relations heavily influences the researcher's ability to collect accurate, truthful information.

Hayano (1982), for instance, became a professional cardplayer (became the phenomenon studied) as part of his participant observational investigation of poker players. Similarly, Sudnow (1978) became a jazz pianist to study improvised conduct. Hayano and Sudnow, it should be noted, were interested in poker playing and jazz piano for important biographical (or personal) reasons not directly related to scholarly concerns. Forrest (1986) used apprenticeship strategically as a participant observer role. Peshkin (1986), on the other hand, nominally participated in activities at a fundamentalist Christian school studied while observing and retaining the identity of a researcher. Likewise, Wallis's (1977) participation in Scientology was limited to a brief training period. Douglas became a nude beacher to study this scene, but he also participated as a member of the home owners' association opposed to the nude beach (Douglas and Rasmussen, with Flanagan, 1977). Hayano, Sudnow, and Wallis participated covertly for the most part, while Peshkin's participant role was entirely overt. Douglas did not reveal his research interests (and certainly not his participation as a nude beacher) to the home owners, but, depending on the circumstances, his everyday life identities sometimes were acknowledged to the nude beachers.

Methods of Collecting Information

Direct observation is the primary method of gathering information, but the participant observer usually uses other strategies. Depending on the nature and extent of participant involvement, the researcher's immediate experience can be an extremely valuable source of data (Cooley, [1930] 1969; Znaniecki, 1934, pp. 157-67). Documents (newspapers, letters, diaries, memoranda), as well as other forms of communication (audio recordings, photography, videotapes, radio, television) and artifacts (art, tools, clothing, buildings) are readily available in many field settings. The researcher may find informants knowledgeable about matters of interest, and gather life histories (Thomas and Znaniecki, 1918-19). Participant observers commonly gather data through casual conversations, in-depth, informal, and unstructured interviews, as well as formally structured interviews and questionnaires (see Fine, 1987; Wallis, 1977).

Participant observation may be conducted by a single researcher. Or researchers may employ a team strategy (see Lynd and Lynd, 1929; Warner and Lunt, 1941, 1942; Warner and Srole, 1945; Warner, 1959; Vidich and Bensman, 1968; Becker et al., 1961). Team strategies offer distinctive advantages, such as the possibility of performing different participant and observer roles simultaneously as well as exploiting various talents and identities (such as gender) of the researchers (see Golde, 1970; Douglas, 1976; Douglas and Rasmussen, with Flanagan, 1977; Warren and Rasmussen, 1977).

It is extremely important that the results of participant observational study be recorded. Participant observers generally keep a diary or log of activities in the field, unique experiences, and other matters of possible interest. The researcher may keep written records or tape-record observations while in the field or shortly after some period of observation. Action may be recorded by way of photographic, audio, and/or audio-video equipment. Increasingly, computers have been employed to record, file, and otherwise assist in the organization and analysis of research materials (see Conrad and Reinhartz, 1984).

Hochschild (1983), to illustrate, used questionnaires, several forms of interviewing, and direct observation in studying emotion work. Wallis (1977) depended extensively on documents, used a questionnaire, conducted informal interviews, and briefly participated as an observer in collecting data on Scientology. Fine (1987) participated and observed among Little Leaguers, and used a questionnaire. Altheide (1976) used direct observation and formal and informal interviewing, collected documents and newscasts, and engaged in natural experiments in studying news making. Hayano (1982), in studying poker players, depended primarily on observation and memory, making records after a period of intense participation. Johnson (1975) recorded the results of direct observation and informal interviews on an audio recording during and after periods of participant observation of welfare workers. Spradley (1970) used direct observation, informal and formal interviews, a life history, and depended on native informants for information on urban alcoholics.

SUMMARY

The methodology of participant observation is appropriate for a wide range of scholarly problems pertinent to human existence. It focuses on human interaction and meaning viewed from the insiders' viewpoint in everyday life situations and settings. It aims to generate practical and theoretical truths formulated as interpretative theories. The methodology of participant observation involves a flexible, open-ended, opportunistic process and logic of inquiry through which what is studied constantly is subject to redefinition based on field experience and observation. Participant observation generally is practiced as a form of case study that concentrates on in-depth description and analysis of some phenomenon or set of phenomena. Participation is a strategy for gaining access to otherwise inaccessible dimensions of human life and experience. Direct observation and experience are primary forms and methods of data collection, but the researcher also may conduct interviews, collect documents, and use other methods of gathering information.

Participant observation is appropriate for a wide range of problems, especially when the meanings people use to define and interact with their ordinary environment are central issues. Though especially useful for exploratory and descriptive research purposes, participant observation results in generalizations useful for forming new theories as well as testing existing ones. The methodology of participant observation differs considerably from positivistic approaches, especially experiments and surveys.

Unlike participant observation, experiments demand control and manipulation of the research environment. Experiments are best suited for testing specific hypotheses and theories conceived in terms of causal relationships among quantitatively measured variables. Unlike participant observation, experiments are highly obtrusive and not especially useful for exploratory purposes. Survey research is best suited for collecting a vast amount of information regarding public opinion as well as basic (demographic) characteristics of populations (see Babbie, 1973; Fowler, 1984).

Survey questionnaires or interviews enable the researcher to collect a standardized set of data, much of it in quantitative form, from relatively small samples of subjects. Probability sampling techniques enable the researcher to generalize these findings to larger populations. Like experiments, survey research is useful for testing theories and providing explanations.

REFERENCES

Adler, P. A. (1985). Wheeling and Dealing. New York: Columbia University Press.

Adler, P. A. & Adler, P. and Rochford, Jr., E.B. (Eds.) (1986). The Politics of Participation in Field Research [Special Issue]. *Urban Life* 14 (4, January).

Agar, M. (1986). Speaking of Ethnography. Beverly Hills, CA: Sage.

Altheide, D. L. (1976). Creating Reality. Beverly Hills, CA: Sage.

_____. (1985). Media Power. Beverly Hills, CA: Sage.

Altheide, D. L. and Snow, R. (1979). Media Logic. Beverly Hills, CA: Sage.

Babbie, E. (1973). Survey Research Methods. Belmont, CA: Wadsworth.

_____. (1968). Social Observation and Social Class Studies. In D. L. Sills (Ed.) *International Encyclopedia of the Social Sciences* (pp. 232-38). New York: Macmillan.

Berger, P. L. & Luckmann, T. (1966). The Social Construction of Reality. New York: Doubleday.

Blalock, H. M., Jr. (1971). Causal Models in the Social Sciences. Chicago: Aldine & Atherton.

Blumer, H. (1969). Symbolic Interactionism. Englewood Cliffs, NJ: Prentice-Hall

Chenitz, W. C. &. Swanson, J.M. (Eds.) (1986). From Practice to Grounded Theory. Menlo Park, CA: Addison-Wesley.

Conrad, P. and Reinhartz, S. (Eds.) (1984). Computers and Qualitative Data [Special issue]. *Qualitative Sociology* 7(2, Spring/Summer).

_____. (1969). Sociological Theory and Social Research. New York: A. M. Kelley. [Original work published 1930]

Denzin, N. K. (1978). The Research Act. New York: McGraw-Hill

Douglas, J. D. (1976). Investigative Social Research. Beverly Hills, CA: Sage.

_____. (1985). Creative Interviewing. Newbury Park, CA: Sage.

Douglas, J. D., Adler, P. A., Adler, P., Adler, A., Fontana, Freeman, J. A. Kotarba. (1980). Introduction to the Sociologies of Everyday Life. Boston: Allyn & Bacon.

Douglas, J. D. (1976). Investigating Social Research: Individual and Team Field Research. Beverly Hills, CA: Sage.

Douglas J. D. & Rasmussen, P. K. with Flanagan, C. A. (1977). The Nude Beach. Beverly Hills, CA: Sage.

Dressler, W. W. (1987). The Stress Process in a Southern Black Community. *Human Organization* 46(3):211-20

Ellis, C. (1986). Fisher Folk. Lexington: University of Kentucky Press.

Emerson, R. M. (1969). Judging Delinquents. Chicago: Aldine.

_____, ed. (1983). Contemporary Field Research. Boston: Little, Brown.

Fine, G. A. (1987). With the Boys. Chicago: University of Chicago Press.

Forrest, B. (1986). Apprentice-Participation.˙ *Urban Life*, 14, 431-53.

Fowler, F. L., Jr. (1984). Survey Research Methods. Beverly Hills, CA: Sage

Fox, K. J. (1987). Real Punks and Pretenders. *Journal of Contemporary Ethnography* 16(3), 344-70.

Gans, H. J. (1962). The Urban Villagers. New York: Free Press.

Gibbs, J. P. (1972). Sociological Theory Construction. Hillsdale, IL: Dryden.

Goffman, E. (1959). The Presentation of Self in Everyday Life. Garden City, NY: Doubleday.

_____. (1961). Asylums. Garden City, NY: Doubleday.

_____. (1974). Frame Analysis. New York: Harper & Row.

Gold, R. L. (1954). Toward a Social Interaction Methodology for Sociological Field Observation. *Ph.D. Dissertation*, University of Chicago, Department of Sociology.

_____. (1958). Roles in Sociological Field Observations. *Social Forces* 36, 217-23.

_____. (1969). Roles in Sociological Field Observations. In G.J. McCall and J.L. Simmons (Eds.), In *Issues in Participant Observation* (pp. 30-39). Reading, MA: Addison-Wesley.

Golde, P., (Ed.) (1970). Women in the Field. Chicago: Aldine.

Hall, E. T. (1959). The Silent Language. New York: Anchor.

_____. (1966). The Hidden Dimension. New York: Anchor.

_____. (1976). Beyond Culture. New York: Anchor.

Hayano, D. H. (1982). Poker Faces. Berkeley: University of California Press.

Hochschild, A. R. (1983). The Managed Heart. Berkeley: University of California Press.

Hockey, J. (1986). Squaddies. Ester: Wheaton.

Irwin, J. (1970). The Felon. Englewood Cliffs, NJ: Prentice-Hall

Johnson, J. M. (1975). Doing Field Research. New York: Free Press.

Junker, B. H. (1960). Field Work. Chicago: University of Chicago Press.

Kaplan, A. (1964). The Conduct of Inquiry. San Francisco: Chandler

Kleinman, S. (1984). Equals Before God. Chicago: University of Chicago Press.

Krieger, S. (1985). Beyond Subjectivity. *Qualitative Sociology* 8, 309-24.

Latour, B. & Woolgar, S. (1979). Laboratory Life. Beverly Hills, CA: Sage.

Lofland, J. (1966). Doomsday Cult. Englewood Cliffs, NJ: Prentice-Hall.

Lyman, S. M. & Scott, M. B. (1970). A Sociology of the Absurd. New York: Appleton-Century-Crofts.

_____. (1975). The Drama of Social Reality. New York: Oxford.

Lynch, M. (1985). Art and Artifact in Laboratory Science. London: Routledge & Kegan Paul.

Lynd, R. S. & Lynd, H. M. (1929). Middletown. New York: Harcourt Brace.

MacIver, R. M. (1942). Social Causation. Boston: Ginn.

Mandell, N. (1988). The Least-Adult Role in Studying Children. *Journal of Contemporary Ethnography* 16(4), 433-67.

Mitchell, R. G., Jr. (1983). Mountain Experience. Chicago: University of Chicago Press.

Peshkin, A. (1986). God's Choice. Chicago: University of Chicago Press.

Polkinghorne, D. (1983). Methodology for the Human Sciences. Albany: State University of New York Press.

Richard, M. P. (1986). Goffman Revisited. *Qualitative Sociology* 9(4), 321-38.

Roethlisberger, F. J. & Dickson, W. J. (1939). Management and the Worker. Cambridge, MA: Harvard University Press.

Sanders, C. R. (1988). Marks of Mischief. *Journal of Contemporary Ethnography* 16(4), 433-67.

Schutz, A. (1967). The Phenomenology of the Social World. Chicago: University of Chicago Press.

Scott, M. (1968). The Racing Game. Chicago:Aldine.

Simmel, G. (1950). The Sociology of George Simmel, translated by K. H. Wolff. New York: Free Press.

Spradley, J. (1980). Participant Observation. New York: Holt, Rinehart & Winston.

Strauss, A. (1987). Qualitative Analysis for Social Scientists. Cambridge: Cambridge University Press.

Sudnow, D. (1978). Ways of the Hand. Cambridge, MA: Harvard University Press.

Suttles, G. D. (1968). The Social Order of the Slum. Chicago: University of Chicago Press.

_____. (1972). The Social Construction of Communities. Chicago: University of Chicago Press.

Thomas, W. I. & Thomas, D. S. (1928). The Child in America. New York: Knopf.

Thomas, W. I. & Znaniecki, F. (1918-19). The Polish Peasant in Europe and America. Chicago: University of Chicago Press.

Wallace, W. (1971). The Logic of Science in Sociology. Chicago: Aldine.

Wallis, R. (1977). The Road to Total Freedom. New York: Columbia University Press.

Warner, W. L. (1959). The Living and the Dead: A Study of Symbolism of Americans. New Haven, CT: Yale University Press.

Warner, W. L. & Lunt, P. (1941). The Social Life of a Modern Community. New Haven, CT: Yale University Press.

Warner, W. L. & Srole, L. (1945). The Social Systems of American Ethnic Groups. Vol. 3, Yankee City. New Haven, CT: Yale University Press.

Warner, W. L. & Rasmussen, P. K. (1977). Sex and Gender in Field Research. Urban Life 6, 349-69.

Weber, M. (1949). The Methodology of the Social Sciences. Glencoe, IL: Free Press.

Whyte, W. F. (1984). Learning from the Field. Beverly Hills, CA: Sage.

Williams, D. D. (Ed.) (1986) Naturalistic Evaluation. San Francisco: Jossey-Bass.

Yin, R. K. (1984). Case Study Research. Beverly Hills, CA: Sage.

Znaniecki, F. (1935). The Method of Sociology. New York: Holt, Rinehart & Winston.

Researchers conducting field studies should be cognizant of the patterns of interaction between themselves and the subjects they are researching. When the fieldworkers become immersed into the group and setting they are studying, they must develop strategies to stay close to the scene without being drawn into the group and affecting its functioning. Participant observation must be perceived as having the consent of those being studied in order to permit the researcher to be physically present but socially marginal. The article further discusses and analyzes fieldwork-subjects' relationships concerning boundary issues, the fieldworkers as a resource for study participants, personal attributes of the fieldworker, and managing the degree of activity and involvement of the fieldworker with the group being researched.

CONSTRUCTING PARTICIPANT/ OBSERVATION RELATIONS

ROBERT M. EMERSON
MELVIN POLLNER

The reflexive thrust of contemporary ethnography has led to ever deepening examination of the tacit practices and presuppositions of fieldwork. Early self-analyses that focused on the (typically practical) problems of accessing and exiting the field, for example, evolved into questioning the very notion of the "field" itself. One strand of this questioning urges "reinventing the field" in order to expand the boundaries of ethnographic attention and to transform ethnographic practice: thus Gupta and Ferguson (1997:4) recommend abandoning a spatial notion of the field as bounded place and its associated practices and presuppositions. A different impulse highlights the socially constructed character of "the field." Clifford (1997) in particular has argued that while movement ("dislocation," "displacement") literally brings the ethnographer to a different place, the critical processes in constituting the field derive from the ethnographer's distinctive "professional habitus" and representational practices. Addressed through disciplinary concerns and methods and culminating in textual representation, the spaces, inhabitants and interactions of one or another "community" are consolidated and transformed into the object and site of ethnographic scrutiny—"the field."

To focus primarily upon ethnographers' practices as field-constituting activities, however, neglects the feature of fieldwork which distinguishes it from most other social science methodologies: *embodied presence in the daily lives of those who host the research*. Some form of immediate presence is the sine qua non of ethnography; some degree of participation is unavoidable in order to establish a place and identity for oneself—and one's research activities—in the local setting or community. Ethnographers must create and maintain this presence in ongoing encounters and negotiations with the people who are both hosts for and objects of research activities. As Atkinson insists: "[t]he boundaries of the field are not given" but are the outcome of what the ethnographer "may negotiate with hosts and informants" (1992:9). In this sense, the ethnographer constructs the field not simply through gaze and representation but also, and more fundamentally, by negotiating interactional presence to local events and scenes that can then be made subject to disciplinary gaze and textual representation.[1]

Not only is "the field" a negotiated construct, so too is the identity of "fieldworker": a researcher seeking to establish a social place from which to do ethnography must secure and sustain categorization and treatment as a "fieldworker" in actual interactions with those whose lives and circumstances are of interest. As the researcher cognitively, interactionally and inscriptively attempts to institute the field and herself as a fieldworker, she does so in the midst of a host able to accept, ignore and resist such impositions. In contrast to other methodologies in which the researcher transforms a domain into a research object merely by intention and inscription, the fieldworker *in situ* must invite, encourage or cajole her hosts to be objects of ethnographic scrutiny—to be the "field"—and to allow the researcher to be a "fieldworker."[2]

Ethnographers have typically addressed these issues within the framework of participant/observation, using the term to identify a tension inherent in their efforts to comprehend and study social life: how to strike a balance between closeness and distance, between involvement and detachment (Reinharz 1992: 67-71). On the one hand, the participant-observer seeks to get close to those studied, to become immersed in their everyday life. The ethnographer desires empathetic understanding of the daily routines and subjective meanings of the researched, seeking, in Goffman's (1989:125-26) terms, to "penetrate" their "circle of response to their social situation" at a depth that brings visceral appreciation of local scenes, smells and standards. On the other hand, the participant-observer must at some point disengage and distance himself from local scenes and relations. In addition to eventually leaving the field, the fieldworker often needs to establish the distance that will allow him to observe (rather than shape or simply experience) the naturally occurring activity. Even Goffman, who seems to have advocated ethnographic involvement until the fieldworker felt able to "settle down and forget about being a sociologist," advised "forcing yourself to be tuned into something that you then pick up *as a witness*—not as an interviewer, not as a listener, but as a witness to how they respond to what gets done to and around them."

Ethnography, then, can be examined for how ethnographers "do closeness" on the one hand and "do distance" on the other. Yet analyses of constructing participant/observer relations are skewed: discussions of fieldwork methods have devoted much attention to the processes of immersing oneself in and getting close to the lifeworlds of others, considering specific strategies for "entering" (Schatzman and Strauss 1973:18-33), sustaining "continuing access" (Lofland and Lofland 1995:53-63), and moving beyond "respectful distance" to intimate closeness (Reinharz 1992:68). It should not be surprising that processes for decreasing distance have tended to preoccupy fieldworkers; this concern mirrors the ordinary sequence of priorities in most fieldwork. The researcher must, after all, get in the door and become welcome before she can begin to do fieldwork in earnest. Distance, especially at the start of the project, is often construed as an obstacle to be overcome, and later, even when desired, appears readily attained. Similarly, "observing" would initially appear to involve an unproblematic, minimalist form of being present in social happenings.

In contrast, the other constituent of participant observation—practices for "doing distance," for staying sufficiently detached to witness what life circumstances do to these others—has received little attention.[3] Reinharz has observed that "general methodological writings about participant observation have an unwarranted (male-oriented?) assumption that the researcher can control his/her stance" (1992:59). While we might have reservations about the imputed source of this assumption, it is indeed clear that researchers must negotiate the boundaries and nature of their involvement with their hosts from *within* the social world of the host. Unlike laboratory researchers whose one-way mirrors provide distance and allow completely unengaged observation, however, fieldworkers cannot necessarily stand back and watch social interaction with absolutely no involvement with those engaged in that interaction. Nor can the fieldworker simply declare a detached position by fiat: host members may resist the researcher's definition of his level of (non-) involvement and even ignore his self-definition as a researcher, analyst or observer. The fieldworker's recurrent problem is to achieve the distance necessary to observe while physically and socially present to those who are the objects of such observation.[4] Thus, constructing distance, though rarely in the methodological spotlight, can be as complex and consequential as the more commonly considered concerns of access and rapport. Turning to "doing distance" as an interactional process, then, corrects the imbalance in the ethnographic literature and contributes to understanding how the boundary between "field" and "fieldworker," so fundamental to the possibility of ethnography, is collaboratively constituted.

BOUNDARY WORK IN PARTICIPANT/OBSERVATION

The slash in participant/observation symbolizes the apportionment of a fieldworker's activities between the two modes of presence in the field: participation and observation. Ethnographic precepts and perspectives encourage the researcher to position the slash at different points on the continuum—some toward the observation pole, others toward the participatory pole.[5] Regardless of whether "participation" or "observation" is emphasized, however, decisions regarding the

distribution of involvement between the two poles are inherent in ethnography. These decisions, as we have suggested, are not unilateral but a collaborative achievement of host and researcher.

From the point of view of the fieldworker, hosts may pose two major challenges: initiating exclusionary pushes to the periphery as the researcher seeks presence at the center of the group, and making inclusionary pulls to the center as he seeks to remain on the margins. Prototypical forms of *exclusion* are initiated by hosts in refusing to allow the fieldworker to enter or remain in the field; a less extreme form of such exclusion involves more partial denials of fieldworker presence on particular occasions. This exclusionary impulse may take more focused, specific form in hosts' efforts to eliminate or remove certain happenings from what is to constitute the field. For example, hosts may attempt to mark certain events as "out of bounds" for observation by asking that the fieldworker not include them in her fieldnotes:

> A field researcher studying divorce mediation had been openly taking notes while interviewing a mediator about a session just completed. "[the mediator] began to apply some eye make-up while I was finishing writing down some observations. She flashed me a mock disgusted look and said, 'Are you writing *this* down too!' indicating the activity with her eye pencil." (Emerson et al. 1995:23)[6]

The fieldworker himself may delimit or restrict his field by self-consciously staying out of certain places and situations, or by deliberately abandoning the position of observer, as Johnson (1975:159) reports doing in deciding not to write notes while in the throes of an emotionally charged moment.[7]

Less appreciated is the second source of threats to "doing observation"—pressures toward increased *inclusion*.[8] Indeed, a major threat to observation is often not that the researcher will be expelled by the observed, but rather that the researcher will be accorded some more consequential presence in ongoing scenes and relations. Such excessive involvement can arise from hosts who entice the researcher into more participatory roles or who engage the researcher other than as "fieldworker." At the extreme, the researcher may be pressured to become a fully committed participant. Or excessive participation can arise from the fieldworker's enthusiastic embrace of opportunities for fuller, more central participation in local life; at an extreme, the researcher may "go native" or "become the phenomenon" (Mehan and Woods 1975). The result in either case is an erosion of the boundary that divides and distinguishes the "field" from the "fieldworker."

Participant/observation stances vary in their direct vulnerability to such challenges and, relatedly, to the task of overtly and interactionally maintaining a boundary in situ. While classic participant-observers routinely adopted more or less detached, witnessing stances toward local happenings, some contemporary ethnographers de-emphasize observation in favor of active participation. In such "complete membership" (Adler and Alder 1987) or "experiential" fieldwork (Reinharz 1979, 1992), the fieldworker seeks to participate as an active or full member in naturally occurring activities and scenes, at the moment abandoning concern with distance and detachment in favor of intense, "natural" involvement. Thus it might appear that detached observation has no place in this approach to fieldwork. But deep immersion and experiential fieldwork do not so much abandon detachment as postpone it; in subsequently writing fieldnotes, for example, the fieldworker will necessarily reflect on and achieve distance from these experiences, turning them into recorded observations. Furthermore, there may be moments and occasions in such an experiential field where the fieldworker decides to forego active participation in order to observe events and actions which she had no direct part in creating, hence having to create and sustain a visible, interactionally managed observational position.[9]

Alternatively, participant/observation may not rely on negotiated arrangements between an identified "researcher" and "research subjects." The clearest instance involves ethnographic accounts based entirely on recollections of events and experiences that were not at that time matters of research interest and concern, as in Turner's (1947) analysis of the work of the navy disbursing officer. Here the field is constituted retrospectively, as past events are remembered and reconstructed as matters for description and analysis in ways that are entirely under the control of the now-ethnographer. At the time these events occurred, of course, there was no research, no field, no ethnography, and indeed, no ethnographer. More mixed examples arise with disguised fieldwork, where the fieldworker pursues research goals while those studied remain unaware that research is taking place. This can occur both in classic covert fieldwork, where the ethnographer reveals neither professional identity nor the existence of a research project to those studied (e.g., *When Prophecy Fails*); and in autoethnography where those encountering the ethnographer in the course of his daily activities have not been informed of the fact of ongoing research. Here the field is actively but asymmetrically constructed by the ethnographer, since those studied do not know there is a field; but this occurs (in the case of covert fieldwork) by means of the interactional moves and stratagems through which the ethnographer "passes" while maneuvering into places yielding the kinds of observations and information desired. Interactional negotiations take place, but what is negotiated is only understood as matters of research by one of the parties.

Our analysis, then, addresses ethnographies involving encounters between a known, identified researcher and hosts who are aware of the fact of being studied—the situation of classic participant observation. Using a variety of accounts of fieldwork experience (including our own), we consider, first, how the distance associated with the position of "observer" is sometimes transgressed or dissolved by the host group. Specifically, we inventory how a host, wittingly or not, may refuse to allow a field researcher to be merely or only a "researcher" or an "observer" (or less an "observer" than the fieldworker would prefer to be) and draw her more deeply into local matters. In contrast to the processes through which individuals are systematically excluded from participation in various settings Lemert described in his classic "Paranoia and the Dynamics of Exclusion" (1962), the practices considered here comprise what might be termed the *dynamics of inclusion*. Second, we survey the ad hoc efforts recounted by fieldworkers to sidestep deeper involvement or to extricate themselves when they find that they have become excessively active participants. Examining the practices for doing, undoing and preserving "observer" highlights the practices through which the central duality of ethnography—"fieldworker" and "field"—is constituted and, from time to time, demolished.

INCLUSIVE OVERTURES

We have argued that while exclusion can in fact be a substantial threat to participant-observation fieldwork, at least as great dangers derive from tendencies toward inclusion, from pressures to become more of a participant, less of a researcher. For although the fieldworker may plan and proffer a distribution of observation and involvement, the host group, pursuing its own concerns and understandings, may disregard or override the projected boundaries. Accounts by fieldworkers suggest three related types of overtures for increased participation that arise with particular frequency: overtures that seek to utilize the fieldworker as a resource; incorporate her as a co-member; or engage her as a person.

Fieldworker as Resource

The ethnographer often brings attributes and possessions useful to the host. The very physical presence of the researcher, for example, may prove to be a resource that the host may incorporate and use in their everyday activities. In a study of police work (Ericson 1981:37), detectives identified the fieldworker as a researcher to citizens except in encounters involving potentially troublesome suspects; here, during search and interrogations detectives remained silent about the researcher's identity, thereby implying that he was a detective in order to increase the aura of intimidation. Researchers may sometimes be identified as a superior, authority, or expert who is then called upon to support the members in dealing with dubious or recalcitrant clients. Gussow (1964:236), for example, describes several incidents in which teachers used fieldworker entry into the classroom to chide classes for their unruly behavior.

The fieldworker provides not only a body whose imputed identity can be incorporated into ongoing activities but also one capable of actual work. With some frequency fieldworkers are used as an extra pair of hands for sundry tasks. Johnson, for example, reports that over the course of his investigations of a social welfare office he served as driver, reader, luggage porter, babysitter, money lender, ticket taker, note taker, phone answerer, book reader, book lender, adviser on automobile purchases, party arranger, bodyguard, letter writer, messenger, and other roles (1975:107). Indeed, fieldworkers occasionally become useful to the hosts as an addition to or substitute for regular workers. In our research on psychiatric emergency teams (see Emerson and Pollner 1976) typically composed of two persons, for example, some team members felt that a second team member was not necessary because one of the researchers could serve as a backup. In fact, at one point it was half-jokingly suggested that, given our experience, we, the two fieldworkers, would comprise the team.

The fieldworker may also bear valued or needed resources. Although money is probably the most common asset lit upon by hosts, anthropologists may be accessible sources of medicine (McCurdy 1976). Close relations with a "key informant" often involves the ethnographer providing a wide range of resources and services; Patricia and Peter Adler (1987:41), for example, report not only having housed their primary drug-trafficking informant for seven months, "but over the six years we were involved in the research we also fed him, clothed him, took care of his children, wrote letters of reference on his behalf, helped to organize his criminal defense, visited him in jail, gave him money, and testified in child support court for him."

The fieldworker may not only be utilized in ongoing concerns and tasks but may also inspire the host to develop projects fitted to the unique possibilities afforded by his presence. In addition to being treated as a "gofer" and extra pair of hands by the residents of the teaching hospital he studied, Bosk (1979) was also enlisted as a source of information from the "outside" world from which houseofficers felt cut off; as a sounding board for various dissatisfactions; as a referee for conflicts; and as an informal group "historian." Or the ethnographer's social capital may make her attractive as an agent or spokesperson for the group. In her study of Alzheimer's day-care centers, Lyman (1993:203) came to feel a sense of responsibility to staff and patients deriving from her insider access and also from the requests made by staff and implicitly by patients; indeed, one staff member told her, "I see you as an advocate."

Fieldworkers, of course, are often willing and even eager to provide desired resources to hosts. But the consequence of doing so may be heightened involvement in activities peripheral or irrelevant to the research project, an involvement which may threaten to overrun fieldwork purposes. McCurdy (1976), for example, found his capacity to conduct his research seriously threatened by villagers who sought his modest supply of antibiotics. The medicines worked so well against local bacteria that he became besieged by requests for treatment, requests that constantly interfered with his opportunities to observe tribal life. "They would catch me," he writes, "as I hurried to meet an informant for an interview, interrupt as I tried to type field-notes, or pull me away from the observation of an interesting religious event" (1976:14). Greater involvement on the hosts' terms, then, directly impinged upon the fieldworker's ability to conduct the kinds of observations he intended.

Fieldworker as Member

While some fieldworkers self-consciously attempt to establish themselves as partial or complete members, even detached participant-observers may find themselves subject to inclusive pressures to become a member of the communities or organizations they study. At the extreme, a host may exert a comprehensive claim on the fieldworker's involvement through overtures to become a full member. This kind of total overture is frequently encountered in proselytizing groups for whom others—virtually any other—are prospective converts. While such groups may be readily approached and "observed," the group may ultimately ask a high price—the fieldworker's total commitment and participation. Lofland's experiences with what proved to be the beginning of the Unification Church are illustrative of how the group may regard the fieldworker first and foremost as a prospective member (1966:274):

[Ms.] Lee [a leader] told me that she was tired of playing the "studying the movement" game. She made it clear that she was very concerned that, after all these months and all that the members had told me, I had not become a convert. I responded that my interest was necessarily professional. Lee expressed regret: "If I had known from the beginning that you only looked at our Precepts as a scientist—why should I have bothered?"

More commonly, hosts may come to accord the fieldworker a quasi-membership role while recognizing that the researcher is not a true member. Leo (1995:121-22), for example, received repeated invitations from detectives to "actively participate in the interrogation process" he attempted to study. Thus:

. . . several of the robbery detectives invited me to step outside of my role as a detached observer and to interrogate suspects myself. In one instance, two detectives loaded me up with a badge, a pair of handcuffs, a beeper and an empty holster.

Beyond total or partial efforts to make a researcher a member, host groups may effect tacit conversions. Simply "hanging around" the local culture often shapes a fieldworker's sensibility and comportment to a greater degree than they initially realize. Just as an observer may surreptitiously infiltrate the host group, the host group may surreptitiously infiltrate the observer. The venerable Evans-Pritchard (1976:244) describes how living among the Azande altered some fundamental beliefs about reality:

Azande were talking about witchcraft daily, both among them and to me; any communication was well nigh impossible unless one took witchcraft for granted. . . . I had to act as though I trusted the Zande oracles and therefore to give assent to their dogma of witchcraft, whatever reservations I might have. If I wanted to go hunting or on a journey, for instance, no one would willingly accompany me unless I was able to produce a verdict of the poison oracle that all would be well, that witchcraft did not threaten our project; and if one goes on arranging one's affairs, organizing one's life in harmony with the lives of one's hosts, whose companionship one seeks and without which one would sink into disoriented craziness, one must eventually give way, or at any rate partially give way. If one must act as though one believed, one ends in believing, or half-believing as one acts.

Clearly the attractions of membership become seductive to many ethnographers, leading to gradually increasing levels of immersion and involvement. Some may indeed ultimately "go native" and abandon the research enterprise; but more common in the fieldwork literature are reports of fieldworkers who, having reached their "personal limits" (Adler and Adler 1987:79), drew back from intense involvement or abandoned the field entirely. "Adopted by" and having functioned as part of a Japanese family, Kondo (1990:17), describes coming to this limit and the subsequent change in her fieldwork:

> As I glanced into the shiny metal surface of the butcher's display case, I noticed someone who looked terribly familiar: a typical young housewife, clad in slip-on sandals and the loose, cotton shifts called "home wear" (*homu wea*), a woman walking with a characteristically Japanese bend to the knees and a sliding of the feet. Suddenly I clutched the handle of the stroller to steady myself as a wave of dizziness washed over me, for I realized I had caught a glimpse of nothing less than my own reflection. Fear that perhaps I would never emerge from this world into which I was immersed inserted itself into my mind and stubbornly refused to leave, until I resolved to move into a new apartment, to distance myself from my Japanese home and my Japanese existence.

Similarly, severe emotional upset when she actually began to see "spirit figures or hallucinations," accompanied by drastic weight loss, led Forrest (1986:445) to abandon completely her full-membership "apprentice-participation" research on spiritualism.[10]

Fieldworker as Person

Frequently, ties with those studied draw heavily upon the fieldworker's personal attributes, particularly congeniality and personal attractiveness. A research procedure relying upon personal ties, fieldwork almost inevitably generates tendencies to expand and deepen these ties in ways that ignore and may ultimately obliterate the fieldworker's research commitments. The researcher may be able to modulate these developing personal relations by limiting intimacy, thus balancing the often conflicting pulls of personal and research relations. But the direction and intensity of a relation are not unilaterally determined and fieldworkers may find that, having taken a step in the level of intimacy, their subjects demand or expect that they will take more. In treating the fieldworker as a "friend," for example, host members may assume a relational reciprocity demanding more self-disclosure than the fieldworker had anticipated:

> And we're rapping about the situation at God's Love (commune) and where her head's at, etc., and the, just as an afterthought, she says, "Are you a Christian?" And I went into my stereotyped song and dance about "This is a study and I can't talk about," etc., and she got furious. She was very angry, and she went on about how she considered me to be a friend, and she had told me intimate things about herself and I had acted friendly and then all of a sudden I had copped out on a friendship whenever she asked a personal question of me. She also said something about how I was trying to cop out of being a Christian by doing a "scientific trip." (taped fieldnote) (Robbins et al. 1973:266)

Hosts may make claims on the personal life of the observer not simply through friendship and praise but also through emotional button-pushing which effectively pulls the researcher into their emotional orbit. Myerhoff (1989:89), for example, describes how the elderly Jewish members of the senior citizen center she studied subjected her to guilt-inducing criticisms:

> After greeting me warmly, Basha would often ask, "Never mind these other things you all the time ask about. Tell me who's with your children?" Men and women alike would admire a new skirt or dress I wore, then turn over my hem for inspection. Nathan remarked, "For a lady professor, you don't do so good with a needle."

This barrage of criticism, combined with the guilt from comparing her youth, strength and future with those of her elderly hosts, led her to consider leaving the field. "It was unbearable to abide the countless ways in which the Center people used guilt, often unconsciously," she writes, "intending not to hurt but only to make themselves feel potent." (1989:89)

Probably one of the more frequent personal overtures involves sex. Fieldwork accounts in the 1960s and 1970s broke the earlier silence about sexual happenings in the field to recount *hosts'* sexual "motivations, imputations, and unwanted overtures" (Warren and Hackney 2000:26), thereby depicting the field as a place generating at least occasional sexual provocations and dangers.[11] More recent discussion of *fieldworkers'* sexual attraction and activities (see Warren and Hackney 2000:26-35) has begun to puncture "the myth of the chaste fieldworker" (Fine 1993), suggesting that neither fieldworkers nor their hosts are exempt from the human condition, that personal relations in the field may well assume sexual dimensions. Indeed, whether or not this occurs is not a unilateral decision under the control of the fieldworker, for members of the host community may well sexualize what had been a research relation in ways that undermine further fieldwork. For example, in responding to the overly enthusiastic used-car salesmen she was studying, Brown found it necessary "to leave the field for a while and let things cool off naturally rather than face a showdown and lose an informant" (1971:78; see also Warren and Hackney 2000:31-35).

MANAGING INCLUSIVE OVERTURES

While fieldworkers frequently feel pulls toward greater involvement, whether from hosts' enticements, the attractions of immersion, or both, the participant-observer generally tries to resist or to accede only in part. The involvement may be emotionally draining, physically dangerous, or ethically and legally problematic. Acceptance of overtures to perform as part of the "team" or to support one or another local faction may delimit access to other factions. Further, increased involvement may affect the very processes one seeks to observe. Thus, in "doing participant-observation" fieldworkers rely on a variety of distancing practices to manage overtures to deeper involvement. We will consider four such practices—interactional efforts to preclude, to finesse, and to decline overtures for greater involvement, and cognitive reminders to retain the "research" framing of one's experiences in the field.

Preempting

From the point of view of sustaining fieldwork distance, the qualities and styles usually considered obstacles to rapport can ward off unwanted overtures before they begin. Many common field relations have this character: A white European among black or brown third-world peoples, women among men, a young graduate student among older, experienced workers, are effectively preempted from certain forms of involvement. The role of novice, initiate, or learner may also serve to preclude inclusionary moves, and some fieldworkers will work long and hard to hold on to their apparent ignorance of local ways exactly in order to enjoy this exemption. In general, if the fieldworker happens to be unattractive or useless in terms of group needs and interests, or can alter or minimize qualities that would attract host interest as resource, member or friend, overtures may be nipped in the bud.

Furthermore, most fieldworkers devote considerable effort right at the start to establishing an implicit contract with their hosts allowing presence at and participation in local happenings but in restricted, limited ways. In initially negotiating access to a setting, for example, fieldworkers often try to set limits on participation, proclaiming their intent to act as only partial and detached participants in these activities. Seeking to avoid involvements that could easily become all encompassing and/or that are personally and morally unacceptable to the fieldworker, the researcher may stipulate the degree of involvement in which he is prepared to indulge. Sanchez-Jankowski (1991:13) notes, for example, that as part of the "mutual understanding" with the many gangs he observed, "it was agreed that I did not have to participate in any activity (including taking drugs) that was illegal."

Within specific interactions, the fieldworker may seek a position at the edges of the unfolding event. Almost by definition, the periphery of whatever focused engagements comprise a setting's main involvement (Goffman 1963b) are attractive niches for observing. Through initial preempting moves, along the lines of "I'm here to watch you do it" and "I'm not qualified or inclined to help you do it," fieldworkers attempt to stay on the periphery, to establish a distinctively nonconsequential presence in these interactions. Johnson (1975: 102), for example, after being frequently drawn into the center of client home visits on being mistaken for a welfare worker, adopted the following strategy with the social workers he accompanied into client homes:

> I would tell them that it appeared that the physical location of the furniture in nearly all the homes included at the minimum a couch and an adjacent chair. From earlier experiences, it seemed inter-action would not focus on the researcher if he was positioned at either end of the couch-chair combi-nation. So the social workers were instructed to "manage" me to one end or the other, out of the direct line of fire, to reduce the chances that my presence in the setting would disturb the ongoing interactions.

Of course, staying on the margins may require active work, and fieldworkers often show great agility in resetting themselves at the outer edge as the fore- and background regions of a setting form and shift. Moreover, sustaining noninvolve-ment at the periphery often requires strategic management of facial expression, eye movements, body direction, and public demeanor to minimize accessibility. In this way, fieldworkers will often employ a "looking at no one in particular" gaze to avoid engulfing engagements, or become immersed in an engrossing side-involvement (jotting fieldnotes provides a convenient one) to preclude an imminent overture.

Principled exemptions and marginal position-ings, however, are never total and absolute, and initial efforts to stake out detached observer pres-ence are precarious and routinely subject to threat and undermining in the flux of field interactions. Just what might be entailed in terms of partici-pation and observation by initial agreements to let a fieldworker "hang out" in the interest of a "study" depends upon subsequent developments. Thus, initially able to sustain research relations with male Chicano gang members by gaining acceptance as a "lady reporter," Horowitz found this arrangement began to dissolve:

> After more than a year of using "lady reporter" as a key identity, some members began to flirt seriously and tried to make passes. They claimed that my age (six to eight years older) did not

constitute a barrier to starting a relationship. The identity of lady reporter was being replaced by my potential as a sexual partner, regardless of my efforts to deemphasize my appearance and emphasize my age and outsider status. (1986:420)

Similarly, an interactional position on the periphery is inherently unstable: a shift in con-cerns, a glance, a turn of the head, may recon-stitute the rim as the center, as in the following fieldnote involving a psychiatric emergency team call:

> I (RME) accompanied a PET team composed of two women, a psychiatric social worker and a public health nurse, to the home of a 21-year-old black ex-mental patient named Albert Roy. The young man's mother had initiated the visit, claim-ing his behavior was extremely disoriented and something had to be done. After introductions and some preliminary talk about Albert's recent prob-lems, I seated myself in an easy chair slightly removed from but with a good view of the couch where the workers and Albert sat talking. I assid-uously observed and took notes on all that was said about Albert's mental condition, efforts to get a job, problems with medication, etc. At various points Albert became somewhat "agitated," at one point getting up and standing two feet away from one of the PET workers, shaking his fist in her face and yelling that he could take care of himself. At this point, his mother, standing in the kitchen area watching all this, pointed toward me (I had said absolutely nothing) and warned her son: "Sit down Albert! Or that man over there will get you. That's what he's here for!"[12]

If overtures are successfully preempted, the host feels no need or desire to incorporate the observer. Once an overture has been made, however, the fieldworker's options change dramatically; any response is now monitored for what it may signify about the fieldworker's character, commitments, and relation to the group. Under these circumstances, the field-worker's distancing options involve either evasion or refusal.

Finessing

Given the potential costs for the research project of direct refusal, it is not surprising to find fieldworkers adept in finessing overtures through evasive or ambiguous replies. In some situations, the overture itself is framed so indirectly that it can be responded to in kind without either party feeling publicly embarrassed or humiliated. Arendell (1997:357), for example, reports that most of the divorced men in her interview study who became interested in her as a "potential date" proceeded cautiously:

> For the most part, inquiries were indirect, such as: "Let me know if you'd like to go to dinner sometime." "What kinds of things do you like to do in your spare time?" "Does a busy woman like yourself have time for a personal life?" Such remarks were sufficiently ambiguous so they could be side-stepped, saving face for both of us: the participant's, if he were suggesting a date which I declined, and mine, if I was misinterpreting his meaning.

In other circumstances, however, overtures may be explicit and responses closely scrutinized. The fieldworker may find her wit and diplomacy tested when she is publicly asked to commit herself to one or another "side," as in the situation described by Bosk (1979:197):

> . . . houseofficers viewed me as a "referee" in conflicts among themselves over patient management, quarrels over the equity of the division of labor, and disputes about whether or not patients understood what was happening. In the midst of such disagreements, one houseofficer would turn to me and ask: "Well, what do you think? Which of us is right?" These were not comfortable situations for me when I could hide behind the observer role. A judgment was demanded as the price for my continued presence. Moreover, any judgment was certain to alienate one of my informants. *I developed tactics for throwing the question back to the disputants or for pointing out the merits of either side, or making a joke of the entire dispute.* (emphasis added)

Evasive responses are a consummate test of the fieldworkers' ethnographic grasp of local culture, for the place that has been established must now to be preserved without wreaking havoc to the relationships that sustain it. Not only must the evasive fieldworker respond, but he must do so in such a way that members do not press for further involvement, are not offended, and do not treat the fieldworker as

evasive. As part of his covert participation in the Children of God, Van Zandt (1991:14) was called upon to "litness" or sell COG literature to the public, a task he found especially odious.

> Fortunately, the structure of litnessing permitted me to develop a number of techniques to avoid these unpleasant interactions. Chief among these was to reduce my activity to the minimum acceptable limit: I litnessed very slowly and approached only a small number of people; I litnessed furiously for a very short time. I took a deep breath, attempted to desensitize my feelings, and rapidly approached people with the same statement. After such a period, I would slip out of view of my litnessing partner and take a rest. Another technique I used was to claim that I needed more "Word Time" or devotional time, and request that we take a break to read a Mo [the leader of COG] letter together. I drew on my status as a neophyte as an excuse to take more and longer breaks than most competent members.

Furthermore, these circumstances permitted a measure of overt role distance: Using devices ranging from facial expressions communicating "Can you believe I'm doing this? I can't" to confessing to those encountered "that I was really a sociologist conducting a covert study" (1991:15), Van Zandt participated by showing that his identity was other than what his activities might imply.

Because of the indexicality of evasions it is not unusual that responses intended as hedges fail. Responses intended to be "neutral" and noncommittal, for example, may be transformed into patently partial statements. *When Prophecy Fails* (1956) provides the prototypical instance:

> At the end of the December 3-4 meeting, Bertha sat for "private consultations" between the individual members and "the Creator" who spoke through her. All the observers dutifully asked a question or two of the Creator and accepted the answers passively, quitting the situation as soon as they politely could. The last observer to go through this ritual was not allowed to be merely passive and nondirective, however. The voice of the medium droned on for a few minutes and then said: "I am the Creator." Next the voice asked our observer: "What do you see when I say 'I am the Creator'?" To this the observer replied, "Nothing," whereupon the medium's voice explained: "That's

not nothing; that's the void." The medium then pressed further: "Do you see a light in the void?" Our observer struggled with this impasse by answering, "A light in the void?" and got, as a reply, a fuller explanation of the "light that expands and covers the void" together with an increasing flood of elaboration that terminated when the medium called other members into the room and asserted that the observer had just been "allowed to witness Creation"! The medium further stated that this "event" was validation of her speaking with the Creator's voice since, every time her voice said "I am the Creator" our observer saw the vision of Creation! (Festinger et al. 1956:242-43)

As these fieldworkers lamented: "Against this sort of runaway invention even the most polished technique of nondirective response is powerless" (243).

Nonetheless, evasive finessing provides one of the foundational skills of participant/ observation fieldwork. Counterposing efforts to draw close and develop rapport, interactional techniques of ambiguity and avoidance, often conveyed through humor and misdirection, are standard ethnographic implements for sustaining nonconsequential presence in the face of inclusive overtures.

Declining and Withdrawing

Overtures may be so sudden and direct that the fieldworker feels compelled to respond with a more or less direct refusal. Often this is an explicit declaration asserting identity as (just) a researcher or unwillingness to participate: When asked by attending physicians for advice on life-and-death decisions on a neonatal intensive care unit, Anspach (1993:203) asserted that "as a sociologist" she "had no special expertise in resolving ethical dilemmas."[13] Such declarations, of course, may be hostilely received, as in the following reaction to Terry Williams' appeal to his researcher identity as a way of declining a sexual overture that arose in his study of cocaine users in after-hours clubs (1989:30):

I was in a club that had been heterosexual until the Thursday night I arrived, which was "gay night." I thought I would take advantage of the situation for sociological purposes, making comparison between heterosexual and homosexual cocaine users. I was wearing black leather (the fashion in New York at the time) not realizing the role of black leather in the gay community. I noticed a group of men sitting in the corner and moved toward them inconspicuously, or so I thought, until I was eight or ten feet away. One of them stared up at me and I of course looked toward him. His sleeves were rolled past his elbows, revealing purple and red tattoos on both arms. After looking at me for a few seconds, he walked over and offered to buy me a drink, asking if this was my first time there. I explained that I had been there before and informed him that I was a researcher and just wanted to talk to as many people as possible. He grew red in the face and said to his companions in a loud voice, hands on his hips, head cocked to one side: "Hey, get a load of this one. He wants to do research on us. You scum bag! What do we look like pal? Fucking guinea pigs? You got some nerve walking in here, talking about doing some research!"

Since declining may give offense and damage rapport, ethnographers often take care to identify indigenous methods for declining to participate in local activities. For example, in seeking to study cocaine culture without using cocaine, Williams (1989:29) "observed several patrons actually refusing cocaine that was offered them, saying 'my nose is out' or 'I'm cocked out' or simply that they did not trust other people's drugs." Relying on these techniques, Williams was able to observe cocaine use in after-hours clubs without arousing suspicion.

In some situations, what is intended as an unequivocal declination by the fieldworker may be understood in an entirely different way by members. Golde (1970) noted, for example, that when her refusals of amorous propositions were filtered through indigenous cultural understandings, their meaning and implications were transformed. "The difficulty was that it was expected of the female always to appear unwilling initially," Golde writes, "so that my lack of interest and my refusals were not always taken at face value but were interpreted as typical female behavior" (1970:86). Indeed, in extreme instances, members may maintain an interpretive frame that deprives the fieldworker of any effective means of declaring distance. Snow's (1980) efforts to terminate his fieldwork in the Nichiren Shoshu Buddhist movement provides a case in point. Committed members of this group responded to those showing signs of disaffection or withdrawal with renewed contact and involvement. Snow, for example, told his group leader about his growing disillusionment only to be congratulated because such feelings were "good signs" and subsequently taken to the Community Center for "guidance." As Snow comments: "While I was thus trying to curtail my involvement and offer what seemed to be legitimate reasons for dropping out, I was yet being drawn back at the same time" (1980:110).

The overtures may be so intense or sustained that despite efforts to preempt, evade or directly decline, the fieldworker may feel that she has no recourse but to withdraw from the field. As Horowitz was increasingly seen as a sexually available "chick" by the Latino gang she observed, for example, she attempted to ward off overtures by not dancing with any of the youths and by making sure that other women were present at meetings. The persistence of the overtures, however, rendered her position as researcher untenable. "As the pressures increased to take a locally defined membership role," Horowitz writes, "I was unable to negotiate a gender identity that would allow me to continue as a researcher" (1986:423).

Subjective Anchoring

A variety of processes may lead fieldworkers to become deeply engulfed by and immersed in the worlds they came to study. Declining overtures to deeper involvement may threaten continued access to the group; as McCurdy noted, for example, refusal to dispense medications would likely have resulted in his exclusion from the village. Detached, passive observation can become strained or boring, making the fieldworker amenable to normalizing his presence by engaging in host activities. Relatedly, fieldworkers may seek opportunities to express their gratitude for what Bosk (1979) refers to as the "gift" of access by doing things with and for his hosts. Finally, deeper involvement may furnish attractive opportunities to construct selves and acquire experiences not possible in other circumstances. As Thorne (1983:222) had

suggested, ethnography affords the researcher "controlled adventure" into exciting, tabooed, dangerous, enticing circumstances, while retaining the ability to control the time, extent, and costs of participation.

On many occasions, when actively involved in host events, distancing, as by establishing a publicly recognized role of "observer," is neither possible nor desired. Instead, composing oneself as an observer is primarily a matter of self-discipline: Unable to preempt, evade, or decline overtures, or to symbolically distance herself from the actions she performs, the fieldworker remains distant from her hosts only through the work whereby she recalls her "researcher" identity and commitments. In one way or another, the researcher reminds (re-minds) herself of her anchorage in the discipline, not in the activities in which she is currently engaged, much less in the host group.[14]

Writing fieldnotes provides one concrete method for re-minding and recommitting to research purposes. The fieldworker may get caught up in the moment-by-moment, day-after-day experience of living in the field, becoming immersed in the rhythms and routines of local life. In simply "participating" and "experiencing," research priorities may recede and disappear. Taking up the task of writing fieldnotes draws the fieldworker back into the space of research and observation, revitalizing fieldworker "commitment to the exogenous project of studying or understanding the lives of others—as opposed to the indigenous project of simply living a life in one way or another" (Emerson et al. 1995:36). And returning to these matters may not be easy: As one anthropological fieldworker observed (Jackson 1990a:18): "I slowed down. More concerned with the hour to hour. You forget to take notes because you feel this is your life."

Other fieldworkers may create devices for immediate self-reminding as their local involvement leads them into activities which create discomfort, anxiety and internal conflict. Van Zandt (1991:181) describes one such device:

I thought if I could keep some perspective on my activity, it would be easier to get by. I carried two index cards. One contained a list of imperatives to help me remember my goals and to keep that perspective. The second held the words to a song that I always found particularly relaxing and reassuring.

The first card included advice such as "1. Maintain 2 distinct positions: don't let them merge and conflict. . . . 3. Maintain distance or perspective. . . . 7. Study what is happening to self" (1991:181).

As the anchorage is attenuated, the distinction between fieldworker and member may dissolve. In a section entitled "'Going Native,' Almost," Van Zandt describes the instant in a conversation with a COG leader when he felt, to invoke Goffman's words, that he "could settle down and forget about being a sociologist":

> I felt a rush to just emotionally fall on him—not Jesus—or not physically—I wanted to rest emotionally on him; things clouded up—and I was unclear about my exact relation—researcher/ member—[it] came after [he] listened and understood my problem about security and answered some questions forthrightly—also after I mentioned some things Roy [Wallis] said [to me about the Family] then I realized I was trapped . . . I thought maybe the Lord was moving me. (1991:16, brackets in original)

Van Zandt tried to hide his emotional reaction and asked the leader "sociological" questions but later that evening and the next morning contemplated the possibility of joining the Family. What kept him from the "brink," as he describes it, was reminding himself not so much of the sociological project per se but of the unacceptability of the COG's overall project.[15]

CONCLUSION

The workaday practices of the human sciences vary in the extent to which the distinction between researcher/observer and subject/ observed is problematic. At one extreme, studies of documents, records, and bones allow examination without fear of rebuff or rejection. In a literal sense the documents and bones are objects indifferent to investigation (though, of course, their keepers and owners may not be). When active human agents comprise the focus of study, however, the epistemological conditions

of research become more problematic. Insofar as the "object" of concern can object—that is, resist or refuse the inquirer's efforts to examine and explore—the subject/object dichotomy is transformed from an abstract philosophical scheme presupposed by the researcher to a relation which must be continually and collaboratively constructed.

Excessive participation in the social world under observation—whether due to engulfment by the host and/or enthusiastic embrace by the researcher—threatens the boundary dividing and constituting the "field" from the "fieldworker." As the boundary is attenuated through enticements to, say, "go native," not only is the "field" vulnerable to dissolution but so too is the identity of the fieldworker. Appreciation of the in-situ co-constitution of fieldworker/field invites attention to the practices through which the very distinction is implicitly or explicitly invoked, used and sustained—or disregarded. As Schegloff (1987:219) notes, the common sociological practice of identifying interactional participants by reference to a particular role or status—e.g., "doctor" and "patient"—assumes that participants are treating one another in that capacity in the course of interaction. Interactants who might be appropriately categorized as "doctor" and "patient" respectively, however, may orient to other dimensions of their relation, e.g., "friends." Thus, in any particular interaction, the identification of situatedly relevant identities awaits establishing the identities to which participants are actually oriented. Similarly, the construction of "fieldworker," "ethnographer," "observer," as well as "observed," as operative categories in relations in the field ultimately refers to whether and how host and researcher collaboratively define and use these categories as a premise of interaction.

The collaborative construction and maintenance of participant/observation fieldwork, we have suggested, can be extremely precarious: any and every transaction between a fieldworker and his hosts can affirm or nullify the stance of "observer." Host actions that ostensibly do not seem to address or implicate the fieldworker—a cold shoulder, as it were— implicitly establish the latter as a non-consequential witness. Alternatively, the observer's seemingly Archimedian perch is eroded as group members find they cannot or do not want to disregard the fieldworker's presence. Thus, "observing" is a continuously negotiated posture in which fieldworker and host orchestrate their activities to allow the researcher to remain on the margins with minimal consequence and involvement. Not a position given or obtained once and for all, "doing observer" is variously reproduced, threatened, and preserved through the particulars of interaction.

Ironically, even hosts' acceptance of the definitions of themselves as observed and observable objects, and of the researcher as their observer/ fieldworker, does not provide a terminal point of negotiation much less a transcendent position allowing unproblematic study. Rather, such acceptance comprises and reflects negotiations in which hosts orchestrate themselves as researchable "objects" and the researcher as "observer." Not only may hosts refrain from what they anticipate might be inappropriately inclusive overtures, but they may monitor and manipulate the researcher to make sure he conducts himself in a manner appropriate to an observer. Thus, in contrast to Kondo's family who attempted to make her look, sound and act Japanese, Whyte's Cornerville hosts cautioned him against becoming like them (1955:304):

> At first I concentrated upon fitting into Cornerville, but a little later I had to face the question of how far I was to immerse myself in the life of the district. I bumped into that problem one evening as I was walking down the street with the Nortons. Trying to enter into the spirit of the small talk, I cut loose with a string of obscenities and profanity. The walk came to a momentary halt as they all stopped to look at me in surprise. Doc shook his head and said: "Bill, you're not supposed to talk like that. That doesn't sound like you."

In doing observed/observer, hosts may invite, solicit and even stage events in which they believe the researcher is interested. Hosts may also impose their version of the appropriate focus of or framing for observable matters. Lomax and Casey (1998, para. 5.13), for example, describe how their efforts to videotape midwife practice[16] were stymied by their hosts' versions of these matters:

Once I had set up the camera I left the room and went downstairs. After about 5-10 minutes Sarina (the midwife) shouted to me "we've finished," a statement which I interpreted as a summons to switch off the video camera, which I did. Reviewing this experience in the context of both the events which occurred during the visit after the camera had been switched off and the consultations videoed so far, it is becoming apparent that there are certain activities which the midwives construe as "midwifery" and that they perceive I will be interested in researching (the physical examination, bathing the baby, helping mum breast-feed) and others which, although observable in each of the visits I will not be interested in ("social" talk occurring at the beginning and end of a visit, making arrangements for a subsequent visit). On this occasion, it being difficult to explain in the context of the visit that in fact I was interested in interaction other than that around the physical examination of the mother and child, I went along with the assumption and switched off the camera.

The host group may even appropriate the ethnographer in his very capacity as observer into its ongoing activity. Consider Bosk's (1992) paradoxical involvement in a project in which he was invited to do an ethnographic study of genetic counseling. Accepted and understood to be an observer of the counseling team's activities, Bosk was often requested to "witness" what the doctors were doing (1992:13): to serve as a "reality check" regarding what transpired in particular cases; to provide some measure of legal protection in complex and contested cases; and to appreciate the existential conundrums confronted by the team. Far from being unilaterally invoked, the observer/observed distinction may be appropriated, cultivated, and used by hosts.

In sum, the ethnographic field is constructed through processes that both organize encounters and relations between researcher and researched, and represent such encounters and relations. While the latter processes involve the largely unilateral constitution of field and fieldworker, the former are essentially and unavoidably mutual and collaborative. Our analysis, however, has by and large addressed the mutual construction of field and fieldworker in one-sided terms, focusing on the interactional work of "doing observer." But as our final series of reflections make clear, the "observation" of ongoing scenes and relationships requires the concerted participation of both the observer and the observed. This collaborative process can and should also be examined specifically from the latter's point of view; thus, the analysis of "doing observer" we provide here should be complemented by consideration of exactly how hosts constitute themselves as objects of study, that is, by full analysis of "doing observed."

NOTES

1. Clifford (1997) certainly recognizes fieldwork as "embodied spatial practice" but subordinates such in-the-field "embodied participation" to subsequent textual representation. For example, he emphasizes how gender, race and sex, while deeply salient in actual field relations, are typically written out of ethnographers' representations of the field (1997: 202), ignoring the processes whereby gender, race and sex enter into and affect actual, ongoing relations in ways that allow and shape the ethnographer's interactional presence with and among host members.

2. Analyses of "the field" as a construct developed by the practices of ethnography often neglect or ignore these processes, instead depicting the field as the essentially *unilateral construction of the fieldworker* Clifford (1997), for example, treats fieldwork as an activity initiated and controlled by the ethnographer, the core terms of his analysis—"practice," "dislocation," "attention"—all refer to actions/mindings originating from and controlled by the ethnographer. On occasion the field may indeed be the solipsistic creation of the ethnographer, arising exactly because the ethnographer thinks, speaks and writes as though it did. But in actual encounters with hosts, in attempting to "make a place" from which to participate and observe, the ethnographer generally lacks unilateral power, and "field" and "fieldworker" are co-constituted by hosts and researcher through processes of negotiation which require some (but not necessarily consistently equal) power on both sides.

3. Discussions of distance and detachment by and large have addressed two standard issues the dangers of "overrapport" (Miller 1952), of too intimate or sympathetic identification with those studied (Douglas 1976); and a recommended sequencing of immersion and withdrawal, the latter to take place after the more active phases of fieldwork have been concluded (e.g., Schwartz and Schwartz 1955).

4. At first glance it might appear that fieldworkers could avoid the interactional conundrums of constructing an observer role simply by seeking out and adopting locally available, indigenous observer roles. Humphreys (1970:27-28) recounts such a procedure in studying sexual activities in men's public toilets: "I assumed the role of the voyeur—a role superbly suited for sociologists and the only lookout role that is not overtly sexual." But such a strategy simply pushes the problem back one step: The sociologist-as-voyeur must still enact and sustain this distanced, nonparticipatory stance in the midst of a variety of cues, invitations and overtly sexual activities.

5. Park's hoary exhortation to get the "seat of your pants dirty" by going out to "observe" neighborhoods in Chicago, for example, yields a marginally involved (i.e., sitting on the side) observer. Reinharz's more recent suggestion of an "openness to intimacy and striving for empathy," which "lays the groundwork for friendship, shared struggle, and identity change" (1992:68), promotes a far more immersed and involved researcher.

6. Often such negotiations are conducted through humor, as in the following instance:

> A fieldworker in a HUD housing office reported: "The workers are talking and laughing as Sam decides where to put his desk in his new office. I hear one of the workers say, 'I hope Bob didn't write that down.' I walked up 'What?' 'Oh, I just told Sam it's good he's got space for his machete behind his desk.' They laugh." (Emerson et al. 1995:220)

7. As Johnson explains (1975:159): "To observe sociologically means that one deliberately cedes experiencing the things in themselves to the members of the setting, observation entails seeing phenomena as 'exhibits' of the things in themselves."

8. For an exception, see Ericson (1981:36), who called attention not only to the efforts of police detectives to exclude fieldworkers from key observational sites, but also to "many attempts at *inclusion* of fieldworkers in policing tasks," notably detectives' efforts "to use fieldworkers as allies" in certain field situations.

9. Similar processes arise in autoethnography, a variant of experiential fieldwork in which circumstances of the researcher's own life are constituted as a field. Again, to the extent that one is a central figure in the focal events, "observation" becomes a form of self-reflection in which distance from events and experiences is achieved conceptually, with the fieldworker bifurcating levels of awareness or consciousness, simultaneously immersing in the activity at hand and sustaining a more detached, observational

standpoint. For example, Adler and Adler (1987:70) provide this description of the complexity of orienting to poker playing while actively participating in the game:

> Hayano, for instance, simultaneously had to play the cards that he was dealt, think about the other cards that had already passed through the deck, observe his fellow players to try to interpret what they were holding, look for general categories or typologies of action through which he could organize and analyze the scene, and look for behaviours that constituted specific examples of these types to draw upn in his future writings as examples.

10. As Bosk (1979:193) suggests: "In the field, the everyday life of his subjects overwhelms the researcher, threatens to obliterate his sense of self, and forces a reconsideration of deeply held personal and intellectual beliefs."

11. As Clifford (1997) emphasizes, classic accounts of fieldwork represented the ethnographer as having a distinctive "disciplined professional body," one in which emotions are restricted, the fieldworker's gender and race are marginalized, and sex with the natives is taboo. This last taboo, Clifford suggests, arose less as a barrier against "'going native' or losing critical distance than against 'going traveling,' violating a professional habitus" (202). As he reports: "In travel practices and texts, having sex, heterosexual and homosexual, with local people was common" (202).

12. Note also that members may perceive and react to a fieldworker's silent,watchful presence in ways that depart radically from the latter's self-understanding as "mere observer," showing once again the collaborative interactional work that underlies observation.

13. It is our impression that such outright denials are relatively hard to find in the fieldwork literature, a fact which may well reflect members' sensitivities in what they will ask of fieldworkers, and fieldworkers' reluctance to make an outright refusal, perhaps thereby risking rapport and access. Supporting this possibility are a number of reports in which fieldworkers failed to say no when, in members' eyes or in their own retrospective evaluations, they should have; Whyte's (1955:312ff) regret for having voted under others' names provides one example. Fieldworkers do report making direct declarations of refusal when asked to report on their observations to outsiders or superordinates, but such refusals, of course, reaffirm ties to those studied by denying any obligation to these other parties.

14. In effect, the interaction that might have been with one's hosts to preserve distance ("I am a sociologist") becomes a private interaction with oneself, in these instances, fieldworkers sustain (or reestablish) their position as "observer" without the complicity of their hosts.

15. A variety of routine operations in the field may contribute to anchoring an individual as a researcher. From this point of view, daily note taking, letters to and from the field, contacts with chairs of dissertation committees and the like, both reflect and remind the fieldworker of her commitments.

16. Videotaping naturally occurring interaction generates many of the same problems as faced by the participant-observer fieldworker. These problems center both around matters of where to place and when to turn on and off the camera, and around interactions between camera person and those being taped; as Lomax and Casey (1998:para 5.2) report: "It is not possible to enter a person's home and set up camera without becoming interactionally involved."

REFERENCES

Adler, P.A., & Adler, P. (1987). Membership Roles in Field Research. Newbury Park, CA: Sage.

Anspach, R.R. (1993). Deciding Who Lives: Fateful Choices in the Intensive-Care Nursery. Berkeley and Los Angeles' University of California Press.

Arendell, Ty. (1997). Reflections on the Researcher-Researched Relationship: A Woman Interviewing Men. *Qualitative Sociology,* 20, 341-68.

Atkinson, P. (1992). Understanding Ethnographic Texts. Newbury Park, CA: Sage.

Bosk, C.L. (1979). Forgive and Remember: Managing Medical Failure. Chicago: University of Chicago Press.

Clifford, J. (1997). Spatial Practices: Fieldwork, Travel, and the Disciplining of Anthropology. In A. Gupta and J. Ferguson (Eds.), *Anthropological Locations: Boundaries and Grounds for a Field Science* (pp. 185-222). Berkeley: University of California Press.

Emerson, R.M., & Fretz, R., Shaw, L.L. (1995). Writing Ethnographic Fieldnotes. Chicago: University of Chicago Press.

Emerson, R.M., & Pollner, M. (1976). Dirty Work Designations: Their Features and Consequences in a Psychiatric Setting. *Social Problems,* 23, 243-55.

Ericson, R.V. (1981). Making Crime a Study of Detective Work. Toronto: Butterworth.

Evans-Pritchard, E.E. (1976). Some Reminiscences and Reflections on Fieldwork. Appendix IV in

Witchcraft, Oracles and Magic among the Azande (Abridged). Oxford: Clarendon Press.

Festinger, L. & Riecken, H.W., Schachter, S. (1956). When Prophecy Fails. New York: Harper and Row.

Fine, G.A. (1993). Ten Lies of Ethnography: Moral Dilemmas in Field Research. *Journal of Contemporary Ethnography*, 22, 267-94.

Forrest, B. (1986). Apprentice-Participation: Methodology and the Study of Subjective Reality. *Urban Life*, 14, 431-53.

Goffman, E. (1963b). Behavior in Public Places: Notes on the Social Organization of Gatherings. New York: Free Press.

Goffman, E. (1989). On Fieldwork. *Journal of Contemporary Ethnography*, 18, 123-32.

Golde, P. Ed. (1986/1970). Women in the Field: Anthropological Experiences. Berkeley: University of California Press.

Gupta, A. & Ferguson, J., (Eds.) (1997a). Anthropological Locations: Boundaries and Grounds for a Field Science. Berkeley and Los Angeles: University of California Press.

Gussow, Z. (1964). The Observer-Observed Relationship as Information about Structure in Small Group Research: A Contemporary Study of Urban Elementary School Classrooms. *Psychiatry*, 27, 230-47.

Horowitz, R. L. (1967). The Rise and Fall of Project Camelot. Cambridge, MA: M.I.T. Press.

Horowitz, R. (1986). Remaining an Outsider: Membership as a Threat to Research Rapport. *Urban Life*, 14, 409-30.

Johnson, J.M. (1975). Doing Field Research. New York: Free Press.

Kondo, D.K. (1990). Crafting Selves: Power, Gender, and Discourses of Identity in a Japanese Workplace. Chicago: University of Chicago Press.

Lemert, E.M. (1962). Paranoia and the Dynamics of Exclusion. *Sociometry*, 25, 2-25.

Leo, R.A. (1995). Trial and Tribulations: Courts, Ethnography and the Need for an Evidentiary Privilege for Academic Researchers. *The American Sociologist*, 26, 113-34.

Lofland, J. (1966). Doomsday Cult: A Study of Conversion. Proselytization, and Maintenance of Faith. Englewood Cliffs, NJ: Prentice-Hall.

Loftland, J. & Lofland, L.H. (1995). Analyzing Social Settings: A Guide to Qualitative Observation and Analysis. Third Edition. Belmont, CA: Wadsworth.

Lomax, H. & Casey, N. (1998). Recording Social Life: Reflexivity and Video Methodology. *Sociological Review Online*, 3(2).

Lyman, K.A. (1993). Day in, Day Out with Alzheimer's: Stress in Caregiving Relationships. Philadelphia: Temple University Press.

McCurdy, M. & Becker, H.S. (1990). Performance Science. *Social Problems*, 37, 117-32.

Mehan, H. & Wood, H. (1975). The Reality of Ethnomerhodology. New York: Wiley.

Myerhoff, B. (1989). So What Do You Want from Us Here? In C. D. Smith and W. Kornblum (Eds.), *In the Field: Readings on the Field Research Experience* (pp. 83-90). New York: Praeger.

Reinharz, S. (1979). On Becoming a Social Scientist: From Survey Research and Participant Observation to Experimental Analysis. San Francisco: Jossey-Bass.

Reinharz, S. (1992). Feminist Methods in Social Research. New York: Oxford University Press.

Robbins, T. & Anthony, D., Curtis, T.E. (1973). The Limits of Symbolic Realism: Problems of Empathetic Field Observation in a Sectarian Context. *Journal for the Scientific Study of Religion*, 12, 259-71.

Sanchez Jankowksi, M. (1991). Islands in the Street: Gangs and American Urban Society. Berkeley and Los Angeles: University of California Press.

Schatzman, L. & Strauss, A.L. (1973). Field Research: Strategies for a Natural Sociology. Englewood Cliffs, NJ: Prentice-Hall.

Snow, D.A. (1980). The Disengagement Process: A Neglected Problem in Participant Observation Research. *Qualitative Sociology*, 3, 100-22.

Thorne, B. (1983). Political Activist as Participant Observer: Conflicts of Commitment in a Study of the Draft Resistance Movement of the 1960s. In R. M. Emerson (Ed.) *Contemporary Field Research: A Collection of Readings* (pp. 216,34). Boston: Little, Brown.

Turner, R.H. (1947). The Navy Disbursing Officer as a Bureaucrat. American *Sociological Review*, 12, 342-48.

Van Zandt, D. E. (1991). Living in the Children of God. Princeton, NJ: Princeton University Press.

Warren, C.A.B. & Hackney, J.K. (2000). Gender Issues in Ethnography. Second Edition. Thousand Oaks, CA: Sage.

Whyte, W.F. (1943/1955/1983/1993). Street Corner Society: The Social Structure of an Italian Slum. Chicago: University of Chicago Press.

Williams, T. (1989). Exploring the Cocaine Culture. In C.D. Smith and W. Kornblum (Eds.), *In the Field: Readings on the Field Research Experience* (pp. 27-32). New York: Praeger.

As an anthropologist, Spradley introduces the very important concept of interviewing as a major qualitative method for the collection of data. Two major themes are involved in this process: developing rapport with those you are interviewing and attaining meaningful information. The rapport process, if developed correctly, has four stages: (1) Apprehension—most interviews have an element of uncertainty that may cause apprehensive feelings, both for the subject being interviewed and the researcher conducting the inquiry; (2) exploration—once rapport begins to be established, the researcher and the subject become more comfortable with each other; (3) cooperation represents the third stage. Here, mutual trust is established between both parties, and as a result, cooperation exists; (4) participation is the last step in gaining rapport. After some time spent together, the informant begins to perceive his or her role as a teacher to the researcher. At this stage, complete participation is achieved. Spradley then goes on to describe and analyze the various types of ethnographic questions that the interviewer asks and elicits answers that have to be drawn from those being questioned. This process should lead to further probing questions and more in-depth information. The author examines numerous descriptive questions. He goes on to offer the novice researcher practical methods in conducting an ethnographic interview.

ASKING DESCRIPTIVE QUESTIONS

JAMES SPRADLEY

Ethnographic interviewing involves two distinct but complementary processes: developing rapport and eliciting information. Rapport encourages informants to talk about their culture. Eliciting information fosters the development of rapport. In this step we will examine rapport and discuss the nature of ethnographic questions, particularly descriptive questions.

THE RAPPORT PROCESS

Rapport refers to a harmonious relationship between ethnographer and informant. It means that a basic sense of trust has developed that allows for the free flow of information. Both the ethnographer and the informant have positive feelings about the interviews, perhaps even enjoy them. However, rapport does not necessarily mean deep friendship or profound intimacy between two people. Just as respect can develop between two people who do not particularly like one another, rapport can exist in the absence of fondness and affection.

It is impossible to identify universal qualities that build rapport because harmonious relationships are culturally defined in every society. And so the ethnographer must pay particular attention to friendly relationships in each cultural scene to learn local, culture-bound features that build rapport. For example, when I interviewed Kwakiutl informants in British Columbia, I observed that friends and kinsmen sat together in long periods of silence. Although difficult, I learned to sit in silence and to converse more slowly. The rapport I gained through adopting these local patterns of interaction contributed to successful interviews. What follows regarding rapport must be taken as general suggestions. Some will work well within our own society in many cultural scenes; other suggestions must be modified to fit local cultural situations as well as the peculiarities of individual informants.

Probably the only universal characteristic of rapport is that it changes and fluctuates over time. On first encounter a potential informant may appear eager and cooperative. During the first interview this same informant appears uncomfortable, anxious, and even defensive. A different informant, after several interviews conducted in a harmonious fashion, becomes suspicious and bored, even discontinuing further contact. Laura Bohannon, in her classic anthropological novel, *Return to Laughter*, graphically describes the fluctuating rapport she experienced with her informants. Yabo, an old man who showed initial antagonism, became the first informant to reveal the secrets of witchcraft. Kako, the chief, took the anthropologist into his homestead and expressed willingness to help from the start. However, circumstances changed and he soon refused to talk of anything significant, influencing others to ignore the anthropologist. Finally, this phase in the relationship passed and Kako again became a willing and helpful informant.

Although sometimes unpredictable, rapport frequently does develop in a patterned way. I want to suggest a model of the *rapport process* in ethnographic interviewing. This model will provide the beginning ethnographer with a kind of compass for recognizing when rapport is developing well and when it has wandered off course. It can provide a basis for identifying and correcting problems that arise in the ethnographer-informant relationship.

The rapport process, in cases where it develops successfully, usually proceeds through the following stages:

APPREHENSION → EXPLORATION → COOPERATION → PARTICIPATION

I want to discuss these stages by focusing on the interaction that goes on *during* interviews. In doing this, however, we should not lose sight of the wider context of field work. Most ethnographers will conduct participant observation at the same time, thus encountering key informants when they are working, visiting friends, enjoying leisure time, and carrying out ordinary activities. These encounters contribute to rapport as much as, or more than, the encounters during actual interviews. Under such conditions, the relationship may move more quickly to full cooperation. However, rapport still goes through a sequence of stages. Many times an ethnographer may want to conduct interviews with people not encountered during participant observation; rapport can still develop in a positive manner.

Apprehension

Ethnographic interviews always begin with a sense of uncertainty, a feeling of *apprehension*. This is true for both experienced ethnographers and the beginner. Every time I contacted a tramp and asked if we could talk, I felt apprehensive and sensed that each potential informant had similar feelings. Sometimes apprehension is slight; at other times informants express deep anxiety and suspicion. I recall one tramp who seemed overly anxious. I explained my purpose and began asking questions but received only brief, curt replies. I felt increasing discomfort and made further attempts to put my informant at ease. "Are you with the F.B.I.?" he finally blurted out. I assured him I was a professor at the nearby medical school and had no connection with the F.B.I. or the local police department. He made me promise that I would not divulge his name to anyone, that all his statements could only be used anonymously.

Such extreme apprehension is rare, but some degree of uncertainty starting with the first contact through one or two interviews is common. The informant doesn't know what to expect, doesn't really understand the purposes and motives of the ethnographer. Both researcher and informant are unsure how the other person will evaluate responses. Informants may fear that they will not meet the expectations of the ethnographer. They may comment: "I don't know if I know enough," or "I'm not sure I can really help you, maybe you ought to talk to someone else about this."

The realization that ethnographic interviews begin with some uncertainty in the relationship can help the beginning ethnographer relax and accept this fact. At the same time, several things can help move the interviews through the stage of apprehension. The most important thing is to get informants talking. As we shall see later in this step, *descriptive questions* are especially useful to start the conversation and keep an informant freely talking. It does not usually matter what a person talks about; it does matter that the informant does most of the talking during the first couple of interviews. When an informant talks, the ethnographer has an opportunity to listen, to show interest, and to respond in a nonjudgmental fashion. These kinds of responses represent the most effective way to reduce an informant's apprehension. They communicate acceptance and engender trust. One of the most important principles, then, for the first interviews is to *keep informants talking*.

Exploration

Apprehension usually gives way quickly to *exploration*. In this stage of the rapport process, both ethnographer and informant begin trying out the new relationship. Together they seek to discover what the other person is like, what the other person really wants from the relationship. Exploration is a time of listening, observing, and testing. What does he want me to say? Can she be trusted? Is she going to be able to answer my questions? What does she really want from these interviews? Am I answering questions as

I should? Does he really want to know what I know? These questions often go unspoken but exist nonetheless.

Apprehension, the first stage, arises in part from simple unfamiliarity with the terrain of ethnographic interviews. Exploration is the natural process of becoming familiar with this new landscape. Although each party begins exploring immediately, there comes a point where they leave behind the feelings of uncertainty and anxiety to enter the fullblown stage of exploration. It may occur when each laughs at something said, when the informant seems to go off on an interesting tangent, or when the ethnographer mentally sets aside prepared questions to talk about something. When a sense of sharing occurs, a moment of relaxation comes. Both can then begin to explore the territory with greater freedom.

Informants need the opportunity to move through the stage of exploration without the pressure to fully cooperate. It takes time to grasp the nature of ethnographic interviews. It takes time to see if the ethnographer's actions will match the explanation offered during the first interview. Valuable data can be collected during this stage if the ethnographer is willing to wait for full cooperation. During this stage a certain tenseness exists and both parties may find the interviews exhausting.

Three important principles facilitate the rapport-building process during this stage. First, *make repeated explanations*. A simple statement may suffice: "As I said earlier, I'm interested in finding out how you talk about things, how you see things. I want to understand things from your point of view." One dare not assume that informants appreciate the nature of ethnographic interviews based only on the first explanation. Repetition before each interview, during interviews, and at the end of each will pay great dividends.

Second, *restate what informants say*. Using this principle, the ethnographer selects key phrases and terms used by an informant and restates them. Restating in this fashion reinforces what has been said by way of explanation. Restating demonstrates an interest in learning the informant's language and culture. Here are three examples of restatements typical of my interviews with tramps:

1. "Then you would say, 'I made the bucket in Seattle.'"

2. "So, if a man was a trustee, he'd do easy time."

3. "Then I might hear another tramp saying, 'He's a bindle stiff.' Is that right?"

Restating embodies the nonjudgmental attitude which contributes directly to rapport. When the ethnographer restates what an informant says, a powerful, unstated message is communicated—"I understand what you're saying; I am learning; it is valuable to me." Restatement must be distinguished from reinterpreting, a process in which the interviewer states *in different words* what the other person said. Reinterpreting prompts informants to translate; restating prompts them to speak in their own ordinary, everyday language.

The third principle states, *don't ask for meaning, ask for use.* Beginning ethnographers often become overconcerned with meanings and motives. They tend to press informants with questions like, "What do you mean by that?" and "Why would you do that?" These questions contain a hidden judgmental component. Louder than words, they seem to shout, "You haven't been clear; you haven't explained adequately; you are hiding the true reasons for what you told me." Ethnographic interviewing differs from most other approaches by the absence of probing "why" and "what do you mean" questions.

Let me constrast the use of *why questions* and *meaning questions* with the strategy of asking informants how they use their ordinary language. An unfamiliar term emerged in my interviews with tramps; it was called "days hanging." I heard an informant say, "I had twenty days hanging so I pled guilty and asked the judge for the alcoholism treatment center." Another recalled, "Well, I left town because I had a lot of days hanging." Tramps could respond to direct questions and at first I asked things like, "Why did you have twenty days hanging?" "Why did you leave town?" and "What do you mean you had twenty days hanging?" However, this kind of questioning led directly to translations for my benefit. "Well, I had twenty days hanging because I'd made the bucket four times in a row." "I left town 'cause I knew I'd do hard time." And such

translations required still more probing "why" questions—"*Why* did you have twenty days?" "What do you *mean*, did hard time?" Such questions communicated to my informants that they had not been clear. In a subtle, unspoken way, these questions pressured informants to use their translation competence.

As time went on I learned that instead of asking for meaning, it worked best to ask for use. Cultural meaning emerges from understanding how people *use* their ordinary language. With tramps, I would restate, then ask how the phrase was used. For example, I would say, "You had twenty days hanging. Could you tell me what you would say to the judge if you had ten or thirty or sixty days hanging?" Or I might ask for the way others used this phrase: "Would tramps generally talk about the days they had hanging before they went into the courtroom? What kinds of things would I hear them saying?" I might be more direct: "What are some other ways you could talk about days hanging?" or "Would someone ever say, 'I had twenty days hanging so I pled *not* guilty?'" Asking for use is a guiding principle that underlies all ethnographic interviewing. When combined with restating and making repeated explanations, ethnographic interviews usually move quickly through the stage of exploration.

Cooperation

In time, the rapport process moves into the next stage—cooperation. Informants often cooperate from the start of the first interview, but this stage involves more complete cooperation based on mutual trust. Instead of uncertainty, the ethnographer and informant know what to expect of one another. They no longer worry about offending each other or making mistakes in asking or answering questions. More and more, both persons find satisfaction in meeting together to talk. Informants may offer personal information and feel free to ask the ethnographer questions. Most important, both share in the definition of the interviews; they both know the goal is to discover the culture of the informant in the language of the informant. Now informants may spontaneously correct the ethnographer: "No, I wouldn't say 'the police arrested me,' but that 'a bull pinched me.'"

Participation

The final stage in the rapport process is *participation*. After many weeks of working closely with an informant, sometimes a new dimension is added to the relationship, one in which the informant recognizes and accepts the role of teaching the ethnographer. When this happens there is a heightened sense of cooperation and full participation in the research. Informants begin to take a more assertive role. They bring new information to the attention of the ethnographer and help in discovering patterns in their culture. They may begin to *analyze* their culture, but always from their own frame of reference. Between interviews they are on the lookout for information relevant to the ethnographic goals. Not all informants progress to this last stage of participation. If they do, they increasingly become participant observers in their own cultural scene. The ethnographer's role is then to help informant/participant-observers record what they know.

Building rapport is a complex process, one that every ethnographer must monitor when doing field work. In conducting ethnographic interviews, this process is facilitated by following certain principles: keep informants talking; make repeated explanations; restate what informants say; and don't ask for meaning, ask for use. When combined with asking ethnographic questions, rapport will usually develop in a smooth way from apprehension through cooperation and even into the stage of participation.

ETHNOGRAPHIC QUESTIONS

In most forms of interviewing, questions are distinct from answers. The interviewer asks the questions, someone else responds with answers. This separation often means that questions and answers come from two different cultural meaning systems. Investigators from one cultural scene draw on their frame of reference to formulate questions. The people who respond are from a different cultural scene and draw on another frame of reference to provide answers. This kind of interviewing assumes that questions and answers are separate elements in

human thinking. In the study of other cultures it frequently leads to distortions.

Ethnographic interviewing, on the other hand, begins with the assumption that the question-answer sequence is a single element in human thinking. Questions always imply answers. Statements of any kind always imply questions. This is true even when the questions and answers remain unstated. In ethnographic interviewing, *both questions and answers must be discovered from informants.* Mary Black and Duane Metzger have summarized this point of view:

> It is basic to communications theory that you don't start getting any information from an utterance or event until you know what it is in response to—you must know what question is being answered. It could be said of ethnography that until you know the question that someone in the culture is responding to you can't know many things about the responses. Yet the ethnographer is greeted, in the field, with an array of *responses*. He needs to know what question people are *answering* in their every act. He needs to know which questions are being taken for granted because they are what "everybody knows" without thinking. . . . Thus the task of the ethnographer is to discover questions that seek the relationship among entities that are conceptually meaningful to the people under investigation (1965:144).

There are three main ways to discover questions when studying another culture. First, the ethnographer can record the questions people ask in the course of everyday life. An ethnographer on a university campus in the United States might hear students asking the following questions about motion pictures: "Who stars in that one?" or "Is it rated R?" Other questions would probably be asked about particular courses such as: "Is that a sluff course?" or "When does it meet?" Some settings offer unique opportunities for discovering questions, as Frake has pointed out:

> The ethnographer can listen for queries in use in the cultural scenes he observes, giving special attention to query-rich settings, e.g., children querying parents, medical specialists querying patients, legal authorities querying witnesses, priests querying the gods (1964a:143).

Second, the ethnographer can inquire directly about questions used by participants in a cultural scene. Black and Metzger have suggested three strategies:

1. To ask the informant, "What is an interesting question about ____?"

2. To ask the informant, "What is a question to which the answer is ____?"

3. To ask the informant to write a text in question-and-answer form on some topic of interest to the investigator (1965:146).

In my ethnographic research with tramps and cocktail waitresses I found it useful to create a hypothetical situation and then ask for questions. For example, I would ask a waitress-informant, "If I listened to waitresses talking among themselves at the beginning of an evening, what questions would I hear them ask each other?" To which they might answer, "Who's the other bartender tonight?" or "Which section would you like to work?"

A third strategy for discovering questions simply asks informants to talk about a particular cultural scene. This approach uses general *descriptive questions* that are less likely to reflect the ethnographer's culture. Answers can be used to discover other culturally relevent questions. This approach is like offering informants a frame and canvas and asking them to paint a word-picture of their experience. "Could you tell me what the jail is like?" and "Could you describe a typical evening at Brady's Bar?" are examples of such *descriptive questions*. A variation on this approach developed by Agar (1969) in his study of heroin addicts in prison, is to ask two or more informants to role-play typical interactions from the cultural scene under consideration. As informants talk to each other, the ethnographer can record questions and answers. In the rest of this chapter I want to discuss in detail several kinds of descriptive questions.

DESCRIPTIVE QUESTIONS

Descriptive questions take "advantage of the power of language to construe settings" (Frake

1. Grand Tour Questions
  1.1 Typical Grand Tour Questions
  1.2 Specific Grand Tour Questions
  1.3 Guided Grand Tour Questions
  1.4 Task-Related Grand Tour Questions
2. Mini-Tour Questions
  2.1 Typical Mini-Tour Questions
  2.2 Specific Mini-Tour Questions
  2.3 Guided Mini-Tour Questions
  2.4 Task-Related Mini-Tour Questions
3. Example Questions
4. Experience Questions
5. Native-Language Questions
  5.1 Direct Language Questions
  5.2 Hypothetical-Interaction Questions
  5.3 Typical-Sentence Questions

Figure 1   Kinds of Descriptive Questions

1964a:143). The ethnographer does need to know at least one setting in which the informant carriers out routine activities. For example, I needed to know my informants spent much of their time in jail to be able to ask, "Could you tell me what the jail is like?" I needed to know that cocktail waitresses worked evenings in Brady's Bar to be able to ask, "Could you describe a typical evening at Brady's Bar?" Because ethnographers almost always know *who* an informant is, they almost always know at least one appropriate setting to be used in a descriptive question. If one is studying air-traffic controllers, it is easy to ask, "What do you do as an air-traffic controller?" If one is studying the culture of housewives, it is easy to ask an informant, "Could you describe a typical day? What do you do as a housewife?"

There are five major types of descriptive questions and several subtypes (Figure 1). Their precise form will depend on the cultural scene selected for investigation. Descriptive questions aim to elicit a large sample of utterances in the informant's native language. They are intended to encourage an informant to talk about a particular cultural scene. Sometimes a single descriptive question can keep an informant talking for more than an hour.

One key principle in asking descriptive questions is that *expanding the length of the question tends to expand the length of the response.* Although a question like, "Could you tell me what the jail is like?" qualifies as a descriptive question, it needs expansion. Instead of this brief form, I might say, "I've never been inside the jail before, so I don't have much of an idea what it's like. Could you kind of take me through the jail and tell me what it's like, what I would see if I went into the jail and walked all around? Could you tell me what it's like?" Expanding descriptive questions not only gives informants time to think, but it says, "Tell me as much as you can, in great detail."

1. Grand Tour Questions

A grand tour question simulates an experience many ethnographers have when they first begin to study a cultural scene. I arrived at the alcoholism treatment center and the director asked, "Would you like a grand tour of the place?" As we walked from building to building, he named the places and objects we saw, introduced me to people, and explained the activities in progress. I could not ask tramps to give me a grand tour of the Seattle City Jail, so I simply asked a grand tour question: "Could you describe the inside of the jail for me?" In both situations, I easily collected a large sample of native terms about these cultural scenes.

A grand tour usually takes place in a particular locale: a jail, a college campus, a home, a factory, a city, a fishing boat, etc. Grand tour questions about a locale almost always make sense to informants. We can now expand the idea of "grand tour" to include many other aspects of experience. In addition to *space*, informants can give us a grand tour through some *time* period: "Could you describe the main things that happen during the school year, beginning in September and going through May or June?" They can take an ethnographer through a sequence of *events*: "Can you tell me all the things that happen when you get arrested for being drunk, from the first moment you encounter the police, through going to court and being sentenced, until you finally get out jail?" An informant can give the ethnographer a grand tour through some group of *people*: "Can you tell me the names of all your relatives and what each one is like?" Some large events such as a ceremony are made up of *activities* that can become the basis for a grand tour question: "What are all the things that you do during the

initiation ceremony for new members who join the fraternity?" Even a group of *objects* offers an opportunity for a grand tour: "Could you describe all the different tools and other equipment you use in farming?" Whether the ethnographer uses *space, time, events, people, activities*, or *objects*, the end result is the same: a verbal description of significant features of the cultural scene. Grand tour questions encourage informants to ramble on and on. There are four different types which vary the way such questions are asked.

1.1. Typical Grand Tour Questions. In this form, the ethnographer asks for a description of how things usually are. "Could you describe a *typical* night at Brady's Bar?" One might ask a secretary informant: "Could you describe a *typical* day at the office?" In studying Kwakiutl salmon fishing, I asked, "Could you tell me how you *usually* make a set?" Typical grand tour questions ask the informant to generalize, to talk about a pattern of events.

1.2. Specific Grand Tour Questions. A specific question takes the most recent day, the most recent series of events, or the locale best known to the informant. "Could you describe what happened at Brady's Bar last night, from the moment you arrived until you left?" An ethnographer might ask a secretary, "Tell me what you did yesterday, from the time you got to work until you left?" "Tell me about the last time you made a set, fishing for salmon." Some informants find it difficult to generalize to the *typical* but can easily describe a recent situation.

1.3. Guided Grand Tour Questions. This form asks the informant to give an actual grand tour. A secretary might be asked: "Could you show me around the office?" The ethnographer might ask a Kwakiutl fisherman, "The next time you make a set, can I come along and could you explain to me what you are doing?" Some subjects, such as a typical year or month, do not lend themselves to a guided tour.

1.4. Task-Related Grand Tour Questions. These questions ask the informant to perform some simple task that aids in the description. For example, I frequently asked tramps, "Could you draw a map of the inside of the Seattle City

Jail and explain to me what it's like?" While performing this task, they added a great deal of verbal description. The map helped informants to remember and gave me a better understanding of the jail as they saw it. In studying the cultural scene of backgammon players, I asked, "Could you play a game of backgammon and explain what you are doing?" When informants perform tasks in the context of grand tour questions, the ethnographer can ask numerous questions along the way, such as, "What is this?" and "What are you doing now?"

2. Mini-Tour Questions

Responses to grand tour questions offer almost unlimited opportunities for investigating smaller aspects of experience. Because grand tour questions lead to such rich descriptions, it is easy to overlook these new opportunities. One ethnographer, investigating the culture of directory assistance operators working for Bell Telephone Co., began with a grand tour question: "Could you describe a typical day in your work as a directory assistance operator?" After a lengthy description, she discovered that one recurrent activity was "taking calls." Each call lasted an average of 37 seconds. This led to a mini-tour question: "Could you describe what goes on in taking a call?" The informant was able to break down that brief period of time into more than a dozen activities, ones that were far more complex than the ethnographer realized when she asked the question.

Mini-tour questions are identical to grand tour questions except they deal with a much smaller unit of experience. "Could you describe what you do when you take a break at Brady's Bar?" "Could you draw me a map of the trusty tank in the Seattle City Jail?" "Could you describe to me how you take phone calls in your work as a secretary?" The four kinds of mini-tour questions (typical, specific, guided, task-related) use the same approaches as their counterparts do with grand tour questions.

3. Example Questions

Example questions are still more specific, in most cases. They take some single act or event identified by the informant and ask for an example. A tramp, in responding to a grand tour question, says, "I was arrested while pooling," and so I would ask, "Can you give me an example of pooling?" A waitress states, "There was a table of guys who really gave me a hard time last night." An example question: "Could you give me an example of someone giving you a hard time?" This type of question can be woven throughout almost any ethnographic interview. If often leads to the most interesting stories of actual happenings which an ethnographer will discover.

4. Experience Questions

This type merely asks informants for any experiences they have had in some particular setting. "You've probably had some interesting experiences in jail; can you recall any of them?" "Could you tell me about some experiences you have had working as a directory assistance operator?" These questions are so open ended that informants sometimes have difficulty answering them. They also tend to elicit atypical events rather than recurrent, routine ones. They are best used after asking numerous grand tour and mini-tour questions.

5. Native-Language Questions

Native-language questions are designed to minimize the influence of informants' translation competence. Because descriptive questions are a first step to discovering more culturally relevant questions, they sometimes contain words and phrases seldom used by informants. This encourages informants to translate. Native-language questions ask informants to use the terms and phrases most commonly used in the cultural scene.

When I first began studying tramps, I only knew they were often incarcerated in the Seattle City Jail. "Could you describe the jail?" was a useful grand tour question, but I still was not sure that "jail" was a commonly used term. And so I asked a native-language question: "How would you refer to the jail?" When informants uniformly said, "Oh, most guys would call it *the bucket*," I was able to use this term in future questions. "How would you talk about getting arrested?" led to the term "made the bucket."

Only then could I ask more meaningful descriptive questions like "Could you describe in detail what happens from beginning to end when you make the bucket?"

Native-language questions serve to remind informants that the ethnographer wants to learn their language. They can be used whenever one suspects an informant is translating for the ethnographer's benefit. They should be employed frequently in early interviews until an informant begins to state voluntarily, "The way we would say it is ____," or "Our term for that is ____." Every ethnographer can develop ways to insert native-language queries into each interview. I want to identify three useful strategies.

5.1. Direct-Language Questions. This type of native-language question simply asks "How would you refer to it?" when an informant uses a term. Sometimes it may take the form "Is that the way most people would say it?" For example, tramps often spoke of trying to find a place to sleep at night, so I would ask: "Would you say, 'I was trying to find a place to sleep?'" "No," they responded. "Probably I would say I was trying to *make a flop*." An ethnographer studying the culture of secretaries might ask the following native-language question:

SECRETARY: When I type letters I have to watch out for mistakes.

ETHNOGRAPHER: How would you refer to *mistakes*?

SECRETARY: Oh, I would call them *typos*.

The more familiar the informant and ethnographer are with each other's cultures, the more important native-language questions become. I asked many direct-language questions of cocktail waitresses for this reason. An informant would say, "These two customers were really hassling me," and I would ask, "How would you refer to them, as *customers*?" To which she would reply: "I'd probably say those two *obnoxos*."

5.2. Hypothetical-Interaction Questions. Speaking takes place between people with particular identities. When an informant is talking to an ethnographer, it may be difficult to recall ways to talk to other people. The ethnographer can

help in this recall by creating a hypothetical interaction. For example, an ethnographer could ask, "If you were talking to another directory assistance operator, would you say it that way?" Tramps not only interact among themselves but with policemen, or *bulls*. I often phrased hypothetical-interaction questions to discover how tramps talked to bulls as well as to other tramps.

Hypothetical-interaction questions can be used to generate many native-language utterances. I have interviewed children about school who could easily recall native usages when placed in situations such as the following: "If I were to sit in the back of your classroom, what kinds of things would I hear kids saying to each other?" "If a friend called on the phone to ask if you were going to bring your lunch, what would that person say?" It is even possible to construct the situation in more detail, as in the following question to a waitress: "Imagine yourself at a table of four male customers. You haven't said anything yet, and you don't know any of them. What kinds of things would they likely say to you when you first walked up to their table?" By being placed in a typical situation and having the identities of speaker and listener specified, most informants overcome any tendency to translate and recall many phrases used in ordinary talk.

5.3. Typical-Sentence Questions. A closely related kind of native-language question, this one asks for typical sentences that contain a word or phrase. "What are some sentences I would hear that include the phrase *making the bucket*," or "What are some sentences that use the term *flop*?" are two examples. The typical-sentence question provides an informant with one or more native terms and then asks that informant to use them in typical ways.

Descriptive questions form the basis of all ethnographic interviewing. They lead directly to a large sample of utterances that are expressed in the language used by informants in the cultural scene under investigation.

All ethnographic questions can be phrased in both personal and cultural terms. When phrasing questions *personally*, the ethnographer asks, "Can *you* describe a typical evening you would have at Brady's Bar?" or "How would *you* refer to the jail?" This tells the informant to present his own point of view or her own particular language usage. When phrasing questions *culturally*, the ethnographer asks, "Can you describe a typical evening for most cocktail waitresses at Brady's Bar?" or "How would most tramps refer to the jail?" An informant is someone who can tell about patterns of behavior in a particular scene, not merely his or her own actions. I recall one novice ethnographer who asked a letter carrier about lunch. "I don't eat lunch" was the reply. The ethnographer later rephrased the question in cultural terms: "What do letter carriers do at lunch time?" This query brought a long response which included those who didn't eat lunch, those who brought lunches and ate together, those who ate at restaurants, and several other variations. The various things letter carriers did at lunch turned out to be important cultural information. But eliciting this information depended on phrasing the question in cultural terms.

In this chapter we have examined the rapport process and some of the principles that will facilitate the development of rapport. In addition, we have examined the nature of ethnographic questions and descriptive questions in particular. Descriptive questions form the backbone of all ethnographic interviews. They will make up most of the questions asked in the first interview and their use will continue throughout all subsequent interviews. With practice, a beginning ethnographer can easily gain skill in asking this type of ethnographic question.

REFERENCES

Agar, M. (1969). The Simulated Situation: A Methodological Note. *Human Organization*, 28, 322-29.

Black, M. & Metzger, D. (1965). Ethnographic Description and the Study of Law. *American Anthropologist*, 67, 145-65.

Frake, C. (1964). Notes on Queries in Ethnography. *American Anthropologist*, 66, 132-45.

A researcher's capacity to transcend differences between the occupational culture of the group being studied from that of the researcher is illustrated by Van Maanen's ability to conduct a participant observation study of police within their own culture. By retrospectively discussing his early field experiences with an urban police department, the author analyzes the different roles he played while conducting his study. Of particular importance is the reciprocal relationship that occurs over time between those being studied and the researcher. Van Maanen explains how the completion of a successful research project is very dependent on the reactions and responses of the subjects being studied to the participation and involvement of the researcher within their social milieu. Last, the author offers advice for fieldworkers. He suggests that when conducting such active research, they should, upon entering the field, attempt to remove themselves from outside distractions that are not part of the research scene. This is the only way to gain access to the study groups' world without imparting the fieldworkers' own values into it.

PLAYING BACK THE TAPE

Early Days in the Field

JOHN VAN MAANEN

It is neatly the case that persons under the eye of an avowed researcher may well act in ways knowledgeable of this fact. This principle has been documented so many times that any statement attesting to its presence is now a methodological cliché. What is often overlooked, however, is the implicit reciprocity embedded in the cliché. That is, while researchers attend to the study of other persons and their activities, these others attend to the study of researchers and their activities. An underlying theme of the confessional and cautionary tale I tell here is that the success of any fieldwork endeavor depends inherently on the results of the unofficial study the observed undertake of the observer.

My own research takes place in police agencies, where for the past 20 years I have been in and out of various research roles. Primarily from the bottom up, I have been trying to make

Reprinted from *Experiencing Fieldwork,* Copyright © 1991 Sage Publications, Inc.

sense out of the police life, its consequences for the people who live it and for those subject to it. Like my own, it is a life patterned by the society in which it is located and by the specific organizations that, in imperfect ways, direct it. Significantly, a large body of writing relevant to the police life, policing as an activity, and police organizations in general has been generated through ethnographic fieldwork of the sort I practice. This chapter is about some of my practices as played out in the early days of my work with the police.

Framing my remarks is the view that social researchers are typically aliens in the worlds they study, if only because of their supposed double-edged and academic interests in these worlds. Fieldwork amplifies such strangeness because the researcher comes into the setting as an uninvited, unknown guest, carrying a suitcase, wearing an uncertain smile, and prepared for a long stay (Sanday, 1979). Moreover, the work routines of a field-worker, what Agar (1980) calls a "professional stranger," are rather unnatural or at least unusual ones in most settings—hanging around, snooping, engaging in seemingly idle chitchat, note taking, asking odd (often dumb) questions, pushing for disclosures on matters that may be a source of embarrassment to some on the scene, and so forth. In image and in fact, the activities that fill out the ethnographic curiosity represent a most uncommon adult role in virtually any social setting.

In strong form, the role carries with it a social stigma that can potentially discredit the fieldworker who embodies the role. Much of a fieldworker's behavior—particularly during the initial stages of a lengthy, live-in project—can be understood as an attempt to manage this stigma so that it does not loom large in everyday interaction and its potential is never fully realized. In weak form, the field-worker is in a betwixt-and-between position, akin to any newcomer on the studied scene who must undergo a shift from outsider to insider, recruit to member, observer to participant. Understanding fieldwork from this angle requires coming to terms with the characteristic problems faced by neophytes everywhere (Jackson, 1990). Both of these perspectives are applied below as I play back some of the actions that marked my initial encounters in the police world.

RATIONALIZING FIELDWORK

My work began with a nine-month stay in the field. From the beginning, my official interest in police organizations has been presented to others in the form of a most practical logic. In 1969, for example, I wrote in my thesis proposal:

> The police are quite possibly the most vital of our human service agencies. Certainly they are the most visible and active institution of social control, representing the technological and organizational answer to the question of social order. Through their exclusive mandate to intervene directly into the lives of the citizenry, the police are crucial actors in both our everyday and ceremonial affairs. As such, they deserve intensive and continual scientific study for their role and function in society is far too important to be taken-for-granted, or worse, ignored.

Such high-sounding sentiment provides a sort of doctrinaire or ideological canopy to cover my work. Although rooted in an appealing common sense, it is a woefully inadequate sociological explanation for my work on at least two counts. First, because I conveniently ignore what is to be explained or how such explanations might be forthcoming, my research (and fieldwork) is being used only rhetorically, to establish my credibility and moral authority. The logic of the statement is Olympian and can be read as an inverted Pogo-like aphorism: "I have found the solution and the solution is me." It is, in brief, a gate-opening ploy designed to persuade, not to establish purpose. Second, research canopies such as my formal statement carefully play down the fact that research is both a social and personal act. It is subject to the same biographically and situationally specific understandings by which any individual act is made sensible.

In my case, I began thinking of the police for a research topic in the late 1960s. Whether damned or praised, the police were then prominently fixed in the public imagination as crucial actors in the dramas of the day. I found the police intriguing in that cultural moment for no doubt the same reasons that had occurred to other intellectual types—journalists, novelists, and historians (e.g., Mailer, 1968; Rubinstein, 1973; Wambaugh, 1970). Nor were the police being ignored by my sociological kin (e.g., Bittner, 1970; Manning, 1972; Reiss, 1971; Skolnick, 1966). The police were, in the vernacular, happening and hot and, therefore, dramaturgically attractive to me. Closer to home, however, I also had grown up subject to what I regarded as more than my share of police attention and hence viewed the police with a little loathing, some fear, and considerable curiosity. Nor were such feelings devoid of analytic supposition. I did not go to the field out of affection for the police. In many ways, I had it in for them as I packed my bags.

The general point here is that despite the conversions sure to occur with field experience, it is important for the would-be (and wanna-be) fieldworker to recognize as legitimate the personal matters that lead one into a project. Moreover, I suspect staying with a lengthy project may have more to do with the emotional pull and attraction of a given setting on the field-worker than with any abstracted notions of disciplinary aims such as the conventional one of "making a contribution to the field." There is always a person standing behind the research project, but the standard vocabularies of motive associated with the social research trades often preclude the public appearance of such a person.

Also at play during the early phases of fieldwork is the emergence of methodological ideals and a heightened self-consciousness. Method textbooks are of some comfort, but perhaps the most helpful advice to be found in print comes from carefully combing the prefaces and personal asides written (occasionally) by those who have field experience in the setting of interest. In my own work, the words of police researcher William Westley (1970) were particularly striking:

> There was a terrible tension in the flow of this semi-participant research, for to understand, he had to sympathize; but, in attempting to sympathize, he wanted to be liked. To be liked, he had to play by their rules and not ask too many questions. Thus, the work went in waves of carefully building up confidences and inevitably becoming involved in their regard, then asking questions, sharp probing questions that soon caused rejection. This proved to be personally painful, in the sense that thereafter he had to push himself on men who he felt disliked and were afraid of

him and, practically disastrous, since if the men refused to talk to him, the research would stop. (p. vii)

The practical significance of such accounts are, I hasten to add, rather slight. Westley's words were riveting only after some of my perhaps overly eager fieldwork gestures failed to open up conversations (or, conversely, worked to close them down). Cautionary tales may alert one to a few of the situational demands of fieldwork, but they hardly offer much guidance as to how one will personally answer and remain alive to such demands. Thus, although Howard Becker's (1965b) classic query, "whose side are you on" (p. 239) went with me to the field, what it meant when I arrived there was entirely another matter.

Two concrete and apparently common problems cast shadows over the early stages of fieldwork in organizational settings. First, because fieldworkers typically force themselves through a third party—in my case, the high officials of the studied police agency—into the life situations of others, they must first disassociate themselves as best they can from the interest and control the third party may have over those who are studied. Second, field-workers must recognize that they cannot offer very much of obvious value to those who are studied. As such, there are few, if any, compelling reasons for people to participate in their studies. I could not reasonably claim to be able to cure police problems, teach the police very much, or influence their respective careers. The problem at both levels is to find people for whom one's practiced cover story for the research makes sense and for whom one's presence is not too great a burden.

To move into the flow of events that characterize the work and social situations of those studied requires the assistance of a few reasonably knowledgeable and reliable guides. They run interference for the fieldworker, provide testimony as to the field-worker's aims and character, and, in general, offer member interpretations for the passing scene such that the field-worker can assume lines of conduct that are more or less acceptable to others in the setting. Securing such assistance is a delicate and never-ending task. It is not a single, immutable role a field-worker builds, but an emergent and many-sided one. With many patrolmen, for example, I wanted to appear as a humble, helpful sort, the proverbial "good guy" who would not be likely to do anyone harm. I did little favors for people, provided a sympathetic ear, and when they discussed the topics to which the men of the police culture invariably turned when filling up their day—sex, sports, cars—I joined in eagerly with my own two cents worth.

I tried also to display a good deal of circumspection in relation to what I heard and saw. I wanted to learn the ordinary standards of performance, not establish, recite, or mock them. In a sense, I sought to be accepted by others in the role of an appreciative student or worthy apprentice and sought explicitly to disclaim the judgmental prerogatives commonly associated with a research or expert role (Van Maanen & Kolb, 1984). Yet any form of sustained inquiry implies an evaluative framework—even if one is no more than a reluctant witness. Distrust, suspicion, and guarded conduct cannot be dispelled simply by assuming a sort of "good guy" stance.

The obvious point here is that fieldwork turns not on claims, candor, or mutual regard per se, but on trust. Conventional theories of trust locate its origins in the person toward whom it is directed rather than in the particular occasions of its appearance. This view is, I think, quite misleading not only because it glosses over the ebb and flow of trust over time, but also because it reduces the field-worker or confidant to something of a doofus or cipher, an altogether accommodating sort of nonperson, totally embraced by a research role. Trust underlies all social interaction. In the field, it is built slowly and comes forth only in particular situations with particular people as the field-worker displays a practical understanding, a partisan stance, and a visible conformance to the forms of conduct followed by those studied.

To demonstrate competence in the performances appropriate to a specific social setting does not mean that the field-worker must engage in some sort of echolalia, imitating gesture for gesture and thought for thought the actions of others on the scene. Nor does it mean that one should take a servile stance toward others. In the police world, both orientations would be inappropriate. The first would be detected quickly

as phony and resented because no one likes to be mimicked. The second would jar the refined sense of propriety among the police, who in general interpret weakness or lack of opinion and judgment on the part of another as a sure sign of moral decay. Competence consists of hanging on to a part of one's own identity and style while staying within the boundaries of tolerable behavior as established by those on the scene. Strategy, however, can go only so far.

Disagreeable and unapproachable people are sure to be among those with whom the field-worker must deal. Not everyone is equally open or receptive to the field-worker's presence. Nor is it the case that relationships in the field should be—even in the ideal—random, representative, or equal. Members of the studied world are hardly equivalent in the knowledge they posses. Field-workers do not want to become close to just anyone, but rather want to count among their associates the more open, knowledgeable, comfortable, good-natured, well-placed, and articulate members of the organization. The fact is, however, that informants probably select the researcher as much as the researcher selects them. There is a rather impenetrable barrier between what a grizzled 58-year old street cop will tell a green pea regardless of whether the green pea is a rookie patrolman or a merry field-worker. Glimpses of these boundaries are provided by some snippets of unambiguous rejection recorded in my fieldnotes:

> What do you expect to learn from me? I'm another cabbage around here just trying to lay low and keep outta trouble. Go talk to the blue-light-and-siren boys, they've got the corner on the action. Me? I don't do any police work anymore, haven't for twenty years I'd say.
>
> Stay outta my life, Van Maanen. I don't have nothing to say to you and you don't have nothing to say to me. I'm putting in my time. . . . I don't know what you want and I wouldn't give a shit even if I did. You mind your business and I'll mind mine.
>
> Sociologists? Shit. You're supposed to know what's going on around here. Christ, you come on asking questions like we're the fucking problem. Why don't you go study the goddamn niggers and find out what's wrong with them? They're the fucking problem, not us. I haven't met a sociologist yet who'd make a pimple on a street cop's ass.

TESTING THE FIELD-WORKER

The field-worker's biographical particulars (both fixed and variable) and the situationally specific suppositions (including the unarticulated sort) carried by those in the setting interact, of course, in uncountable ways. Moreover, the biographical particulars and situationally specific suppositions that matter most to others are precisely what the fieldworker has gone into the field to locate. Understanding why and where one's presence is likely to bring forth an "oh fuck, here he comes again" response on the part of others is not merely a tactical consideration. A good part of fieldwork is simply paying attention to the impressions one's vocation, words, and activities cast off. Being out of line or, more crudely, making an ass of oneself is an operational indicator of subjecting oneself to the life situation of others. From this perspective, field-workers are concerned not only with what is revealed explicitly by others but also with the conditional properties that appear to lubricate (or jam) such revelations. Sharpening one's character in the field is both a means of inquiry and, when recognized, an end. Consider now some setting-specific features of my fieldwork with the police.

My entrance into the police world was intended to be similar to that of any recruit. I made no effort to conceal my identity or the general purposes behind my work—although the meaning of this work for those who knew me or of me was no doubt highly variable. In the beginning, I was provided a uniform, a reservist badge and number, a departmental-issue .32-caliber revolver, and a slot in the police academy training class. From an insider's perspective, passage through the academy represents the first common and fundamental test of membership. Few fail, although reputations can be earned in the academy that live long lives. For a field-worker as for a recruit, academy life provided an instant set of cohorts, a source and sense of identification with the agency, and a few but precious friends.

Following graduation, I moved to the street and assumed a less participative role, though on my body I still carried a badge and gun. These symbols of membership signified to others my public commitment to share the risks of the police life. Aside from a few special events, parades, and civic ceremonies where uniformed bodies were in short supply, I was, as the police said, out of the bag. I dressed for the street as I thought plainclothes officers might—heavy and hard-toed shoes, slit or clip-on ties, and loose-fitting jackets that would not make conspicuous the bulge of my revolver. I carried with me chemical Mace, handcuffs, assorted keys, extra bullets, and sometimes a two-way portable radio and a concealed two-inch revolver loaned to me by co-workers who felt that I should be properly prepared.

My plainclothes but altogether coplike appearance created some status confusion for citizens who took me for another officer, perhaps a ranking one. On the streets, citizens would often direct their comments to me. I usually deflected these comments back toward my police companions. On occasion, however, there was no one to deflect such comments back to because my companions were busy elsewhere. At such moments, I more or less bumbled through the encounter by doing what I thought would be approved by my workmates. Mistakes were common.

Crucial to the matter of gaining some acceptance within the agency is what both the police and I have labeled a "balls test"—an assessment made by veteran police officers as to the willingness of a rookie, gender notwithstanding, to support a fellow officer physically. Although all policemen accept colleagues *whom they criticize for their odd views, dishonesty, personal habits, or character, they will not tolerate a colleague in their midst whom they consider dangerous to their health and safety.*

For a field-worker alongside the police, this test was, without doubt, far less extreme than it was for the fully committed. There were instances, however, where I felt it necessary to assist—in police parlance, to back up—the patrolmen whom I was ostensibly observing. At such moments, I was hardly making the rational, reasoned choice in light of the instrumental research objectives I had set. I was reacting as the police react to the unavoidable contingencies of unfolding events. Whether or not I passed these tests with colors flying or dragging is a matter of retrospective opinion. I can say that after a time, most men seemed to accept my presence in the department and appeared at ease when I worked a shift with them.

It is also worth noting that the height of moral duplicity would be to create this sort of partnership impression among the people one studies and then refuse to act in line with the implicit bargain such an impression conveys. For me to pose as a friend of the police and then not back them up on a potentially risky encounter, an encounter they may well have undertaken only because of the additional safety they believed my presence provided, would be to violate the very premises of field research and the importance that human relationships play in its enactment.

Prudence is another tested aspect of the research role. Virtually all policemen have engaged in activities that, if known to some, could get them fired, or, worse, land them in jail. A field-worker who spends more than a trivial amount of time among the police quickly discovers this. A glib statement attesting to one's (confidential intents) will not be taken at face value. Polite acceptance or even deep friendship is not sufficient to get one into the back regions of police departments. Only practical tests will demonstrate one's trustworthiness; liking a person is no guarantee that one can also trust them.

I was party to much discrediting information regarding the legality and propriety of police action. On occasion, I was present when illegal acts took place and, as such, I was as culpable legally as any witness to such actions. One tactic of neutralizing the power of observation is to involve the faultless in potentially embarrassing acts, thus making the faultless as vulnerable to sanction as others. Debts and obligations are, therefore, equalized and discretion becomes almost a structural and taken-for-granted matter. On and following these troublesome incidents, the choices I made followed police custom: *I kept my mouth shut.*

Less crucial perhaps were other rather individually tailored forms of character testing. Early in my police academy days, for example, I was given a series of "gigs"—punitive assignments—for what I took to be fabricated offenses: jogging, not running, from the parking lot to the academy classroom; yawning, stretching, and not paying attention in class; whispering to others; and presenting a dirty weapon at morning inspection. In a short time, I had amassed enough gigs relative to others

in the class to convince myself that the academy staff was pushing to find out just how attached I was to my studies. Privately bitching, I plodded through without great clamor and, by so doing, rediscovered the universal irony of direct social control. By serving as the target for discipline administered by one group, I became entrenched more firmly within the protective circle of another group, thus making control, in the end, far more problematic.

As one might surmise, I think neutrality in fieldwork is an illusion. Neutrality is itself a role enactment and the meaning of such a role to people will, most assuredly, not be neutral. Only by entering into the webs of local associations does the field-worker begin to understand the distinctive nature of what lies within and without these webs. The field-worker's initial tasks involve finding out what classes of people are present on the scene and trying to figure out the cleavages that operate within these classes. There is unlikely to be much of a honeymoon period in fieldwork, for in short order the field-worker will have to decide which of the inner circles and classes to accept as his or her own.

By staking out a particular research patch, a field-worker soon learns that much of the concern and information in one segment of the organization is about another segment. Even among my confidants, talk was more readily forthcoming about someone else's patrol unit, squad, shift, or division. People apparently are far more willing to hold forth on the alleged secrets of others than they are their own. By collecting such tales and noting the regions within which they fell, I was, of course, far more worried about marking the boundaries than with assessing the truth of any given story. Truth in fieldwork, as in life, lies in the eyes of the beholder. The beholders of my work have been, by and large, street cops for whom the adage "there ain't that much truth around" represents the human condition.

In sum, the majority of my time in the police field has been spent within the patrol division and, in particular, with specific squads and shifts within the division. Moreover, I have spent far more time with some squad members than others. These officers were my guides in both the sponsorship and informational senses of the term. They positioned me in the department and suggested to others where precisely my loyalties and sentiments lay. The ecological rights to be close to them, in a sense, were gained early on but had to be sustained continually. A good part of this proximity was attributable to a novitiate's willingness to live with all the good and bad things that took place within this distinct work circle. Understanding, from this perspective, is not mysterious or analytic but rather pragmatic and empathetic. It comes largely from being caught up in the same life situation and circumstances as those one studies. One knows how others feel because one feels it, too.

The Field-Worker's Conceit

This last point is, alas, a conceit. Although field-workers attempt to get as close to others as possible and then stay there for awhile, it is the case that they can pick up and go whenever they choose. Though they may act as though this is impossible, such restraint is always an act. This reflects a basic distinction between the member's "native understanding" and the field-worker's "specimen understanding" of the social world they both share for a time (Bittner, 1973). Although I believe I have learned to think like a cop, I still can stand back and critique that particular frame of mind from another—safe—position. This is a curious and privileged state of mind, not at all characteristic of many men and women I know in the police world who, of practical necessity, take for granted as fact much of what I regard as relative matters. To suggest that I have come to understand the police world as the police themselves do would be a grave error. I do not have to live with the results of police action in the same way as those I study must. The result is that field-workers, by moving in and out of distinct social worlds, come to regard the factual validity of the studied worlds as far more subjective and conjured than many members do.

Not all members fit this rather vulgar characterization. Certainly some are tuned as finely, if not more so, to the stranger's perspective as the field-worker. Double agents, immigrants, marginal members, skeptical tourists, spies, missionaries out to make over the organization, inside theorists and critics, court jesters, and even fellow sociologists (in and out of uniform) often are not hard to locate within a studied scene. In many respects, they all share a common project with the field-worker—spoken or not—which is to question and thus undermine the reality claims made by other more central, self-satisfied, and powerful organizational members, both high caste and low. Fieldwork as practiced at home in familiar institutions is almost inevitably a subversive and, to a degree, collective project.

There is a final irony worth noting in this respect because I have come to believe that successful fieldwork depends on being able for a time to forget (or, at least, overcome) this standard fieldwork plot. Indeed, one implication to be drawn from the body of this chapter is that field-workers should cut their lives down to the bone on entrance to a field setting by removing themselves from resources—physical, social, and intellectual—outside the studied scene. Every social world provides something of a distinctive life for people and the best way to gain access to such a life is to need it by not importing a life of one's own (Goffman, 1989). Cutting one's self off for a time and looking to build a life with one's new colleagues means that penetration is achieved when the field-worker puts down the subversive project, the notebook and pen, the decentered attitude carried into the scene and begins to anticipate as unremarkable and welcome the daily sights and sounds, to appreciate, if not enjoy, life among the studied, to joke back and forth across the membership, to move at the same tempo as his or her companions, to find comfort in work routines established by others, and to not be sought out by would-be donors of trade secrets or critical tales.

All of this unfolds as a highly personal, contingent, temporal process. If one were to wind the tape back to the early days of my fieldwork and let it play again from an identical starting point, I think the chances are astonishingly low that anything like the same study would grace the replay. Obviously, with the luxury of hindsight, sweet reason and rule can be marshaled out to frame much of my actions in the field. Yet reader beware: Self-justification and surely self-parody lurk just beneath the surface in confessional tales. When called on to scrutinize our past, we quite naturally merge the question of what we did with the question of what we should have done, and the answer to one becomes the answer to the other. There is no way to duck this matter and no way to calibrate just how self-serving we have been until perhaps our written-about natives decide to start writing about us and putting on display some of our own odd and exotic ways. At that point, the subjective and conjured features of our own research world and work can come to be appreciated.

REFERENCES

Agar, M. (1980). The Professional Stranger. New York: Academic Press.

Becker, H.S. (1965b). Whose Side Are We On? *Social Problems*, 14, 239-247.

Bittner, E. (1970). Objectivity and Realism in Sociology. In G. Psathas (Ed.), *Phenomenological Sociology* (pp. 108-125). New York: John Wiley.

Goffman, E. (1989). On Fieldwork. [Transcribed and edited by Lyn H. Lofland]. *Journal of Contemporary Ethnography*, 18, 123-132.

Mailer, N. (1968). The Armies of the Night. New York: New American Library.

Manning, P.K. (1972). Observing the Police. In J.D. Douglas (Ed.), *Research on Deviance* (pp. 213-268). New York: Random House.

Reiss, A.J. (1971). The Police and the Public. New Haven, CT: Yale University Press.

Rubenstein, J. (1973). City Police. New York: Farrar, Straus & Giroux.

Sanday, P. (1979). The Ethnographic Paradigm(s). *Administrative Science Quarterly*, 24, 482-493.

Skolnick, J. (1966). Justice Without Trial. New York: John Wiley.

Van Maanen, J. & Kolb, D. (1984). The Professional Apprentice. In S.B. Bacharach (Ed.), *Perspectives in Organizational Sociology* (pp. 1-33). Greenwich, CT: JAI.

Wambaugh, J. (1970). The New Centurions. New York: Norton.

Westley, W.A. (1970). Violence and the Police. Cambridge: MIT Press.

II

POLICE

The articles in this section are representative of qualitative studies that have been conducted on police. Because police are the most visible criminal justice agency, they are frequently in the public eye. Interest in their role within society has long been popularized by movies and television shows, which obviously have enjoyed wide audiences on a national level. The popularity of police issues holds true for the news media, both print and television, and is reflective of the public's fascination with this occupation. I believe that much of the curiosity about the world of law enforcement also has had an effect on social science research. I would venture to speculate that there has been more research and published journal articles, academic books, journalistic accounts, and movies about the police profession than any other component of the criminal justice system. In short, much of the research interest in the police role is mirrored by the public's image of the occupation. In this respect, those who have studied various aspects of policing are not that different from the citizenry we live among.

The seven articles that constitute the police section of this anthology offer a wide array of subjects within the police occupation. Each article consists of a field study project that lasted from months to over 1 year, which involved a particular type of police organization. It is necessary to discuss the actual qualitative approach each researcher utilized in order to better understand how the study was

formulated and completed. This allows readers to determine for themselves the quality and the contributions of the studies' findings.

In the first article, Van Maanen's study of police socialization provides an analysis of the novice police officers' learning process by the author actually attending a 3-month police academy. Following his formal training after graduating from the academy, Van Maanen spent 5 more months of fieldwork, 6 days a week, working in patrol cars with recruits and their training officers. By using a participant observation method of study (although not undertaking the official role as police officer), he was privy to the socialization process of rookie cops who were learning the ropes of police work on a daily basis. Because he spent a great deal of time in the training academy and stayed with one urban police department, Van Maanen was offered the opportunity to see firsthand the ways rookies learn on-the-job training skills necessary to function as a police officer. From his research in Union City, Van Maanen analyzed many other aspects of policing and published some of the best and most academically cited articles on the subject.

The article by Pogrebin and Poole is a good example of how a qualitative research study was formulated by happenstance. The authors were conducting an organizational development consultation for a suburban police department, which required them to spend approximately 1 year riding with patrol officers on all three work shifts. By doing this, they spent the beginning and the end of each shift with the officers in the briefing room. It was at these briefing room sessions that they began to notice insider jokes among the officers that the researchers often found to be sarcastic and offensive. The insider-outsider reactions to the jokes being told peaked their interest, and so the study began. This qualitative-observational study used a grounded theory–inductive approach, in which the researchers began to analyze the strategic uses that insider-organizational employees use for various utilitarian purposes. They based their theoretical perspectives for the uses of humor among police by building on the data they acquired in the field; in this case, the briefing room. As they began to group the meanings the humor provided for the police, they were able to translate these meanings into theoretical perspectives for the various types of humor situations they encountered.

Relying on participant-observation research with an investigation bureau of a city police department, Waegel spent 9 months studying the handling and integration of criminal cases that were assigned to the unit. A great deal of his data were derived from observing investigator-victim interviews and from written case reports. It is important to note that Waegel had to be perceived as a trusted, empathetic person by the detectives he observed or they never would have permitted him to participate in their working lives. Relying on conventional research strategies would have limited his understanding of how detectives handled cases. Instead, Waegel used a qualitative approach for studying the processing of cases and their outcomes by focusing on the shared professional methods used by detectives in organizing their daily activities.

Stenross and Kleinman used interviews with investigative staff from a sheriff's department in a county with about 40,000 people and a mid-size city detective bureau with a similar population. They conducted semistructured, in-depth interviews to collect their data. They taped their interviews and believed that the detectives in both agencies were candid and often unflattering to themselves, because they admitted not working very hard on crimes they felt were unsolvable. Because one of the researchers was married to a sheriff's deputy, the study respondents felt comfortable with the interviewer

and her questions. Having an inside agency connection can be very helpful in studying police, where outsiders' research intentions are frequently suspect. In this particular case, having a relative on the inside most likely saved the researchers an enormous amount of time ingratiating themselves with the study participants. The usual practice is to spend an adequate period of time establishing a rapport between the researcher and respondents before in-depth interviews can elicit credible information, but that obviously was not necessary in this case.

Drawing on interviews with undercover police from three federal and eight municipal police departments, Pogrebin and Poole structured their study population by approaching the agencies for former and current undercover operatives who would be willing and available for personal interviews. The selection of study participants was stratified according to length of time in undercover operations and present assignment. They interviewed twenty former undercover agents and twenty current operatives. Normally, being so selective in a qualitative research project would not be necessary. Because of the secretive nature of undercover work, the authors thought it best to contact the various agencies and have their request for names of current and former undercover officers be provided by them. This allowed each participant to volunteer for the study. The researchers used a grounded theory approach with a semistructured, in-depth interview format, which relied on sequential probes to pursue leads provided by the study subjects. Their advantage to entree for most of the police agencies was due to their ongoing relationships they established with police graduate students as well as those former police students who had maintained a relationship with the authors. They believe that without these established relations, conducting undercover police research would have proved very difficult at best.

In examining community policing by studying law enforcement practices in rural areas, Weisheit and his colleagues utilized data that were based on a larger research project on crime in rural areas. It is a common practice among researchers conducting large data collection studies to find smaller theoretical issues to analyze and write about. This practice holds true for both qualitative and quantitative researchers. In this particular article, the authors interviewed 6 rural sheriffs and 28 police chiefs from small towns. Only 13 interviews, or 18%, were actually face-to-face; the rest of the interview data were collected by telephone. Interviewing by phone is a useful technique to acquire data when those participating in the study live long distances from the researcher. Although face-to-face interviews are the preferred methodological technique to use in conducting qualitative studies, phone interviews represent a legitimized practice of data collection under these circumstances. The authors point out that this was an exploratory study that focused on finding police administrators from the widest range of social and physical environments, due to their understanding of the varied differences across rural areas. Weisheit et al. focused their interviews on police managers in 18 states who were identified as predominantly rural and looked for common themes among the various organizations.

In their study of police lying, Hunt and Manning utilize data that were collected by Hunt's research on police training in a large metropolitan police department. Hunt completed a fieldwork approach by spending 18 continuous months as a participant observer, focusing her efforts on the differences and similarities of the occupational socialization process between male and female police recruits. Like Van Maanen, she participated in a police academy class, used observation and participation, and tape-recorded interviews. The taped interviews occurred in informal settings, away from the department, and with informants selected for their cooperation in providing lengthy interviews. Other data were collected from personnel files of all 200 officers who began their police career during the 18-month period she was there. To gain more insight into the socialization process, she participated in many different off-duty social events and activities with members of the force. This study on police deviancy, collected primarily from taped interviews, represents only one of the articles Hunt produced from her research on police.

SOCIALIZATION

In this article, Van Maanen examines the process by which rookie police recruits attain the motives, sentiments, and behavioral characteristics of the occupational culture as perceived by the recruits attempting to become police officers. The development of a community of purpose is defined by four distinct processual stages. The following socialization begins with four stages: (1) choice, (2) introspection, (3) encounter, and (4) metamorphosis. These stages serve as temporary occupational points for describing the processual movement that recruits follow. New recruits' early police experiences and adventures result in their becoming part of the occupational culture shared by police in general. The ongoing socialization process of becoming an officer causes a gradual incorporation of a police collective consciousness that can be characterized as emphasizing a "we against them" working philosophy.

OBSERVATIONS ON
THE MAKING OF POLICEMEN

JOHN VAN MAANEN

In recent years the so-called "police problem" has become one of the more institutionalized topics of routine conversation in this society. Whether one views the police as friend or foe, virtually everyone has a set of "cop stories" to relate to willing listeners. Although most stories dramatize personal encounters and are situation-specific, there is a common thread running through these frequently heard accounts. In such stories the police are almost always depicted as a homogeneous occupational grouping somehow quite different from most other men.

Occupational stereotyping is, of course, not unknown. Professors, taxicab drivers, used-car salesmen, corporate executives all have mythological counterparts in the popular culture. Yet, what is of interest here is the recognition by the police themselves of the implied differences.

Policemen generally view themselves as performing society's dirty work. As such, a gap is created between the police and the public. Today's patrolman feels cut off from the mainstream culture and unfairly stigmatized. In short, when the policeman dons his uniform, he enters a distinct subculture governed by norms

Reprinted from *Human Organization*, 32, 1973 (407–418). Reprinted by permission.

and values designed to manage the strain created by an outsider role in the community.[1]

To classify the police as outsiders helps us to focus on several important things: the distinctive social definitions used by persons belonging to such marginal subcultures (e.g., "everybody hates a cop"); the outsider's methods for managing the tension created by his social position (e.g., "always protect brother officers"); and the explicit delineation of the everyday standards of conduct followed by the outsider (e.g., "lay low and avoid trouble"). Furthermore, such a perspective forces a researcher to delve deeply into the subculture in order to see clearly through the eyes of the studied.

CONTEXT

While observation of the police in naturally occurring situations is difficult, lengthy, and often threatening, it is imperative. Unfortunately, most research to date relies almost exclusively upon interview-questionnaire data (e.g., Bayley and Mendelsohn 1969; Wilson 1968), official statistics (e.g., Webster 1970; President's Commission on Law Enforcement and the Administration of Justice 1967), or broad-ranging attitude surveys (e.g., Sterling 1972; McNamara 1967). The very few sustained observational studies have been concerned with specific aspects of police behavioral patterns (e.g., Skolnick 1966—vice activities; Reiss 1971—police-citizen contacts; Bittner 1967, Cicourel 1967—police encounters with "skid row alcoholics" and juveniles, respectively). This is not to say these diverse investigations are without merit. Indeed, without such studies we would not have even begun to see beneath the occupational shield. Yet, the paucity of in-depth police-related research—especially from the outsider perspective—represents a serious gap in our knowledge of a critical social establishment.[2]

In particular the process of becoming a police officer has been neglected.[3] What little data we presently have related to the police socialization process come from either the work devoted to certain hypothesized dimensions of the police personality (e.g., dogmatism, authoritarianism, cynicism, alienation, etc.) or cross-sectional snapshots of police attitudes toward their public audiences. Using a dramaturgic metaphor, these studies have concentrated upon the description of the actors, stage setting, and "on stage" performance of the police production. Little attention has been paid to the orientation of the performers to their particular role viewed from "backstage" perspective. Clearly, for any performance to materialize there must be casting sessions, rehearsals, directors, stagehands, and some form(s) of compensation provided the actors to insure their continued performance. Recognizing that to some degree organizational socialization occurs at all career stages, this paradigm focuses exclusively upon the individual recruit's entry into the organization. It is during the breaking-in period that the organization may be thought to be most persuasive, for the person has few guidelines to direct his behavior and has little, if any, organizationally based support for his "vulnerable selves" which may be the object of influence. Support for this position comes from a wide range of studies indicating that early organizational learning is a major determinant of one's later organizationally relevant beliefs, attitudes, and behaviors (Van Maanen 1972; Lortie 1968; Berlew and Hall 1966; Evan 1963; Hughes 1958; Dornbush 1955). Schein (1971) suggested perceptively that this process results in a "psychological contract" linking the goals of the individual to the constraints and purposes of the organization. In a sense, this psychological contract is actually a modus vivendi between the person and the organization representing the outcomes of the socialization process.

METHOD

The somewhat truncated analysis that follows was based upon the observation of novice policemen in situ. The study was conducted in Union City over a nine-month period.[4] Approximately three months of this time were spent as a fully participating member of one Union City Police Academy recruit class. Following the formal training phase of the initiation process, my fully participating role was modified. As a civilian, I spent five months (roughly eight to ten hours a day, six days a week) riding in patrol units operated by a recruit and his FTO (i.e., Field Training Officer charged with imputing "street sense" into the neophyte) as a back-seat observer.

From the outset, my role as researcher-qua-researcher was made explicit. To masquerade as a regular police recruit would not only have been problematic, but would have raised a number of ethical questions as well (particularly during the field training portion of the socialization sequence).[5]

The conversational data presented below are drawn primarily from naturally occurring encounters with persons in the police domain (e.g., recruits, veterans, administrators, wives, friends, reporters, court officials, etc.). While formal interviews were conducted with some, the bulk of the data contained here arose from far less-structured situations.

THE MAKING OF A POLICEMAN: A PARADIGM

For purposes here, the police recruit's initiation into the organizational setting shall be treated as if it occurred in four discrete stages. While these stages are only analytically distinct, they do serve as useful markers for describing the route traversed by the recruit. The sequence is related to the preentry, admittance, change, and continuance phases of the organizational socialization process and are labeled here as choice, introduction, encounter, and metamorphosis, respectively.

Preentry: Choice

What sort of young man is attracted to and selected for a police career? The literature notes that police work seems to attract local, family-oriented, working-class whites interested primarily in the security and salary aspects of the occupation. Importantly, the authoritarian syndrome which has popularly been ascribed to persons selecting police careers has not been supported by empirical study. The available research supports the contention that the police occupation is viewed by the recruits as simply one job of many and considered roughly along the same dimensions as any job choice.

While my research can add little to the above picture, several qualifications are in order which perhaps provide a greater understanding of the particular choice process. First, the security and salary aspects of the police job have probably been overrated. Through interviews and experience with Union City recruits, a rather pervasive *meaningful work theme is apparent as a major factor in job choice.* Virtually all recruits alluded to the opportunity afforded by a police career to perform in a role which was perceived as consequential or important to society. While such altruistic motives may be subject to social desirability considerations, or other biasing factors, it is my feeling *that these high expectations of community service are an important element in the choice process.*

Second, the out-of-doors and presumably adventurous qualities of police work (as reflected in the popular culture) were perceived by the recruits as among the more influential factors attracting them to the job. With few exceptions, the novice policemen had worked several jobs since completing high school and were particularly apt to stress the benefits of working a non-routine job.

Third, the screening factor associated with police selection is a dominating aspect of the socialization process. From the filling out of the application blank at City Hall to the telephone call which informs a potential recruit of his acceptance into the department, the individual passes through a series of events which serve to impress an aspiring policeman with a sense of being accepted into an elite organization. Perhaps some men originally take the qualifying examination for patrolman lightly, but it is unlikely many men proceed through the entire screening process—often taking up to six months or more—without becoming committed seriously to a police career. As such, the various selection devices, if successfully surmounted, increase the person's self-esteem, as well as buttress his occupational choice. Thus, this anticipatory stage tends to strengthen the neophyte's evaluation of the police organization as an important place to work.

Finally, as in most organizations, the police department is depicted to individuals who have yet to take the oath of office in its most favorable light. A potential recruit is made to feel as if he were important and valued by the organization. Since virtually all recruitment occurs via generational or friendship networks involving police officers and prospective recruits, the individual receives personalized encouragement and support which helps sustain his interest during the arduous screening procedure. Such links begin to attach the would-be policeman to the organization long before he actually joins.

To summarize, most policemen have not chosen their career casually. They enter the department with a high degree of normative identification with what they perceive to be the goals and values of the organization. At least in Union City, the police department was able to attract and select men who entered the organization with a reservoir of positive attitudes toward hard work and a strong level of organizational support. What happens to the recruit when he is introduced to the occupation at the police academy is where attention is now directed.

Admittance: Introduction

The individual usually feels upon swearing allegiance to the department, city, state, and nation that "he's finally made it." However, the department instantaneously and somewhat rudely informs him that until he has served his probationary period he may be severed from the membership rolls at any time without warning, explanation, or appeal. It is perhaps ironic that in a period of a few minutes, a person's position vis-à-vis the organization can be altered so dramatically. Although some aspects of this phenomenon can be found in all organizations, in the paramilitary environment of the police world, the shift is particularly illuminating to the recruit.

For most urban police recruits, the first real contact with the police sub-culture occurs at the academy. Surrounded by forty to fifty contemporaries, the recruit is introduced to the harsh and often arbitrary discipline of the organization. Absolute obedience to departmental rules, rigorous physical training, dull lectures devoted to various technical aspects of the occupation, and a ritualistic concern for detail characterize the academy. Only the recruit's classmates aid his struggle to avoid punishments and provide him an outlet from the long days. A recruit soon learns that to be one minute late to a class, to utter a careless word in formation, or to be caught walking when he should be running may result in a "gig" or demerit costing a man an extra day of work or the time it may take to write a long essay on, say, "the importance of keeping a neat appearance."

Wearing a uniform which distinguishes the novices from "real" policemen, recruits are expected to demonstrate group cohesion in all aspects of academy life. The training staff actively promotes solidarity through the use of group rewards and punishments, identifying garments for each recruit class, interclass competition, and cajoling the newcomers—at every conceivable opportunity—to show some unity. Predictably, such tactics work—partial evidence is suggested by the well-attended academy class reunions held year after year in the department. To most veteran officers, their police academy experiences resulted in a career-long source of identification. It is no exaggeration to state that the "in-the-same-boat" collective consciousness which arises when groups are processed serially through a harsh set of experiences was as refined in the Union City Police Department as in other institutions such as military academies, fraternities, or medical schools.[6]

The formal content of the training academy is almost exclusively weighted in favor of the more technical aspects of police work. A few outside speakers are invited to the academy (usually during the last few weeks of training), but the majority of class time is filled by departmental personnel describing the more mundane features of the occupation. To a large degree, the formal academy may be viewed as a didactic sort of instrumentally oriented ritual passage rite. As such, feigning attention to lectures on, for example, "the organization of the Administrative Services Bureau" or "state and local traffic codes" is a major task for the recruits.

However, the academy also provides the recruit with an opportunity to begin learning or, more properly, absorbing the tradition which typifies the department. The novices' overwhelming eagerness to hear what police work is really like results in literally hours upon hours of war stories (alternately called "sea stories" by a few officers) told at the discretion of the many instructors. One recruit, when asked about what he hoped to learn in the academy, responded as follows:

> I want them to tell me what police work is all about. I could care less about the outside speakers or the guys they bring out here from upstairs who haven't been on the street for the last twenty years. What I want is for somebody who's gonna level with us and really give the lowdown on how we're supposed to survive out there.

By observing and listening closely to police stories and style, the individual is exposed to a partial organizational history which details certain personalities, past events, places, and implied relationships which the recruit is expected eventually to learn, and it is largely through war stories that the department's history is conveyed. Throughout the academy, a recruit is exposed to particular instructors who relate caveats concerning the area's notorious criminals, sensational crimes, social-geographical peculiarities, and political structure. Certain charismatic departmental personalities are described in detail. Past events—notably the shooting of police officers—are recreated and informal analyses passed on. The following excerpt from a criminal law lecture illustrates some of these concerns.

> I suppose you guys have heard of Lucky Baldwin? If not, you sure will when you hit the street. Baldwin happens to be the biggest burglar still operating in this town. Every guy in this department from patrolman to chief would love to get him and make it stick. We've busted him about ten times so far, but he's got an asshole lawyer and money so he always beats the rap. . . . If I ever get a chance to pinch the SOB, I'll do it my way with my thirty-eight and spare the city the cost of a trial.

The correlates of this history are mutually held perspectives toward certain classes of persons, places, and things which are the objective reality of police work. Critically, when war stories are presented, discipline within the recruit class is relaxed. The rookies are allowed to share laughter and tension-relieving quips with the veteran officers. A general atmosphere of camaraderie is maintained. The near lascivious enjoyment accompanying these informal respites from academy routine serve to establish congeniality and solidarity with the experienced officers in what is normally a rather harsh and uncomfortable environment. Clearly, this is the material of which memories are made.

Outside the classroom, the recruits spend endless hours discussing nuances and implications of war stories, and collective understandings begin to develop. Via such experiences, the meaning and emotional reality of police work starts to take shape for the individual. In a sense, by vicariously sharing the exploits of his predecessors, the newcomer gradually builds a common language and shared set of interests which will attach him to the organization until he too has police experience to relate.

Despite these important breaks in formality, the recruits' early perceptions of policing are overshadowed by the submissive and often degrading role they are expected to play in the academy. Long, monotonous hours of class time are required, a seemingly eternal set of examinations are administered, meaningless assignments consume valuable off-duty time, various mortifying events are institutionalized rituals of academy life (e.g., each week, a class "asshole" was selected and received a trophy depicting a gorilla dressed as a policeman), and relatively sharp punishments enacted for breaches of academy regulations. The multitude of academy rules make it highly unlikely that any recruit can complete the training course unscathed. The following training division report illustrates the arbitrary nature of the dreaded gigs issued during the academy phase.

> You were observed displaying unofficerlike conduct in an academy class. You openly yawned (without making any effort to minimize or conceal the fact), (this happened twice), you were observed looking out the window constantly, and spent time with your arms lying across your desk. You will report to Sergeant Smith in the communications division for an extra three hours of duty on August 15 (parentheses theirs).

The main result of such stress training is that the recruit soon learns it is his peer group rather than the "brass" which will support him and which he, in turn, must support. For example, the newcomers adopt covering tactics to shield the tardy colleague, develop cribbing techniques to pass exams, and become proficient at constructing consensual ad hoc explanations of a fellow-recruit's mistake. Furthermore, the long hours, new friends, and ordeal aspects of the recruit school serve to detach the newcomer from his old attitudes and acquaintances. In short, the academy impresses upon the recruit that he must now identify with a new group— his fellow officers. That this process is not complete, however, is illustrated by the experience of one recruit during this last week of training before his introduction to the street. This particular recruit told his classmates the following:

> Last night as I was driving home from the academy, I stopped to get some gas. . . . As soon as I shut off the engine some dude comes running up flapping his arms and yelling like crazy about being robbed. Here I am sitting in my car with my gun on and the ole buzzer (badge) staring him right in the face. . . . Wow!. . . I had no idea what to do; so I told him to call the cops and got the hell away from there. What gets me is that it didn't begin to hit me that I WAS A COP until I was about a mile away (emphasis mine).

To this researcher, the academy training period serves to prepare the recruits to alter their initially high but unrealistic occupational expectations. Through the methods described above, the novices begin to absorb the subcultural ethos and to think like policemen. As a fellow recruit stated at the end of the academy portion of training:

> There's sure more to this job than I first thought. They expect us to be dog catchers, lawyers, marriage counselors, boxers, firemen, doctors, babysitters, race-car drivers, and still catch a crook occasionally. There's no way we can do all that crap. They're nuts!

Finally, as in other highly regulated social systems, the initiate learns that the formal rules and regulations are applied inconsistently. What is sanctioned in one case with a gig is ignored in another case. To the recruits, academy rules become behavioral prescriptions which are to be coped with formally, but informally dismissed. The newcomer learns that

when The Department notices his behavior, it is usually to administer a punishment, not a reward. The solution to this collective predicament is to stay low and avoid trouble.

Change: Encounter

Following the classroom training period, a newcomer is introduced to the complexities of the "street" through his Field Training Officer (hereafter referred to as the FTO). It is during this period of apprenticeshiplike socialization that the reality shock encompassing full recognition of being a policeman is likely to occur. Through the eyes of his experienced FTO, the recruit learns the ins and outs of the police role. Here he learns what kinds of behavior are appropriate and expected of a patrolman within his social setting. His other instructors in this phase are almost exclusively his fellow patrolmen working the same precinct and shift. While his sergeant may occasionally offer tips on how to handle himself on the street, the supervisor is more notable for his absence than for his presence. When the sergeant does seek out the recruit, it is probably to inquire as to how many hazardous traffic violations the "green pea" had written that week or to remind the recruit to keep his hat on while out of the patrol car. As a matter of formal policy in Union City, the department expected the FTO to handle all recruit uncertainties. This traditional feature of police work—*patrolmen training patrolmen— insures continuity from class to class of police officers regardless of the content of the academy instruction.* In large measure, the flow of influence from one generation to another accounts for the remarkable stability of the pattern of police behavior.

It was my observation that the recruit's reception into the Patrol Division was one of consideration and warm welcome. As near as interviewing and personal experience can attest, there was no hazing or rejection of the recruit by veteran officers. In all cases, the recruits were fully accepted into the ongoing police system with good-natured tolerance and much advice. If anyone in the department was likely to react negatively to the recruits during their first few weeks on patrol, it was the supervisor and not the on-line patrolmen. The fraternal-like regard shown the rookie by the experienced officers stands in stark contrast to the stern greeting he received at the police academy. The newcomer quickly is bombarded with "street wise" patrolmen assuring him that the police academy was simply an experience all officers endure and has little, if anything, to do with real police work. Consequently, the academy experiences for the recruits stand symbolically as their rites de passage, permitting them access to the occupation. That the experienced officers confirm their negative evaluation of the academy heightens the assumed similarities among the rookies and veterans and serves to facilitate the recruit's absorption into the division. As an FTO noted during my first night on patrol:

> I hope the academy didn't get to you. It's something we all have to go through. A bunch of bullshit as far as I can tell. . . . Since you got through it all right, you get to find out what it's like out here. You'll find out mighty fast that it ain't nothing like they tell you at the academy.

During the protracted hours spent on patrol with his FTO, the recruit is instructed as to the real nature of police work. To the neophyte, the first few weeks on patrol is an extremely trying period. The recruit is slightly fearful and woefully ill-prepared for both the routine and eccentricities of real police work. While he may know the criminal code and the rudimentaries of arrest, the fledgling patrolman is perplexed and certainly not at ease in their application. For example, a two-day veteran told the following story to several of his academy associates.

> We were down under the bridge where the fags hang out and spot this car that looked like nobody was in it. . . . Frank puts the spot on it and two heads pop up. He tells me to watch what he does and keep my mouth shut. So I follow him up to the car and just kind of stand around feeling pretty dumb. Frank gives 'em a blast of shit and tells the guy sitting behind the wheel he's under arrest. The punk gets out of the car snivelling and I go up to him and start putting the cuffs on. Frank says, "just take him back to the car and sit on him while I get the dope on his boyfriend here." So I kind of direct him back to the car and stick him in the backseat and I get in the front. . . . While Frank's filling out a FIR (Field Investigation Report) on

the other guy, the little pansy in the backseat's carrying on about his wife and kids like you wouldn't believe. I'm starting to feel sorta sorry for arresting him. Anyway, Frank finishes filling out the FIR and tells the other guy to get going and if he ever sees him again he'll beat the holy shit out of him. Then he comes back to the car and does the same number on the other fag. After we drove away, I told Frank I thought we'd arrested somebody. He laughed his ass off and told me that that's the way we do things out here.

To a recruit, the whole world seems new, and from his novel point of view it is. Like a visitor from a foreign land, the daily events are perplexing and present a myriad of operational difficulties. At first, the squawk of the police radio transmits only meaningless static; the streets appear to be a maze through which only an expert could maneuver; the use of report forms seems inconsistent and confusing; encounters with a hostile public leave him cold and apprehensive; and so on. Yet, next to him in the patrol unit is his partner, a veteran. Hence, the FTO is the answer to most of the breaking-in dilemmas. It is commonplace for the rookie to never make a move without first checking with his FTO. By watching, listening, and mimicking, the neophyte policeman learns how to deal with the objects of his occupation—the traffic violator, the hippie, the drunk, the brass, and the criminal justice complex itself. One veteran reflected on his early patrol experiences as follows:

> On this job, your first partner is everything. He tells you how to survive on the job . . . how to walk, how to stand, and how to speak and how to think and what to say and see.

Clearly, it is during the FTO phase of the recruit's career that he is most susceptible to attitude change. The newcomer is self-conscious and truly in need of guidelines. A whole folklore of tales, myths, and legends surrounding the department is communicated to the recruit by his fellow officers—conspicuously by his FTO. Through these anecdotes—dealing largely with mistakes or "flubs" made by policemen—the recruit begins to adopt the perspectives of his more experienced colleagues. He becomes aware that nobody's perfect and, as if to reify his police academy experiences, he learns that to be protected from his own mistakes, he must protect others. One such yarn told to me by a two-year veteran illustrates this point.

> Grayson had this dolly he'd been balling for quite a while living over on the north side. Well, it seemed like a quiet night so we cruise out of our district and over to the girl's house. I baby-sit the radio while Grayson goes inside. Wouldn't you know it, we get an emergency call right away. . . . I start honking the horn trying to get the horny bastard out of there; he pays me no mind, but the neighbors get kind of irritated at some cop waking up the nine-to-fivers. Some asshole calls the station and pretty soon Sparky and Jim show up to find out what's happening. They're cool but their Sergeant ain't, so we fabricate this insane story 'bout Sparky's girlfriend living there and how he always toots the horn when passing. Me and Grayson beat it back to our district and show up about 45 minutes late on our call. Nobody ever found out what happened, but it sure was close.

Critical to the practical learning process is the neophyte's own developing repertoire of experiences. These events are normally interpreted to him by his FTO and other veteran officers. Thus, the reality shock of being "in on the action" is absorbed and defined by the recruit's fellow officers. As a somewhat typical example, one newcomer, at the prodding of his patrol partner, discovered that to explain police actions to a civilian invited disrespect. He explained

> Keith was always telling me to be forceful, to not back down and to never try and explain the law or what we are doing to a civilian. I didn't really know what he was talking about until I tried to tell some kid why we have laws about speeding. Well, the more I tried to tell him about traffic safety, the angrier he got. I was lucky to just get his John Hancock on the citation. When I came back to the patrol car, Keith explains to me just where I'd gone wrong. You really can't talk to those people out there, they just won't listen to reason.

In general, the first month or so on the street is an exciting and rewarding period for the recruit. For his FTO, however, it is a period of appraisal. While the recruit is busy absorbing many novel experiences, his partner is evaluating the newcomer's reaction to certain situations. Aside from assisting the recruit with the routines of patrol work, the training officer's main concern is in how the recruit will handle the "hot" or, in the contemporary language of the recruits, the "heavy" call (i.e., the in-progress, or on-view, or help the officer situation which the experienced officer knows may result in trouble). The heavy call represents everything the policeman feels he is prepared for. In short, it calls for police work. Such calls are anticipated by the patrolmen with both pleasure and anxiety, and the recruit's performance on such calls is in a very real sense the measure of the man. A Union City Sergeant described the heavy call to me as follows:

> It's our main reason for being in business. Like when somebody starts busting up a place, or some asshole's got a gun, or some idiot tries to knock off a cop. Basically, it's the situation where you figure you may have to use the tools of your trade. Of course, some guys get a little shaky when these incidents come along, in fact, most of us do if we're honest. But, you know deep down that this is why you're a cop and not pushing pencils somewhere. You've got to be tough on this job and situations like these separate the men from the boys. I know I'd never trust my partner until I'd seen him in action on a hot one.

While such calls are relatively rare on a day-to-day basis, their occurrence signals a behavioral test for the recruit. To pass, he must have "balls." By placing himself in a vulnerable position and pluckily backing-up his FTO and/or other patrolmen, a recruit demonstrates his inclination to share the risks of police work. Through such events, a newcomer quickly makes a departmental reputation which will follow him for the remainder of his career.

At another level, testing the recruit's propensity to partake in the risks which accompany police work goes on continuously within the department. For example, several FTO's in Union City were departmental celebrities for their training techniques. One officer made it a ritual to have his recruit write parking citations in front of the local Black Panther Party headquarters. Another was prominent for requiring his recruit to "shake out" certain trouble bars in the rougher sections of town (i.e., check identifications, make cursory body searches, and possibly roust out customers, a la *The French Connection*). Less dramatic, but nonetheless as important, recruits are appraised as to their speed in getting out of the patrol car, their lack of hesitation when approaching a suspicious person, or their willingness to lead the way up a darkened stair-well. The required behaviors vary from event to event; however, contingent upon the ex post facto evaluation (e.g., Was a weapon involved? Did the officers have to fight the suspect? How many other patrolmen were on the spot?), a novice makes his departmental reputation. While some FTO's promote these climactic events, most wait quietly for such situations to occur. Certainly varying definitions of appropriate behavior in these situations exist from patrolman to patrolman, but the critical and common element is the recruit's demonstrated willingness to place himself in a precarious position while assisting a brother officer. In the police world, such behavior is demanded.

Although data on such instances are inherently difficult to collect, it appears that the behaviorally demonstrated commitment to one's fellow officers involved in such events is a particularly important stage in the socialization process. To the recruit, he has experienced a test and it provides him with the first of many shared experiences which he can relate to other officers. To the FTO, he has watched his man in a police work situation and now knows a great deal more about his occupational companion.

Aside from the backup test applied to all recruits, the other most powerful experience in a recruit's early days on patrol is his first arrest. Virtually all policemen can recall the individual, location, and situation surrounding their first arrest. One five-year veteran patrolman stated:

> The first arrest is really something. I guess that's because it's what we're supposedly out here for. . . . In my case, I'd been out for a couple of weeks but we hadn't done much. . . . I think we'd made some chippies, like stand-ups, or DWI's, but my partner never let me handle the arrest part. Then one night he tells me that if anything happens, I've got to handle it. Believe me, I'll never forget that first arrest, even if it was only a scumbag horn (wino) who had just fallen through a window. . . . I suppose I can remember my first three or four arrests, but after that they just start to blur together.[7]

It is such occurrences that determine the recruit's success in the department. To some extent, both the back up test and the first arrest are beyond the direct control of the newcomer. The fact that they both take place at the discretion of the FTO underscores the orderliness of the socialization process. In effect, these climactic situations graphically demonstrate to the recruit his new status and role within the department. And after passing through this regulated sequence of events, he can say, "I am a cop!"

Continuance: Metamorphosis

This section is concerned broadly with what Becker et al. (1961) labeled the final perspective. As such, the interest is upon the characteristic response recruits eventually demonstrate regarding their occupational and organizational setting. Again, the focus is upon the perspectives the initiates come to hold for the backstage aspect of their career.

As noted earlier, one of the major motivating factors behind the recruit's decision to become a policeman was the adventure or romance he felt would characterize the occupation. Yet, the young officer soon learns the work consists primarily of performing routine service and administrative tasks—the proverbial clerk in a patrol car. This finding seems well-established in the pertinent literature and my observations confirm these reports (e.g., Wilson 1968; Webster 1970; Reiss 1971). Indeed, a patrolman is predominantly an order taker—a reactive member of a service organization. For example, most officers remarked that they never realized the extent to which they would be "married to the radio" until they had worked the street for several months.

On the other hand, there is an unpredictable side of the occupation and this aspect cannot be overlooked. In fact, it is the unexpected elements of working patrol that provides self-esteem and stimulation for the officers. This unpredictable feature of patrol work has too often been understated or disregarded by students of police behavior. To classify the police task as bureaucratically routine and monotonous ignores the psychological omnipresence of the potential "good pinch." It is precisely the opportunity to exercise his perceived police role that gives meaning to the occupational identity of patrolmen. Operationally, this does not imply patrolmen are always alert and working hard to make the "good pinch." Rather, it simply suggests that the unexpected is one of the few aspects of the job that helps maintain the patrolman's self-image of performing a worthwhile, exciting, and dangerous task. To some degree, the anticipation of the "hot call" allows for the crystallization of his personal identity as a policeman. One Union City patrolman with ten years' experience commented succinctly on this feature. He noted:

> Most of the time being a cop is the dullest job in the world . . . what we do is pretty far away from the stuff you see on Dragnet or Adam 12. But, what I like about this job and I guess it's what keeps me going, is that you never know what's gonna happen out there. For instance, me and my partner will be working a Sunday first watch way out in the north end and expecting everything to be real peaceful and quiet like; then all of a sudden, hell breaks loose . . . Even on the quietest nights, something interesting usually happens.

Reiss noted perceptually the atypical routine enjoyed by patrolmen. After examining the police "straight eight"—the tour of duty—he stated:

> No tour of duty is typical except in the sense that the modal tour of duty does not involve the arrest of a person (Reiss 1971:19).

Still, one of the ironies of police work is that recruits were attracted to the organization by and large via the unrealistic expectation that the work would be adventurous and exciting. In the real world such activities are few and far between. Once a recruit has mastered the various technical and social skills of routine policing (e.g., "learning the district," developing a set of mutual understandings with his partner, knowing how and when to fill out the myriad of various report forms) there is little left to learn about his occupation which can be transferred by formal or informal instruction. As Westley (1951) pointed out, the recruit must then sit back and wait, absorb the subjective side of police work and let his experiences accumulate. The wife of one recruit noted

this frustrating characteristic of police work. She said:

> It seems to me that being a policeman must be very discouraging. They spend all that time teaching the men to use the gun and the club and then they make them go out and do very uninteresting work.

It has been suggested that for a newcomer to any occupation, "coping with the emotional reality of the job" is the most difficult problem to resolve (Schein 1963). In police work, the coping behavior appears to consist of the "learning of complacency." Since the vast majority of time is spent in tasks other than real police work, there is little incentive for performance. In other words, the young patrolman discovers that the most satisfying solution to the labyrinth of hierarchy, the red tape and paperwork, the plethora of rules and regulations, and the "dirty work" which characterize the occupation is to adopt the group norm stressing staying out of trouble. And the best way in which he can stay out of trouble is to minimize the set of activities he pursues. One Union City veteran patrolman explained:

> We are under constant pressure from the public to account for why we did or did not do this or that. It's almost as if the public feels it owns us. You become supersensitive to criticisms from the public, almost afraid to do anything. At the same time, the brass around here never gives a straightforward answer about procedures to anyone and that creates a lot of discontent. All communication comes down. But, try and ask a question and it gets stopped at the next level up. It gets to the point where you know that if you don't do anything at all, you won't get in trouble.

In a similar vein, another veteran officer put it somewhat more bluntly. He suggested caustically:

> The only way to survive on this job is to keep from breaking your ass . . . if you try too hard you're sure to get in trouble. Either some civic-minded creep is going to get outraged and you'll wind up with a complaint in your file; or the high and mighty in the department will come down on you for breaking some rule or something and you'll get your pay docked.

These quotations suggest that patrolman disenchantment has two edges. One, the police with the general public—which has been well-substantiated in the literature—and two, the disenchantment with the police system itself. In short, a recruit begins to realize (through proverb, example, and his own experience) it is his relationship with his fellow officers (particularly those working the same sector and shift—his squad) that protects his interests and allows him to continue on the job—without their support he would be lost.[8]

To summarize, the adjustment of a newcomer in police departments is one which follows the line of least resistance. By becoming similar in sentiment and behavior to his peers, the recruit avoids censure by the department, his supervisor and, most important, his brother officers. Furthermore, since the occupational rewards are to be found primarily in the unusual situation which calls for "real" police work, the logical situational solution is for the officers to organize their activities in such a way as to minimize the likelihood of being sanctioned by *any* of their audiences. The low visibility of the patrolman's role vis-à-vis the department allows for such a response. Thus, the pervasive adjustment is epitomized in the "lie low, hang loose, and don't expect too much" advice frequently heard within the Union City Police Department. This overall picture would indicate that the following tip given to me by a Union City veteran represents a very astute analysis of how to insure continuance in the police world. He suggested:

> There's only two things you gotta know around here. First, forget everything you've learned in the academy' cause the street's where you'll learn to be a cop; and second, being first don't mean shit around here. Take it easy, that's our motto.

The above characterization of the recruit socialization process, while necessarily a drastic condensation of a much more complex and interdependent process, does delineate the more important aspects of becoming a policeman. Furthermore, this descriptive narrative hints that many of the recent attempts to alter or reform police behavior are likely to meet with frustration and failure.

A CODA FOR REFORMERS

Most police reformers view the behavior of individual patrolmen as a problem for the department or society, not vice versa. I have, in a small way, tried to correct this bias by describing the point of view of the entering recruit. This emphasizes the intelligibility of the newcomer's actions as he works out solutions to his unique problems. In short, we "looked up" at the nature of the network above the recruit rather than using the usual approach which, in the past, has "looked down" on the "outsider." Perhaps this approach indicates the dilemma in which our police are indeed trapped.

In a very real sense, this article suggests a limit upon the extent to which the police can be expected to solve their own problems. Regardless of how well-educated, well-equipped, or professional the patrolman may become, his normative position and task within society will remain unchanged. From this perspective, the characteristic response of police officers to their present situation is indeed both rational and functional. Clearly, the police subculture—like subcultures surrounding bricklayers, lawyers, or social workers—will probably exist in even the most reformed of departments. To change the police without changing the police role in society is as futile as the labors of Sisyphus.

The long-range goal should be a structural redefinition of the police task and a determination of ways in which the external control principle—so central to the rule of law—may be strengthened. Of course, ways must be found to make the policeman's lot somewhat more tolerable, both to him and to the general citizenry. Organizational change can aid this process by designing training programs which place less stress on the apprenticeship relationship. However, it is doubtful that without profound alterations in the definition and structural arrangement of the police task (and in the implied values such arrangements support), significant change is possible.

Thus, plans to increase the therapeutic and operational effectiveness of police institutions by "in-house" techniques must be judged in terms of what is being done now and what might be done—and, given the features of the police institution as described here, the difference is painfully small. The particular pattern of police practices is a response to the demands of the larger complex and, as such, reflects the values and norms prevalent throughout society. The extent to which the police system undermines the rule of law; the extent to which the public is willing to alter the crime fighter image of police; the extent to which the police bureaucracy will allow change; and ultimately, the extent to which the police system as presently constructed can operate under strict public accounting—these are the major issues confronting the police, not the degree to which the individual policeman can be professionalized.[9]

NOTES

1. The use of the term "outsider" in the above context is not intended to invidiously portray the police. Rather, the term simply connotes the widespread conviction carried by the police themselves that they are, of necessity, somehow different, and set-off from the larger society. To most police observers, isolationism, secrecy, strong in-group loyalties, sacred symbols, common language, and a sense of estrangement are almost axiomatic subcultural features underpinning a set of common understandings among police in general which govern their relations with one another as well as with civilians (Bayley and Mendelsohn, 1969; President's Commission, 1967; Skolnick, 1966). Such a perspective emphasizes the necessity to view the world from the eyes of the outsider—a perspective which ideally is empathetic but neither sympathetic or judgmental.

2. If one takes seriously research findings regarding esoteric subcultures, social scientists interested in police behavior are limited in their choice of methodological strategy. If we are to gain insight into the so-called police problem, researchers must penetrate the official smoke screen sheltering virtually all departments and observe directly the social action in social situations which, in the last analysis, defines police work.

3. One exception is Westley's (1951) insightful observational study of a midwestern police department. However, his research was devoted mainly to the description of the more salient sociological features of the police occupation and was concerned only peripherally with the learning process associated with the police role.

4. Union City is a pseudonym for a sprawling metropolitan area populated by more than a million people. The police department employs well over 1,500 uniformed officers, provides a salary above the national average, and is organized in the classic pyramidal arrangement (see Van Maanen, 1972). Based on interviews with police personnel from a number of different departments and, most importantly, critical readings of my work by policemen from several departments, the sequence of events involved in recruit socialization appears to be remarkably similar from department to department. This structural correspondence among recruit training programs has been noted by others (see Ahern, 1972; Berkeley, 1969; Neiderhoffer, 1967).

5. While it cannot be stated categorically that my presence had little effect upon the behavior of the subjects, I felt I was accepted completely as a regular group member in my particular police academy class and little or no behavior was (or, for that matter, could be) altered explicitly. Furthermore, the lengthy, personal, and involving nature of my academy experiences produced an invaluable carry-over effect when I moved to the street work portion of the study. The importance of continuous observation and full participation as an aid for minimizing distortions and behavior change on the part of social actors has been strikingly demonstrated by a number of social scientists (e.g., see Whyte, 1943; Becker, 1963; Dalton, 1964; Greer, 1964; and, most recently, Schatzman and Strauss, 1973).

6. Significantly, a recruit is not even allowed to carry a loaded weapon during the classroom portion of his academy training. He must wait until graduation night before being permitted to load his weapon. To the recruit, such policies are demeaning. Yet, the policies "stigmatizing" the recruits-as-recruits (e.g., different uniforms, old and battered batons, allocation of special parking spaces, special scarfs, and name plates) were exceedingly effective methods of impressing upon the recruits that they were members of a particular class and were not yet Union City Police Officers.

7. By "chippies," the officer was referring to normal arrests encountered frequently by patrolmen. Usually, a chippie is a misdemeanor arrest for something like drunkenness. The chippie crimes the officer noted in the quotation, "stand-up" and "DWI's," refer to drunk-in-public and driving-while-intoxicated, respectively.

8. In most ways, the patrolmen represent what Goffman (1959) calls a team. In Goffmanesque, a team is "a set of individuals whose intimate co-operation is required if a given projected definition of the situation is to be maintained" (1959:104). The situational definition to be sustained in the patrol setting is that "all-is-going-well-there-are-no-problems." The covert rule for patrolmen is to never draw attention to one's activities. An analysis I conducted on written

weekly FTO progress reports illustrates this point convincingly. Of over 300 report forms, only one contained an even slightly negative evaluation. Uniformly, all forms were characterized by high praise for the recruit. The topics the FTO's chose to elaborate upon were typified by such concerns as the recruit's driving skill, the recruit's pleasing personality, the recruit's stable home life, and so on. The vast majority of reports contained no reference whatsoever to the types of activities engaged in by the recruits. The point is simply that in no case was an FTO report filed which might result in departmental attention. It should be clear that such behavior does not pass unnoticed by the recruit. Indeed, he learns rapidly the importance and value of his team as well as the corresponding definition of the police situation.

9. I have attempted to suggest in this article that the intelligibility of social events requires they be viewed in a context which extends both spatially and in time. Relatedly, social actors must be granted rationality for their behavior. Given the situational imperatives faced by patrolmen, is it any wonder our police recoil behind a blue curtain? Perhaps we have reached what R.D. Laing (1964) calls the "theoretical limit of institutions." According to Laing, this paradoxical position is characterized by a system which, when viewed as a collective, behaves irrationally, yet is populated by members whose everyday behavior is eminently rational.

REFERENCES

Ahern, J. F., (1972) Police in Trouble. New York: Hawthorn Books.

Bayley, P. H., and H. Mendelsohn, (1969) Minorities and the Police. New York: The Free Press.

Becker, H. S. (1963) Outsiders: Studies in the Sociology of Deviance. New York: The Free Press.

Becker, H. S., B. Greer, E. C. Hughes, and A. Strauss (1961) Boys in White: Student Culture in Medical School. Chicago: University of Chicago Press.

Berkeley, G. E., (1969) The Democratic Policeman. Boston: Beacon Press.

Berlew, D. E., and D. T. Hall, (1966) The socialization of managers: effects of expectations on performance. Administrative Science Quarterly 11:207-23.

Bittner, E., (1967) The police on skid row. American Sociological Review 21:699-715.

Cicourel, A. V., (1967) The Social Organization of Juvenile Justice. New York: John Wiley and Sons.

Dalton, M., (1964) Preconceptions and methods in men who manage. In Sociologists at Work, P. Hammond, ed. New York: Doubleday.

Dornbush, S. M., (1955) The military academy as an assimilating institution. Social Forces 33:316-21.

Evan, W. M., (1963) Peer group interaction and organizational socialization: a study of employee turnover. American Sociological Review 28: 436-40.

Goffman, E., (1959) The Presentation of Self in Everyday Life. New York: Doubleday.

Greer, B., (1964) First days in the field. In Sociologists at Work, P. Hammond, ed. New York: Doubleday.

Hughes, E. C., (1958) Men and their Work. Glencoe, Illinois: The Free Press.

Laing, R. D., (1964) The obvious. In Dialectics of Liberation, D. Cooper, ed. London: Institute of Phenomenological Studies.

Lortie, D. C., (1968) Shared ordeal and induction to work. In Institutions and the Person, H. S. Becker, B. Greer, D. Riesman, and R. T. Weiss, eds. Chicago: Aldine.

McNamara, J., (1967) Uncertainties in police work: the relevance of police recruits' background and training. In The Police: Six Sociological Essays, D. J. Bordura, ed. New York: John Wiley and Sons.

Neiderhoffer, A., (1967) Behind the Shield. New York: Doubleday.

President's Commission on Law Enforcement, (1967) Task Force Report: The Police. Washington, D.C.: Government Printing Office.

Reiss, A. J., (1971) The Police and the Public. New Haven: Yale University Press.

Schatzman, L., and A. Strauss, (1973) Field Research: Strategies for a Natural Sociology. Englewood Cliffs, New Jersey: Prentice-Hall.

Schein, E. H., (1963) Organizational socialization in the early career of industrial managers. Paper presented at the New England Psychological Association, Boston, Massachusetts, (1971). Organizational socialization and the profession of management. Industrial Management Review 2:37-45.

Skolnick, J., (1966) Justice Without Trial: Law Enforcement in a Democratic Society. New York: John Wiley and Sons.

Sterling, J. W., (1972) Changes in Role Concepts of Police Officers. Washington, D.C.: International Association of Chiefs of Police.

Van Maanen, J., (1972) Pledging the police: a study of selected aspects of recruit socialization in a large, urban police department. Ph.D. Dissertation,

University of California, Irvine. (1976) Breaking-in: socialization to work. *In* Handbook of Work, Organization, and Society, R. Dubin, ed. Chicago: Rand-McNally.

Webster, J. A., (1970) Police task and time study. Journal of Criminal Law, Criminology and Police Science 61:94-100.

Westley, W. A., (1951) The police: a sociological study of law, custom and mortality. Ph.D. Dissertation, University of Chicago, Chicago, Illinois.

Whyte, W. F., (1943) Street Corner Society. Chicago: University of Chicago Press.

Wilson, J. Q., (1968) Varieties of Police Behavior. Cambridge, Massachusetts. Harvard University Press.

In this article, Pogrebin and Poole explored the strategic uses of humor in the police organization in a year-long ethnographic study of a suburban police department. They examined four types of humor characteristics of the work relations among patrol officers: jocular aggression, audience degradation, diffusion of danger/tragedy, and normative neutralization. Humor allows for a wide range of creative expressions by which specific ideas, attitudes, and behaviors may be tested. Through humor, patrol officers relate and interpret work experiences to reinforce their own perspective of policing. Institutionalized humorous communication also contributes to the maintenance of organizational relationships.

HUMOR IN THE BRIEFING ROOM

A Study of the Strategic Uses of Humor Among Police

MARK R. POGREBIN

ERIC D. POOLE

Within various occupational groups humor represents a symbolic resource through which social meanings are created (Zijderveld, 1968). Certain types of humor actually come to characterize members of these groups. As part of the group subculture, humor entails a set of joking relations that support group values, beliefs, and behaviors.

First, through humorous exchanges group members find that they share common experiences and that they can raise a variety of both individual and group concerns that could not otherwise be addressed (Fine, 1983). Humor represents a strategic tool in testing the attitudes, perceptions, or feelings of other group members. By exploring some issue or concern through humor, people can gauge others' positions without having to take a stance themselves (Emerson, 1969).[1]

Second, humor promotes social solidarity. Through mutual ribbing, teasing, or pulling pranks, group members recognize that they can

Reprinted from *Journal of Contemporary Ethnography*, Vol. 17, No. 2, July 1988, 183–210. Copyright © 1988 Sage Publications, Inc.

laugh at each other with no ill intent since they share a communal relationship (Coser, 1959, 1960). Shared laughter reflects a social benchmark of the group's common perspective. Joking relations among peers generate feelings of implicit understanding and camaraderie, thus strengthening group norms and bonds. Similarly, solidarity may be enhanced by directing humor at out-group members. This "laughter of inclusion" (Dupreel, 1928) affirms the group's social boundaries and moral superiority (Davies, 1982).

Third, groups utilize humor as a coping strategy in managing a variety of forces beyond their direct control. For example, gallows humor represents an attempt to transform crises or tragic situations into ones that are less threatening and thus more tolerable (Orbdlik, 1942). Although the humor may be morbid and cynical, group members are able to laugh at their plight, demonstrating *communities* and reinforcing group cohesion. Humor also helps to normalize crises by couching the threatening situations as routine occurrences; that is, as just part of the job. In this way humor fosters a sense of confidence that these problems can be handled (Holdaway, 1984).

In this article we extend the previous works on the role of humor in groups by exploring how police patrol officers incorporate humor as a strategic activity to ensure the integrity of their occupational work group. We seek to identify how various types of humor are used to define situations salient to police work; that is, we attempt to show how humor is situationally grounded in the social construction of reality of the police occupation. First, we describe our research methods. Second, we examine the strategic uses of four types of humor among patrol officers. Third, we discuss the role of institutionalized humorous communication in maintaining organizational relationships.

METHODS

We collected data for the project during a year-long ethnographic study of a medium-sized metropolitan police department in Colorado. Our study began in June 1985 and ended in June 1986. Our objective was to examine the nature of interpersonal relations among patrol officers. We focused on humor and joking relations as complex, patterned constructions of interpersonal behavior and as strategic activities serving various functions for the group. We attempted to interpret and assign meaning to police humor by identifying how it was both responsive to a specific contextual situation and consistent with normative properties of the more general occupational structure.

Research Setting

The police department we observed is located in a community of approximately 90,000, part of the Denver Metropolitan Statistical Area. During the study there were 135 sworn personnel on the force, with 83 officers attached to uniformed street patrol. Patrol officers were assigned to one of three shifts for a 12-month tour, working a 10-hour day and a 4-day week. At the end of that time, a complex bidding process, based on seniority, was used to reassign officers across the three shifts; moreover, departmental policy prohibited any officer from serving more than two consecutive years on the same shift.

Every month we each took a different shift, rotating through all three shifts during the year. This procedure allowed us to return to the same shift every three months and provided the opportunity for both of us to spend four full months on each shift. It also ensured a more representative sampling of police activities across shifts and patrol assignments throughout the 12-months study. As observers, we kept field diaries, reviewed daily police logs, and conducted informal interviews. Our monthly rotating shift procedure provided the means by which we cross-checked our independent observations and field notes.

Our daily observations began in the briefing room, where all patrol officers met at the beginning of their shift. Based on officer deployment plans, we implemented a procedure whereby we rode with a different patrol officer every other day. Since we covered each shift on a three-month rotation, we were able to schedule our ride-along assignments so that both of us spent time on patrol with every officer during the year. On many occasions we spent the entire shift with the assigned patrol officer; on others, we were able to spend only a few hours on patrol. Our daily observations concluded with the debriefing sessions when the officers returned to the station house to complete their reports. Since our emphasis was on the role of humor among patrol officers, we focused our attention on the group interactions during the briefing and debriefing sessions.

Field Relations

We made an intensive effort to get to know all patrol officers during the study. First, we sought to earn their respect through our personal commitment of time and energy in their organization. Second, we sought to gain their acceptance through our sustained collegiality and professional relations. As confidants, many officers kept us informed about the latest organizational rumor or personnel gossip, offered their personal views and assessments, and provided a wealth of "war stories"; others sought us out for information. While we gratefully acknowledged receipt of information, we were insistent that the code of ethics that governed our research prohibited our divulging any information that we received in confidence. This explanation was generally satisfactory to most officers; moreover, it reinforced the trust element that we worked hard to ensure in our field relations.

During the project we developed a working camaraderie with the officers, so that our presence on patrol or in the station house was taken for granted. We were viewed as part of the social organization of the department, having personally participated in the "routine" experiences of policework. Our personal acceptance in the police organization also led to our being invited by officers to off-duty social gatherings. The extension of these social relationships allowed us access to the private lives and personal histories of the officers. The mutual rapport and understanding that arose from such associations further supported our position in the police organization as "insiders." As a result, we feel confident that our observations and interpretations are reliable and valid representations of the phenomena under study.

Backstage Behavior in the Briefing Room

While we were able to ride with and observe each officer on patrol, it was in the social context of the briefing room that groups of officers routinely exhibited the types of humor we focus on as part of the police occupation. The briefing room served as the primary setting where officers engaged in backstage behavior, that is, where the officers were not performing to a public or providing stereotyped scripts to outsiders (Goffman, 1959; Punch, 1979).

The briefing room represented what Lyman and Scott (1967: 270) have defined as a "home territory . . . where regular participants have a relative freedom of behavior and a source of intimacy and control over the area." Ardrey (1966) has argued that control of territory is associated with maintaining identity. Backstage behavior reflects the subcultural group identity in contrast to the front-stage identity managed in public. As Goffman (1959) has noted, backstage identities are revealed in territories that are separated from public view.

In the station house a formal reception area served as a staging place where police appearance was managed for the public. It represented a screen or barrier for the backstage area where police could act in an uninhibited manner and not concern themselves with outside scrutiny. For each shift of officers, the briefing area offered a collective arena where they could talk about their street experiences to others who understood and appreciated their feelings and perceptions. Still, as members of a paramilitary bureaucracy, officers had to be careful to ensure that their manner of expressing these experiences was organizationally acceptable or tolerable. Humor provided a wide range for creative expressions within such organizational constraints.

The Briefing Room Routine

When police officers arrived at the station house, they usually went directly to the locker room to change into their uniforms. The officers working a particular shift then proceeded to the briefing room for roll call and patrol assignments. During the 15-to-20-minute briefing session, officers also received current information on previous shift activities and communications on policy from the command staff. At times the shift sergeant cautioned the officers about some present dangers in the community, praised officers for their exceptional performance or related accomplishments, or called attention to particular problems officers might be experiencing.

At the end of a shift, officers returned to the station house briefing room to complete their paperwork. During this debriefing session, the sergeant reviewed the officers' reports, cleared up any questions that might arise, and offered officers constructive advice. The time required for debriefing all shift officers could range from a few minutes to over an hour, with officers leaving when their reports were filed and approved; however, officers typically remained in the briefing room long after their official duties were completed.

This informal period of officer interaction came to serve as a forum for officers to swap stories about individual work experience, allowing officers to "cool out" from a rough shift, to vicariously experience the highlights of fellow officers' calls, or to wind down before going home. It also provided an opportunity to discuss department policies, politics, and personalities. Rumors made their rounds at this time—with a few being squelched, several being started, and many being embellished. As Hannerz (1969) has observed, such informal gatherings of police officers foster highly stylized exchanges of information and forms of communication.

Like most groups characterized by informality, patrol officers have developed a set of joking references that require "insider" knowledge to be fully understood and appreciated as humorous.[2] After several weeks of riding with patrol officers and attending briefing and debriefing sessions, we began to discern distinct functions of joking relationships. The forms of humor we have identified are grounded in the natural work experiences of policing. We have classified police humor into four types: jocular aggression, audience degradation, diffusion of danger/tragedy, and normative neutralization.

STRATEGIC USES OF HUMOR AMONG POLICE

In this section we will explore the strategic uses of the four types of humor. We begin our assessment of each type with a view of its functions in general; we then illustrate and examine the way each manifests itself within specific contexts of police work.

Jocular Aggression

Jocular aggression represents a humorous attack against supervisory or management personnel. It is a way subordinates in a group can collectively denounce departmental policies and regulations or the directives and orders of superiors in an acceptable manner. Jocular aggression thus avoids a direct confrontation with a superior that could lead to organizational sanctions.

Blau (1955) has contended that within bureaucracies individual complaints are often expressed and explored through joking relations in an informal work group. Jocular aggression reflects this type of joking relation in which discontent can be vented in a safe manner; that is, individuals are able not only to get their complaints out in the open but also to displace latent frustration and aggression via humorous expressions. In addition, jocular aggression serves to translate an individual concern into a group issue. In the group context the expression of an individual concern brings to bear the collective experience and advice of fellow workers. Individual problems may then be viewed from the perspective of the group.

The following problem incident involved a shift lieutenant who persisted in stopping drunk drivers and then calling for a patrol officer to respond to the scene and make the arrest. Such action involved the administration of a breathalyzer test, forced the officer to wait at the station until someone could come and take the drunk driver home, and required the completion of a lengthy offense report.

Did you hear our favorite lieutenant on the radio tonight? He tied the fucking thing up so long we couldn't get through to anyone. Here we got both DUI cars tied up and that nut is running around catching four DUI's. It's dangerous to leave him out on the street. Why doesn't he sit on his ass in the station and pretend he's busy like the rest of the lieutenants do?

Another problem incident arose from the chief's new policy concerning relations with the minority community, whose spokespersons had met with the chief to complain about their treatment by patrol officers. The chief videotaped his new policy on minority-police relations and had it played for all shifts during briefing sessions. At one of the shift viewings, we observed the following. The officers were all seated, waiting for the tape to be played. One officer yelled out, "It's the Chief Marty Show; let's get some popcorn." As the tape played, officers made wisecracks, hissed, booed, and laughed; moreover, several officers threw paper airplanes at the screen. At the end of the video presentation, there was sporadic applause, and one policeman yelled out:

This show was boring. . . . They should have sex flicks and make the Chief's show more interesting. Hell, I almost fell asleep.

Another officer joined in the chorus of criticism with a rather sarcastic observation:

Now that was really a useful piece of shit. We all need to improve our community relations skills. Next thing they'll have us doing is asking a suspect for his permission before we can arrest him.

Jocular aggression reinforces the solidarity of the individuals within the group because it is based on shared experiences of the membership. Like jokes, it causes a collectivity of laughter that strengthens the group's social cohesion (Martineau, 1972). One such incident: An officer saw a young woman's car stuck in the snow and, after attempting to push her out, told the woman that he could do no more for her. After a short discussion in which the woman berated the officer for refusing to use his patrol car to pull her car from the snow drift, the officer told the woman to calm down and call a tow truck.

The woman subsequently filed a formal complaint against the officer with the department. Even though departmental policy prohibits the use of a police vehicle to remove a civilian's car (unless the car is impeding traffic), the officer received a three-day suspension without pay for the way he handled the incident. In assessing the implications of this administrative action, a fellow patrol officer presented his position to the shift:

The next time it snows I'm going to help every goddam person stuck. Then when the dispatcher calls me on a case, I'm going to just say the chief wants us to help citizens get their cars out of the snow. I really have no time for the call.

Another officer followed up on this statement:

And don't forget to tell them how grateful you are that you could be of help. You wouldn't want to leave a poor citizen stranded two blocks from home with groceries to carry.

The stories told in the briefing room tend to mediate the hierarchy of authority within the bureaucratic structure of the department. Such stories relate the patrol officer's perception of what "real" police work is all about. These humorous tales often reflect frustrations experienced by officers who must rely on their own common sense in working patrol and then have their decisions second-guessed by a supervisor later on. Jocular aggression affirms the patrol officer's perceived superiority to management personnel who are far removed from the realities officers face on the street.

Because they must often deviate from administrative policies and procedural regulations in order to perform order-maintenance functions, patrol officers guard their autonomy and discretionary decision making. New sergeants have to adjust to this informal work norm. For these supervisors, learning the nuances of the shift's personality is critical to their success in effectively managing the officer's activities on patrol (Van Maanen, 1984).

Officers want and expect the sergeant to act in a consultative manner. They feel that because of the nature of their front-line work, they should initiate the bulk of their contacts with a supervisor as they deem necessary. As the following example reveals, supervisors must learn to accept and support the autonomy and discretion so valued by patrol officers. A new sergeant had been assigned to the swing shift (4 p.m. to 2 a.m.). Because he had worked for the preceding five years in the detective bureau, he had limited contact with those working patrol. Thus, the new sergeant was known to patrol officers only by reputation, although there were a few veteran officers who had worked with him when he was on the street in uniform.

Most officers contend that new supervisors have a tendency to become involved in too many radio-dispatched calls to patrol. On a busy night it is not uncommon for a rookie sergeant to be running from one side of town to another for what he believes to be necessary supervision of his shift. Since officers resent close scrutiny, they attempt to socialize new shift sergeants to the patrol norms stressing laissez faire supervision.

An example of this process took place in the briefing room after a busy Saturday night of calls for service. The new sergeant was obviously fatigued from attempting to be with his patrol officers at every call. He was seen as constantly invading officers' territory and interfering with the tactics each officer had developed for handling interactions with suspects and citizens. Jocular aggression was abundant that night, as evidenced in the remarks of one officer during debriefing:

> Hey, Sarge! Where were you when I got that call on those bikers' loud music complaint over on the East Side? I figure you could have made it there if you used your lights and siren. It was only about five miles from where you were. Hell, if you ran hot at 90 miles an hour, you could have been there to help me.

A veteran officer also raised the issue of the sergeant's intrusion into patrol work during that shift. He described an incident in which a male suspect placed under arrest for possession of an illegal weapon was refusing to come peacefully with his younger partner. The rookie sergeant arrived, took charge of the scene, and tried to convince the suspect to come to the station. All attempts by the sergeant failed to resolve the situation, and the suspect became more agitated. At this point the veteran officer decided to intervene. He simply picked up the suspect and

carried him back to the sergeant's car for transport to the station. At the debriefing, the officer gave the sergeant some friendly advice:

> Well, Sergeant, the reason I picked up that asshole at the apartment house and carried him to your car was that the bullshit that guy was giving you would have gone on forever. I figured you and Sam had talked enough; I just got tired of that runt's smartass manner. We got better things to do than listen to pukes like him. . . . Now don't you think I was professional?

In the following remark, we see how jocular aggression is used to address the larger issue of the new sergeant's attempts to supervise shift officers at every call:

> Now we all know that the city wants us to cut down on our driving time to save on gas expenses. Sarge, you must have put on over a thousand miles tonight. You better be careful or the city manager is going to get on your ass. You know you've got to help the city save money in these times of cutback management.

In short, jocular aggression provides a means by which subordinates can express dissatisfaction with superior officers or with the organization itself. However, those in subordinate positions must maintain the lines of authority that define the police structure. They must be careful not to cross the communicative boundary where jocular aggression becomes directly offensive to a superior, lest they suffer the consequences for violating organizational status (e.g., being perceived as insubordinate and sanctioned).

Audience Degradation

As we noted earlier, debriefing sessions present the opportunity for discussion of problems officers faced during the shift and feedback on how they were handled. Swapping stories about citizen encounters offered officers a chance to exploit the humor in the troubles and foibles of the public in general. Because the police saw themselves frequently called to intervene in conflicts between equally disreputable parties, they came to view the public in rather cynical terms. That is, they often failed to differentiate citizens in need of police services from individuals suspected of criminal involvement.

"Naming" refers to the process by which police classify people as social objects having certain stereotypical attributes and then act toward them on the basis of the identifying label (Lindesmith et al., 1977). Such standardized characterizations provide a common argot among police for conjuring up the appropriate images (e.g., demeanor, dress, speech, attitude) of individuals encountered. There is no need for further explanation when an officer refers to various persons contacted during the shift as "scumbag," "asshole" "puke," "bimbo," or other equally graphic appellations. One officer described his contact with a drunk couple as follows:

> I had a real good DUI tonight. I pulled behind a couple parked on the side of the road and they were drunk as well. When the driver got out, this bimbo also got out of the car and started yelling at me to leave the driver alone. There she is yelling at me about harassment, shit-faced and all, with her dress wide open. When I finally pointed this out to her, she sure as shit quieted down.

The use of the disparaging reference to the female suspect in this incident also reflects the frustration that officers experience in trying to protect citizens from themselves. Similarly, humorous remarks are used to belittle those individuals who create the "dirty work" that officers are called upon to perform. For example, one officer described the following encounter:

> A mental starts talking to me outside the station when I was coming to briefing. I can't understand what he's saying, but the next thing I know he pulls his pants down and exposes himself. At the same time all these women are coming out of city hall leaving work. . . . Hell, I don't know why he did that; there wasn't that much to show.

While most opportunities for backstage humor occur in the briefing room, many humorous stories about citizen encounters are told during slow times of a shift when patrol officers know that the supervisor is at the station or otherwise indisposed. These exchanges usually take place in isolated areas secluded from

public view. A favorite spot for patrol officers to, as they put it, "shoot the shit" is behind shopping centers late at night. Usually two or three patrol cars will be parked parallel to one another, and officers will converse without leaving the vehicles. Such impromptu meetings of a few officers allow for more individualized sharing of work experiences that would not be suitable for collective discussion in the briefing room; moreover these brief storytelling sessions help break up the routine of a tedious shift. Comic relief provided by these occasions is illustrated in the following exchange among three officers:

Officer Able: What was that call for over at the Sandstone apartments? It sounded like a good one.

Officer Baker: There were some teenagers swimming naked in the pool, raising a lot of hell. When we rolled up, the boys ran but the chicks stayed. They came over stark naked and began to talk with Brewer and me; shit, they didn't bat an eye. It was hard not to look, believe me. . . .

Officer Cruz: Damn, I never get good calls like that. If I did, by the time I was on the scene they'd probably be dressed.

The access the police had to individuals' personal problems caused them to make moral judgments on a regular basis. They were more often called on to perform social-service functions than law enforcement duties. They had to be counselors, mediators, arbitrators, referral agents, power brokers, and all-purpose consultants. To patrol officers oriented to "real" police work, many citizens calls for service seemed trivial, mundane, or unfounded. Officers came to view complainants as people who were too weak or ineffectual to handle their own problems. Responding to their calls was viewed as a waste of time and effort. In order to manage such distasteful situations, police recounted their encounters with citizens in humorously degrading ways, often poking fun at complainant misfortunes. As Goffman (1959: 175) has pointed out, "Backstage derogation of the audience is another strategy that performance teams employ in order to maintain morale."

Humorous putdowns of complainants served to promote the police sense of moral superiority and to maintain the dichotomy between police and policed.

Diffusion of Danger/Tragedy

Police are expected not to show fear in dangerous situations. Even to admit being afraid after threatening encounters is taboo. Displays of fear, although quite understandable under such conditions, are viewed as a sign of weakness. It is through humor that police can empathize with each other's feelings of fear and vulnerability. Joking relations concerning dangerous interactions provide a way for officers to express their emotions without damaging their professional image as confident and fearless. As Fine (1983: 175) has argued, such humor fosters "a sense of social control for the participants on how to deal with these threatening or embarrassing topics."

In the following example, an officer conveyed the fear brought about by a highly threatening situation using joking references implicitly understood by other members of the group. The incident involved five patrol officers and one lieutenant who responded to a residential burglary-in-progress call. The six officers positioned themselves around the perimeter of the house and waited for the suspect to exit. An account of what occurred was provided by one of the patrol officers during the shift's debriefing session:

> There were six of us on the scene. The perpetrator is in the house and we've got the area covered. Everyone is in position waiting for the thief to come out. I'm in some bushes about 10 feet behind the lieutenant, who's standing behind a tree. The dude comes running out the back door, and the lieutenant is in the firing position and yells at the top of his lungs, "Hit the ground or I'll blow your fucking head off!" I thought the lieutenant was going to come in his pants right there. I couldn't tell who was more afraid—the bad guy or the lieutenant.

Every police officer is aware of the danger inherent in such incidents; moreover, apprehension is heightened by the possibility that the suspect is armed. The following incident illustrates how officers humorously reflect upon their own vulnerability in precarious situations. The call involved an officer dispatched to a residence for what was thought to be a minor domestic disturbance. Upon his arrival at the residence, the officer was met by a highly agitated male suspect wielding a shotgun. The officer immediately radioed for backup, took his shotgun from the cruiser, and positioned himself behind a tree in the front yard of the residence. The suspect demanded that the officer "get the hell off my property"; the officer ordered the suspect to put down his weapon. Neither complied, but the officer continued to talk to the suspect in an effort to calm him down. The backup officers arrived within minutes and assumed tactical positions behind their cars. After a 10-minute standoff, the suspect finally dropped his shotgun and surrendered to the first officer. At the debriefing one of the backup patrolman began gibing his officer:

> I thought you were going to be behind that tree all goddam night. That asshole didn't give a shit if you blew him to hell. I was going to bet Alex that you would shoot first. But you know him, he never carries more than a quarter when he's on duty.

Another backup officer joked about what could have happened:

> It's a good thing Wayne didn't have to shoot that scumbag, because we haven't qualified with the shotgun for I don't know how long. He would have shot and probably hit the front window, and that son of a bitch would have opened up on all of us.

This example reveals the importance of the officer maintaining control over his emotions; for had he "lost it" and overreacted, the consequences could have been disastrous. Yet the reality of such threatening situations cannot be denied, and the intense emotions must eventually be dealt with. Jokes can be used to focus on the uncomfortable topic of fear, allowing the group to deal collectively with an emotion that could not be expressible otherwise. When a fellow officer has confronted a life-threatening situation, the backstage humor of the briefing room promotes shared understanding of the experience and identification with the feelings of the officer. In this way, humorous debriefings help to manage the danger that is a part of police work.

Similarly to the way humor is used to diffuse emotions accompanying dangerous situations, joking relations also serve to temper tragic events experienced on the job. As trained professionals, police officers are expected to maintain a poised presence even under the most tragic circumstances. Their authority and effectiveness in handling such events would be compromised if officers could not control their own emotions. In the face of tragedy (e.g., victims of child abuse, rape, accidents), officers must maintain their composure, distancing themselves from the intense emotional reactions evoked in such encounters. To an outsider, the jokes that are told to diffuse tragedy may not seem humorous at all. In fact they can be perceived as cruel and insensitive; however, for patrol officers the callousness of such jokes actually helps lessen the emotional intensity elicited by tragic events. In this way humor allows the police to handle situations that would emotionally paralyze others.

One tragic event that occurred during our observational study involved the arrest of a middle-aged, white male suspect for driving under the influence of alcohol. After being brought to the police station and given a breathalyzer test, the suspect requested to see his "good friend" on the force, Lieutenant Williams. Although it was 2 a.m., the lieutenant was called to the station. When the lieutenant arrived, he briefly talked with the suspect, explaining the procedures to be followed in DUI cases, then drove the suspect home. A few hours later the suspect committed suicide.

When the graveyard shift came off the street at 8 a.m., Lieutenant Williams was in the briefing room and the discussion focused immediately on the suicide. It was soon learned that the suspect was not the lieutenant's close friend; rather, he was at best a casual acquaintance whom the lieutenant saw infrequently at a local stable where they both kept their horses. Once the relationship had been clarified, the patrol officers saw the opportunity to diffuse the tragic elements of the case for the lieutenant:

I saw the guy in here when he was waiting to blow in the machine. He didn't look depressed.

What the hell did you say to him to depress him to the point he blew himself away? You didn't bore him to death with all those horse stories you always tell?

After a few more speculative gibes concerning the role of the lieutenant in the suspect's demise, one officer offered the lieutenant some final advice:

I tell you, Lieutenant, you really have to pick your friends more carefully in the future. You know, you could give the department a bad name.

In another tragic incident we observed during our study, a middle-aged white man walked into the police station around 3 a.m. on a Saturday and reported that he had just murdered his live-in girlfriend. When the graveyard shift returned for debriefing later that morning, the officers shared what they had learned about the bizarre event:

The guy comes into the station, hardly anyone is around, and tells the desk clerk he needs to see a cop. I happen to pass the front desk and am told . . . that there is a man here who wants to speak to an officer. I take him back to the briefing room and he tells me he murdered his girlfriend and gives me the details. Then he says as calmly as hell he wants to speak to a priest, not a lawyer, but a priest! That's when I figure this guy's for real. Hell, it's too late to get religion.

One of the officers dispatched to the crime scene then described what he found:

The door to the house was open and there to the left of the front door was the .22 [-caliber] rifle, just like we were told by dispatch.

We know right away this guy was not a mental. We go to the master bedroom and there is this broad with covers over her. We pull them back and, man, there are about five holes in her chest. She's deader than hell. Looks like the guy was trying to make her look like Swiss cheese.

The casual observer is likely neither to understand nor to appreciate the humorous social meanings created by these stories. But the appropriateness of joking depends on the situation; that is, there are contextual rules for joking that are often not explicit or even consciously recognized. They represent intricate functions of group processes. It is through the shared experiences of group activity that the standards by which humor is judged and interpreted evolve.

For police, backstage humor represents a strategic means of managing the consequences of tragic events. First, jokes allow officers to vent feelings in an acceptable manner. Second, joking relations provide for a collective diffusion of emotional responses (e.g., outrage, disgust, horror) to tragedies. Third, the humorous treatment of tragedy promotes its normalization as just part of the job. Humor thus supports emotional distancing, allowing officers to perform their jobs regardless of the situation.

Normative Neutralization

According to Reuss-Ianni (1983), the street-officer culture supports bending formal rules and procedures that may impede officers from doing their job as they deem necessary. Sometimes the law itself is seen by the police as getting in the way of the administration of justice (Skolnick, 1966); thus legislative and judicial constraints may have to be sidestepped by officers. When police "know" a suspect is guilty (i.e., factual guilt), they feel justified in violating procedural rules in order to obtain evidence that may better ensure a conviction. Similarly, if police perceive that a suspect who they feel deserves punishment is unlikely to be prosecuted or convicted, they may impose "street justice" (e.g., verbal or physical abuse). Street justice is also administered to belligerent suspects whom the police lack probable cause to arrest but whom the police feel need to be taught a lesson in proper respect for police authority.

We found patrol officers quite candid in describing street-justice incidents to their peers. They often swapped humorous stories about these encounters during debriefing sessions, although they were discreet in the presence of certain supervisors. Such humorous accounts help to define the working ideology of patrol officers, providing examples of informal standards and expectations for behavior by which officers may be judged.

The following example shows how legal guidelines were compromised by one officer in adhering to the principle of street justice. This incident involved a veteran officer who was dispatched to a residence for a family disturbance call. After restraining the couple involved in the dispute, the officer learned that the wife had just returned home, having left her husband and two small children for a two-month hiatus with another man. This man had accompanied the wife to the home and was present when the officer arrived. The situation was further aggravated by the woman's agitated state and violent demeanor, a condition the officer judged to be drug-induced. Demanding that the officer arrest her husband, the woman then produced a court order awarding her temporary custody of the children, enjoining the husband to leave the home, and denying him child visitation rights until a subsequent court hearing was held.

The officer felt that the judge who issued the injunction was not fully cognizant of all the facts in the case; consequently he decided to ignore the court order. Instead, he lectured the woman on parental responsibility, told her and her boyfriend to leave the house without the children, and advised her to get an attorney. The officer then warned the woman that if she caused any more trouble that night, he would have her arrested for suspected drug use. The next day the woman filed a formal complaint against the officer at police headquarters.

When questioned about the incident by his fellow officers during the debriefing session, the veteran officer provided the following insight to his application of street justice:

No sooner do I arrive on the scene when this hysterical asshole starts screaming at me to get her husband out of the house. There she is waving a court order in my face, screaming the judge wants him out. Then I heard from her old man that she returned after deserting the family for two months, leaving the two small kids at home with him and never leaving a note to explain where she was going and never contacting her husband while being gone. I told her what she could do with the court order. Then she gets real loud and starts cussing me out, all the while threatening to sue my ass. "Lady," I said, "you're high on drugs and I'm going to haul your ass in if you don't shut up and get out of here now." She saw I was pissed and she leaves with her boyfriend. No way I was going to throw that guy out and let that bitch stay with the kids, especially not in her condition. I just can't believe the judge knew what this case was about. But what the hell do they know anyway. When was the last time you saw a judge handle a domestic?

The working ideology of patrol officers is premised on the inherent superiority of their decision making and commonsense understandings that determine the appropriate course of action to be taken. By humorously degrading the demeanor of the wife and the wisdom of the judge, the officer justified both his negative assessment of her moral character and his refusal to abide by the court order. In this case, ensuring street justice was more important than abiding by the law. The legal constraints were thus neutralized by an appeal to higher loyalties (Sykes and Matza, 1957).[3] Although every shift member knew the officer would be subject to departmental disciplinary action, his example reinforced the preeminence of autonomy and discretion within the occupational ideology.

In addition to their resentment of legal constraints, patrol officers express frustration in following operational policies and procedures formulated by police administrators. Patrol officers often assert that management has lost touch with the realities of real police work and complain that many administrative directives are either intrusive or useless. Because officers view certain managerial policies as obstacles preventing them from being effective, they bend the rules and follow those procedures that have worked best for them.

In the following example one officer administered street justice to a suspect in direct contradiction to departmental policy concerning the handling of intoxicated individuals. The incident involved a routine investigation of a suspicious vehicle parked on the shoulder of a major thoroughfare early on a Saturday morning. The officer described the circumstances to the shift at the debriefing session:

It's almost 2 a.m. and I came across this '85 Olds Cutlass on the side of Sheridan. The dome light is on and the driver's door is open, with a guy's legs hanging out. I wake up the dumb shit who's been sleeping one off and order him out of the car. Immediately he starts mouthing off, and really goes bat shit when I tell him I'm taking him to detox. . . . I told the asshole three times to shut up, but he keeps running his mouth. Fuck it. The puke goes to the county jail. . . . After I checked his license, I noticed it was his birthday and started feeling a little sorry for the guy. But I'm sure some of the inmates will have a few surprises for him this weekend.

In almost all cases when a person is found to be intoxicated but not driving a vehicle, departmental policy instructs that suspects be taken to the detoxification center, a county facility that holds drunken individuals for 24 hours and provides treatment on a voluntary basis. The policy calls for the use of the detoxification center in such situations in order to prevent the individual from getting injured or harming others.

In this case, the officer felt that the suspect had exceeded the bounds of acceptable demeanor to be exhibited in such encounters. He thus decided to arrest the suspect on a drunk and disorderly charge and have him jailed. In taking this action, the officer ensured a punishment more commensurate with the seriousness of the suspect's disregard for police authority. The officer's humorous account of the incident at the debriefing session served to justify his discretionary street justice superseding the departmental policy. Through humor the police reinforce their work perspective and organizational status, promoting a collective self-confidence conducive to the maintenance of group autonomy and the exercise of individual discretion.

DISCUSSION

The four types of humor we have examined—jocular aggression, audience degradation, diffusion of danger/tragedy, and normative neutralization—reflect rather serious issues in policing. In considering the strategic uses of humor, we must address why officers choose to express such serious content in unserious forms. As noted above, joking relations provide a socially acceptable means to test the feelings of group members, one that allows denial of the serious implications of the humorous message if challenged. But the expression of serious concern in a humorous form may ensure more than a defensible posture in gauging others' sentiments.

First, a serious theme expressed in jest, rather than in earnest, may actually dramatize its message. The humorous expression, by providing amusement and eliciting overt reactions of smiling or laughter, symbolically commits the group to the position of the humorist. The impact of the message is also increased with the weight of consensual acknowledgement implicit in group laughter. If an overtly serious comment is offered, the group's response may be concealed by ambiguous silence or equivocally impassive faces.

Second, humor provides a forum for presentation of concerns without directly threatening the system that fosters them; that is, unlike the formal repercussions that could result from taking a serious position on an issue, humor affords expression (or even diffusion and defusion of concerns) without changing the terms of the organizational relationships. To this extent, then, the medium is the message. Humor is communicated and interpreted within the existing subcultural context (e.g., ideology, power, status, morality, norms, and values) of the police organization. Both the individual officers and the police organization benefit from institutionalized humorous communication. The status quo is preserved.

A final consideration of our findings deals with the use of jocular aggression aimed at superiors. We focus on this type of humor since previous studies have indicated that jocular aggression is directed either laterally or downwards through the organizational hierarchy; that is, individuals jokingly attack their equals or subordinates, but not their superiors. In two observational studies of joking relations in work settings, both Bradney (1957) and Coser (1959, 1960) reported no instance in which a subordinate worker used humor to express aggression or hostility to a superior face-to-face; humorous derision of superiors occurred only in their absence. In contrast, superiors publicly, as well as privately, ridiculed subordinates for their failings or inadequacies.

The similarity of these findings, obtained in markedly different work settings (Bradney studied interactions of department store staff; Coser observed psychiatric staff meetings), supports the notion of asymmetrical access to jocular aggression. As the object of the hostile joking by subordinates, superiors have the authority to make reprisals. Subordinates subjected to humorous derision by superiors do not. Yet, in our observations of jocular aggression among police we have noted numerous occasions on which nonranking patrol officers directly ridiculed their first-line supervisors, the shift sergeants. To account for this joking relationship, we must examine the nature of the sergeant's position in the police organization.

Observational studies of police work have revealed that the exercise of authority in law enforcement agencies is primarily based on personal relationships with subordinates (Rubinstein, 1973; Muir, 1977; Van Mannen, 1984). This is because all supervisory personnel must rise from line-level positions in the police organization. The common occupational socialization experiences in the street culture of patrol work provided the basis for group solidarity and informal relations across departmental ranks.

At the same time, Van Maanen (1984) has pointed out that senior police administrators seek to promote individuals who are less likely to bring the "patrolman's mentality" to the supervisory role. The purpose of this selection strategy is to ensure that supervisors will supervise from a formal administrative, rather than an informal line-level perspective. Success in rising through the ranks is dependent, in part, on shedding the "street-cop" mentality. This promotional process thus serves to increase tension and social distance between supervisory and line staff.

Police sergeants, as first-line supervisors, occupy rather incongruous positions in the police organization. First, they are at the bottom of the supervisory hierarchy where policy and procedures developed from above must be implemented at the line level. But the ability of sergeants to implement policies and procedures is largely determined by the actions of line officers (Van Maanen, 1984). Sergeants have to earn the respect of their subordinates; it is not granted on the basis of rank alone.

Second, the relations between sergeants and patrol officers reflect a structured ambiguity. There is a mixture of camaraderie and antagonism, identification and rejection, and trust and suspicion. This ambiguity lends itself to a mutual testing of the boundaries of acceptable behavior in the roles of superior and subordinate. Under these conditions, subordinates are provided greater latitude in the expression of jocular aggression. For example, Radcliffe-Brown (1940) has argued that such joking relations are premised on institutionalized social ambiguity. That is, jocular aggression arises among individuals whose relationship is simultaneously conjunctive and disjunctive—having grounds for both solidarity and separation and reflecting "a peculiar combination of friendliness . . . [and] hostility" (Radcliffe-Brown, 1940: 195). The terms of the joking relation allow a person to make fun of another who, in turn, is expected to take no offense. Since the police organization provides an analogous relation between sergeants and line officers, we can account for why, contrary to previous research, the subordinates in our study could direct jocular aggression at their superiors.

In this article we have explored the strategic uses of humor among patrol officers. We have emphasized the contextual aspect of humor; that is, we have focused on specific types of humor in relation to the distinctive nature of patrol work. It is hoped that future ethnographic research will build upon our efforts and move toward identifying the roles of individuals in the social organization of humor and the role of groups as humor repositories. In this way, a better understanding of the rules governing humorous interaction, communication, and transmission of group culture may be obtained.

NOTES

1. If the humorous remarks produce a positive response, one may assume that others share, or at least sympathize with, one's own viewpoint. On the other hand, if the humor is rejected, one may suffer the embarrassment of having told a bad joke but risk very little else, since the joker was, after all, only kidding.

2. This is particularly important in relation to humor premised on an understanding of historical events within the department. Subtle or indirect remarks linking past experiences to present situations would be unrecognizable to those outside the work group. During the debriefing sessions, oral histories of the department are passed along to successive cohorts of police officers. Much of the localized culture is embodied in humorous stories and jokes that capture different aspects and reflect various versions of the department's history.

3. One may argue that the officer also employed another technique of neutralization, denial of victim harm, in ignoring the court order; that is, the officer felt that the wife deserved the kind of street justice meted out because she had acted so irresponsibly.

REFERENCES

Ardrey, R. (1966) The territorial imperative. New York: Dell.

Blau, P. M. (1955) The Dynamics of Bureaucracy. Chicago: Univ. of Chicago Press.

Bradney, P. (1957) "The joking relationship in industry." Human Relations 10:179-187.

Coser, R. L. (1959) "Some social functions of laughter." Human Relations 12:171-182.

Coser, R. L. (1960) "Laughter among colleagues." Psychiatry 23:81-95.

Davies, C. (1982) "Ethnic jokes, moral values and social boundaries." British J. of Sociology 33: 383-403.

Dupreel, E. (1928) "Le probleme sociologique du rise." Revue Philosophique 106:213-260.

Emerson, J. P. (1969) "Negotiating the serious import of humor." Sociometry 32:169-181.

Fine, G. A. (1983) "Sociological approaches to the study of humor," pp. 159-181 in P. E. McGhee and J. H. Goldstein (eds.) Handbook of Humor Research, Vol. 1. New York: Springer-Verlag.

Goffman, E. (1959) The Presentation of Self in Everyday Life. Garden City, NY: Anchor.

Hannerz, U. (1969) Soulside: Inquiries into Ghetto Culture And Community. New York: Columbia Univ. Press.

Holdaway, S. (1984) Inside the British Police. Oxford: Basil Blackwell.

Lindesmith, A. R., A. L. Straus, and N. K. Denzin (1977) Social Psychology. New York: Holt, Rinehart & Winston.

Lyman, S. M. and M. B. Scott (1967) "Territoriality: a neglected sociological dimension." Social Problems 15:236-249.

Martineau, W. H. (1972) "A model of the social functions of humor," pp. 101-125 in J. H. Goldstein and P. E. McGhee (eds.) The Psychology of Humor. New York: Academic Press.

Muir, W. K. (1977) Police: Streetcorner Politicians. Chicago: Univ. of Chicago Press.

Orbdlik, A. J. (1942) "Gallows humor: a sociological phenomenon." Amer. J. Soc. 47:709-716.

Punch, M. (1979) "The secret social service," pp. 102-117 in S. Holdaway (ed.) The British Police. Beverly Hills, CA: Sage.

Radcliffe-Brown, A. R. (1940) "On joking relationships." Africa 13:195-210.

Reuss-Ianni, E. (1983) Two Cultures of Policing. New Brunswick, NJ: Transaction Books.

Rubinstein, J. (1973) City Police. New York: Farrar, Strauss & Giroux.

Skolnick, J. H. (1966) Justice Without Trial. New York: John Wiley.

Sykes G. M. and D. Matza (1957) "Techniques of neutralization: a theory of delinquency." Amer. J. of Soc. 22:664-670.

Van Maanen, J. (1984) "Making rank: becoming an American police sergeant." Urban Life 13:155-176.

Zijderveld, A. C. (1968) "Jokes and their relation to social reality." Social Research 35:268-311.

In his study of police detectives, Waegel discusses the process for the typification of crimes, which involves particular types of offenders. This categorization comprises a large part of the investigator's working knowledge of criminals and their activities. The case routinization process used by investigators reflects their shared knowledge of what constitutes typical crimes, typical offenders, typical people involved in the criminal activity, and predicted behavior of the various types of citizens residing in an urban environment.

CASE ROUTINIZATION IN INVESTIGATIVE POLICE WORK*

WILLIAM B. WAEGEL

Discretionary decision making and the nature of the processes by which legal agents structure and manage their handling of persons and events have become central concerns in recent studies of the criminal justice system. Much traditional research on this system has focused on discretion in the context of race and class discrimination. The image is often that of one-person legal units making decisions, but this individualistic conception appears to be substantially misleading. A recent study by Swigert and Farrell (1977) highlights the inadequacy of the use of ostensibly objective criteria of race and class in the analysis of legal processing: they found that social and demographic attributes are filtered through stereotypic conceptions held by legal agents. Their work suggests that conventional research strategies will continue to produce a mass of contradictory findings regarding legal decision making.

Discretion is an irreducible element in the behavior of legal agents. In police work, as in other socially organized activities, members do not always have a set of formal rules which provide an adequate decision-making base for organizing their conduct. Bittner put this succinctly:

The domain of presumed jurisdiction of a legal rule is essentially open-ended. While there may

*An earlier version of this paper was presented at the annual meeting of the Society for the Study of Social Problems, Boston, 1979. The author would like to thank Gerry Turkel for his helpfupl comments.

be a core of clarity about its application, this core is always and necessarily surrounded by uncertainty. . . . No matter how far we descend on the hierarchy of more and more detailed formal instruction, there will always remain a step further down to go, and no measure of effort will ever succeed in eliminating, or even meaningfully curtailing, the area of discretionary freedom of the agent whose duty it is to fit rules to cases (1970:4).

Police investigators, prosecutors, public defenders, and presentence caseworkers typically must process a steady stream of cases or clients under rather rigid time constraints. In their normal day-to-day activities, these agents do not generally proceed by following a set of codified rules and procedures. However, their discretion is not unlimited nor are their decisions most usefully viewed as individualistic "free choices." The organizational setting in which the work is performed places distinctive constraints and demands on legal agents, producing a specific orientation to case handling and a set of largely shared formulas for dealing with different types of cases.

A more promising approach for understanding legal decision making assigns central importance to occupational typifications and common social stereotypes. Under pressure to observe court schedules or meet paperwork deadlines, and in an effort to reduce problematic features of their tasks at hand, legal agents typically rely on shorthand methods for reaching required decisions.

Typical or "normal case" conceptions have been found to act as a central basis for client treatment in a variety of organizational settings. Sudnow's (1965) study of case processing in a public defender's office found that attorneys did not handle clients and cases in terms of their unique features, but rather used typifications of the normal offense and normal offender as a basis for understanding particular cases and deciding how to handle them. For cases reasonably conforming to a familiar pattern, specific plea bargaining formulas were routinely employed. Stereotypic conceptions have been found to act as guiding imageries for action in the treatment of skid-row residents by patrolmen (Bittner, 1967), in police encounters with juveniles (Piliavin and Briar, 1964) and a "suspect population" (Skolnick, 1967), and in responses to shoplifters

(Steffensmeier and Terry, 1973). Swigert and Farrell's (1977) study of the processing of homicide defendants found that critical legal decisions regarding bail, the assignment of counsel, and plea bargaining were based upon the extent to which the person involved conformed to popular criminal stereotypes.[1]

The theoretical implication of these studies is that the decisions made in dealing with a person or event are based not so much on specific features of the actor or situation at hand, but upon the recognition of the person or event as properly belonging to a familiar and typical category and the taken-for-granted understandings built into that category. Stokes and Hewitt (1976) argue for a reflexive relationship between such social constructions and conduct. While meaning structures are a *product* of social action, it is also the case that:

A great many of the objects that constitute the human world have a 'pre-existing' meaning, in the sense that people confront such objects with a set of assumptions about them—with a particular preparedness to act in routine, familiar and unquestioned ways (Stokes and Hewitt, 1976:841).

Typifications of others and events serve to structure interaction in a provisional way, rendering it more predictable, minimizing its problematic character, and enabling the actor to better manage an ambiguous social environment. Typificatory schemes are used as resources from which to construct a practical solution to the problem at hand.

The corresponding implication for research is that conventional research strategies focusing on decision-making variations between individuals and between functionally similar organizations have severe limitations. A more fruitful approach for studying processing outcomes takes as its focus the shared categorization schemes used by members in organizing their day-to-day activities.

WORKING CASES: AN OVERVIEW

In the police department studied,[2] detectives face two practical problems which substantially shape the manner in which cases are handled. They must satisfy the paperwork demands of the organization (referred to as "keeping the red numbers down") by classifying each case and producing a formal investigative report within two weeks after the case is assigned. Sanctions may be applied to those who fail to meet deadlines and who thus accumulate too many "red numbers."

At the same time, the detectives are under the same pressure as other employees: they must produce. Specifically, detectives believe they must produce an acceptable level of arrests which will enhance their chances of remaining in the detective division and gaining promotion. While no arrest quota is formalized in the division, there is a shared belief that one should produce roughly two to three lock-ups per week. This arrest level is a practical concern for the detective because most wish to remain in the division and avoid transfer "back to the pit" (i.e., back into uniform in the patrol division). Moreover, the position of detective holds the highest status of any assignment in the department, and a transfer, therefore, generally entails a loss of status.

For the vast majority of cases handled, no explicit procedures exist to indicate what must be done on the case and how to go about doing it. As detectives go about the ordinary business of investigating and processing cases, they can select strategies ranging from a *pro forma* victim interview comprising the total investigative activity devoted to the case, to a full-scale investigation involving extensive interviewing, physical evidence, the use of informants, interrogation, surveillance and other activities. The selection of a particular handling strategy in most cases is an informal process and not the direct result of formal organizational policy or procedure. This process of selection is grounded in practical solutions to concrete problems faced by the detective; it consists of an assignment of meaning to persons and events in ways that are regarded as proper because they have "worked" in previous cases.

A great deal of actual detective work may thus be seen as a process of mapping the features of a particular case onto a more general and commonly recognized *type* of case. The present work suggests that a detective's interpretation, classification, and handling of cases

is guided by a set of occupationally shared typifications. The categorization schemes used by detectives center around specific configurations of information regarding the victim, the offense, and possible suspects. Information pertaining to these three elements constitutes the meaningful unit that detectives deal with: the case.

The most basic dimension of case categorization is that of the routine versus the nonroutine. Where a particular configuration of information regarding the victim, the offense, and possible suspects appears, the competent detective understands the case as a routine one— as an instance of a familiar type—and particular handling strategies are deemed appropriate. Such cases contrast with those which are viewed as nonroutine: that is, where no general type is available to which the case reasonably corresponds, and where the case is vigorously investigated and the detective attends to the unique features of the case. Case routinization is most characteristic for burglaries, which comprise the bulk of cases handled by detectives, but it is also exhibited in the handling of many assault, robbery, rape and homicide cases.

The categorization schemes used by detectives are derived from concrete experiences in working cases and are continually assessed for their relevance, adequacy, and effectiveness in handling one's caseload. It is because typificatory schemes serve as a solution to practical problems commonly faced by all detectives that they learn to share most of the content of these schemes. Both through direct experience in working cases and through interaction with other members, the detective learns to categorize and handle cases in ways that are regarded as proper by other detectives.

Routine case imageries serve as resources upon which detectives may draw to construct a solution to their problem of interpreting, investigating, and resolving their cases. The features of a specific case are compared with routine case imagery in a process of interpretive interplay. In some instances a correspondence is readily apparent, in others a fit is forced by the detective, and in still others the features of a specific case render the use of the typical imagery inappropriate. The interpretation and handling of a case may also change over the case's history; a routine case may come to be treated as nonroutine upon the receipt of additional information, and vice-versa.

THE ORGANIZATIONAL CONTEXT OF CASE ROUTINIZATION

In the department studied, detectives have no formal guidelines for allocating time and effort to different cases and there is little effective monitoring of daily activities by supervisors.[3] In conducting their work, detectives are, however, guided and constrained by two organizational imperatives: 1) the requirement to submit investigative reports, and 2) the requirement to produce arrests. In other words, the work is not organized by formal rules, but rather by the kinds of outcomes that are expected. Both of these expected outcomes generate practical problems leading to routinized solutions.

An investigative report must be produced for each case assigned, and its submission within the prescribed time limit is viewed as a fundamental constraint on how vigorously different cases can be investigated. Departmental policy indicates that each investigative report submitted must be reviewed and signed by a supervisory lieutenant. However, in practice, these reports are often given only a cursory glance, and seldom is the content of a report questioned or challenged by a lieutenant.

The potential a case appears to hold for producing an arrest also has an important impact on how the case will be handled. Most detectives believe that the number of arrests they produce will be used as a basis for evaluating performance and, therefore, will affect decisions regarding promotions and transfers. Attempts to cope with the practical problems of meeting paperwork demands, while at the same time producing a satisfactory number of arrests, creates a situation in which one burglary case involving a $75 loss may receive less than five minutes investigative effort, yet another case with an identical loss may be worked on exclusively for two or three full days. These two concerns constitute central features of the work setting which structure case handling.

Paperwork

Formal organizational procedure demands that a case be investigated, classified, and a report produced within a specified time period after it is assigned. Detectives experience paperwork requirements and deadlines as central sources of pressure and tension in their job, and stories abound concerning former detectives who "could handle the job but couldn't handle the paperwork."

Most cases are assigned during the daily roll-call sessions. At this point, the information about the incident consists of an original report written by a patrol officer and any supplemental reports submitted by personnel in the evidence detection unit. Each case is stamped with a "red number" which supervisors use to monitor compliance with report deadlines.

Ordinary cases require the submission of two reports within specific time periods. A brief first-day report, consisting essentially of an interview with the victim, is formally required the day after the case is assigned. However, this deadline is generally ignored by supervisors and first-day reports are seldom submitted. The more meaningful deadline for detectives is the fourteen day limit for the submission of an investigative report. Here, the detective must provide a detailed accounting of the activities undertaken in investigating the incident and assign an investigative status to the case. Compliance with this second deadline is closely monitored; every Sunday a lieutenant draws up a list of each detective's overdue red numbers, and this list is read at the next roll call along with a caution to keep up with one's paperwork.

In the investigative report, the detective must classify the status of the investigation as suspended, closed arrest, or open. The ability to manipulate information about cases to fit them into these categories is of the utmost importance to detectives, for it is through such strategic manipulations that they are able to manage their caseloads effectively.

Of the total cases handled by a detective, a substantial majority are classified as suspended. This means that the steps already taken in the investigation (which may consist merely of a telephone interview with the victim) have not uncovered sufficient information to warrant continued investigation of the incident. Any number of acceptable reasons for suspending a case may be offered, ranging from a simple statement that the victim declines to prosecute up to a fairly elaborate report detailing contacts with the victim, the entry of serial numbers of stolen articles into the computerized crime files, the usefulness of evidence obtained from the scene, and a conclusion that the case must be suspended because there are no further investigative leads. Over 80 percent of the burglary cases assigned in the city are suspended; this percentage drops considerably for robbery cases and even more for assault, rape and homicide cases.[4]

An investigation is classified as closed when one or more arrests have been made pertaining to the incident and the detective anticipates no additional arrests. A case is classified as open when an investigation extends beyond the fourteen day limit but it is expected that an arrest eventually will be made. Generally, only major cases may remain classified as open after the fourteen day investigative period.

Producing Arrests

As organizations become more bureaucratized and their procedures more formalized, there evolves a general tendency to develop quantitative indices or measures of individual performance. In the department studied, most detectives believed that the crude number of lock-ups they make is used as a basis for assessing their performance and competence in doing investigative work. Every arrest a detective makes is entered into a logbook, which is available for inspection by superiors and from which they can compare each detective's arrest level with that of others.

Ambitious detectives in particular are very conscious of producing a steady stream of arrests, feeling that this is an effective way to achieve recognition and promotion. One young detective boasted:

> I've made over forty lock-ups since the beginning of the year and eleven in April alone. Since I don't really have a godfather in here, I gotta' depend on making good lock-ups if I'm gonna' make sergeant.

This detective's use of the term "godfather" reveals a widely shared belief that some individuals are promoted not because of their performance but because they have a friend or relative in a position of power within the department.

Skimming off selected cases from one's workload is widely practiced as a means of achieving a steady stream of arrests. The practice of skimming refers to 1) selectively working only those cases that appear potentially solvable from information contained in the original report, and 2) summarily suspending the remainder of one's ordinary cases. Supervisors are certainly aware of both aspects of this practice, but they recognize its practical value in producing arrests. Moreover, supervisors, to a greater extent than working detectives, find their performance assessed in crude quantitative terms, and they are likely to be questioned by superiors if arrest levels begin to drop sharply. Supervisors support the practice of skimming even though they recognize that it ensures that a majority of ordinary cases will never receive a thorough investigation. The pragmatic work orientation of detectives is further revealed in the lack of attention given to conviction rates both by detectives and supervisors. Competence and productivity are judged by the arrests made, not by the proportion of cases which survive the scrutiny of the judicial process.

The recognition of potentially productive cases and of their utility in effectively managing one's caseload are among the earliest skills taught to the neophyte in the detective division. Moreover, newcomers are taught that their work on burglary cases is the primary basis upon which their performance will be judged. In a sizeable percentage of crimes against persons, the perpetrator is readily identified from information provided by the victim. Since no great investigative effort or acumen is involved, the same credit is not accorded an arrest in this type of case as in burglary cases. Detectives are expected to produce a steady flow of "quality" arrests: that is, arrests involving some effort and skill on the part of the investigator. Straightforward assaults cases involving acquainted parties, for example, are often handed out by supervisors along with a remark such as "Here's an easy one for you."

INTERPRETING CASES

The preceding observations have suggested that detectives are constrained in their conception and handling of cases not by the formal organization of their work or by supervisory surveillance, but rather by the bureaucratic pressure of writings reports and producing the proper number and quality of arrests. The process of interpreting cases in accordance with these pragmatic concerns may now be considered.

Data derived from observation of detective-victim interviews and from written case reports provide a basis for examining the interpretive schemes used by detectives. In the victim interview, the kinds of questions asked and the pieces of information sought out reveal the case patterns recognized as routine for the different offenses commonly encountered.[5] However, in attempting to make sense of the incident at hand, detectives attend to much more than is revealed in their explicit communications with the victim. Interpretation of the case is also based upon understanding of the victim's lifestyle, racial or ethnic membership group, class position, and possible clout or connections—especially as these factors bear upon such concerns as the likelihood of the victim inquiring into the progress of the investigation, the victim's intentions regarding prosecution, and the victim's competence and quality as a source of information.

The interpretive schemes employed also receive partial expression in the written investigative reports which must be produced for each case. These reports contain a selective accounting of the meaning assigned to a case, the information and understandings upon which this interpretation is based, and the reasonableness of the linkage between this particular interpretation of the case and the handling strategy employed.[6]

Several important features of the process of interpreting cases as routine or nonroutine may be seen in the following incidents.

Case 1: Attempted Homicide

A radio call was broadcast that a shooting had just occurred on the street in a working-class residential area. The victim, a white male, was still conscious when the detectives arrived, although he had been severely wounded in the face by a shotgun blast. He indicated that he had been robbed and shot by three black males, and provided a vague description of their appearance and clothing. This description was broadcast, an area search was initiated, the crime scene was cordoned off, and a major investigation was begun.

The following morning, the victim's employer brought into question the account of the incident that has been provided. He indicated his belief that the incident involved a "lover's triangle" situation between the victim, a male acquaintance of the victim, and a woman. All three were described as "hillbillies." The three parties were interviewed separately and each denied this version of the incident. After further questioning, the victim finally admitted that the story concerning three black males was false, but would say nothing more about the incident. Articles of the woman's clothing believed to show bloodstains and a weapon believed to have been used were obtained, but crime lab analysis would take at least three weeks. The case was now interpreted as a routine "domestic shooting" and little additional effort was devoted to it.

Case 2: Burglary

A detective parked his car in front of an address in a public housing project and pulled out the original burglary report. A new member of the prosecutor's office was riding along to observe how detectives work. The detective read over the report, and after hesitating for awhile decided to go into the residence. He explained to the prosecutor that the loss was an inexpensive record player and added, "This one's a pork chop, like most of the burglaries we get. But we gotta' go and interview the victim before suspending it." The detective asked the victim if she knew who might have committed the burglary or if she had heard about anyone committing burglaries in the area. Negative replies followed both questions. The entire encounter with the victim lasted less than two minutes.

Case 3: Assault and Robbery

A robbery squad detective was waiting for two victims to come in the hall to be interviewed. Both were black, middle-aged, center-city residents who were described by the detective as "dead-end alcoholics." They had been robbed in their residence by a young male who had forced his way in, taken $20 from the pair, and cut the female victim on the hand with a knife. The victims were able to provide the detective with the name of their assailant, and they both picked his photograph out of a number of pictures they were shown. Several minutes later the detective handed them a photograph of a different individual, asking, "Are you sure this is the guy who robbed you?" After inspecting the picture they replied that they knew this person as well but he had not been the one who robbed them. At this point, the detective sat down and took a formal statement from the victims.

When the victims had left, the detective explained his views and usual handling of such "ghetto robberies": "In a case like this, what can we do? To tell you the truth, the only way this kind of thing is going to stop is for the victims or somebody they know to kill this guy off. My involvement in this case is minimal. If the two victims, those two old drunks, if they sober up and if they show up in court, we'll see how they do there. It's up to them here and not up to me."

Case 4: Burglary

A detective entered the center-city residence of a burglary victim in a block where about one-fourth of the row houses were vacant. He examined a large hole in a basement wall that had been made to gain entry, and then sat down to compile a list of articles that had been stolen. The victim had literally been cleaned out, losing every easily transportable item of value she had owned. The woman explained that she worked during the day, that this was the fifth time she had been burglarized in the past four years, and that her coverage had been dropped by the insurance company. She added that she lived in the house for 21 years and was not about to move, and then asked, "What can I do to keep this from happening again?" The detective replied: "Ma'am, I don't know what to tell you. You're the only white family on this block. Most of the people around here work during the daytime, and a lot of these people, even if they saw somebody coming out of your house with

some of your stuff, they're not going to call the cops anyhow. That's the way it is around here. It's a shame, but that's the way it is." The detective entered the serial numbers of some of the stolen articles into the computerized stolen property files, "to cover myself, just in case." The written report indicated that the pawn shop sheets had been checked but in fact this step was not taken. When the report deadline approached, the case was suspended.

Case 5: Homicides

Two homicides had occurred over the weekend. On Monday morning two detectives who were working on the different cases were discussing the status of their investigations. One detective, who was investigating a shooting death that occurred in a crowded bar in the presence of 100 persons noted that he was on the verge of making a lock-up even though none of the witnesses present had voluntarily come forward. The other detective was investigating the bludgeoning death of a male homosexual whose body had been found by firemen called to extinguish a small fire in the victim's residence. There were as yet no suspects in the case. The second detective took offense to remarks made by the other comparing the lack of progress in the second case to the nearly completed investigation in the barroom case. The second detective remarked, "Anybody can handle a killing like you've got. What we've got here is a murder, not a killing."

The above incidents illustrate detectives' use of a body of accumulated knowledge, beliefs, and assumptions which lead to the interpretation of certain case patterns as common, typical and routine. Cases are interpreted primarily using conceptions of (1) how identifiable the perpetrators seem to be; (2) the normal social characteristics of the victims; and (3) the settings involved, and behavior seen as typical in such settings. A detective's initial efforts on a case tend to focus on these three aspects, in the process of assigning meaning to the case and selecting an appropriate strategy for handling it.

1. Conceptions of how different kinds of offenses are typically committed—especially how identifiable the perpetrators seem to be—are

routinely used in interpreting incidents. These imageries are specifically relevant to a detective's practical concerns. The ordinary burglary (Cases 2 and 4) is seen as involving a crude forced entry at a time of day or at a location where it is unlikely that anyone will witness the perpetrator entering or exiting. A burglary victim's ability or inability to provide information identifying a probable perpetrator constitutes the single feature of burglary cases which is given greatest interpretive significance. In roughly ten percent of these cases, the victim provides the name of a suspected perpetrator (commonly an ex-boyfriend, a relative or a neighboring resident), and vigorous effort is devoted to the case. For the remaining burglary cases, the initial inclination is to treat them as routine incidents deserving of only minimal investigative effort. In these routine cases the victim's race and class position have a decisive impact on whether the case will be summarily suspended or whether some minor investigative activities will be undertaken to impress the victim that "something is being done."

On the other hand, assault, rape, and homicide cases commonly occur in a face-to-face situation which affords the victim an opportunity to observe the assailant. Further, detectives recognize that many personal assault offenses involve acquainted parties. The earliest piece of information sought out and the feature of such cases given the greatest interpretive significance is whether the offense occurred between parties who were in some way known to one another prior to the incident. The interpretation and handling of the shooting incident in Case 1 changed markedly when it was learned that the victim and suspect were acquainted parties and that the offense reasonably conformed to a familiar pattern of domestic assaults. Where the victim and perpetrator are acquainted in assault, rape and homicide cases, the incident is seen as containing the core feature of the routine offense pattern for these cases. In such incidents a perfunctory investigation is usually made, for the identity of the perpetrator generally is easily learned from the victim or from persons close to the victim.

The barroom homicide in Case 5 was termed a "killing" and viewed as a routine case because the victim and perpetrator were previously acquainted and information linking the perpetrator to the crime could be easily obtained. The term "murder" is reserved for those homicides which do not correspond to a typical pattern.

A somewhat different pattern follows in the category of incidents which detectives refer to as "suspect rapes." Victims having certain social characteristics (females from lower-class backgrounds who are viewed as having low intelligence or as displaying some type of mental or emotional abnormality) are viewed as most likely to make a false allegation of rape. Where a victim so perceived reports a sexual assault by a person with whom she had some prior acquaintance, the initial orientation of the detective is to obtain information which either negates the crime of rape (the complainant actually consented) or warrants reducing the charge to a lesser offense. Where the victim and assailant were not previously acquainted, the case receives a vigorous investigative effort. The level of police resources devoted to the case varies according to the race and social standing of the victim.

2. Conceptions of the normal social characteristics of victims are also central to case routinization. Victims having different social characteristics are regarded as being more or less likely to desire or follow through with prosecution in the case, to be reliable sources of information about it, and to inquire as to the outcome of the investigation.

The treatment of the assault and robbery in Case 3 illustrates how a case may be interpreted and handled primarily in terms of the victim's class position, race, and presumed lifestyle and competencies. The case was cleared by arrest on the basis of information provided by the victims, but the handling of this "ghetto robbery" involved little actual police effort. No attempt was made to locate witnesses, gather evidence from the crime scene, or otherwise strengthen the case against the accused.

Poor and working-class people who are regarded as unlikely to make inquiries regarding the handling and disposition of the case are seen as typical of victims in the category of routine burglaries. Case 2 illustrates how the interpretation of an incident may be accomplished solely on the basis of information contained in the patrol report and prior to an actual interview with the victim. The interview was structured in this case by the detective's expectation of its outcome.

Case 4 illustrates how inconsistent elements in an otherwise routine pattern (in this instance the victim's social status and apparent interest in the handling of the case) are managed to suit the purposes of the detective. Detectives speak of a case "coming back on them" if a respectable victim contacts superiors regarding progress in the case when the incident has received little or no investigative effort. Informing the victim that the case was not solvable largely because of her neighbor's attitudes enabled the detective to suspend the case with minimal problems.

3. Routinization formulas, finally, contain conceptions of the settings in which different kinds of offenses normally occur and the expected behavior of inhabitants of those settings. While assumptions about victims and perpetrators are derived in part from the nature of the offense involved, the physical and social setting where the incident occurred also contributes to a detective's understanding of these parties. The fact that the burglary in Case 2 occurred in a particular public housing project told the detective much of what he felt he had to know about the case. It should be noted that none of these perceptions were communicated to the prosecutor observing the detective work; they were part of the taken-for-granted background upon which the detective based his handling of the case.

With regard to actual and potential *witnesses*, however, a detective's assumptions and beliefs are based primarily on the offense setting, if the witness is seen as a normal inhabitant of that setting. (This latter qualification simply recognizes that detectives attribute different inclinations and sentiments to social workers or salesmen who may have witnessed an incident than to residents of the area who may have witnessed a crime.)

The impact of territorial conceptions may be seen in the handling of Case 4. Routine burglaries occur mainly in low-income housing projects, residences in deteriorating center-city areas or, less frequently, in commercial establishments in or near these locations. Residents of these areas are considered unlikely to volunteer that they have witnessed a crime. Although official investigative procedure dictates that neighboring residents be interviewed to determine whether they saw or heard anything that might be of value to the investigation, this step was not undertaken in Cases 2 or 4 because it was assumed that the residents would be uncooperative.

Routine cases, then, may be seen as having two components, one at the level of consciousness and cognition, and the other at the level of observable behavior. A detective's interpretation of a case as routine involves an assessment of whether sufficient correspondence exists between the current case and some typical pattern to warrant handling it in the normal way. The criterion of sufficient correspondence implies that not all the elements of the typical pattern need be present for a detective to regard a case as a routine one. Common elements are viewed and used as resources which may be drawn upon selectively in accordance with one's practical concerns and objectives. Further, when certain elements in a case appear inconsistent with the typical pattern, there is a tendency to force and manage a sufficient fit between the particular and the typical in ways that help detectives deal with their caseload management problems and constraints.

These features of the interpretation process mean that the assessments of the routine or nonroutine nature of a case take on more of the character of a dichotomy than a continuum. Once an assessment is made, the case will be handled by means of prescribed formulas unless additional information changes the interpretation. It must be emphasized that the routinization process is not a matter of automatic or unreflective mapping of case features onto more general conceptions of criminal incidents. The interpretation of any particular case is shaped by a detective's understandings of what is required and expected and of how to manage these concerns effectively.

CASE HANDLING

Case handling normally proceeds in accordance with informal understandings shared among detectives. Routine case patterns are associated with prescribed handling recipes. It is critical to an understanding of investigative police work that interpretation of criminal incidents as routine or nonroutine largely determines which cases will be summarily suspended, which will be investigated, and how vigorous or extensive that investigation will be.

The characteristic behavioral element of a routine case is an absence of vigorous or thorough investigative effort. Two distinct sets of circumstances are ordinarily encountered in routine cases which lead to such a superficial or cursory investigate effort. The first, most common in burglary and robbery cases, is that the available information concerning the incident is seen as so meager or of so little utility that the possibility of making a quick arrest is virtually nonexistent. Viewing the case as nonproductive, and not wishing to expend effort on cases for which there are no formal rewards, the detective produces a brief investigative report detailing the routine features of the incident, concludes the case summary with "N.I.L." (no investigative leads were found), and classifies it as a suspended case.

The second set of circumstances associated with an absence of vigorous investigative effort involves assault, rape, and homicide cases which require some investigation because of their seriousness and the possibility of scrutiny by the judicial process. However, in many such incidents the facts of the case are so obvious and straightforward that little actual investigative work needs to be done. In these three types of offenses the victim and perpetrator are often known to one another, and it is not at all uncommon for the victim to name the assailant as soon as the police arrive. Cases in which a spouse or lover is still standing by the victim with weapon in hand when the police arrive, or in which the victim names the perpetrator before expiring, are not unusual. In essence, such cases are solved without any substantial police investigation. The detective is obligated to produce a comprehensive report on the incidence, and the investigation is generally classified as closed in this report if the perpetrator has been apprehended. Indeed, in such obvious and straightforward cases the detective's only difficult task may be that of locating the perpetrator.[7]

Handling recipes associated with routine cases have a practical and instrumental character, reflecting the objective circumstances surrounding the investigation of many criminal events. After all, in the great majority of burglary cases the probability of ascertaining the identity of the perpetrator is rather small. Yet, handling recipes reflect certain *beliefs* and *assumptions* on the part of detectives concerning such matters as a victim's willingness to cooperate fully in the case, whether persons in particular sections of the city are likely to volunteer information about a crime, or the kind of impression a victim or witness would make in court. Such beliefs and assumptions constitute integral features in the construction of cases as routine or nonroutine, and they represent a pivotal linkage between specific features of cases and particular handling recipes.

The following incident illustrates the extent to which case handling may be guided by the detective's beliefs and assumptions about the nature of an incident and the parties involved:

Case 6

A detective was assigned a case in which a man had stabbed his common-law wife in the arm with a kitchen knife. The patrol report on the incident indicated that the woman had been taken to City Hall to sign an arrest warrant, while the man had been arrested by patrol officers on the charge of felony assault and released on his own recognizance. Nominally, the detective was required to collect additional information and evidence relating to the incident and to write a detailed and comprehensive report which would be used in prosecuting the case. However, the detective's interpretation of the incident, based on his understanding of the area in which it occurred and the lifestyles of the persons involved, led him to view any further investigative effort on his part as futile. He remarked: "These drunks, they're always stabbing one another over here. Then you see 'em the next day and they're right back together again. She won't show up in court anyhow. Why waste my time and everybody else's on it." The handling of the case involved only the production of a brief report which concluded: "The victim in this complaint wishes no further investigation by the police department. This complaint is to be classified as closed."

The interpretive schemes used by detectives are not based solely on their experiences as police investigators, but also on their accumulated experiences as everyday social actors; they thus reflect commonsense social knowledge. Categorizations made by detectives about race, class, ethnicity, sex, and territory parallel wider cultural evaluations of morality and worth. None of the features of the formal organization of detective work substantially reduce this reliance on commonsense knowledge and its typical biases, prejudices and interpretations.

SUMMARY AND IMPLICATIONS

Some general features of case routinization may now be noted in an attempt to clarify the interpretive activities through which detectives achieve order and predictability in their handling of cases and their encounters with victims and other relevant actors.

1. Shortly after receipt of a case, specific pieces of information are sought out and attended to for use in assessing the typicality of the incident. That is, the fundamental case-working orientation of detectives involves an attempt to establish commonalities between an actual case and typical case patterns. Incidents having typical features are interpreted and constructed as some variety of routine case. The orientation to typify and routinize cases is partly traceable to bureaucratic pressures and constraints to meet paperwork deadlines and produce a certain quantity and quality not of convictions but of arrests.

2. The interpretation of an incident is accomplished by attending to case features having commonly recognized utility as indicators of the type of case at hand. Detectives use such routinization schemes unless some problematic feature of an actual case brings into question their applicability and appropriateness. The interpretation of a case as routine or nonroutine essentially determines whether the case will be quickly closed or suspended or whether it will receive a more vigorous and extensive investigation. However, this initial assignment

of meaning is provisional and subject to revision or modification upon receipt of additional information. Most importantly, the handling of cases is directed by these informal categorization schemes, and is not the result of formal organizational policy or procedures. These schemes constitute a taken-for-granted background of decision making.

3. The interpretive schemes shared by detectives represent "successful" solutions to common practical problems, based on experience and shared understandings about the nature of urban crime and about types of urban residents, lifestyles and territories. These understandings are rooted in socially distributed as well as role-specific knowledge, for both provide a basis for constructing solutions to work problems. Occupationally specific knowledge provides a set of instructions for interpreting case patterns in ways which enable a detective to successfully manage organizational constraints and demands. Commonsense social knowledge provides an understanding of the typical characteristics, attitudes and action patterns of persons encountered. Identities may be readily assigned to persons by drawing on this stock of knowledge. Such identity assignments structure case handling along race, class, age, sex and territorial lines in ways that are intended to minimize case handling problems. Because of this reliance on general social knowledge, the treatment of different types of urban residents tends to reflect wider cultural evaluations of social worth.

4. The essential nature of these interpretive processes is phenomenological rather than mechanical or rule-guided. In formulating a particular case, the operative process involves a determination of whether sufficient correspondence exists between the actual case and the paradigmatic case to warrant handling the incident in routine, low-effort ways. Sufficient correspondence assessments are accomplished in ways that serve the practical purposes of detectives, especially those of paper-work compliance and productivity.

5. Accordingly, routine cases are not constituted as a single determinant pattern. A variety of combinations of case features may result in routine handling of the case. For each offense, a

core feature or set of features gets maximum interpretive significance. When a core feature is recognized in a particular case, other features which are ambiguous or even contradictory tend to be interpreted in a manner consistent with the identified core feature. Additional interpretive features, particularly the social status of the victim, are used as resources in selecting a safe and workable handling strategy.

6. In highly routinized case patterns, there is a tendency to squeeze great indicativeness out of a few case features. Detectives often rely upon assumptions to add detail to a case rather than actually gather information to further specify the type of case at hand. In other words, it is frequently taken for granted that certain investigate procedures will have predictable outcomes. Frequently, this process manifests itself in the fudging, doctoring and manipulation of formal organizational reports.

It is likely that interpretive schemes having similar features will be found in all bureaucratically organized enterprises where large numbers of clients or cases are processed (e.g., social service centers, public hospitals, and other agencies in the criminal justice system). Whenever we find an organizational setting where members deal with similar events time and again, and where there are no features in the formal organization of the work which act to counter stereotyping, we may expect to find routinization schemes in use. These schemes will be used to categorize the population and apply standard patterns of treatment to each category.

These observations have significant implications for the study of decision making by legal agents. Decision making by bureaucratic agents inevitably involves discretion on the part of the agent who must fit general rules to particular cases. This discretionary latitude will be reflected in different forms of decision making in different kinds of organizational settings. The work of Roth (1977), Scheff (1978), Sudnow (1965) and others suggests that caseload size, amount of information readily available about the person or event, the nature of the body of knowledge used, and the expectation of future interaction with the person are crucial features governing the nature of the decision-making

process. Where caseloads are high, continued interaction is not anticipated, minimal information is available, and the body of knowledge used by the agent is imprecise—stereotypes tend to become the operative and binding basis for decision making. Accordingly, detective work, presentence casework, public defender work, and medical practice in clinics or emergency rooms may be seen as lying toward the end of a continuum where typifications act as essentially final judgments.

At the other end of the continuum are settings where caseload sizes are smaller, more detailed information about the person is available, future interaction is anticipated, and decision making is grounded in a more substantial body of knowledge. In such settings, typificatory schemes are likely to be used only as provisional hypotheses, to be amplified and modified over the course of the encounter. Thus in probation work, some types of social service work, and the practice of general medicine, we might expect to find interaction only tentatively structured by stereotypic understandings. As interaction proceeds in these latter settings, typifications will begin to fade in importance as the basis for decision making.

NOTES

1. The use of shared typificatory schemes to make required decisions appears to be a pervasive phenomenon not only in social control organizations, but in other organizations which process large numbers of people as well. Roth (1977) observed the same basic process in the evaluation, categorization, and treatment of patients by hospital personnel. The differential treatment of clients of public service bureaucracies was likewise found to be rooted in occupational typifications (Gordon, 1975).

2. The description and the analysis presented here are based on nine months of participant observation field work in a city police detective division. Further information about access agreements, characteristics of the city and department, the field role adopted, and problems encountered during the research is available from the author.

3. An exception to this general observation occurs where a supervisor imposes a "major case" definition on an incident. In highly publicized or non-routine homicide or rape cases, especially those

involving higher status victims, a supervisor frequently takes an active part in the investigation and more closely monitors and directs the activities of detectives. With regard to the influence of the victim's social status on case handling, see Wilson's (1968: 27) analysis of police perceptions of the legitimacy of complaints made by middle-class versus lower-class victims.

4. Official nationwide clearance rates are listed as 17.6% for burglary, 27.3% for robbery, 63.4% for felonious assault, 51.1% for rape, and 79.9% for homicide (Hindelang *et al.*, 1977).

5. Cf. Sudnow's (1965) argument that public defenders use their first interview with a client to gain an initial sense of the defendant's place in the social structure as well as the typicality or lack thereof of the offense with which the person has been charged.

6. Garfinkel (1967:186-207) argues that organizational records are not to be treated as accurate or mirror reflections of the actual handling of a client or case by organizational members. However, these records can be employed to examine how members go about constructing a meaningful conception of a client or case and use it for their own practical purposes. Any valid sociological use of such records requires detailed knowledge on the part of the researcher regarding the context in which the records are produced, background understandings of members, and organizationally relevant purposes and routines.

7. Reiss (1971) makes a similar observation. He found that a great deal of detective work in the department studied merely involves attempting to locate identified perpetrators. The Rand survey of investigative practices in 153 police departments draws conclusions similar to those presented here. It was found that substantially more than half of all serious reported crimes receive no more than superficial attention from investigators (Greenwood and Petersilia, 1975).

REFERENCES

Bittner, Egon. 1967 "The police on skid row: A study of peace keeping." American Sociological Review 32(October): 699-715.

Bittner, Egon. 1970 The Functions of the Police in Modern Society. Chevy Chase, Maryland: National Institute of Mental Health.

Garfinkel, Harold. 1967 Studies in Ethnomethodology, Englewood Cliffs, N.J.: Prentice-Hall.

Gordon, Laura. 1975 "Bureaucratic competence and success in dealing with public bureaucracies." Social Problems 23 (2):197-208.

Greenwood, Peter W. and Joan Petersilia. 1975 The Criminal Investigation Process, Volume I. Santa Monica, Calif.: The Rand Corporation.

Hindelang, M., M. Gottfredson, C. Dunn and N. Parisi. 1977 Sourcebook of Criminal Justice Statistics. Washington, D.C.: National Criminal Justice Information and Statistics Service.

Piliavin, Irving and Scott Briar. 1964 "Police encounters with juveniles." American Sociological Review (70):206-214.

Reiss, Albert. 1971 Police and the Public. New Haven: Yale University Press.

Roth, Julius. 1977 "Some contingencies of the moral evaluation and control of clients." American Journal of Sociology 77 (October):830-56.

Scheff, Thomas. 1978 "Typification in rehabilitation agencies." Pp 172-175 in E. Rubington and M.S. Weinberg (eds.), Deviance: The Interactionist Perspective. New York: Macmillan.

Skolnick, Jerome. 1967 Justice Without Trial. New York: Wiley.

Steffensmeier, D. and R. Terry. 1973 "Deviance and respectability: An observational study of reactions to shoplifting." Social Forces 51:417-426.

Stokes, Randall and John Hewitt. 1976 "Aligning actions." American Sociological Review 41: 838-849.

Sudnow, David. 1965 "Normal crimes: Sociological features of the penal code in a public defender's office." Social Problems 12 (3):255-276.

Swigert, Victoria and Ronald Farrell. 1977 "Normal homicides and the law." American Sociological Review 42:16-32.

Wilson, James Q. 1968 Varieties of Police Behavior. Cambridge, Mass.: Harvard University Press.

Social scientists have conceived of emotional labor as alienating for those occupations that experience a high degree of emotional work on a daily basis. Stenross and Kleinman studied this phenomenon with police detectives and found that even within the same occupation, workers may find some emotional labor alienating, but that other types of emotional labor were enjoyable. The investigators in their study disliked their interactions with victims of crime, but were very favorable toward their encounters with criminal suspects. The detectives discounted criminals' emotional appeals and untruths and perceived their emotional labor as necessary to apprehend suspects. Often, they would turn these interactions into a game for purposes of attaining a positive outcome, that of arrest. However, they were not able to transform their uncomfortable emotional encounters with victims into a positive experience.

THE HIGHS AND LOWS OF EMOTIONAL LABOR

Detectives' Encounters with Criminals and Victims

BARBARA STENROSS

SHERRYL KLEINMAN

With the shift from a production to a service economy, increasing numbers of Americans have jobs that require them to manage their own and others' feelings. Workers who do "emotional labor" often experience burnout and become estranged from their feelings (Hochschild, 1983). Those called upon to make clients feel good (e.g., flight attendants) must suppress their own feelings of anger; those called upon to make others

Authors' Note: This research was supported in part by a grant from the University Research Council of the University of North Carolina at Chapel Hill. We thank Howard Aldrich, Howard Becker, Carolyn Ellis, Peter Hall, Arlie Hochschild, Arne Kalleberg, Michael Russell, Richard Simpson, Robert Wilson, the editors of the *Journal of Contemporary Ethnography* and three anonymous reviewers for their comments on drafts of this paper. A version of this article was presented at the Conference on Ethnography, University of Waterloo, Ontario, Canada, May 1986.

Reprinted from *Journal of Contemporary Ethnography*, Vol. 17, No. 4, January 1989, 435–452, Copyright © 1989 Sage Publications, Inc.

feel bad (e.g., bill collectors) must suppress their own feelings of compassion. Emotional labor, Hochschild argues, may alienate workers more than the oppressive manual labor of the factory worker. Manual laborers must bend their body to the task, but emotional laborers must surrender their heart.

Some workers find their emotional labor bearable because they have "status shields" (Hochschild, 1983) that protect them from others' emotional onslaughts. For example, the high status of career diplomats, doctors, and judges makes others less likely to challenge them.

What happens to lower-status emotional laborers, those who lack a status shield? The detectives we interviewed considered their "core task" (Hughes, 1958) to be solving crimes and arresting criminals (see also Sanders, 1977; Skolnick, 1966; Waegel, 1981). Yet emotional labor became a part of their work as they faced the outbursts of criminals and victims. Since victims and detectives are on the same side, we expected the detectives to get along well with victims. Perhaps victims would even look up to those who are in a position to help them. And we expected the detectives to find their interactions with criminals a trying experience. Instead, we found the opposite: The detectives felt burdened by victims and energized by criminals. Why?

The detectives lacked a status shield, but they protected themselves from criminals' abusive language and scornful gestures by denying the authenticity of these expressive displays. In addition, criminals gave the detectives opportunities to do "real detective work," to redefine their emotional labor as higher status mental work, and to derive an emotional high from it. Detectives viewed victims' emotional displays as genuine and thus they could not discount them. In addition, victims vented their feelings of frustration on the detectives and expected them to do the kind of emotional labor the detectives could not transform into anything better.

We will examine differences in detectives' emotional labor with criminals and with victims, outlining the strategies that those without status shields may use to transform emotional labor into engaging work. Our study suggests that emotional labor need not be alienating. Even within the same occupation workers may find some emotional labor

alienating but other emotional labor bearable or even satisfying.

RESEARCH SETTING AND METHODS

We interviewed the investigative staffs of a police and a sheriff's department located in adjacent counties in the southeast. The departments served similar jurisdictions of about 40,000 people. The sheriff's department employed seven investigators and a department head who worked mainly as an administrator. The police department employed six investigators and a department head who also investigated crimes. The detectives, all men, came from both working and middle class backgrounds. Most were born and raised in the South. Five of the detectives were black; about half had attended college.

The detectives began their days by reporting for duty and receiving their new case assignments. When assigned a case, the detectives received the investigative report form that had been filed by the officer on duty when the crime was reported. Those forms included the complainant's (usually the victim's) statement, as well as other details about the crime. The detective's job was to do the follow-up investigation on the cases for which a suspect was not already apprehended. (In violent crimes the dispatcher notified the detective division immediately, and a detective usually joined the patrol officer at the crime scene.) Property crimes, including breaking and enterings, larcenies, and vandalism, made up 89% of the incoming cases in the sheriff's department and 87% in the police department. The average case load per detective was approximately 25 to 30 cases per month.

We conducted semistructured, in-depth interviews to study detectives' interpretations of their work. The interviews took place in the detectives' offices or in interrogation or briefing rooms at the department. Questions included how many cases detectives worked, how they spent their days, how they solved crimes, how their job varied by shift and type of crime, and how they felt about their encounters with criminals, victims, witnesses, and informants. We also asked the detectives to tell us about any matters we overlooked. Each interview ranged from 45 minutes to two and one-half hours. The interviews were tape-recorded, transcribed, and analyzed with the methods outlined in Glaser and Strauss's (1967) discussion of grounded theory.

Since the police are open to public scrutiny and criticism, we expected them to hold back information during interviews. But we found that the detectives' statements were candid and not particularly flattering to themselves or their occupation. For example, the detectives admitted that they did little or no work on many reported crimes, and they were also critical of programs popular among the public, such as community watch and routine dusting for prints. The detectives may have felt comfortable with the interviewer because they knew her husband was a sheriff's deputy. Manning (1967) has suggested that respondents will participate more fully in an interview when they feel they don't have to ingratiate themselves to the interviewer.

Detectives interact with many members of the public. We will limit our discussion to detectives' relations with criminals and victims because these are the audiences the detectives talked about the most and regarded as most important in making them feel good or bad about their work.

Detectives And Criminals

Doing Real Detective Work

The detectives considered themselves crime-solvers and thief-takers (Klockars, 1985). Yet most of the leads the detectives followed led nowhere, and the detectives spent much of their time writing reports and sitting in court (see also Greenwood et al., 1977). Against this background of boredom and bureaucratic routine, their encounters with criminals felt like a breath of fresh air. Criminals gave the detectives opportunities to learn many things street cops and bureaucrats do not know: how criminals commit crimes, how the "criminal mind" works, what criminals do with stolen property, and how they enter the "world of crime." The detectives felt that handling criminals was "real detective work" (see also Van Maanen, 1974: 97), and looked forward to their encounters with them.

All of the detectives believed that burglars and other criminals have particular methods of operation, often specializing in certain kinds of crime. During interviews and interrogations, the detectives tried to get inside information about criminal methods from the criminals themselves. Most criminals did not readily volunteer information about their own or others' crime techniques. But in return for an actual or expected favor (e.g., a lower bond), or by getting the criminal to boast about the crime, the detectives often finagled such information out of them. A novice detective revealed his excitement at learning the ins and outs of how a burglary was committed:

> So he [the burglar] looked in and saw all this [alarm system], so he just took something and popped the glass and knocked it out, reached in and pulled himself in, never set the alarm off! [laugh] He broke into five houses right there in that neighborhood.

The detectives used their familiarity with criminals and criminal techniques to develop notions of "normal crimes" (Sudnow, 1965; Waegel, 1981) and to build suspect pools for future crime-solving. As a veteran detective in the sheriff's department explained,

> You look for patterns of previous break-ins to try to tie them into the same people.

The detectives especially liked to deal with "seasoned" criminals. These criminals were often recalcitrant, but the detectives thought of them as a knowledgeable audience who could evaluate their growing expertise and insights. The detectives believed that seasoned criminals "knew the law" and would only confess to a crime or plead guilty if the detective had built a solid case:

> People that've been through the system won't tell you much unless you got something on them. If you got them *dead right*, got enough on them, they'll do a little talking. They don't want to go back to prison again.

Criminals, then, not only gave the detectives insights into the world of crime, but also served as an audience that could put the stamp of approval on the work they did.

Shielding Themselves

The detectives wanted to solve crimes and put criminals away, so it made sense that they enjoyed arresting suspects and bringing them in for interviews or interrogations. Arrests and interrogations were occasions when the detectives' work finally came to a head. Success was now assured or at least within reach. But criminals did not make things easy for detectives. Brought in for arrest, criminal suspects often yelled at the detectives, cursed them, or refused to talk. At times they cried or became hysterical.

Yet the detectives found a way to let the criminals' emotional outbursts or stubborn silences roll off their backs. They discounted criminals' expressive displays by interpreting them as feigned rather than genuine. The detectives believed that criminals would fake almost any emotion to shake the detective's composure. An older detective who now heads a detective division explained:

A lot of times they [criminal suspects] are trying to get you angry so that you make a mistake, and that becomes one of the hardest parts of the job.

The detectives dismissed the criminals' emotional displays by conceiving of them as "strategic interaction" (Goffman, 1969), or part of a game. They considered criminals' expressive displays moves, not real emotions. Hence, the criminals' barbs did not go deep. Workers will only take others' emotional displays to heart when they view the emotions as genuine.

The Fun Of Mental Work

By regarding criminals as gamesmen, the detectives also set the frame for reinterpreting the emotional labor they did with criminals as mental work. The detectives clearly performed emotional labor with criminals, but their redefinition of it as higher status mental work enabled them to *enjoy* it, thinking of their encounters with criminals as challenging intellectual games.

The detectives liked interrogating suspects because it was their chance to match wits with, and win out over, their archrivals in crime. Until detectives have enough evidence to make an arrest, one young detective explained, "the criminal has

the upper hand." But during interrogation, he added with a smile, "the tables are turned." The detectives used information and evidence to "show up" the criminal and control him. The detectives found it exciting to con those whose business is conning:

You're giving him [the suspect] something he's going to get anyway [a reduced charge], but he doesn't know that yet, and he thinks he's got it because of your, ah, being benevolent, or your influence with other officers. So you use him, you're conning him at the same time they're going to try to con you. And they're going to con you every chance they get.

In face-to-face encounters with criminals the detectives played their hands with cunning and care. For example, when the detectives did not have all the evidence they wanted, they often bluffed, making the suspect believe they had more evidence than they did:

It depends on how much information you have on the suspect as to which way you would go. You can bluff 'em, of course, make them think you have more than you *do*. Sometimes then they'll reveal a lot more information.

Or, they got the suspect to tell a lie and used the suspect's mistake to "catch him." For example, one detective said he often asked suspects the same questions over and over until they tripped up:

You ask a lot of questions and you bring this guy in for interrogation. And then you start checking him, checking him, and you can pass him the same questions over and over and over until he just makes some mistakes. Then you know you've got him!

The detectives believed that "psyching out" their opponent was crucial for successful interrogation. Before they brought a suspect in for questioning, the detectives tried to find out as much as possible about him so they could "plan what [they're] going to do as far as the suspect." For example, one older black detective said he often tried to talk with the suspect's mother, his high school teacher, or people in the neighborhood before he brought the suspect in for interrogation. But sometimes detectives had to size up suspects they had never met. They found this work challenging:

> You have to *learn* the person that you are dealing with, even though you may have just picked him up on the street. . . . But right then and there begin formulating a picture of this person so you can interview him more intelligently and approach him in a way that he will be more willing to tell you things.

The detectives believed that each suspect required a different style of interrogation (as suggested in textbooks on the interrogation process, e.g., Inbau and Reid, 1953). For example, a veteran detective said he varied his style with suspects. He claimed that some suspects responded well to a "straightforward approach," but others required "playing John Wayne" :

> For instance, a 16-year-old boy who has had no experience with the law and has perceived the law in a certain light, if you approach him like a teacher—very honest, straightforward—he may respond. But he'll be more likely to respond if he perceives you as Kojak or John Wayne.

Detectives and Victims Hand-Holding Victims

The detectives said that victims were often distraught, upset, or angry. Some victims cried or became too upset to endure the interview; others complained endlessly about the crime. A young black detective who had worked for years with the state bureau of investigation complained about an encounter he had just had:

> I went to the house and the man talked two hours. I just couldn't turn him off. He wanted to show me where this happened. He wanted me to talk to this individual.

Another detective said he disliked working the "first part" of rape cases because of the uncomfortable feelings the crime evoked in himself and others:

> don't like to see anybody beat, or well, maybe she don't have to be beat—crying, you know. You gotta go home and tell her husband, or you gotta

tell her mother, and you gotta sit up with her. It's just, I don't like that part.

Even workers who are trained as counselors find it difficult to deal with clients who flood out and lose control (Joffe, 1978). The detectives often felt powerless before victims' emotional outbursts.

The detectives dismissed criminals' emotional displays by viewing them as moves in a game. But the detectives could not use the same strategy with victims. They felt that most victims' emotional displays were authentic, not phony, and even justified. Hence, the detectives thought they *should* feel sympathy for crime victims. Although crime was a routine even for the detectives, they knew it was traumatic for the victim.

In addition, the detective said their superiors *expected* them to cool victims out as a matter of public relations. Police and sheriff's departments are political organizations. Top officials can get ahead only if they maintain good relations with the public (Reiss and Bordua, 1967; Wilson, 1968: 69-70). Consequently, detectives and other subordinates receive pressure from the top to take citizens' complaints seriously. The detectives said they worried that they would get into trouble with the sheriff or police chief if a crime victim complained about lack of attention:

> You really try to go out here and do a job, but you forgot about this one guy over here. I mean, you're really doing a good job for 90% of the people, but this one guy calls the sheriff, "I ain't seen him out here but one time, and blah, blah, blah, blah, blah." And then you got to catch it.

Several detectives talked about pacifying victims as a department policy:

> You can't do anything [on the case], you *know* you can't do anything, you got other things you *can* do, but you go talk to this man [the victim], pacify him, tell him you're going to do something.

The detectives often had a hard time acting sympathetic when people had their microwaves or stereos stolen (a common crime they regarded as not very serious). But they knew that if they did not seem upset, victims might accuse them of indifference and complain to their superiors. This added to the anxiety they felt in encountering victims. A middle-aged detective complained bitterly:

> If they're [victims] excited and they're upset, some people resent the fact that the officer doesn't seem to be as bent out of shape as they are about it. People just accuse us of being hard-hearted or say we just don't give a damn.

The detectives found their interactions with victims emotionally trying. They had empathy for victims, but they still resented having to "hold their hands." Moreover, they were supported in their view by the masculine—even macho—ethic of the police culture. Within that occupational culture (Manning, 1979), nurturing others is regarded as low-status women's work (Hunt, 1984). Yet the police are not alone in regarding sympathetic emotional labor as low status. Within the helping professions (such as medicine and law), the highest prestige goes to those who do the *least* nurturing (Abbot, 1974). For example, surgery has the highest prestige in medicine, while psychiatry has the lowest. And corporate tax law has high status, while family law has low status. Although victims were often high-status clients, the detectives disliked dealing with them because they still had to do low-status emotional labor.

Fighting For Autonomy

Many victims usurped the detectives' investigative role, telling them how to solve the case. The detectives felt that their supervisors had the right to direct them. But they resented victims—people without authority or expertise—who told them what to do (see also Mennerick, 1974).

The detectives complained that victims often "played detective." Burglary victims believed they knew who committed the crime, claiming that someone who had recently been to their house (e.g., an electrician or exterminator) had "cased the place" and then returned to steal their property. The detectives were reluctant to follow these suggestions, but knew that many victims would check on whether they had. Also, since following *any* lead is central to solving

crimes, the detectives halfheartedly thought of ways to approach those accused by victims. A detective explained:

> A lot of times we have people who are trying to do investigation, they'll give us suspects, and you know, the suspects, their reasons for being suspects are, "He was here, ah, the other day with my son," or something like that. But that's the only reason they got for him being a suspect and they want you to watch him, talk to him, and all this stuff.

The detectives said that victims often demanded that they dust for fingerprints (see also Sanders, 1977: 98). The detectives knew that fingerprints could not be lifted off all surfaces, and that even good prints rarely helped them solve cases that have no suspect leads. As one detective put it, "If you don't have any idea of who that person is to compare those fingerprints with, fingerprints aren't worth a dime to you." When the detectives believed prints would help them make an arrest or pacify a victim they tried to get an identifications expert or patrol officer to do it. Because this was not always possible and victims often demanded prints, the detectives sometimes ended up dusting for prints themselves—a task they regarded as dirty and unpleasant. For example, one detective described his efforts to lift prints in a house trailer:

> It's a real messy job. A lot of us don't like it because that dust goes everywhere. It gets up in your nose, in your face. I did it with a white shirt on not too long ago, and it's sort of greasy . . . There was a trailer broken into and the man had a window open on one side and the door on the other and I was spreading the stuff and someone says, "It's all over your back" [laugh].

The detectives felt even more insulted by victims who suggested that they take suspects aside and beat them up. The detectives disliked this perception of them as "heavies" in the war on crime, and resented having to explain that such behavior was in fact illegal:

> [Victims] think that you can just run out there and kick doors in, arrest people for no reason, grab a suspect and smash him up, beat him up and make him tell you that he's been in your house. I

mean, you know, "I think if you *lean* on him a little, he'll tell you what you want to know"—I've had people *say* that!

The detectives believed that victims got their ideas about detective work from television. Since TV crimes are solved within the hour, detectives complained that victims often expected quick results. As one detective put it, "Victims feel that we can do a lot more than we can right off the bat, and it's not that simple." Yet the detectives could not easily put victims off. Some victims called the police station if they did not get results soon enough or felt the detective was ignoring their case. The detectives felt hounded by victims:

> Some people, when you've done all you can really do, and you're getting nowhere and you don't have any suspects, you're not going to get their property back, uh, you just can't *do* any more, and they still keep on saying: [in a whisper] "Whatcha gonna do? Whatcha gonna do?" I tell them I've done all I can, but they don't want to hear that. They won't let you rest with that.

Ingratitude

The detectives might have felt more charitable toward victims if they believed that victims did *their* part. But the detectives said that many victims let them down and were ungrateful. For example, theft cases require a lot of legwork: Detectives must enter property descriptors into the state computer system, visit pawnshops in search of the stolen items, ask their informants about the crime, and go through case files looking for similar methods of operation or similar thefts. Yet few victims had information about their property that would make the detectives' efforts worthwhile. Detectives said that few people mark their property or keep a record of serial numbers for such frequently stolen items as televisions and stereos. Some victims even give the wrong information about their property, reporting the theft of a Magnavox TV when they actually owned a Panasonic. Without good property descriptions, detectives complained, they could not identify and locate victims' property. One disgruntled detective said:

People don't understand that if you can't identify your property, there's nothing I can do about it.

When the detectives did recover stolen property, their work was often futile, because victims could not conclusively identify the item as theirs. Pointing in the direction of the room where the department stored recovered property, one detective said in frustration:

> A lot of people can't identify their property. Our property room can be loaded with a hundred thousand dollars, but we can't do anything with it.

The detectives also learned that they could not rely on victims to appear in court. Once victims got their property back or received their insurance money, many no longer cared about catching the criminal. One detective mimicked an ungrateful victim:

> I got my stuff back, I don't care what you all do with him, don't call me no more. I'm not coming to court.

The detectives had sympathy for victims' plight, but felt that victims became an emotional burden. Victims took out their anger and frustration on the detectives, misinterpreted the detectives' role as "heavies" or counselors, and abandoned them in their hour of need. The detectives knew the department could not ignore crime victims. But they wished that they weren't the ones who had to keep seeing them. As one detective put it, "Hopefully, someday, we'll have someone right here in the bureau that can sit at a desk and call these people." Other detectives agreed. They thought the department should hire *other* workers to visit or call victims, to free them to do real detective work:

> I think it would take a lot off the investigator if we had someone contact the victim. So the investigator could go out and make the contacts he needs to make in order to solve some of the crimes.

Ironically, they would then be free to spend time with the very people one would expect them to abhor: criminals.

DISCUSSION AND CONCLUSION

The case of the detectives suggests that emotional labor need not be alienating. Even in the same occupation, some emotional labor will be satisfying or at least bearable, while other emotional labor will be alienating.

The detectives' encounters with victims suggest (by their absence) two conditions that may make emotional labor bearable for *other* workers: organizational shields provided by the organization, and status shields provided by prestige.

First, some organizations provided workers with an organizational status shield. For example, bosses can rely on secretaries to field requests and complaints, screen callers and visitors, and serve as the "human face" (Kanter, 1977) of the corporation. The detectives longed for their organization to provide a buffer between themselves and victims. In fact, police and sheriff's organizations do send patrol officers out to take victims' initial complaints. Yet the detectives wanted their departments to hire workers to do all the public relations work the departments expected of them.

Second, prestigious positions offer status shields for workers. For example, doctors, lawyers, and other professionals have acquired the license and mandate (Becker, 1970; Hughes, 1958) to answer to themselves rather than to others. In addition, students in professional schools learn to distance themselves emotionally from their clients (e.g., Haas and Shaffir, 1977; Kleinman, 1984; Smith and Kleinman, 1988). This "affectively neutral" stance (Parsons, 1951) keeps professionals from feeling put upon by clients' threats or emotional displays. Also, by cultivating a demeanor that people associate with authority, clients often feel too intimidated by professionals to complain to them face-to-face. Affective neutrality sets up an emotional distance in the relationship that clients, having less power and feeling vulnerable, are likely to go along with. This "professional demeanor" may well cut down on the amount of emotional labor a professional will have to do.

Despite these shields, clients may on occasion challenge professionals. Yet the case of the detectives suggests that workers who lack status shields (and those who temporarily find themselves without one) may discover ways to make their work bearable or even enjoyable.

Workers will make work bearable if they can convince themselves that client's emotions are phony. The detectives felt that criminals feigned emotions in order to protect themselves. Similarly, teachers psych out students, judging between those whose tears are genuine and those whose are ploys to get their grades raised.

Workers will make emotional labor enjoyable if they redefine that work as relevant to the task they value the most. The detectives wanted to solve crimes. Since they defined their encounters with criminals as a way to catch more criminals, the detectives turned an emotionally trying experience into a valuable learning experience. Such positive redefinition enabled the detectives to regard the encounters with criminals as a challenging and exciting intellectual game. They enjoyed delving into the "criminal mind" and figuring out which interactional style would best elicit information from particular suspects. By reframing their emotional labor as mental work, they transformed these encounters into fun.

This study suggests that a "qualitative," inductive approach is especially useful for understanding worker alienation and job satisfaction. By uncovering the meanings the workers give to their tasks, we may find that alienation occurs where we expect workers to feel satisfied, and enjoyment occurs where we expect workers to feel alienated.

REFERENCES

Abbott, A (1974) "Status and status strain in the professions." Amer. J. Sociology 86: 819-835.

Becker, H. S. (1970) "The nature of a profession," pp. 87-103 in H. S. Becker (ed.) Sociological Work: Method and Substance. Chicago: Aldine.

Glaser, B. and A. Strauss (1967) The Discovery of Grounded Theory. Chicago: Aldine.

Goffman, E. (1969) Strategic Interaction. Philadelphia: Univ. of Pennsylvania Press.

Greenwood, P. J., J. M. Chaiken, and J. Petersilia (1977) The Criminal Investigation Process. Lexington, MA: D. C. Heath.

Haas, J. and W. Shaffir (1977) "The professionalization of medical students: developing competence and a cloak of competence." Symbolic Interaction 1: 71-88.

Hochschild, A. R. (1983) The Managed Heart: Commercialization of Human Feeling. Berkeley: Univ. of California Press.

Hughes, E. C. (1958) Men and Their Work. Glencoe, IL: Free Press.

Hunt, J. (1984) "The development of rapport through the negotiation of gender in field work among police." Human Organization 43: 283-296.

Inbau, F. E. and J. E. Reid (1953) Lie Detection and Criminal Investigation (3rd ed.). Baltimore: Williams and Watkins.

Joffe, C. (1978) "What abortion counselors want from their clients." Social Problems 26: 112-121.

Kanter, R. M. (1977) Men and Women of the Corporation. New York: Basic Books.

Kleinman, S. (1984) Equals Before God: Seminarians as Humanistic Professionals. Chicago: Univ. of Chicago Press.

Klockars, C. B. (1985) The Idea of Police. Beverly Hills, CA: Sage.

Manning, P. K. (1967) "Problems in interpreting interview data." Sociology and Social Research 51: 302-316.

Manning, P. K. (1969) "Organization and environment: influences on police work," pp. 98-123 in R.V.G. Clark and J. M. Hough (eds.) The Effectiveness of Policing. Westmead, England: Gower.

Mennerick, L. A. (1974) "Client typologies: a method of coping with conflict in the service worker-client relationship." Soc. of Work and Occupations 1: 396-418.

Parsons, T. (1951) The Social System. Glencoe, IL: Free Press.

Reiss, A. J., Jr., and D. J. Bordua (1967) "Environment and organization: a perspective on the police," pp. 25-55 in D. J. Bordua (ed.) The Police: Six Sociological Essays. New York: John Wiley.

Sanders, W. B. (1977) Detective Work: A Study of Criminal Investigation. New York: Free Press.

Skolnick, J. H. (1966) Justice Without Trial. New York: John Wiley.

Smith, A. C. and S. Kleinman (1988) "Managing emotions in medical school: students' contacts with the living and the dead." Presented at the annual meeting of the American Sociological Association, Atlanta, Georgia.

Sudnow, D. (1965) "Normal crimes: sociological features of the penal code." Social Problems 12: 255-270.

Van Maanen, J. (1974) "Working the street: a developmental view of police behavior," pp. 83-130 in H. Jacob (ed.) The Potential for Reform of Criminal Justice. Beverly Hills, CA: Sage.

Waegel, W. B. (1981) "Case routinization in investigative police work." Social Problems 28: 263-275.

Wilson, J. Q. (1968) Varieties of Police Work. New York: Atheneum.

Criminal activities, including the use of narcotics, prostitution, and gambling, have few, if any, complaining witnesses and victims that will aid the police in their investigations of these types of crimes, forcing the police to become more proactive. Often they use undercover operations and confidential informants. Pogrebin and Poole researched the occupational and social consequences of working undercover. They found that undercover police needed to maintain two separate identities—one in which they must act as if they are part of the criminal lifestyle, and the other in which the undercover operant is part of the law enforcement world. Attempting to separate these two identities is often very difficult to do, especially for those who work deep undercover for very long periods of time. The longer they are separated from family, co-workers in the department, friends, and others who have a conventional lifestyle, the more these two roles become strained. Police supervisors and administrators need to carefully monitor those working in undercover operations, and the police working in this type of enforcement need to be cognizant of changes over time in their own behavior and outlook outside the world of undercover work.

VICE ISN'T NICE

A Look at the Effects of Working Undercover

MARK R. POGREBIN

ERIC D. POOLE

Undercover police operations have increased greatly since the 1970s (Marx, 1988). An extensive body of work has addressed a variety of issues involving covert police activities, such as deceptive tactics (Skolnick, 1982), criminal inducements and entrapment (Marx, 1988; Stitt and James, 1985), corruption (Pogrebin and Atkins, 1979), and moral dilemmas and ethical decisionmaking (Schoeman, 1986). These studies generally have dealt with criminal justice policy implications of undercover operations; little attention has

Reprinted from the *Journal of Criminal Justice*, Vol. 21, pp. 383–394, © 1993. Reprinted by permission of Elsevier Science, Ltd.

focused on the effects of undercover work on the officers themselves (Girodo, 1984; 1985).

In this study undercover work was defined as assignments of police officers to investigative roles in which they adopt fictitious civilian identities for a sustained period of time in order to discover criminal activities that are not usually reported to police or to infiltrate criminal groups that are normally difficult to access (see Miller, 1992). This study examined the consequences of working undercover for police officers. Focusing on role dynamics and situated identity in undercover assignments, it explored the impact of work experiences on officers with respect to their interaction with informants and suspects, interpersonal relations with family and friends, and readjustment to routine police activities.

THE NATURE OF UNDERCOVER WORK

Assignments to undercover units are avidly sought and highly valued. The selection process typically is intense and very competitive. Most undercover police units require interested officers to make application in the form of a request to transfer, which is followed by a series of rigorous interviews and assessments to screen out all but the best qualified for the specialized unit. Since an elite few are actually selected for undercover assignments, these officers enjoy a professional mystique associated with the unique nature of their work.

Undercover assignments allow officers wide discretionary and procedural latitude in their covert roles. This latitude, coupled with minimal departmental supervision, allows the undercover agent to operate with fewer constraints, exercise more personal initiative, and enjoy greater professional autonomy than regular patrol officers. Manning (1980) cautioned that such conditions may lessen officer accountability, lower adherence to procedural due process, and undermine normative subscription to the rule of law.

Marx (1988) further argued that police subcultural norms of suspicion and solidarity may take a conspiratorial turn as undercover agents adopt a protective code of silence not unlike that characteristic of organized crime. Covert intelligence gathering procedures and processes become highly insular, almost peripheral to routine police operations. There develops a need-to-know doctrine in which information is strictly guarded and selectively shared. The secrecy required for clandestine police work offers rich opportunities for self-aggrandizement, with many agents developing an exaggerated sense of power. As Marx (1988:161) concluded, "the work has an addictive quality as [officers] come to enjoy the power, intrigue, excitement and their protected contact with illegality."

The undercover agent typically must operate alone; moreover, the deeper the level of cover required in the investigation, the more isolated the officer becomes (Williams and Guess, 1981). Direct and sustained management of covert activities is practically impossible because of the solitary nature of the work. When supervision is lax or nonexistent, undercover officers are prone to cut corners, which may lead to an end-justifies-the-means type of attitude (Manning, 1980). In addition to the inadequate supervision, often there are no written departmental policy guidelines covering undercover operations for officers to rely on in lieu of direct supervisory control. Even when policies are explicated in departmental operations manuals, typically they are neither known nor followed by officers (Farkas, 1986).

Lack of supervision and effective policy guidelines diminish operational accountability and responsibility at the department level, leaving officers in the field to fend for themselves. Consequently, undercover agents often devise their own operational procedures in order to accomplish unit objectives. These officers develop individualized styles of working, relying on personal expertise and judgment (Marx, 1985; 1988).

METHODS

Three federal law enforcement agencies and eight municipal police departments located in the greater Denver metropolitan area participated in the present study. The researchers approached each agency with a request to obtain the names of officers who were presently or formerly assigned to undercover operations and who would be available for personal interviews with the researchers. Utilizing the lists of study volunteers provided by the respective agencies, the researchers contacted each officer initially to determine his or her length of undercover experience and present assignment. The officers were then stratified according to these two variables so that a wide range of work experiences, from entry to termination of undercover work, would be tapped. Next, 20 officers who currently were working undercover were selected—ten having less than three years and ten having three or more years of undercover experience, and 20 officers who were not presently assigned to undercover operations also were selected—ten having less than three years and ten having three or more years of prior undercover experience. The sample of 40 officers was comprised of 35 men and 5 women. Their ages ranged from 28 to 45 (mean = 37), and their undercover experience ranged from one to seven years (mean = 4).

All interviews were conducted at the respective agencies in either subject offices, private conference rooms, or interrogation rooms. Each interview lasted approximately two hours and was tape-recorded with the subject's consent. An unstructured in-depth interview format was used, which relied on sequential probes to pursue leads provided by subjects. This allowed the subjects to identify and elaborate on important domains they perceived to characterize their experiences in undercover work, rather than the researchers eliciting responses to structured questions. The interview tapes were subsequently transcribed for qualitative data analysis.

Qualitative data analysis involved a search for general statements about relationships among categories of observations. As Schatzman and Strauss (1973:110) noted, "the most fundamental operation in the analysis of qualitative data is that of discovering significant classes of things, persons or events and the properties that characterize them." Employing grounded theory techniques similar to those suggested by Glaser and Strauss (1967), the researchers categorized the data into primary conceptual themes to reflect the experiential domains of undercover work identified by the officers.

THE IMPACT OF UNDERCOVER WORK

Informant Relations

Since officers must learn to operate on their own much of the time and since undercover work is proactive, one of the most critical requirements is the ability to cultivate informants for information on illegal activities and for contacts with active criminals. The relationship between an officer and an informant is to a great extent symbiotic, for they come to rely upon one another for services they can obtain only from each other. The cooperation of informants in supplying information is fundamental in most police intelligence-gathering operations. Deals and bargains must be struck and honored for cases to be made. Informant relations are really exchange relations. For example, Skolnick (1975) noted that at each link in the chain of a narcotics investigation officers must make arrangements with suspects in order to move to the next higher level in the criminal organization responsible for the purchase, manufacture, and distribution of the narcotics. According to one federal agent,

> An informant is the easiest, quickest way to do police work.... [He] can walk you in the front door and take you directly to the crook and introduce you face-to-face.

Officers must develop and maintain stable relations with informants who can provide reliable information over time. The incentives that officers can offer informants to secure their cooperation or compliance often involve a carrot-and-stick approach. One officer provided several examples of the tactics he has used with his informants:

> Getting cases dropped . . . or dealing with probation officers for not going hard on them. Lobbying district attorneys or city attorneys about the cases or getting bonds reduced so that they can bond out of jail. . . . Getting their cars released from the pound so they can get their wheels back. I have even loaned them money out of my own pocket.

The handling of informants may be highly individualized. Since interpersonal styles vary, relations with informants may be idiosyncratic and thus not transferable across officers.

> I developed my own informants who got to trust me and take me at my word. My word was gospel to them. . . . They literally wouldn't talk to anybody else. When they got into trouble, they called me. And they would do anything for me.

Left to their own personal devices in working with informants, however, some officers may resort to questionable practices:

> We would have the person arrested by other officers, not knowing why they were involved. They usually were arrested for misdemeanor warrants. We would then get them out of jail in return for information. It would appear to the informant that we were doing him a favor.

A related problem involves officers' discretion to overlook illegal activities of informants in order to preserve access to information. This practice may cause agents to lose their sense of perspective regarding the relative importance of their operations in crime control; that is, these officers may come to believe that the types of crimes they are fighting pose a greater public safety concern than the offenses committed by their informants. The immediate justice meted out through arrests of informants for their crimes seems to be far outweighed by the long-term crime control benefits that may be realized only through the use of information these individuals provide. This utilitarian view may be advanced even by police administrators, who emphasize the larger public safety view of crime control; that is, these administrators convey the view that the activities of street criminals may be ignored for the purpose of getting at the "heavy hitters" who run criminal organizations. As one officer observed.

> You see captains and lieutenants using people and not putting them in jail for certain warrants so that they can get more information. . . . You see there is no problem doing it even though it was a violation of the operations manual. We feel if the captain can do it, and do it in front of us like that, then we can do it.

This reliance on active criminals for information about other active and ostensibly more serious criminals creates a variety of challenges to the integrity of police work. For example, informants are not bound by procedural due process constraints. Moreover, the tolerance of informant lawlessness by law enforcement officials in the interest of securing information may blur the line between legal and illegal police practices.

> [Informants] . . . are going to screw up, so you've got to cover their ass. I've had to do things on several occasions, like setting up some guy, just to clear an informant. . . . You just know that when they screw up . . . they're always able to turn around and offer something that makes up for that.

On the other hand, many officers are sensitive to the risks involved in depending on informants for information to do their jobs. Informant information may be faulty and, if acted upon, could jeopardize, compromise, or embarrass the officer. One federal agent illustrated the problem:

> The main basis for our intelligence and what we go by in initiating investigations usually is a confidential informant, who are criminals themselves, which makes their motives suspect. I have seen cases where we were sure as we could be about a suspect, and we have been wrong. Our information came from an informant who had been corroborated in the past and had been pretty trustworthy, and you still get burned.

The officer-informant relationship is driven by reciprocity but grounded in deceit. Both the agent and the informant must create illusions in the dual roles they play—both pretend to be people they are not. Credibility and reliability are tenuous commodities where misrepresentation of self is the key to continued relations.

Informants, as active participants in illicit enterprises, are part of the cover that affords police access to criminals (Manning, 1980); however, the illegal activities informants engage in while working for the police pose a problem of control. Police undercover operations must not disrupt routine criminal processes, which include illegal behavior by informants. Thus, it is not uncommon for informants to take advantage of their protected status by pursuing more criminal opportunities.

For police, it is imperative that informants' motivations for cooperation be judged and their roles in undercover operations be monitored. Assessing informant motivation and directing informant participation are critical in managing undercover operations. The observations of three officers typify this perspective:

> A guy that is motivated by money is pretty easy to control. The ones that are into revenge are also easy to control, because if they think they are getting back at someone, or as long as you keep them thinking that you are doing this to get back at so-and-so, they are okay. . . . The hard ones to control are the ones who are doing it because it's fun or a game to them. They think they are smarter than you. . . . You control snitches by strength of personality—letting them know your rules and . . . knowing their motivation.

> The trick is being able to place the proper weight on the informant's credibility. What is his motive? That's the rule in dealing with these people.

> You never take anything they [informants] do for granted. I put myself in their position and ask, "What's in it for me?" You then get a feeling for what they're doing and why. What you don't want is surprises.

As Levine (1990:45) noted, "Never trust a snitch' . . . is one of the most important proverbs in the unwritten bible of a narc." Many undercover officers have echoed this sentiment, often adding that informants do not deserve to be treated well. After all, informants typically commit a range of criminal acts, and they may be perceived as no different than the offenders who are being targeted. Two agents sized up their informants as follows:

> [Y]ou can't turn your back on them for a second or they will bite you. They lie to you all the time. They are untrustworthy. They have the morals of an alley cat.

> [I]nformants are some of the sorriest excuses for human beings imaginable—like sociopaths, no conscience. They're just looking out for themselves. . . . I have dealt with some real scum bags, and you can feel awfully dirty later on. . . .

Informants are generally considered a necessary evil. This view is typified in the observation that it often "takes a crook to catch a crook." The work ideology prevailing among undercover officers reflects a rather matter-of-fact dissonance reduction in managing relationships with informants, as the following two accounts illustrate:

> You'll always have informants in this kind of work. There's just no other way . . . to do the job. . . . [T]hat old saying, "You can't live with 'em, you can't live without 'em"—I think it applies to informants as well.

> We're not dealing with saints here. We see it all . . . , so you get used to just about anything after awhile. . . . [Y]ou can't let it get to you, because if you do, then you have a big problem. . . . What's important is control—you have to be able to control your informant. You must be a good manipulator.

From such sentiments arise purely utilitarian justifications for the manipulation of informants and their treatment as disposable byproducts of undercover operations. For example, several officers noted that it would be counterproductive to become too concerned about the personal well-being of an informant simply because informants are expendable; that is, once a police operation concludes, an informant may be cut off from the department or, in some cases, arrested and prosecuted. For many veteran officers, informants become almost invisible, blending into the background of the criminal environment. There is no affect associated with their dealings with informants; personal relations are feigned for instrumental purposes. One officer summed up this approach:

> Informants can appear to be our friends and we can appear to be theirs; however, they are a necessary tool of our trade and must be treated that way. . . .

In contrast, some officers experience genuine feelings of concern for informants as individuals. They point out that they frequently must establish and nurture relationships with key informants over extended periods of time. Such relations inevitably lead to a mutual exchange of personal information. It is not surprising that these relationships may foster conflicting emotions among officers:

I have sympathy for some of my informants. . . . You spend a great deal of time working with them and listening to their problems. Basically, you are their keeper while they are working for you. You start to feel responsible for what they do. You wonder why their life is such a mess. I try to keep that separate, but you really can't. . . .

While relations with informants pose significant problems for officers, close association with targeted criminals heightens the challenges of the undercover role considerably. As the next section shows, the stakes are higher and the costs of deception are greater.

Identification with Criminals

As noted previously in this article, undercover infiltration into criminal networks requires the use of techniques that include presenting a false identity in interaction with offenders in their environment. However, the agent is not feigning his or her entire presentation of self. Much of his or her genuine self is actually incorporated into the false identity created. After all, he or she is playing a role, and, like a method actor, the officer actually strives to identify personally with the part:

You have to learn to be an actor because you're pretending to be somebody you're not. . . . [Y]ou're pretending to be a crook, and the crook thinks you're a crook, so you must rely on personal experience.

The officer's job is actually made easier through incorporating much of himself or herself into the performance. As one undercover agent observed:

It's best to tell as few lies as possible. The fewer lies you tell, the easier the lies are to remember and keep straight. And your lies should be related to your personal life experiences. This makes recall easier. . . . You should not attempt to change your life history . . . because you are likely to confuse what you said to each crook.

Undercover officers who must sustain a deceptive front over extended periods of time face increased risk of stress-induced illness, physical harm, or corruption (Girodo, 1991;

Carter, 1990; Manning and Redlinger, 1991). For example, Girodo (1991) noted that the more undercover assignments undertaken, the more drug, alcohol, and disciplinary problems experienced by federal agents during their careers. In a report on drug trafficking and police corruption, the International Association of Chiefs of Police (1989:74-75) warned of the negative impact on officers working covert narcotics operations:

[O]fficers who do come into continuous contact with criminals while in an undercover capacity are more vulnerable to temptation. In most cases, long-term undercover assignments . . . are not worthwhile, considering the jeopardy to an officer's well being.

Most subjects in the present study readily identified a host of temptations endemic to undercover work. As one officer attested,

It's unlike anything else in law enforcement. There is a great deal of hours that are spent alone. There is a great deal of pressure. . . . There are a great many temptations out there involving money, narcotics, alcohol . . . [and] women.

In a Federal Bureau of Investigation study of its special agents who were involved in deep undercover operations, many operatives were found to experience profound changes in their value systems, often resulting in overidentification with criminals and a questioning of certain criminal statutes they were sworn to enforce (U.S. Department of Justice, Federal Bureau of Investigation, 1978). Two federal agents in the present study reported these types of problems in their long-term undercover assignments:

I identified very strongly with the bad guys. . . . Even though these people were breaking the law, they had some fairly good reasons for doing it. . . . I realized everything wasn't black and white. Everything became kind of gray. . . .

It didn't take me long to get into the way of thinking like the crooks I was running with. I started identifying with these people very quickly. . . . [P]art of it was identifying with them and part of it was trying to fit in with them.

The deep undercover operative who lives under false pretenses for months or years necessarily forms close relationships with those under investigation, as well as with their associates, friends, or families. There are subtle assimilation processes involved in undercover work since officers must adjust and adapt to an unfamiliar criminal subculture; consequently, officers may take on, in greater or lesser degree, the folkways, mores, and customs of that criminal subculture. For some, the net result is having their conventional outlook undermined and conventional bonds of social control weakened. Such processes free the officer to engage in nonconventional activities characteristic of the criminal primary group with which he or she affiliates, as illustrated in the following two reports:

> You get into a case where you are undercover for a very long period of time, where you are acting like a puke-ball for a year or more in order to make a huge case. I mean, you start hanging around these guys and start picking up their bad habits . . . , doing things that are not really related to the case and hanging out with people you shouldn't be with.

> I had an undercover apartment where I would stay a good amount of time. I soon met and started to run around with some groups. They were a segment of society that I didn't have a whole lot of experience with. All of a sudden they became the whole focus of my life. They were my social life. They were my work life. They were everything.

Undercover operatives come to share many experiences with those under investigation in order to be perceived as authentic. While this sharing heightens officer credibility, it also promotes bonding, which in turn fosters understanding of and sympathy for the targeted individuals.

> You are only human and you get to know and like a lot of people. When you're a year with these people, they become your friends. You share your problems with them . . . [and] they make sacrifices for you. . . .

Prolonged and intense interaction within a criminal network leads to emotional conflicts. Since deception requires a dual self-identity for the agent, there is constant tension between loyalty and betrayal in performing an undercover role and an uneasy moral ambiguity, as revealed in the following remarks of two narcotics officers:

> There are cases that you don't want to see come to an end because you don't want to arrest them. You like the people. You hate to see their lives ruined. You hate to think about what they are going to think about you. . . . You would like to just slide out of the picture and never be seen again.

> I can remember very distinctly going out and arresting these same people that had become my friends. I can't even talk about it now without getting emotional. They had trusted me. And all of a sudden I was the police and I'm testifying in court . . . against them. It took a long time to get over that.

The observations of the next two officers indicate that they felt morally tainted by the undercover experience.

> It is something that you have to live with that just doesn't go away. It nags and eats at you. You feel really bad about it—all the people that got caught up . . . [in the operation], and their lives were ruined and their kids' lives.

> Knowing what I know now, I don't think I could ever work narcotics again. . . . I know I've changed. Certainly more cynical about what we're doing. . . . And for what? To dirty ourselves like the crooks?

The work orientations and habits developed by undercover officers often have spillover effects on their interpersonal relations with family and friends. These problems are described in the next section.

Relations with Family and Friends

Undercover assignments may disrupt or interfere with an officer's family relationships and activities. As Marx (1988:166-67) observed, undercover work exerts pressure on interpersonal relations because of "the odd hours, days, weeks away from home, unpredictability of work schedules, concern over safety, late night temptations and partying that the role may bring, and personality and life style changes that the agent may undergo."

Some undercover officers have difficulty separating the traits and attributes associated with their deceptive criminal roles from their normal demeanor in conventional social roles. They experience role strain in shifting between the criminal identity at work and the conventional identity at home.

> Trying to be what the crooks were caused me some real problems with my wife right off the bat. We would go to a social gathering and I would end up off in some corner staring into the back yard and probably drinking too much, because I didn't like the pressure. People would come up and ask me what I did for a living and I had some cockamamie story I would give . . .; it was always some lie.

For some officers, adopting a deceptive criminal identity for an undercover assignment essentially precludes their assuming their conventional identity while off-duty. As a veteran agent observed,

> There are a lot of guys who I don't think have been able to put their undercover role aside when they go home. When they work undercover, they are always undercover.

One officer who apparently adopted this work strategy provided additional insight into the demands of the undercover role:

> For me, at least, working undercover is not something that can easily be turned on and off again at will. You get into character and start thinking and acting like the crooks you're hanging with. . . . You can't afford to be yourself because it's hard to keep who you are and your stories straight. . . . I think it's dangerous if you let yourself slip back and forth.

In Farkas's (1986) study of former and current undercover police officers in Honolulu, 41 percent reported adverse changes in interpersonal relations with family and friends, 37 percent experienced stress in associating with family and friends in public, and 33 percent expressed anxiety over not being able to discuss their assignments with family and friends. In the following observations, officers in the present study have provided first-hand accounts of the types of problems revealed in

the research by Farkas (1986). First, an officer described some of the disruptive effects of his work on family relationships:

> [A] lot of times I was involved in undercover operations where I would spend so much time away from home. . . . Then you go home grumpy. You don't feel like doing anything with the family. They want to go out for a burger. I just got through eating fifty burgers in the last two weeks. . . . The last thing I want to do is go out and get in the car. So, undercover work messes up your family life a lot.

Second, being in an active undercover role often can cause officers to worry about the safety of their families when they are with them in public; there is concern about the possibility of chance encounters with suspects or criminal associates who know the officers by undercover identities:

> [W]e may have gone to a shopping mall or somewhere with my family and see somebody who may be involved in a case or may know who you are, so you wouldn't want your family to be part of it. So, I found myself limiting my activities . . . to pretty much just staying at home with the family. Or when I did go out, not taking them with me. This isolation was definitely stressful for all of us.

Third, the need to maintain secrecy in covert operations restricts communication with family and friends, heightening feelings of uncertainty and danger associated with the work:

> I was totally isolated from my family and friends. I couldn't tell them where I was. . . . how [I was] doing or what [I was] working on. . . . [It] was extremely painful and upsetting [and frightening] to them. . . . My whole family really took a beating over that period of time.

Law enforcement organizations rarely prepare officers or their families for the kinds of interpersonal problems they are likely to face as a result of an undercover assignment. Two former narcotics officers in the present study lamented the negative effects in hindsight:

> I would give anything if prior to working undercover I would have known some of the pitfalls and

some of the pressures that were going to be put on my family situation.

Things got kind of crazy. . ., out of control, really. I lost perspective on a lot of things, including my wife and kids, and she ended up divorcing me. . . . I should have seen it coming, but I was so into my work that it didn't matter at the time. Nothing mattered at the time.

A common theme of undercover work that runs through the dramatic life-style changes revealed above is a "separation of self." Undercover work typically requires officers to adopt a criminal persona, distancing themselves from a conventional life style. This transformation involves isolation from police peers, family members, and friends, as well as from conventional places where activities with these individuals normally occur. These people and places provide the emotional, psychological, social, and moral bearings for conventional living. To a great extent, these bearings reflect and reinforce one's personality, a part of the self; thus, the separation of that part of the self is akin to a loss of identity. Officers working undercover are expected to seem to be people they are not through role-playing; however, their isolation in those roles actually may foster real changes in attitudes, values, beliefs, manner, habits, demeanor, character, and identity (Strauss, 1988). Operatives may begin to think and feel like the criminals they are impersonating. Who they are, or are becoming, may be confusing to family, friends, and colleagues. These individuals are perceived as different. The relational landscapes are altered, and the situations are disorienting.

Return to Routine Police Work

Ending an undercover assignment and returning to patrol duty can be awkward for many officers. These former operatives often experience difficulty in adjusting to the everyday routine of traditional police work. Farkas (1986) reported that former undercover agents frequently suffer from such emotional problems as anxiety, loneliness, and suspiciousness; moreover, they experience disruptions in marital relations. Similarly, Girodo (1984) noted that the return to regular police duties after a lengthy

assignment as an undercover operative is analogous to coming down from an emotional high. Officers in this situation often report feeling lethargic and depressed as well as experiencing self-estrangement in their new assignments. After six years in an undercover unit, this former narcotics agent described his adjustment problems:

I was well trained for something else. What am I doing here? At times it hits you hard. For three months on graves I didn't want to hear about vice and narcotics. I didn't want to see them, hear about them, or know anything about them. I just didn't want any contact because it was painful. . . . I don't blame anybody. I knew I was going to be rotated out. . ., but yet I feel cheated somehow.

Two former undercover officers commented on the psychological impact of being transferred back to patrol:

I was really pissed off. I had a short fuse and would go off for no reason at all. I guess I was even trying to provoke some sort of response. . . .

I was bored and restless and resented what I was doing. I just didn't feel good about myself and was mad at everybody. I didn't feel anybody understood what I was going through because they hadn't done the things I had.

Many of the problems associated with reassignment to patrol duties can be attributed to decreased autonomy and diminished personal initiative in job performance. For example, working a certain geographic area of the community, responding primarily to radio-dispatched calls for service, handling noncriminal cases, and being subject to closer supervisory monitoring of activities all make for less exciting work experiences than those enjoyed in undercover assignments (Marx, 1988). A veteran officer reflected upon what he missed the most following his transfer to patrol after five years in an undercover unit:

The excitement in undercover work is, to me, the ultimate. An officer is actually doing something and creating things that are happening. He comes back on the street and back to a daily routine. . . . I still miss the closeknit unit and having the kind of freedom and control we did.

Former undercover agents generally see themselves as having developed and honed special skills as a result of their undercover experiences; consequently, they feel that their talents and abilities are wasted in routine assignments. As the following comments show, officers view their return to patrol as the functional equivalent of a demotion:

> It's like stepping backwards. I mean, you have accomplished a lot of things . . . [in] seven years in undercover. You get better and better over time and suddenly you're sent back to where you were seven years ago—right back at the bottom.

> Narcotics is not a glamorous job. You got to be tough mentally. You get that only from experience. . . . Narcotics officers should be assigned on a permanent basis and not rotated out after a set number of years. . . . I'll never be able to adjust to patrol: my career is ruined.

For several former narcotics officers, the return to routine police duties was even more devastating; they expressed deeply held personal beliefs and commitment concerning the societal importance of their undercover work. As undercover narcotics agents, they saw themselves not just on the "front lines" fighting the war on drugs; they felt they had assumed even greater risks by going undercover "behind enemy lines" to infiltrate and destroy criminal networks. Their experiences were intense, inherently dangerous, and exciting. Some of these officers actually perceived themselves as engaged in a perverse form of trench warfare, as soldiers whose mission was to win the war on drugs one dealer at a time. The following comment is representative of this sentiment:

> Highly committed members of an elite narcotics unit want no part of ordinary police duties . . ., handling DUIs, domestics, and noise complaints. . . . Drugs are our number one problem, and I got tremendous satisfaction getting drug traffickers off the street. . . . There is a drug war going on out there, and it bothers me a lot I'm no longer . . . doing my part.

Finally, Girodo (1985) noted that some attributes thought to be beneficial in an undercover assignment (e.g., deceptive, manipulative, inclined toward risk taking) may have adverse consequences in routine police work. For example, ex-undercover officers tend to adopt a more proactive approach to policing, with an emphasis on the "strategic management" of suspects. As one former undercover investigator explained:

> I talk to arrestees differently. I am always looking for what information they can give me as opposed to throwing them in jail and forgetting about them like I did before I was in undercover. Now all I think about is, "Can I get something out of them?"

Undercover officers are likely to have developed a different working style and demeanor—often characterized by heightened suspicion, cynicism, and caution—that may escalate conflict in interaction with suspects or undermine citizen satisfaction and confidence in service calls. Such consequences have led several officers to stress the need for a decompression period; that is, former operatives need time off for gradual reentry into their new assignments:

> I think it's extremely dangerous to go back on the street in uniform and deal with citizen complaints just off a long undercover assignment. You're just not ready to handle those types of problems. . . . I mean, you're not comfortable or as confident as you should be. And I guess you try to make up for that with a lot of bravado. . . . You really need some time away to get things straight again.

For many officers, an understanding of the dramatic changes they have undergone as a result of their undercover experiences arises only in retrospect, after they have had time to appreciate the stark contrast between the demands of their former and present work assignments fully.

CONCLUSIONS

Unlike police officers with conventional assignments, undercover agents tend to operate primarily within criminal networks. The agent's ability to blend in—to resemble and be accepted by criminals—is critical for any undercover operation. Deception is continuous and must be adhered to consistently for the illusion to be maintained; that is, the officer's appearance and demeanor must seem natural and genuine.

An operative is required to adopt an alternate identity. The undercover officer must be a good improviser in order to perform convincingly in accordance with the role demands of a false identity. When a person's identity is changed, even for the temporary purpose of acting a part, the individual comes to view himself or herself differently; he or she is not the same person as before. This identity transformation helps the officer to fit in with those of the criminal world in which he or she now operates. It is not unexpected, then, that prolonged participation in a criminal subculture may create role conflicts for the officer.

In addition, the officer must manage a split between conventional and nonconventional identities. Typically, undercover work requires the officer to obtain new identification documents, to change appearance (e.g., clothes, hair style, beard, made-up, etc.), and to alter demeanor, speech, and life-style in order to fit in with suspects. Over an extended period of time, undercover pursuits tend to isolate the officer from contact with friends and relatives, thus limiting or precluding participation in conventional activities. The undercover officer is often far removed, both physically and emotionally, from support systems and institutional symbols that serve to define his or her conventional self. Without such relational ties to reinforce his or her normal identity, sustained interaction with law violators threatens to undermine the maintenance of a conventional self concept. The line separating the self concept associated with the role of an undercover cop and the self concept tied to the responses of deviant others who reinforce the role performances becomes increasingly blurred. The norms of police ethics may thus be turned upside down in undercover work.

Undercover operatives face both professional and personal risks in the deceptive roles they assume in their assignments. From an operational standpoint, police administrators must formulate and implement organizational guidelines and procedures to monitor the activities of undercover agents within the rules and regulations of the department and the laws governing the jurisdiction. First, these procedures will promote constitutional due process protections. Second, these procedures will govern the parameters of the investigation, the assessment of intelligence information, and the gathering of evidence, and thus they will minimize tactical and legal pitfalls that could threaten the success of the operation. Third, these procedures will gauge the impact of undercover work experiences on the operative.

The monitoring of an undercover officer throughout an assignment requires regular supervisory meetings with the agent to discuss problems or issues that arise. These concerns may involve the array of adverse consequences identified in the present study, which have been shown to pose various moral, ethical, legal, professional, and personal dilemmas related to the unique roles officers have assumed in particular undercover operations or to reentering traditional assignments. Moreover, debriefing sessions may be made mandatory following the termination of every undercover assignment or as part of a periodic rotation out of undercover assignments or part of a reorientation training in preparation for the transition from operative to traditional police officer. The emphasis shifts from managing undercover activities to monitoring the ability of operatives to function within the undercover role and to return as normal, functional members of the department and the community, that is, to ensure their capacity to resume their responsibilities as law enforcement officers, spouses, parents, friends, etc.— the whole complex of roles and identities that make them who they really are, not who they have pretended to be.

REFERENCES

Carter, D. L. (1990). An overview of drug-related misconduct of police officers: Drug abuse and narcotics corruption. In *Drugs, crime and the criminal justice system*, ed. R. Weisheit. Cincinnati, OH: Anderson Publishing Co.

Farkas, G. (1986). Stress in undercover policing. In *Psychological services for law enforcement*, ed. J. T. Reese and H. A. Goldstein. Washington, DC: U.S. Government Printing Office.

Girodo, M. (1984). Entry and re-entry strain in undercover agents. In *Role transitions: Explorations and explanations*, ed. V.L. Allen and E. van de Vliert. New York: Plenum Press.

____. (1985). Health and legal issues in narcotics investigations: Misrepresented evidence. *Behavioral Sciences & the Law* 3:299-308.

____. (1991). Drug corruption in undercover agents: Measuring the risk. *Behavioral Sciences & the Law* 9:361-70.

Glaser, B. G., and Strauss, A. L. (1967). *The discovery of grounded theory: Strategies for qualitative research*. Chicago: Aldine Publishing Co.

International Association of Chiefs of Police (1989). *Building integrity and reducing drug corruption in police departments*. Gaithersburg, MD: IACP.

Levine, M. (1990). *Deep cover*. New York: Delacorte Press.

Manning, P. K. (1980). *The narc's game: Organizational and informational limits on drug enforcement*. Cambridge, MA: MIT Press.

Manning, P. K., and Redlinger, L. J. (1991). Invitational edges. In *Thinking about police*, ed. C. B. Klockars and S. Mastrofski. New York: McGraw-Hill.

Marx, G. T. (1985). Who really gets stung? Some issues raised by the new police undercover work. In *Moral issues in police work*, ed. F.A. Elliston and M. Feldberg. Totowa, NJ: Rowman and Allanheld.

____. (1988). *Undercover: Police surveillance in America*. Berkeley: University of California Press.

Miller, G. I. (1987). Observations on police undercover work. *Criminology*, 25(1): 27-46.

Pogrebin, M. R., and Atkins, B. (1979). Some perspectives on police corruption. In *Legality, morality and ethnics in criminal justice*, ed. N.N. Kittrie and J. Susman. New York: Praeger Publishers.

Schatzman, L., and Strauss, A. L. (1973). *Field research: Strategies for a natural sociology*. Englewood Cliffs, NJ: Prentice-Hall.

Schoeman, F. (1986). Undercover operations: Some moral questions about S. 804. *Crim Just Ethics* 5:16-22.

Skolnick, J. H. (1975). *Justice without trial: Law enforcement in democratic society*, 2nd ed. New York: John Wiley and Sons.

____. (1982). Deception by police. *Crim Just Ethics* 1:40-54.

Stitt, B. G., and James, G. (1985). Entrapment: An ethical analysis. In *Moral issues in police work*, ed. F.A. Elliston and M. Feldberg. Totowa, NJ: Rowman and Allanheld.

Strauss, A. L. (1988). Turning points in identity. In *Social interaction*, ed. C. Clark and H. Robboy. New York: St. Martin's Press.

U.S. Department of Justice, Federal Bureau of Investigation (1978). *The special agent in undercover investigations*. Washington, DC: U.S. Department of Justice.

Williams, J., and Guess, L. (1981). The informant: A narcotics enforcement dilemma. *Journal of Psychoactive Research* 13:235-45.

In recent years, the concept of community policing has become a new method of law enforcement nationally, especially among urban police departments. The authors argue that small town and rural law enforcement agencies have a long history of a policing style that corresponds directly to the principles of community policing and have performed problem-solving activities that have frequently involved community members. The authors point out the irony of researchers historically looking at large city police departments for examples of community policing involvement, when they have rarely looked to small town and rural police for ways to make police more effective and responsive using the community policing model.

COMMUNITY POLICING IN SMALL TOWN AND RURAL AMERICA

RALPH A. WEISHEIT

L. EDWARD WELLS

DAVID N. FALCONE

In recent years, American policing has seen the emergence of a new vocabulary and, some would argue, a new philosophy of policing. The *idea* of community policing has swept the country, although in practice the term has been defined in many ways, some of them seemingly contradictory. At the heart of community policing is the idea that police departments must be more responsive and connected to the communities they serve, that policing is properly a broad problem-solving enterprise that includes much more than reactive law enforcement, and that individual line officers on the street and in the community should have a major role in this process.

Reprinted from *Crime & Delinquency*, Vol. 40, No. 4, October 1994, 549–567. Copyright © 1994 Sage Publications, Inc.

This manuscript was prepared with the support of the National Institute of Justice (Grant No. 92-IJ-CX-K012). The views presented here are those of the authors and do not necessarily reflect those of NIJ. An earlier version of this article was presented to the Academy of Criminal Justice Sciences' Annual Meeting in Chicago on March 10, 1994.

Community policing by no means represents an isolated development. Rather, it seems to have emerged as a correlate of various social trends and movements, particularly the victim's rights and civil rights movements, each of which has organized citizens to demand that police be more accountable to the public (Karmen 1990). Similarly, such grassroots organizations as Mothers Against Drunk Driving (MADD) have focused on monitoring criminal justice agencies and have demanded that they be more accountable to the public for their decisions. The interest in community policing among police administrators also parallels general management trends that have emerged in the business world. Total quality management (TQM), for example, concerns itself with reducing layers of bureaucracy, empowering line employees, and increasing responsiveness to customers (e.g., Walton 1986)—ideas that have figured prominently in discussions of community policing. Health care and medicine have shown parallel developments, particularly in the growing trend toward medicine as proactive wellness production, rather than simply reactive disease treatment. The result is an emphasis on holistic, coproductive, general practitioner, and family practice medicine, as contrasted with segmented, specialty-oriented medicine. Given the developments in policing's recent past, the greater organization of citizens, and management trends more generally, it would have been surprising if some form of community policing had *not* become a dominant philosophy among police administrators.

Although community policing clearly has roots in earlier police strategies, as an organizational philosophy, its boundaries, implications for specific programs, and the circumstances under which it might be effective are still being explored. This article examines the idea of community policing by considering the fit between police practices in rural areas and the philosophy of community policing as an urban phenomenon. We suggest that experiences in rural areas provide examples of successful community policing, but the comparison also raises questions about the simple applicability of these ideas to urban settings.

WHAT IS COMMUNITY POLICING?

Although a relatively new idea, the concept of community policing has already generated a sizable and rapidly growing body of literature (e.g., Brown 1989; Goldstein 1987; Greene and Mastrofski 1988; Moore 1992; Trojanowicz and Bucqueroux 1990; Wilson and Kelling 1989). Although there is agreement on some broad dimensions of the concept, there is substantial variability in the types of program activities included under this conceptual umbrella and in the presumed central focus of the approach. Some discussions depict community policing as primarily a matter of reorganizing the nature of *police work*, from reactive law enforcement to proactive policing (in the classical sense of that term), order maintenance, and problem solving. At other times, the emphasis is on the implications of community policing for the *organizational structure* of police agencies as formal organizations. These discussions suggest that community policing is primarily a move from segmented, hierarchical, paramilitary bureaucracies that flatter, to more participatory and flexible organizations. Still other discussions of community policing stress the *community* half of the term and center on the idea that social order is most effectively a coproduction by police and the community, where police-citizen connections and cooperation are essential to doing the job effectively and properly.

The focus here is not on the organizational structure of police departments, although the rural setting does provide opportunities to study the issue of formal organization variability. Most rural municipal police departments are small and have simple organizational structures; however, it is possible for sheriff's departments to be rather large and organizationally complex while still serving a predominantly rural area. Rather than organizational structures, this study focuses on the relationship between the community and the police in rural areas and how this relationship affects police practices.

It is possible to extract three broad themes from the literature on community policing that are relevant to the relationship. The first has to do with the police being *accountable* to the community as well as to the formal police hierarchy. The second is that police will become more *connected* with and integrated into their communities, which means that police will interact with citizens on a personal level, will be familiar with community sentiments and concerns, and will work *with* the community to address those concerns. A third and final theme requires that police will be oriented to *solving general problems*, rather than only responding to specific crime incidents. The discussion that follows reflects each of these broad themes and how it plays out in rural areas. First, however, we will describe the existing literature that can also be used to build our arguments.

Existing Evidence

We begin with the simple observation that community policing looks and sounds a great deal like rural and small town policing, as it has been practiced for a long time. Although there have been no studies that directly examine the extent to which rural policing reflects many key elements of community policing, there are many scattered pieces of evidence with which one can make this case.

In his study of tasks regularly performed by police in 249 municipal agencies of differing sizes, Meagher (1985) found that small agencies were more concerned with crime prevention, medium-sized agencies showed the greatest concern for providing noncrime services, and large agencies focused on enforcing criminal laws and controlling crime through arrests. Similarly, Flanagan (1985) examined public opinion data about the police role. He found that the larger and more urban the community, the more citizens were likely to believe that police should limit their role to enforcing criminal laws. Conversely, people from smaller communities were more likely to want police to perform a wide variety of problem-solving and order-maintenance functions. Gibbons (1972) also saw evidence of this emphasis on order maintenance in his study of "crime in the hinterland." In the sheriff's department in rural Pine County (a pseudonym), Decker (1979) observed that

the police were called upon and *expected* to render services for a wide variety of irregular occurrences, only a few of which were statutorily defined as law enforcement responsibilities. For example, the deputies complied with a request to inspect a boundary line between two farmers' property that was only accessible by tractor. In a related incident, the same mode of transportation was used to check on a foundered cow. Many instances required the symbolic presence of a sheriff's deputy to legitimate its occurrence in the citizen's eyes. (p. 104)

In many rural areas, police *must* provide a wide range of services because other social services are either nonexistent or are more remote than the police. Marenin and Copus (1991) observed that in rural Alaska, where all types of social services are scarce, traditional law enforcement is a relatively small part of the service police are expected to perform: "Village policing is not normal policing, in the sense of law enforcement or crime control, but is much more of a social work kind of job" (p. 16), which includes fire fighting, emergency medical services, and rescue operations.

A number of researchers have observed that styles of policing are partly a reflection of the relationship between police and the community. Although police in many urban areas may be viewed as outsiders, in rural areas they are viewed as an integral part of the community (Decker 1979). In interviews with officers from one rural department and several urban departments, Kowalewski, Hall, Dolan, and Anderson (1984) found that whereas officers in rural and urban departments had many similar concerns, they differed in several interesting respects. Urban officers thought they were less respected and less supported by citizens, whereas police in rural communities felt more public support for being tough, particularly with juveniles. Dealing with juveniles is an important function for rural police because this is often a major concern for rural community members (Decker 1979).

Consistent with the greater informality of social interaction processes in rural areas, rural and urban officers believed they were given public respect for different reasons (Decker 1979). In urban areas, respect went to the *position*, the role, or the badge, and it was believed that a good way to improve public respect was through professionalizing the department. In contrast, respect was thought to be given to rural officers as *individuals*, who had to prove that respect was *personally* deserved. This was often done by establishing a reputation for toughness and fairness early in their career.

Given the nature of rural culture and of social interactions in rural areas, police-community relations probably will be very different in rural and urban departments. In rural areas, officers are likely to know the offenders, the victims, and their families, just as the officer and his family will be known by the community. Rural officers are also more likely to know and appreciate the history and culture of an area and to use that information in their work, something observed by Weisheit (1993) in his study of rural marijuana growers. Given the close social ties between police and the community, it should be expected that rural officers will use policing styles that are responsive to citizens in their area and that, in turn, local residents should be supportive of the police. In fact, a 1991 Gallup survey found measurable rural-urban differences in the support that citizens show for the local police. In urban areas, 54% of the citizens reported having a great deal of respect for the local police, contrasted to 61% of rural citizens. The differences were even more pronounced when asked about police brutality and the discretionary use of force by police. In the survey, 59% of urban residents thought that there was police brutality in their area, but only 20% of rural residents believed this to be the case ("Americans Say Police Brutality Frequent" 1991).

The same features of rural policing that compel officers to be more responsive to the public also mean that rural police may have relatively less discretion because their work is more visible to the public:

> A major explanation for the high degree of police discretion found in urban areas is the *low visibility* of police actions. In smaller communities the actions of police officers are known to most of the population thanks to the effectiveness and extensiveness of informal communication networks; there they are more highly visible. As a result, small town police enjoy less latitude in deviating from dominant community values. (Eisenstein 1982, p. 117)

Consistent with this idea, Crank (1990) found that organizational and community factors had a different impact on the adoption of a legalistic police style in rural and urban areas. In urban areas, characteristics of the police organization, such as the number of ranks or the ratio of administrators to sworn officers, were better predictors of police style than were characteristics of the community, such as percentage Black or level of economic distress. In rural areas, these relationships were reversed, with community factors being more important than organizational ones. As might be expected, Crank's data suggested that rural departments are more responsive to the local community, whereas urban departments may be more sensitive to the dynamics of the police organization. Or, as a publication of the International Association of Chiefs of Police (IACP) put it, "The urban officer answers to the police department. The rural or small town officer is held accountable for his actions by the community" (IACP 1990, p. 9).

In many ways, rural departments are positioned to be the very embodiment of community policing. According to the IACP document,

> Rural and small town police are closer to their community than are urban police. Rural and small town police are a part of the local culture and community, whereas urban police tend to form a subculture and move apart from the community. . . . Urban police tend to be efficient; rural police tend to be effective. (IACP, 1990, p. 8)

These scattered pieces of evidence suggest it would be fruitful to more fully examine the link between rural policing and community policing. They also suggest that rather than modifying rural departments to fit an urban definition of good policing, or of community policing, urban departments might well look to rural areas for insights into policing in general and community policing in particular.

THE STUDY

The information presented here is drawn from a larger study of rural crime and rural policing funded by the National Institute of Justice. The larger study involves collecting and reviewing relevant literature, conducting a focus group with rural sheriffs, locating and cataloging data sets relevant to rural crime, and, finally, interviewing officials familiar with rural crime and rural policing. This article is based on information from interviews conducted to date. The larger study was not specifically designed to study community policing but to consider rural crime and rural policing issues more generally. In the course of reviewing the literature and in interviews with rural police, we were continuously presented with ideas that paralleled those raised in discussions of community policing in urban areas. Thus what follows explores one dimension of a larger study which is itself exploratory. The purpose is not to reach definite conclusions but to stimulate thinking and suggest patterns that merit further study.

Although over 100 people from a variety of perspectives have been interviewed thus far, this discussion is based on interviews with 46 rural sheriffs and with 28 police chiefs in small towns. Of these 74 interviews, 13 (18%) were face-to-face, and the remainder were by telephone. Although we wanted to include jurisdictions of varying sizes, the focus was on the most rural jurisdictions. Among interviewed municipal chiefs, their community ranged in size from 900 to 50,000 people, with an average of 7,500 persons. Departments ranged in size from 1 to 66 uniformed officers, with an average of 17 officers. The departments of the interviewed county sheriffs ranged in size from 1 to 182 uniformed officers, with an average of 23 officers. This figure is a very rough approximation because sheriff department size is difficult to compute due to sometimes high numbers of part-time employees, jail staff who are sometimes also sworn officers, and some counties having a large number of reserves. The county populations served by these sheriffs ranged from 2,100 to 712,000 people, with only 8 of the 46 sheriffs working in a county of more than 50,000.

As an exploratory study, locating subjects for interviews focused on identifying individuals from the widest possible range of social and physical environments, rather than on studying "average" rural settings. Indeed, the differences across rural areas are so substantial that speaking of averages is probably misleading and is certainly of limited use for policy. Rural

Montana and rural Delaware, for example, probably are as dissimilar as they are similar. To capture as much of this range as possible, we selected police officers from across the country, attempting to include every state, while giving particular attention to the 18 states identified as predominantly rural by the federal General Accounting Office (1990).

Because we are engaged in an exploratory study, we felt it important to use largely unstructured interviews. Appreciating rural variation, and always keeping it in mind, we were still interested in identifying common themes. Thus we used the available literature and information gathered from a series of preliminary interviews to develop a list of question areas to be covered in the course of the interviews, but we also encouraged subjects to explore other areas they thought were important. Question areas included crime concerns, police-citizen interactions, police practices, and the working relationship between police and other criminal justice agencies. The length of interview ranged from 20 minutes to 2 hours but was typically about 40 minutes long.

OBSERVATIONS

There was general agreement among the interviewed rural police that their long-standing police practices fit well into what has been termed community policing. However, the concept of community policing is a broad one, encompassing a variety of ideas. Consequently, we focus here on more specific ways in which rural police practices seem to mirror the principles of community policing.

Community Connections

A key element of community policing is police-citizen familiarity and interaction. For example, having officers walk through neighborhoods and talk with people means that more citizens will know officers personally, and, at the same time, officers will come to know many individuals in a neighborhood. The bonds between rural police and the community are also strengthened by the practice of hiring local citizens in police agencies. Thus the officers not only know the community and share many of the values of its members, they are also members of that community and are often involved in community activities. As Decker (1979) noted:

All members of the sheriff's department had biographies not uncommon to those of the community. The sheriff and his three deputies were all born and educated in the county. Prior to joining the force, every member was involved in an agricultural form of employment, the dominant form of employment for the county. There is evidence of integration into the community in other ways. Each member participates in an important community function; i.e., the softball team, Jaycees, Rotary, Elk's Club, etc. (p. 105)

Many urban departments have recently tried, with varying degrees of success, to induce individual officers to live in their work area, sometimes even providing financial incentives for them to do so. Living in the areas they patrol, however, has been a long-standing practice in rural and small town agencies that has occurred naturally and without special effort. Through increased citizen-police interactions, it is believed that citizens will be more likely to cooperate with the police, and police, in turn, will be more sensitive to the community.

Sheriffs and chiefs with whom we spoke frequently saw what they had been doing in rural areas as community policing and believed they were well ahead of urban areas in this regard. One sheriff's comments are typical:

Yes, there's far more community policing taking place in rural agencies than urban. We have been doing community policing since time began, I believe. We have always stopped and talked with the ranchers, the businessmen. We have walked the streets, rattled doors, and checked on sick folks. We know the various workers in the community and what they do. We see the kid delivering papers at 6:00 a.m. and talk with him. We have always done that. We are much closer to the people. Consequently, your whole mode of operation changes. Our method of gathering information derives from our personal contact on a day-to-day or minute-to-minute basis. In an urban setting, you're out "developing informants." We do that too, but the vast majority of our information comes from regular folks on a regular basis.

I'm a believer in scanners. That would cause cardiac arrest in a lot of agencies. We have gotten more help from folks that have heard us out on a chase and we have lost the guy. They call up and say, "He's two blocks away going down this street." Plus, it tells them we are on the job, what we're doing.

This illustration shows how a strong bond between police and the community in rural settings is helpful in enforcing the law. It is also true, however, that rural police themselves act differently when such a bond exists:

You cannot call somebody an SOB on the street here because the next day you could be buying tires from him or going in to eat in his restaurant. You've got to know these people because you deal with them day after day. I worked in Fort Worth, Texas. You get into a row with some guy down there—he's smart mouthing you, bad mouthing you. You can give it right back because you're not going to see that man again, except in court. After court, you'll never lay eyes on him again. Here, he's the cousin of the deputy who works the night shift.

Knowing their citizens well also allows rural officers greater latitude in disposing of cases informally:

The street officer sees ol' Joe on the street and waves to him. When Joe gets drunk and gets into a row, he can just grab him and stuff him into the car. If he doesn't need to go to jail, he can just take him home and turn him over to Martha. She's going to straighten him out.

In smaller communities, particularly with juveniles, which is most of the crime problem in small communities, in my experience, the parents were not some faceless, mythical creatures from the middle of nowhere. I could grab up little Johnny by the scruff of his neck or whatever and we would go talk to Mommy and Daddy, who also knew me. We could work things out a lot easier, without having to get involved in the formal justice system. . . . The small communities, at least where I worked, generally if we had to make an arrest, it was the exception rather than the norm. We almost looked at arrests as a last resort. Everything else either has not worked or will not work. If I had to make an arrest, it was almost as if I'd done something wrong further back down the line.

These close personal interactions also mean that citizens expect more of their police, both in the range of services offered and in the personal attention that will be paid to individual cases:

> The city residents expect the man in blue to come by and be very perfunctory, a Joe Friday. We're expected to do the follow-up and a lot more caring. People expect caring from rural law enforcement. We're not there to just take the reports of crimes; we also scoot the kiddies across crosswalks. It's an obligation. We have to wave at everybody we pass by. We have to be more caring.
>
> We've had a lot of examples. An officer might go to a domestic one night and he'll stop by the next night and see how things are going. It's not uncommon for an officer, where a couple of juveniles have gotten into trouble, the next day he's got off to go get 'em and take them fishing. They try and get involved personally and make a difference.

In rural areas, police are highly visible members of the community, and it is not unusual for citizens to know individual officers by name. It also appears rather common for a citizen to consider a particular police officer *his* or *her* officer and to request him or her by name when problems arise. Although this also happens to some extent in urban areas, it appears to be far more common in rural communities.

These examples illustrate how close police-citizen interactions in rural areas shape the nature of police work in those areas. For the most part, the features of rural policing described above arise quite naturally and spontaneously and are not the result of formal policies or of specific community policing *programs*.

General Problem Solving

Another central characteristic of community policing is the focus on general problem solving, rather than more narrowly on reactive law enforcement. That is, officers not only respond to specific criminal incidents, but, more importantly, they recognize and respond to more general problems that set the stage for specific criminal acts. These problems are not be limited to "crimes" and the solutions need not involve arrests.

This lady just recently passed away. We've changed light bulbs for people. She called up, she's old, she's not very mobile, she's scared. The power went off, and now she's hearing things. Tell us the name, we know we're going to change a light bulb, talk to her for five or ten minutes and everything's fine. That is a service that fortunately we can still do—spend the time, especially on some of the older residents. Everything is OK, we're here. You call, we're going to be there.

When asked about the kinds of problems to which his department was expected to respond, one small-town chief responded:

> Everything, including the kitchen sink. I've had people in here to counsel families on their sex life because they think I'm the Almighty and can do that. I've had people come in who are having problems making ends meet, and we intercede for them in getting assistance, helping them file for welfare. We do a lot of service-oriented work. I consider it non law enforcement. Somebody needs a ride, like an elderly lady needs a ride to the doctor. We'll take her to the doctor or go get her groceries for her.

Because they are closer to the public they serve, and because they are often the only 24-hour service providers in rural areas, rural police receive calls for a wide range of services. If they respond to a wider variety of non-police problems than do urban police, it is not because they are required to do so by statute or because written departmental policies demand it. Rather, it is because they define police work differently, perhaps because the people they serve are neighbors and fellow community members, rather than nameless, faceless citizens. As such, it is not a conscious formal decision but a necessity arising from the social context.

Rural Versus Urban Policing

We found some of the most telling evidence that rural and urban policing styles are very different in the experiences of rural sheriffs and chiefs who had previously worked outside of rural areas or who hired officers with such experiences:

> Their [police and citizens'] kids go to the same school. You see them on the street. You see

them in the grocery store. It isn't like a city. In fact, I've worked with several cities and their officers are cold. They treat the good people the same way they treat the bad people. They are callous.

If you hire somebody from a larger agency who has been in a situation where they specialized, they tend to look at a "hay seed" operation and say things need to be done in a different way ... We've had some real problems with them having personality conflicts with the public in general because they are used to dealing with people as faces and not as neighbors or friends or relatives.

I'm willing to be shown that I'm wrong, but it's a lot harder being a sheriff of a small rural county than it is to be the sheriff of [a city] with a population of 250,000 because everybody in that [rural] county—they want to be able to pick up that phone, whether it be Saturday night at 2:00 in the morning and they have a problem. They want to be able to pick up that phone and call that sheriff. They don't want to talk to a deputy, or the dispatcher. They want the sheriff, "I have a problem." It may be dogs barking.

One officer who had worked in an urban department and then moved to a rural part of Alaska declared:

If there's a bar fight and I get involved, and somebody comes toward me with the intent of attacking me, I've had several bar patrons jump on them and take them down and even put their hands behind their back so I can handcuff them. It's not like a bar in the lower 48. You still have to watch your back, but we're a part of the community here more than you are there. In an urban area, the police officer is not part of the community. Here, a police officer is a part of the community. We live here, we work here, our kids run around with their kids, date their kids, and go to basketball games. I encourage my officers, and I do it by example, to participate as much as possible in all community functions. ... But we just don't have problems that we can't take the time to sit down and talk it over with them. In the lower 48, I never had time. At the end of my shift, I was handing call cards out for burglaries in progress and rapes to the following shift. I had already worked 2 hours overtime and I couldn't get to all of them. But here, we have time to take care of the problems. I don't know if they would even use it [the time] if they had it in the lower 48.

Another chief who was asked if he thought rural police had to be more sensitive to the public than urban police responded:

Absolutely, I come from a bigger agency. In the bigger agencies, you lose that personal day-to-day touch with the actual citizenry, unless you're there for a specific reason. Here, we're very close to these people. There's not too many of us, so they all get to know you. They come in all the time with their problems, and not just law enforcement-related problems. Yes, we're extremely sensitive. It's a very close-knit operation.

These comments repeat many of the contrasts between rural and urban policing noted in earlier sections. Routine personal contact between the police and the policed changes the relationship between the two. And the fact that many rural officers live in the communities they police seems to further strengthen the ties between the two groups.

Effectiveness

Aside from being good public relations, it has also been argued that community policing is more effective. The idea that rural departments may be more effective is not consistent with stereotypes of rural police, and there may be some disagreement about what constitutes effective. One bit of evidence about the relative effectiveness of rural police comes from the *Uniform Crime Reports*, which report the percentage of crimes cleared by arrest by size of the community served. As Table 1 shows, agencies in rural counties have consistently higher clearance rates than departments in cities of 250,000 or more. This pattern holds for every index crime except rape, for which the clearance rates are essentially the same.

The gap in clearance rates between rural and urban areas shown in Table 1 is particularly marked for violent crimes. Some of the rural-urban differences might be attributable to differences in reporting and recording practices. Rural police might, for example, be less likely to write up a report on a larceny if there are no suspects. However, this cannot explain the very large rural-urban difference in clearance rates for homicides. Homicides will almost certainly

Table 1   Percentage of Index Crimes Cleared by Arrest, 1992

Crime Type	Cities 250,000+	Rural Counties
Violent	38.5	60.7
Murder	59.6	74.5
Rape	53.4	53.0
Robbery	21.4	38.1
Aggravated Assault	53.2	63.4
Property	14.3	18.4
Burglary	11.3	16.4
Larceny	16.9	18.3
Vehicle theft	10.3	32.4
Arson	9.2	21.8
All Index Crimes	18.8	23.0

SOURCE: *Uniform Crime Reports* 1992, Table 25, Pp. 208-9.

be recorded regardless of whether there are suspects. It is also possible that the close social networks in rural areas make it easier to solve crimes. One police chief told us:

> You've got a specific number of kids who are committing things and it's very easy after a crime to determine who did it here. The closeness of the community and the wide variety of MOs, when something happens they usually leave enough of a telltale sign that we know exactly who committed it. We only have one school that we have to listen to for rumors and things. We've got a lot of law-abiding kids that let us know what they are hearing. We solved almost every one of our crimes here. For every one of our thefts, burglaries, we know who has done it.

A county sheriff echoed this view by noting:

> For example, my secretary's husband owns the tire store. His tire store got burglarized. People know him and they know her, so they come and tell me "I know who did it." All we have to do is prove it. In some place like Fort Worth [Texas], that's not going to happen—ever. The people on the street don't know the cop; the cop doesn't know the person on the street. They don't intermix too much.

Finally, when one chief was asked if knowing people in the community made his job easier, he replied:

> Yeah, I'll give you an example. I live on a road, and when I heard on the squawk box here of a burglary at a neighbor's house three doors down, I immediately called my neighbor across the street, because I knew the two girls were home at that time. I just asked them, "Did you see anything?" They said, "Yeah, I saw this person that was passing around." We picked them up and recovered the goods. Because we are small, my neighbors saw the car and recognized the person, the thief. It happens with some frequency because of the fact that people know each other.

The circumstantial evidence presented here suggests that rural police are more effective than urban police, and that effectiveness may be related to the close bonds among community members and between the community and the police. This was also suggested by Cordner (1989), who found that rural departments were more effective investigators, and this was in part due to the close social networks in those areas:

> Consider two small police departments, one located in a rural area and the other in a metropolitan area. Although the residential populations served by the two agencies may be the same size, the investigators in the rural departments have some natural advantages. They actually know, by name, by sight, and/or by reputation, a much greater proportion of the people in their jurisdiction and its surrounding area than the metropolitan agency investigators know of theirs. The witnesses that they deal with are much more likely to have recognized suspects they observed. Also, the rural investigator has only a few neighboring jurisdictions to keep in contact with, whereas the metropolitan investigator may have a dizzying array of other police departments in close proximity. (p. 153)

Factors in the rural environment that seem to make rural police more effective are those interpersonal networks that community policing tries to foster in urban areas. Thus a better understanding of how rural departments use these networks may have implications for community policing in urban areas.

Other Issues

Looking at policing in rural areas leads one to think about community policing in other ways, particularly to adopt a more elaborate conception of *the community* than is common in discussions of community policing. For example, community policing discussions often allude to the community in terms of lay citizens or nonpolice agencies that might be helpful to citizens. In the rural environment, however, the community in which the police officer works includes not only citizens but other criminal justice officials as well. As one sheriff describes it:

> I tell the guys, we are as much social workers as we are law enforcement officers—community policing. We are expected to work for solutions for these people—what brought them to our attention. When these cases are brought to court, myself, the state public defender, the chief deputy, the prosecutor, and the judge have all set [sic] around a table and discussed what actions we're going to do to this guy, what treatment program we can come up with to keep him from becoming a repeater. I think that's probably unusual, even in rural areas. We take an interest. At court time, it's not unusual for the officer working the case, the prosecutor, and the public defender to go over here to the restaurant and get in the back corner where you have some privacy, and try to work out a solution to the case. What's best for him and what's best for the community?

It is easy to see how this informal approach can be a two-edged sword. In many cases it can render justice in the very best sense of the word. At the same time, however, it is less clear what happens to justice when the defendant is an outsider, such as a migrant worker, or an insider who is simply disliked, or when rural officers do not use good sense or sound judgment.

Accordingly, it is easy to see why some critics are concerned that community policing can shift away from something that is *for* the good of the public to a technique for manipulating the public and doing things *to* it (see Bayley 1988). After all, the development of the formal, militarized style of modern urban police was itself a response to corruption and misbehavior by police, arising from informality that also meant a lack of control (Klockars 1988). Although our study was not designed to examine misconduct or corruption among rural police, such a study would provide insights into

problems that arise when the police and the community are *too* close.

Policing in rural areas can also illustrate the idea of decentralizing police department activities. One municipal chief, who previously had been a police officer in a large city, suggested that as generalists, rural police do not simply involve themselves in a variety of nonpolice functions, but they also have to be generalists within policing:

> In a rural area, you do everything yourself. You do the fingerprinting, the pictures, the interviews, the crime scene, everything. In a big department in an urban area, you specialize. As a patrolman in an urban area, I would simply secure the scene of a crime. Once the detective arrived, it was theirs. The detective called in whoever they [sic] needed. Here, there's one officer on duty; he's the primary officer. If he calls for a backup and I come out, he is still the primary officer. The future of policing is where a complete, mature, well-rounded police officer can step into a situation and handle it, or call for the necessary elements to handle it. The day will come in this country . . . where all police officers, no matter where they are stationed, they're it. . . . There won't be chiefs and things like that. There might be supervisors, but they'll be stationed in one place where they can respond to many, many officers from many, many areas.

Rural police practices also raise questions about the nature of police accountability to the public and highlight the difference between *formal* and *informal* accountability. Formal accountability is more explicit but less direct, being concentrated through specific established channels of communication and authority within the organization. In contrast, informal accountability is diffused through multiple channels spread throughout the community, which are also more direct. For example, under formal accountability, the officer is accountable through the organization, and citizens make their complaints through formal channels. Their complaints are processed and eventually fed back to the officer. In contrast, informal accountability means that officers are more directly and immediately aware of citizen concerns and may hear about those concerns from a variety of people, both inside and outside the police organization, in a variety of social settings.

We have argued throughout that as a result of close social ties between police and community in rural settings and in the absence of organizational buffers in small rural departments, rural police are more accountable and responsive to local citizens than are urban police. Although this appears to be true of rural police as a group, rural sheriffs with whom we spoke were emphatic that, as *elected* officials, they were compelled to be much more sensitive to citizen concerns than were municipal chiefs. *If* their perceptions are accurate, and *if* accountability to the public is a worthwhile goal, then it is interesting to speculate what might happen if municipal departments shifted to a system in which chiefs were elected officials.

DISCUSSION

We have argued that modern community policing draws heavily on ideas and practices that have long been traditions in rural areas, although this link is rarely made explicit. It is important to understand the rural dimensions that matter most. What makes the rural community unique in the examples given here is not simply low population density, but also relatively dense social networks. Even among rural areas there is variation in the density of these networks, and it is possible to police rural areas without having the kinds of experiences described here. State police, for example, may operate in rural areas but have relatively little connection to local social networks. As one sheriff observed about his own prior experience as a state trooper:

> I was in 11 stations in 25 years with the state police. I worked all over the place. You see a group of young state troopers come in, they work there for a very short period of time, they go out, they don't care about the individual population. They're statistically oriented—A, B, C—so they are out to make numbers. I think your [sheriffs'] deputies are there for life. They develop a better relationship with the people, on the whole, where they are *their* cop.

Similarly, one may be an officer whose background and/or personality make it difficult for him or her to fit in with the local culture—and it is our experience that such officers have a particularly difficult time doing their work. Thus a rural area is not simply a physical place but a *social place* as well. This is something community policing advocates in urban areas recognize when they suggest that beats cover *natural* (i.e., social) neighborhood boundaries, rather than those created for bureaucratic expediency. Of course, the social characteristics of crime and policing in rural areas are shaped by the size of the population and the size of the department. We do not know the threshold size for either departments or communities, that is, the size at which they cease to be clearly *rural*. However, we did encounter a number of departments in which rapid population growth had transformed their rural conditions and eroded the police-community networks that once characterized their community:

> That is the one thing that I'm crying about. We are now responding to in excess of 3,000 calls for service in a year. We are losing some of that personal contact. [His city] and some of the urban areas are having to limit the types of calls they will respond to, such as whether they will do funeral escorts. It's a Catch 22; when you become incident driven, the community plays a less active role, and it's a downward spiral.

Although we have gone to great lengths to show themes common to community policing and rural policing, we would argue that community policing is *not* simply and invariably identical to rural policing. Rather, community policing is a formalized and rationalized version of small town policing—where the purpose is to introduce accountability and provide a measure of legal rationality to what, in rural areas, is a much more spontaneous and informal process. Thus community policing and rural policing are not identical. Community policing is small town policing set in a rational framework that attempts to formalize the spontaneous acts of good sense and good citizenship found in many rural officers into a *program* that can be taught and that can be monitored and evaluated. This observation suggests a fundamental paradox of community policing—in many ways it is the formalization of informal custom and the routinization of spontaneous events.

It is also true that rural policing is not homogenous across the country. One implication of this is that, to be effective, there can be no *one* program of community policing. Effective community policing must be tailored to the needs and wishes of each individual community, just as rural police tailor their activities to their local communities.

Further, what we have learned about community policing in rural departments suggests there are elements of the model that chiefs and line officers in urban departments might *not* find attractive or acceptable. For example, the closeness between citizens and police in rural areas may have many benefits for both groups, but it also comes at the expense of the privacy of rural chiefs and line officers. We have observed there are very few rural chiefs or rural sheriffs whose home telephone numbers are unlisted—and many reported that citizens were more than willing to call them at home at any hour, even regarding minor problems. In many communities, line officers could also expect to routinely be contacted at home on police business. One rural chief provided a particularly telling example, an example that is unlikely to be duplicated by any large urban chief:

> In a small town you lose your private life, too. It has taken a toll on my wife and our kids. Two years ago on Thanksgiving we had our family over and then we had a domestic that ended up on my front porch. The husband came over to tell me the problem and then she came over. . . . It was pretty embarrassing. I have since put a sign up on my porch that says this is not the police department, it is our home. Dial 911 if you have an emergency. It hasn't worked. The amount of calls that you get at your house, and . . . if you get an unlisted number, they will come by your house. I would rather have them call me.

This chief, and a number of others, also observed that when off duty they could not have a beer at the local bar without starting rumors in the community. In such cases it is not unusual for chiefs, sheriffs, and their officers to go to nearby towns if they wish to have a quiet evening or if they wish to have a drink. How many urban chiefs and line officers are willing to "live" their jobs to this extent?

Another feature common to rural policing that may not be welcomed by urban officers is the high level of community involvement expected of rural officers. In most rural areas, officers live in the community in which they work. Beyond that, it is our impression that rural police are more involved in civic organizations than are urban police. In most rural communities this is voluntary. One sheriff was more explicit, expressing his philosophy this way:

> I tell them [deputies] before they are ever employed that I want my people involved in the community in some way. It may be a service club, a fraternal organization, your church—I don't care what it is. But I don't want you and your partner to just work together all day and drink together all night. When you deal with the rear end of society, and the majority of our work deals with those kinds of people, it's awful easy to build a negative, horrible attitude where everybody is a SOB or a jerk. . . . Some kind of community activity, but in some way to deal with real people, just like themselves and see that they are not all criminals. If they'll do that, then they try to make their community a better place rather than just through law enforcement.

In summary, rural policing presents an *ideal type* example of community policing. A more extensive study of rural policing should allow us to determine which aspects of the rural police experience can be applied to urban models of community policing. At the same time it is important to determine if there are key elements of successful rural policing that will *never* fit the urban setting. By improving our understanding of these contrasting areas, the study of rural policing can also provide a better understanding of community policing's potential and its limitations.

REFERENCES

"Americans Say Police Brutality Frequent." 1991. *The Gallup Poll Monthly* 306:53-56.

Bayley, David H. 1988. "Community Policing: A Report From a Devil's Advocate." Pp. 225-37 in *Community Policing: Rhetoric or Reality,* edited by J. R. Greene and S. D. Mastrofski. New York: Praeger.

Brown, Lee P. 1989. *Community Policing: A Practical Guide for Police Officials.* Washington, DC: National Institute of Justice.

Cordner, Gary W. 1989. "Police Agency size and Investigative Effectiveness," *Journal of Criminal Justice* 17:145-55.

Crank, John P. 1990. "The Influence of Environmental and Organizational Factors on Police Style in Urban and Rural Environments." *Journal of Research in Crime and Delinquency* 27: 166-89.

Decker, Scott. 1979. "The Rural County Sheriff: An Issue in Social Control." *Criminal Justice Review* 4:97-111.

Eisenstein, James. 1982. "Research on Rural Criminal Justice: A Summary." Pp. 105-43 in *Criminal Justice in Rural America,* edited by S. Cronk, J. Jankovic, and R. K. Green. Washington, DC: U.S. Department of Justice.

Flanagan, Timothy J. 1985. "Consumer Perspectives on Police Operational Strategy." *Journal Of Police Science and Administration* 13:10-21.

General Accounting Office. 1990. *Rural Drug Abuse: Prevalence, Relation to Crime, and Programs.* Washington, DC: U.S. General Accounting Office.

Gibbons, Don C. 1972. "Crime in the Hinterland." *Criminology* 10:177-91.

Goldstein, Herman. 1987. "Toward Community-Oriented Policing: Potential, Basic Requirements, and Threshold Questions." *Crime & Delinquency* 33:6-30.

Greene, Jack R. and Stephen D. Mastrofski, eds. 1988. *Community Policing: Rhetoric or Reality,* New York: Praeger.

International Association of Chiefs of Police (IACP). 1990. *Managing the Small Law Enforcement Agency.* Dubuque, IA: Kendall/Hunt.

Karmen, Andrew. 1990. *Crime Victims: An Introduction to Victimology,* 2nd ed. Pacific Grove, CA; Brooks/Cole.

Klockars, Carl B. 1988. "The Rhetoric of Community Policing." Pp. 239-58 in *Community Policing: Rhetoric or Reality,* edited by J. R. Greene and S. D. Mastrofski. New York: Praeger.

Kowalewski, David, William Hall, John Dolan, and James Anderson. 1984. "Police Environments and Operational Codes: A Case Study of Rural Settings." *Journal of Police Science and Administration* 12:363-72.

Marenin, Otwin and Gary Copus. 1991. "Policing Rural Alaska: The Village Public Safety Officer (VPSO) Program." *American Journal of Police* 10:1-26.

Meagher, M. Steven. 1985. "Police Patrol Styles: How Pervasive is Community Variation?" *Journal of Police Science and Administration* 13:36-45.

Moore, Mark Harrison. 1992. "Problem-Solving and Community Policing." Pp. 99-158 in *Modern Policing,* edited by M. Tonry and N. Morris. Chicago University of Chicago Press.

Trojanowicz, Robert and Bonnie Bucqueroux. 1990. *Community Policing: A Contemporary Perspective.* Cincinnati, OH: Anderson.

Walton, Mary. 1986. *The Deming Management Method.* New York: Perigee.

Weisheit, Ralph A. 1993. "Studying Drugs in Rural Areas: Notes from the Field." *Journal of Research in Crime and Delinquency* 30:213-32.

Wilson, James Q. and George L. Kelling. 1989. "Making Neighborhoods Safe." *Atlantic Monthly* 263:46-52.

This study illustrates the organizational constraints that result in deviant occupational behavior among police. Hunt and Manning systematically show how officers are taught to tell nontruths as part of their everyday work. Being taught to lie has its beginnings in an officer's training at the police academy. As rookies on the street, they are socialized by veteran officers to ignore the "by the book" techniques they learned while attending the academy and are taught that the realities of police work include lying. The authors found that lying begins with the police officers having to account for their behavior to supervisors. This deception can extend to lying in court about the extent of actual probable cause to conduct a search of a citizen, the seizure of illegal items, and finally, the actual arrest. The authors document the cultural norms of police that justify and excuse lying in order to accomplish departmental goals of apprehending criminals, rather than this behavior being perceived as illegal and dishonest.

THE SOCIAL
CONTEXT OF POLICE LYING

JENNIFER HUNT
PETER K. MANNING

INTRODUCTION

Police, like many people in official capacities, lie. We intend here to examine the culturally grounded bases for police lying using ethnographic materials.[1]

Following the earlier work of Manning (1974), we define lies as speech acts which the speaker knows are misleading or false, and are intended to deceive. Evidence that proves the contrary must be known to the observer.[2] Lying is not an obvious matter: it is always socially and contextually defined with reference to what an audience will credit; thus, its meaning changes and its effects are often ambiguous (Goffman 1959, Pp. 58-66). The moral context of lying is very important insofar as its definition may be relative to membership status. The outsider may not appreciate distinctions held scrupulously within a group; indeed, differences between what is and is said may constitute a lie to an outsider, but these distinctions

©1991 by JAI Press. Reprinted by permission of University of California Press. From *Symbolic Interaction* (14)1. Pp. 1-20, by permission.

may not be so easily made by an insider. In a sense, lies do not exist in the abstract; rather they are objects within a negotiated occupational order (Maines 1982). In analytic terms, acceptable or normal lies become one criteria for membership within a group, and inappropriate lying, contextually defined, sets a person on the margins of that order.

The structural sources of police lying are several. Lying is a useful way to manipulate the public when the applying the law and other threats are of little use (see Bittner 1970; Muir 1977; Westley 1970; Skolnick 1966; Klockars 1983, 1984; Wilson 1968; Stinchombe 1964). The police serve as gatherers and screeners of facts, shaping them within the legal realities and routines of court settings (Buckner 1978). The risks involved in establishing often problematic facts and the adversarial context of court narratives increases the value of secrecy and of concealing and controlling information generally (Reiss 1974). Police are protected for their lies by law under stipulated circumstances (see McBarnett 1981; Ericson and Shearing 1986).[3] The internal organization of policing as well as the occupational culture emphasize control, punishment, and secrecy (Westley 1970; Manning 1977). Some police tasks, especially those in specialized police units such as vice, narcotics and internal affairs, clearly require and reward lying skills more than others, and such units may be subject to periodic scandals and public outcry (Manning 1980). The unfilled and perhaps impossible expectations in drug enforcement may escalate the use of lies in the "war on drugs," further reducing public trust when officers' lies are exposed. Most police officers in large forces at one time or another participate in some form of illicit or illegal activity, from the violation of departmental morals codes to the use of extra-legal force. Perhaps more importantly, there is an accepted view that it is impossible to "police by the book;" that any good officer, in the course of a given day, will violate at least one of the myriad rules and regulations governing police conduct. This is certain; what is seen as contingent is when, how and where detection by whom will take place.

Lying is a sanctioned practice, differentially rewarded and performed, judged by local occupationally-grounded standards of competence.[4]

However, it is likely that these standards are changing; as police claims to professional competence and capacity to control crime and incivilities in cities are validated, and absent any changes in internal or external sources of control and accountability (Cf. Reiss 1974), police may encounter less external pressure and public support in routine tasks and are less likely to be called into account. Policing has emerged as a more "professional" occupation and may be less at risk generally to public outcry. One inference of this line of conjecture is that lying is perceived as less risky by police. The occupational culture in departments studied by researchers contains a rich set of stories told to both colleagues and criminals. However, like the routinely required application of violence, some lies are "normal," and acceptable to audiences, especially colleagues, whereas others are not.

Given the pervasiveness of police lies, it is surprising that no research has identified and provided examples of types of lies viewed from the officers' perspective. We focus here on patrol officers' lies and note the skill with which they cope with situations in which lies are produced. Some officers are more frequently in trouble than others, and some more inclined to lie. We suggest a distinction between lies that excuse from those that justify an action, between troublesome and non-troublesome lies, and between case and cover lies. Lies are troublesome when they arise in a context such as a courtroom or a report in which the individual is sworn to uphold the truth. In such a context, lying may risk legal and/or moral sanctions, resulting in punishment and a loss in status. *Case lies* and *cover stories* are routinely told types of troublesome lies. Case lies are stories an officer utilizes systematically in a courtroom or on paper to facilitate the conviction of a suspect. Cover stories are lies an officer tells in court, to supervisors, and to colleagues in order to provide a verbal shield or mitigation in the event of anticipated discipline.

METHODOLOGY

The senior author was funded to study police training in a large Metropolitan police department ("Metro City"). Continuous fieldwork, undertaken as a known observer-participant for eighteen months, focused on the differences and similarities in the socialization experiences of young female and male officers.[5] The fieldwork included observation, participation in training with an incoming class in the police academy, tape-recording interviews in relaxing informal settings with key informants selected for their verbal skills and willingness to give lengthy interviews. The social milieu encouraged them to provide detailed and detached stories. The observer had access to the personnel files of the two hundred officers who entered the force during the research period. She attended a variety of off-duty events and activities ranging from meetings of the Fraternal Order of the Police, sporting events, parties, and funerals (For further details see Hunt 1984). The data presented here are drawn primarily from tape recorded interviews.

Learning to Lie

In the police academy, instructors encouraged recruits to lie in some situations, while strongly discouraging it in others. Officers are told it is "good police work," and encouraged to lie, to substitute guile for force, in situations of crisis intervention, investigation and interrogation, and especially with the mentally ill (Harris 1973).[6] During classes on law and court testimony, on the other hand, students were taught that the use of deception in court was illegal, morally wrong, and unacceptable and would subject the officer to legal and departmental sanctions. Through films and discussions, recruits learned that the only appropriate means to win court cases was to undertake and complete a "solid," "by the books" investigation including displaying a professional demeanor while delivering a succinct but "factual" narrative in court testimony.

Job experience changes the rookies' beliefs about the circumstances under which it is appropriate to lie. Learning to lie is a key to membership. Rookies in Metro City learn on the job, for example, that police routinely participate in a variety of illicit activities which reduce the discomfort of the job such as drinking, sleeping on duty, and staying inside during inclement

weather. As these patterns of work avoidance may result in discovery, they demand the learning of explanatory stories which rationalize informal behavior in ways that jeopardize neither colleagues nor supervisors (Cain 1973; Chatterton 1975). Rookies and veteran police who demonstrate little skill in constructing these routine lies were informally criticized. For example, veteran officers in Metro City commented sympathetically about rookies who froze on footbeats because they were too green to know that "a good cop never gets cold or wet. . ." and too new to have attained expertise in explaining their whereabouts if they were to leave their beats. After a few months in the district, several veteran officers approvingly noted that most of the rookies had learned not only where to hide but what to say if questioned by supervisors.

Rookies also learn the situational utility of lying when they observe detectives changing reports to avoid unnecessary paperwork and maintain the clearance rate. In the Metro City police department, some cases defined initially as robberies, assaults, and burglaries were later reduced to less serious offenses (Cf. Sudnow 1965). Police argued that this practice reduced the time and effort spent on "bullshit jobs" little likely to be cleared. Rookies who opposed this practice and insisted on filing cases as they saw fit were ridiculed and labeled troublemakers. As a result, most division detectives provided minimal cooperation to these "troublemakers." This added the task of reworking already time-consuming and tedious reports to the workload of young officers who were already given little prospective guidance and routine assistance in completing their paperwork.

Young police also observe veterans lying in court testimony regarding, for example, the presence of probable cause in situations of search, seizure and arrest (see, for example, McClure 1986, Pp. 230-232).

There are also counter-pressures. While learning to lie, rookies also recognize that the public and court officials disapprove of lying, and that if caught in a serious lie, they may be subject to either legal sanctioning and/or departmental punishment. But recognizing external standards and their relevance does not exhaust the learning required. There are also relevant tacit rules within the occupational culture about what constitutes a normal lie. Complexity and guile, and agile verbal constructions are appreciated, while lying that enmeshes or makes colleagues vulnerable or is "sloppy" is condemned. Lying is judged largely in pragmatic terms otherwise. Soon, some rookies are as skillful as veterans at lying.[7]

POLICE ACCOUNTS OF LYING

Lies are made normal or acceptable by means of socially approved vocabularies for relieving responsibility or neutralizing the consequences of an event. These accounts are provided *after* an act if and when conduct is called into question (See the classic, Mills 1940; Sykes and Matza 1957; Scott and Lyman 1968). Police routinely normalize lying by two types of accounts, excuses and justifications (Van Maanen 1980; Hunt 1985; Waegel 1984). These accounts are not mutually exclusive, and a combination is typically employed in practice. The greater the number of excuses and justifications condensed in a given account, the more the police officer is able to reduce personal and peer related conflicts. These accounts are typically tailored to an audience. A cover story directed to an "external" audience such as the district attorneys, courts, or the media is considered more problematic than a lie directed to supervisors or peers (Manning 1974). Lies are more troublesome also when the audience is perceived as less trustworthy (Goffman 1959, p. 58).

Excuses deny full responsibility for an act of lying but acknowledge its inappropriateness. Police distinguish passive lies which involve omission, or covering oneself, from active lies such as a "frame," of a person for a crime by, for example, planting a gun, or the construction of a sophisticated story. The latter are more often viewed as morally problematic.

Justifications accept responsibility for the illegal lie in question but deny that the act is wrongful or blameworthy. They socially construct a set of justifications, used with both public and other police, according to a number of principles (These are analogous to the neutralizations found by Sykes and Matza 1957 in another context). When lying, police may appeal to "higher" loyalties that justify the means used or deny that anyone is truly hurt or a victim of the lies. Police may also deny injury by claiming that court testimony has little consequence as it is merely an extension of the "cops and robbers" game. It is simply a tool in one's repertoire that requires a modicum of verbal skill (see Sudnow 1965; Blumberg 1967). Finally, as seen in "cover stories," officers justify lies instrumentally and pragmatically (see Van Maanen 1980; Waegel 1984).

LYING IN ACTION

Case Stories and the Construction of Probable Cause

The most common form of case lying, used to gain a conviction in court, involves the construction of probable cause for arrest, or search and seizure in situations where the legally required basis in the street encounter is weak or absent.[8] Probable cause can be constructed by reorganizing the sequence of events, "shading" or adding to the facts, omitting embarrassing facts, or entering facts into a testimony that were not considered at the time of arrest or while writing the report.

The following is a typical case story-account chosen from a taped interview in which probable cause was socially constructed. The officer was called to a "burglary in progress" with no further details included and found a door forced open at the back of the factory.

> So I arrive at the scene, and I say, I know: I do have an open property and I'm going in to search it. And I'm looking around, and I hear noise. Then, I hear glass break. And I run to the window, and obviously something just jumped out the window and is running and I hear skirmishing. So I run, and I still don't see anyone yet. I just hear something. I still haven't seen anyone. You hear a window, you see a window and you hear footsteps running. Then you don't hear it anymore. I don't find anybody. So I say to myself "whoever it is around here somewhere." So, fifteen minutes go by, twenty go by. The job resumes.
>
> One cop stays in the front and about a half an hour or forty-five minutes later, low and behold, I see someone half a block away coming out of a

field. Now, the field is on the other side of the factory. It's the same field that I chased this noise into. So a half hour later I see this guy at quarter to four in the morning just happened to be walking out of this field. So I grab him. "Who are you? What are you doing?" Bla bla bla... And I see that he has flour on him, like flour which is what's inside of this factory. So I say to myself, "you're the suspect under arrest for burglary." Well, I really, at this point it was iffy if I had probable cause or not ... a very conservative judge would say that that was enough... but probably not, because the courts are so jammed that that weak probable cause would be enough to have it thrown out. So in order to make it stick, what I said was "As I went to the factory and I noticed the door open and I entered the factory to search to see if there was anybody inside. Inside, by the other side of the wall, I see a young black male, approximately twenty two years old, wearing a blue shirt and khaki pants, jump out of the window, and I chase him and I lost him in the bushes. An hour later I saw this very same black male walking out of the field and I arrested him. He was the same one I saw inside." O.K.?...

What I did was to construct probable cause that would definitely stick in court and I knew he was guilty. So in order to make it stick ... That's the kind of lies that happen all the time. I would defend that.[9]

The officer's account of his activity during the arrest of a suspect and subsequent testimony in court reveals a combination of excuses and justifications which rationalize perjury. He clearly distinguishes the story he tells the interviewer from the lie he told in court. Near the end of the vignette, by saying "O.K.?," he seeks to emphasize phatic contact as well to establish whether the interviewer understood how and why he lied and how he justified it. Within the account, he excuses his lies with reference to organizational factors ("conservative judges"-those who adhere to procedural guarantees—and "overcrowded courts"), and implies that these are responsible for releasing guilty suspects who should be jailed. These factors force the officer to lie in court in order to sustain an ambiguous and weak probable cause. The officer further justifies his lies by claiming that he believes the suspect to be guilty, and is responsible for perpetrating crime more serious than the lie used to convict him. He ends by claiming

that such lies are acceptable to his peers—they "happen all the time"—and implicitly appeals to the higher goal of justice. As in this case, officers can shape and combine observed and invented facts to form a complex, elaborate yet coherent, picture which may help solve a crime, clear a case, or convict a criminal.

Case Stories and the Manipulation of the Court as an Informal Entity

As a result of community pressure in Metro City, a specialized unit was created to arrest juveniles who "hung out" on street corners and disturbed neighborhoods. The unit was considered a desirable assignment because officers worked steady shifts and were paid overtime for court appearances. They were to be judged by convictions obtained, not solely upon their arrests. An officer in this unit explains some of the enforcement constraints produced by the law and how they can be circumvented:

Legally ... when there's any amount of kids over five there is noise, but it's not really defined legally being unruly even though the community complains that they are drunk and noisy. Anyway, you get there, you get their, you see five kids and there's noise. It's not really criminal, but you gotta lock them up, particularly if someone had called and complained. So you lock them up for disorderly conduct and you tell your story. If they plead not guilty then you have to actually tell a story.

... It's almost like a game. The kids know that they can plead guilty and get a $1250 fine or a harder judge will give them a $30.50 fine or they can plead not guilty and have the officer tell their story of what occurred which led to the arrest.

... The game is who manipulates better, the kid or the cop? The one who lies better wins.

Well, the kids are really cocky. I had arrested this group of kids, and when we went to court the defense attorney for the kids was arguing that all of the kids, who I claimed were there the first time that I warned them to get offa the corner, weren't there at all. Now, you don't really have to warn them to get offa the corner before you arrest them, but the judge likes it if you warn them once.

Meanwhile, one of the kids is laughing in the courtroom, and the judge asks why he's laughing in her courtroom and showing disrespect.

At this point, the kid's attorney asks me what the kid was wearing when I arrested him. I couldn't remember exactly what he had on so I just gave the standard uniform; dungarees, shirt, sneakers . . . Then, the defense attorney turns around and asks the kid what he was wearing and he gives this description of white pants with a white sports jacket. Now, you just know the kid is lying because there ain't a kid in that neighborhood who dresses like that. But, anyway, I figure they got me on this one.

But then I signal the District Attorney to ask me how I remembered this kid outta the whole bunch who was on the corner. So the District Attorney asks me, "Officer, what was it that made you remember this male the first time?" And I said, "Well, your honor, I referred this one here because the first time that I warned the group to get offa the corner, this male was the one that laughed the hardest." I knew this would get the Judge because the kid has pissed her off in the first place by laughing in the courtroom. Well, the judge's eyes lit up like she knew what I was talking about.

"Found guilty . . . 60 dollars." (The Judge ruled).

In this case, the officer believed the boy was guilty because he "hung out" regularly with the juvenile corner group. Although the officer forgot the boy's dress on the day he was arrested, he testifies in court that it was the "standard [juvenile] uniform." The boy, however, claims he wore pants and a sport jacket. The officer was in a potentially embarrassing and awkward spot. In order to affirm the identification of the suspect and win the case, the officer constructs another lie using the District Attorney's question. He manipulates the emotions of the judge whose authority was previously threatened by the boy's disrespectful courtroom demeanor. He claims that he knows this was the boy because he displayed arrogance by laughing when arrested just as he had in court.

The officer's account of the unit's organization, the arrest, and his courtroom testimony reveals a combination of excuses and justifications. He justifies his lie to make the arrest without probable cause and to gain a conviction citing the organizational and community pressures. He also justifies perjury by denying the reality and potential injury to the suspect caused by his actions. He sees courtroom communications as a game, and argues that the penalty is minor in view of the offense and the age of the suspect. The officer argues instrumentally that the lie was a means to gain or regain control as well as a means to punish an offender who has not accepted the police definition of the situation. The latter is evident in the officer's assertion that the boys are "really cocky." Their attempts to question the police version of the story by presenting themselves as clean cut children with good families is apparently viewed as a demonstration of deliberate arrogance deserving of retaliation in the form of a lie which facilitates their conviction.

Another officer from the same unit describes a similar example of case construction to gain a conviction. The clumsy character of the lie suggests that the officer believes he is at little risk of perjury. According to a colleagues account:

We arrested a group of kids in a park right across from the hospital. They all know us and we know them, so they are getting as good as we are at knowing which stories go over better on the judge. So the kids in this instance plead not guilty which is a real slap in the face because you know that they are going to come up with a story that you are going to have to top [That is, the case will go to court and require testimony].

So, the kids' story was that they were just sitting in the park and waiting for someone and that they were only having a conversation. [The police officer's testimony was]: "The kids were making so much noise, the kids were so loud . . . They had this enormous radio blasting and the people in the hospital were so disturbed that they were just hanging outta the windows. And some nuns, some of the nuns that work in the hospital, they were coming outside because it was so loud." And the thing that appalled the officer the most was that this was going on right in front of the entrance to the hospital. The kids were acting in such a manner that the officer immediately arrested them without even a warning.

Well, the kid, when he hears this, likely drops dead. He kept saying "what radio, what radio?" The funny part of it was that the other police officers who were in the back of the courtroom watching the cop testify kept rolling their eyes at him. First of all, because when he said that the people were hanging outta the hospital windows, the windows in that hospital don't open. They're sealed. Another thing was that the cop said this occurred at the entrance of the hospital. Two years ago this was the entrance to the hospital. But it's not the entrance now. Another thing was that there never was a radio. But when the officer testified regarding the radio, he got confused. He actually did think there was one but in fact, the radio blasting was from another job. The cop realized after he testified that the kid didn't have a radio blasting.

The lies are described as instrumental: they are designed to regain control in court and to punish the offender for violating the officer's authority by verbally "slapping him in the face." In addition, the court-as-a-game-metaphor is evident in the notion that each participant must top the other's story in court. The amused reaction evidenced by peers listening to what they viewed as absurd testimony, rolling their eyes, also suggests their bemused approval. The informant's ironic identification of his colleague's factual errors points out the recognized and displayed limits and constraints upon lying. The officers recognized the difference between a rather sloppy or merely effective lie and an admired lie that artfully combines facts, observations, and subtle inferences. Perhaps it is not unimportant to note that the police engaged in the first instance in a kind of social construction of the required social order. The police lied in virtually every key facet of this situation because they believed that the juveniles should be controlled. What might be called the police ordering of a situation was the precondition for both of these court lies. Such decisions are potentially a factor in community policing when police define and then defend in court with lies their notions of public order (See Wilson and Kelling 1982).

Cover Stories

A cover story is the second kind of legal lie that police routinely tell on paper, in court, and to colleagues. Like most case stories, cover stories are constructed using sub-cultural nuances to make retelling the dynamics of encounters legally rational. Maintaining the capacity to produce a cover story is viewed as an essential skill required to protect against disciplinary action.

A cover story may involve the manipulation of legal and departmental rules, or taken-for-granted-knowledge regarding a neighborhood, actions of people and things. A common cover story involves failure to respond to a radio call.

Every officer knows, for example, that some districts have radio "dead spots" where radio transmissions do not reach. If "radio" (central communications) calls an officer who doesn't respond or accept, "pick up the job," radio will usually recall. If he still doesn't respond, another officer typically takes the job to cover for him, or a friendly dispatcher may assign the job to another unit. However, if radio assigns the same job to the same car a third time and the unit still doesn't accept the job, the officer may be subject to formal disciplinary action. One acceptable account for temporary unavailability (for whatever reason) is to claim that one's radio malfunctioned or that one was in a "dead spot" (see Rubinstein 1973; Manning 1988).

The most common cover stories involving criminal matters are constructed to protect the officer against charges of brutality or homicide. Such cover stories serve to bridge the gap between the normal use of force which characterizes the informal world of the street and its legal use as defined by the court.

Self protection is the presumed justification for cover stories. Since officers often equate verbal challenges with actual physical violence, both of which are grounds for retaliatory violence, either may underlie a story.[10] Threats of harm to self, partner, or citizens are especially powerful bases for rationalizations. Even an officer who is believed by colleagues to use brutal force and seen as a poor partner as a result, is expected to lie to protect himself (see Hunt 1985; Waegel 1984). He or she would be considered odd, or even untrustworthy, if he or she did not. There is an interaction between violence and lying understood by police standards.

In the following account, the officer who fired his weapon exceeded "normal" force, and committed a "bad shooting" (see Van Maanen 1980). Few officers would condone the shooting of an unarmed boy who they did not see commit a crime. Nevertheless, the officers participate in the construction of a cover story to protect their colleague against disciplinary action and justify it on the basis of self-defense and loyalty. Officers arrived at a scene that had been described mistakenly in a radio call as a "burglary in progress" (in fact, boys were stripping a previously stolen car). Since this is a call with arrest potential, it drew several police vehicles and officers soon began to chase the suspect(s):

> Then they get into a back yard chasing one kid. The kid starts running up a rain spout like he's a spider man, and one of the cops took a shot at him. So now they're all panicky because the kid made it to the roof and he let out a scream and the cops thought that they hit him. And that was a bad shooting! What would you think if you was that kid's mother? Not only did they not have an open property, but they don't know if it's a stolen car at all. Well, when they shot the kid I gave them an excuse by mistake, inadvertently. I was on the other side of the place with my partner when I heard the one shot. [The officer telling the story is on one side of an iron gate, and another officer J.J. was on the other side. He kicks open the gate, thinking it is locked. It is not locked and swings wildly open, striking J.J. in the head].
>
> J.J. keeps stepping backward like he wanted to cry . . . . . . like he was in a daze. "It's all right, it's not bleeding." I says to him . . . like he was stunned.
>
> So then the Sergeant gets to the scene and asks what happened, cause this shot has been fired, and the kid screamed, and you figure some kid's been hit and he's up on the roof.
>
> They gotta explain this dead kid and the shot to the sergeant when he gets there. So J.J. and Eddy discuss this. Eddy was the cop who'd fired the shot at the kid climbing up the rain spout, and all of a sudden they decide to claim he got hit with something in the head, and J.J yells, "I'm hit, I'm hit." Then Eddy, thinking his partner's been shot, fires a shot at the kid. So they reported this all to the Captain and J.J. gets reprimanded for yelling "I'm shot" when he said, "I'm hit."
>
> J.J. was never involved at all, but he just says this to cover for Eddy.
>
> Meanwhile, the fire department is out there looking on the roof for the kid and they never found him so you figure he never got hit.

Here, the officer telling the story demonstrates his solidarity with colleagues by passively validating (refusing to discredit) the construction of an episode created by collusion between two other officers. The moral ambiguity of participation in such a troublesome lie is recognized and indicated by the interviewed officer. He disclaims responsibility for his involvement in the lie by insisting that he was not at the scene of the shooting and only "by

mistake. . . . inadvertently. . . . gave them [the other officers] an excuse" used to create the cover story. In such morally ambiguous situations, individual officers remain in some moral tension. Note the officers' role-taking capacity, empathy and concern for the generalized other when he asks in the vignette what the interviewer's thoughts would be if ". . . you was that kid's mother?" Such views may conflict with those of peers and supervisors. Moral tensions also arise in situations producing case stories.

The Morally Ambiguous Lie in a Case Story

Occasionally, officers cannot fully neutralize their sense of self-responsibility in the context of the police role. Their lies remain troubling in a moral sense. Such lies suggest the moral limits of pragmatism within the police, but in this case, the lie may be also a sign of the youth and gender of the officer involved. In the following example, a five year veteran police officer experiences a profound moral dilemma as a result of pressures to frame a boy for a burglary she did not see him commit and did not believe he had committed. She refuses, even under peer and supervisory officers' pressure to do so, to produce a case story lie. Refusing to lie in this instance does not constitute a violation of police officers' sense of mutual obligation since she does not jeopardize peers. She sets the scene by noting that she and her partner are talking to John near his butcher shop when Frankie, a powerful and well-connected community member, approaches her and wants her to watch his shop. He claims a guy is trying to pass a bad check. She continues:

> Well, Frankie's a close friend of the Police Commissioner and his sister's married to the owner of a drug manufacturing company. He donated a lot of money to the mayor's political campaign. . . . The police commissioner vacations at Frankie's sister's summer home in [an elite resort location]. . . . Frankie has "a lot of pull" and we [the police] sometimes call ourselves "Frankie's private little army."
>
> Anyway, I tell Frankie, "O.K. I'll watch the store." But I don't think anything's really gonna

happen. Frankie's just jealous because I'm spending more time with John than with him. Anyway, I go in the butcher shop and talk to John and when I come out, I hear Frankie screaming, "Stop him, stop him!" I respond, "Stop who?" Frankie says, "Stop the guy walking with the bag." I see a black kid walking away from the store with a bag in his hand and I call him over. I ask Frankie, "What's going on?" He responds, "Something's fishy, something fishy's going on." At this point, the kid opens the bag in front of me and there's nothing in it and I search the kid. . . . The so called bad check that the kid was trying to cash at Frankie's store turned out to be a valid money order. I ask the kid to come over to the car and make out a ped stop. Thank God, I made up a good ped stop . . . I got all the information on the kid.

At this point a "man with a gun" [call] comes over the radio. As no one else picks up the job, we take it. It was unfounded and I tell my partner that we'd better go back and check on Frankie because there might be trouble. When we return I ask Frankie, "Is everything all right?" He responds, "No it isn't." I say, "What's wrong?" Frankie says, "I told you he took something." I say, "That's not good enough, you have to tell me what he took. . . . not that 'something's fishy and he must have taken something'. . . . Did you see him take anything?" Frankie responds, "Three radios."

I go inside the appliance store to see the missing radios and there are a number of radios on a shelf way above the counter where it would be difficult for anyone to reach them, particularly a kid. I ask Frankie if he wants me to take the report or if he would prefer a regular district car to do it. He tells me, "You take it!" I take the report and right away call a 43rd district car to take it into the detectives.

An hour later, I got a call to go to the district. The captain asks me "What did you do to Frankie?" I tell him, "nothing." The captain asks me again, "What did you do to Frankie?" I say "nothing," and tell him exactly what had occurred at the incident. The captain says, "Did you run him [the suspect] through the computer?" I say, "No, I didn't . . . because he had legitimate identification." The captain then tells me, "Well, you better get your story together because Frankie's going before the Board of Inquiry. You fucked up. Now, tomorrow you're gonna apologize!" I say, "But if I apologize, it makes it seem like I did something wrong. I did nothing wrong." The captain adds, "Don't argue with me, I told you what you're gonna do."

An hour later, I receive a call from the Division detective and he wants to know my side of the story. I tell him what happened. The detective says, "Well, we have to put out a warrant for the kid's arrest." I say, "For what?" The detective explains, "Believe me, the only reason this kid is getting locked up is because it's Frankie. . . . Have you ever been burnt by Frankie? Do you know who Frankie is?"

The detective then asks, "Will you go to court?" I say, "why should I go to court, I didn't make the arrest." The detective says, "Well, you're the key to the identification of the kid." I respond, "O.K. you send me to court and I'll make the asshole out of him that he is." The detective then says, "O.K. if I'm not man enough to stand this up in court, then I won't ask you to do it. . . . Let the old bastard do it himself."

Later, I'm called back into the Captain's office . . . and he tells me that "You're in for it now . . . the detectives have put out a warrant for the kid's arrest and that makes you look foolish . . ." He then orders me to tell my story again. I tell it again. Finally, I say, "I didn't lock the kid up because I had no probable cause and to this day, I have no probable cause." The Captain warns me, "Well, you're going to the Board of Inquiry and there's nothing you can say that will get you out of this one . . . I hope your partner's a good front man." I told him, "My partner don't need to lie."

In this incident, the officer is unwilling, in spite of quite direct threats and pressures, to neutralize her felt responsibility by constructing a case story lie. She believed that the boy was innocent and did not believe that "higher truth" was served by participating in a lie that would have framed the boy and saved Frankie's face. She also thought her lie would facilitate the conviction of the boy for burglary, an offense that was so serious that injury to him could not be denied. The officer not only refused to lie but agreed to testify for the boy if subpoenaed to appear in court.

This ambiguous lie highlights several important subpoints. The officer clung to a version of the situation that denied the relevance of lying, and featured her view of the facts, her duty and her distrust of Frankie. The pressure to lie illustrated here makes evident some divergence of opinions about what is acceptable practice by rank and function. She refuses to lie in part because neither she nor her partner were at fault in her eyes (in contrast to the other examples in this article in which officers understood that both the public and themselves viewed a story as a lie), and her refusal does not jeopardize other officers. The officer first is confronted by her Captain who tells her she "fucked up" and should apologize. He implies that she should agree with Frankie's view (which she, in turn, views as a lie), be prepared to apologize, and to go before a Board of Inquiry. The division detective is ambivalent and unsure of what to do, and passes responsibility on to her. He asks her if she will go to court. The Captain again calls her in and by telling her that a warrant has been issued by detectives i.e. that there is probable cause in the case, and that she will look foolish for persisting in her story. He does not go into the details of the case with her, just listens to her story and then implies that she is lying and that her partner will have to lie for her before the Board of Inquiry.

While officers are oriented to peers and their sergeants, and are sensitive to those loyalties (Cain 1973), administrative officers may justify their actions with regard to higher political obligations, organizational pressures or even loyalty to the Police Commissioner or the Mayor (even though such politicians may have no direct involvement in the case). If a case involves for an officer such higher loyalties and patronage as well as political corruption, there is more to be lost by *not* lying.[11] Detectives are more cynical and view their role as mediating between the street realities and those of the courtroom. Their standards for judging normal lies differ from those of uniformed officers. This patrol officer, however, defined her loyalties in terms of her immediate peers and the public rather than officials whom she viewed as corrupt. Rank, age and other factors not explored here may mediate an officer's relationship with the community, his/her allegiance to the police department and sense of right and wrong.

CONCLUSION

This ethnographic analysis relies principally upon the perspective of the officers observed and interviewed. It draws, however, on broad ethnographic accounts or general formulations of the police mandate and tasks. We attempt to integrate the pressures inherent in the inevitable negotiation within hierarchical systems between official expectations and roles, and one's individual sense of self. Officers learn how to define and control the public and other officers, and to negotiate meanings. The social constructions or lies which arise result from situational integration of organizational, political and moral pressures. These are not easily captured in rules, norms, or values. Repeatedly, officers must negotiate organizational realities *and* maintain self-worth. Police lies, serving in part to maintain a viable self, are surrounded by cultural assumptions and designations, a social context which defines normal or acceptable lies and distinguishes them from those deviant or marginal to good practice. The meanings imputed to the concepts "lie," "lying" and "truth" are negotiated and indicate or connote subtle intergroup relationships. In a crisis, ability to display solidarity by telling a proper and effective lie is highly valued and rewarded. The ironic epithet "police liar" is neutralized. Subtle redefinition of truth includes forms of group-based honesty that are unrecognized by legal standards or by the standards of outsiders. These findings have implications that might be further researched.

Lying is a feature of everyday life found in a variety of personal, occupational and political interactions. Although telling the full truth may be formally encouraged throughout life, it is not always admired or rewarded. Neither truth nor lies are simple and uniform; cultural variation exists in the idea of normal lying and its contrast conception. Those who continue to tell the truth and do not understand communications as complex negotiations of formal and informal behavioral norms, find themselves in social dilemmas, and are vulnerable to a variety of labels used in everyday life like "tactless," "undersocialized," "deviant," or "mentally ill." The application of the label is contingent upon taken-for-granted modes of deception that structure interpersonal relations. As the last few years have shown, given the impossible mandate of the police, certain police tasks are more highly visible e.g. drug enforcement, and even greater pressure to lie may emerge. Thus, the mandate is shaped and patterned by tasks as well as general social expectations, and the sources of lying may differ as well.

The cultural grounds explored here are features of any organization which lies as a part of its routine activities, such as government agencies carrying out domestic intelligence operations and covert foreign activities. Standards of truth and falsehood drawn from everyday life do not hold here, and this shifting ground of fact and reality is often difficult to grasp and hold for both insiders and outsiders. As a result, organization members, like the police, develop sophisticated and culturally sanctioned mechanisms for neutralizing the guilt and responsibility that troublesome and even morally ambiguous lying may often entail. In time, accounts which retrospectively justify and excuse a lie may become techniques of neutralization which prospectively facilitate the construction of new lies with ready-made justifications. When grounds for lying are well-known in advance, it takes a self-reflective act to tell the truth, rather than to passively accept and use lies when they are taken-for-granted and expected. Police, like politicians, look to "internal standards" and practices to pin down the meaning of events that resonate with questions of public morality and propriety (Katz 1977). When closely examined in a public inquiry, the foreground of everyday internal standards may become merely the background for a public scandal. Normal lies, when revealed and subjected to public standards, can become the basis for scandals. This may be the first occasion on which members of the organization recognize their potential to be seen in such a fashion.

Finally, the extent to which an organization utilizing lies or heavily dependent upon them perceives that it is "under seige" varies. In attempts to shore up their mandate, organizations may tacitly justify lying. As a result, the organization may increase its isolation, lose public trust and credibility, and begin to believe its own lies. This differentially occurs within policing, across departments, and in agencies of control generally. Such dynamics are suggested by this analysis.

Acknowledgment

20 June 89. Revision of a paper presented by the senior author to The Society for the Study of Social Problems, New York, 1986. We acknowledge the very useful comments from this journal's reviewers as well as from Betsy Cullum-Swan, Peter and Patti Adler.

Notes

1. The many social functions of lying, a necessary correlate of trust and symbolic communication generally, are noted elsewhere (Ekman 1985; Simmel 1954; Manning 1977). Our focus is restricted. We do not discuss varieties of concealment, falsification and leakage (Ekman 1985, Pp. 28-29), nor interpersonal dynamics, such as the consequence of a sequence of lies and cover lies that often occur. We omit the case in which the target, such as a theater audience or someone conned, is prepared in advance to accept lies (Ekman 1984, p. 28). Nor do we discuss in detail horizontal or vertical collusions within organizations that generate and sustain lying (e.g. Honeycombe 1974).

2. We do not distinguish "the lie" from the original event, since we are concerned with verbal rationalizations in the sense employed by Mills (1940), Lindesmith and Strauss (1956) and Scott and Lyman (1968). We cluster what might be called accounts for lies (lies about lies found in the interview material included here) with lies, and argue that the complexity of the formulations, and their embeddedness in any instance (the fact that a story may include several excuses, and justifications, and may include how these, in turn, were presented to a judge) makes it misleading to adhere to a strict typology of lies such as routine vs. non-routine, case lies, (both justifications and excuses) vs. cover stories (both justifications and excuses), and troublesome vs. not troublesome lies. If each distinction were worked out in a table, as one reader noted, omitting ambiguous lies, at least 16 categories of lies would result. After considering internal distinctions among lies in policing, we concluded that a typology would suggest a misleading degree of certainty and clarity. More ethnographic material is required to refine the categories outlined here.

3. Police organization, courts and the law permit sanctioned freedom to redefine the facts of a case, the origins of the case, the bases of the arrest and the charge, the number of offenders and the number of violations. Like many public officials, they are allowed to lie when public well-being is at issue (for example, posing as drug dealers, buying and selling drugs, lying about their personal biographies and so on. See Manning 1980; Hellman 1975). Officers are protected if they lie in order to enter homes, to encourage people to confess, and to facilitate people who would otherwise be committing

crimes to commit them. They have warrant to misrepresent, dissemble, conceal and reveal as routine aspects of an investigation.

4. Evidence further suggests, in a point we do not examine here, that departments differ in the support given for lies. This may be related to legalistic aspects of the social organization of police departments (Cf. Wilson 1968, ch. 6). Ironically, for members of specialized units like "sting operations" or narcotics, the line between truth and lies becomes so blurred that according to Ekman's definition (the liar must know the truth and intend to lie), they are virtually always "telling the truth." Furthermore, as noted above, such units are more vulnerable to public criticism because they are held to unrealistic standards, and feel greater pressure to achieve illegally what cannot be accomplished legally. Marx (1988) argues that increased use of covert deceptive operations leads to further penetration of private life, confusion of public standards, and reduced expectations of police morality.

5. She spent some 12 weeks in recruit classes at the academy. For fifteen months, she rode as a non-uniformed research observer, usually in the front seat of a one officer car, from 4-midnight and occasionally on midnight to eight shifts. Although she rode with veteran officers for the first few weeks in order to learn official procedures, the remainder of the time was spent with rookie officers. Follow-up interviews were conducted several years after the completion of the initial 18 months of observation.

6. Typically, recruits were successful in calming the "psychotic" actor when they demonstrated convincingly that they shared the psychotic's delusion and would rescue him/her from his/her persecutors by, for instance, threatening to shoot them. Such techniques were justified scientifically by trained psychologists who also stressed their practical use to avoid violence in potentially volatile situations.

7. Previous research has shown how detailed the knowledge is of officers of how and why to lie, and it demonstrates that trainees are taught to lie by specific instructions and examples (See Harris 1973; McClure 1984; Fielding 1988).

8. Technically, adding facts one recalls later, even in court, are not the basis for lies. Lies, in our view, must be intended.

9. This is taken verbatim from an interview, and thus several rather interesting linguistic turns (especially changes in perspective) are evidenced. Analysis of this sociolinguistically might suggest how this quote replicates in microcosm the problem officers have in maintaining a moral self. They dance repeatedly along the edges of at least two versions of the truth.

10. Waegel (1984) explores the retrospective and prospective accounts police use to excuse and justify the use of force. However, he does not distinguish accounts told by colleagues which are viewed as true by the speaker and those told to representatives of the legal order which are viewed as lies and fit the description of a cover story. For example, the account of accidental discharge which Waegel perceives as a denial of responsibility may also be a cover story which itself is justified as "self defense" against formal reprimand. In contrast, other police excuses and justifications invoked to account for the use of force are often renditions of events that present the officer in a morally favorable light rather than actual lies (see Van Maanen 1980; Hunt 1985; Waegel 1984). Whether the police categorize their use of force as "normal" or "brutal" (Hunt 1985) also structures the moral assessment of a lie, a point which Waegel also overlooks. Thus, acts of normal force which can be excused or justified with reference to routine accounting practices may necessitate the construction of cover stories which became morally neutral by virtue of the act they disguise. Other acts of violence viewed as demonstrating incompetence or brutality may not be excused or justified according to routine accounting practices. Although cover stories in such cases are perceived as rational, they may not provide moral protection for the officer because the lie takes on aspects of the moral stigma associated with the act of violence which it conceals.

11. Supervisors and higher administrators, of course, collude in maintaining the viability of lies because they share the beliefs of officers that it is not possible to police by the book, and that one should not rock the boat and should keep your head down (Van Maanen 1975). It is viewed as impossible to manage routine tasks without lying both to colleagues and supervisors (Punch 1985). The working bases of corruption are thus laid, as well as the potential seen in so many corruption scandals of cover-ups, lies about lies, and vertical and horizontal collusion in lying as seen in both the Watergate and the Iran-Contra affairs.

REFERENCES

Bittner, E. 1970. *Functions of The Police in an Urban Society.* Bethesda: NIMH.

____. 1974. "A Theory of Police: Florence Nightingale in Pursuit of Willie Sutton." In *The Potential for Reform of Criminal Justice,* edited by H. Jacob. Beverly Hills: Sage.

Blumberg, A. 1967. *Criminal Justice.* Chicago: Quadrangle Books.

Buckner, H.T. 1978. "Transformations of Reality in the Legal Process," *Social Research,* 37:88-101.

Cain, M. 1973. *Society and the Policeman's Role.* London: Routledge, Kegan Paul.

Chatterton, M. 1975. "Organizational Relationships and Processes in Police Work: A Case Study of Urban Policing." Unpublished Ph.D. thesis, University of Manchester.

____. 1979. "The Supervision of Patrol Work Under the Fixed Points System." in *The British Police,* edited by S. Holdaway, London: Edward Arnold.

Ekman, P. 1985. *Telling Lies.* New York: W.W. Norton.

Ericson, R. and C. Shearing. 1986. "The Scientification of the Police." in *The Knowledge Society,* edited by G. Bohme and N. Stehr. Dordrecht and Boston: D. Reidel.

Fielding, N. 1988. *Joining Forces.* London: Tavistock.

Goffman, E. 1959. *The Presentation of Self in Everyday Life.* New York: Doubleday Anchor Books.

Harris, R. 1973. *The Police Academy.* New York: Wiley.

Honeycombe, G. 1974. *Adam's Tale.* London: Arrow Books.

Hunt, J.C. 1985. "Police Accounts of Normal Force." *Urban Life* 13:315-342.

____. 1984. "The Development of Rapport Through the Negotiation of Gender in Fieldwork among the Police." *Human Organization.*

Katz, J. 1977. "Cover-up and Collective Integrity: on the Natural Antagonisms of Authority Internal and External to Organizations." *Social Problems* 25:3-17.

Klockars, C. 1983. "The Dirty Harry Problem." *Annals of the American Academy of Political and Social Science.* 452 (November):33-47.

____. 1984. "Blue Lies and Police Placebos." *American Behavioral Scientist* 27:529-544.

Lindesmith, A. and A. Strauss. 1956. *Social Psychology.* New York: Holt, Dryden.

McBarnett, D. 1981. *Conviction.* London: MacMillan.

McClure, J. 1986. *Cop World.* New York: Laurel/Dell.

Maines, D. 1982. "In Search of Mesostructure: Studies in the Negotiated Order" *Urban Life* 11:267-279.

Manning, P.K. 1974. "Police Lying." *Urban Life* 3:2830306.

____. 1977. *Police Work.* Cambridge: MA: M.I.T. Press.

____. 1980. *Narc's Game.* Cambridge: MA: M.I.T. Press.

____. 1988. *Symbolic Communication: Signifying Calls and the Police Response.* Cambridge, MA: M.I.T. Press.

Marx, G. 1988. *Undercover: Policework in America: Problems and Paradoxes of a Necessary Evil.* Berkeley: University of California Press.

Mills, C.W. 1940. "Situated Actions and Vocabularies of Motive." *ASR* 6 (December): 904-913.

Punch, M. 1985. *Conduct Unbecoming.* London: Tavistock.

Reiss, A.J., Jr. 1971. *The Police and the Public.* New Haven: Yale University Press.

____. 1974. "Discretionary Justice." Pp. 679-699 in *The Handbook of Criminal Justice,* edited by Daniel Glaser. Chicago Rand-McNally.

Rubinstein, J. 1973. *City Police.* New York: Farrar, Straus and Giroux.

Scott, M.B. and S. Lyman. 1968. "Accounts." *American Sociological Review.* 33:46-62.

Simmel, G. 1954. *The Society of Georg Simmel,* edited by Kurt Wolff. Glencoe: Free Press.

Skolnick, J. 1966. *Justice Without Trial.* New York: Wiley.

Stinchcombe, A. 1964. "Institutions of Privacy in the Determination of Police Administrative Practice." *American Journal of Sociology* 69:150-160.

Sykes, G.M. and D. Matza. 1957. "Techniques of Neutralization: A Theory of Delinquency." *American Sociological Review* 22:664-670.

Van Maanen, J. 1974. "Working the Street . . ." in *Prospects for Reform in Criminal Justice,* edited by H. Jacob, Newbury Park, CA: Sage.

____. 1975. "Police Socialization: A Longitudinal Examination of Job Attitudes in an Urban Police Department." *Administrative Science Quarterly* 20 (June):207-228.

____. 1978. "The Asshole." in *Policing: A View From the Street,* edited by P.K. Manning and J. Van Maanen, New York: Random House.

____. 1980. "Beyond Account: The Personal Impact of Police Shootings." *Annals of the American Academy of Political and Science* 342:145-156.

Waegel, W. 1984. "How Police Justify the Use of Deadly Force." *Social Problems* 32:144-155.

Westley, W. 1970. *Violence and the Police.* Cambridge: MA: M.I.T. Press.

Wilson, James Q. 1968. *Varieties of Police Behavior.* Cambridge: Harvard University Press.

Wilson, J.Q. and G. Kelling. 1982. "The Police and Neighborhood Safety: Broken Windows." *Atlantic* 127 (March):29-38.

JUDICIAL

Where the police are highly visible in the community, the opposite is true for the criminal courts. The media image of actors in the judicial arena is one characterized by frequent criminal trials, with each side battling for truth within an adversarial environment. Although this image may be true on occasion, it is not the way the adjudicative process operates in reality. Over 90% of criminal cases are officially disposed of by plea bargaining agreements that take place between the prosecutor's office and defense attorneys. Often these behind-the-scenes deliberations take a very short period of time, although not always, as one of the authors in this section points out.

Conducting qualitative research in courthouses, prosecutors' and public-supported defense attorneys' offices, and judges' chambers is no easy task. But studies conducted through painstaking observation and interviewing over lengthy periods of time has lifted the hidden operational process of decision making that, for most outsiders, has never been well understood. Ingratiating oneself with the courthouse work group and developing rapport for purposes of gaining entree over a sustained time frame is an absolute necessity if one is to be permitted to attain some degree of insider status. It is only by being there and witnessing firsthand the way criminal cases are handled can a researcher begin to formulate theoretical propositions that attempt to explain the informal judicial decision-making process that affects every criminal case.

The articles selected for this chapter represent qualitative approaches that analyze some of the most important issues facing the criminal courts today. The discretionary process of decision making of whether to prosecute a case or not and the decisions affecting guilty pleas remain controversial. Each actor involved in the plea arrangement is presented by a particular study. And although they may overlap somewhat, these articles provide a close-up opportunity for the reader to see and understand why the adjudication process operates the way it does. Social class and its effects on adjudication, the judges' role, and probation recommendations are inclusive in the qualitative approaches presented here. Although not completely comprehensive, I have chosen research studies that cover most of the important issues dealing with due process questions and the court systems' treatment of criminal defendants. It is through these field study efforts that we have come to better comprehend the practices of actors in our criminal courts.

Frohmann's analysis of prosecutorial discretion to reject a case from continuing beyond the arrest stage of the legal process is demonstrated by her ethnographic field study of the refusal of assistant district attorneys to prosecute certain sexual assault crimes. Two branch offices of a prosecutor's office in a metropolitan area on the West Coast provided the study site for this research. The author spent 9 months on a full-time basis in one study site and 8 months in the other. The data were collected from 17 months of observation of over 300 prosecutorial screenings of sexual assault cases in the two offices. Frohmann observed discussions between the police detectives and prosecutors, interviews with victims by district attorneys about the assault, and discussions between prosecutors regarding the filing status of the police report. Because tape recording was prohibited, Frohmann took extensive field notes. Open-ended interviews were conducted with prosecutors in the sexual assault units and with detectives who were assigned to sexual assault cases. All accounts of case rejections were collected and compared, which then were analyzed through the development of a coding schema. Frohmann's research provides a good example of observation over a long period of time at two district attorneys' study sites, together with extensive interviews with the decision-making actors in the legal system.

Based on data collected from 155 defense attorneys from nine felony trial courts, Flemming studied defense lawyers' thoughts about their relationships with the criminal clients they represent. Because he had preconceived ideas about what the study was attempting to explain, Flemming tailored his interview questions toward these ends. Here, as in a few previously discussed articles, the interview data were part of a larger research project that focused on justice in felony courts in nine medium-sized counties located in three states. Private attorneys, public defenders, and assigned counsel comprised this study population. Semistructured interviews were tape-recorded and analyzed. Flemming's participants consisted of 29 full-time public defenders, 34 part-time public defenders, 44 court-appointed attorneys, and 48 private lawyers over a 2-year period. Last, the reader will notice that Flemming uses two tables with quantitative data to illustrate information in numerical form. The use of both quantitative and qualitative data is used most often when the research population is large enough for comparative purposes. This study is representative of both forms of data analysis.

Emmelman's two articles in this judicial chapter demonstrate how two different studies can be completed while researching similar social phenomena. The first study examined the effects of social class on criminal case

outcome, and the second focused on plea bargaining as a recursive process for deciding whether a criminal case should be immediately settled or should proceed further into the judicial system. Emmelman began this 4-year project as a graduate student intern and law clerk with a private, nonprofit legal corporation that defended indigent criminal defendants. She studied a population of fifteen attorneys at one branch of the corporation by using a participant observation technique for 8 hours per week over a 4-year period of time. Because she was a student intern and law clerk, she was permitted to observe all behind-the-scenes interactions with defense lawyers, prosecutors, and judges in their working environments. In sum, she was accepted as an insider, which afforded her the opportunity to observe close up and gain firsthand knowledge of the informal operations of the criminal court process. She recorded extensive field notes throughout the study period, and she conducted in-depth interviews near the end of the project that were tape-recorded, transcribed, and analyzed.

This selection on plea bargaining and the socialization process that novice prosecutors learn to adapt to represents only one aspect of plea bargaining process that Heumann studied. His article comes from a book he wrote based on the experiences of all parties involved in the plea decision. Heumann collected data for this study by interviewing 71 crucial players in the plea bargaining process in six criminal courts of one state. They consisted of judges, prosecutors, and defense attorneys. Heumann also used observation, participant observation, and analysis of court records to supplement his interview data. He was permitted to follow prosecutors around on the job and was allowed to observe plea bargaining discussions after a sufficient period of fieldwork, which resulted in his acquiring insider status. This status applied to public defenders as well and provided him access to them for interview purposes. Heumann conducted this study while attending graduate school and, remarkably, was one of the first to view informal, behind-the-scenes workings of the criminal court that few outsiders have ever had access to: the plea bargaining process itself.

Drawing on observations of 236 criminal defendants over a 2-year period in a large city's guilty plea court, where cases are only resolved through nontrial dispositions, McConville and Mirsky present a most unique qualitative method for presenting their findings. Because they believe that it is not possible to present more than a small portion of their large body of qualitative data, they reveal the fundamental process of the guilty plea court operation by using a model case study of one criminal defendant to illustrate the normative case processing procedure of this judicial tribunal. By presenting an exemplary case, the researchers hoped to produce insight into the punitive process of discipline that this court metes out to criminal defendants. Although an unusual way to present a large amount of qualitative data, the authors, by utilizing a single case study approach, were able to capture the normative people-processing methods of a guilty plea court as well as provide an analysis of its true functional purposes.

Rosencrance offers an example of a researcher who worked in a probation agency, returning to it years later for study purposes. One great advantage of having experienced firsthand that which the researcher is studying is the previously acquired knowledge one processes about the organization, which should enable the researcher to better understand the functioning of the agency and the people who are employed in it. Here Rosencrance theorizes that probation officer sentencing recommendations are subordinate to that of the prosecutor, and that all of probation, functioning at this stage of the judicial process, is actually ceremonial at best. To study this theoretical proposition, Rosencrance interviewed probation officers who wrote presentence reports in two county probation departments and utilized his prior probation officer experience to analyze the data. Rosencrance points out that his prior job in probation greatly enhanced the interview process due to his ability to empathize with those officers he interviewed. He further conducted interviews with a number of probation supervisors and judges to ascertain their perceptions of how presentence reports were conducted. Last, Rosencrance explains how the utilization of the grounded theory method of data collection allowed him to remain cognizant of the effects his prior probation experiences could have had in biasing his data analysis.

Complaint filing is an extremely important stage in the prosecution of a case, for it is at this stage that the district attorney decides which cases will be filed for adjudication by the courts. Frohmann describes and analyzes the organizational dynamics of the district attorney's office, researching the ways in which sexual assault cases and victims are often made to feel devalued if their sexual assault case did not fall into a stereotypical norm and was rejected for prosecution. The author examined prosecutorial accounts for case rejection and the organizational structure of the district attorney's office in which decisions to not proceed with the filing of cases were made.

DISCREDITING VICTIMS' ALLEGATIONS OF SEXUAL ASSAULT

*Prosecutorial Accounts of Case Rejections**

LISA FROHMANN

Case screening is the gateway to the criminal court system. Prosecutors, acting as gatekeepers, decide which instances of alleged victimization will be passed on for adjudication by the courts. A recent study by the Department of Justice (Boland et al. 1990) suggests that a significant percentage of felony cases never get beyond this point, with only cases characterized as "solid" or "convictable" being filed (Stanko 1981, 1982; Mather 1979). This paper will examine how prosecutors account for the decision to reject sexual assault

*An earlier version of this paper was presented at the American Sociological Association, August 1990. I want to thank Jack Katz, Janet A. Gilboy, Elizabeth A. Stanko, Nancy A. Matthews, James A. Holstein, Timothy Diamond, Kate Gilbert, and the anonymous reviewers of *Social Problems* for their comments on earlier drafts. I am indebted to Robert M. Emerson for his reading of numerous drafts, ever insightful comments, and continuing guidance and support.

cases for prosecution and looks at the centrality of discrediting victims' rape allegations in this justification.

A number of studies on sexual assault have found that victim credibility is important in police decisions to investigate and make arrests in sexual assault cases (LaFree 1981; Rose and Randall 1982; Kerstetter 1990; Kerstetter and Van Winkle 1990). Similarly, victim credibility has been shown to influence prosecutors' decisions at a number of stages in the handling of sexual assault cases (LaFree 1980, 1989; Chandler and Torney 1981; Kerstetter 1990).

Much of this prior research has assumed, to varying degrees, that victim credibility is a phenomenon that exists independently of prosecutors' interpretations and assessments of such credibility. Particularly when operationalized in terms of quantitative variables, victim credibility is treated statistically as a series of fixed, objective features of cases. Such approaches neglect the processes whereby prosecutors actively assess and negotiate victim credibility in actual, ongoing case processing.

An alternative view examines victim credibility as a phenomenon constructed and maintained through interaction (Stanko 1980). Several qualitative studies have begun to identify and analyze these processes. For example, Holmstrom and Burgess's (1983) analysis of a victim's experience with the institutional handling of sexual assault cases discusses the importance of victim credibility through the prosecutor's evaluation of a complainant as a "good witness." A "good witness" is someone who, through her appearance and demeanor, can convince a jury to accept her account of "what happened." Her testimony is "consistent," her behavior "sincere," and she cooperates in case preparation. Stanko's (1981, 1982) study of felony case filing decisions similarly emphasizes prosecutors' reliance on the notion of the "stand-up" witness—someone who can appear to the judge and jury as articulate and credible. Her work emphasizes the centrality of victim credibility in complaint-filing decisions.

In this article I extend these approaches by systematically analyzing the kinds of accounts prosecutors offer in sexual assault cases to support their complaint-filing decisions. Examining the justifications for decisions provides an understanding of how these decisions appear rational, necessary, and appropriate to decision-makers as they do the work of case screening. It allows us to uncover the inner, indigenous logic of prosecutors' decisions and the organizational structures in which those decisions are embedded (Garfinkel 1984).

I focus on prosecutorial accounting for case rejection for three reasons. First, since a significant percentage of cases are not filed, an important component of the case-screening process involves case rejection. Second, the organization of case filing requires prosecutors to justify case rejection, not case acceptance, to superiors and fellow deputies. By examining deputy district attorneys' (DDAs') reasons for case rejection, we can gain access to what they consider "solid" cases, providing further insight into the case-filing process. Third, in case screening, prosecutors orient to the rule—when in doubt, reject. Their behavior is organized more to avoiding the error of filing cases that are not likely to result in conviction than to avoiding the error of rejecting cases that will probably end in conviction (Scheff 1966). Thus, I suggest that prosecutors are actively looking for "holes" or problems that will make the victim's version of "what happened" unbelievable or not convincing beyond a reasonable doubt, hence unconvictable (see Miller [1970], Neubauer [1974], and Stanko [1980, 1981] for the importance of conviction in prosecutors' decisions to file cases). This bias is grounded within the organizational context of complaint filing.

DATA AND METHODS

The research was part of an ethnographic field study of the prosecution of sexual assault crimes by deputy district attorneys in the sexual assault units of two branch offices of the district attorney's offices in a metropolitan area on the West Coast.[1] Research was conducted on a full-time basis in 1989 for nine months in Bay City and on a full-time basis in 1990 for eight months in Center Heights. Three prosecutors were assigned to the unit in Bay City, and four prosecutors to the unit in Center Heights. The data came from 17 months of observation of more than three hundred case screenings. These screenings involved the presentation and assessment of a police report by a sexual assault detective to a prosecutor, conversations between detectives and deputies regarding the "filability"/reject status of a police report, interviews of victims by deputies about the alleged sexual assault, and discussions between deputies regarding the file/reject status of a report. Since tape recordings were prohibited, I took extensive field notes and tried to record as accurately as possible conversation between the parties. In addition, I also conducted open-ended interviews with prosecutors in the sexual assault units and with investigating officers who handled these cases. The accounts presented in the data below include both those offered in the course of negotiating a decision to reject or file a case (usually to the investigating officer [IO] but sometimes with other prosecutors or to me as an insider), and the more or less fixed accounts offered for a decision already made (usually to me). Although I will indicate the context in which the account occurs, I will not emphasize the differences between accounts in the analysis.

The data were analyzed using the constant comparison method of grounded theory (Glaser and Strauss 1967). I collected all accounts of case rejection from both offices. Through constant comparison of the data, I developed coding schema which provide the analytic framework of the paper.

The two branches of the district attorney's office I studied cover two communities differing in socioeconomic and racial composition. Bay City is primarily a white middle-to-upper-class community, and Center Heights is primarily a black and Latino lower-class community. Center Heights has heavy gang-drug activity, and most of the cases brought to the district attorney were assumed to involve gang members (both the complainant and the assailant) or a sex-drug or sex-money transaction. Because of the activities that occur in this community, the prior relationships between the parties are often the result of gang affiliation. This tendency, in connection with the sex-drug and sex-money transactions, gives a twist to the "consent defense" in "acquaintance" rapes. In Bay City, in contrast, the gang activity is much more limited and the majority of acquaintance situations that came to the prosecutors' attention could be categorized as "date rape."

THE ORGANIZATIONAL CONTEXT OF COMPLAINT FILING

Several features of the court setting that I studied provided the context for prosecutors' decisions. These features are prosecutorial concern with maintaining a high conviction rate to promote an image of the "community's legal protector," and prosecutorial and court procedures for processing sexual assault cases.

The promotion policy of the county district attorney's (DA) office encourages prosecutors to accept only "strong" or "winnable" cases for prosecution by using conviction rates as a measure of prosecutorial performance. In the DA's office, guilty verdicts carry more weight than a conviction by case settlement. The stronger the case, the greater likelihood of a guilty verdict, the better the "stats" for promotion considerations. The inducement to take risks—to take cases to court that might not result in conviction—is tempered in three ways: First, a pattern of not-guilty verdicts is used by the DA's office as an indicator of prosecutorial incompetency. Second, prosecutors are given credit for the number of cases they reject as a recognition of their commitment to the organizational concern of reducing the case load of an already overcrowded court system. Third, to continually pursue cases that should have been rejected outright may lead judges to question the prosecutor's competence as a member of the court.

Sexual assault cases are among those crimes that have been deemed by the state legislature to be priority prosecution cases. That is, in instances where both "sex" and "nonsex" cases are trailing (waiting for a court date to open), sexual assault cases are given priority for court time. Judges become annoyed when they feel that court time is being "wasted" with cases that "should" have been negotiated or rejected in the first place, especially when those cases have been given priority over other cases. Procedurally, the prosecutor's office handles sexual assault crimes differently from other felony crimes. Other felonies are handled by a referral system; they are handed from one DDA to another at each stage in the prosecution of the case. But sexual assault cases are vertically prosecuted; the deputy who files the case remains with it until its disposition, and therefore is closely connected with the case outcome.

ACCOUNTING FOR REJECTION BECAUSE OF "DISCREPANCIES"

Within this organizational context, a central feature of prosecutorial accounts of case rejection is the discrediting of victims' allegations of sexual assault. Below I examine two techniques used by prosecutors to discredit victim's complaints: discrepant accounts and ulterior motives.

Using Official Reports and Records to Detect Discrepancies

In the course of reporting a rape, victims recount their story to several criminal justice officials. Prosecutors treat consistent accounts of the incident over time as an indicator of a victim's credibility. In the first example two prosecutors are discussing a case brought in for filing the previous day.

DDA Tamara Jacobs: In the police report she said all three men were kissing the victim. Later in the interview she said that was wrong. It seems strange because there are things wrong on major events like oral copulation and intercourse . . . , for example whether she had John's penis in her mouth. Another thing wrong is whether he forced her into the bedroom immediately after they got to his room or, as the police report said, they all sat on the couch and watched TV. This is something a cop isn't going to get wrong, how the report started. (Bay City)

The prosecutor questions the credibility of the victim's allegation by finding "inconsistencies" between the complainant's account given to the police and the account given to the prosecutor. The prosecutor formulates differences in these accounts as "discrepancies" by noting that they involve "major events"—events so significant no one would confuse them, forget them, or get them

wrong. This is in contrast to some differences that may involve acceptable, "normal inconsistencies" in victims' accounts of sexual assault. By "normal inconsistencies," I mean those that are expected and explainable because the victim is confused, upset, or shaken after the assault.

The DDA also discredited the victim's account by referring to a typification of police work. She assumes that the inconsistencies in the accounts could not be attributed to the incorrect writing of the report by the police officer on the grounds that they "wouldn't get wrong how the report started." Similarly, in the following example, a typification of police work is invoked to discredit the victim's account. Below the DDA and IO are discussing the case immediately after the victim interview.

DDA Sabrina Johnson: [T]he police report doesn't say anything about her face being swollen, only her hand. If they took pictures of her hand, wouldn't the police have taken a picture of her face if it was swollen? (Bay City)

The prosecutor calls the credibility of the victim's complaint into question by pointing to a discrepancy between her subsequent account of injuries received during the incident and the notation of injuries on the police reports taken at the time the incident was reported. Suspicion of the complainant's account is also expressed in the prosecutor's inference that if the police went to the trouble of photographing the victim's injured hand they would have taken pictures of her face had it also shown signs of injury.

In the next case the prosecutor cites two types of inconsistencies between accounts. The first set of inconsistencies is the victim's accounts to the prosecutor and to the police. The second set is between the account the victim gave to the prosecutor and the statements the defendants gave to the police. This excerpt was obtained during an interview.

DDA Tracy Timmerton: The reason I did not believe her [the victim] was, I get the police report first and I'll read that, so I have read the police report which recounts her version of the facts but it also has the statement of both defendants. Both defendants were arrested at separate times and give[n] separate independent statements that were virtually the same. Her story when I had her recount it to me in the DA's office, the number of acts changed, the chronological order of how they happened has changed. (Bay City)

When the prosecutor compared the suspects' accounts with the victim's account, she interpreted the suspects' accounts as credible because both of their accounts, given separately to police, were similar. This rests on the assumption that if suspects give similar accounts when arrested together, they are presumed to have colluded on the story, but if they give similar accounts independent of the knowledge of the other's arrest, there is presumed to be a degree of truth to the story. This stands in contrast to the discrepant accounts the complainant gave to law enforcement officials and the prosecutor.

Using Official Typifications of Rape-Relevant Behavior

In the routine handling of sexual assault cases prosecutors develop a repertoire of knowledge about the features of these crimes.[2] This knowledge includes how particular kinds of rape are committed, post-incident interaction between the parties in an acquaintance situation, and victims' emotional and psychological reactions to rape and their effects on victims' behavior. The typifications of rape-relevant behavior are another resource for discrediting a victim's account of "what happened."

Typifications of Rape Scenarios. Prosecutors distinguish between different types of sexual assault. They characterize these types by the sex acts that occur, the situation in which the incident occurred, and the relationship between the parties. In the following excerpt the prosecutor discredits the victim's version of events by focusing on incongruities between the victim's description of the sex acts and the prosecutor's knowledge of the typical features of kidnap-rape. During an interview a DDA described the following:

DDA Tracy Timmerton: [T]he only act she complained of was intercourse, and my experience has been that when a rapist has a

victim cornered for a long period of time, they engage in multiple acts and different types of sexual acts and very rarely do just intercourse. (Bay City)

The victim's account is questioned by noting that she did not complain about or describe other sex acts considered "typical" of kidnap-rape situations. She only complained of intercourse. In the next example the DDA and IO are talking about a case involving the molestation of a teenage girl.

DDA William Nelson: Something bothers me, all three acts are the same. She's on her stomach and has her clothes on and he has a "hard and long penis." All three times he is grinding his penis into her butt. It seems to me he should be trying to do more than that by the third time. (Center Heights)

Here the prosecutor is challenging the credibility of the victim's account by comparing her version of "what happened" with his typification of the way these crimes usually occur. His experience suggests there should be an escalation of sex acts over time, not repetition of the same act.

Often the typification invoked by the prosecutor is highly situational and local. In discussing a drug-sex-related rape in Center Heights, for example, the prosecutor draws on his knowledge of street activity in that community and the types of rapes that occur there to question whether the victim's version of events is what "really" happened. The prosecutor is describing a case he received the day before to an investigating officer there on another matter.

DDA Kent Fernome: I really feel guilty about this case I got yesterday. The girl is 20 going on 65. She is real skinny and gangly. Looks like a cluckhead [crack addict]—they cut off her hair. She went to her uncle's house, left her clothes there, drinks some beers and said she was going to visit a friend in Center Heights who she said she met at a drug rehab program. She is not sure where this friend Cathy lives. Why she went to Center Heights after midnight, God knows? It isn't clear what she was doing between 12 and 4 a.m. Some gang bangers came by and offered her a ride. They picked her up on the corner of Main and Lincoln. I think she was turning a trick, or looking for a rock, but she wouldn't budge from her story. . . . There are lots of conflicts between what she told the police and what she told me. The sequence of events, the sex acts performed, who ejaculates. She doesn't say who is who. . . . She's beat up, bruises on face and a laceration on her neck. The cop and doctor say there is no trauma—she's done by six guys. That concerns me. There is no semen that they see. It looks like this to me—maybe she is a strawberry, she's hooking or looking for a rock, but somewhere along the line it is not consensual. . . . She is [a] real street-worn woman. She's not leveling with me—visiting a woman with an unknown address on a bus in Center Heights— I don't buy it. . . . (Center Heights)

The prosecutor questioned the complainant's reason for being in Center Heights because, based on his knowledge of the area, he found it unlikely that a woman would come to this community at midnight to visit a friend at an unknown address. The deputy proposed an alternative account of the victim's action based on his knowledge of activities in the community—specifically, prostitution and drug dealing—and questioned elements of the victim's account, particularly her insufficiently accounted for activity between 12 and 4 a.m., coming to Center Heights late at night to visit a friend at an unknown address, and "hanging out" on the corner.

The DDA uses "person-descriptions" (Maynard 1984) to construct part of the account, describing the complainant's appearance as a "cluckhead" and "street-worn." These descriptions suggested she was a drug user, did not have a "stable" residence or employment, and was probably in Center Heights in search of drugs. This description is filled in by her previous "participation in a drug rehab program," the description of her activity as "hanging out" and being "picked up" by gang bangers, and a medical report which states that no trauma or semen was found when she was "done by six guys." Each of these features of the account suggests that the complainant is a prostitute or "strawberry" who came to Center Heights to

trade sex or money for drugs. This alternative scenario combined with "conflicts between what she told the police and what she told me" justify case rejection because it is unlikely that the prosecutor could get a conviction.

The prosecutor acknowledges the distinction between the violation of women's sexual/physical integrity—"somewhere along the line it wasn't consensual"—and prosecutable actions. The organizational concern with "downstream consequences" (Emerson and Paley, forthcoming) mitigate against the case being filed.

Typifications of Post-Incident Interaction. In an acquaintance rape, the interaction between the parties after the incident is a critical element in assessing the validity of a rape complaint. As implied below by the prosecutors, the typical interaction pattern between victim and suspect after a rape incident is not to see one another. In the following cases the prosecutor challenges the validity of the victims' allegations by suggesting that the complainants' behavior runs counter to a typical rape victim's behavior. In the first instance the parties involved in the incident had a previous relationship and were planning to live together. The DDA is talking to me about the case prior to her decision to reject.

DDA Sabrina Johnson: I am going to reject the case. She is making it very difficult to try the case. She told me she let him into her apartment last night because she is easily influenced. The week before this happened [the alleged rape] she agreed to have sex with him. Also, first she says "he raped me" and then she lets him into her apartment. (Bay City)

Here the prosecutor raises doubt about the veracity of the victim's rape allegation by contrasting it to her willingness to allow the suspect into her apartment after the incident. This "atypical" behavior is used to discredit the complainant's allegation.

In the next excerpt the prosecutor was talking about two cases. In both instance the parties knew each other prior to the rape incident as well as having had sexual relations after the incident. As in the previous instance, the victims' allegations are discredited by referring to their atypical behavior.

DDA Sabrina Johnson: I can't take either case because of the women's behavior after the fact. By seeing these guys again and having sex with them they are absolving them of their guilt. (Bay City)

In each instance the "downstream" concern with convictability is indicated in the prosecutor's talk—"She is making it very difficult to try the case" and "By seeing these guys again and having sex with them they are absolving them of their guilt." This concern is informed by a series of common-sense assumptions about normal heterosexual relations that the prosecutors assume judges and juries use to assess the believability of the victim: First, appropriate behavior within ongoing relationships is non-coercive and nonviolent. Second, sex that occurs within the context of ongoing relationships is consensual. Third, if coercion or violence occurs, the appropriate response is to sever the relationship, at least for a time. When complainants allege they have been raped by their partner within a continuing relationship, they challenge the taken-for-granted assumptions of normal heterosexual relationships. The prosecutors anticipate that this challenge will create problems for the successful prosecution of a case because they think that judges and jurors will use this typification to question the credibility of the victim's allegation. They assume that the triers of fact will assume that if there is "evidence" of ongoing normal heterosexual relations—she didn't leave and the sexual relationship continued—then there was no coercive sex. Thus the certitude that a crime originally occurred can be retrospectively undermined by the interaction between complainant and suspect after the alleged incident. Implicit in this is the assumed primacy of the normal heterosexual relations typification as the standard on which to assess the victim's credibility even though an allegation of rape has been made.

Typifications of Rape Reporting. An important feature of sexual assault cases is the timeliness in which they are reported to the police (see Torrey, forthcoming). Prosecutors expect rape victims to report the incident relatively promptly: "She didn't call the police until four hours later. That isn't consistent with someone who has been raped." If a woman reports "late," her motives for reporting and the sincerity of her allegation are questioned if they fall outside the typification of officially recognizable/explainable reasons for late reporting. The typification is characterized by the features that can be explained by Rape Trauma Syndrome (RTS). In the first excerpt the victim's credibility is not challenged as a result of her delayed reporting. The prosecutor describes her behavior and motives as characteristic of RTS. The DDA is describing a case to me that came in that morning.

DDA Tamara Jacobs: Charlene was in the car with her three assailants after the rape. John (the driver) was pulled over by the CHP [California Highway Patrol] for erratic driving behavior. The victim did not tell the officers that she had just been raped by these three men. When she arrived home, she didn't tell anyone what happened for approximately 24 hours. When her best friend found out from the assailants (who were mutual friends) and confronted the victim, Charlene told her what happened. She then reported it to the police. When asked why she didn't report the crime earlier, she said that she was embarrassed and afraid they would hurt her more if she reported it to the police. The DDA went on to say that the victim's behavior and reasons for delayed reporting were symptomatic of RTS. During the trial an expert in Rape Trauma Syndrome was called by the prosecution to explain the "normality" and commonness of the victim's reaction. (Bay City)

Other typical motives include "wanting to return home first and get family support" or "wanting to talk the decision to report over with family and friends." In all these examples, the victims sustained injuries of varying degrees in addition to the trauma of the rape itself, and they reported the crime within 24 hours. At the time the victims reported the incident, their injuries were still visible, providing corroboration for their accounts of what happened.

In the next excerpt we see the connection between atypical motives for delayed reporting and ulterior motives for reporting a rape allegation. At this point I focus on the prosecutors' use of typification as a resource for discrediting the victim's account. I will examine ulterior motives as a technique of discrediting in a later section. The deputy is telling me about a case she recently rejected.

DDA Sabrina Johnson: She doesn't tell anyone after the rape. Soon after this happened she met him in a public place to talk business. Her car doesn't start, he drives her home and starts to attack her. She jumps from the car and runs home. Again she doesn't tell anyone. She said she didn't tell anyone because she didn't want to lose his business. Then the check bounces, and she ends up with VD. She has to tell her fiance so he can be treated. He insists she tell the police. It is three weeks after the incident. I have to look at what the defense would say about the cases. Looks like she consented, and told only when she had to because of the infection and because he made a fool out of her by having the check bounce. (Bay City)

The victim's account is discredited because her motives for delayed reporting—not wanting to jeopardize a business deal—fall outside those considered officially recognizable and explicable.

Typifications of Victim's Demeanor. In the course of interviewing hundreds of victims, prosecutors develop a notion of a victim's comportment when she tells what happened. They distinguish between behavior that signifies "lying" versus "discomfort." In the first two exchanges the DDA and IO cite the victim's behavior as an indication of lying. Below, the deputy and IO are discussing the case immediately after the intake interview.

IO Nancy Fauteck: I think something happened. There was an exchange of body language that makes me question what she was doing. She was yawning, hedging, fudging something.

DDA Sabrina Johnson: Yawning is a sign of stress and nervousness.

IO Nancy Fauteck: She started yawning when I talked to her about her record earlier, and she stopped when we finished talking about it. (Bay City)

The prosecutor and the investigating officer collaboratively draw on their common-sense knowledge and practical work experience to interpret the yawns, nervousness, and demeanor of the complainant as running counter to behavior they expect from one who is "telling the whole truth." They interpret the victim's behavior as a continuum of interaction first with the investigating officer and then with the district attorney. The investigating officer refers to the victim's recurrent behavior (yawning) as an indication that something other than what the victim is reporting actually occurred.

In the next excerpt the prosecutor and IO discredit the victim's account by referencing two typifications—demeanor and appropriate rape-victim behavior. The IO and prosecutor are telling me about the case immediately after they finished the screening interview.

IO Dina Alvarez: One on one, no corroboration.

DDA William Nelson: She's a poor witness, though that doesn't means she wasn't raped. I won't file a one-on-one case.

IO Dina Alvarez: I don't like her body language.

DDA William Nelson: She's timid, shy, naive, virginal, and she didn't do all the right things. I'm not convinced she is even telling the truth. She's not even angry about what happened to her. . . .

DDA William Nelson: Before a jury if we have a one on one, he denies it, no witnesses, no physical evidence or medical corroboration they won't vote guilty.

IO Dina Alvarez: I agree, and I didn't believe her because of her body language. She looks down, mumbles, crosses her arms, and twists her hands.

DDA William Nelson: She has the same mannerisms and demeanor as a person who is lying. A jury just won't believe her. She has low self-esteem and self-confidence. . . . (Center Heights)

The prosecutor and IO account for case rejection by characterizing the victim as unbelievable and the case as unconvictable. They establish their disbelief in the victim's account by citing the victim's actions that fall outside the typified notions of believable and expected behavior—"she has the same mannerisms and demeanor as a person who is lying, and I'm not convinced she is even telling the truth. She isn't even angry about what happened." They assume that potential jurors will also find the victim's demeanor and post-incident behavior problematic. They demonstrate the unconvictability of the case by citing the "holes" in the case—a combination of a "poor witness" whom "the jury just won't believe" and "one on one, [with] no corroboration" and a defense in which the defendant denies anything happened or denies it was nonconsensual sex.

Prosecutors and investigating officers do not routinely provide explicit accounts of "expected/honest" demeanor. Explicit accounts of victim demeanor tend to occur when DDAs are providing grounds for discrediting a rape allegation. When as a researcher I pushed for an account of expected behavior, the following exchange occurred. The DDA had just concluded the interview and asked the victim to wait in the lobby.[3]

IO Nancy Fauteck: Don't you think he's credible?

DDA Sabrina Johnson: Yes.

LF: What seems funny to me is that someone who said he was so unwilling to do this talked about it pretty easily.

IO Nancy Fauteck: Didn't you see his eyes, they were like saucers.

DDA Sabrina Johnson: And [he] was shaking too. (Bay City)

This provides evidence that DDAs and IOs are orienting to victims' comportment and could provide accounts of "expected/honest" demeanor if necessary. Other behavior that might be included in this typification are the switch from looking at to looking away from the prosecutor when the victim begins to discuss the specific details of the rape itself; a stiffening of the body and tightening of the face as though to hold in tears when the victim begins to tell about the particulars of the incident; shaking of the body and crying when describing the details of the incident; and a lowering of the voice and long pauses when the victim tells the specifics of the sexual assault incident.

Prosecutors have a number of resources they call on to develop typification related to rape scenarios and reporting. These include how sexual assaults are committed, community residents and activities, interactions between suspect and defendants after a rape incident, and the way victims' emotional and psychological responses to rape influence their behavior. These typifications highlight discrepancies between prosecutors' knowledge and victims' accounts. They are used to discredit the victims' allegation of events, justifying case rejection.

As we have seen, one technique used by prosecutors to discredit a victim's allegations of rape as a justification of case rejection is the detection of discrepancies. The resources for this are official documents and records and typifications of rape scenarios and rape reporting. A second technique prosecutors use is the identification of ulterior motives for the victim's rape allegation.

ACCOUNTING FOR REJECTION BY "ULTERIOR MOTIVE"

Ulterior motives rest on the assumption that a woman consented to sexual activity and for some reason needed to deny it afterwards. These motives are drawn from the prosecutor's knowledge of the victim's personal history and the community in which the incident occurred. They are elaborated and supported by other techniques and knowledge prosecutors use in the accounting process.

I identify two types of ulterior motives prosecutors use to justify rejection: The first type suggests the victim has a reason to file a false rape complaint. The second type acknowledges the legitimacy of the rape allegation, framing the motives as an organizational concern with convictability.

Knowledge of Victim's Current Circumstances

Prosecutors accumulate the details of victims' lives from police interviews, official documents, and filing interviews. They may identify ulterior motives by drawing on this information. Note that unlike the court trial itself, where the rape incident is often taken out of the context of the victim's life, here the DDAs call on the texture of a victim's life to justify case rejection. In an excerpt previously discussed, the DDA uses her knowledge of the victim's personal relationship and business transactions as a resource for formulating ulterior motives. Drawing on the victim's current circumstances, the prosecutor suggests two ulterior motives for the rape allegation—disclosure to her fiance about the need to treat a sexually transmitted disease, and anger and embarrassment about the bounced check. Both of these are motives for making a false complaint. The ulterior motives are supported by the typification for case reporting. Twice unreported sexual assault incidents with the same suspect, a three-week delay in reporting, and reporting only after the fiance insisted she do so are not within the typified behavior and reasons for late reporting. Her atypical behavior provides plausibility to the alternative version of the events—the interaction was consensual and only reported as a rape because the victim needed to explain a potentially explosive matter (how she contracted venereal disease) to her fiance. In addition she felt duped on a business deal.

Resources for imputing ulterior motives also come from the specifics of the rape incident. Below, the prosecutor's knowledge of the residents and activities in Center Heights supply the reason: the type of activity the victim wanted to cover up from her boyfriend. The justification for rejection is strengthened by conflicting accounts between the victim and witness on the purpose for being in Center Heights. The DDA and IO are talking about the case before they interview the complainant.

DDA William Nelson: A white girl from Addison comes to buy dope. She gets kidnapped and raped.

IO Brandon Palmer: She tells her boyfriend and he beats her up for being so stupid for going to Center Heights. . . . The drug dealer positively ID'd the two suspects, but she's got a credibility problem because she said she wasn't selling dope, but the other two witnesses say they bought dope from her. . . .

LF: I see you have a blue sheet [a sheet used to write up case rejections] already written up.

IO Brandon Palmer: Oh yes. But there was no doubt in my mind that she was raped. But do you see the problems?

DDA William Nelson: Too bad because these guys really messed her up. . . . She has a credibility problem. I don't think she is telling the truth about the drugs. It would be better if she said she did come to buy drugs. The defense is going to rip her up because of the drugs. He is going to say, isn't it true you had sex with these guys but didn't want to tell your boyfriend, so you lied about the rape like you did about the drugs, or that she had sex for drugs. . . . (Center Heights)

The prosecutor expresses doubt about the victim's account because it conflicts with his knowledge of the community. He uses this knowledge to formulate the ulterior motive for the victim's complaint—to hide from her boyfriend the "fact" that she trading sex for drugs. The victim, "a white woman from Addison," alleges she drove to Center Heights "in the middle of the night" as a favor to a friend. She asserted that she did not come to purchase drugs. The DDA "knows" that white people don't live in Center Heights. He assumes that whites who come to Center Heights, especially in the middle of the night, are there to buy drugs or trade sex for drugs. The prosecutor's scenario is strengthened by the statements of the victim's two friends who accompanied her to Center Heights, were present at the scene, and admitted buying drugs. The prosecutor frames the ulterior motives as an organizational concern with defense arguments and convictability. This concern is reinforced by citing conflicting accounts between witnesses and the victim. He does not suggest that the victim's allegation was false—"there is no doubt in my mind she was raped"; rather, the case isn't convictable—"she has a credibility problem" and "the defense is going to rip her up."

Criminal Connections

The presence of criminal connections can also be used as a resource for identifying ulterior motives. Knowledge of a victim's criminal activity enables prosecutors to "find" ulterior motives for her allegation. In the first excerpt the complainant's presence in an area known by police as "where prostitutes bring their clients" is used to formulate an ulterior motive for her rape complaint. This excerpt is from an exchange in which the DDA was telling me about a case he had just rejected.

DDA William Nelson: Young female is raped under questionable circumstances. One on one. The guy states it is consensual sex. There is no corroboration, no medicals. We ran the woman's rap sheet, and she has a series of prostitution arrests. She's with this guy in the car in a dark alley having sex. The police know this is where prostitutes bring their customers, so she knew she had better do something fast unless she is going to be busted for prostitution, so, lo and behold, she comes running out of the car yelling "he's raped me." He says no. He picked her up on Long Beach Boulevard, paid her $25 and this is "where she brought me." He's real scared, he has no record. (Center Heights)

Above, the prosecutor, relying on police knowledge of a particular location, assumes the woman is a prostitute. Her presence in the location places her in a "suspicious" category, triggering a check on her criminal history. Her record of prostitution arrests is used as the resource for developing an ulterior motive for her complaint: To avoid being busted for prostitution again, she made a false allegation of rape. Here the woman's record of prostitution and the imminent possibility of arrest are used to provide the ulterior motive to discredit her account. The woman's account is further discredited by comparing her criminal history—"a series of prostitution arrests" with that of the suspect, who "has no record," thus suggesting that he is the more credible of the two parties.

Prosecutors and investigating officers often decide to run a rap sheet (a chronicle of a person's arrests and convictions) on a rape victim. These decisions are triggered when a victim falls into certain "suspicious" categories, categories that have a class/race bias. Rap sheets are not run on women who live in the wealthier parts of town (the majority of whom are white) or have professional careers. They are run on women who live in Center Heights (who are black and Latina), who are homeless, or who are involved in illegal activities that could be related to the incident.

In the next case the prosecutor's knowledge of the victim's criminal conviction for narcotics is the resource for formulating an ulterior motive. This excerpt was obtained during an interview.

DDA Tracy Timmerton: I had one woman who had claimed that she had been kidnapped off the street after she had car trouble by these two gentlemen who locked her in a room all night and had repeated intercourse with her. Now she was on a cocaine diversion [a drug treatment program where the court places persons convicted of cocaine possession instead of prison], and these two guy's stories essentially were that the one guy picked her up, they went down and got some cocaine, had sex in exchange for the cocaine, and the other guy comes along and they are all having sex and all doing cocaine. She has real reason to lie, she was doing cocaine, and because she has then violated the terms of her diversion and is now subject to criminal prosecution for her possession of cocaine charge. She is also supposed to be in a drug program which she has really violated, so this is her excuse and her explanation to explain why she has fallen off her program. (Bay City)

The prosecutor used the victim's previous criminal conviction for cocaine and her probation conditions to provide ulterior motives for her rape allegation—the need to avoid being violated on probation for the possession of cocaine and her absence from a drug diversion program. She suggests that the allegation made by the victim was false.

Prosecutors develop the basis for ulterior motives from the knowledge they have of the victim's personal life and criminal connections. They create two types of ulterior motives, those that suggest the victim made a false rape complaint and those that acknowledge the legitimacy of the complaint but discredit the account because of its unconvictability. In the accounts prosecutors give, ulterior motives for case rejection are supported with discrepancies in victims' accounts and other practitioners' knowledge.

CONCLUSION

Case filing is a critical stage in the prosecutorial process. It is here that prosecutors decide which instances of alleged victimization will be forwarded for adjudication by the courts. A significant percentage of sexual assault cases are rejected at this stage. This research has examined prosecutorial accounts for case rejection and the centrality of victim discreditability in those accounts. I have elucidated the techniques of case rejection (discrepant accounts and ulterior motives), the resources prosecutors use to develop these techniques (official reports and records, typifications of rape-relevant behavior, criminal connections, and knowledge of a victim's personal life), and how these resources are used to discredit victim's allegations of sexual assault.

This examination has also provided the beginnings of an investigation into the logic and organization of prosecutor's decisions to reject/accept cases for prosecution. The research suggests that prosecutors are orienting to a "downstream" concern with convictability. They are constantly "in dialogue with" anticipated defense arguments and anticipated judge and juror responses to case testimony. These dialogues illustrate the intricacy of prosecutorial decision-making. They make visible how prosecutors rely on assumptions about relationships, gender, and sexuality (implicit in this analysis, but critical and requiring of specific and explicit attention) in complaint filing of sexual assault cases. They also make evident how the processes of distinguishing truths from untruths and the practical concerns of trying cases are central to these decisions. Each of these issues, in all its complexity, needs to be examined if we are to understand the logic and organization of filing sexual assault cases.

The organizational logic unveiled by these accounts has political implications for the prosecution of sexual assault crimes. These implications are particularly acute for acquaintance rape situations. As I have shown, the typification of normal heterosexual relations plays an important role in assessing these cases, and case conviction is key to filing cases. As noted by DDA William Nelson: "There is a difference between believing a woman was assaulted and being able to get a conviction in court." Unless we are able to challenge the assumptions on which these typification are based, many cases of rape will never get beyond the filing process because of unconvictability.

NOTES

1. To protect the confidentiality of the people and places studied, pseudonyms are used throughout this article.

2. The use of practitioners' knowledge to inform decision making is not unique to prosecutors. For example, such practices are found among police (Bittner 1967; Rubinstein 1973), public defenders (Sudnow 1965), and juvenile court officials (Emerson 1969).

3. Unlike the majority of rape cases I observed, this case had a male victim. Due to lack of data, I am unable to tell if this made him more or less credible in the eyes of the prosecutor and police.

REFERENCES

Bittner, Egon A. 1967 "The police on skid-row: A study of peace keeping." American Sociological Review 32:699-715.

Boland, Barbara, Catherine H. Conly, Paul Mahanna, Lynn Warner, and Ronald Sones. 1990 The Prosecution of Felony Arrests, 1987. Washington, D.C.: Bureau of Justice Statistics, U.S. Department of Justice.

Chandler, Susan M., and Martha Torney. 1981 "The decision and the processing of rape victims through the criminal justice system." California Sociologist 4:155-69.

Emerson, Robert M. 1969 Judging Delinquents: Context and Process in Juvenile Court. Chicago: Aldine Publishing Co.

Emerson, Robert M., and Blair Paley. Forthcoming "Organizational horizons and complaint-filing." In The Uses of Discretion, ed. Keith Hawkins. Oxford: Oxford University Press.

Garfinkel, Harold. 1984 Studies in Ethnomethodology. Cambridge, Eng.: Polity Press.

Glaser, Barney, and Anselm Strauss. 1967 The Discovery of Grounded Theory. Chicago: Aldine Publishing Co.

Holmstrom, Lynda Lytle, and Ann Wolbert Burgess. 1983 The Victim of Rape: Institutional Reactions. New Brunswick, N.J.: Transaction Books.

Kerstetter, Wayne A. 1990 "Gateway to justice: Police and prosecutorial response to sexual assaults against women." Journal of Criminal Law and Criminology 81:267-313.

Kerstetter, Wayne A., and Barrik Van Winkle. 1990 "Who decides? A study of the complainant's decision to prosecute in rape cases." Criminal Justice and Behavior 17:268-83.

LaFree, Gary D. 1980 "Variables affecting guilty pleas and convictions in rape cases: Toward a social theory of rape processing." Social Forces 58:833-50.

LaFree, Gary D. 1981 "Official reactions to social problems: Police decisions in sexual assault cases." Social Problems 28:582-94.

LaFree, Gary D. 1989 Rape and Criminal Justice: The Social Construction of Sexual Assault. Belmont, Calif.: Wadsworth Publishing Co.

Mather, Lynn M. 1979 Plea Bargaining or Trial? The Process of Criminal-Case Disposition. Lexington, Mass.: Lexington Books.

Maynard, Douglas W. 1984 Inside Plea Bargaining: The Language of Negotiation. New York: Plenum Press.

Miller, Frank. 1970 Prosecution: The Decision to Charge a Suspect with a Crime. Boston: Little, Brown.

Neubauer, David. 1974 Criminal Justice in Middle America. Morristown, N.J.: General Learning Press.

Rose, Vicki M., and Susan C. Randall. 1982 "The impact of investigator perceptions of victim legitimacy on the processing of rape/sexual assault cases." Symbolic Interaction 5:23-36.

Rubinstein, Jonathan. 1973 City Police. New York: Farrar, Straus & Giroux.

Scheff, Thomas. 1966 Being Mentally Ill: A Sociological Theory. Chicago: Aldine Publishing Co.

Stanko, Elizabeth A. 1980 "These are the cases that try themselves: An examination of the extra-legal criteria in felony case processing." Presented at the Annual Meetings of the North Central Sociological Association, December. Buffalo, N.Y.

Stanko, Elizabeth A. 1981 "The impact of victim assessment on prosecutor's screening decisions: The case of the New York District Attorney's Office." Law and Society Review 16:225-39.

Stanko, Elizabeth A. 1982 "Would you believe this woman? Prosecutorial screening for "credible" witnesses and a problem of justice." In Judge, Lawyer, Victim, Thief, ed. Nicole Hahn Rafter and Elizabeth A. Stanko, 63-82. Boston: Northeastern University Press.

Sudnow, David. 1965 "Normal crimes: Sociological features of the penal code in a public defenders office." Social Problems 12:255-76.

Torrey, Morrison. Forthcoming "When will we be believed? Rape myths and the idea coming of a fair trial in rape prosecutions." U.C. Davis Law Review.

Waegel, William B. 1981 "Case routinization in investigative police work." Social Problems 28: 263-75.

Williams, Kristen M. 1978a The Role of the Victim in the Prosecution of Violent Crimes. Washington D.C.: Institute for Law and Social Research.

Williams, Kristen M. 1978b The Prosecution of Sexual Assaults. Washington D.C.: Institute for Law and Social Research.

This study focuses on the relations between private- and public-supported criminal defense lawyers and their clients' attitude toward each of them, based on the attorneys' perspective of the relationship. Flemming found that public-supported defendants are more skeptical and less willing to accept their professional authority than are private clients and that public-supported attorneys need to take extra steps to gain cooperation from indigent defendants. The accountability of public defense lawyers is explored in relationship to the necessity for client control. Resolution for this attorney-client problem is accomplished through shared decision-making power between both parties.

CLIENT GAMES

Defense Attorney Perspectives on Their Relations with Criminal Clients

ROY B. FLEMMING

This article was prepared for presentation at the annual meeting of the Midwest Political Science Association, Chicago, Illinois, April 10-12, 1986. The research for this study was made possible by the National Institute of Justice (79-NI-AX-0062) and by the National Science Foundation (SES-8309609). The views expressed herein are those of the author and do not necessarily represent the views of the sponsoring agencies. The author also thanks the Institute of Government and Public Affairs at the University of Illinois for its hospitality and generous support as well as his collaborators, James Eisenstein and Peter F. Nardulli, on the larger project from which this study is derived.

INTRODUCTION

Lawyer-client relations substantially define the reality of law in society. It is through these

Reprinted from *American Bar Foundation Research Journal*, Spring 1986, 253–277.

interactions and encounters that the legal system takes on form and substance for both parties. What clients learn of the reality of their rights, the operation of courts, and the inner workings of the law, and whether they feel they are treated fairly or justly are all colored by their experiences with attorneys. By the same token, the satisfactions and disappointments, financial rewards and social returns of lawyering strongly reflect the kinds of clients attorneys represent. Moreover, as professionals, lawyers presumably have considerable latitude in choosing how to relate to clients, raising concerns over their accountability to clients and equal treatment of them.

The social preconditions for traditional lawyer-client relationships that putatively foster accountability are often missing in the practice of criminal law, however. Criminal clients express deep misgivings about attorneys assigned to them by courts, reactions to a policy reform not anticipated at the time of its adoption. While attention to the client's or defendant's perspective on attorneys has not languished for this reason, the attorney's view of clients has been neglected. And, yet, a fuller understanding of this relationship obviously demands an exploration of the attorney's side. This study takes this tack and looks at how attorneys feel they are seen by their clients and the implications of client reactions for how they practice criminal law. In this sense it adds another dimension toward a more complete view of the professional behavior of criminal attorneys, a dimension that stresses the difference between public and private clients in affecting the accountability or, at least, responsiveness of attorneys to their clients.

Skepticism about the accountability of criminal defense attorneys is not a new concern. Some 20 years ago Blumberg described the private practice of criminal law as a "confidence game."[1] The intangible quality of the attorney's work, the concern over fees, and the need to prepare clients for guilty pleas or trial convictions while satisfying the interests of the court system all came together as ingredients in this game. A few years later, however, it became clear that clients distrust their public defenders and court-appointed attorneys and hold them in low esteem. Casper neatly captured their views and caught the tone of subsequent studies with the title of his seminal article, "Did You Have a Lawyer When You Went to Court? No, I Had a Public Defender."[2] A rather substantial body of research agrees that in contrast with their attitudes toward privately retained attorneys, criminal defendants see publicly paid and assigned counsel as part of the "system"—overly eager to plead them guilty, disinclined to give them much time, and little concerned about their welfare.[3]

Doubts about a lawyer's professional skills and fears of not being faithfully represented raise questions about the attorney's role as described in Blumberg's "confidence game." For what kind of game is it if clients do not trust their attorneys? And how do lawyers cope with this problem? Without the aura of professional legitimacy, do they dominate their clients to the degree found in civil cases? And how do they gain control of them?[4] When faced with these problems plus the social, racial, and economic differences that usually separate them from criminal defendants, how can they function as "translators" of their needs as they apparently do in civil matters, where the social gap between lawyer and client is often narrower?[5]

This study offers answers to these questions. Specifically it reports how attorneys feel they are viewed by their clients, how they try to develop working relationships with them, and what roles they think are most useful in dealing with criminal clients. Interviews with 155 defense attorneys provide the data for this study, and excerpts are presented to establish their concerns and views. The study concludes by placing the defense attorney's relations with criminal clients in a perspective that extends and revises Blumberg's notion of a "confidence game" between attorneys and their clients to show how attorney accountability arises in a situation characterized by mistrust.

The interviews were conducted as part of a larger research project on felony justice in nine medium-sized counties located in three states.[6] The attorneys, almost all of whom were white males, were "regulars": they generally handled substantial portions of the local circuit court felony caseload in the period centering around 1980-81 as public defenders, assigned counsel, or private attorneys. Because of their pivotal positions in the courts, sizeable caseloads, and usually long tenure in the jurisdictions, they were well-versed, knowledgeable informants. The interviews were semi-structured, recorded, and covered a variety of topics; this study draws on those segments dealing with their encounters with clients.

Overall, 29 full-time public defenders, 34 part-time defenders, 44 court-appointed or -assigned attorneys, and 48 private attorneys were interviewed. The value of including the latter three groups of attorneys is that they had experience with both public and private clients. Table 1 indicates the number of attorneys interviewed, their practice type, and the proportion of the sampled felony cases they handled in each court. This table also shows the proportions of the sampled cases in the nine courts in which defendants were assigned to an attorney by the court or through a public defender's office. As these proportions indicate, public clients often constitute a large proportion of the local felony caseloads in the courts.

PROBLEMATICAL
AUTHORITY AND PUBLIC CLIENTS

Attorneys with public clients labor in the shadow of the "public defender" stereotype. Whether they actually work as public defenders makes no difference; their clients give them little respect and distrust them. A sampling of the attorneys' comments illustrates their problem.[7]

The standard joke around this county is, "Do you want a public defender or a real attorney?" (1303)

* * * * *

Well, I think the general impression is, "I don't have the money to hire a real attorney, so I have you." We get a lot of that. (3303)

* * * * *

A lot of times they don't respect you as an attorney because you accepted this court appointment, and that creates a problem. (6437)

* * * * *

It's very tough being an appointed defense attorney. I think a lot of the clients . . . really don't trust you. (5419)

* * * * *

They think because you're free, you're no good. (2306)

* * * * *

Because you're part of the system, your indigent client doesn't trust you. (6451)

Public clients have doubts about the status of their lawyers, are skeptical about their skills as advocates, and are worried about whose side the lawyers are on. These attitudes complicate the attorneys' work. They cannot assume their clients respect them professionally, and they do not presume that they have their trust or confidence. Thus, perhaps even before procedural or substantive issues can be thrashed out, attorneys need to establish relationships with public clients that will quiet their qualms. Attorneys with private clients run into these problems less often.

Private clients accept that you are going to do a good job or you know what you're doing. Public defender clients have no idea where you come from; no idea of your background, no idea of whether you've ever done another criminal case in your life. (2303)

* * * * *

A guy that comes in here and pays $5,000 in cash wants to believe you're good, I guess. He handles you with a lot of respect and is less likely to call you everyday with some bullshit question. He's more likely to treat you as you want to be treated as an attorney, that you're representing him as best as you can, and you have his interests in mind always. (6437)

A third attorney explained why he refused to take any further public defender cases after a client questioned his professional judgment.

Well, I like to be my own man, and I was assigned to represent this black man who was caught stone cold in a robbery. I filed a habeas corpus petition, and I took it over to him to show him.

He said, "Not good enough, man." It was fine. It was enough to get me where I wanted to go. It was fine. So I said, "Well, why don't you do this? Why don't you go to law school and learn? And then take my petition and stick it up your ass." I quit. That was the end of it.

I certainly believe you should take your client's interest to heart and do the best job you

Table 1   Characteristics of Interviewed Attorneys and Trial Court Caseloads

	Illinois			Michigan			Pennsylvania		
Type of Lawyer	*DuPage*	*Peoria*	*St.Clair*	*Oakland*	*Kalamazoo*	*Saginaw*	*Montgomery*	*Dauphin*	*Erie*
Public defender Full time	6	–	6	–	–	–	2	10	5
Part time	2	6	3	–	–	–	15	–	8
Court-appointed or private attorney	14	8	10	19	12	13	4	6	6
Total	**22**	**14**	**19**	**19**	**12**	**13**	**21**	**16**	**19**
Proportion of cases handled by interviewed attorneys	36.1%	66.6%	55.7%	18.6%	74.3%	26.8%	24.5%	59.1%	47.6%
Proportion of all sampled cases with public clients	41.6%	70.0%	51.6%	56.2%	79.0%	73.1%	26.5%	47.0%	43.8%
No. of sampled felony cases	649	930	996	900	681	650	673	1,063	588

possibly can, but I'm not going to have some idiot tell me that my paperwork is wrong when it's not. (9427)

Client disrespect dismays and irritates attorneys; it sours associations with clients and makes the job less pleasant. A public defender (1303) complained, "It's frustrating to have to constantly sell yourself" to clients. Moreover, the etiquette of normal client-professional relations seems weaker to public attorneys who find that their clients or family and friends freely criticize them and treat them cavalierly. When asked what makes their work unsatisfying, attorneys often point to their public clients.

Sometimes we aren't treated the best by our clients. . . . I had someone this morning whose father was yelling about how bad the public defender was right when I was appointed. That wasn't exactly thrilling. (1302)

* * * * *

I think my dissatisfaction with being a public defender is that the people don't appreciate you. They figure they have a right to an attorney, and you can't really say, "Hey, look. Take a hike. Just get out of here. I don't want to talk to you anymore." There really is a lot of personal abuse, a lot of stuff that gets on my nerves. (3310)

* * * * *

They tend to feel that since they're getting a lawyer for free that they sometimes can be abusive if that's their personality. (2306)

Mistrust compounds these problems. According to an attorney (6451) who represented both kinds of clients, public clients see him as part of the courthouse machinery: "They just figure that if the prosecutor is part of the system, the judge is part of the system; then, as an attorney, you're part of the system too." Another also said his public clients think he would work more diligently if he were retained. Allaying their suspicions took time and patience: "In three-quarters of the cases, there is an immediate skepticism where they say, 'Well, I suppose if I were paying you, you'd probably be cutting a little better deal.' Or, 'I suppose if I were paying, you wouldn't hesitate to go dig these witnesses up.' Overcoming their skepticism is a very slow process" (4410). Such

anxieties, a public defender (3310) stated, "just put that much more pressure on you when you can't get along with the person." They also stymie communication between attorneys and their clients.

I had one guy who told me, "I don't like public defenders. All they do is plea bargain. They don't protect your interests." And it was obvious to me that no matter what I said to this guy, he wasn't gonna listen to me. And he was stuck with me, and I was stuck with him. (9307)

* * * * *

One guy wouldn't even talk to me when I went into the jail. He wouldn't tell me his name or his birth date. "Because you're the public defender, I'm not talking to you." So, we do have problems with that. (3303)

Distrust undermines the chances for cooperation. "Because they think you're part of the system, you end up doing all the worrying, you end up doing all the scrambling around, and your client could really care less," an attorney (6451) quoted earlier concluded. Another (2303) said a "prime frustration" in representing public clients was the feeling that "basically you're out there by yourself because you don't have a client along with you." Finally, trust matters because disgruntled clients can make trouble for attorneys later on. The prospects of facing grievances or appeals loom too large for an attorney to shrug off a client's distrust.

Doing so much appointed work, you've got to really cover your rear end. These guys, if they're gonna turn on anybody when nothing else is left, they're gonna turn on you. (5519)

* * * * *

I have to watch myself more with a public defender case because I can't kick the guy out. And if I am nasty to him, he'll complain and make my life miserable later. So I swallow my pride a lot more with a public defender case. (9324)

Attorneys see client disrespect and mistrust as inherent to indigent defense systems. Few mentioned that racial or class differences impede empathy or communication. Still, one attorney (2303) confided, "I don't really identify with my clients. I'm not from that level of society." Three others also commented on this problem.

> I'm an attorney, live in a nice neighborhood. I'm white. I don't know whether the black defendant in particular trusts me as much as he would a black lawyer. (5406)

* * * * *

> In a lot of ways our clientele is our worst enemy. . . . We get quite a few poverty cases in here. Guys come in, they're on welfare. You sit down and work with them. You say, "You're going to trial. I want you dressed like you're going to church." Because I've had guys come in for trial dressed in T-shirts. I say, "Hey, are you crazy?" It's really difficult for me to comprehend. (9304)

* * * * *

> It seems that most attorneys, a lot of them, are dealing with appointed cases. . . . The defendants maybe are repulsive people. They may not even like these guys, but they're representing them. And it's difficult for them. (6437)

Attorneys' perceptions of public clients do not rest on vague, unsubstantiated notions that the grass is greener on the private side of the legal fence; many handled both kinds of clients, and their perceptions corresponded with those of attorneys who had never practiced privately. Attorneys' experience of day-to-day defense work, then, divides sharply according to this public-private dimension and may be underlined by racial or class differences. Attorneys find publicly assigned clients to be more skeptical, less deferential, and less trusting. These perceived qualities are more than mere irritations or inconveniences for attorneys, however, because when they perceive an absence of client respect and trust, they feel that their professional authority is weakened. Consequently, as long as clients question or reject this authority, "client control" remains problematical.

CLIENT CONTROL: GAINING THE CLIENT'S RESPECT AND TRUST

The attorney's craft rests on knowing how to persuade clients who have the most to lose from tactical miscues or strategic errors to listen to them. When considering the stakes involved, an attorney (1310) admitted, "I suppose it's natural to feel like you want to be in control of your own destiny." Nonetheless, attorneys try to disabuse clients of this desire as well as of other misconceptions of their role. As one attorney (4412) put it, "I'm not gonna let any guy [client] tell me how to try my case. . . . So I think client control is a key." In addition, they drive home to them that they are neither novices in the courthouse nor naive about criminal defendants.

> A lot of these defendants are very street-wise, and they will try to manipulate the system and their lawyer. And they look at the lawyer as someone who is going to get them off, as opposed to protect their rights. And that's a problem. You have got to establish yourself from the outset with them, so that they don't take advantage of you. (3401)

* * * * *

> The problem most often is that they want to control their own case. . . . They have a hard time because most are incarcerated on felony cases, and they get a lot of jailhouse talk. I think the biggest problem is that they think they know all the answers. (1310)

* * * * *

> I've been through the system ten damn years, and I know the ins and outs. . . . And this schmuck doesn't know from nothing. He wants to run some bullshit by you. He didn't do it. Well, maybe he didn't. But in my experience there's damn few of them like that. When a dude just says, "I didn't do it," white or black, because they're too smart to admit to anything, you got problems. (4415)

* * * * *

> If you're slipshod from the beginning, he's not gonna trust you, he's not gonna do what you say. You've gotta develop trust as soon as possible, get control of the client as much as you can. It's still their decision to make, but they gotta trust you. And once they trust you then they'll work with you, and they'll tell you the truth. (8301)

Client control requires respect and trust for the lawyer. Without respect from the client, the attorney's advice or suggestions may be ignored. Without the client's trust, the attorney may not be believed; in turn, attorneys are not always sure if they can trust their clients. Once attorneys secure their clients' confidence, they can exercise their judgment and satisfy a desire for professional autonomy.

Spending time with clients, attorneys claim, can help win their confidence. Yet time, a limited resource, also carries opportunity costs. Time spent with clients favorably influences their reactions to attorneys, but its effects on case outcomes are questionable.[8] Moreover, client demands are not always reasonable and, because attorneys have no way of knowing in advance which ones deserve attention, time spent with clients may be wasted. Attorneys grow weary of listening to clients if what they say has little bearing on their case; moreover, indigent clients are often detained, which means visiting the jail—an unpleasant chore. Finally, because actions usually speak louder than words, the exchange value of time when purchasing a client's confidence is weak compared with what is gained when the client actually sees the attorney at work in the courtroom.

> The most common complaint of prisoners is that they don't see their attorney enough. The problem frankly is that a lot of the things they want to tell us are irrelevant. It depends on the client. But a lot of times they want to tell you things that are totally irrelevant to your presentation of the case. (1310)

* * * * *

> I don't know how it works in other public defender's offices, but you won't find people here running out to the jail to calm a guy down because he might have a question. More times than you'll just say, "Ah, shit, let him stew." The only time you see your client is either at arraignment or just before trial. Most of the time you have, maybe, one or two visits of no more than 15 or 20 minutes with your client. And they have to be wondering, "What the fuck is that guy doing?" (9321)

* * * * *

> There are cases where the stigma [of being an assigned attorney] is really strong and where they [the clients] think they're gonna get railroaded. I literally go out of my way to do things. I'll go out there and see them at the jail once a week if that's what it takes. And to be honest with you, I found that it's not all that successful. I think, if they distrust you, you can be out there every week, and, until they see you do something, you can sit there and talk with them every night for three months and it makes no difference to them. (4210)

"Being honest" also can settle client misgivings because, according to one attorney (4417), "The biggest problem with court-appointed counsel is the credibility factor. . . . So you go out to the jail, and you try to be up front and candid with him right off the bat." By extending candor, attorneys hope to purchase their clients' trust, honesty, and cooperation. This overture counters their suspicions that they will not be dealt with squarely. Moreover, by telling them what they think of their stories, what their chances look like, and how the case will be handled in court, attorneys flourish their insider's knowledge, which bolsters efforts to win the clients' respect as well. During these encounters, attorneys who are skilled at impression management take the opportunity to portray themselves as competent, concerned, and not easily fooled or buffaloed. As one attorney (5423) pointed out:

> You can waste a lot of time with criminal defendants unless they have enough confidence in you to skip all the baloney right from the beginning. I think that one of the ways to develop that kind of confidence is to present yourself in a manner so that they think that this time their court-appointed attorney may really know what he or she is doing.

Once again, however, client reactions reflect whether or not the lawyer is privately retained; attorneys believe that deference and honesty are inherent in relations with private clients but not with public ones. Still, regardless of the type of client, attorneys first feel them out so that they can adopt the right manner to elicit the respect, cooperation, and frankness they need.

Respondent: When I'm retained, there is a certain rapport immediately. That means that person paid me for my experience and my judgment. When I'm appointed to a case, generally there is no rapport whatsoever. So in an appointed case, the first that I have to do is establish that rapport and convince my client (1) I'm being truthful with him, and (2) I'm a good lawyer.

Interviewer: How do you do it?

Respondent: Well, sometimes you don't. It's difficult. A valuable way of doing it is by going to the jail to see your client ahead of time. But that's not always easily done, since you've got a law practice, and time and economics don't allow you to go to the jail and sit down with your client. . . .

I find it absolutely invaluable to be honest. I will not tell my client a fib. These people are far more intelligent than we generally give them credit for. Plus, they have a disbelief in what you're telling them; so if you're honest, you at least don't have anything to worry about. They check out everything you tell them. So you'd better tell them the truth.

And later on when I have to say to him, "Now, look. You make the decision, but here are your alternatives, and you know I've never lied to you." He at least will say, "Well, I don't like Mr. Smith, and I don't like what he's telling me, but the guy's always been honest with me." (5431)

* * * * *

Respondent: It's difficult to establish yourself with the client.

Interviewer: So how do you do that?

Respondent: Well, I think what you do is wait and see what the client is like. You look at the case before you go over and see him. Then you just start to feel the client out. Find out what his thoughts are. Review what his prior record is. And feel him out. If he's the kind of person who, because you're an attorney, is gonna listen to you right off the bat, then you have no problem. You can sit there and say, "Okay. Now this is what I think we should do." Boom, boom, boom.

But if you sit down and the guy starts throwing all kinds of things at you right away, then you just have to sit back and, again, it's hard to give a concrete method of procedure, but you have to determine whether or not this guy is being uncooperative, or is he just concerned with his case?. . . If he's just being plain uncooperative, well, then you've got another problem. Then you have to maybe speak a little louder, you know. Speak with a little bit more authority.

Interviewer: In well-modulated, middle-class tones, or what?

Respondent: I've been able to modify my vocabulary to the point where I can usually get the point across no matter who I'm speaking to. I know how to talk to them so that they know I'm not just some clown out of law school who doesn't know anything about what's going on. (9317)

"Client control" too bluntly describes the complex, often-subtle relationships attorneys try to arrange to gain their clients' confidence. Once it is established, they feel they are less likely to be surprised by a sudden balkiness or by unexpected revelations of something the client concealed from them. Again, this task is harder in public cases than in private ones, and it affects the manner in which attorneys approach clients when making decisions about the dispositions and handling of their cases.

STYLES OF CLIENT CONTROL: ADVISING AND RECOMMENDING

If attorneys prepare the ground well enough by giving clients time, frank assessments of their situations, and the impression they can be trusted, and if the clients respond by listening and offering to cooperate, the attorney's authority takes root in the nascent relationship. This social exchange nurtures and, in effect, legitimates their status with public clients, while with private clients, professional legitimacy generally accompanies the retainer or fee. In either instance, legitimation forms the basis for client control and allows attorneys to moderate their clients' demands and adjust their expectations to courthouse realities. The styles they use, however, range from a soft "advising" approach to a more forceful "recommending" posture,[9] with finer gradations in between. Advising can consist of simply listing the options facing clients and leaving the decision in their hands, or it can mean providing much blunter appraisals that, even without explicit recommendations, make the attorneys' preferences clear. Similarly, recommendations can be made in ways that give clients room to disagree or that present little more than a "take it or leave it" proposition.

A public defender described a situation that approximates the latter extreme of the recommending approach. With the plea conditions set before-hand, the lawyer relies on four factors to convince the client to take the plea offer: a lenient sentence (11 1/2 to 23 months in the local jail), the favorable reactions and support of his client's detained colleagues, the client's doubts about the fairness of the court, and the odds against getting a better sentence.

> Most times I've struck a deal before I even talk to my client. You know pretty well what the hell went on without talking to your guy. I think I've run across three people who I believe to be innocent since I've been here, and that's five years.
>
> If I get a good deal, then I'll go over to the guy, and I'll say, "Look, here's the way it is. That's the best I could get from the D.A. I think you ought to take it." And then I go over the case, you know, what the strong points are, what the weak points are, etc., etc. . . . And then I say, "11 1/2 to 23." The guy says, "No, man, I'm not going to do any time. I want to go to court. you know, I'm gonna take this up to the Supreme Court."
>
> So, you say, "Fine, are you prepared to spend 10 months in jail asserting your rights?" They aren't completely stupid, you know. They come around. I'll say, "OK, I'll see you tomorrow. Talk to your guys in the joint because they know what's good and what isn't."
>
> I never really pressure them per se, but I guess you could say that I use some influence upon them. Most of our people are black, and I think they realize they just really aren't going to get that great a shake out here. Either with the jury or with the judge. And most of our guys have street sense. They know what the hell is going on. (9321)

In contrast with this attorney, who exerts "some influence" and orchestrates his client's decision, others adopt a softer, more indirect "advising" style for reasons of effectiveness and professional ethics. As one of these lawyers explained

> I find that if they are actively involved at all points in the proceedings, they'll give you more help, you'll find out things about the case that you wouldn't have known. And it isn't so much that when they get into court that they're gonna balk at what happened or say "I didn't expect this to happen," it's just keeping them involved at all times is vitally important to your own role as a defense attorney. Also, I don't think it's ethically proper for an attorney to make decisions

for his client, especially in a criminal defense situation. (5404)

Attorneys generally prefer this lawyer's advising approach when representing public clients. An emphatic stance and urgent recommendations strain fragile relationships with wary clients and raise the possibility of problems farther down the road. As two lawyers quoted earlier mentioned, attorneys must "cover" their "rear end" and perhaps "swallow" their pride to avoid having public clients "turn on" them. Another attorney underscored the need for caution and the importance of letting public clients make the key decisions in their cases.

> Certainly I'm not gonna twist an arm. If anything, I'm very, very cautions with these guys. I was warned about that when I first took it over. Be very specific that any decision is their decision. Because a lot of times they'll plead, they'll go through it, they'll get sentenced. And they'll immediately say, "My attorney forced me into it." So you try to be very cautious. It puts the burden on them. (4411)

Some attorneys learn the hard way about advising public clients: they discover that even though recommending a course of action may seem more professional, clients may react strongly against what they see as overbearing attitudes. A headstrong style can provoke a client's anger, reawaken suspicions, and undermine an attorney's tentative authority. In private cases, where clients are more accepting of professional authority, attorneys feel freer to recommend what their clients should do, and they push more vigorously those dispositions they see as in their clients' interests. Being privately retained also means that if significant or unresolvable differences arise, clients can go elsewhere for an attorney. The odds, however, of clients switching attorneys after paying non-refundable fees or retainers undoubtedly are slim, and perhaps these "sunk costs" add to the clients' willingness to listen to and follow their attorney's recommendations. Nevertheless, for attorneys, the ability of their clients to go elsewhere for service (however chimerical it may be for private clients) represents a psychological escape hatch their public clients do not have at all. As a public defender concluded, the "psychology of representation" in private cases was "totally different" from that of private cases.

The longer you're [in the public defender's office], the more you get into the psychology of representation. It's totally different than private representation. In private you always have the threat of, "Look, if you don't want to follow my advice, go down the road." Here you don't have that luxury. . . . I think we've learned to deal with the type of client that we're dealing with. But, you know, if we're not dealing with a client who is willing to listen to us, we're not like the private bar. If the guys says, "I want you to file an X, Y, Z motion," you're gonna have to file it. (9318)

* * * * *

When I started, I found myself getting upset with my clients because they wouldn't settle, and I was just determined I was going to eliminate that. Now I don't force them to do anything. And I find if you put that burden on them and don't give them any reason to get pissed off at you, then they have to start thinking about this thing and making their own decisions. A lot of them turn pretty reasonable the morning of the trial. And, you know, I don't have that many problems with my clients anymore. (2303)

* * * * *

It used to be I would argue with a client on why he should take the plea. Now, somewhat to his disadvantage, I have said, "Screw him." I just thought, "Why get in an argument with this guy and really lean on him because I know he's gonna be convicted?" . . .

I'm not gonna fight with him and tell him he's gonna plead. Because over and over again you see cases in which the defendant is appealing. And one of the grounds is—"I told the lawyer I wasn't guilty, but all he ever wanted to talk about was how I should plead guilty to this charge." That's on appointed. Now in private cases, I will lean on him. That is the difference that comes out in a private case. If he doesn't like the advice, it's sure easy enough to hire somebody else. But on an appointed case it doesn't work that way. (5406)

* * * * *

If you walk in and say, "Mr. Jones, I want you to handle my case," then I will talk to you about the facts, I will consider all the alternatives. I will see what it's gonna take in time and money, and I will quote you a fee. And I will decide ahead of time whether or not I'm gonna be able to call the shots with you and if you're gonna listen to

me. . . . On an indigent case, I'm assigned by the court. I'm out of the blue, he doesn't trust me, he's not paying me, there's no rapport between us. I may have to try that case, even though it's absolutely deadly. (5431)

As a matter of style, if not substance, attorneys who "advise" public clients seek to impress on them that they sit in the driver's seat, that they are the arbiters of strategy in their cases. Two purposes lie behind this approach. First, advising invites client participation, or at least a *feeling* of participation that counteracts client apprehensions about being railroaded by an attorney. Second, by placing the burden for decisions on their clients' shoulders, attorneys hope to extract a measure of personal commitment to their decisions that will facilitate the handling of cases and forestall later complaints about their performance.

It is not easy to measure the effects of these two styles on case outcomes. Indeed, it may be preferable to view the quality or nature of relationships between attorneys and clients as dependent on "procedural" rather than "substantive" justice. Both Casper and Tyler, for example, offer evidence that perceptions of fairness—and not just the outcomes of their cases—matter greatly to defendants in appraising their treatment in court.[10] The larger study from which this study derived its data did not have information regarding the nature of attorney-client relations and client reactions to their attorneys on a case-by-case basis. Nonetheless, a useful purpose can be served by looking at three selected facets of how public and private cases were handled by attorneys in each of the nine courts. Table 2 compares the proportions of preliminary hearings held, mean or average number of due process-related motions (e.g., suppression of statements or exclusion of evidence) filed per case, and the proportion of trials in public and private cases.

In general, the data suggest that public and private clients were treated rather similarly by attorneys in these courts. With respect to preliminary examinations, statistically significant differences existed between the two types of cases in four of the nine courts. But after taking into account the severity of trial court charges lodged against defendants and their prior criminal

Table 2   Preliminary Hearings, Motions, and Trials by Type of Attorney

	Illinois			Michigan			Pennsylvania		
	DuPage	Peoria	St.Clair	Oakland	Kalamazoo	Saginaw	Montgomery	Dauphin	Erie
Preliminary Hearings Held									
Public cases	90.4%	34.1%	98.0%	58.3%	34.6%	73.1%	95.4%	71.0%	68.6%
Private cases	85.3%	41.8%	96.5%	69.8%**	48.1%	64.3%	95.4%	70.2%	66.5%
Attorney effect	-.09*	.05	-.04	.13***	.13***	-.08	.00	.01	.03
Mean No. of Motions Per Case									
Public cases	0.64	0.77	2.36***	0.43	0.20	0.46	1.16***	0.15	0.65***
Private cases	1.08***	0.69	1.56	0.43	0.52***	0.41	0.63	0.16	0.36
Attorney effect	.22***	-.04	-.23***	-.01	.19***	.00	-.09*	.02	-.07
Bench or Jury Trials									
Public cases	4.1%	5.4%	9.7%	4.1%	5.0%	4.4%	5.1%	8.6%**	8.5%**
Private cases	4.1%	4.1%	7.3%	4.5%	7.5%	7.1%	5.2%	4.0%	4.2%
Attorney effect	.02	-.02	-.03	.02	.06	.05	.04	-.09**	-.02

Note: Attorney effect is the standardized regression coefficient for the dummy variable "type of attorney," where 0 = public defender or assigned counsel and 1 = privately retained attorney, in a multiple regression equation using severity of the trial charge and criminal record of the defendant as control variables.

*$p < .05$ **$p < .01$ ***$p < .001$

records, the type of attorney mattered only in DuPage, where public defenders requested preliminary hearings more often than private attorneys, and in Oakland and Kalamazoo, where the pattern reversed itself and attorneys in private cases held these examinations more frequently than when they were appointed by the courts.[11]

A mixed pattern also exists for the mean number of motions. In five of the courts, no statistically significant differences emerged. However, in two (DuPage and Kalamazoo) private attorneys filed more motions than did attorneys with public clients; in two others (St. Clair and Montgomery), motion activity in public cases exceeded that in private cases after controlling for charge and record. In Erie, these control variables erased an apparent difference between types of attorneys. This also happened in the comparison of Erie's trial rates, so that no significant differences were found in eight of the nine trial courts. Only in Dauphin were public defenders significantly more likely to go to trial than were private attorneys.

To the extent overall patterns can be found in this table, Kalamazoo is one court where public cases apparently were handled differently than private ones were: In public cases preliminary hearings were less frequent, fewer motions were filed, and while not statistically significant, trial rates were lower than in private cases. However, St. Clair and Erie displayed reverse images of Kalamazoo, with higher, but statistically insignificant, preliminary hearing and trial rates in public cases along with significantly greater motion activity. For the remaining six courts, no consistent patterns emerged.

This short analysis is not definitive. Yet, when viewed in light of systematic, comparative analyses of the impact of defense attorneys on other measures of case outcomes such as sentencing, the evidence indicates that public clients do not fare more poorly in court than their peers who retain private counsel.[12] Although the sampling of attorney complaints about public clients clearly shows that their dealings with these clients are often contentious and at times disagreeable, with few notable exceptions in the nine counties, public clients are not treated in significantly different ways than are private clients. In this sense, attorney-client relations may be best viewed as part of procedural justice,

in which style, approach, rapport, attitudes, and perception define "fairness." Thus, in games between attorneys and clients, clients perceive fairness if they trust their attorneys and believe they have a say or voice in the handling of their cases.

CLIENT GAMES: CONCLUDING THOUGHTS, A PARADOX, AND POLICY QUESTIONS

This exploration of attorney-client relations in criminal cases relied on the comments of "regular" attorneys. The picture that emerges reflects their particular angle of vision and exposes only certain aspects of lawyer relationships with criminal clients.[13] For example, in their eyes, public clients were skeptical and uncooperative, but by the same token, some frankly admitted they did not give these clients much of their time. Thus, they stressed the resistance of public clients while downplaying their own actions or inactions that may have played a part in their clients' negative responses.[14]

Most also felt their difficulties with public clients were institutionally rooted in the fact that indigent defense systems rarely allow criminal defendants to choose their lawyers. This fact, when combined with the commonly held precept that "you get what you pay for," suggests that the public client's lack of trust and respect is neither peculiar to certain programs nor characteristic of particular kinds of clients. Instead, these responses are intrinsic to an involuntary relationship in which the client holds no readily available, easily employed, and culturally sanctioned lever to assure professional accountability.

The attorneys quoted in this study worked in a wide variety of settings. The indigent defense systems differed considerably from each other, for instance. Only Dauphin County had a traditional, full-time public defender office in which the attorneys could not practice privately on the side; Peoria used a part-time public defender staff; and the others had mixes of full-time and part-time defenders with different rules regarding private practices. As for the Michigan counties, Oakland and Saginaw used assigned counsel programs of different designs, but Kalamazoo had a contract-attorney system that closely resembled Peoria's program. These systems also followed varying operating practices; some, for example, had horizontal or "zone" representation, in which clients had different attorneys at each stage of the disposition process; others provided vertical representation, in which clients had the same attorney from beginning to end. Finally, without going into further detail, plea negotiation policies and customs as well as sentencing practices varied widely across these nine courts.[15]

The point here is that attorneys' comments about their relations with public and private clients revealed the same basic themes despite the many dissimilarities of policy and politics in the courts in which they worked. Casper found the same thing to be true for Baltimore, Detroit, and Phoenix, where relationships between client views and type of attorney held across the three different cities.[16]

A few attorneys felt that race and class affected their relations with public clients. According to the case data for the nine counties, 43.6% of the public clients were black, whereas the proportion of private clients who were black was 26.8%. It is also worth mentioning that public clients were more likely to have prior criminal records (59.0%) than were private clients (38.6%). Finally, 35.3% of the public clients were detained prior to trial, while only 10.7% of the private clients were in jail, a reflection of their different economic statuses as well as their criminal histories.

According to Casper, a prior criminal record, but not a defendant's race, has a consistent, eroding effect on defendants' views of public attorneys.[17] Incarceration also diminishes their trust. With the data available for this study, it is not possible to compare the effect of these factors on client behavior with the effect of the institutional factors that most attorneys offered as explanations for client behavior. Undoubtedly these factors combine and possibly interact with one another to exacerbate attorneys' problems with public clients. Although sorting out their relative impacts remains an unresolved problem, the literature provides little evidence that differences between public and private clients can totally replace the fundamental institutional reasons for client mistrust and lack of confidence.

Attorneys in this study say they generally "advised" their public clients, while they "recommended" what their private clients should do. Casper, however, found that most criminal defendants felt public defenders told them what to do instead of offering advice, giving information, or making suggestions. Defendants with private attorneys, in contrast, did not think their lawyers "muscled" them even when they insisted on something. Casper suggests these different views rested on more than just the attorney's behavior.

> The nature of the transaction between attorney and client provides a context for *interpreting* the behavior of the attorney. In part because the defendant (or his family) was paying the attorney, the whole tone of the relationship was altered. For example, insistence upon a particular course of action by a street [private] lawyer (e.g., pleading guilty, commitment for observation to a hospital) is interpreted differently by his client. Similar "advice" from a public defender might well be interpreted as giving orders, as telling the client what to do rather than discussing it with him. With a street lawyer insistent advice is only the lawyer's "proper" role and the exercise of the expertise that he is supposed to possess.[18]

Defense attorneys work in a social setting where expectations and interpretations of their behavior count as much as what they actually do. Their role, then, is symbolic as well as substantive because they need the respect and trust of clients before they enter the courtroom or do anything on a case. When combined with its intangible qualities, this inherently political side of lawyering produces, as Blumberg argued, a "confidence game" with clients. But it is a confidence game in the literal sense, since attorneys must win the confidence of clients who do not initially recognize or accept their professional authority before they can gain their cooperation. Client control, therefore, is a confidence game in which cooperation between lawyers and mistrustful clients is at stake.

Clients refuse to cooperate in various ways. Some have mild consequences for attorneys, others do not. For instance, attorneys said that public clients were discourteous or that they refused to talk to them, which made their work unpleasant and more arduous. An attorney lamented earlier that some clients were so alienated that "You don't have a client along with you," while another complained that attorneys "end up doing all the worrying" and "doing all the scrambling around" because "your client could really care less." Clients may also spurn advice or balk at suggestions, which not only increases the lawyers' work but threatens their reputation for client control within the courthouse community.

Deception, dishonesty, and a lack of candor are equally serious problems. Clients, especially public ones, were described as "street-wise," often manipulative, sometimes "too smart to admit anything," less than candid "at least 50% of the time," and reluctant to talk openly with their lawyer, according to one attorney (5425) whose remarks echoed those made by others.[19] The attorneys' difficulty is that evasion and deception can affect tactical and strategic decisions.[20] Mather describes a case in which a public defender went to trial at the request of a client who claimed she had no prior record. Expecting a sentence of no more than probation if she were found guilty, the defender went through a five-day jury trial that ended in a conviction. To his surprise the defendant's presentence report revealed that she had a five-year history of similar crimes. She was sentenced to the state prison. The public defender said his client "fooled everyone."[21]

By the same token public clients hold serious reservations as to how vigorously attorneys will represent client interests if it means sacrificing their own longer term interests within the court system—and the attorneys know the clients are thinking this. As one attorney (3310) put it, "You know, the scuttlebutt goes around the jail, 'Hey, the public defender, they get along well with the state's attorney. They're gonna send you down the river.'" And, as another (5406) explained, "If you say to an indigent client, 'I think you should plead,' and he doesn't want to plead, he'll say, 'See, that proves it. They appointed him to lean on me.'"

By substantial margins, defendants interviewed by Casper and others think public attorneys are less likely to fight hard for them and are more concerned about wrapping up their cases quickly than in getting justice; defendants also doubt whether public attorneys will be honest with them. Overwhelmingly, they believe private attorneys work for their clients, but that public attorneys do not.[22] Indeed, concern that defense attorneys are coopted by the court system has been a staple of contemporary research on defense attorneys. As "repeat players" with "oneshotter" clients, defense attorneys presumably rely on cooperative relations within the courthouse that would be jeopardized by aggressive advocacy.[23] More generally, Carlin suggested some time ago that "clients are expendable" whenever their lawyers do not depend on them for their fees or future business.[24]

Attorneys acknowledge how they are perceived. Thus, in their relations with clients, they are enmeshed in perceptions and expectations running along the lines of "If he thinks I am thinking of selling him out, he will not trust me even though I am not thinking of that, and if he knew this, he would go along with what I say." Attorneys fear their clients will not cooperate because they think they will be deceived. They fear deceit by clients just as much. Attorneys consequently fret over what kind of game their clients may be playing and whether they will find out soon enough to know if they should try to change their minds or take other precautions. As their comments amply suggested, however, attorneys make important distinctions between public and private clients.

Attorneys claim that because private clients pick them and pay them a fee, these clients respect and trust them, believe they are good, have faith in what they are doing, and are willing to accept a "certain rapport" so that matters can be discussed frankly. One attorney (5406) summed it up by saying, "There is a difference, I think, in the relationship—as far as openness and working together for the same goal—between being an appointed attorney and a retained attorney." Attorneys perceive private clients as generally more cooperative. Even if they encounter fee problems later on or discover a private client is less candid than they thought at first, they nevertheless see private clients as generally more trusting than public clients, largely because of the nature of their contractually based relationship. Private clients choose their attorneys, pay them a fee and, however remote the chance, can replace them. Similarly, attorneys can nip problems in the bud by declining to accept cases.[25] As a private attorney (9427) said, "I blow them out of here" if potential clients refused to heed his directions. In public cases, where this option is usually missing for both parties, a lawyer (3310) described the relationship as a "shot-gun wedding."

The ambivalence in attorney-client relationships is cleared away in private criminal cases because the retainer or fee reflects the attorneys' assessment of cases and how they should be handled. Consequently, clients have both an idea and a commitment from their attorneys about their intentions; at the same time, attorneys assume that the fees signal the clients' good faith. Neither expects deception by the other. In public cases, clients have no immediate leverage at hand to assure themselves that their attorneys will serve their interests and, indeed, see them as having long-term commitments to the courts, not to them. Attorneys sense this mistrust and wonder if their clients will cooperate with them. With no easy way of ascertaining, measuring, or purchasing each other's commitment, proclamations of honesty and dependability may be viewed as trying to pull the wool over one another's eyes. From the attorneys' perspective, public clients often act as if they need to avoid being taken advantage of by their attorneys or try to exert misguided efforts to take control of their cases. Their immediate problem focuses on changing these perceptions. Their task with private clients is much easier; the attorneys only have to keep their clients' confidence while making sure that they are not gulled by the appearance of client comity.

Because private clients come to attorneys in an apparently cooperative frame of mind, the attorneys' goal in this client game boils down to simply keeping their trust.[26] Because attorneys first must win the confidence of public clients, the game changes and is more involved. "You've really got to earn their trust," an attorney (5419) declared, but "sometimes you do, sometimes you don't." In attorneys' eyes, clients are the chief losers if they refuse to cooperate; but they also know from personal experience what clients suspect they might do to them under the guise of representing them before the court. Consequently, they face the

critical, interrelated problems of not only gaining their confidence but dispelling thoughts that they will desert them.

In this situation, where each side is skeptical of the other's intentions but mutual cooperation is required, attorneys can take the first step by "being honest" and by trying to assure clients that mutual trust is necessary. As an attorney (9307) warned, "If you get to a point where the two of you really can't talk with each other, you're both losing." In addition to being honest, visiting with clients and engaging in courtroom activities are "moves" in this confidence game. These moves give clients a chance to assess their attorneys' preferences and commitments. In turn, through these moves, attorneys try to rid themselves of the public defender stereotype so their clients can see that "this time their court attorney may really know what he or she is doing," as another lawyer quoted earlier said. This helps to counteract the effects of self-confirming labels that impede cooperation. The advising style also reinforces these moves, since it encourages clients to feel they have a say in the handling of their cases.

The decision to cooperate depends lastly on its rewards and costs. If clients believe that confiding in their lawyers will not penalize them, they will be more likely to cooperate. Sentencing weighs heavily in this equation. Client concerns and uncertainties over this issue offer attorneys another opening to persuade them to cooperate, since they are the ones with knowledge of what is likely to occur and the ability to do something about it. The attorney's chore is lightened especially if the client is faced with a lenient sentence on the one hand and the specter of more severe punishment for going to trial on the other. For the nine courts taken as a whole, nearly two-thirds (65.8%) of the 4,100 sampled cases that ended in guilty pleas received probation.[27] Defendants who went to trial and were convicted, however, fared worse—even after controlling for relevant sentencing variables.[28] First offenders less often received probation after a jury trial, and repeat offenders were sentenced more severely than comparable defendants who plead guilty.[29]

The mere threat of trial penalties probably eases the attorney's efforts. The prospect of more severe punishment, for whatever reason, usually chills a client's desire to go to trial rather than to plead guilty. Similarly, the price for deceiving an attorney may be a stiffer sentence if the client miscalculates and the deception is uncovered as in the case Mather described.[30] The upshot is that if attorneys succeed in convincing their public clients to trust them and persuade them to listen to them, they successfully convert the public client confidence game into something more like the cooperative game attorneys perceive to exist with private clients.

A paradox may exist in this confidence game between suspicious public clients and wary attorneys who are involuntarily joined in an association from which they generally cannot exit until the case is over. Rosenthal distinguished between "traditional" and "participatory" models of lawyer-client relations. In the traditional model, "the client who is passive, follows instructions, and trusts the professional without criticism, with few questions or requests, is preferable, and will do better than the difficult client who is critical and questioning."[31] Conversely, the participatory model stresses an active, skeptical client who shares the responsibility for making choices with an attorney who must be patient and earn the client's cooperation. Many criminal attorneys who handle public cases may prefer the traditional model, particularly younger or less experienced ones who are insecure about their professional status and react to questioning clients as though their self-esteem and pride were threatened; but with practice, others learn to adopt more participatory styles because of the suspiciousness of their public clients. The need to win their confidence means attorneys must persuade their clients that they can be trusted or else they may fail to gain control of them.

The paradox here is twofold. First, the mistrust public clients hold for their attorneys may force them to bow more to their clients' wishes than one might expect from folk wisdom or from arguments like Carlin's about "client expendability." Because of their clients' qualms, attorneys may find the advisory role more palatable, with the result that clients participate more actively in the progress of their cases. By including clients in decisions and restraining their own urge to make them alone, attorneys hope to prove that they are not trying to stampede their

clients into decisions contrary to their interests. The second aspect involves the involuntary nature of their relationship. The public client's reluctance to recognize an attorney's professional authority denies the lawyer a major resource in gaining the client's compliance and acquiescence, yet the attorney cannot refuse to handle the case as easily as one who is privately retained. The lawyer's overtures and advice also can be shunned, which threatens his or her reputation for "client control," and unless matters between them get totally out of hand, little can be done but to try again. This involuntary relationship means the client gains a measure of power in dealings with the attorney, a certain equalization of positions buttressed further by the client's ability to file grievances or appeal cases. Together these add yet other incentives to adopt the participatory mode—advising public clients about their options and letting them bear the responsibility for making decisions. The paradox, then, is that those things which irritate attorneys about public clients foster what many observers consider a more appropriate professional role, though clients evidently do not see it this way. They still prefer fee arrangements with private lawyers where, ironically, according to the lawyers in this study, more traditional lawyer-client relationships prevail because they have their clients' confidence.

The institutional basis of client estrangement from court-appointed counsel and public defenders calls into question the design of indigent defense policies. In all nine courts, felony defendants deemed to be indigent and eligible for publicly paid counsel had no say in the selection of their attorneys. In one court (Oakland), the judges appointed specific lawyers to handle these cases; in seven of the others (the Illinois and Pennsylvania courts plus Kalamazoo), the public defenders or contract attorneys allocated the cases among themselves; while in the ninth (Saginaw), a court official chose counsel to represent indigent defendants. In each instance, criminal defendants were expected to live with the lawyer assigned to them.

In the eyes of criminal clients, professional accountability hinges on a market conception and fee-for-service definition of lawyer responsibility. They place little faith in the notion that ethical concerns and feelings of professional obligation by themselves are sufficient guarantees that a lawyer picked seemingly "out of the hat" will adequately represent their interests. Post-conviction proceedings offer them something of a retributive stick, but by that time they already have paid a price for what they feel was mistakenly listening to their lawyers; moreover, the prevalence of guilty pleas removes many grounds for appeal and grievances. Stuck with their attorneys, and their attorneys stuck with them, they are caught up in a confidence game in which competing interests and the need for accommodation are resolved in ways that are not as self-evidently effective as choosing and paying a lawyer to represent them.

Given the finding of this and other studies that public clients fare no worse but are treated no better than private clients, the policy implications of client mistrust and disrespect reported by attorneys depend on (1) whether an equivalence of outcomes and attorney behavior is a satisfactory standard for evaluating attorney performance and (2) what weight is given to "procedural justice" in designing indigent defense policies. Comparisons of how attorneys treat public and private clients are necessary but limited indicators of substantive fairness because, while feasible, they also leave the criteria of accountability undefined. Equivalence in and by itself necessarily adopts the outcome of either private or public cases as a benchmark to gauge the other, without stating explicitly whether this benchmark might itself be too high or too low; indeed, it is likely that both are inadequate and that some other criterion is required.

Without alternative evaluation standards, and in the absence of readily apparent, substantive differences in the treatment of publicly and privately represented criminal defendants, changes in the provision of indigent defense counsel may seem unwarranted. Public client mistrust and the problems attendant on the assignment of attorneys may be viewed as the inevitable but nonetheless harmless consequence of an otherwise beneficent policy that, thus, can be safely ignored. A concern for procedural justice, however, suggests that the perceptions, reactions, and feelings of clients regarding policy and institutional arrangements ought to matter as much as substantive effects in prompting reform or change.

From this perspective, it can be asked whether indigent defense systems might be designed to allow criminal defendants to select their own attorneys. If organized along the lines of a voucher system, attorney fees and costs would still be paid publicly, but defendants could, if they wished, select an attorney from among those who wanted to represent indigent criminal clients. Indigent defendants with the freedom to choose might express fewer apprehensions about their attorneys. The disappearance, or at least amelioration, of these fears as public policy is brought into line with client conceptions may however weaken the apparent paradox that client mistrust fosters attorney accountability and client participation in public cases.

NOTES

1. Abraham Blumberg, The Practice of Law as a Confidence Game: Organizational Cooptation of a Profession, 1 Law & Soc'y Rev. 15 (1967).

2. Jonathan D. Casper, Did You Have a Lawyer When You Went to Court? No, I Had a Public Defender, 1 Yale Rev. L. & Soc. Action 4 (1971).

3. Jonathan D. Casper, American Criminal Justice: The Defendant's Perspective (Englewood Cliffs, N.J.: Prentice-Hall, 1972); *id.*, Criminal Courts: The Defendant's Perspective (Washington, D.C.: Government Printing Office, 1979); Glen Wilkerson, Public Defenders as Their Clients See Them, 1 Am. J. Crim. L. 141 (1972); Antoinette N. Hetzler & Charles H. Kanter, Informality and the Court: A Study of the Behavior of Court Officials in the Processing of Defendants, *in* Sawyer F. Sylvester, Jr., & Edward Sagarin, eds., Politics and Crime (New York: Praeger, 1974); F. Arcuri, Lawyers, Judges, and Plea Bargaining, 4 Int'l. J. Criminology & Penology 177 (1976); Burton M. Atkins & E. W. Boyle, Prisoner's Satisfaction with Defense Counsel, 12 Crim. L. Bull. 427 (1976); Geoffrey P. Alpert & Donald A. Hicks, Prisoners' Attitudes Toward Components of the Legal System, 14 Criminology 461 (1977); Stewart O'Brien, Steven Pheterson, Michael Wright, & Carl Hosticka, The Criminal Lawyer: The Defendant's Perspective, 5 Am. J. Crim. L. 283 (1977); Geoffrey P. Alpert & C. Ronald Huff, Defending the Accused: Counsel Effectiveness and Strategies, *in* William F. McDonald, ed., The Defense Counsel (Beverly Hills, Cal.: Sage Publications, 1983).

4. Carl Hosticka, We Don't Care About What Happened, We Only Care About What Is Going to Happen, 26 Soc. Probs. 599 (1979); Douglas E. Rosenthal, Lawyer and Client: Who's In Charge? (New York: Russell Sage Foundation, 1974).

5. Maureen Cain, The General Practice Lawyer and the Client, 7 Int'l. J. Soc. L. 331 (1979).

6. The counties were chosen on the basis of social, economic, and political criteria that produced diverse triplets of counties within each state while forming roughly comparable triplets of matched counties across states. There were three suburban "ring" counties that were primarily middle class and Republican; three "autonomous" counties; and three declining industrial, Democractic counties. More detailed information on the methods and scope of the larger project can be found in Peter F. Nardulli, Roy B. Flemming, & James Eisenstein, The Tenor of Justice: Criminal Courts and the Guilty Plea Process (Champaign: University of Illinois Press, forthcoming).

7. The numbers shown in parentheses after each interview excerpt are codes assigned to assure anonymity to each attorney.

8. Casper, Criminal Courts, *supra* note 3, at 83.

9. This distinction parallels the two meanings of "representation" identified by Skolnick: in one, an attorneys accepts a client's view of how the case should be handled and provides counsel as to how to implement the strategy; in the other the attorney takes the responsibility for both strategy and tactics. Jerome Skolnick, Social Control in the Adversary System, 11 J. Conflict Resolution 52, 65 (1967).

10. Jonathan D. Casper, Having Their Day in Court: Defendant Evaluations of the Fairness of Their Treatment, 12 Law & Soc'y Rev. 237 (1978); Tom R. Tyler, The Role of Perceived Injustice in Defendants' Evaluations of Their Courtroom Experience, 18 Law & Soc'y Rev. 51 (1984).

11. For a more detailed examination of the preliminary hearing decision in these nine courts, see Roy B. Flemming, Elements of the Defense Attorney's Craft: An Adaptive Expectations Model of the Preliminary Hearing Decision, 8 Law & Pol'y 33 (1986).

12. R. Hermann, E. Single, & J. Boston, Counsel for the Poor: Criminal Defense in Urban America (Lexington, Mass.: Lexington Books, 1977). An analysis of "regular" defense attorneys, their "styles," and their negligible impact on case outcomes and sentencing in these nine courts can be found in Peter F. Nardulli, "Insider's" Justice: Defense Attorneys and the Handling of Felony Cases (paper presented at annual meeting of Law and Society Association, San Diego, Cal., June 6-9, 1985).

13. For a discussion of the problems in more direct observation of lawyer-client interaction, see Brenda Danet, Kenneth B. Hoffman, & Nicole C. Kermish, Obstacles in the Study of Lawyer-Client Interaction: The Biography of a Failure, 14 Law & Soc'y Rev. 905 (1980); Douglas E. Rosenthal, Comment on "Obstacles to the Study of Lawyer-Client Interaction: The Biography of a Failure," 14 Law & Soc'y Rev. 923 (1980); Stewart Macaulay, Law and Behavioral Sciences: Is There Any There There? 6 Law & Pol'y 149 (1984). These problems may not be insurmountable, however; e.g., see Hosticka, *supra* note 4, and Cain, *supra* note 5.

14. Casper found that privately retained lawyers spent dramatically different, more extensive periods with their clients; 47% of 132 defendants with private lawyers said they saw their attorneys for more than 3 hours. In contrast, 59% of the 463 defendants with public attorneys reported that their attorneys spent a half hour or less with them. Casper, Criminal Courts, *supra* note 3, at 35.

15. See Nardulli et al, *supra* note 6, for further descriptions of the nine courts.

16. Casper, Criminal Courts, *supra* note 3, at 12.

17. *Id*. at 22-23.

18. Casper, American Criminal Justice, *supra* note 3, at 117-18 (emphasis in original).

19. In autobiographies of their work and careers, defense attorneys frequently bemoan their clients' lack of veracity. For example, Moldovsky states, "I know that clients lie to me . . . I just don't know which ones are the liars." Joel Moldovsky & Rose DeWolf, The Best Defense 76 (New York: Macmillan Publishing Co., 1975). Wishman also recalls, "It didn't take me long to realize that nearly every client had lied to me." Seymour Wishman, Confessions of a Criminal Lawyer 81 (New York: Times Books, 1981). Finally, Kunen describes the awkward situation a new client created for him when he asked, "Do you believe me?" "I didn't want to say I didn't believe him, because then it would seem I wasn't on his side. But I didn't want to say I did believe him, because then he'd think I was a fool." James S. Kunen, How Can You Defend Those People? The Making of a Criminal Lawyer 187 (New York: Random House, 1983).

20. Alan M. Dershowitz, The Best Defense (New York: Vintage Books, 1983), recounts his shock at discovering his client was a stool pigeon for the prosecution: "After all, when I agreed to become his lawyer I had taken his case to defend a *landsman*, a fellow Boro Parker, a kid from the old neighborhood—not a stool pigeon. How could I ever trust Seigel again? For months he had tricked me and my colleagues into believing that he was a murder

suspect, when all the while he was working for the other side, probably reporting every detail of our strategy right back to the prosecutor" (at 21).

21. Lynn Mather, The Outsider in the Courtroom: An Alternative Role for Defense, *in* Herbert Jacob, ed., The Potential for Reform of Criminal Justice 283 (Beverly Hills, Cal.: Sage Publications, 1974).

22. Casper, Criminal Court, *supra* note 3, at 16.

23. Marc Galanter, Why the "Haves" Come Out Ahead: Speculations on the Limits of Legal Change, 9 Law & Soc'y Rev. 95 (1974).

24. Jerome E. Carlin, Lawyers on Their Own 161-62 (New Brunswick, N.J.: Rutgers University Press, 1962).

25. In an early study, Arthur Lewis Wood, Criminal Lawyer 101 (New Haven, Conn.: College and University Press, 1967), found that of 93 criminal lawyers, all of whom were private practitioners, 21 said they refused to accept clients who would not follow their advice.

26. This means that attorneys who are successful in this respect can play the kind of "confidence game" Blumberg describes. Blumberg, *supra* note 1.

27. See Nardulli et al., *supra* note 6, for an analysis of the guilty plea processes in the nine courts.

28. See *id.* regarding trial penalties in these courts. For other analyses, see Thomas M. Uhlman & N. Darlene Walker, He Takes Some of My Time: I Take Some of His: An Analysis of Sentencing Patterns in Jury Cases, 14 Law & Soc'y Rev. 323 (1980); David Brereton & Jonathan D. Casper, Does It Pay to Plead Guilty? Differential Sentencing and the Functioning of Criminal Courts, 16 Law & Soc'y Rev. 45 (1981-82).

29. While sentences are important components of the client's decision, grievances and appeals are part of the attorney's choice and concerns. Between 1973 and 1983 criminal appeals more than doubled in Michigan and rose by 80% in Illinois. U. S. Department of Justice, Bureau of Justice Statistics, The Growth of Appeals: 1973-1983 Trends (Feb. 1985). However, all appeals do not center on the attorney's performance, and success rates for defendants are not high. Thomas Y. Davies, Affirmed: A Study of Criminal Appeals and Decision-Making Norms in a California Court of Appeals, 1982 A.B.F. Res. J. 543.

30. See text accompanying note 21.

31. Rosenthal, *supra* note 4, at 13.

Criminal case outcomes and the effects of the defendants' social status are addressed in this field study. Emmelman asserts that her data support Donald Black's position that a criminal defendant's social class directly affects the amount of law applied to cases. This influence occurs through the interpretive procedures of important court personnel involved in criminal proceedings. Many court-appointed lawyers have a tendency to link behavior to various social class types. These tendencies are expressed through "common sense"—a system of knowledge that is called forth throughout all types of judicial proceedings. Criminal lawyers' expectations of court actors influence their behavior. In those criminal court cases in which the social status of persons associated with the defense side are lower than those participants involved in the case, more law will be applied than in cases where the opposite is true.

THE EFFECT OF SOCIAL CLASS ON THE ADJUDICATION OF CRIMINAL CASES

Class-Linked Behavior Tendencies, Common Sense, and the Interpretive Procedures of Court-Appointed Defense Attorneys

DEBRA S. EMMELMAN

INTRODUCTION

Research findings concerning the effect of social class upon the adjudication of criminal cases are mixed: Willick, Gehlker, and McFarland-Watts (1975) found that social class and severity of sanctions for homosexual offenses are not related when controlling for

Acknowledgements: A previous version of this article was presented at the Annual Meetings of the Midwest Sociological Society, Kansas City, Missouri, April 1-4, 1992. The author would like to thank Joseph R. Gusfield, Jacqueline P. Wiseman, Michael E. Butler, Donald D. Landon, and John D. Hillebrand for their helpful comments. Any errors of fact or interpretation are, however, the author's sole responsibility.

previous convictions. Holmes, Daudistel, and Farrell (1987) found that social status has only little direct effect on charge reductions and that this effect is not in the direction which would be expected. Instead, minorities receive less severe responses.[1] In contrast, Clarke and Koch (1976) found that although defendants' incomes do not effect the likelihood of their being convicted of crimes, their incomes do effect the likelihood of their getting prison sentences. Similarly, Jankovic (1978) found that socioeconomic status affects the punishment received by persons convicted of drunken driving, and Lizotte (1978) found that laborers and non-whites are more likely to be incarcerated between arrest and final disposition as well as given longer prison sentences than those from higher socioeconomic groups. (See also Farrell [1971]; Hagan [1974]; Kruttschnitt [1980]; and Swigert and Farrell [1977] for similar discussions on this issue.)

More recently, Donald Black (1989) has argued that many sociologists have improperly conceptualized the manner by which social class (as a component of social status) influences criminal case outcomes. As stated by Black (p. 9):

> Some [observers] claim . . . that poor and black defendants in American courts receive more severe treatment than those who are wealthy and white, but others insist this is not true. What legal sociologists have learned, however, is that both of these popular views are wrong. A sizeable body of evidence from a number of societies and historical periods indicates that, by itself, the social status of a defendant tells us little or nothing about how a case will be handled. Instead, we must consider simultaneously each adversary's social status *in relation to the other's* [emphasis added].

According to Black, variations in the social characteristics of people involved in legal cases affect the quantity of law applied to cases. In legal cases where the statuses of persons associated with the defense side are lower than those of other persons involved in the case, more law as well as more severe law is applied than in those cases where the opposite is true.

While Black generated a number of noteworthy propositions, he failed to specify how social class influences case outcomes as a component of consciousness (cf. Hawkins 1990; Nelson 1990; Sarat 1989). In other words, like the former researchers, Black provided no insight into the interpretive process through which social class "causes" a greater or lesser quantity of law to be applied in legal cases.

The findings presented in this paper support Black's argument that court actors' relative social classes affect the quantity of law applied to legal cases. I find, however, that this influence occurs through the interpretive procedures of key actors involved in criminal cases. Specifically, I find that one group of court-appointed defense attorneys link behavior tendencies to court actors characterized as certain social class types. These tendencies are expressed through the grammar and rhetoric of "common sense" —a knowledge system which is evoked throughout all types of judicial proceedings. The attorneys' expectations of these court actors influence their behavior such that lower-class defendants are likely to endure a greater quantity of law.

An Overview of the Research Setting and the Methods for Research

Between September of 1984 and September of 1988, I conducted field research on a private, nonprofit corporation for the defense of indigent criminal defendants. (Henceforth, this corporation will be referred to as "Defense Alliance" and its attorneys will be referred to as "Defenders.") Until the corporation went out of business in September of 1988, it was located in a large, well-populated urban area whose basic industries are tourism and military-industrial activities. The overall system for defending indigent persons in the area entailed a limited Public Defender's Office, a Central Office of Defense Services, and a private contract system. Defense Alliance was one of many private contract groups in the area.

Defense Alliance differed from other contract groups in the area in at least three ways. First, it was the largest such group. It had four different offices that covered three different jurisdictions, and it employed approximately 36 attorneys overall at any given time. Second, unlike the other contract groups, Defense Alliance was a nonprofit corporation of court-appointed defense attorneys. Third, Defense Alliance had a reputation for providing high quality defense services to indigent defendants.

For approximately eight hours a week between September 1984 and January 1986, I observed as a student intern the Defenders' behavior at the downtown branch of Defense Alliance. Throughout this period, approximately 15 attorneys were employed at this office; this number was about average for that branch. Approximately half of these attorneys were men and half were women. The attorneys' ages ranged from their early '30s to their early '50s; the average age was in the late '30s. With the exception of one black man, who worked at the downtown office only part of the time in which I observed the Defenders' behavior, all the attorneys employed at this office were white. Throughout the observation period, field notes were recorded and then later analyzed through a grounded theory methodology (for further details on the use of this methodology, see Glaser and Strauss 1967; Lester and Hadden 1980.)

Upon completing my preliminary analysis, I interviewed in depth a total of 13 Defenders and ex-Defenders. The interviews took place in August and September of 1988. The respondents were comprised of seven men and six women. Nine attorneys were currently employed in the downtown office as it prepared to close its doors. Four attorneys had worked previously in that office but currently were employed elsewhere. One attorney was in private practice; the other three were working for the Public Defender's office. Of all attorneys interviewed, four men and six women had worked at the downtown branch of Defense Alliance throughout my previous period of observation.

Among the attorneys who were interviewed (excluding the director), the average length of employment was four-and-one-half years. The average age was in the late '30s; the modal age was the early '40s. The men's and the women's average ages were about be the same.

THE THEORETICAL FRAMEWORK: AN INTERPRETIVE APPROACH TO SOCIAL CLASS

The interpretive tradition in sociology maintains that society is created in and through the interpretive behavior of social actors (e.g., Berger and Luckmann 1967; Blumer 1978; Cicourel 1968, 1974; Garfinkel 1967; Mehan and Wood 1975). This is a study on social class in the interpretive tradition: one consequence is that "social class" is viewed here as a reality that is somehow produced and transmitted through interpretive behavior.

Social class influenced the Defenders' behavior through their images of court actors who were involved in adjudication proceedings. The most critical among these actors were judging authorities (i.e., judges and juries), witnesses, and indigent defendants.[2] The Defenders' images of these actors were configured—in a largely tacit, taken-for-granted manner—by three major types of behavior patterns: (1) role prerequisite behaviors; (2) structurally linked behavior tendencies; and (3) any actor's typical usage of certain knowledge systems.

Like incorrigible propositions (see Pollner 1974; Mehan and Wood 1975), role prerequisite behaviors are behaviors implicit in the very roles of social actors: any actor who plays a role is assumed to perform at least some cursory prerequisite behaviors. Otherwise, the role ceases to have any reality. For the Defenders, this meant that such actors as defense attorneys, District Attorneys, judges, juries, witnesses, and defendants all performed certain predictable role behaviors. The D.A. brought cases against (or prosecuted) defendants, for example, whereas defense attorneys provided at least some modicum of advocacy on behalf of defendants.

Structurally linked behavior tendencies are behavior patterns which actors themselves link to (or believe stem from) social practices and conditions deemed to exist beyond their immediate situations. For our purposes, the most important type that shaped the Defenders' images of judging authorities, witnesses, and indigent defendants were class-linked behavior tendencies.

Class-linked behavior tendencies correspond to one of Randall Collins's four types of "macro references." This reference is what Collins called "situational macro views." According to Collins (1981, p. 97):

> Micro-principles often refer to people in situations who take account of the macro structure itself, whether they do this by referring to other micro-situations or to more reified macro-concepts.

As a type of situational macro view, the Defenders' perspective on social class involved a macro concept that is similar to the sociological concept of "socioeconomic status." It is perceived as a type of ranking system that stratifies our entire society and that is based upon levels of wealth, income, occupational prestige, and educational attainment, as well as race. However, unlike some sociological conceptions, it is critical to realize here that the Defenders assigned individuals into categories of social class on the basis of perceived socioeconomic factors that indicated "types" of people. Specifically, on the basis of socioeconomic factors that the Defenders evidenced through visual as well as verbal cues, the Defenders characterized individuals as "upper-class" (meaning wealthy), "middle-class" (which means both upper-middle-class as well as working class), and "lower-class" (meaning the underclass) types of people.

The Defenders' situational macro view on social class also entailed references as well as linkages to other micro-situations: they expected a person's social class to influence virtually all aspects of his or her social life. It influenced, for example, friendship networks, places of residence, modes of articulation, material possessions, and physical appearances as well as personal experiences and general perspectives. In addition and perhaps most importantly, the Defenders expected certain social class types of court actors to behave in typical manners throughout judicial proceedings.

The Defenders' characterization of social class types of court actors should not be confused with that of persons involved in "normal crimes." As explained by Sudnow (1965), "normal crimes" involve typical offenders who commit certain types of crimes in typical manners, in typical places, that often involve typical victims.

The Defenders' characterization of social class types of court actors, on the other hand, was more general and broadly conceived. It was based solely on socioeconomic information that actually varied somewhat from person to person. In addition, these characterizations influenced the Defenders' behavior throughout all types of judicial proceedings regardless of whether the crime at issue was considered "normal."[3]

The Defenders' images of court actors were also shaped by expectations concerning any actor's typical usage of knowledge systems. "Knowledge systems" are cultural domains of meaning. They both prescribe as well as circumscribe the ways in which social actors are able to understand their world. Actors also use them to communicate with others. As such, they constitute what Kenneth Burke (1989) has called the "grammar and rhetoric of social action."

Although knowledge systems are shared by social actors, the extent to which they are shared by all social actors varies. Some people, for example, possess expertise concerning matters about which others know little. Knowledge systems may also be employed differently by social actors. While most of us know how to steal, for example, many choose not to employ that knowledge by committing theft. The knowledge which one expects certain actors to possess and the manner in which one expects them to employ it also has important implications for one's interaction with those actors. One does not visit an attorney for medical care, for example, and one does not usually let suspected thieves into one's home.

Among the different knowledge systems which the Defenders expected social actors to employ was "common sense." Simply defined, common sense is the largely shared and usually taken-for-granted value and belief system of our society (cf. Berger and Luckmann 1967; Gusfield 1981, p. 9). Although it is largely shared, the Defenders expected certain types of actors to employ this knowledge system differently. How they were expected to employ it had important implications for the Defender's advocacy behavior. The Defenders' expectations concerning any actor's typical use of common sense is especially critical in this analysis because it is through the use of common sense that class differences are expressed.

THE DEFENDERS' IMAGE OF JUDGING AUTHORITIES

The role prerequisite behavior of judging authorities is that of "pronouncing judgment." While judges typically decide certain legal issues that arise between prosecuting and defense attorneys, both judges and juries are sometimes called upon to judge the evidence in criminal cases.

A judging authority's role prerequisite behavior was especially important to the Defender because it had important potential consequences for the final dispositions of criminal cases. Therefore, the Defenders often postulated their typical point of view toward criminal cases when they evaluated cases in terms of defense strategies (cf. also Mather 1979; Neubauer 1974). This meant that whether they were present physically or only conceptually, judging authorities also acted as a reference group for the Defenders.

Typical judging authorities are deemed to be middle-class. They are also expected to have experiences typical of the middle-class and, therefore, to judge issues in cases from a typical middle-class point of view.[4] In this sense, these actors are politically and economically, as well as culturally, the "status quo" and uphold the values of the status quo in their decision-making.

The bias of typical judging authorities is expressed through their traditional use of "common sense." In other words, these court actors are expected not only to know the commonly shared values and beliefs of society, but also to accept them and impose them in their assessments of situations. (Hence, the traditional, one-dimensional use of common sense can also be seen as the grammar and rhetoric of the status quo.)[5]

The behavior patterns that configured the Defenders' images of typical judging authorities are illustrated in the following comments:

Nora (a seven-year veteran in her early forties who was certified to handle serious felony cases): [The typical jury is] middle-class. Very different from our clients in lifestyle, experiences, with the justice system, experience with crimes—they've never been accused of crimes usually. The biggest problem I guess is that they're too far removed from our clients. I mean, our clients are not really judged by their peers, but another social strata up. . . . [Judges are influenced by their] career. Desire for advancement. Judges have to be approved by the voters. And they really don't want to do anything that puts them in the public's eyes. They don't want to make waves, first of all. And secondly, they are concerned about their own advancement.

Kathy (a six-and-three-quarters-year veteran in her early forties who was certified to handle serious felony cases): [What is the "right frame of reference" for the jury?] I had a client—a cute little white kid who was 22, and he was charged with battery on his wife's lesbian lover. Well, now, all I had to do—there was a fight and he told the lesbian lover to get out of the house, and she basically told him to fuck off, and so he threw her out. And I think technically he was guilty of a battery. But all I had to do was give the jury something they could use to acquit him with, and they did. . . . Now it's hard for a jury—if you've got a crime that none of them can really feel strong about, negatively. . . . If I can't put the act into some kind of frame of reference to make it acceptable. [Are they behaving on the basis of certain traditional values?] Right. [One is that a woman shouldn't have a lesbian lover?] Right. [And the other one is that . . . sort of working-class, conservative type values?] I don't know if they're working-class, conservative, but yeah, I know what you mean. Yes, traditional values.

(From the researcher's field notes dated 1-7-85): I began the day with Karl [a six-and-a-half-year veteran who was certified to handle any type of criminal case except death penalty cases] . . . and two law interns. He called the day "orientation day" and began by telling us about organization of his daily calendar and case files. He had a total of three appearances today—two of which were scheduled at the same time in two different courts. He told us that judges were "prima donnas" [meaning that they are elitist and extremely sensitive to social proprieties] and that he would have to figure out a way not to upset the two judges.

THE DEFENDERS' IMAGE OF WITNESSES

The witness's role prerequisite behavior is that of providing evidence: every witness in a criminal case is one who "bears witness" or testifies to some matter in a criminal case. These matters often pertain to a defendant's innocence or guilt of alleged criminal conduct. However, they may also pertain to such issues as sentencing as well as due process procedures.

Because it affects the character of a witness's testimony, a witness's credibility is linked to a great extent to his or her social class. Social class affects a witness's testimony by influencing such factors as his or her credentials, articulation, demeanor, and physical appearance as well as other personal experiences and situations which could be brought to bear upon an issue at hand. Typically, the higher a witness's social class, the more credible he or she is expected to be.

A witness's credibility is expressed through the grammar and rhetoric of common sense. The more a witness manifests the traditional values and beliefs of typical judging authorities (or, the values and beliefs of the status quo), the more credible he or she is expected to be.

The comments of three Defenders illustrate the behavior patterns thought to be typical of witnesses:

> *Kathy (a six-and-three-quarters-years veteran in her early forties who was certified to handle serious felony cases)*: [How would you describe a good witness?] The more middle-class your witness is, the more effective the testimony. The more articulate the witness is, the more effective the testimony. The more sophisticated or well-educated the witness is, the more effective his testimony is gonna be.

> *LuAnn (a three-and-one-half-year veteran in her mid-thirties who was certified to handle medium-range felony cases. She is discussing the role of witnesses)*: The witness is . . . a vehicle by which evidence is admitted into court . . . it's also part of your selling. Because that person's credibility—everything that person brings into the courtroom is scrutinized. So that if you have a person who's telling the truth but looks like a slob, you have a problem with the case. . . . I mean I could say to my clients, for example, that, "Yeah. I understand that you have a witness who saw it happen this way. But he's got a record." Or, "She's a prostitute. Who's gonna believe them?" . . . [and] you have to work with [these types of] witnesses cause you never know what's gonna come out of their mouths. . . . But these are the [types of] people my clients live with. . . . Sometimes that is very very hard to get across to the jury—even with your witnesses because they

come from this other world. It's like having an alien being in court when it's someone from [the poorest residential area] who comes in to testify. All your jurors come from [a working-class residential area].

> *Tom (a four-year-veteran who was certified to handle medium-range felony cases)*: [Do indigent defendants make good witnesses?] No. [Why?] 'Cause poor people in our society are disadvantaged people, and the coin of the realm in this country is education. And if you're disadvantaged in many instances it's because you lack the education to be otherwise. And a lot of them have emotional problems. Some of them have physical problems. Many of them simply are not intelligent—they're developmentally disabled. Others are just people who have had very unhappy, unpleasant, and sad lives. Most of them don't have much experience being in court. Nervousness is extremely common. They're very afraid to testify. They have no experience at it. And as a result, they require a great deal of preparation to get it done right. . . . Police officer witnesses you'll find are experienced after a time and some of them are very good. Some are superb witnesses. Best one I ever saw was a guy who had been a building contractor for years who got a job as an undercover police cop. He looked like Santa Claus. He was the most benevolent, warm, charming guy you ever met in your life. He got up there and lied his head off.

The Defenders' Image of Indigent Defendants

The defendant's role prerequisite behavior is that of "the accused," who requires professional legal counsel and advocacy. Among other things, this meant that the Defender and the defendant worked together as a team in which the defendant assisted the Defender with his or her defense.

Typical indigent defendants are lower-class. Because most of their personal allies are also lower-class, this greatly affects the credibility of the witnesses they are able to provide on their own behalf. In addition, these defendants are somewhat noncredible "testaments" to themselves throughout court proceedings regardless of their official decisions to testify. Due to their social class, typical indigent defendants are therefore handicapped in their ability to assist with their own defenses.

A typical indigent defendant's handicap is expressed through what may be termed the "incompetent" use of common sense. Indigent defendants as well as their personal allies tend to employ a culturally deviant knowledge system. This means they are unable to manifest many of the traditional values and beliefs of the status quo throughout court proceedings. Because they are largely unable to portray such values and beliefs, typical indigent defendants are less able than other types of defendants to convince typical judging authorities that they are virtuous persons.

The Defenders' image of typical indigent defendants is illustrated in the following comments made by two Defenders in response to the question, "How do you think the typical indigent defendant tends to differ from other types of defendants?":

Robert (an attorney in his early forties who was previously employed as a Public Defender in another city and who was certified to handle non-serious felony cases): Well, he is almost definitionally a member of the underclass. Which means that he is under or uneducated. Likely to be illiterate. He is typically inarticulate. He is often—usually a racial minority. All those things are important factors in how his case is gonna be heard and looked upon, and what the final determination is gonna be for his case . . . The fact that a defendant is inarticulate limits his ability to get on the witness stand and express himself to the jury. That goes hand-in-hand with his educational background. Members of the underclass [also] have—it is a subculture in which certain things are accepted or tolerated which may not be tolerated by jurors who come from more of a mainstream kind of background. Living together with girlfriends, children out of wedlock, situations like that which may not be as well accepted by jurors. Those kinds of factors play heavily. . . . And if you're able to present to the jury a defendant who is a working stiff, that makes him a much more loveable kind of person, a sympathetic kind of person, a person more like the jurors, and is a great advantage. And if the defendant is truly indigent, that's not something you can do for him. You can't present that.

Ingmar (a one-and-three-quarter-years veteran in his early thirties, certified to handle medium-range criminal cases, who was previously employed as a Public Defender for juvenile

cases in another city): I think in general they have a lot more difficult cases to defend. I mean, there's certain things you don't have. You don't have wonderful character witnesses for them because you can't bring in all these members of the business community, and politics, and what have you to come in and testify that this person's character is unimpeachable.

The Influence of Social Class on the Defenders' Routine Decision-Making and Defense Tactics

The Defenders' images of typical judging authorities, witnesses, and indigent defendants influenced their routine decision-making and defense tactics throughout virtually the entire process for litigating criminal cases. It influenced, for example, their decision making and tactics concerning pretrial release for defendants, motions to exclude or suppress evidence, plea bargaining, and trial as well as sentencing. Moreover, these images influenced the Defenders' behavior not only as extralegal considerations but also as components of legal considerations. Most illustrative of these influences is how the Defenders assessed the value (or "worth") of criminal cases.

Consistent with other research findings on defense attorneys' behavior (i.e., Heumann 1975; Mather 1979; McDonald 1985; Neubauer 1974; Rosett and Cressey 1976), the Defenders' decision making concerning plea bargaining was based largely on their assessments of the value of individual criminal cases: When the value of a case was high, the Defenders expected the defendant to receive considerable incentive to plea bargain. Conversely, when the value of a case was low, they expected the defendant to receive little or no incentive. Perhaps ironically, cases that had little or no value typically resulted in trials, whereby the defendant was likely to be convicted of more serious crimes as well as receive more severe sentences than he or she would have through a plea bargain.[6]

The Defenders' assessments were based upon three factors: (1) the seriousness of the crime(s) with which the defendant was charged (which means both how serious the charge itself was as well as how serious or atypical the actual crime was); (2) the strength of the evidence (which means how strong or weak the evidence was on both sides of the issue); and (3) the defendant's background characteristics (which included but were not limited to the defendant's prior criminal record) (cf. the findings of Heumann 1975; Mather 1979; McDonald 1985; Neubauer 1974; Rosett and Cressey 1976).

With the exception of the defendant's prior criminal record, perhaps the most obvious way in which social class affected the Defenders' assessments was through the defendant's background characteristics. This influence was illustrated in three Defenders' comments concerning plea bargain negotiations:

Mindy (a six-years veteran in her mid-thirties who was certified to handle medium-range felony cases): I go to the dispo department, you wait your turn, you go in and talk to the D.A. and the judge at the same time. The D.A. makes you an offer— and I do different things . . . I usually "puff" [i.e., inflate the value of the case] if I want to settle the case, and I make the D.A. think his case is not as good as he thought. And sometimes they come down. . . . Sometimes I'll do things like, "Hey, my guy's got a great military record" or—sometimes I'll do my sentencing stuff—I'll say, "Hey, look at this medal of honor he has, look at this and that." . . . Sometimes they'll buy into it and say, "Yeah you're right. This isn't your average schlock."

Steve (a three-year veteran who was approximately 40 years old and who was certified to handle non-serious criminal cases): Sometimes I might be able to get a little better deal on some type of charges than they originally offered. . . . [An example of how you might do this?] Right now, their offers on petty theft are $300 and 10 days public service work. You have a client who has a clean record and he [stole] a shirt from Nordstroms. And you talk to your client and you find out he's got a job which requires a security clearance. You go to [the prosecutor] the first time and say, "My client has a job which requires a security. Look at him, he's got a clean record. He admits he did it. It seems like he did it. But it's only a $20 shirt and it was an impulse-type thing. Will you reduce it to a trespass?"

Kathy: [You said you know what a case is worth beforehand, then you go into the judge's chambers and talk to the D.A., and then the D.A. makes you an offer?] Right. I go in and say, "What's the offer on this case, Rick?" He tells me, and I usually respond "Geez Rick! You can give

me something better than that!" And [then I] give the D.A. information about the client, information about the case—mitigating factors in essence. [Example?] The client has no record. The client is young. Actually—to be quite truthful—the client's white. [Actually?!] I do indeed. If I've got a young blonde kid out there, you think I'm not gonna tell the D.A. that I've got a young blonde kid out there? You better believe I do! [Wow!] I tell the D.A., "This kid's really middle-class." Or, "This man's worked all his life and now after 20 years this whatever—this embezzlement happened," or y'know, "This woman was going through medical problems." Mitigating factors.

As should be evident from the above discussions, lower-class defendants are less able than other types of defendants to portray in their social histories and current situations the traditional values and beliefs of typical judging authorities. This means that the Defenders were less able to portray these defendants as generally upright, moral people who had perhaps suffered temporary lapses and who warranted more consideration with regard to sentencing.

Not so obvious was the manner in which social class affected the Defenders' assessments of the strength of the evidence. Consider, for example, the following incidents in which three Defenders considered taking certain cases to trial:

(*10-1-84*) [An] investigator [working for Nora] asked me to analyze or map out a particular case for him that was getting ready to go to trial from the available police and investigative reports. It was regarding a young male (approximately 21) accused of stealing and pawning about $15,000 worth of gold jewelry from a residence in [a wealthy community]. According to the police reports, the victim's son broke into their home while they were on vacation (he was barred from the home and spending time in an [out-of-state] home for delinquent children) and had a party with about 8 people—most of whom he was not acquainted with. . . . This particular defendant (not the son) was being charged with the theft because several people had supplied the police with a description of a male accompanied by another male of very similar characteristics who sold the stolen gold jewelry at two pawn stores (i.e., white male, early 20s, approximately 5'6" to 5'8," 160-170 lbs., light brown or blonde hair).

The defendant, who insisted he is innocent and had no previous record, had pointed out another person as the actual thief. He had provided a picture of the alleged thief and the two were amazingly similar in looks. . . . The problem for the Defender, then, appeared to be pointing out possible contradictions and faulty assumptions made by the witnesses. [The investigator] also told me that Nora's defendant had a job (and therefore less reason to steal) and that during the time he was supposed to have been pawning the jewelry, the defendant was also at work—where he was not permitted to leave the premises. The alleged thief, however, had no job and therefore more reason to have committed the theft. [The investigator] said he would keep me posted regarding this case. [The charges against the defendant were ultimately dropped.]

(10/12/84) [Betty's] second case [in court] involved [possession of cocaine]. [The case was scheduled for trial]. According to Betty, the arresting police officer in this case said he pulled the defendant over—along with several other males in a car—in an attempt to protect the defendant. [She stated that] the defendant was associated with the Navy and looked the part (although he was actually only a civilian employee of the Navy), and the other males in the car were known by the police officer to take advantage of military personnel. According to the police officer, he was politely questioning the suspects outside of their car when he noticed that the defendant dropped about a gram of cocaine from his pocket. . . . The defendant, on the other hand . . . [stated that] the officer in fact ordered the suspects out of the car. . . . Betty and the investigator also discussed some trial tactics for this case. Betty said she hoped there were some Black jurists in the trial. The investigator agreed that would be a good idea: "You get some Black people on the jury and they'll know how Black people are treated by the police." (The defendant was Black.) Betty said that because the defendant was well-spoken and clearly not a criminal, that would be a plus for him, too.

(1/11/85) After lunch, Karl had a case where a defendant (who was on probation for previous crimes) was charged with [four drug crimes]. [The defendant was a Black, medium-built, rather muscular male in his mid-20s who wore his hair in short braids.] This was a preliminary hearing. According to the police report, the police spotted the defendant and noted that he was making slow and rigid movements and was expressionless. The police suspected he might be under the influence

of PCP because the area was known for PCP usage. When approached [by the police], the defendant apparently acted confused, spoke slow and deliberately, and smelled of an odor "which I generally associated with PCP usage" [i.e., ether]. The police administered a [field test] and the defendant apparently didn't pass. They then arrested the defendant, patted him down for weapons, took him to the station for a blood test (he flunked again), and then noted that 5 PCP cigarettes had been dropped beside the defendant before he was actually given the blood test. [It is important to note here that the results of such "hard evidence" as blood tests are often found by defense attorneys to be consistent with other, legal behavior in which defendants engage]. . . . Karl first told the defendant that he could get the charges reduced to one count of "under the influence of PCP" [with local jail time]. He noted that the defendant had a previous record [and] that the prosecution did have some proof problems (i.e., 5 PCP cigarettes are not enough for "possession for sale"). . . . The defendant then asked about the chances of fighting the charges. Karl told him that he had a chance, but that possession for sale was a big issue. The defendant was not going to win the case [altogether] because he had 5 "sherms" (PCP cigarettes) on him. The defendant stated that the police did not find the five sherms on him but beside him at the jail. He indicated that they had only found one sherm on him. Karl said that although the police had already patted him down before the sherms were found beside him, they would just say that they had only done a weapons check—not a thorough one, which would suggest that the sherms really were not on him. Karl also told him that the police do lie. He then told the defendant about other problems concerning a jury trial: there was a problem with status; that is, the judge and jury would be primarily white, middle-class. The jury was usually composed of white, middle-class, aged people—people who were retired from the Navy or who worked in the aerodynamics field. He would be lucky if he got one or two Black people. He also said the police are expert witnesses who would be acting like "Mr. Nice Guy"—not like they usually acted out in the streets. The defendant would also have problems testifying in court because he would be in custody—not free to roam around and let the jury know him during recesses but with a bailiff breathing down his neck. The jury would only see a rather formal and contrived performance of him during the trial. The cards were stacked against the defendant, according to Karl.

As apparent in the above examples, the Defenders expected such class-linked information as employment situation, job status, credentials, mode of articulation, demeanor, and physical appearance to influence—either positively or negatively—typical judging authorities' assessments of situations. It is critical to realize here, however, that this information was expected to influence their assessments not merely through the defendant's physical appearance in the court room. Instead, it was also expected to influence them through "facts" that would be presented as evidence by witnesses who themselves evoked more or less credibility due to their class-linked behaviors.

Because typical indigent defendants are likely to have less credible witnesses (or by the same token, less convincing "facts" to present) than the prosecution or other types of defendants, they tend to have weaker evidence to present on their behalf. As suggested by the latter Defender, the cards are generally stacked against such defendants.

As suggested previously, the manner in which social class influences the value of a criminal case does not mean that lower-class defendants are any more likely to be plea-bargained than other types of defendants. On the contrary, it means that their cases tend to have little value and that they frequently have less to lose by going to trial. This does indicate, however, that lower-class defendants are more likely to be convicted, more likely to be convicted of serious crimes, and more likely to receive harsh sentences than other types of defendants. With regard to the former, this means that lower-class defendants are also more likely to have prior convictions—a factor which weighs heavily in future decision making in the adjudication of criminal cases.

While the defendants' background characteristics, as well as the seriousness of the crime(s) with which they had been charged, influenced the value assigned to their cases, these two factors also influenced decision making concerning pretrial release. As explained by the Defenders, the major issue in a bail review hearing is whether or not the defendant can be counted upon to show up at court hearings. Because many lower-class defendants do not have a permanent residence, a job, or other "socially acceptable" ties to the community, they are generally deemed high risks for pretrial release and the Defenders were constrained in their ability to make a viable pitch to judges for a bail reduction. Compare, for example, the different manners in which the same Defender handled bail review hearings for two different defendants:

(4/23/85) Karl asked [the defendant] how much bail he could afford. . . . The defendant told Karl he could afford somewhere between $2,000 and $3,000 bail—$200-$300 actual amount paid. [In the Bail Review hearing] Karl . . . told the judge that the defendant's father was in the courtroom in support of his son, emphasized the amount of time the defendant had spent in [the area], and that the defendant had only one count alleged against him. [In essence, it appeared Karl was emphasizing all the positives regarding a release on bail.] The judge reduced the bail to $1500 after having asked the D.A. if he had any objections. The D.A. said "no"—but added that the defendant had used five or six other names.

(4/19/85) Karl had only one bail review hearing which involved a man charged with burglary. . . . The defendant had only been in [the area] about two weeks, had no job and no relatives in the area (he was from another state) [and was homeless]. Karl told him there was little hope he would be released from custody because of this. [Karl did not make a bail pitch in this case. He simply removed the issue from the court calendar.]

SUMMARY AND CONCLUSION

The findings reported in this article support Black's contention that the relative social class of the individuals involved in criminal cases affects the quantity of law applied to those cases. I find, however, that this influence occurs through the interpretive procedures of key court actors involved in criminal cases. More specifically, I find that social class influences the behavior of one group of court-appointed defense attorneys in the following manner:

The Defenders' behavior was influenced by their images of judging authorities, witnesses, and indigent defendants. In a largely tacit, taken-for-granted manner, three major types of behavior patterns comprised these images: (1) role prerequisite behavior patterns; (2) structurally linked (including, most importantly, "class-linked") behavior tendencies; and (3) any actor's typical usage of certain knowledge systems.

Overall, role prerequisite behaviors bring about a set of relationships whereby some persons (i.e., judging authorities) are relegated the authority to assess and judge others (i.e., witnesses and defendants). This set of relationships does not itself dictate that social class intercede, however. Instead, social class biases are introduced into these relationships through "class-linked behavior tendencies." Class-linked behavior tendencies are behavior patterns that the Defenders themselves link to the social class of court actors characterized as middle- or lower-class types. Their class-linked behavior tendencies are expressed through the grammar and rhetoric of "common sense"—a knowledge system which is apparently evoked among all these actors throughout courtroom procedures.

The latter two types of behavior patterns shaped the Defenders' perceptions such that witnesses and defendants of higher social class were assumed to reap some benefits of doubt which those of lower class did not: typical indigent defendants and their personal allies, as well as lower-class witnesses, are often deemed to lack the political, economic, and cultural resources with which to present themselves as socially acceptable and morally upright individuals to typical judging authorities.[7] In essence, the Defenders expected lower-class persons to be judged as low-class, noncredible, and morally suspect people more than people of other social classes.[8] These tendencies influence virtually all aspects of adjudicative processes and indicate that lower-class defendants are ultimately more likely to be convicted, more likely to be convicted of serious crimes, and more likely to receive harsh sentences. In other words, these findings support Black's (1989, p. 11) contention that "downward law is greater than upward law."

Clearly, the findings reported in this study are not without certain limitations: While they do substantiate that social class influenced the Defenders' behavior through their interpretive procedures, they do not substantiate whether other important court actors behave similarly or in the manner that the Defenders allege (but see Wiseman 1970). Neither do they indicate how

the Defenders' own social class might have influenced their behavior (but see Feeley 1986; Hermann, Single, and Boston 1977; McIntyre 1987; Wheeler and Wheeler 1980 for discussions on how publicly provided defense attorneys behave similarly to other types of defense attorneys). Finally, these findings do not substantiate the precise extent to which social class influences criminal case outcomes through interpretive procedures.

This study invites further research to compensate for the shortcomings described above. However, before other studies can do so, the analysis presented here exhorts researchers to seriously reconsider the manner in which a defendant's social class is conceived to influence criminal case outcomes.

One important refinement concerns the method in which social class is specified as a variable. The findings reported here indicate that social class should be studied as a type of nominal variable that encompasses distinctions made among persons of different social classes by the social actors themselves. While certainly some researchers have specified variables in manners that appear to encompass some interpretive nuances (e.g., Jankovic 1978; Lizotte 1978; Kruttschnitt 1980), other studies preclude them (e.g., Clarke and Koch 1976; Holmes, Daudistel, and Farrell 1987).

This study also indicates that social class influences adjudication outcomes not only as an extralegal variable but also as a component of legal variables. It affects some court actors' assessments not only of a defendant's social history and background but also the strength of the evidence.[9] Consequently, social class can also be seen to affect conviction rates and the severity of sentences received, as well as prior records. Although several researchers have stated that they suspected such influences (i.e., Jankovic 1978; Lizotte 1978; Swigert and Farrell 1977), most research has controlled for "strength of the evidence" and/or "prior convictions" (e.g., Clarke and Koch 1976; Farrell 1971; Hagan 1974; Holmes, Daudistel, and Farrell 1987; Jankovic 1978; Kruttschnitt 1980; Lizotte 1978; Swigert and Farrell 1977; Willick, Gehlker, and McFarland-Watts 1975). Unless researchers consider these influences more seriously, however, they may exclude from their findings some very important effects of social class itself!

Finally, the findings reported here indicate that a lower-class defendant's failure to obtain pretrial release may occur at least partially because his/her class-linked behavior is not conducive to making a favorable impression on judges. Like the Defenders, all attorneys for the poor may be constrained in their ability to make viable bail pitches on behalf of such clients. Thus, while some researchers (e.g., Swigert and Farrell 1977; Holmes, Daudistel, and Farrell 1987) have found that social class affects case outcomes only in an indirect manner (i.e., through type of attorney procured which then influences pretrial release and the defendant's ability to assist with his or her defense), this study indicates that at least some of this influence may actually be the direct result of social class.

I conclude by urging researchers to undertake studies that compensate for all the shortcomings described above. By so doing, we might find not only that social class has some definite influence on criminal case outcomes, but also that its influence is considerably greater than any of us have realized.

NOTES

1. The authors hypothesized that this was due to some initial overcharging by the prosecutor.

2. I am not intending to suggest here that the Defenders' image of D.A.s is not also important. On the contrary, it is quite important. However, because the Defenders expect D.A.s to prosecute (or aggravate) cases against defendants to the fullest extent, they generally view judges and juries as constraints upon the D.A.s' power. In fact, the Defenders often appeal to the authority of these latter actors—if only hypothetically—in attempting to reason with D.A.s. For this reason, the Defenders' images of judging authorities—as well as witnesses and defendants—are viewed as more critical components in this analysis.

3. Farrell (1971) found that lower-class defendants accused of homosexual offenses were more likely to be detained and treated harshly by criminal justice officials than their upper-class counterparts. Farrell attributed a great deal of this tendency both to the lower-class defendant's greater likelihood of conforming to the stereotype of homosexuality and to the upper-class defendant's greater ability to elicit sympathy from middle-class judging authorities. Somewhat like Farrell, Swigert and Farrell (1977) maintained that homicide suspects' conformity to a popular stereotype of criminality (i.e., the "normal primitive") as well as their low social class were related to more severe conviction rates. One way in which the findings of this study differ from those of these other researchers is that they indicate that lower-class defendants are less likely to be sympathetic to (or respected by) judging authorities due to behavior tendencies that are directly linked to their low social class. Any stereotype of criminality implied here should therefore be seen as one that is created by typical lower-class persons, or, the types of people in our society who have the lowest socioeconomic status. It should also be made clear here that unlike stereotypes discussed by other researchers (e.g., Sudnow 1965; Farrell 1971; and Swigert and Farrell 1977), this image is not specific to certain types of crimes.

4. In her study on skid row alcoholics, Wiseman (1970) found that judges imposed middle-class values in their sentencing decisions. This suggests both that the Defenders were not mistaken in their image of typical judges and that such class bias is pervasive.

5. It is important to note here that I am not suggesting that the Defenders' own social class had no influence whatsoever on their behavior. However, because the Defenders viewed judges and juries as important constraints upon their ability to protect their clients' interests, the class biases of these latter actors were less taken for granted and influenced the Defenders' behavior regardless of their own class biases. This is somewhat supported in others' findings (e.g., Feeley 1986; Hermann, Single, and Boston 1977; McIntyre 1987; Wheeler and Wheeler 1980) that criminal case outcomes are about equivalent for publicly provided and retained attorneys.

6. One way in which the Defenders determined whether the value of a case was high or low was by comparing the offer they expected to receive with those they normally received for cases of a particular type. It is here that the Defenders' concepts of "normal crimes" came into play. For the Defenders, a case was "normal" when it conformed to what was typical with regard to the three factors discussed below. In cases involving normal crimes, they expected typical reductions. When a case did not conform, however, they expected atypical reductions—which meant either greater-than-average incentive or lower-than-average incentive to plea bargain. The Defenders did not encourage their clients to plea bargain when the value of a case was low because they believed their clients had little or nothing to lose through a trial. For

this reason, defendants whose cases had little or no value were likely to be convicted of more serious crimes as well as to receive more severe sentences through a trial than other types of defendants.

7. This somewhat substantiates Hawkins (1990, p. 318) assertion that "Black gives too little credit to lawyers for being able to distinguish cases sociologically as well as technically." I would add here, however, that attorneys often make such "sociological" distinctions in a tacit, taken-for-granted manner through the use of "common sense."

8. This also suggests that any person's social rank, class or status—as long as it is incorporated into interpretive procedures and viewed as relative to other ranks—is also implicitly associated with some type of moral rank or assessment (e.g., a low-status person is always somehow "lower" and therefore less inherently valuable than other types of people). In other words, the social structure—as a system of statuses and roles—also appears to be a type of moral structure or hierarchy. Therefore, contrary to what Black (1976, p. 1989) argued, this suggests that it is not possible to study either the behavior of law or the social structure of the case without also being somehow moral or valuation. To not make explicit such implicit assessments is simply to accept or condone one set of moral standards as legitimate (cf. Hawkins 1990; Nelson 1990; Sarat 1989).

9. Because these findings indicate that social situations are inherent features of evidence (i.e., it is not possible to attempt to prove a case without also introducing into evidence such facts as "who" did what or perhaps could not have done something because of their social situation), this also makes Black's (1989) concept of "the desocialization of law" problematic (cf. Cotterrell 1991).

REFERENCES

Berger, Peter L., and Thomas Luckmann, 1967. *The Social Construction of Reality.* New York: Doubleday.

Black, Donald. 1976. *The Behavior of Law.* New York: Academic.

____. 1989. *Sociological Justice.* New York: Oxford University Press.

Blumer, Herbert. 1978. "Society as Symbolic Interaction." Pp. 97-103 in *Symbolic Interaction,* edited by Jerome G. Manis and Bernard N. Meltzer. Boston: Allyn and Bacon.

Burke, Kenneth. 1989. *The Heritage of Sociology: Kenneth Burke on Symbols and Society.* Edited and with an introduction by Joseph R. Gusfield, Chicago; University of Chicago Press.

Cicourel, Aaron. 1968. *The Social Organization of Juvenile Justice.* New York: Crane, Russak & Company.

____. 1974. *Cognitive Sociology.* New York: The Free Press.

Clarke, Stevens H., and Gary G. Koch. 1976. "The Influence of Income and Other Factors on Whether Criminal Defendants Go to Prison." *Law and Society Review* 11(1, Fall): 57-92.

Collins, Randall. 1981 "Micro-Translation as a Theory-Building Strategy." Pp. 81-108 in *Advances in Social Theory and Methodology,* edited by K. Knorr-Cetina and A.V.Cicourel, Boston: Routledge & Kegan Paul.

Cotterrell, Roger. 1991. "The Durkheimian Tradition in the Sociology of Law." *Law and Society Review* 25(4):923-945.

Farrell, Ronald A. 1971. "Class Linkages of Legal Treatment of Homosexuals." *Criminology* 9 (May): 49-68.

Feeley, Malcolm. 1986. "Bench Trials, Adversariness, and Plea Bargaining: A Comment of Schulhofer's Plan" (Symposium titled "Effective Assistance of Counsel for the indigent Criminal Defendant: Has the Promise Been Fulfilled?"). *Review of Law and Social Change* 14:173.

Garfinkel, Harold. 1967. *Studies in Ethnomethodology.* Englewood Cliffs, NJ: Prentice-Hall.

Glaser, Barney, and Anselm Strauss. 1967. *The Discovery of Grounded Theory.* Chicago: Aldine Publishing Company.

Gusfield, Joseph R. 1981. *The Culture of Public Problems.* Chicago: The University of Chicago Press.

____. 1989. "Introduction." Pp. 1-49 in *The Heritage of Sociology: Kenneth Burke on Symbols of Society,* edited by Joseph R. Gusfield. Chicago: University of Chicago Press.

Hagan, John. 1974. "Extra-Legal Attributes and Criminal Sentencing: An Assessment of a Sociological Viewpoint." *Law and Society Review* 8: 357-383.

Hawkins, Darnell F. 1990. A Review of "Sociological Justice." *Social Forces* 69(1): 316-318.

Hermann, Robert, Eric Single, and John Boston. 1977. *Counsel for the Poor.* Lexington, MA: Lexington Books.

Heumann, Milton. 1975. "A Note on Plea Bargaining and Case Pressure." *Law and Society Review* 9(3, Spring): 515-528.

Holmes, Malcolm D., Howard C. Daudistel, and Ronald A. Farrell. 1987. "Determinants of Charge Reductions and Final Dispositions in Cases of Burglary and Robbery." *Journal of*

Research in Crime and Delinquency 24(3, August): 233-254.

Jankovic, Ivan. 1978. "Social Class and Criminal Sentencing." *Crime and Social Justice* 10(Fall-Winter): 9-16.

Kruttschnitt, Candace. 1980. "Social Status and Sentences of Female Offenders." *Law and Society Review* 15(2, Winter): 247-265.

____. 1982. "Respectable Women and the Law." *Sociological Quarterly* 23(2, Spring): 221-234.

Lester, Marilyn, and Stuart C. Hadden. 1980. "Ethnomethodology and Grounded Theory Methodology: An Integration of Perspective and Method." *Urban Life* 9(1): 3-33.

Lizotte, Alan J. 1978. "Extra-Legal Factors in Chicago's Criminal Courts: Testing the conflict Model of Criminal Justice." *Social Problems* 25(5, June): 564-580.

Mather, Lynn M. 1979. *Plea Bargaining or Trial?* Lexington, MA: Lexington Books.

McDonald, William F. 1985. *Plea Bargaining: Critical Issues and Common Practices.* Washington, DC: U.S. Department of Justice.

McIntyre, Lisa J. 1987. *The Public Defender.* Chicago: The University of Chicago Press.

Mehan, Hugh, and Houston Wood. 1975. *The Reality of Ethnomethodlogy.* New York: John Wiley & Sons.

Nelson, Robert L. 1990. A Review of "Sociological Justice." *American Sociological Review* 95: 1095-1097.

Neubauer, David W. 1974. *Criminal Justice in Middle America.* Morristown, NJ: General Learning Press.

Pollner, Melvin. 1974. "Mundane Reasoning." *Philosophy of the Social Sciences* 4: 35-54.

Rosett, Arthur, and Donald Cressey. 1976. *Justice by Consent.* New York: J. B. Lippencott.

Sarat, Austin. 1989. "Donald Black Discovers Legal Realism: From Pure Science to Policy Science in the Sociology of Law." *Law and Social Inquiry* 14(4): 765-785.

Sudnow, David. 1965. "Normal Crimes: Sociological Features of the Penal Code in a Public Defender Office." *Social Problems* 2: 255-275.

Swigert, Victoria Lynn, and Ronald A. Farrell. 1977. "Normal Homicides and the Law." *American Sociological Review* 42(1, February): 16-32.

Wheeler, Gerald R., and Carol L. Wheeler. 1980. "Reflections on Legal Representation of the Economically Disadvantaged: Beyond Assembly Line Justice." *Crime and Delinquency* 26(3, July): 319-332.

Willick, Daniel H., Gretchen Gehlker, and Anita McFarland-Watts. 1975. "Social Class as a Factor Affecting Judicial Disposition Defendants Charged with Criminal Homosexual Acts." *Criminology* 13(1, May): 57-77.

Wiseman, Jacqueline P. 1970. *Stations of the Lost.* Chicago: The University of Chicago Press.

Prosecutors are a key component to case processing in the criminal courts. Heumann analyzes the way new prosecutors learn to adapt to this practice. Both the defense lawyer and the assistant district attorney agree upon a plea, which will determine the sentence the defendant will receive. Because 90% or more of criminal cases are decided by plea bargaining, the prosecutor becomes the key power broker in the bargaining process, usurping many of the judges' responsibilities in their sentencing role. The author presents an analysis for the realities of plea bargaining and the politics and conflicts that are often involved in these proceedings.

ADAPTING TO PLEA BARGAINING

Prosecutors

MILTON HEUMANN

The new prosecutor shares many of the general expectations that his counterpart for the defense brings to the court. He expects factually and legally disputable issues, and the preliminary hearings and trials associated with these. If his expectations differ at all from the naive "Perry Mason" orientation, it is only to the extent that he anticipates greater success than the hapless Hamilton Burger of Perry Mason fame.

The new prosecutor's views about plea bargaining parallel those of the defense attorney.

He views plea bargaining as an expedient employed in crowded urban courts by harried and/or poorly motivated prosecutors. He views the trial as "what the system is really about" and plea bargaining as a necessary evil dictated by case volume. The following exchange with a newly appointed prosecutor is illustrative.

Q: Let's say they removed the effects of case pressure, provided you with more manpower. You wouldn't have that many cases. . . .

Reprinted from *Plea Bargaining* by Milton Heumann (by permission of The University of Chicago Press and the author). © 1978 by The University of Chicago Press.

Editor's note: This study is based on data from Connecticut, where, until a reorganization of the court system in July 1978, prosecution was conducted by state's attorneys in the supreme court and by prosecutors in the circuit court. Readers should understand that the powers of each office are essentially the same; only the workplace is different.

A: Then everybody should go to trial.

Q: Everybody should go to trial?

A: Yeah.

Q: Why?

A: Because supposedly if they're guilty they'll be found guilty. If they're not guilty they'll be found not guilty. That's the fairest way . . . judged by a group of your peers, supposedly.

Q: So you think that plea bargaining is a necessary evil?

A: Yeah.

Q: Would justice be better served if all cases went to trial?

A: That's the way it's supposed to be set up. Sure. Why wouldn't it?

Q: Would prosecutors be more satisfied?

A: Probably.

Q: If cases went to trial?

A: Sure.

Q: Why?

A: Because they could talk in front of twelve people and act like a lawyer. Right. Play the role.

It should be emphasized that these expectations and preferences of the new prosecutor are founded on the minimal law school preparation. . . . The newcomers simply do not know very much about the criminal justice system.

Unlike defense attorneys, however, the new prosecutor is likely to receive some form of structured assistance when he begins his job. The chief prosecutor or chief state's attorney may provide this aid, if the prosecutor's office is staffed by a number of prosecutors or state's attorneys—that is, if the newcomer is not the only assistant prosecutor—it is more common for the chief prosecutor to assign to one or more of his experienced assistants the responsibility for helping the newcomer adjust. Since the newcomer's actions reflect on the office as a whole, it is not surprising that this effort is made.

The assistance the newcomer receives can be described as a form of structured observation.

For roughly two weeks, he accompanies an experienced prosecutor to court and to plea-bargaining sessions and observes him in action. The proximity of the veteran prosecutor—and his designation as the newcomer's mentor—facilitates communication between the two. The experienced prosecutor can readily explain or justify his actions, and the newcomer can ask any and all relevant questions. Certainly, this is a more structured form of assistance than defense attorneys receive.

However, new prosecutors still feel confused and overwhelmed during this initial period. Notwithstanding the assistance they receive, they are disoriented by the multitude of tasks performed by the prosecutor and by the environment in which he operates. This is particularly true in the circuit court, where the seemingly endless shuffling of files, the parade of defendants before the court and around the courtroom, the hurried, early-morning plea-bargaining sessions all come as a surprise to the new prosecutor.

Q: What were your initial impressions of the court during this "orientation period?"

A: The first time I came down here was a Monday morning at the arraignments. Let's face it, the majority of people here, you don't expect courts to be as crowded as they are. You don't expect thirty to thirty-five people to come out of the cell block who have been arrested over the weekend. It was . . . you sit in court the first few days, you didn't realize the court was run like this. All you see, you see Perry Mason on TV, or pictures of the Supreme Court, or you see six judges up there in a spotless courtroom, everyone well dressed, well manicured, and you come to court and find people coming in their everyday clothes, coming up drunk, some are high on drugs, it's . . . it's an experience to say the least.

Q: Could you describe your first days when you came down here? What are your recollections? Anything strike you as strange?

A: Just the volume of business and all the stuff the prosecutor had to do. For the first week or two, I went to court with guys who had been here. Just sat there and watched. What struck me was the amount of things he [the prosecutor] has to do in the courtroom. The prosecutor runs the courtroom. Although the judge is theoretically in charge, we're standing there plea bargaining and calling the cases at the same time and chewing gum and telling people to quiet down and setting bonds, and that's what amazed me. I never thought I would learn all the terms. What bothered me also was the paperwork. Not the Supreme Court decisions, not the *mens rea* or any of this other stuff, but the amount of junk that's in those files that you have to know. We never heard about this crap in law school.

As suggested in the second excerpt, the new prosecutor is also surprised by the relative insignificance of the judge. He observes that the prosecutor assumes—through plea bargaining—responsibility for the disposition of many cases. Contrary to his expectations of being an adversary in a dispute moderated by the judge, he finds that often the prosecutor performs the judge's function.

It is precisely this responsibility for resolving disputes that is most vexing to the new superior court state's attorney. Unlike his circuit court counterpart, he does not generally find hurried conferences, crowded courts, and so on. But he observes that, as in the circuit court, the state's attorney negotiates cases, and in the superior court far more serious issues and periods of incarceration are involved in these negotiations. For the novice state's attorney, the notion that he will in short order be responsible for resolving these disputes is particularly disturbing.

Q: What were your initial impressions of your job here [as a state's attorney]?

A: Well, I was frightened of the increased responsibility. I knew the stakes were high here. . . . I didn't really know what to expect, and I would say it took me a good deal of time to adapt here.

Q: Adapt in which way?

A: To the higher responsibilities. Here you're dealing with felonies, serious felonies all the way up to homicides, and I had never been involved in that particular type of situation. . . .

I didn't believe that I was prepared to handle the type of job that I'd been hired to do. I looked around me and I saw the serious charges, the types of cases, and the experienced defense counsel on the one hand and the inexperience on my part on the other, and I was, well. . . .

Q: Did you study up on your own?

A: No more than. . . . Before I came over here I had done some research and made a few notes, et cetera, about the procedures. I think I was prepared from the book end of things to take the job, but, again, it was the practical aspects that you're not taught in law school and that you can only learn from experience that I didn't have, and that's what I was apprehensive about.

These first weeks in the court, then, serve to familiarize the newcomer with the general patterns of case resolution. He is not immediately thrust into the court but is able to spend some time simply observing the way matters are handled. The result, though, is to increase his anxiety. The confusion of the circuit court and the responsibilities of a state's attorney in the superior court were not anticipated. The newcomer expects to be able to prepare cases leisurely and to rely on the skills learned in law school. Yet he finds that his colleagues seem to have neither the time nor the inclination to operate in this fashion. As the informal period of orientation draws to a close, the newcomer has a better perspective on the way the system operates, but still is on very uneasy footing about how to proceed when the responsibility for the case is his alone. In short, he is somewhat disoriented by his orientation.

The Prosecutor on his Own: Initial Firmness and Resistance to Plea Bargaining

Within a few weeks after starting his job, the prosecutor and the state's attorney are expected to handle cases on their own. Experienced personnel are still available for advice, and the newcomer is told that he can turn to them with his problems. But the cases are now the newcomer's, and, with one exception, he is under no obligation to ask anyone for anything.

The new prosecutor is confronted by a stream of defense attorneys asking for a particular plea bargain in a case. If the prosecutor agrees, his decision is irreversible. It would be a violation of all the unwritten folkways of the criminal court for either a defense attorney or a prosecutor to break his word. On the other hand, if the prosecutor does not plea bargain, offers nothing in exchange for a plea, he at least does not commit himself to an outcome that may eventually prove to be a poor decision on his part. However, a refusal to plea bargain also places him "out of step" with his colleagues and with the general expectation of experienced defense attorneys.

Like the new attorney, the new prosecutor is in no hurry to dispose of the case. He is (1) inclined toward an adversary resolution of the case through formal hearings and trial, (2) disinclined to plea bargain in general, and (3) unsure about what constitutes an appropriate plea bargain for a particular case. Yet he is faced with demands by defense attorneys to resolve the case through plea bargaining. The new defense attorney has the luxury of postponing his decision for any given case. He can seek the advice of others before committing himself to a particular plea bargain in a particular case. For the new prosecutor, this is more difficult, since he is immediately faced with the demands of a number of attorneys in a number of different cases.

When the new prosecutor begins to handle his own cases, then, he lacks confidence about how to proceed in his dealings with defense attorneys. He often masks his insecurity in this period with an outward air of firmness. He is convinced that he must appear confident and tough, lest experienced attorneys think they can take advantage of him.

Q: What happened during your first few days of handling cases on your own?

A: Well, as a prosecutor, first of all, people try to cater to you because they want you to do favors for them. If you let a lawyer run all over you, you are dead. I had criminal the first day, on a Monday, and I'm in there [in the room where cases are negotiated], and a guy comes in, and I was talking to some lawyer on his file, and he's just standing there. Then I was talking to a second guy, and he was about fourth or fifth. So he looked at me and says: "When the hell you going to get to me?" So I says: "You wait your fucking turn. I'll get to you when I'm ready. If you don't like it, get out." It's sad that you have to swear at people, but it's the only language they understand—especially lawyers. Lawyers are the most obstinate, arrogant, belligerent bastards you will ever meet. Believe me. They come into this court—first of all—and we are really the asshole of the judicial system [circuit court], and they come in here and don't really have any respect for you. They'll come in here and be nice to you, because they feel you'll give them a *nolle*. That's all. Lawyers do not respect this court. I don't know if I can blame them or not blame them. You can come in here and see the facilities here; you see how things are handled; you see how it's like a zoo pushing people in and out. . . . When they do come here, lawyers have two approaches. One, they try to soft-soap and kiss your ass if you give them a *nolle*. Two, they'll come in here and try to ride roughshod over you and try to push you to a corner. Like that lawyer that first day. I had to swear at him and show him I wasn't going to take shit, and that's that. The problem of dealing with lawyers is that you can't let them bullshit you. So, when I first started out I tried to be. . . . It's like the new kid on the block. He comes to a new neighborhood, and you've got to prove yourself. If you're a patsy, you're going to live with that as long as you're in court. If you let a couple of lawyers run over you, word will get around to go to ____, he's a pushover. Before you know it, they're running all over you. So you have to draw a line so they will respect you.

At first I was very tough because I didn't know what I was doing. In other words, you have to be very wary. These guys, some of them, have been practicing in this court for forty years. And they'll take you to the cleaners. You have to be pretty damn careful.

The new prosecutor couples this outward show of firmness toward attorneys with a fairly rigid plea-bargaining posture. His reluctance to offer incentives to the defendant for a plea or to reward the defendant who chooses to plead is, at this point in the prosecutor's career, as much a function of his lack of confidence as it is a reflection of his antipathy toward plea bargaining. During this very early stage he is simply afraid to make concessions. Experienced court personnel are well aware that new prosecutors adopt this rigid stance.

Q: Have you noticed any differences between new prosecutors and prosecutors that have been around awhile?

A: Oh, yes. First of all, a new prosecutor is more likely to be less flexible in changing charges. He's afraid. He's cautious. He doesn't know his business. He doesn't know the liars. He can't tell when he's lying or exaggerating. He doesn't know all the ramifications. He doesn't know how tough it is sometimes to prove the case to juries. He hasn't got the experience, so that more likely than not he will be less flexible. He is also more easily fooled. [Circuit court judge]

I can only answer that question in a general way. It does seem to me that the old workhorses [experienced prosecutors] are more flexible than the young stallions. [Superior court judge]

Q: You were saying about the kids, the new prosecutors, the new state's attorneys. Are they kind of more hard-assed?

A: They tend to be more nervous. They tend to have a less well defined idea of what they can do and what they can't do without being criticized. So, to the extent that they are more nervous, they tend to be more hard-assed. [Private criminal attorney]

Q: What about new prosecutors? Do they differ significantly from prosecutors who have been around awhile?

A: Initially a new prosecutor is going to be reluctant to *nolle*, reluctant to give too good a deal because he is scared. He is afraid of being taken advantage of. And if you are talking about the circuit court, they've got the problem that they can't even talk it over with anybody. They've got a hundred fifty cases or whatever, and they make an offer or don't make an offer, that's it. Maybe at the end of the day they may get a chance to talk it over and say: "Gee, did I do the right thing?" The defense attorney, when the offer is made, has the opportunity to talk to somebody plus his client before making a decision. So I think it takes the prosecutor a longer time to come around and work under the system. [Legal aid attorney]

It is not difficult to understand why the new prosecutor is reluctant to plea bargain and why he appears rigid to court veterans. Set aside for the moment the prosecutor's personal preference for an adversary resolution and consider only the nature of the demands being made on him. Experienced attorneys want charges dropped, sentence recommendations, and *nolles*. They approach him with the standard argument about the wonderful personal traits of the defendant, the minor nature of the crime, the futility of incarceration, and so on. When the new prosecutor picks up the file, he finds that the defendant probably has an extensive prior criminal record and, often, that he has committed a crime that does not sound minor at all. Under the statute for the crime involved, it is likely that the defendant faces a substantial period of incarceration, yet in almost all circuit court cases and in many superior court cases, the attorneys are talking about a no-time disposition. What to the new prosecutor frequently seems like a serious matter is treated as a relatively inconsequential offense by defense attorneys. And, because the newcomer views the matter as serious, his resolve to remain firm—or, conversely, his insecurity about reducing charges—is reinforced.

Illustrations of this propensity for the new prosecutor or state's attorney to be "outraged" by the facts of the case, and to be disinclined to offer "sweet" deals, are plentiful. The following comments by two circuit court prosecutors and a superior court state's attorney, respectively, illustrate the extent to which the newcomer's appraisal of a case differed from that of the defense attorney and from that of his own colleagues.

Q: You used to go to ____ [chief prosecutor] for help on early cases. Were his recommendations out of line with what you thought should be done with the case?

A: Let's say a guy came in with a serious crime . . . a crime that I thought was serious at one time, anyway. Take fighting on ____ Avenue [a depressed area of Arborville]. He got twenty-five stitches in the head and is charged with aggravated assault. One guy got twenty-five stitches, the other fifteen. And the attorneys would want me to reduce it. I'd go and talk to ____ [chief prosecutor]. He'd say: "They both are drunk, they both got head wounds. Let them plead to breach of peace, and the judge will give them a money fine." Things like that I didn't feel right about doing, since, to me, right out of law school, middle class, you figure twenty-five stitches in the head, Jesus Christ.

Q: How did you learn what a case was worth?

A: What do you mean, what it's worth?

Q: In terms of plea bargaining. What the going rate. . . .

A: From the prosecutors and defense attorneys who would look at me dumbfounded when I would tell them that I would not reduce this charge. And then they would go running to my boss and he'd say, "Well, it's up to him." Some would even go running to the judge, screaming. One guy claimed surprise when I intended to go to trial for assault in second, which is a Class D felony. Two counts of that and two misdemeanor counts. It was set for jury trial. His witnesses were there. His experience in this court, he said, having handled two or three hundred cases, was that none has ever gone to trial. So he claimed surprise the day of trial. He just couldn't believe it.

Q: Were you in any way out of step with the way things were done here when you first began handling cases on your own?

A: In one respect I was. I evaluated a case by what I felt a proper recommendation should be, and my recommendations were almost always in terms of longer time. I found that the other guys in the office were breaking things down more than I expected. As a citizen, I couldn't be too complacent about an old lady getting knocked down, stuff like that. I thought more time should be recommended. I might think five to ten, six to twelve, while the other guys felt that three to seven was enough.

Implicit in these remarks are the seeds of an explanation for a prosecutor's gradually becoming more willing to plea bargain. One can hypothesize that as his experience with handling cases increases, he will feel less outraged by the crime, and thus will be more willing to work out a negotiated settlement. One assistant state's attorney likened his change in attitude to that of a nurse in an emergency room.

It's like nurses in emergency rooms. You get so used to armed robbery that you treat it as routine, not as morally upsetting. In the emergency room, the biggest emergency is treated as routine. And it's happening to me. The nature of the offense doesn't cause the reaction in me that it would cause in the average citizen. Maybe this is a good thing; maybe it isn't.

Though there is merit in this argument— prosecutors do become accustomed to crime—it is hardly a sufficient explanation of prosecutorial adaptation to plea bargaining. Other factors, often far more subtle, must be considered if we are to understand how and why the novice prosecutor becomes a seasoned plea bargainer.

LEARNING ABOUT PLEA BARGAINING

In the preceding sections I have portrayed the new prosecutor as being predisposed toward an adversary resolution of a case, uncertain about his responsibilities, rigid in his relations with defense attorneys, reluctant to drop charges and to plea bargain in cases that he considers serious, and anxious to try out the skills he learned in law school. This characterization of the newcomer contrasts sharply with that of the veteran prosecutor. [The veteran prosecutor takes] an active role in plea bargaining—urging, cajoling, and threatening the defense attorney to share in the benefits of a negotiated disposition.

How is the veteran prosecutor to be reconciled with the new prosecutor . . . ?

Prosecutors and state's attorneys learn their roles primarily entail the processing of factually guilty defendants. Contrary to their expectations that problems of establishing factual guilt would be central to their job, they find that in most cases the evidence in the file is sufficient to conclude (and prove) that the defendant is factually guilty. For those cases where there is a substantial question as to factual guilt, the prosecutor has the power – and is inclined to exercise it – to *nolle* or dismiss the case. If he himself does not believe the defendant to be factually guilty, it is part of his formal responsibilities to filter the case out. But, of the cases that remain after the initial screening, the prosecutor believes the majority of defendants to be factually guilty.

Furthermore, he finds that defense attorneys only infrequently contest the prosecutor's own conclusion that the defendant is guilty. In their initial approach to the prosecutor they may raise the possibility that the defendant is factually innocent, but in most subsequent discussions their advances focus on disposition and not on the problem of factual guilt. Thus, from the prosecutor's own reading of the file (after screening) and from the comments of his "adversary," he learns that he begins with the upper hand: more often than not, the factual guilt of the defendant is not really disputable.

Q: Are most of the defendants who come to this court guilty?

A: Yeah, or else we wouldn't have charged them. You know, that's something that people don't understand. Basically the people that are brought here are believed very definitely to be guilty or we wouldn't go on with the prosecution. We would *nolle* the case, and, you know that is something, when people say, "Well, do you really believe. . . ." Yeah. I do. I really do, and if I didn't and we can clear them, then we *nolle* it, there's no question about it.

But most cases are good, solid cases, and in most of them the defendant is guilty. We have them cold-cocked. And they plead guilty because they are guilty . . . a guy might have been caught in a package store with bottles.

Now, he wasn't there to warm his hands. The defendant may try some excuse, but they are guilty and they know they are guilty. And we'll give them a break when they plead guilty. I don't think we should throw away the key on the guy just because we got him cold-cocked. We've got good cases, we give them what we think the case is worth from our point of view, allowing the defendant's mitigating circumstances to enter.

Q: The fact that you're willing to offer a pretty good bargain in negotiations might lead a person to plead guilty even if he had a chance to beat it at trial. But if he was found guilty at the trial he might not get the same result?

A: That's possible. I mean, only the accused person knows whether or not he's committed the crime, and. . . . It's an amazing thing, where, on any number of occasions, you will sit down to negotiate with an accused's attorney . . . and you know [he will say]: "No, no, he's not guilty, he wants his trial." But then if he develops a weakness in the case, or points out a weakness to you, and then you come back and say: "Well, we'll take a suspended sentence and probation," suddenly he says, "Yes, I'm guilty." So it leads you to conclude that, well, all these people who are proclaiming innocence are really not innocent. They're just looking for the right disposition. Now, from my point of view, the ideal situation might be if the person is not guilty, that he pleads not guilty, and we'll give him his trial and let the jury decide. But most people who are in court don't want a trial. I'm not the person who seeks them out and says, "I will drop this charge" or "I will reduce this charge, I will reduce the amount of time you have to do." They come to us, so, you know, the conclusion I think is there that any reasonable person could draw, that these people are guilty, that they are just looking for the best disposition possible. Very few people ask for a speedy trial.

In addition to learning of the factual culpability of most defendants, the prosecutor also learns that defendants would be hard-pressed to raise legal challenges to the state's case. As was discussed earlier, most cases are simply barren of any contestable legal issue, and nothing in the prosecutor's file or the defense attorney's arguments leads the prosecutor to conclude otherwise.

The new prosecutor or state's attorney, then, learns that in most cases the problem of establishing the defendant's factual and legal guilt is non-existent. Typically, he begins with a very solid case, and, contrary to his expectations, he finds that few issues are in need of resolution at an adversary hearing or trial. The defendant's guilt is not generally problematic; it is conceded by the defense attorney. What remains problematic is the sentence the defendant will receive.

Distinguishing Among The Guilty Defendants

Formally, the prosecutor has some powers that bear directly on sentence. He has the option to reduce or eliminate charges leveled against the defendant; the responsibility for the indictment is his, and his alone. Thus, if he *nolles* some of the charges against the defendant, he can reduce the maximum exposure the defendant faces or ensure that the defendant is sentenced only on a misdemeanor (if he *nolles* a felony), and so forth. Beyond these actions on charges, the formal powers of the prosecutor cease. The judge is responsible for sentencing. He is supposed to decide the conditions of probation, the length of incarceration, and so on. Notwithstanding this formal dichotomy of responsibility, prosecutors find that defense attorneys approach them about both charge and sentence reduction.

Since charge reduction bears on sentence reduction, it is only a small step for defense attorneys to inquire specifically about sentence; and, because there is often an interdependence between charge and sentence, prosecutors are compelled at least to listen to the attorney's arguments. Thus, the prosecutor finds attorneys parading before him asking for charge and sentence reduction, and, in a sense, he is obligated to hear them out.

It is one thing to say that prosecutors and state's attorneys must listen to defense attorneys' requests about disposition and another to say that they must cooperate with these attorneys. As already indicated, new prosecutors feel acutely uneasy about charge and sentence reduction. They have neither the confidence nor the inclination to usurp what they view as primarily the judge's responsibility. Furthermore, one would think that their resolve not to become involved in this area would be strengthened by their learning that most defendants are factually and legally guilty. Why should they discuss dispositions in cases in which they "hold all the cards?"

This query presupposes that prosecutors continue to conceive of themselves as adversaries, whose exclusive task is to establish the defendant's guilt or innocence. But what happens is that as prosecutors gain greater experience handling cases, they gradually develop certain standards for evaluating cases, standards that bear not just on the defendant's guilt or innocence, but, more importantly, on the disposition of the defendant's case. These standards better explain prosecutorial behavior in negotiating dispositions than does the simple notion of establishing guilt or innocence.

Specifically prosecutors come to distinguish between serious and nonserious cases, and between cases in which they are looking for time and cases in which they are not looking for time. These standards or distinctions evolve after the prosecutor has processed a substantial number of factually and legally guilty defendants. They provide a means of sorting the raw material—the guilty defendants. Indeed, one can argue that the adversary component of the prosecutor's job is shifted from establishing guilt or innocence to determining the seriousness of the defendant's guilt and whether he should receive time. The guilt of the defendant is assumed, but the problem of disposition remains to be informally argued.

Prosecutors and state's attorneys draw sharp distinctions between serious and nonserious cases. In both instances, they assume the defendant guilty, but they are looking for different types of dispositions, dependent upon their classification of the case. If it is a nonserious matter, they are amenable to defense requests for a small fine in the circuit court, some short, suspended sentence, or some brief period of probation; similarly, in a nonserious superior court matter the state's attorney is willing to work out a combination suspended sentence and probation. The central concern with these nonserious cases is to dispose of them quickly. If the defense attorney requests some sort of no-time disposition that is dependent upon either a prosecutorial reduction of charges or a sentence recommendation, the prosecutor and state's attorney are likely to agree. They have no incentive to refuse the attorney's request, since the attorney's desire comports with what they are "looking for." The case is simply not worth the effort to press for greater penalty.

On the other hand, if the case is serious, the prosecutor and state's attorney are likely to be looking for time. The serious case cannot be quickly disposed of by a no-time alternative. These are cases in which we would expect more involved and lengthy plea-bargaining negotiations.

Whether the case is viewed as serious or nonserious depends on factors other than the formal charges the defendant faces. For example, these nonformal considerations might include the degree of harm done the victim, the amount of violence employed by the defendant, the defendant's prior record, the characteristics of the victim and defendant, the defendant's motive; all are somewhat independent of formal charge, and yet all weigh heavily in the prosecutor's judgment of the seriousness of the case. Defendants facing the same formal charges, then, may find that prosecutors sort their cases into different categories. Two defendants charged with robbery with violence may find that in one instance the state's attorney is willing to reduce the charge and recommend probation, while in the second case he is looking for a substantial period of incarceration. In the former case, the defendant may have simply brushed against the victim (still technically robbery with violence), whereas in the second, he may have dealt the victim a severe blow. Or possibly, the first defendant was a junkie supporting his habit, whereas the second was operating on the profit motive. These are, of course, imperfect illustrations, but the point is that the determination as to whether a case is serious or not serious only partially reflects the charges against the defendant. Often the determination is based on a standard that develops with experience in the court, and operates, for the most part, independently of formal statutory penalties.

The following excerpts convey a sense of the serious/nonserious dichotomy and also support the argument that charge does not necessarily indicate seriousness.

Q: How did you learn what cases were worth?

A: You mean sentences.

Q: Yeah.

A: Well, that's a hit-or-miss kind of an experience. You take a first offender; any first offender in a nonviolent crime certainly is not going to jail for a nonviolent crime. And a second offender, well, it depends again on the type of crime, and maybe there should be some supervision, some probation. And a third time, you say, well now this is a guy who maybe you should treat a little more strictly. Now, a violent crime, I would treat differently. How did I learn to? I learned because there were a few other guys around with experience, and I got experience, and they had good judgments, workable approaches, and you pick it up like that. In other words, you watch others, you talk to others, you handle a lot of cases yourself.

Q: Does anybody, the public, put pressure on you to be tougher?

A: Not really.

Q: Wouldn't these sentences be pretty difficult for the public to understand?

A: Yeah, somewhat. . . . Sure, we are pretty easy on a lot of these cases except that. . . . We are tough on mugging and crimes by violence. Say an old lady is grabbed by a kid and knocked to the ground and her pocketbook taken as she is waiting for the bus. We'd be as tough as anybody on that one, whether you call it a breach of peace or a robbery. We'd be very tough. And in this case there would be a good likelihood of the first offender going to jail, whatever the charge we give him. The name of the charge isn't important. We'd have the facts regardless.

Q: So you think you have changed? You give away more than you used to?

A: I don't give away more. I think that I have reached the point where. . . . When I started I was trying to be too fair, if you want to say that, you know, to see that justice was done, and I was severe. But, you know, like ____ [head prosecutor] says, you need to look for justice tempered with mercy, you know, substantial justice, and that's what I do now. When I was new, a guy cut [knifed] someone he had to go to jail. But now I look for substantial justice—if two guys have been drinking and one guy got cut, I'm not giving anything away, but a fine, that's enough there.

Q: But you are easier now? I mean, you could look for time?

A: Look, if I get a guy that I feel belongs in jail, I try to sentence bargain and get him in jail. We had this one guy, ____. He was charged with breach of peace. We knew he had been selling drugs but we couldn't prove anything. He hits this girl in ____'s parking lot [large department store], and tried to take her purse. She screams and he runs. This was a real son-of-a-bitch, been pimping for his own wife. On breach of peace I wanted the full year, and eventually got nine months. Cases like that I won't give an inch on. And the lawyer first wanted him to plead to suspended sentence and a money fine. I said this guy is a god-damned animal. Anybody who lets his wife screw and then gets proceeds from it, and deals in drugs . . . well, if you can catch the bastard on it, he belongs behind bars.

* * *

The second standard used by prosecutors and state's attorneys in processing factually and legally guilty defendants is the time/no-time distinction. There is an obvious relationship between the serious/nonserious standard and this one: in the serious case time is generally the goal; whereas in the nonserious case, a no-time disposition is satisfactory to the prosecutor. But this simple relationship does not always hold, and it is important for us to consider the exceptions.

In some serious cases, the prosecutor or state's attorney may not be looking for time. Generally, these are cases in which the prosecutor has a problem establishing either the factual or legal guilt of the defendant, and thus is willing to settle for a plea to the charge and offer a

recommendation of a suspended sentence. The logic is simple: the prosecutor feels the defendant is guilty of the offense but fears that if he insists on time, the defense attorney will go to trial and uncover the factual or legal defects of the state's case. Thus, the prosecutor "sweetens the deal" to extract a guilty plea and to decrease the likelihood that the attorney will gamble on complete vindication.

Of the prosecutors I interviewed, a handful expressed disenchantment with plea bargaining. They felt that their associates were being too lenient, giving away too much in return for the defendant's plea. They argued that the prosecutor's office should stay firm and go to trial if necessary in order to obtain higher sentences. They were personally inclined to act this way: they "didn't like plea bargaining." But when pushed a bit, it became clear that their antipathy to plea bargaining was not without its exceptions. In the serious case with factual or legal defects they felt very strongly that plea bargaining was appropriate. The sentiments of such an "opponent" to plea bargaining are presented below.

Q: So you are saying that you only like some kinds of plea bargaining?

A: I like to negotiate cases where I have a problem with the case. I know the guy is guilty, but I have some legal problem, or unavailability of a witness that the defendant doesn't know about that will make it difficult for us to put the case on. I would have trouble with the case. Then it is in my interest to bargain; even in serious cases with these problems, it is in the best interests of the state to get the guy to plead, even if it's to a felony with suspended sentence.

Q: If there was no plea bargaining, then the state would lose out?

A: Yes, in cases like these. These would be cases that without plea bargaining we would have trouble convicting the defendant. But this has nothing to do with the defendant's guilt or innocence. Yet we might have to let him go. It is just to plea bargain in cases like this. It is fair to get the plea from the defendant, since he is guilty. Now, there is another situation; whereas in the first situation, I have no philosophical problems with plea bargaining. We may have a weak case factually. Maybe the case depends on one witness, and I have talked to the witness and realized how the witness would appear in court. Maybe the witness would be a flop when he testifies. If I feel the defendant is guilty, but the witness is really bad, then I know that we won't win the case at trial, that we won't win a big concession in plea bargaining. So I will evaluate the case, and I will be predisposed to talking about a more lenient disposition.

* * *

The other unexpected cross between the standards—nonserious case/looking for time—occurs in several types of situations. First, there is the case in which the defendant has a long history of nonserious offenses, and it is felt that a short period of incarceration will "teach him a lesson," or at least indicate that there are limits beyond which prosecutors cannot be pushed. Second, there is the situation where the prosecutor holds the defense attorney in disdain and is determined to teach the attorney a lesson. Thus, though the defendant's offense is nonserious, the prosecutor would generally be amenable to a no-time disposition, the prosecutor chooses to hold firm. It is precisely in those borderline cases that the prosecutor can be most successful in exercising sanctions against the uncooperative defense attorney. The formal penalties associated with the charges against the defendant give him ample sentencing range, and by refusing to agree to a no-time disposition, the costs to the defense attorney become great. The attorney is not able to meet his client's demands for no time, and yet he must be leery about trial, given the even greater exposure the defendant faces. These borderline decisions by prosecutors, then, are fertile grounds for exploring sanctions against defense attorneys. It is here that we can expect the cooperative defense attorney to benefit most, and the recalcitrant defense attorney to suffer the most. Relatedly, one can also expect prosecutors to be looking for time in nonserious offenses in which the defendant or his counsel insists on raising motions and going to trial. These adversary activities may be just enough to tip the prosecutor into looking for time.

In addition to its relationship to the serious/nonserious standard, the time/no-time standard bears on prosecutorial plea-bargaining behavior in another way. As prosecutors gain experience in the plea-bargaining system, they tend to stress "certainty of time" rather than "amount of time." This is to say that they become less concerned about extracting maximum penalties from defendants and more concerned with ensuring that in cases in which they are looking for time, the defendant actually receives some time. Obviously, there are limits to the prosecutor's largesse—in a serious case 30 days will not be considered sufficient time. But prosecutors are willing to consider periods of incarceration substantially shorter than the maximum sentence allowable for a particular crime. In return, though, prosecutors want a guarantee of sorts that the defendant will receive time. They want to decrease the likelihood that the defendant, by some means or other, will obtain a suspended sentence. Thus, they will "take" a fixed amount of time if the defendant agrees not to try to "pitch" for a lower sentence, or if the defendant pleads to a charge in which all participants know some time will be meted out by the judge. In the latter instance, the attorney may be free to "pitch," but court personnel know his effort is more a charade for the defendant than a realistic effort to obtain a no-time disposition. The following excerpts illustrate prosecutorial willingness to trade off years of time for certainty of time.

> I don't believe in giving away things. In fact ____ [a public defender] approached me; there's this kid ____, he has two robberies, one first degree, one second, and three minor cases. Now, this kid, I made out an affidavit myself for tampering with a witness. This kid is just n.g. ____ came to me and said, "We'll plead out, two to five." He'll go to state's prison. I agreed to that—both these offenses are bindovers. These kids belong in jail. I'd rather take two to five here than bind them over to superior court and take a chance on what will happen there. At least my two to five will be a year and three-quarters in state's prison. The thing is, if I want to get a guy in jail for a year, I'll plea bargain with him, and I'll take six months if I can get it, because the guy belongs in jail, and if I can get him to jail for six months why should I fool around with that case, and maybe get a year

if I am lucky? If I can put a guy away for six months I might be cheated out of six months, but at least the guy is doing six months in jail.

What is a proper time? It never bothers me if we could have gotten seven years and instead we got five. In this case, there was no violence; minor stuff was stolen. We got time out of him. That is the important thing.

A: It makes no difference to me really if a man does five to ten or four to eight. The important thing is he's off the street, not a menace to society for a period of time, and the year or two less is not going to make that great a difference. If you do get time, I think it's . . . you know, many prosecutors I know feel this way. They have achieved confinement, that's what they're here for.

Q: Let's take another example. Yesterday an attorney walked in here when I was present on that gambling case. He asked you if it could be settled without time?

A: And I said no. That ended the discussion.

Q: What will he do now?

A: He'll file certain motions that he really doesn't have to file. All the facts of our case were spelled out; he knows as much about our cases as he'll ever know. So his motions will just delay things. There'll come a point, though, when he'll have to face trial; and he'll come in to speak with us, and ask if we still have the same position. We'll have the same position. We'll still be looking for one to three. His record goes back to 1923, he's served two or three terms for narcotics, and he's been fined five times for gambling. So we'd be looking for one to three and a fine. Even though he's in his sixties, he's been a criminal all his life, since 1923. . . .

Q: But if the attorney pushes and says, "Now look. He's an old guy. He's sixty-two years old, how about six months?"

A: I might be inclined to accept it because, again, confinement would be involved. I think our ends would be met. It would show his compadres that there's no longer any immunity for gambling, that there is confinement involved. So the end result would be achieved.

Justice Holmes, who is supposed to be the big sage in American jurisprudence, said it isn't the extent of the punishment but the certainty of it. This is my basic philosophy. If the guy faces twelve years in state's prison, I'm satisfied if on a plea of guilty he'll go to state's prison for two or three years.

The experienced prosecutor, then, looks beyond the defendant's guilt when evaluating a case. He learns—from a reading of the file and from the defense attorney's entreaties—that most defendants are factually and legally guilty and that he generally holds the upper hand. As he gains experience in processing these cases, he gradually begins to draw distinctions within this pool of guilty defendants. Some of the cases appear not to be serious, and the prosecutor becomes willing to go along with the defense attorney's request for no-time dispositions. The cases simply do not warrant a firmer prosecutorial posture. In serious cases, when he feels time is in order, he often finds defense attorneys in agreement on the need for some incarceration.

In a sense, the prosecutor redefines his professional goals. He learns that the statutes fail to distinguish adequately among guilty defendants, that they "sweep too broadly," and give short shrift to the specific facts of the offense, to the defendant's prior record, to the degree of contributory culpability of the victim, and so on. Possessing more information about the defendant than the judge does, the prosecutor—probably unconsciously—comes to believe that it is his professional responsibility to develop standards that distinguish among defendants and lead to "equitable" dispositions. Over time, the prosecutor comes to feel that if he does not develop these standards, if he does not make these professional judgments, no one else will.

The prosecutor seems almost to drift into plea bargaining. When he begins his job he observes that his colleagues plea bargain routinely and quickly finds that defense attorneys expect him to do the same. Independent of any rewards, sanctions, or pressures, he learns the strengths of his cases, and learns to distinguish the serious from the nonserious ones. After an initial period of reluctance to plea bargain at all (he is fearful of being taken advantage of by defense attorneys), the prosecutor finds that he is engaged almost unwittingly in daily decisions concerning the disposition of cases. His obligation to consider alternative charges paves the way for the defense attorney's advances; it is only a small jump to move to sentence discussions. And as he plea bargains more and more cases, the serious/nonserious and time/no-time standards begin to hold sway in his judgments. He feels confident about the disposition he is looking for, and if a satisfactory plea bargain in line with his goals can be negotiated, he comes to feel that there is little point to following a more formal adversary process. . . .

Case Pressure and Potential Backlog

Though they may do so during the first few weeks, the newcomer's peers and superiors do not generally pressure him to move cases because of volume. Instead, he is thrust in the fray largely on his own and is allowed to work out his own style of case disposition. Contrary to the "conspiratorial perspective" of the adaptation process, he is not coerced to cooperate in processing "onerously large caseloads."

The newcomer's plea-bargaining behavior is conditioned by his reactions to particular cases he handles or learns about and not by caseload problems of the office. The chief prosecutor within the jurisdiction may worry about his court's volume and the speed with which cases are disposed, but he does not generally interfere with his assistant's decision about how to proceed in a case. The newcomer is left to learn about plea bargaining on his own, and for the reason already discussed, he learns and is taught the value of negotiating many of his cases. The absence of a direct relationship between prosecutor plea bargaining and case pressure is suggested in the following remarks.

Q: Is it case pressure that leads you to negotiate?

A: I don't believe it's the case pressure at all. In every court, whether there are five cases or one hundred cases, we should try to settle it. It's good for both sides. If I were a public defender I'd try to settle all the cases for my guilty clients. By negotiating you are bound to

do better. Now take this case. [He reviewed the facts of a case in which an elderly man was charged with raping a 7-year-old girl. The defendant claimed he could not remember what happened, that he was drunk, and that, though the girl might have been in the bed with him, he did not think he raped her.] I think I gave the defense attorney a fair deal. The relatives say she was raped, but the doctor couldn't conclusively establish that. I offered him a plea to a lesser charge, one dealing with advances toward minors, but excluding the sex act. If he takes it, he'll be able to walk away with time served [the defendant had not posted bail and had spent several months in jail]. It's the defendant's option though. He can go through trial if he wants, but if he makes that choice, the kid and her relatives will have to be dragged through the agonies of trial also. Then I would be disposed to look for a higher sentence for the defendant. So I think my offer is fair, and the offer has nothing to do with the volume of this court. It's the way I think the case—all things considered—should be resolved.

Q: You say the docket wasn't as crowded in 1966, and yet there was plea bargaining. If I had begun this interview by saying why is there plea bargaining here. . . .

A: I couldn't use the reason there's plea bargaining because there are a lot of cases. That's not so; that's not so at all. If we had only ten cases down for tomorrow and an attorney walked in and wanted to discuss a case with me, I'd sit down and discuss it with him. In effect, that's plea bargaining. Whether it's for the charge or for an agreed recommendation or reduction of the charge or what have you, it's still plea bargaining. It's part of the process that has been going on for quite a long time.

Q: And you say it's not because of the crowded docket, but if I gave you a list of reasons for why there was plea bargaining and asked you to pick the most important. . . .

A: I never really thought about the. . . . You talk about the necessity for plea bargaining, and you say, well, it's necessary, and one of the reasons is because we have a crowded docket, but even if we didn't we still would plea bargain.

Q: Why?

A: Well, it has been working throughout the years, and the way I look at it, it's beneficial to the defendant, it's beneficial to the court, and not just in saving time but in avoiding police officers coming to court, witnesses being subpoenaed in, and usually things can be discussed between prosecutors and defense counsel which won't be said in the open court and on the record. There are many times that the defense counsel will speak confidentially with the prosecutor about his client or about the facts or about the complainant or a number of things. So I don't know if I can justify plea bargaining other than by speaking of the necessity of plea bargaining. If there were only ten cases down for one day, it still would be something that would be done.

Maybe in places like New York they plea bargain because of case pressure. I don't know. But here it is different. We dispose of cases on the basis of what is fair to both sides. You can get a fair settlement by plea bargaining. If you don't try to settle a case quickly, it gets stale. In New York the volume probably is so bad that it becomes a matter of "getting rid of cases." In Connecticut, we have some pretty big dockets in some cities, but in other areas—here, for example—we don't have that kind of pressure. Sure, I feel some pressure, but you can't say that we negotiate our cases out to clear the docket. And you probably can't say that even about the big cities in Connecticut either.

Prosecutors, then, do not view their propensity to plea bargain as a direct outcome of case pressure. Instead, they speak of "mutually satisfactory outcomes," "fair dispositions," "reducing police overcharging," and so on. We need not here evaluate their claims in detail; what is important is that collectively their arguments militate against according case pressure the "top billing" it so often receives in the literature.

Another way to conceptualize the relationship between case pressure and plea bargaining is to introduce the notion of a "potential backlog." Some prosecutors maintain that if fewer cases were plea bargained, or if plea bargaining were eliminated, a backlog of cases to be disposed of would quickly clog their calendars.

A potential backlog, then, lurks as a possibility in every jurisdiction. Even in a low-volume jurisdiction, one complex trial could back up cases for weeks, or even months. If all those delayed cases also had to be tried, the prosecutor feels he would face two not-so-enviable options. He could become further backlogged by trying as many of them as was feasible, or he could reduce his backlog by outright dismissal of cases. The following comments are typical of the potential backlog argument.

Q: Some people have suggested that plea bargaining not be allowed in the court. All cases would go to trial before a judge or jury and. . . .

A: Something like that would double, triple, and quadruple the backlog. Reduce that 90 percent of people pleading guilty, and even if you were to try a bare minimum of those cases, you quadruple your backlog. It's feasible.

Well, right now we don't have a backlog. But if we were to try even 10 percent of our cases, take them to a jury, we'd be so backed up that we couldn't even move. We'd be very much in the position of. . . . Some traffic director in New York once said that there will come a time that there will be one car too many coming into New York and nobody will be able to move. Well, we can get ourselves into that kind of situation if we are going to go ahead and refuse to plea bargain even in the serious cases.

Though a potential backlog is an ever-present possibility, it should be stressed that most prosecutors develop this argument more as a prediction as to the outcome of a rule decreasing or eliminating plea bargaining than as an explanation for why they engage in plea bargaining. If plea bargaining were eliminated, a backlog would develop; but awareness of this outcome does not explain why they plea bargain.

Furthermore, prosecutors tend to view the very notion of eliminating plea bargaining as a fake issue, a straw-man proposition. It is simply inconceivable to them that plea bargaining could or would be eliminated. They maintain that no court system could try all of its cases, even if huge increases in personnel levels were made; trials consume more time than any realistic increase in personnel levels could manage.

They were willing to speculate on the outcome of a rule proscribing plea bargaining, but the argument based on court backlog that they evoked was not a salient consideration in understanding their day-in, day-out plea-bargaining behavior.

It is, of course, impossible to refute with complete certainty an argument that prosecutors plea bargain because failure to do so would cause a backlog of unmanageable proportions to develop. However, the interviews indicate other more compelling ways to conceptualize prosecutorial adaptation to plea bargaining, and these do not depend on a potential backlog that always can be conjured up. Though the backlog may loom as a consequence of a failure to plea bargain, it—like its case-pressure cousin—is neither a necessary nor sufficient explanatory vehicle for understanding the core aspects of prosecutorial plea-bargaining behavior.

A Perspective on Prosecutorial Adaptation

Perhaps the most important outcome of the prosecutor's adaptation is that he evidences a major shift in his own presumption about how to proceed with a case. As a newcomer, he feels it to be his responsibility to establish the defendant's guilt at trial, and he sees no need to justify a decision to go to trial. However, as he processes more and more cases, as he drifts into plea bargaining, and as he is taught the risks associated with trials, his own assumption about how to proceed with a case changes. He approaches every case with plea bargaining in mind, that is, he presumes that the case will be plea bargained. If it is a "nonserious"

matter, he expects it to be quickly resolved; if it is "serious" he generally expects to negotiate time as part of the disposition. In both instances, he anticipates that the case will eventually be resolved by a negotiated disposition and not by a trial. When a plea bargain does not materialize, and the case goes to trial, the prosecutor feels compelled to justify his failure to reach an accord. He no longer is content to simply assert that it is the role of the prosecutor to establish the defendant's guilt at trial. This adversary component of the prosecutor's role has been replaced by a self-imposed burden to justify why he chose to go to trial, particularly if a certain conviction— and, for serious cases, a period of incarceration—could have been obtained by means of a negotiated disposition.

Relatedly, the prosecutor grows accustomed to the power he exercises in these plea-bargaining negotiations. As a newcomer, he argued that his job was to be an advocate for the state and that it was the judge's responsibility to sentence defendants. But, having in fact "sentenced" most of the defendants whose files he plea bargained, the distinction between prosecutor and judge becomes blurred in his own mind. Though he did not set out to usurp judicial prerogatives—indeed, he resisted efforts to engage him in the plea-bargaining process—he gradually comes to expect that he will exercise sentencing powers. There is no fixed point in time when he makes a calculated choice to become adjudicator as well as adversary. In a sense, it simply "happens" ; the more cases he resolves (either by charge reduction or sentence recommendations), the greater the likelihood that he will lose sight of the distinction between the roles of judge and prosecutor.

Plea bargaining by court-appointed criminal lawyers is examined in this article. Emmelman discusses and analyzes how cases are settled and concludes that the plea-bargaining process is comprised of multiple stages of negotiating behavior and also involves a wide range of formal litigation proceedings. The decision-making process consists of three types of activities: assessing the offender for a plea of guilty, negotiating the terms of a plea, and discussing a course of action with the defendant. Because many cases do not result in a plea agreement during the first negotiation, defense attorneys' recursive consideration of whether the case should be settled or processed further until an acceptable plea is attained is common practice. By litigating throughout various court hearings until a plea is decided, defense lawyers go through multiple negotiations as well as formal litigation proceedings for their clients.

TRIAL BY PLEA BARGAIN

Case Settlement as a Product of Recursive Decision Making

DEBRA S. EMMELMAN

A great deal of research has focused on the settlement of criminal cases through guilty pleas.[1] Among this research, the vast majority portrays plea bargaining primarily as a single episode of negotiating behavior.[2] Scant attention is paid to the facts that many criminal cases are not immediately plea bargained, that attorneys often negotiate plea bargains numerous times on behalf of a single client, or that plea bargaining may at times actually parallel the adversarial proceedings of trial.[3]

Reprinted by permission from *Law & Society Review,* Vol. 30, No. 2 (1996). Copyright © The Law and Society Association.

A previous version of this article was presented at the Annual Meetings of the Midwest Sociological Society in Chicago, 8 April 1993. I thank Joseph R. Gusfield, Jacqueline P. Wiseman, Michael E. Butler, Theodore T. Smith, the Spring '93 feminist support group in the Sociology and Anthropology Department at Southwest Missouri State University, as well the anonymous reviewers of *Law & Society Review* for helpful comments. Any errors of fact or interpretation are, however, the author's sole responsibility.

By focusing on findings generated through ethnographic research on a private, nonprofit corporation of court-appointed defense attorneys (hereinafter referred to as "Defenders"),[4] this article examines plea bargaining as part of the defense attorney's recursive consideration of whether a case should be settled immediately or proceed further. "Proceeding further" means that, until an attorney achieves an acceptable plea bargain, s/he proceeds to litigate a case throughout various court hearings that could ultimately lead to a jury trial and sentencing. Viewed in this manner, plea bargaining can be seen to encompass not only multiple episodes of negotiating behavior but also a wide range of formal litigation proceedings. As such, distinctions made between plea bargaining and taking a case to trial can actually be seen as relatively minor.

METHODS

This study was part of a larger study that focused on the everyday defense behavior of a private, nonprofit corporation of court-appointed defense attorneys situated in a southern California location I refer to as "Smith County." The study was conducted between September 1984 and September 1988. The data were collected through qualitative research techniques.

At the time, the system for defending indigent persons in the area consisted of a limited Public Defender's Office, a Central Office of Defense Services, and a private contract system. The corporation studied was one of the many private contract groups in the area. It differed from the others, however, in at least one crucial way: This corporation had a reputation in the criminal justice community for providing high-quality defense service to indigent persons (for further discussion on this issue, see Emmelman 1993).

The population studied consisted of all the attorneys employed at the downtown branch of this corporation. About 15 attorneys were employed at any given time in that office. Approximately half of the attorneys were men and half were women. Their ages ranged from the early 30s to the early 50s; the average age was in the late 30s. With the exception of one African American attorney, who worked at this office for only a brief time, all the attorneys were white. All but one of the attorneys handled felony cases.

Entry into the setting was gained through an internship program carried out between the university and the defense corporation. (I was a graduate student at the time.) Once permission had been received to conduct research, both formally (from the university's Human Subjects Committee) as well as informally (from the attorneys who participated in the study), I initially collected data through participant observation: For an average of about eight hours per week, I observed the Defenders' behavior while serving as a student intern and law clerk.

As a student intern and law clerk, I was permitted to observe virtually every aspect of the Defenders' behavior—including that which occurred in such behind-the-scenes places as the attorneys' offices, judges' chambers, and jail. I was also accepted by these attorneys as an "insider" to the extent that some invited me to their homes for parties or other get-togethers. Only one attorney appeared to regard me with any suspicion.

Throughout the observation period, I recorded field notes, which I later analyzed through a grounded theory methodology (see Glaser & Strauss 1967 and Lester & Hadden 1980 for further details on the use of this methodology). To clarify and refine these preliminary research findings, I conducted in-depth interviews toward the end of the study.

The interviews were designed to ascertain the manner in which the Defenders routinely defend criminal cases. To avoid predisposing responses and thereby biasing the findings, questions were open-ended and phrased as neutrally as possible. After some preliminary questions regarding attorneys' background and general perceptions of other court actors, for example, I began the interview with "What do you typically do with a case once you have received it? How do you typically handle it?"

All the attorneys who were then employed by the corporation (five men and six women) as well as four former Defenders (three men and one woman) participated in the interviews. The interviews lasted between three and a half and four hours. About half of this time was devoted to the topic of plea bargaining. All the interviews were taped, transcribed, and then later analyzed.

The importance of these interviews in the research process and especially their value in this study cannot be overemphasized. While I *observed* cases being plea bargained at virtually every point in the career of criminal cases, it never occurred to me that such apparent irregularity in plea bargaining was actually part of the Defenders' plea bargaining strategy. It was only while interviewing that I discovered that the Defender's decision to plea bargain a criminal case is always tentative, frequently recurring, and may actually result in a completed jury trial! The interview material presented in this study reveals this silent, taken-for-granted plea bargaining strategy that transcended the researcher's observations.

Clearly, a major weakness in this study is that the research population is not representative of either all criminal defense attorneys or even all criminal defense attorneys who represent indigent persons. However, an important strength of the study is that it sheds light on a largely elusive and previously unstudied decision-making process that may very well be prevalent among a substantial number of other defense attorneys. It is hoped that this study will inspire further and more systematic research on larger, more representative samples of attorneys.

AN OVERVIEW OF SMITH COUNTY'S PLEA BARGAINING SYSTEM

In Smith County, a "plea bargain" is an agreement made between the prosecuting attorney and the defendant (usually through the defendant's attorney) which stipulates that the defendant will plead guilty to or not contest a fixed number of criminal charges in exchange for some sort of reduction in the number and/or the seriousness of the original criminal charges. Although the Smith County District Attorney maintains that s/he does not do sentence bargaining, one stipulation frequently added to plea bargains refers to the District Attorney's lack of opposition to time in custody being spent in the local jail rather than in the state prison. This stipulation is represented in agreements by the acronym "N.O.L.T.," which means "no opposition to local time."

Unlike judges in some other jurisdictions, Smith County judges are encouraged to facilitate case settlements (see also Maynard 1988; Ryan & Alfini 1979). Consequently, when the prosecutor and Defender agree on the terms of plea bargains, judges generally accept those terms (cf. Skolnick 1967)).[5] When the attorneys encounter problems in reaching agreements, however, judges act as arbiters. In this arbitration, the judge typically exerts pressure on, or makes promises regarding sentencing to, either attorney in order to reach a settlement.

As may be apparent, plea bargain negotiations in Smith County typically involve the defense attorney, the prosecuting attorney, the judge, and the defendant. They may at times also involve co-defendants and (even more rarely) an alleged victim.

Regardless of who they involve, however, rarely if ever do the Defenders carry out all aspects of plea bargaining in the presence of all the actors involved. Instead, their activity among prosecution allies and the judge is usually separated in time and space from their activity among defense allies.

Plea bargains in Smith County are also negotiated almost anywhere and at almost any time throughout the life of an ongoing criminal case. It most obviously occurs on the date of scheduled settlement hearings when one can observe blatant negotiating behavior in the judge's chambers, in the hallways outside of courtrooms, and/or in the courthouse "holding tanks" where incarcerated defendants await scheduled court appearances. However, as will be discussed below, plea bargains may also be deliberately and sometimes clandestinely negotiated before, during, or after other types of court hearings.

Wherever or whenever plea bargaining takes place, the successful negotiation is always followed by a public hearing wherein the agreement is formalized and officially sanctioned.

FINDINGS

The Defenders' goal throughout the course of any criminal case is to mitigate the harm that could befall a defendant (for further discussion on this issue, see Emmelman 1990, 1993). The Defenders maintain that because the prosecutor is unlikely to file charges in cases where the evidence is weak, trials are rare and plea bargains are the most likely method through which they seek their goal. Nevertheless, although plea bargaining is the most common method for case disposal, *it is always considered in light of the alternative of proceeding further with the case.*[6] This ultimately means that many cases are not immediately plea bargained, that some cases involve multiple episodes of plea bargaining, and that the negotiation of plea bargains sometimes entails a wide range of formal litigation proceedings.

The process of deciding whether a case should be settled immediately or proceed further involves three types of activities. These are (1) assessing the offer for a guilty plea, (2) negotiating the terms of a plea bargain, and (3) counseling the defendant and deciding on a course of action. While these activities are interrelated, they do not necessarily emerge in the sequence presented here and they may be more apparent at some times than at others. Sometimes the Defender counsels the defendant prior to intercepting an actual offer, for example, and sometimes the attorneys negotiate the terms of a plea bargain before conferring with the defendant. In addition, sometimes the Defender makes an offer and the DA's acceptance of it precludes any subsequent need for assessment as well as perhaps any further negotiation. Regardless of the order in which the types of activities occur, however, the Defenders always consider the bid for a guilty plea, always confirm the terms of a plea bargain through some type of negotiation technique, and are obligated to counsel the defendant prior to deciding on a course of action.

The discussion below examines the details of this decision-making and how it can lead to multiple episodes as well as rather unique modes of plea bargaining.

Assessing the Offer for a Guilty Plea

Assessing the offer for a guilty plea entails two types of evaluations. The first involves the Defenders' understanding of the "value of a case." The second involves matters associated with the temporary postponement of settlement. Ultimately, both types of evaluations involve consideration of whether a case should proceed further. Thus, while Maynard (1984b) argues that case disposition delays are bargaining strategies, they can also constitute part of the defense attorney's tacit repertoire of strategies which they contemplate *prior to and apart from* interactional negotiation.

Assessing the Offer in Light of "the Value of a Case"

In assessing the offer for any defendant's guilty plea, the Defenders rely on their understanding of "the value of a case." The value of a case is determined by (1) the seriousness of the crime (which means both how serious the charge itself is as well as how serious or atypical the actual crime is), (2) the strength of the evidence (which entails an evaluation of the evidence on both sides of the issue), and (3) the defendant's background characteristics (which include but are not limited to the defendant's prior criminal record) (cf. Eisenstein & Jacob 1977; Maynard 1984a; McDonald 1985; Neubauer 1974; Rosett & Cressey 1976; Utz 1978).

In determining the value of a case, the Defenders distinguish between cases they believe might be won at trial, those in which the evidence against the defendant appears quite strong, and those that have some weaknesses but not enough to completely win a case (cf. Emmelman 1996; Mather 1979). These estimates result in tentative conclusions that some cases should be plea bargained immediately, others should proceed further, and others should be tried. This was explained by Kathy in the following comments:

> There are cases that you know [in the beginning] are gonna settle. . . . You know that there's simply no defense to the case—not a defense that's gonna be worthwhile in terms of having, exposing the person to a state prison sentence and drawing out the procedures for three to six months. . . . There's [another] category of case where it's not a triable case. You see it's not a triable case. However, the [first] offer is bad. Something may shake out at the [preliminary hearing] that is useful. Or the offer may be better in Superior Court than in Municipal Court. Or there's a motion that needs to be run . . . you do whatever needs to be done and you settle the case in Superior Court. But all along you know this case isn't going to trial. . . . The

third case is the case you know is going to go to trial. You know from the day that you get the case that it's going to be tried. That's because your client has no record and it's clear from talking to the client and reading the discovery that a jury could acquit.[7]

Although the Defenders tentatively conclude at this juncture how cases might best be handled, they reach no final conclusion yet. Instead, they are obliged to consider further the virtues of plea bargaining and to relay that information to their clients (cf. American Bar Association 1986:70). In carrying out this task, the Defenders consider what offer for a guilty plea they should expect to receive in a case.

The value of a criminal case indicates to the Defenders what offer or reduction in penalties they should expect to receive for their client's guilty plea (cf. Feeley 1979; Mather 1979; McDonald 1985; Neubauer 1974; Rosett & Cressey 1976). As Ingmar explained,

> The factors that you take [into account when deciding if the District Attorney's offer is good] are what did the client really do. Did he do anything that terrible? What's his record like? Is he on probation? Are there evidentiary issues in the case that you can point out to the DA maybe sometime later—that you can show him his case isn't that good even though you know you'll probably lose at trial? Will the case look better or worse after the preliminary hearing? And the other thing is just having been there before and knowing what you're probably gonna get offered. And if you haven't been there before, you've talked to other people. You say "I got this case, and these are the facts, and this is his record, and what do you think a good offer is?"

Based on their understanding of what offer or penalty a case is worth (i.e., the value of a case), the Defenders assess the DA's *actual* offer for a guilty plea. The issue in this assessment is *not* whether the DA offers any reduction in potential costs to the defendant but instead whether the reduction is "fair" or "reasonable" given the value of the case (cf. Feeley 1979; Mather 1979; McDonald 1985; Neubauer 1974). If it is not, Defenders deem it unacceptable. As Mindy explained,

> [A] first time [auto theft] is worth a misdemeanor. They might not give it to you. They might not offer it to you. But that's all its worth. . . . If [the DA says] we'll offer you a felony and we won't oppose local time, that's an offer where you can say "stuff it." Because there's no reason not to go to trial on that offer. Because if your guy loses after trial, if he's a first time offender he's not gonna be hurt. So they haven't offered you anything. [Interviewer: How do you know he's not going to be hurt?] Because there's not a judge around here who's gonna give prison on first offense auto theft.

As Mindy's comments suggest, when an offer is deemed "unreasonable," the Defenders tentatively conclude that a case should proceed further rather than settle immediately.

Assessing the Offer in Light of Temporary Postponement

Even when the DA makes a reasonable offer for a guilty plea, the Defenders consider whether an offer might get better further along in the adjudication process. Among other matters, the Defenders consider whether a subsequent DA or judge is more lenient (cf. McDonald 1985; Utz 1978). As Janet explained:

> If the offer can't get worse—and you know that because you've been doing [plea bargains] for awhile [and] you know what the standard offers are—the question then sometimes becomes are you judge shopping. Is it better to take the offer now because you have this particular judge that you're in front of, or is it better to wait 'til later when they're probably gonna make you the same offer, and have that judge sentence you? . . . It also depends on who the District Attorney is in that department who's settling the cases. I think I mentioned before that sometimes that District Attorney who is kind of like a boss—a higher-up person in the DA's office who's handing out all the offers—gets burned-out and the offers get real bad.

All other things being equal, the Defenders generally believe that unless an initial offer is better than average, offers for guilty pleas will not get any worse and could become more favorable to the defendant further along in the adjudication process. They explain that this occurs because either the prosecutor loses witnesses or better evidence eventually turns up on behalf of the defense. As Robert explained,

> [Plea bargaining is] pretty similar [in municipal and superior courts]. Personalities are different. You have a different prosecutor and a different judge. And that often makes a difference. . . . Then there's always the possibility that you've developed some additional information during the interim that affects how you're gonna plead. First, what the offer might be, then also evaluating the offer. . . . [W]hat the prosecutor tells you is that the deals are never going to get any better. [That the] inducement to plead early is that that's the best deal you're going to get, and it's going to get tougher on you if you proceed further. In fact, it doesn't seem to be the case. The defendant can get pretty much the same deal [in superior court]—although there are no guarantees about that.

Nevertheless, sometimes the prosecution case gets stronger further along in the litigation process, and the prosecutor will offer a defendant less incentive to plead guilty than previously. In response to my question. "Do plea bargains tend to get better in superior court?" Janet lamented,

> It depends. . . . For example, I have a case now, I think the client was offered local time [in municipal court]. They just came up with 2 prison priors on this guy. He swears they aren't his. I don't believe him. I think they're his. I'm afraid they're his. In which case the deal's gonna get a lot worse. So he's gonna go to trial. And that's okay. But a lot of times they do get better. [Interviewer: Most of the time?] They don't usually get worse. They very rarely get worse. They usually either stay the same or get better.

When the Defenders deduce that the offer for a guilty plea either will not or could not get any worse but could get better, they tentatively conclude that the defendant should proceed further with the case. No final conclusion is reached until after they counsel the client, however. The details of this interaction and its possible outcomes are discussed later.

Negotiating the Terms of Plea Bargains

Before any decision is actually made either to settle a case immediately or to proceed

further with a case, the actual terms of a plea bargain are somehow corroborated or confirmed. The Defenders do this through various types of negotiation techniques.

In his study on misdemeanor plea bargaining, Maynard (1984a, 1984b) examines plea bargain negotiations as a discourse phenomenon. He finds that some negotiations (i.e., unilateral opportunity negotiations) involve very little verbal maneuvering and appear to involve a "concerting of expectations" or the ability of participants to read situations similarly and infer mutually acceptable resolutions. Other negotiations (i.e., bilateral opportunity and compromise negotiations) involve less consensus and more verbal maneuvering. In addition, delays through continuances or the setting of trial dates are important bargaining strategies used by attorneys to mitigate or enhance a defendant's penalty.

In another related study, Maynard (1988) finds that some negotiations involve no narratives (or storytelling). These cases result in routine processing. Others include narrative components or subcomponents which assess character, dispute facts, or argue subjectivity.

Although the Defenders handle primarily felony cases, their negotiating behavior appears to be largely consistent with Maynard's characterizations of misdemeanor plea bargaining: Many of their negotiations involve no narrative and an apparent concerting of expectations, while other negotiations entail less consensus and more narrative. The Defenders also use impending litigation proceedings as a bargaining strategy.

However, the Defenders' behavior appears to diverge from Maynard's characterization of plea bargaining in three ways. First, the Defenders' *tacit, taken-for-granted understanding of the value of a case* structures their negotiation techniques. As discussed below, this may also be the case among the attorneys studied by Maynard (1984a, 1984b, 1988). Second, instead of continuances and the setting of trial dates, the Defenders use the somewhat veiled threat of proceeding further as a bargaining tool *during* negotiations. In other words, issues related to further case litigation are incorporated into their discourse as caveats to increase bargaining leverage. Third, the Defenders also negotiate the terms of plea bargains by making good on their threats and using other types of litigation proceedings to engender more acceptable terms of guilty pleas.

When an offer for a guilty plea is better than expected, the Defenders typically engage in "routine processing" (Maynard 1988) or "consensus bargaining" (cf. Eisenstein et al. 1988): They accept the offer with little or no comment. However, as suggested in the earlier discussion, there is an unspoken understanding that the offer is acceptable *given the value of the case*. As Robert explained in response to my question, "How do you typically plea bargain a case?"

> Well, it depends on what the offer is and what the case of the DA is and who the judge is. But having said all that, essentially the DA makes you an offer. It is rare, but on occasion the offer is much lower, a better offer *than you expected*. In which case, grab it. Usually, almost always you hope that it could be better. (Emphasis added)

When an offer for a guilty plea is not better than average, the Defenders typically engage in "explicit bargaining." Explicit bargaining means that attorneys openly negotiate the terms of plea bargains (cf. Eisenstein et al. 1988; Mather 1979; McDonald 1979).

The Defenders' goal in explicit bargaining is to persuade the prosecutor and perhaps the judge to make a more acceptable offer for a guilty plea. One way in which they do this is by *negotiating the value of a case*.

Negotiating the value of a case does not mean that negotiation participants review all information pertinent to determining the value of a case or that specific information is always discussed (cf. Maynard 1984a:108). Instead, it means that the Defenders engage in a type of "information control" (Goffman 1963) in order to evoke a more positive assessment of the value of their client's case. More specifically, they informally emphasize, overstate, deemphasize, ignore, or perhaps even put forth new information concerning any of the factors (i.e., the seriousness of the crime, the strength of the evidence, and the defendant's background characteristics) pertinent to determining the value of a case. This strategy appears to be consistent with the narrative structure Maynard (1988) found to characterize misdemeanor plea bargaining. However,

"negotiating the value of a case" is perhaps best viewed as the largely tacit, *general* principle (or strategy) that underlies discourse. This principle is illustrated in the following elaborations:

Kathy: I go in [to the judge's chambers] and say [to the prosecutor] "What's the offer on this case, Rick?" He tells me, and I usually respond "Geez, Rick! You can give me something better than that!" And give the DA information about the client, information about the case—mitigating factors in essence. [Interviewer: For example?] . . . "This man's worked all his life and now after 20 years this whatever, this embezzlement happened." Or y'know, "This woman was going through medical problems." [or] "There was spousal abuse."

[Interviewer: What is your typical case like in the disposition department?] Mindy: I go to the dispo department, you wait your turn, you go in and talk to the DA and the judge at the same time. The DA makes you an offer. And I do different things: If I want my client to take the offer, I think he's got a lousy case and he's not gonna be able to win, sometimes what I'll do is I'll puff [i.e., inflate the value of] my case. You say "Hey, these are the weaknesses in your case, and I think I could win at trial and this is the reason why." Or "this is a lousy search issue, and I'm gonna get the evidence suppressed. Give me some reason not to do the suppression motion"—which in the back of my mind I'm saying there's no way I'm ever gonna win this case. But you kind of puff it, and then maybe the DA will come down a little bit.

As apparent in the latter attorney's comments, the Defenders often attempt to coerce DAs and judges into making more acceptable offers by insinuating that they might proceed further with a case. This is also clear in two other Defenders' comments:

Robert: Generally speaking, [in plea bargaining] you try and point out certain advantages that you may have in a case, exploit whatever leverage you have. [For example,] "It's in everybody's best interest to get this thing over with and couldn't they do a little better for a defendant?" Hope that the judge is listening while you're talking.

[Interviewer: How does the offer change?] LuAnn: Well, the DA will try to get you to plead to something worse if they have you by the balls. [And then I say,] "We can win this case, your Honor. Why should we even plead this case out?" [or] "So, okay, if you want to clutter up the courts with cases, that's fine. Make me an offer that I won't go to trial."

It should be noted here that the Defenders' use of veiled threats to proceed further as a bargaining tactic presupposes the understanding that other court actors, if not the Defenders as well, prefer plea bargaining over other types of litigation procedures. One explanation frequently offered for this apparent preference is "case pressure." Specifically, either the overwhelming volume of cases the criminal court handles is said to precipitate plea bargaining or (conversely) plea bargaining is said to alleviate such case pressure (e.g., Alschuler 1968; Blumberg 1967a; Church 1976; Holmes et al. 1992; Kingsnorth & Jungsten 1988; Padgett 1990; Utz 1978).

While most Defenders indicated that judges and DAs experience a great deal of case pressure to plea bargain, only one Defender admitted to feeling any such pressure himself. Consistent with studies arguing that other, more ethical factors take precedence in decisions to plea bargain (e.g, Feeley 1973, 1979; Heumann 1975, 1978; McDonald 1985; Skolnick 1967), the remaining Defenders argued that the primary reason they plea bargain cases is simply because it is in the client's best interest. As two Defenders explained,

[Interviewer: Why not take every case to trial?]

Nora: Because most people are guilty. And it's overwhelmingly evident. And a lot of defendants just want out as fast as possible. . . . The courts couldn't accommodate them all either.

[Interviewer: Are you limited by your resources here?]

We can get as much resources as we need. If we had more cases going to trial, we could get more resources. The county would have to pay for it if we went to trial. It's just that they don't have the courtrooms and the judges to accommodate it. . . . That's why the DA's office pleads as well as overcharges.

[Interviewer: Why not take every case to trial?]

Mindy: Because it's not in the client's best interests.

[Interviewer: Why not?]

Because if the defendant has no good case and he's gonna be found guilty, and—say he's charged with a whole bunch of forgery counts, and he's got ten counts, and he's gonna be found guilty of all of them, and the DA says instead of taking this case to trial, I'll give you one count. Obviously it's better to have him plead guilty to one count and have the others dismissed than to go down on all counts. . . . [In addition,] not that many are going to go to trial because the District Attorney can't try everything. And they have an incentive to offer you something because they can't try everything.

In spite of the facts that they handled the largest percentage of criminal cases in the jurisdiction and that they believed judges and DAs experienced a great deal of case pressure to plea bargain cases, the Defenders never threatened DAs or judges with the peril of taking *all* their cases to trial. This may have been because, unlike the public defenders studied by Skolnick (1967) and McDonald (1985), the Defenders represented a smaller percentage of the criminal caseload in their jurisdiction than Skolnick's public defenders and they consequently had fewer resources and less power to muster (cf. Utz 1978). Nevertheless, they did employ the threat of proceeding further *with individual cases* to increase their leverage during informal negotiations.

When the Defenders are unable to negotiate acceptable plea bargain terms through the techniques described above, they *actually* proceed further with a case. In the next scheduled hearing, they may then attempt again to negotiate informally a more acceptable offer prior to the formal proceeding. If unsuccessful, they attempt to negotiate an acceptable offer during the formal litigation proceeding.

Plea bargain negotiations conducted during litigation proceedings intended for other purposes actually parallel the adversarial proceedings that ordinarily occur in these hearings. However, the Defenders keep in mind the goal of achieving an acceptable plea bargain. Consequently, they often put forth information in these hearings that affects the value of a case but may not be entirely relevant to the formal issue at hand (e.g., present sentencing information at a preliminary hearing).[9] They also continue informally to solicit an incentive to settle. This negotiation strategy was revealed by two Defenders in the following comments:

Tom: [S]ometimes I will look at a case and say, "This is a case which I want to settle," and I will be pushing for settlement [throughout] the entire [litigation process]. I will try to put enough equitable information before the judge during prelim just so the DA gets the idea. I will file motions in Superior Court sometimes . . . knowing that the purpose of that motion is twofold: Trying to get the charge dismissed— which is probably unlikely given the way the [law] is interpreted, and to . . . educate the deputy [i.e., Assistant District Attorney] on the upper level [i.e., in superior court] that he's dealing with a shitty case. . . . And sometimes I'll get better offers.

William: I will research [search and seizure issues] for the preliminary hearing with the hopes that I can beat the DA's case or at least parts of it. Again, *that will affect the value of the case as it goes through the system.* . . . [During preliminary hearings, I will try to undermine the DA's case as much as I can. Try to nip and tuck any evidence that I can. Try to get rid of it. Try to show the DA that his witnesses have problems. Try to set the scene for my theory of the defense later on, and at the same time, try to make that transcript stand out [with problems] so my plea bargain later will be the best one that I can get. (Emphasis added)

As the above discussion indicates, important issues in plea bargaining emerge during litigation proceedings formally intended for other purposes. This suggests a reciprocal relationship between plea bargaining and other pretrial and trial proceedings. It also lends credence to Neubauer's (1974) depiction of plea bargaining as a "mini-trial" and Maynard's (1984b:114)

suggestion that plea bargain negotiations "are rehearsals of scenes that participants would be willing to portray before a jury." Perhaps most important, it makes the distinctions between plea bargaining and trial seem less significant.

The latter in particular is apparent in Kathy's discussion on how she handles settlement cases differently from trial cases. Although she states clearly in this discussion that *some* type of distinct difference exists in the way she handles the various types of cases, it is not entirely obvious even to her what that difference always is. On final analysis, it would appear that the difference is related to the differing strengths of evidence in the cases—a difference that influenced the Defender's original opinion of whether a case is triable or should be plea bargained in the first place! In other words, the only real difference appears to be that which made plea bargaining desirable initially.

Kathy: I think basically for an experienced attorney, you basically know what kind of case you've got when you see it. You say this is a negotiation case, this case is gonna cop out. And some cases you look at them, and after you interview the client, you know this case is gonna be tried. Those cases you know are on a trial track, I handle differently. Other cases, you basically go through the same steps, but for a different reason. A case that's on a trial track, you'll do a different kind of investigation. The other cases, basically you're planning the sentencing from the day you get the case because you know the guy's gonna cop out. Trial track cases you're not looking so much *just for* mitigating sentencing issues [but instead are] thoroughly investigating the facts of the case. *Now you do that with the other cases too*, but for some reason—basically the evidence of the case and a clear showing of guilt on part of the defendant—you realize that this is not a case that can be tried. But trial track cases, you do a much more involved investigation [and] you do the prelim differently. I do extensive prelims on trial track cases. I subpoena witnesses which I do not ordinarily do—although I have been subpoenaing witnesses in to get sentencing issues in on the preliminary transcript so that they're on the record. That's a new technique—I don't do it real often, but sometimes I do. If it's a complicated case or a very serious case, then I will call witnesses in for the prelim just for purposes of mitigating circumstances. But the trial track cases, you're doing comprehensive preliminary hearings to find out what the witnesses are gonna say. *You also sometimes do that on negotiating cases* so that the DA will know the problems with the case—putting people on notice. (Emphasis added)

To what extent the Defender actually proceeds further with a case depends on when or whether s/he receives an acceptable offer for a guilty plea. The role the defendant plays in this decision-making is discussed below.

Counseling the Defendant and Deciding on a Course of Action

On developing a professional opinion of an offer for a guilty plea, the Defenders proceed to advise their clients. The Defender's primary goals in this interaction are to educate (or counsel) the defendant concerning what s/he can reasonably expect in the case and to ascertain the defendant's desires concerning the ultimate outcome of the case. *Never* do the Defenders insist that a defendant accept or reject an offer for a guilty plea, and any final decision to plea bargain or proceed further with a case *always* rests with the client.

For the most part, the Defender's stance while counseling defendants appears to be consistent with that which Flemming (1986) found to be typical of other defense attorneys who represent public clients. Specifically, Flemming found that in order to win their clients' confidence as well as to avoid allegations of professional incompetence, attorneys who represent public clients play an advisory rather than a stronger, more insistent recommendatory role. This actually results in public clients' greater involvement in the development of their cases.

Similarly, the Defenders are careful never to dictate to their clients, to assume they have complete control over their clients' cases, or to assume that their clients trust them (cf. also Skolnick 1967). Indeed! Their approach may be best described as conciliatory. This is apparent in Ingmar's discussion of how he counsels defendants. In this discussion, it appears that Ingmar seeks not merely to instill trust and confidence among his clients but more- over to circumvent any possible claim of unethical conduct. He does this by meticulously if not too eagerly asserting

through conversational techniques his role, their rights, and the status of their cases. In particular, he is especially careful not to suggest plea bargaining too strongly.

I don't have a set function, but I don't say, "Did you do it?" I do say, "What happened? What do you know about all this? They say you did it. And they charged you with such and such. What do you know about it?" Before that, I preface it with a lot of stuff. I make sure that he understands his rights and that he understands what my place is— why I'm there . . . in terms of that I'm here, I'm on your side, I'm your advocate, what I'm gonna do, what I see my role as, that everything he tells me is confidential and that it's best if he tells me everything he knows about the case. . . . Some cases where you see that it's not gonna do this guy any good to plead out, you don't want necessarily to hear that he's guilty—unless he's ready to tell you. You don't want to—you're not the prosecutor. You've got to have a good relationship with this guy. And you don't want to come on strong and say, "I want to know if you're guilty or not guilty" because he's gonna think, "Well, you're supposed to defend me whether I'm guilty or not guilty, and if you're asking me that question right away, you're just a prosecutor. You're just gonna dump me." That's what they're gonna think, so you don't want to come on that way. You say, "Tell me what you know." And maybe later in the case you say, "Look, I've got this, that, and the other thing, and you say this, and nothing makes sense. All the evidence that comes up points to such and such. I think *maybe* you should be taking the deal. And if you are guilty, you're *probably* better off to admit it right now. Here's why." . . . [I explain to defendants my] evaluation of the case, and what all the possible things that could happen to him are. What the sentence ranges are. What I would expect that he would get within a range— usually. There's no guarantee. And what I think he should do. Then I ask him what he thinks and what questions he has. (Emphasis added)

While the Defenders are careful to maintain an advisory stance toward their clients, they often find themselves confronted with clients who have slightly different agendas and are especially resistant to their advice. In these cases, the Defenders appear to behave much like the divorce attorneys studied by Sarat and Felstiner (1986). Specifically, the Defenders employ discourse as well as other strategies which conduce

Table 1   Types of Defender-Client Input and Outcomes to Plea Bargaining Episodes

Defender's Recommendation	Client's Desire	Actual Outcome
Plead	Plead	Settlement
Proceed further	Plead	Settlement
Plead	Different terms	Settlement or proceed further
Plead	Trial	Proceed further
Proceed further	Proceed further	Proceed further

to the choices they deem appropriate. As acknowledged by two Defenders:

[Interviewer: How do you counsel the defendant regarding the offer?]

Janet: Well I usually tell them, "Look. This is the offer. And this is a good offer or this is a bad offer. It's your choice whether you plead guilty or not." That's—there's certain things that only the defendant decides. One of them is whether or not to plead guilty. . . . Sometimes you have to put it stronger than that because the guy may be looking at ten more years if he goes on. He's got all these priors—prior convictions that are gonna [inaudible] later on. So you say, "You know, these priors are gonna come in against you if you testify. And if you're convicted, it's gonna make this burglary sixteen years instead of six. So they're offering you six now so maybe you should seriously think about it."

Steve: The people in custody are the ones that have a lot of runin's with the law. [Sometimes] they think you're a public defender and you're gonna try to force them into taking a quick deal. . . . You have a different attitude with them. Your gesture, your approach to them in your attitude—not in what you *do* for them, but in how you explain what their options are. Sometimes using reverse psychology if you think a person should take the deal. . . . You explain the reality of the situation as I just did to you, and you say, "but I'm ready to go to trial." Once they realize you're not resisting their demand to go to trial and their demand that they pay you some attention, and you indicate to them by whatever way that you'll take their case to trial and that's why you're doing this type of work—because you like to do trial

work and that's more fun than filling out a change of plea form, then they will drop their resistance to a plea bargain based specifically on you as the dump truck who doesn't care about them.

Contingent on the defendant's expressed desires after being counseled, the Defender then commences to finalize a plea bargain, to negotiate further the terms of a plea bargain, or to "proceed further" with the case. If successful in the second instance, a plea bargain agreement proceeds to final form. Otherwise, the case proceeds further.

As outlined in Table 1, there are five possible combinations of Defender-client input that result in one of two actual outcomes to a plea bargaining episode. I observed all these combinations in use to some extent. The following discussion provides rough estimates of their prevalence and describes at least some of their essential ingredients.

Both Defender and Client Agree on Plea Bargain

The easiest and probably most frequent mode of interaction is when the Defender establishes that the defendant should accept an offer and the defendant agrees. In these instances, the case is settled immediately.

A case that illustrates this type was one involving a male defendant charged with burglary and providing false identification to a police officer. The defendant was apprehended inside the bathroom of a restaurant; two other co-defendants were caught outside the building. The only things found missing were donuts. The defendant wanted to take full responsibility for the crimes, but the Defender told him that a plea bargain meant that all three defendants would have to admit some sort of guilt. The Defender also stated that all the defendants *could* be sent to prison for burglary if found guilty by a jury. All three defendants ultimately decided they would plea bargain to second-degree burglary as a misdemeanor—the standard offer. I helped the defendant complete a plea agreement form while the Defender negotiated the terms with the DA. The defendants were then sentenced the same day.

Defender Recommends Proceeding Further and Client Desires a Plea Bargain

Another frequent mode of interaction is when the Defender recommends proceeding further with a case and the defendant desires to plea bargain. As Feeley (1979) has found, many defendants are not interested in taking their cases to trial because it entails costs that otherwise would not be incurred. For the Defenders' clients, these costs are typically believed to be increased jail time. As stated by two Defenders:

Karl: Sometimes—it's usually me coming to [defendants] with an offer. [However,] there are many clients that realize that they are in a very bad situation factually—versus the prosecution. And they bring up plea bargaining. I had a client bring up plea bargaining to me just yesterday, wanted to know what kind of deal we could get real quick.

[Interviewer: What was he interested in?]

He was interested in getting out of jail.

[Interviewer: Why not take every case to trial?]

Nora: . . . [A] lot of defendants just want out [of jail] as fast as possible. They don't want to stay in as long as possible. They want out faster. They want to get rid of it, be done with it, serve the time, and get out.

One case which illustrates this type of interaction involved a defendant charged with commercial burglary. The Defender believed the defendant had a triable case because (arguably) the alleged victim had actually reneged on a business deal in which he had agreed to sell some merchandise for the defendant. The Defender believed he could assert that the defendant was merely attempting to regain control over his own merchandise. However, the defendant did not want a trial because he feared public humiliation and because he wanted to go home to another state. Consequently, the case was settled immediately.

In another case of commercial burglary, however, the defendant insisted that all he wanted was to get out of jail and go home (again, to another state) as soon as possible. Although this case was eventually dismissed, the prosecutor later refiled the charges when more evidence and a rather serious prior record was discovered. Thus, in retrospect, it appeared that this defendant's desire to dispose of the case as quickly as possible was actually motivated by the desire to avoid more serious penalties.

Regardless of the defendant's actual reasons for desiring to plea bargain, in cases where the defendant wants to plea bargain in spite of the Defender's advice to proceed further, the case is settled immediately.

Defender Recommends Plea Bargain and Client Desires Different Terms

If not the most typical, another very frequent mode of interaction is when the Defender recommends plea a bargain but the defendant prefers plea agreement terms of other than those initially offered. When this occurs, the Defenders usually engage in explicit negotiations in order to make a guilty plea acceptable.

A case characteristic of this type of input involved a defendant who was initially charged with using force and inflicting injury on a police officer and obstructing a public officer in the discharge of his duty. The defendant was offered a felony which would be reduced to a misdemeanor after a year's successful probation and up to one year in jail. The defendant bemoaned having a felony on his record and worried about losing his job by spending time in jail. The Defender in this case returned to the judge's chambers and reported that the defendant did not want the deal. The Defender argued that the defendant did not *intend* to harm anyone (the prosecutor was responsible for proving intent). The judge then intervened by promising to give the defendant a misdemeanor at sentencing if he paid restitution beforehand. (The Defender later informed me that he knew the defendant would also get work furlough because "this judge would not want the defendant to lose his job.")

If a Defender is unsuccessful in negotiating more acceptable plea bargain terms in these cases, the defendant then decides whether to accept the offer for a guilty plea anyway (which often occurs) or to "proceed further" with the case (which usually occurs because the Defender concludes that a different DA or judge will be more amenable). If the latter occurs, another decision making process occurs again later on and another episode of plea bargaining takes place. If an acceptable offer is ever made to the defendant, a plea bargain agreement proceeds to be finalized. Otherwise, the attorney could engage in *rounds* of plea bargain gaining[10] and ultimately litigate the case completely in front of a jury.

Defender Recommends Plea Bargain and Client Desires Trial

When counseled about the small chance they have of winning their cases, some defendants *insist* not merely that they are innocent but also on taking their cases to trial. Among those cases that I observed taken to trial, this type of case appeared to be the most frequent. These defendants fall into that category described by Sudnow (1965) and Neubauer (1974) as "stubborn."

These cases typically proceed further down the litigation path toward trial. However, as the case proceeds, the Defenders remain open to and may actively pursue offers for guilty pleas. They also continue to advise their clients about the virtues of plea bargaining. If an acceptable offer is ever made to the defendant, the case proceeds to settlement. This usually occurs when the defendant concedes that s/he could suffer more severe consequences by being found guilty through trial.

A case illustrating this mode involved a defendant charged with three counts of burglary. The defendant insisted that he was innocent in spite of his previous confession and other very incriminating evidence against him. Convinced that the defendant would be seriously hurt through trial, the Defender went directly into the judge's chambers immediately prior to the preliminary hearing

in order to negotiate a plea bargain. The Defender then met with the defendant and told him the offer (i.e., one count of aiding and abetting credit card forgery, reduced to a misdemeanor in 18 months).

Although the defendant in this case continued to resist plea bargaining initially, the Defender reiterated the strong evidence against him and the possible penalties associated with a plea bargain versus a trial. Eventually, the defendant requested and accepted slightly revised plea bargain terms (i.e., receiving stolen property instead of aiding and abetting credit card forgery).

If a defendant in such a case is never convinced that plea bargaining is desirable, the Defender engages in rounds of plea bargaining episodes and the case is completely litigated in front of a jury. And although I never actually witnessed such an instance, I heard several horror stories about defendants who got seriously hurt by severe sentences after trial because they refused to plea bargain.

Defender Recommends Proceeding Further and Client Desires to Proceed Further

A final mode of interaction occurs when the Defender advises the defendant to proceed further with the case and the defendant agrees. This usually occurs because the DA does not make the defendant a "reasonable" offer for a guilty plea (cf. also Utz 1978).[11] This appeared to be the second most likely type of case to go trial.[12] Like the former type, the Defenders in such cases remain open to and may actively pursue guilty plea offers. If an acceptable offer is ever made to the defendant, the case is settled. Otherwise, these cases may be completely litigated in front of a jury.

One example of such a case involved a defendant accused of two counts of assault with a deadly weapon, one count of brandishing a weapon against a police officer, and one count of being under the influence of PCP. According to the Defender, the DA would not offer the defendant anything due to the seriousness of the crime and the defendant's prior record. On the day of the preliminary hearing, the DA asked that the case be "trailed" (a shorter and more tentative delay than a continuance) because two of her witnesses had not shown up. Fearing that a dismissal would result simply in the case being refiled again later, the Defender seized the opportunity to pursue a plea bargain. To the Defender's dismay, the DA refused to deal and the two missing witnesses showed up while other witnesses were testifying. The case did ultimately plead out, however, when the formerly missing witnesses became reluctant to testify against the defendant, who was one's brother and the other's friend.

A final note should be added here regarding interaction in which the Defender advises an agreeable client to take a case to trial because the case is actually triable. This is the rarest mode of interaction and is often said to bypass plea bargaining altogether (see, for example, Kathy's earlier discussion on types of cases and Mather's 1979 discussion on the decision to plea bargain versus taking a case to trial). However, I observed that these cases rarely proceed to trial completion because the DA either drops the charges against the defendant or offers the defendant "a very good deal" (see also Farr 1984:311). Consequently, even when the Defenders advise their clients to take their cases to trial and they agree, it is perhaps better viewed as simply another instance of "proceeding further."

Summary, Evaluation, and Conclusion

This article has examined plea bargaining as a component of the Defender's recursive decision making either to settle a case immediately or to proceed further. It has been found that this decision making consists of three types of activities: (1) assessing the offer for a guilty plea, (2) negotiating the terms of a plea bargain, and (3) counseling the defendant and deciding on a course of action.

The Defenders assess the offer for a guilty plea in light of the value of a case as well as the potential costs of temporary delay. In both instances, the Defenders interject factors related to impending litigation proceedings into their evaluations. Specifically, they compare the costs associated with the current offer with those the defendant is likely to incur after a trial,

after other pretrial litigation proceedings, and/or from another DA or judge. If they foresee that the defendant is not likely to be hurt by such action, they tentatively conclude that the defendant should proceed further with the case.

Before any decision is actually made, the Defenders corroborate or confirm the actual terms of an offer. They do this through various types of negotiation techniques. Underlying the use of all these techniques is the Defenders' understanding regarding "the value of a case."

When offers are better than average, the Defenders typically engage in "routine processing" (Maynard 1988) or "consensus bargaining" (Eisenstein et al. 1988): They accept an offer with little or no comment. However, it also means an offer is acceptable given their understanding of the value of the case.

When an offer is not better than average, the Defenders typically engage in "explicit bargaining" (cf. Eisenstein et al. 1988): They attempt to engender desirable plea bargain terms by asserting information that leads to an increased valuation of the case. In addition, they often employ somewhat veiled threats of proceeding further to increase their bargaining leverage.

When unsuccessful in negotiating acceptable terms through either consensus or explicit bargaining techniques, the Defenders proceed to negotiate plea bargains through litigation proceedings intended for other purposes. In these negotiations, the Defenders once again put forth information that will conduce to a higher valuation of their cases. Perhaps ironically, it appears that such a tactic actually results in only minor modifications from that which would otherwise occur in the proceeding. In other words, plea bargaining increasingly comes to resemble the actual trial of a case. If the case proceeds long enough, the jury renders a verdict and plea bargaining actually becomes trial.

While the Defenders possess the expertise and skill to assess and negotiate plea bargains, it is ultimately the defendant who decides whether a case will be settled immediately or proceed further. Consequently, prior to their decisions, the Defenders carefully counsel their clients regarding their rights and the status of their cases. Whether or not the clients heed the Defenders' advice, the Defenders then proceed to carry out the clients' wishes.

Ultimately, there are two types of outcomes to any plea bargaining episode: immediate settlement or proceeding further. When the defendant opts for immediate settlement, a plea bargain agreement proceeds to final form. Otherwise, the case proceeds to the next scheduled hearing as if it were bound for trial. On the date of that hearing, another decision-making process occurs. If at the end of that plea bargaining episode the defendant again decides to proceed further with the case, yet another decision-making process occurs on the date of the next scheduled hearing. Unless an acceptable offer is at some point made to the defendant, the case proceeds until the defendant is ultimately tried before a jury and then sentenced or acquitted.

Viewed as a component of recursive decision making, plea bargaining can be seen as including multiple episodes of negotiating behavior as well as a wide range of litigation proceedings. Perhaps most important, plea bargaining and trial can actually be seen to converge: not only are plea bargain negotiations "rehearsals of scenes that participants would be willing to portray before a jury" (Maynard 1984b:114), but pretrial and trial proceedings are oftentimes precursors for case settlement.

This article has elucidated a mode of plea bargaining that can provide defendants with a great deal of latitude in deciding their own fates. Not only are defendants' rights to due process protected, but they are also provided with numerous opportunities to limit what may be unwarranted penalties.[13] Consequently, this mode of plea bargaining can be not merely an effective method for representing defendants but also a method perhaps equally as effective or more effective than trial.

An important limitation of this research, however, is that the number of attorneys studied is quite small and hardly representative of the entire population of defense attorneys. Consequently, although Utz (1978) finds that plea bargaining is clearly more adversarial in one city than another, it cannot be stated with any great precision how extensive this decision-making process is. Future research should consider whether or to what extent other defense attorneys make decisions similarly.

Nor do the findings presented here take into account what organizational conditions engender this type of decision making. Certainly, some studies have made inroads regarding this matter. Utz (1978), for example, finds that a poorly organized, relatively powerless, and private system of criminal defense appears to result in adversarial plea bargaining. Similarly, Eisenstein and Jacob's (1977) study suggests that an adversary spirit is the result of a more anonymous, less cohesive courtroom climate. In addition, I have argued elsewhere (Emmelman 1993) that this plea bargaining posture is encouraged by the very organizational structure of the defense corporation I studied. However, more information is still required if such a plea bargaining system is to be reproduced on a larger scale.

Finally, this study does not—and cannot—address the issue of whether this type of decision making is actually desirable. From the standpoint of those who fear tyranny from the powerful (or from what Packer (1968) might call the "Due Process" perspective on justice), such a system of plea bargaining may seem warranted. From the standpoint of those who fear abuse from the disaffected (or from what Packer might call the "Crime Control" perspective on justice), this system might seem only to bring about greater injustice. From the standpoint of those who completely trust neither, however, this system offers only a partial solution; more research needs to be conducted on the problem of bringing about justice for everyone.

NOTES

1. E.g., Albonetti 1992; Alschuler 1975; Blumberg 1967a, 1967b; Farr 1984; Feeley 1979; Harris & Springer 1984; Heumann 1975, 1978; Holmes, Daudistel, & Taggart 1992; LaFree 1985; Mather 1979; Maynard 1984a, 1984b, 1988; McConville & Mirsky 1990; McDonald 1985; Mileski 1971; Neubauer 1974; Padgett 1990; Pritchard 1986; Rosett & Cressey 1976; Ryan & Alfini 1979; Skolnick 1967; Sudnow 1965; Uhlman & Walker 1979; Utz 1978.

2. E.g., Albonetti 1992; Alschuler 1975; Blumberg 1967a 1967b; Church 1976; Eisenstein & Jacob 1977; Eisenstein, Flemming, & Nardulli 1988; Farr 1984; Feeley 1979; Mather 1979; McConville & Mirsky 1990; McDonald 1985; Mileski 1971; Rosett & Cressey 1976; Skolnick 1967; Sudnow 1965; Uhlman & Walker 1979.

3. One exception to this is Maynard's (1984a, 1984b) discourse analysis on misdemeanor plea bargaining. He finds that delays through continuances or the setting of trial dates are used in some negotiations as important bargaining strategies to mitigate or enhance a defendant's penalty. He also notes (1984b:101) that requests for delays often result in *rounds* of negotiation that usually produce guilty pleas or dismissals. Precisely how Maynard's study differs from or is similar to the current one is discussed throughout this article.

4. The names of individual Defenders as well as the county in which the studied corporation is located are pseudonyms.

5. On those rare occasions when a judge rejected a plea bargain agreed on by the prosecutor and the Defender, the two attorneys generally took the case before another judge who presided over court hearings further along in the adjudication process (cf. Utz 1978). Rarely if ever did the Defenders challenge judges for plea bargaining issues. This was because attorneys are allowed only one preemptory challenge to a judge per case and the Defenders usually wanted to save that challenge in case they were forced to take the case to trial in front of an unfavorable trial judge.

6. In discussing misdemeanor plea bargaining, Maynard (1984b:78) states: "For each case, the defense and prosecution must determine some disposition (which may be anything from a dismissal to a jail sentence), or must agree to a trial date, or must agree to continue the case for reconsideration at a later time." The concept of "proceeding further" differs in that it is a less formal outcome of a plea bargaining episode and does not specifically mean that a case will be scheduled for trial or that another settlement hearing will be scheduled. (All the Defenders' cases have tentative trial dates when they are received, and nonserious felonies have two settlement hearings scheduled automatically.) Instead, it means that a case will simply proceed to whatever formal proceeding it ordinarily would *if* it had been scheduled for trial.

7. Indented excerpts are transcripts of taped interviews. Because this is not a conversational analysis, however, I have omitted such things as silences and overlapping talk as well as nonessential repetitive or digressive comments (these are indicated by ellipses). Information in brackets refers to interviewer comments (as noted), to information translated from the Defenders' somewhat opaque argot (e.g., references to a "459" has been translated into "burglary" where appropriate) or to other contextual information necessary to understand certain comments.

8. Sudnow (1965) found that public defenders employ concepts of "normal crimes" which signify "typical reductions" (or offers for guilty pleas) during plea bargaining. The Defenders employ similar concepts. However, the Defenders' concept of a "normal" crime is equivalent to their understanding of a case *whose value* is average or typical. This understanding presupposes and is juxtaposed beside their understanding of cases whose values are "better" or "worse" than average and thus signify better or worse offers for guilty pleas.

9. It is important to distinguish this type of plea bargaining technique from that of the "slow plea" described by Mather (1979). In "slow pleas," the outcome of the court hearing is predetermined by the judge, the prosecutor, and the defense attorney in the case. This does not occur when the Defenders "proceed further" with a case and subterraneously attempt to negotiate plea bargains through other types of court hearings.

10. Maynard (1984b:101) makes this observation about the attorneys he studied. The primary difference here is that rounds of negotiation occur not because the attorneys have continued a settlement hearing but because the Defenders continue to solicit others and negotiate plea bargains as a case proceeds further.

11. This also includes cases in which the DA refuses to plea bargain. In these instances, the defendant does not have any choice but to take the case to trial. See Pritchard (1986) for a discussion regarding the effect of crime news on prosecutors' decisions to plea bargain cases. Also see Farr (1984) for a discussion regarding the effect of certain policies in the DA's office on plea bargaining.

Another relevant observation that should be made here concerns the more serious sentences that defendants receive after convictions at trials than for the same offenses after plea bargaining. Although LaFree (1985) and Uhlman & Walker (1979, 1980) found that defendants who plea bargain generally receive less severe sentences than those who are convicted after trial, the findings reported in this study suggest that perhaps the latter defendants sometimes receive more severe sentences, not as punishment for taking their case to trial, but because the defense attorneys were for some reason unsuccessful in negotiating more acceptable offers.

12. This is somewhat supported by Harris and Springer's (1984) finding that attorneys who represent clients with serious prior records will be more likely to go to trial than to plea bargain. Their finding may reflect the fact that for defendants whose cases have little value, prosecutors offer little incentive to plea bargain. Consequently, these defendants have little or nothing to lose by taking their case to trial.

13. It is important to note here McConville's (1986) contention that trials do not guarantee that

truth (or perhaps "justice") will prevail. Insofar as adversarial procedures do not guarantee that the guilty will be convicted or the innocent set free, and because our judicial system holds that defendants should be given the benefit of doubt (i.e., presumed innocent until proven guilty), it seems this type of plea bargaining system can ensure justice as much or more than trials.

REFERENCES

Albonetti, Celesta A. (1992) "Charge Reduction: An Analysis of Prosecutorial Discretion in Burglary and Robbery Cases." 8 *J. of Quantitative Criminology* 317.

Alschuler, Albert W. (1968). "The Prosecutor's Role in Plea Bargaining." 36 *Univ. of Chicago Law Rev.* 51.

____. (1975). "The Defense Attorney's Role in Plea Bargaining." 84 *Yale Law J.* 1179.

American Bar Association (1986) *Standards for Criminal Justice: The Defense Function.* 2d ed. Boston: Little, Brown & Co.

Blumberg, Abraham. (1967a). *Criminal Justice.* Chicago: Quadrangle Books.

____ (1967b) "The Practice of Law as a Confidence Game: Organizational Co-optation of a Profession." 1 *Law & Society Rev.* 15.

Church, Thomas, Jr. (1976) "Plea Bargains, Concessions and the Courts: Analysis of a Quasi-Experiment," 10 *Law & Society Rev.* 377.

Eisenstein, James, & Herbert Jacob (1977). *Felony Justice.* Boston: Little, Brown & Co.

Eisenstein, James, Roy B. Flemming, & Peter F. Nardulli. (1988). *The Contours of Justice: Communities and Their Courts.* Boston: Little, Brown & Co.

Emmelman, Debra S. (1990) "Defending Indigents: A Study of Criminal Defense Work." Ph.D. diss., University of California, San Diego.

____. (1993). "Organizational Conditions that Facilitate an Ethical Defense Posture among Attorneys for the Poor: Observations of a Private Nonprofit Corporation," 18 *Criminal Justice Rev.* 223.

____. (1996) "Assessing the Strength of Evidence: The Interpretive Practices of a Private, Nonprofit Corporation of Court-appointed Defense Attorneys." Dept. of Sociology & Anthropology, Southern Connecticut State Univ.

Farr, Kathryn Ann. (1984) "Administration and Justice: Maintaining Balance through an Institutionalized Plea Negotiation Process," 22 *Criminology* 291.

Feeley, Malcolm (1973) "Two Models of the Criminal Justice System: An Organizational Perspective," 7 *Law & Society Rev.* 407.

____ (1979) *The Process Is the Punishment.* New York: Russell Sage Foundation.

Flemming, Roy B. (1986) "Client Games: Defense Attorney Perspectives on Their Relations with Criminal Clients," 1986 *American Bar Foundation Research J.* 253.

Glaser, Barney, & Anselm Strauss (1967) *The Discovery of Grounded Theory.* Chicago: Aldine Publishing Co.

Goffman, Erving (1963) *Stigma: Notes on the Management of Spoiled Identity.* Englewood Cliffs, NJ: Prentice-Hall.

Haris, Ronald A., & J. Fred Springer (1984) "Plea Bargaining as a Game: An Empirical Analysis of Negotiated Sentencing Decisions," 4 *Policy Studies Rev.* 245.

Heumann, Milton (1975) "A Note on Plea Bargaining and Case Pressure," 9 *Law & Society Rev.* 515.

____ (1978) *Plea Bargaining: The Experiences of Prosecutors, Judges, and Defense Attorneys.* Chicago: Univ of Chicago Press.

Holmes, Malcolm D., Howard C. Daudistel, & William A. Taggart (1992) "Plea Bargaining Policy and State District Court Caseloads: An Interrupted Time Series Analysis," 26 *Law & Society Rev.* 139.

Kingsnorth, Rodney, & Michael Jungsten (1988) "Driving under the Influence: The Impact of Legislative Reform on Court Sentencing Practices," 34 *Crime & Delinquency* 3.

LaFree, Gary D. (1985) "Adversarial and Non-adversarial Justice: A Comparison of Guilty Pleas and Trials," 23 *Criminology* 289.

Lester, Marilyn, & Stuart C. Hadden (1980) "Ethnomethodology and Grounded Theory Methodology: An Integration of Perspective and Method," 9 *Urban Life* 3.

Mather, Lynn M. (1979) *Plea Bargaining or Trial?* Lexington, MA: Lexington Books.

Maynard, Douglas W. (1984a) *Inside Plea Bargaining.* New York: Plenum Press.

____ (1984b) "The Structure of Discourse in Misdemeanor Plea Bargaining," 18 *Law & Society Rev.* 75.

____ (1988) "Narratives and Narrative Structure in Plea Bargaining," 22 *Law & Society Rev.* 449.

McConville, Michael (1986) "Dilemmas in New Models for Indigent Defense" (Effective Assistance of Counsel for the Indigent Criminal Defendant: Has The Promise Been Fulfilled? New York University, March 23 1985), 14 *Rev. of Law & Social Change* 179.

McConville, Michael, & Chester L. Mirsky (1990) "Understanding Defense of the Poor in State Courts: The Sociolegal Context of Nonadversarial Advocacy," 10 *Studies in Law, Politics, & Society* 217.

McDonald, William F. (1979) "From Plea Negotiation to Coercive Justice: Notes on the Respecification of a Concept," 13 *Law & Society Rev.* 385.

_____ (1985) *Plea Bargaining: Critical Issues and Common Practices.* Washington, DC: National Institute of Justice, U.S. Dept. of Justice.

Mileski, Maureen (1971) "Courtroom Encounters: An Observation Study of a Lower Criminal Court," 5 *Law & Society Rev.* 473.

Neubauer, David W. (1974) *Criminal Justice in Middle America.* Morristown, NJ: General Learning Press.

Packer, Herbert (1968) *The Limits of the Criminal Sanction.* Palo Alto, CA: Stanford Univ. Press.

Padgett, John F. (1990) "Plea Bargaining and Prohibition in the Federal Courts, 1908-1934," 24 *Law & Society Rev.* 413.

Pritchard, David (1986) "Homicide and Bargained Justice: The Agenda-setting Effect of Crime News on Prosecutors," 50 *Public Opinion Q.* 143.

Rosett, Arthur & Donald Cressey (1976) *Justice by Consent.* Philadelphia: J. B. Lippincott Co.

Ryan, John Paul, & James J. Alfini (1979) "Trial Judges" participation in Plea Bargaining: An Empirical Perspective," 13 *Law & Society Rev.* 479.

Sarat, Austin, & William L.F. Felstiner (1986) "Law and Strategy in the Divorce Lawyer's Office," 20 *Law & Society Rev.* 93.

Skolnick, Jerome H. (1967) "Social Control in the Adversary System," 11 *J. of Conflict Resolution* 52.

Sudnow, David (1965) "Normal Crimes: Sociological Features of the Penal Code in a Public Defender Office," 12 *Social Problems* 255.

Uhlman, Thomas M., & N. Darlene Walker (1979) "A Plea Is No Bargain: The Impact of Case Disposition on Sentencing," 60 *Social Science Q.* 218.

_____ (1980) 'He Takes Some of My Time: I Take Some of His': An Analysis of Judicial Sentencing Patterns in Jury Cases," 14 *Law & Society Rev.* 323.

Utz, Pamela J. (1978) *Settling the Facts: Discretion and Negotiating in Criminal Court.* Lexington, MA: Lexington Books.

An analysis of the social construction for guilty pleas was the focus of this research. The examination of the judges' role in pressuring defendants to plead guilty for bureaucratic efficiency (that is, keeping the court dockets moving) illustrates the conflict between the due process model and what the authors term "a social discriminatory model of justice." In this legal environment, the judges rather than the defense attorneys are the very people who persuade the accused, through their lawyers, to plead guilty. This action fulfills the social discriminatory objectives of subordination and maintaining order over indigent clients who are labeled dangerous, while simultaneously providing a façade of legitimacy for judicial decision making that in reality lacks legal rationality.

GUILTY PLEA COURTS

*A Social Disciplinary Model of Criminal Justice**

MIKE MCCONVILLE

CHESTER MIRSKY

INTRODUCTION

The majority of routine felony cases, the day-to-day workload of criminal courts, are settled by guilty pleas.[1] Traditional accounts assume that those actually guilty of criminal acts adopt a cost-efficient method of confronting their guilt, make deals, and plead guilty (Alschuler 1976). Implicit in these accounts is the notion that the decision to offer or accept a plea is based on the weight of the evidence against the accused and the presence or absence of a viable legal

*We wish to thank the Filomen D'Agostino and Max E. Greenberg Research Fund, the Center for Research in Crime and Justice of the New York University School of Law, and the University of Warwick Research and Innovation Fund, all of whom provided generous financial support for this study. Special thanks to David Garland for having read and critiqued an earlier version of this article, to Malcolm Spector, whose incisive editing contributed greatly to the final manuscript, and to Hidelgaida Ortiz.

©1995 by The Society for the Study of *Social Problems. Reprinted from Social Problems (42)*2, pp. 216-234, by permission.

defense (Walker 1993). Nardulli, Eisenstein, and Flemming (1988:210) contend, for example, that the "absence of factual ambiguity in most cases looms large as an explanation for the defendant's decision to plead guilty." The guilty plea is usually both inevitable and just (Feeley 1979; Maynard 1984).

Analysts and ideologues (defenders and supporters of the system) recognize that, without a trial, there is a risk that rights guaranteed to a criminal defendant may not be protected and that the factually innocent may be convicted. The assignment of legal counsel to all criminal defendants, guaranteed by *Gideon vs. Wainwright* (1963), is supposed to ensure the protection of individual rights and adequate scrutiny of the police evidence against a criminal defendant. In spite of legal representation, most criminal defendants still plead guilty because "[c]ourt personnel simply recognize the factual culpability of many defendants and the fruitlessness, at least in terms of case outcome, of going to trial" (Heumann 1978:156).

Indeed, many courtroom observers who defend the current system point to colloquies such as the following (which ended one of the cases discussed below), in which judges question defendants before allowing them to plead guilty, to show that factually guilty defendants' legal rights are respected and protected, even as they forego a public trial. (All names in this paper are pseudonyms.)

Q: "Have you had an opportunity to consult with your lawyer, Mr. Gartenstein, and to discuss the matter with him before choosing to plead guilty?"

A: "Yes."

Q: "Do you understand that by pleading guilty you have given up your right to trial by jury?"

A: "Yes."

Q: "Do you understand that by pleading guilty you have given up your right to confront and cross-examine witnesses against you, to testify, and to call witnesses on your own behalf?"

A: "Yes."

Q: "Do you understand that you have given up your right to remain silent and your privilege against self-incrimination?"

A: "Yes."

Q: "Do you understand that at a trial you are presumed innocent and that the prosecution has to prove your guilt beyond a reasonable doubt?"

A: "Yes."

Q: "Has anybody threatened or coerced you?"

A: "No."

Q: "Is your plea voluntary and of your own free will?"

A: "Yes."

Q: "Do you understand that in pleading guilty you have given up all these rights and that the conviction entered is the same as a conviction after trial?"

A: "Yes."

Q: "Did you along with McBride and Hervey forcibly steal property from the person of the complaining witness and possess what appeared to be a gun."

A: "Yes."[2]

The research reported in this paper comes to a different conclusion. We conclude that in large urban areas guilty pleas are part of a vertically integrated system of imposing control and discipline on highly visible sections of society, those who are perceived as dangerous because of their lack of involvement in an acceptable labor market and the intensity of their involvement with the criminal justice system (Simon 1993). This system often begins with proactive "sweeps" by specialized police units (such as narcotics control units); it extends through the system of assigning counsel to indigent defendants, and it concludes with a highly coercive drama in which defendants are first shown (by being made to watch others) that they will suffer greatly increased penalties if they refuse to plead guilty, and in which they are then given their 15 seconds to accept or reject the pleas and sentences offered to them by calendar judges.

We call this a social disciplinary model, a form of substantive rationality committed to achieving order through surveillance and control of the urban underclass (Simon 1993; Smith and Visher 1981; Smith, Visher, and Davidson 1984). Substantive rationality is concerned with "impact, effect, and ends" served by the criminal justice system (Savelsberg 1992:1348; Weber 1968). It involves "an intrusion of the state into society" and the "opening of state decision making to social (extralegal) criteria" (Savelsberg 1992:1348; Teubner 1987:10-12). As a form of substantive rationality, social discipline has little commitment to traditional notions of crime control through proof of either factual or legal guilt. The latter, often equated with legal rationality, furthers individual autonomy (Nonet and Selznick 1978) and is achieved through an analysis of the state's burden of proof, either informally at settlement conferences (Blumberg 1967a; Mnookin and Kornhauser 1979), or formally at hearings, motions, and trials. By contrast, a social disciplinary model, concerned with containment rather than crime control (Simon 1993), imposes judgments of conviction without restraint on how police power may be exercised against the individual.

In this paper we first describe our research methods and our perhaps unusual way of presenting our results. We then turn to 1) the significance of proactive policing; 2) the relation between the assigned counsel and the indigent criminal defendant; and 3) the educational and disciplinary scripts of pleading guilty.

Research Methods

This essay is part of a study of the provision of defense services to the poor in New York City. In 1984 and 1985, with the permission of the court and the parties, we observed 236 defendants in more than 150 felony cases in guilty plea court, i.e., calendar "parts" (Luskin 1989) as they are called in New York, where cases can only be resolved through non-trial dispositions. We observed more than 650 court appearances along with the activities at central booking and at lawyer interviews in the court pens. We received a copy of all relevant court papers for each case, and we interviewed the prosecutors, judges, defense attorneys, and, whenever possible, the defendants in each case. We recorded all

our observations in field notes made during or immediately after a court proceeding. In 1986 and 1987, we supplemented our sample with an additional 100 felony cases.

In addition to these qualitative materials, we analyzed the statistical reports put out by the Office of Court Administration from 1986 through 1993 (New York State Supreme Court 1984-1994; Office of Court Administration 1986-1993). These contain monthly ratings that show the number of guilty plea dispositions achieved by all judges as well as detailed comparisons among judges. We also assembled quantitative data on the vouchers submitted for payment by assigned counsel that indicated how frequently court-appointed lawyers claimed expenses for investigation and for witness interviews. The historical and quantitative aspects of our research have been reported earlier (McConville and Mirsky 1986-87, 1988, 1989, 1990).

In one brief article it is not possible to present more than a minute sample from our body of qualitative data. Our aim is to present observations that both 1) reveal the fundamental processes at work in the guilty plea system, and 2) represent the central tendencies or model case from our data. Here we focus on one defense lawyer, Emerson, one criminal defendant, Roberto Santiago, and the events, including other cases heard that Emerson represented or that Santiago observed, that preceded Santiago's decision to plead guilty. A closer look at these actors and their cases produces a deeper understanding of the social disciplinary processes at work than a more circumscribed sample of data from a slightly larger number of cases.

Roberto Santiago was arrested as he left his apartment at 1:30 a.m. by police officers engaged in a sweep of the neighborhood. Before the arrest, undercover officers toured Santiago's neighborhood and radioed descriptions of suspected drug dealers to backup units whose officers swept the street for people they believed fit the descriptions. The sweep occurred once the police had decided to complete an operation in which undercover officers, posing as gypsy cab drivers, purchased cocaine and other drugs from street-level dealers. When Santiago was held later in a precinct, an undercover officer, looking through a two-way mirror, identified him as a person from whom the officer had purchased cocaine six months earlier.

By 1989, with the advent of the crack epidemic, drug arrests, often initiated by non-individuated sweeps, produced more than 50 percent of all superior court indictments in New York City (Division of Criminal Justice Services 1989). Santiago, along with more than 56 percent of those arrested who were indicted, pleaded guilty after appearing only before a calendar judge (Office of Court Administration 1984-1985; Miller, McDonald, and Cramer 1978).[3] Santiago was a person of color, and, during our observations, more than 80 percent of all arrested defendants were people of color (New York City Department of Corrections 1984; McConville and Mirsky 1986-87; Division of Criminal Justice Services 1989). Santiago was 21, and more than half of all arrested defendants were below age 30 (New York City Department of Corrections 1984). Santiago, with more than three-quarters of arrested defendants, was represented by a court-assigned lawyer (McConville and Mirsky 1986-87). Santiago, along with more than half of the arrested defendants we observed, was represented by a number of different court-assigned attorneys during several months (McConville and Mirsky 1986-87; Gilboy and Schmidt 1979).

PROACTIVE POLICE WORK

A long-term secular trend away from reactive police work toward proactive police work has shifted the fundamental institutional assumptions of the criminal justice system. Increasingly, police work seeks to impose order in areas of the inner city that the police and the wider society view as dangerous (Pepinsky 1975; Wilson 1987; Jaynes and Williams 1988). When the generation of criminal cases is part of the quest to impose order, arrests and guilty pleas become symbolic tests of police authority (Mann 1993; Balbus 1973). In this model, the police work proactively (Sykes 1986). They reach out into the community, creating and discovering crimes through sting operations and buys and sells, to which police officers and undercover agents are almost invariably the only witnesses. In New York City,

sweeps directed at drug dealers and prostitutes have become increasingly common in many areas. The occupants and inhabitants of these "public" spaces are generically placed at risk (Sherman 1990; Zimmer 1987; Criminal Justice Agency 1984, 1985).

Proactive policing influences how the justice system as a whole responds to crime. When proactive cases become the typical and then the model case, the system itself, regardless of the nature of the case, abandons the traditional assumption that expects police to respond to crimes reported by the public, in which 1) the major witnesses are either the victims or other members of the public, and 2) questions regarding witness reliability, and the sufficiency and persuasiveness of the evidence, are legitimately subject to testing.

In the enterprise of social discipline, based on proactive policing, the only credibility contest pits a team of undercover police officers against people of color who are ghetto dwellers. Here the outcome is predetermined and the message is understood by everyone. Judges, under great pressure to clear their calendars, do not tolerate "obstructive" lawyers who pursue "technical defenses" or insist upon trials (McConville and Mirsky 1986-87:837-38). Defense lawyers rarely conduct in-depth interviews with their clients. In one of the cases discussed here, when the defendant, Hickson, protested that he had not sold any narcotics, his lawyer replied:

> I'm not interested in that. Do you understand? It doesn't matter whether you are innocent or guilty: It doesn't matter because the cops are making out a case.

This was the lawyer's way of saying that when the only potential witnesses are police officers, the idea of denying the charge or insisting upon a hearing or trial is not worth considering.

For the same reason, defense lawyers rarely make independent investigations or use the services of investigators. Court-appointed lawyers may request expense money for conducting investigations and interviewing potential witnesses. However, our analysis of a sample of vouchers submitted by assigned counsel in felony cases (whether proactive or reactive) showed that they rarely do this. There are no vouchers submitted at all for investigation in 73 percent of all homicide cases. The figure was 88 percent for all other felonies. No witness interviews were claimed in 80 percent of all homicides or 90 percent of all other felonies. No motions were filed in 75 percent of all homicide cases or 90 percent for other felonies (McConville and Mirsky 1986-87).

Social discipline eliminates any inquiry into the reliability of the officer's identification, and it informs the actions of the police in their subsequent dealings with those arrested. Thus, the court papers assembled in the case of *People vs. Santiago* contained the only "facts" (Smith 1974:8) upon which his case would be decided. The uniformed officer who signed Roberto Santiago's complaint lacked personal knowledge of the allegations. What the uniformed officer swore to was a conclusionary assertion based upon statements made by the undercover officer after viewing the defendant at the precinct. No police officer questioned Santiago or asked him to provide an explanation of his conduct. The complaint contained no information regarding the undercover officer's opportunity to observe the person selling drugs, how the officer later came to identify the defendant, or the presence of any corroborating evidence.

The remaining court papers, prepared at central booking, included the "RAP sheet," a narcotics addiction form, a "wanted statement," and the Pre-Trial Services Agency form. The RAP sheet, a computerized print-out of a defendant's prior criminal record, generated from a fingerprint comparison, revealed that Santiago did not have any previous arrests, while the narcotics form (from physical observations) indicated only that he was not a drug user. The wanted statement, based upon a name and date-of-birth comparison, however, indicated that someone by the name of Santiageles, with the same date of birth as Santiago, was wanted by the Navy for desertion.

The Pre-Trial Services Agency form indicated that Santiago had "insufficient community ties" and therefore was a risk of flight. At central booking, Santiago had informed an agency representative that he was employed, that he had lived with his mother and sister at his current address for the past ten years and at his previous address for ten years, and that he had never been arrested before. The agency could not verify the information Santiago provided, because Santiago's family did not have a telephone and his employment was "off-the-books."

THE ASSIGNMENT OF COUNSEL

Once Roberto Santiago's court papers were assembled, he was transferred to a holding cell behind the arraignment court to await the assignment of an attorney. A copy of the papers was first placed in a basket designated for the Legal Aid Society, the City's public defender agency (McConville and Mirsky 1986-87). The uneven work patterns of the Legal Aid Society staff attorneys, the number of staff attorneys at arraignment, and the availability of "18-B attorneys,"[4] however, often provoked judges to assign Legal Aid cases to 18-B regulars. These lawyers represented almost as many indicted defendants (roughly 30 percent) as the Legal Aid Society (roughly 40 percent) (McConville and Mirsky 1986-87). The regulars were solo practitioners; some subsisted on court assignments, while others prospered on these cases, earning more than $100,000 from court assignments (McConville and Mirsky 1986-87; Assael 1989; Fritsch and Purdy 1994). They stationed themselves in the court building, expecting to obtain case assignments on a moment's notice.

While Roberto Santiago sat in the court pen, the sight of Legal Aid staff attorneys in court chatting among themselves provoked Judge Lorraine to order the court captain to "find an 18-B who can help clear the docket." Lorraine was a Criminal (inferior) Court calendar judge who routinely processed more than 100 cases in an eight-hour arraignment shift, disposing of 50 percent through guilty pleas.

At the court captain's instigation, Emerson, the 18-B attorney assigned for the day to conflict cases, began to thumb through cases the clerk had placed in the basket. Emerson was a solo practitioner who came to criminal law practice after attending a local law school at night and working as a court officer in guilty plea court (Abel 1989; Wice 1978; Wood 1976). His practice was almost entirely court-assigned.

Emerson picked out some case files, briefly looked at the names and said: "I'm not interested in this, it's a burglary, and this is a robbery, a chain snatch. I can't stand these robberies, it's a horrible crime. I like narcotics, let's see." Then he found a case file that attracted him, looked through it quickly, and said, "I'll take this one." Soon, he had gathered three cases and walked away from the Legal Aid basket. Emerson had chosen the cases of Danny James, Monroe Hickson, and Roberto Santiago.

Emerson proceeded first with the case of Danny James, whose file had been placed in the Legal Aid basket by Jim, a staff attorney, after having interviewed the defendant. When Emerson attempted to dispose of James's case through a guilty plea, Jim intervened shouting, "What's going on it's my case. What's happening?" Lorraine said: "I don't know anything about this." Each pressed the file on the other, but eventually Emerson handed the file over to Jim and said: "It's your case, you keep it. I was helping out. I didn't want it anyway." A second call was ordered so that Jim could resume representation of Danny James.

Emerson's selection of cases was typical of the process we observed. Assignments depended on case backlog and the take-up rate of Legal Aid staff attorneys and 18-B regulars. A successful lawyer, one who received many arraignment assignments, was a lawyer who enabled the calendar judge either to immediately enter a guilty plea or to adjourn the case to another date. This was evident in the initial client interviews Emerson conducted of Hickson and Santiago before the court proceedings.

Emerson briefly interviewed Monroe Hickson, another defendant awaiting arraignment on a street-level drug sale. Emerson flicked through the file; as he picked up the last sheet, a great deal of writing appeared on the jacket containing the notes of an earlier interview of Hickson conducted by a Legal Aid attorney, before Emerson had removed Hickson's file from the Legal Aid basket. Emerson glanced at the writing and let the papers drop back into the file.

When Hickson's case was called, an Assistant District Attorney (ADA) served Emerson with notice that the case was about to be presented to a grand jury. Emerson interjected immediately: "May we approach?"

Lorraine: "Yes."

Emerson: "Is there an offer [guilty plea] in this case?"

ADA: "There is a warrant on him and we need to check."

Emerson: "Where? It's not in my papers."

Lorraine: "It's right there on the first sheet."

Emerson: "No it's not. There's nothing about it."

A court officer showed Emerson the warrant among Hickson's papers. Because of the confusion caused by the appearance of the warrant, the judge ordered a short second call. Emerson spoke to one of the authors at side-bar and said: "Fuck it. It's not such a good case." In Emerson's view, the only alternative was to adjourn the case to another date. At a later call on the calendar, Hickson appeared only to learn that, in his absence, Emerson had adjourned the case, while Lorraine had remanded him to jail.

Emerson began to work on the case of Roberto Santiago. As Santiago pulled on a cigarette and nervously moved around the pen, he looked drawn and frightened.

Emerson: "Okay. They say you sold some cocaine but here's the good news."

A voice from inside the pen intervened and said: "It's your first offense."

Emerson: "That's right it's your first offense, and second, it happened six months ago. No there is no way in which you are going to be convicted by any jury on this. What happened, did you just get picked up? Were they just flushing the area?"

Santiago: "I don't know what happened, man. Oh, man! I was just coming out of my building and I was just grabbed, told to stand up against the wall. I've been here three days . . ."

Emerson: "Okay. So you were just grabbed. They grabbed everyone right?"

The "voice" appeared again (a white male aged about 35, blond with a mustache) and said:

"Look, they picked up the whole neighborhood."

Emerson then left to telephone Santiago's aunt to verify the information Santiago had provided concerning his employment and ties to the community. But the line was always busy and Emerson returned to speak with Santiago again. As he was speaking he flicked through the papers; he suddenly stopped and yelled, "What the fuck is this? There's a warrant out for you."

Santiago: "A warrant? It's not for me. Oh, no!"

Emerson: "The Navy, the Navy wants you. You are wanted by the Navy on a warrant. Did you quit before you did your time with them?"

Santiago: "I've never been in the Navy."

Emerson: "It must be a mistake. There are lots of Santiagos, but it will have to be checked. I'll go and see."

Emerson's interviews with Hickson and Santiago were perfunctory and public. Emerson spoke through the cell bars in the presence of other defendants and uniformed officers. As he returned to court after speaking to Santiago, Emerson said to us: "This [the Navy warrant] could screw it up today but he'll get an acquittal. They will never convict on this evidence." Emerson did not review the physical description of Santiageles to determine whether the warrant referred to someone else.[5]

Nor did Emerson obtain information from Santiago regarding his community ties and whether his family or friends had the capacity to post bail. Similarly, when a cell mate emphasized the non-individuated nature of Santiago's arrest, Emerson responded by referring to the date of the alleged sale as the important factor in determining whether the case would result in a conviction. Emerson never questioned the outcome of a case; he was able to attempt a guilty plea within moments of meeting a defendant or to adjourn cases without further delay.

ARRAIGNMENT—THE COMMENCEMENT OF JUDICIAL REVIEW

At arraignment, his first appearance before a judge, Roberto Santiago saw the futility of any legal challenge to the police case. When

Santiago was produced before Judge Lorraine, Emerson's first act was to respond affirmatively to the court officer's request: "Do you waive the reading of the rights and charges?" Lorraine then asked the Assistant district Attorney (ADA) to address Santiago's release status:

ADA: "This case involves a sale of cocaine. The sale was hand to hand. It is a B felony, quite serious, and the Pre-Trial Services sheet indicates that this defendant has insufficient community ties to warrant parole at this point without a substantial cash bail. Therefore the People ask $3,000 cash bail."

Lorraine: "Mr. Emerson, you may be heard."

Emerson: "This is like when you go into a store to buy olives and someone tells you that there might be more than one quality of olives. You can get big olives or you can get giant olives or you can get absolutely colossal huge olives. Here the District Attorney's office is telling you they have giant olives, but in reality the olives in this case are very small ones. In fact I don't see how they are going to prosecute at all in this case because the sale took place so long ago. The sale took place almost six months ago, and I simply don't see how the state will bring charges successfully in this case. The identification evidence will never stand up. How are they going to produce a lab test? He has no prior arrests. I called his home phone number and it was busy."

Lorraine: "You obviously don't know anything about the Special Narcotics Prosecutor's Office."

Emerson: "They'll never make 180.80."[6]

Lorraine: "I don't think you understand how an undercover investigation works, Mr. Emerson. This is not abnormal at all. In fact, most undercover investigations work like this when the arrest occurs some times after the original sale. But you can keep the case and fight it as much as you want. I'll set bail at $1,500 cash or bond."

Lorraine set bail in an amount that a defendant requiring the assignment of counsel would be unlikely to post (Nagel 1983) without inquiring into the factual-legal basis for the undercover officer's identification (*Manson vs. Brathwaite* 1977), i.e., the opportunity to observe the person selling drugs, the cause for delay in arrest, or its effect on the reliability of the undercover officer's later identification of Santiago. Neither Emerson nor the judge made any reference to Roberto Santiago's community ties, and Emerson failed to challenge the ADA's repetition of the Pre-Trial Services finding of "insufficient community ties," other than to state that Santiago's phone was busy.

Emerson never discussed with Hickson or Santiago the rights that attach to arraignment. Nor did Lorraine inform either defendant that he had a right to remain silent, the right to a prompt hearing on the charges, the right to counsel, or the right to proceed without a lawyer and to represent himself (Criminal Procedure Law Sec. 180.10 [1985]). Instead, Emerson's presence satisfied legal formalism; it signified that a lawyer had so advised the defendants, that each defendant had asserted his right to silence and had requested the assignment of counsel, and that Emerson had agreed to act as the attorney-of-record.

Unless the ADA reduced the charge to a misdemeanor, Lorraine lacked jurisdiction to accept a guilty plea in Santiago's case (Criminal Procedure Law Sec. 10.30(2) [1982]). However, she could have required the ADA to amend the complaint to provide some basis for the undercover officer's identification. She also could have inquired into Santiago's community ties and employment history to determine whether Santiago should be released or detained. In addition, she could have refused to continue Emerson as Santiago's attorney, had she concluded that the lawyer's understanding was so flawed as to disable him from providing competent representation. Instead, Lorraine made no effort to expand the record or to provide a legal basis for her actions. Lorraine adjourned the case to another date without delay.

While in jail following the arraignment, Santiago called a neighbor who made contact with his family. His mother responded and, within a day, posted $1,500 to obtain his release. Santiago thereafter made three court appearances with a family member. Each time he waited until mid-afternoon to discover that the judge had adjourned his case because the grand jury had not yet indicted him. When the grand jury did act, the indictment alleged that the drug sale occurred *eighteen months*, not sixth months, before Santiago's arrest. However, Emerson had not attempted to reconstruct the events in question through an in-depth interview with the defendant, nor had he undertaken any independent factual and legal inquiry.

PUBLIC EDUCATION IN THE COURTROOM AND GUILTY PLEA SCRIPTS

When Roberto Santiago first appeared in Supreme Court, 20 months had expired between the alleged incident and the filing of the indictment. Under formal legal rationality, the delay in arrest and indictment was reason enough to dismiss the charges, upon a showing that the delay was intentional, attributable to the police, and prejudicial to the defendant (*United States vs. Lovasco* 1977; Criminal Procedure Law Sec. 210.20(h) [1980]). Should Santiago refuse to plead guilty and insist upon litigating the propriety of the delay, however, Judge Roger, a calendar judge in guilty plea court with an intolerance for "dilatory tactics" would rule on the challenge. Roger was the calendar judge with the highest rate of dispositions and the largest caseload; his daily calendar often contained more than 50 indicted defendants.

All judges are rated according to their ability to dispose of large caseloads without hearing or trial. The calendar judges we observed in guilty plea court were those with the highest rate of disposition measured in terms of total caseload.[7] These judges were fixtures in guilty plea court, while judges who compared unfavorably were routinely assigned to hearing and trial courts (Luskin 1989; Heydebrand and Seron 1987). During a one-year period of our observations, six calendar judges disposed of approximately 11,600 indictments, of which 4,126 (35 percent) were disposed of within 60 days and 3,581 (31 percent) between 61 and 135 days (Office of Court Administration 1984-85). These judges educated defendants and others present in their courtroom that the opportunity to contest the police case was limited (Pollner 1979; Resnick 1982).

As Roberto Santiago waited for his case to be called, he, along with other defendants, lawyers, and families and friends assembled, listened to the bench conferences Judge Roger conducted with prosecutors and defense attorneys, most of which led to guilty pleas. To be sure Roger appeared to comply with formal legal rationality, the defendants "voluntarily" waived their rights on the record. However, Roger relied upon police interrogation practices to ensure that defendants would become compliant (Rossett and Cressey 1976; Leo 1994). He manipulated the bail status of released defendants (Inciardi 1984)[8] by jailing those defendants who refused to plead guilty, despite the fact that a defendant who had been released at arraignment had voluntarily appeared on several adjourned dates. By contrast, Roger rewarded defendants who pleaded guilty by allowing them to remain free on bail, although they were now convicted and awaiting sentence. Roger raised the stakes on defendants who refused to admit guilt by threatening them with a greater sentence on any subsequent adjourned date (Brereton and Casper 1981; Uhlman and Walker 1980; National Minority Advisory Council 1980). Initial offers of probation, if refused, would later become fixed jail time, whereas offers of jail time once refused, would be increased into indeterminate state prison sentences. In the event of a conviction after a trial, Roger would impose a sentence that greatly exceeded the last guilty plea offer made.

These encounters, which Roger described to the authors as "tests of strength," placed a premium on the defendant's resolve, pitted against the judge's power to control the outcome. At these conferences, Roger reduced cases to skeletal outlines—a "chain snatch," and "undercover drug sale," a "break-in" (Sudnow 1965). All conversations at the bench and all statements made by Roger to lawyers and defendants were "off-the-record." Only the formal setting of bail, the adjourn date, and the entry of the guilty plea and sentence were "on-the-record."[9]

Roger first read a write-up of the state's evidence supplied by the ADA stationed in the calendar part. The central feature of the summary sheet was the prosecution's charge and sentence offer. Should the offer be acceptable to Roger, he would immediately repeat it to the defense lawyer. If Roger believed that the prosecution's offer failed to serve as adequate inducement for a plea, or if he believed it to be too generous, Roger would alter either the charge or the sentence. Should the ADA object, Roger would threaten the prosecution with an immediate trial (for which police and civilian witnesses were never immediately available), or he would insist that the ADA who presented the case to the grand jury or a supervisor immediately appear in court to defend the original offer. When confronted with Roger's displeasure, the ADA usually agreed to Roger's demands, after which Roger would describe the offer to the defense lawyer. Roger then would tell the lawyer to speak to the defendant about pleading guilty.

In Judge Roger's court, the advice that lawyers gave their clients occurred under the judge's watchful eye, at the defense table some 15 feet from the bench. Should the defendant exhibit a facial grimace or utter a hostile response, Roger would raise the guilty plea offer and jail the defendant, while loudly repeating to those assembled the consequences that flow from such resistance. This display of force enabled Roberto Santiago and other defendants sitting in the courtroom to appreciate Roger's displeasure at recalcitrance and the power that the judge could bring to bear on any person who persisted in pleading not guilty (Dumm 1990).

On the day Santiago sat awaiting his turn, the first case conference involved two defendants, Hall and Powell. Both defendants had been released on money bail by another judge. The defendants were initially charged in a complaint of robbery and possession of a weapon. In Supreme Court, the robbery charges were dropped because the complaining witness had not appeared in the grand jury. This left the police as the witnesses to the sole remaining offense — possession of a weapon. As 18-B attorneys Graf and Novick entered the well of the courtroom, Roger stated: "This is the first time on; all of you come up." He began the "off-the-record" case conference:

Roger: "I see there is a predicate felony statement[10] on Powell, and Hall has a pending King's County robbery. [Then loudly addressing himself to the court officers] Heads up on this fellas, please.[11] [Roger then reverted to addressing the lawyers in derisive tones] King's County set $200 bail!

[Referring to a pending charge against Hall] Unbelievable! Of course there could have been a better write up on this . . ."

Graf: "That [referring to the $200 bail] indicates that it wasn't much of a case."

Roger: "Unbelievable! What's the offer?"

ADA: "It's a 'D' to each.[12] Powell had the gun on him. We are asking $7,500 as to Powell and $2,500 as to Hall."

Roger: [Reading from the prosecutor's summary]: "The complaining witness approaches a police officer and tells him that the defendants had harassed him, and robbed him in the past. The officer took him into the patrol car and the complainant pointed out the defendants. The officer recovered a gun from Powell. There's a dispute as to whose gun it is. Hall says 'Why can't you just charge me?' Powell says, 'I was simply keeping it.' Well, that puts both of them in it squarely. Now, let's see, Powell has a second violent felony. [Then addressing the whole courtroom] Bail is going up. It's going up."

Graf: "What is the basis for the stop and search when . . ."

Roger: "Look, make your motions but you have nothing to complain about, nothing to suppress. Nothing was seized from your guy . . ."

Graf: "I think there is an issue . . ."

Roger: "Make your motions. I'd like to see that. [Seeing the DA assigned to this case, Roger called out] There's Seifman; come up."

Roger [to Seifman]: "What's going on? You told me [in prosecution summary] he has a second felony: In fact he is a second *violent* offender.[13] [Loudly] Let's arraign these defendants; they are going in."

The defendants were then arraigned on the indictment by the clerk's on-the-record reading of the charges and by asking the defendants how they pleaded: guilty or not guilty.

The Hall and Powell conference first demonstrates Roger's power to limit the opportunity for defendants to rely on an assertion of rights

(Casper 1972). Hall's statement "Why can't you just charge me?" may have been suppressible as the "fruits" of the illegal arrest (*Wong Sun vs. United States* 1963). (This was what Graf sought to determine when he awkwardly asked Roger about the basis for the "search," i.e., arrest.) Roger's response trivialized Graf's inquiry by informing Graf that "nothing was [actually] seized from your guy . . ." and by daring Graf to assert Hall's rights by making a motion to suppress. Should Graf have insisted on a hearing upon the grounds that the arrest violated his client's rights, Hall would have paid the price by remaining in jail until Roger conducted a hearing to determine whether Hall's statement should have been suppressed. Given Roger's admonition that Hall had "nothing to complain about, nothing to suppress," the time spent in detention and the likely denial of the motion to suppress would have served to reinforce the notion that reliance on formal legal rights was pointless. By contrast, Roger's substantive power to control the defendants' release through the pronouncement that "they are going in" was immediately effective, and it preempted any legal argument.

The case conference further demonstrates Roger's power to manipulate the bail of released defendants in pursuit of a guilty plea. Once Hall and Powell had entered not guilty pleas, Hall's lawyer made the following bail application "on the record:"

Roger: "On Powell, I'm going to exonerate bail and fix it at $7,500/7,500. I'll hear you counsellor."

Novick: "My client is 21. He has voluntarily returned to court. He has lived at the same address for 20 years and is currently employed with [a named business]. I would ask that bail be the same."

Roger: "He has two violent felony convictions. He was found with the gun, and under these circumstances and having regard to the fact that he is facing a minimum of 2 years-5 years, $7,500 is, therefore, reasonable. With regard to Hall, bail is $2,500."

Graf: "My client qualified for parole [release on his recognizance based upon verified community ties]. He was released and came back. He has no prior convictions. He is not facing any state time. His record does not reflect he was arrested in King's County."

Roger: "But the detective was present [on a previous occasion when Hall appeared] to take him there."

ADA: "This will be confirmed on the NICIS [RAP] sheet."

Graf: "This is pending in Criminal Court in King's on $200 bail and the best person to set that was the judge who must have had all the facts . . ."

Roger: "I'm fixing bail . . ."

Graf: "He is not facing mandatory prison."

Roger: "The Gun Statute does contemplate one year but not in state prison. That is, after conviction. It is not mandatory until after conviction."

Graf: "He has returned here . . ."

Roger: "That's the second time you are telling me the purpose of bail. I understand you are frustrated . . ."

Graf: "I'm not frustrated, I'm trying to . . ."

Roger: "OK. $2,500/2,500. Ask the DA to get more facts on the King's County case."

Once Roger told the court officers to keep their "heads up," the judge indicated his intent to have the officers handcuff and remove the defendants to the court pens, even though both had previously appeared while on bail. This punitive rhetoric (Garland 1991) redefined the role of court personnel, from officers to jailers.

The next case demonstrated how respect for law became a function of the extent to which Roger was capable of instilling fear in the individual. Here, Roger threatened to increase the sentence to show defendants that law is "a compelling and powerful force" (Dumm 1990:30). As the court clerk called out the names of Leng, McBride, and Hervey, the defendants, who appeared to be about age 18, were escorted by officers from the court pen to stand behind the defense table. As they did so, three lawyers, Sherr, a Legal Aid attorney, and Gartenstein and Rucker, 18-B attorneys, entered the well of the courtroom and stood facing Roger. The ADA addressed Roger saying: "May we approach the

bench?" Roger told all the lawyers to come up. The ADA then handed Roger a sheet that contained a short summary of the charges, the guilty plea and sentence offer, and a recommendation to continue to detain the defendants in lieu of $10,000 bail.

Roger read aloud the one-line statements of facts disclosed in the prosecutor's summary. As soon as the reading was completed, Roger glanced at the defendants' RAP sheets and made the following remark off the record: "Here's the offer." Before he said anything further, Gartenstein said: "Judge, he [Leng] said he made YO."[14]

Roger: "It is not so on the sheet."

Gartenstein: "He tells me he did or at least I think that's what he says.

Roger: "Check it out."

Gartenstein went to speak to Leng and returned a few seconds later saying: "I've checked and he did make YO." Roger continued: "Here's the offer. McBride 4 to 8 [years] [mandatory minimum sentence for a predicate felon], Leng and Hervey [not predicate felons] 1 to 4 and no YO." All three attorneys went back to inform their clients of the likely consequences of refusing Roger's guilty plea offer.

When Sherr told his client of Roger's offer, McBride recoiled, frowned, and made a dismissive gesture towards Sherr. Roger noticed this immediately and spoke in resonant off-the-record tones to the whole courtroom. Roger's speech enabled Roberto Santiago and others present to hear his contempt for the defendant's response, while it demonstrated that in Roger's court, a lawyer is little more than a formal appendage whose function is easily made redundant:

> McBride doesn't appear to like it. Tell him, Mr. Sherr, that I remember him and it's not good for a calendar judge to remember someone. Tell him it is going to go up next time, 6 to 12. It is not going to stay. It is going up. McBride is going to get 4 to 8 if he is smart, 6 to 12 if he is dumb. [McBride put his face into a nervous smile] I like his attitude. Tell McBride it is *now* 6 to 12 [Roger's emphasis]. If he wants to play hard ball, let's play hard ball. Tell the others it will go to 3 to 9 if they don't want the offer.

Within a few seconds, the lawyers returned to the bench and stated that the defendants were unwilling to accept the judge's offer. Thereafter, Roger showed everyone that the judge, as chief constable and jailor, was neither neutral with regard to the question of guilt or innocence nor powerless to ensure a guilty plea. Roger, speaking over the lawyers and directly to the defendants said: "All right, the offers are now 6 to 12 for McBride and 3 to 9 for Leng and Hervey." The effectiveness of Roger's actions was vividly demonstrated when Leng returned from the court pens moments later and pleaded guilty.

After the court officers had escorted the defendants to the court pen, Gartenstein had further opportunity to speak with Leng. He then asked the clerk to recall Leng's case so that Leng could accept Roger's initial offer of 1 to 4 years. Upon Gartenstein's statement that Leng was now willing to accept the offer, Roger spoke to Leng on the record, allowing him to waive his rights and to plead guilty. The transcript of this colloquy was quoted in the introduction to the article.

Santiago's Guilty Plea

Unknown to Roberto Santiago, Roger had decided to replace Emerson with another attorney, should Emerson appear again before him. Roger's decision was based upon Emerson's performance in an earlier case, when the lawyer had rejected, out-of-hand, Roger's guilty plea offer and had insisted that the defendant could not be convicted on the identification of a stranger. Roger later informed one of the authors that Emerson was an "incompetent lawyer" who acted "obstructively" when confronted with evidence which, in Roger's view, was sufficient to convict the defendant.

When the court clerk called out Roberto Santiago's name, Emerson entered the well of the courtroom along with the defendant. The clerk informed Santiago that he had been indicted for the sale of cocaine and asked Santiago: "How do you plead?" Santiago responded immediately and firmly: "Not guilty." Roger than asked Emerson to approach the bench and said: "I do not want you to appear again in my court. I am going to relieve you of this assignment."

Emerson turned and left the courtroom, leaving Santiago standing alone at the defense table.

Roger's dismissal of Emerson demonized the only individual the court had earlier assigned to protect Santiago. Roger did this without consulting Santiago. To ensure the entry of Santiago's guilty plea, Roger continued the process without a moment's hesitation. He asked Richard Sartag to "accept the court's assignment" and to substitute for Emerson. Sartag, an 18-B regular who had positioned himself in the first row of the courtroom, nodded his assent. Thereafter, he approached the bench, after which Roger read the prosecution's summary of the case:

Roger: "The defendant is a first offender who was one of a group of people who sold drugs to an undercover officer over an 18-month period. The officer positively identified the defendant at the precinct after he was arrested."

Roger then turned to Sartag and stated the offer:

Roger: "Tell him in return for a plea to attempted criminal sale of a controlled substance in the third degree, I'll give him a split sentence [time already served and five years probation].[15] Tell him should he go to trial and be convicted of the sale, he would be facing at least 2 to 6 years."

Neither Roger nor Sartag said anything about whether the twenty-month delay in indictment had prejudiced the defendant's opportunity to receive a fair trial, the reliability of the undercover officer's identification, or the availability of any corroborative evidence to independently connect the defendant to the drug sale. No reference was made to the original allegation that the sale occurred six months before Roberto Santiago's arrest. Instead, Sartag conveyed Roger's offer to Santiago in a momentary conversation. Thereafter, Sartag advised Santiago to "plead guilty in return for a promise of probation." Santiago agreed, after which the formal guilty plea colloquy ensued, on the record. When Roger solicited Santiago's waiver of the rights associated with a jury trial, Santiago responded "yes" to each of the judge's inquiries. Thereafter, Roger asked Santiago two leading questions to provide a *prima facie* basis, in law, to legitimate the entry of the guilty plea:

Q: "Did you, on May 27 (past year), near the northeast corner of 106 Street and Amsterdam Ave., sell a controlled substance, to wit crack cocaine, to an individual then known to you?"

A: "Yes."

Q: "Did you, in exchange, receive $100 in U.S. currency?"

A: "Yes."

Roger directed the court clerk to enter Santiago's guilty plea and to adjourn the case for sentencing, while he rewarded Santiago by permitting him to remain free on bail. Sartag returned to the court benches.

After the court appearance, Santiago stood in the hallway of the courthouse visibly upset. When one of the authors asked him why he pleaded guilty, Santiago said he was "frightened" and that he feared he would have to "flee to Puerto Rico or some other island" to avoid "getting sent to prison." Santiago approached Emerson, who remained in the hallway, and asked: "What is going to happen next?" Emerson replied: "I am no longer your lawyer, and I don't know."

CONCLUSION: LEGAL AND SOCIAL ORDER

Our research shows that guilty pleas in New York City are a part of a vertical process: What will happen later at the court stage influences what happens earlier at the police stage (cf. Maynard 1984:69-75). Routine case processing in court, through guilty pleas, reinforces the actions and expectations of the police and defendants, thereby encouraging sweeps, dragnets and other non-individuated arrests. This integral feedback loop, in which facts are of little consequence and in which witnesses are not called at either hearings or trials (and the propriety of policing and the reliability of police evidence are untested), institutionalizes domination (Savelsberg 1994). Subordination and degradation (Garfinkel 1956; Freeman 1993) are thereafter employed to reinforce the substantive objectives of proactive policing.

Each stage of the criminal process, from arrest and court papers to arraignment and

guilty plea court, displays the contrast between social discipline and a crime control system based upon factual or legal guilt. In a social disciplinary process, defendants charged with felonies, whom a judge has detained, may be released later because the setting of bail relates only to the initiating acts of the police and omits consideration of the sufficiency and persuasiveness of the evidence or the circumstances of the accused. Thereafter, while the subsequent entry of a guilty plea, even with the carrot of probation, may ensure social discipline, it is without any assurance that criminal activity occurred in the first instance or will cease thereafter.

In this setting, the judges, rather than the lawyers (Cain 1979, 1994), are the "conceptive ideologists" whose mission it is to translate the demands of social discipline into the language of the street—and to thereby persuade defendants, through their lawyers, of the desirability and inevitability of pleading guilty. If judges are key courtroom actors in securing guilty pleas, defense lawyers are structurally unable to exercise a meaningful influence on the process, except in relation to defendants. While it is the lawyer's task to convey to the defendant, in no uncertain terms, the wishes of the court (Blumberg 1967b), should the defendant reject the offer, the judge may speak directly to the defendant, further marginalizing the attorney. This hierarchy of power reduces what some commentators in other settings describe as a consensus model (Nardulli, Flemming, and Eisenstein 1985) to a formalistic canopy.

In New York City and other large urban settings, reliance on guilty pleas occurs because of three major structural features endemic to the justice system itself. First, judges proceeded on the assumption that their courtroom practices, while at variance with due process, were consonant with the perceived wishes of the wider society. While the general public observed guilty plea court at a distance, its impressions are created through accounts associated with the "common knowledge" (Garland 1991:206; Savelsberg 1994) that those arrested are guilty, and that when confronted with the moment of truth they will confess their guilt. Second, disciplinary practices regularly occurred in the presence of disempowered people, who expect nothing more from a system in which the objectives of policing define the process (Schur 1971; Taylor, Walton, and Young 1973). It is this audience that was first "taught . . . [the] lesson" (Garland 1991:202). Third, in employing domination, the actors exploited the political space provided by malleable legal rules in an attempt to validate the initiating acts of the police, and to thereby overcome law's perceived failure to arrive at a satisfactory strategy for social control (Simon 1993).

In achieving wider social disciplinary objectives, however, the actors discarded the criminal justice system's crime control objectives, except in so far as they happened to have been fulfilled by the police at the arrest stage. In guilty plea courts, law and legality took on a meaning separate from a crime control system based upon factual guilt or principles of proof associated with legal guilt. Law became redefined and reordered to validate substantive outcomes obtained through methods that subordinate and maintain order over groups society has labeled dangerous. Thus, even in guilty plea court, where the politics of social discipline were ascendant and a reality, order was not finally severed from law.

NOTES

1. In the United States, more than 90 percent of state criminal cases and 85 percent of all federal cases are disposed of without trial, mostly through guilty pleas (United States Department of Justice 1990).

2. The leading question is directed to the definition of robbery in the second degree as contained in Penal Law Sec. 160.10 (1973). It tracks the elements of the offense and it provides a factual basis for the guilty plea. Upon the defendant's response, Judge Roger instructed the clerk to enter defendant Leng's guilty plea in the court record.

3. In New York City, between 1984 and 1990, guilty pleas accounted for between 76 and 84 percent of all dispositions. Trials account for between 7 and 10 percent and dismissals for between 8 and 10 percent (Office of Court Administration 1984-1990).

4. Under New York City's scheme, should a Legal Aid lawyer decline the assignment because of a professional conflict of interest (usually involving representation of more than one defendant in the same case), a court officer would assign a private lawyer compensated by the city. These are known as "18-B attorneys" because of the law that provides for

their appointment and compensation. (New York County Law Article 18-B [1972]; McConville and Mirsky 1986-87).

5. Before the case was called, the ADA reviewed the Navy warrant and determined, from a comparison of the physical descriptions, that Santiago and Santiageles were not the same person. Thereafter, no further mention was made of the warrant.

6. The section of the Criminal Procedure Law (1982) requires the prosecution to present the case to a grand jury within 120 hours of the time of arrest or, if witnesses were unavailable or memories unrefreshed, to release the defendant.

7. Monthly ratings are published that show the number of guilty plea dispositions for all judges over an equivalent number of judge work days, and all judges are compared against the judge with the highest disposition rate and the largest case load (New York State Supreme Court 1984-1994; Office of Court Administration 1986-1993).

8. Roger's use of the power to detain individuals, in lieu of money bail, occurred despite New York's statutory scheme (Criminal Procedure Law Sec. 530.40 [1971]), which first required a finding that the conditions of pre-trial release set by the arraignment judge were inadequate to secure the defendant's further appearance.

9. Off-the-record remarks were publicly uttered and audible to all but were not transcribed by the court stenographer, who waited for something official to occur before placing any words on the record.

10. The predicate felony statement notifies the defendant that the prosecutor will request that the defendant be sentenced as a second felony offender (Penal Law Sec. 70.06 [1987]).

11. "Heads up" is a term Roger used to inform the uniformed court officers that he was about to jail a defendant who had appeared in court on bail.

12. Possession of a weapon in the third degree is a D felony under the Penal Law Sec. 265.02 (1987).

13. A defendant who has been previously convicted of a violent felony offense is eligible for a more severe sentence than a defendant whose previous felony conviction was for a non-violent offense (Penal Law Sec. 70.04 [1987]). However, a judge is not bound to sentence a defendant as a second violent felony offender unless the prosecution serves notice that the defendant was previously convicted of such an offense (Criminal Procedure Law Sec. 240.20 [1982]).

14. People who are judged Youth Offenders (YO) have not been convicted of a crime despite the fact that they may have committed a criminal act. Hence, they may not be sentenced as predicate felons (Criminal Procedure Law 720.35 [1979]).

15. Criminal sale of a controlled substance is a class B felony with a maximum term of 8 1/3 to 25 years (Penal Law 70.02 [1979]). However, a defendant, like Santiago, pleading guilty to an attempt (a lesser class C felony) may receive a split sentence of imprisonment not in excess of 60 days followed by probation of 5 years (Penal Law Sec. 60.01, 60.05 [1979]).

REFERENCES

Abel, Richard L. 1989. American Lawyers. New York: Oxford Press.

Alschuler, Albert W. 1976. "The trial judge's role in plea bargaining." Columbia Law Review 76:1059.

Assael, Shawn 1989. "18-B counsel made $17.5 million in '88." Manhattan Lawyer 49:1.

Balbus, Isaac. 1973. The Dialectics of Legal Repression. New York: Russell Sage.

Blumberg, Abraham. 1967a. Criminal Justice. Chicago: Quadrangle.

Blumberg, Abraham. 1967b. "The practice of law as confidence game: Organizational cooptation of the profession." Law & Society Review 1:15.

Brereton, David, and Jonathan D. Caspar. "Does it pay to plead guilty? Differential sentencing and the functioning of criminal courts." Law and Society Review 16:1.

Cain, Maureen. 1979. "The general practice lawyer and the client: Towards a radical conception." International Journal of the Sociology of Law 7:331.

Cain, Maureen. 1994. "The symbol traders." In Lawyers in a Postmodern World, eds. Maureen Cain and Christian B. Harrington, 15-48. New York: University

Caspar, Jonathon. 1972. American Criminal Justice. Englewood Cliffs, N.J.: Prentiss Hall.

Criminal Justice Agency. 1984. Final Report. New York: Criminal Justice Agency.

Criminal Justice Agency. 1985. Follow-Up Report. New York: Criminal Justice Agency.

Division of Criminal Justice Services. 1989. Crime and Justice Annual Report. Albany: New York State.

Dumm, Thomas L. 1990. "Fear of law." In Studies in Law, Politics and Society, eds. Austin Sarat and Susan Silbey, 10:29. Greenwich, Conn: JAI Press.

Feeley, Malcolm. 1979. The Process Is The Punishment. New York: Russell Sage.

Feeley, Malcolm. 1982. "Plea bargaining and the structure of the criminal process." Justice System Journal 7:338.

Freeman, Jody. 1993. "The disciplinary function of race representation: Lessons from the Kennedy Smith and Tyson trials." Law and Social Inquiry 517-546.

Fritsch, Jane, and Matthew Purdy. 1994. "Lawyers for New York poor: A program with no monitor." New York Times CXLIII:1.

Garfinkel, Harold. 1956. "Conditions of successful degradation ceremonies." American Journal of Sociology 61:420.

Garland, David. 1991. "Punishment in culture: The symbolic dimension of criminal justice." In Studies in Law, Politics and Society, eds. Austin Sarat and Susan Silbey, 11:191. Greenwich, Conn.: JAI Press.

Gilboy, Janet, and John R. Schmidt. 1979. "Replacing lawyers: A case study of the sequential representation of criminal defendants." Journal of Criminal Law and Criminology 70:1.

Heumann, Milton. 1978. Plea Bargaining: The Experiences of Prosecutor, Judges and Defense Attorneys. Chicago: University of Chicago Press.

Heydebrand, Wolf, and Carol Seron. 1987. "The organizational structure of courts: Toward the technocratic administrators of justice." International Review of Sociology 2:63.

Inciardi, James A. 1874. Criminal Justice. Orlando, Fla.: Academic Press.

Jaynes, Gerald D., and Robbin Williams, Jr., eds. 1988. A Common Destiny: Blacks in American Society. Washington, D.C.: National Academy Press.

Leo, Richard A. 1994. "Police interrogation and social control." Social and Legal Studies 3:93-120.

Luskin, Marie. 1989. "Making sense of calendaring system: A reconsideration of concept and measurement." Justice System Journal 13:240.

Mann, Coramae Richey. 1993. Unequal Justice. Bloomington: Indiana University Press.

Maynard, Douglas. 1984. Inside Plea Bargaining: The Language of Negotiation. New York: Plenum Press.

McConville, Michael and Chester L. Mirsky. 1986–1987. "Criminal defense of the poor in New York City." Review of Law and Social Change 15:582.

McConville, Michael and Chester L. Mirsky. 1988. "The state, the legal profession and the defense of the poor." Journal of Law and Society 15: No. 4.

McConville, Michael and Chester L. Mirsky. 1989. "Criminal defense of the poor in New York City." In Occasional Papers From the Center for Research in Crime and Justice, ed. Graham

Hughes, 1-42. New York: New York University School of Law.

McConville, Michael and Chester L. Mirsky. 1990. "Understanding defense of the poor in state courts: The socio legal context of non-adversarial advocacy." In Studies in Law, Politics and Society, eds. Austin Sarat and Susan Silbey, 10:217. Greenwich, Conn: JAI Press.

Miller, Herbert S., William F. McDonald, and James A. Cramer. 1978. Plea Bargaining in the United States. Washington, D.C.: National Institute of Law Enforcement and Criminal Justice.

Mnookin, Robert H., and Lewis Kornhauser. 1979. "Bargaining in the shadow of the law: The case of divorce." Yale Law Journal 88:950.

Nagel, Ilene. 1983. "The legal/extra-legal controversy: Judicial decisions in pre-trial release." Law and Society Review 17:481-515.

Nardulli, Peter F., Roy B. Flemming, and James Eisenstein. 1985. "Criminal courts and bureaucratic justice: Concessions and consensus in the guilty plea process." Criminal Law and Criminology 79:1103-1131.

Nardulli, Peter F. James Eisenstein, and Roy B. Flemming. 1988. Tenor of Justice. Chicago: University of Illinois Press.

National Minority Advisory Council on Criminal Justice. 1980. The Inequality of Justice. Washington, D.C.: U.S. Department of Justice.

New York City Department of Corrections. 1984. Admission Report. New York: New York.

New York State Supreme Court. 1984–1994. New York County Criminal Term—The Week's Summary of Judicial Proceedings. New York: New York.

Nonet, Philippe, and Philip Selznick. 1978. Law and Society in Transition: Toward Responsive Law. New York: Octagon Books.

Office of Court Administration. 1984–1990. Supreme Court Caseload Activity Reports. Albany: New York State.

Office of Court Administration. 1984–1985. Supreme Court Criminal Term—Disposition Report. Albany: New York State.

Office of Court Administration. 1986–1993. Report of Dispositions and Other Activity by Judge. Albany: New York State.

Pepinsky, Harold E. 1975. "Police decision-making." In Decision Making in the Criminal Justice System, ed. Donald M. Gottfredson, Washington, D.C.: U.S. Government Printing Office.

Pollner, Melvin. 1979. "Explicative transactions: Making and managing meaning in traffic court." In Everyday Language: Studies in Ethnomethodology, ed G. Pasathas, 227-255. New York: Irvington.

Resnick, Judith. 1982. "Managerial judges." Harvard Law Review 96:374.

Rosett, Arthur, and Donald R. Cressey. 1976. Justice By Consent. Philadelphia: J. B. Lippincott Co.

Savelsberg, Joachim J. 1992. "Law that does not fit society: Sentencing guidelines as a neoclassical reaction to the dilemmas of substantive law." The American Journal of Sociology 97: 1346-1381.

Savelsberg, Joachim J. 1994. "Knowledge, domination and criminal punishment." The American Journal of Sociology 99:911-943.

Schur, Edward. 1971. Labeling Deviant Behavior. New York: Harper and Row.

Sherman, Lawrence W. 1990. "Police crackdowns: Initial and residual deterrence." In Crime and Justice: A Review of Research 12, eds. Michael Tonry and Norvbal Morris, 159-230. Chicago: University of Chicago Press.

Simon, Jonathan S. 1993. Poor Discipline: Parole and the Social Control of the Underclass. Chicago: University of Chicago Press. Smith, Dorothy "Women's perspective as a radical critique of sociology." Sociological Inquiry 44:7-14.

Smith, Douglas A., and Christy A. Visher. 1981. "Street level justice: Situational determinants of police arrest decisions." Social Problems 29: 167-177.

Smith, Douglas A., Christy A. Visher, and Laura A. Davidson. 1984. "Equity and discretionary justice: The influence of race on police arrest decisions." Journal of Criminal Law and Criminology 75:234-249.

Sudnow, David. 1965. "Normal crimes: Sociological features of the penal code in a public defender's office." Social Problems 12:255.

Sykes, Gary W. 1986. "Street justice: A moral defense of order maintenance policing." Justice Quarterly 3:497-512.

Taylor, Ian, Paul Walton, and Jock Young. 1973. The New Criminology. London: Routledge and Kegan Paul.

Teubner, Gunther. 1987. "Juridification: Concepts, aspects, limits, solutions." In Juridification of Social Spheres: A Comparative Analysis in the Areas of Labor, Corporate, Antitrust and Social Welfare Law, ed. Gunther Teubner, 3-48. Berlin/N.Y.: Walter de Gruyter.

Uhlman, Thomas M., and N. Darlene Walker. 1980. "He takes some of my time; I take some of his: An analysis of sentencing patterns in jury cases." Law and Society Review 14:323.

United States Department of Justice. 1990. Sourcebook of Criminal Justice Statistics, eds. Kathleen

McGuire and Timothy J. Fannagan. Washington, D.C.: United States Government Printing Office.

Walker, Samuel. 1993. Taming the System: The Control of Discretion in Criminal Justice 1950-1990. New York: Oxford University Press.

Weber, Max. 1968. Economy and Society. Berkeley: University of California Press.

Wice, Paul B. 1978. Criminal Lawyers. Beverly Hills, Calif.: Sage.

Wilson, William J. 1987. The Truly Disadvantaged: The Inner City, The Underclass, and Public Policy. Chicago University of Chicago Press.

Wood, Arthur. 1976. Criminal Lawyer. Connecticut: College and University Press.

Zimmer, Lynn. 1987. "Operation pressure point: The disruption of street-level drug trade on New York's Lower East Side." In Occasional Papers from the Center for Research in Crime and Justice, ed. Graham Hughes, 1-26. New York: New York University School of Law.

STATUTES CITED

New York County Law Article 18-B (McKinney 1972).

New York Criminal Procedure Law Sec. 10.30(2) (McKinney 1982).

New York Criminal Procedure Law 180.10 (McKinney 1985).

New York Criminal Procedure Law Sec. 180.80 (McKinney 1982).

New York Criminal Procedure Law Sec. 210.20(h) (McKinney 1980).

New York Criminal Procedure Law Sec. 240.20 (McKinney 1982).

New York Criminal Procedure Law Sec. 530.40 (McKinney 1971).

New York Criminal Procedure Law Sec. 720.35 (McKinney 1979).

New York Penal Law Sec. 60.01 (McKinney 1979).

New York Penal Law Sec. 60.05 (McKinney 1979).

New York Penal Law Sec. 70.02 (McKinney 1979).

New York Penal Law Sec. 70.04 (McKinney 1987).

New York Penal Law Sec. 70.06 (McKinney 1987).

New York Penal Law Sec. 265.02 (McKinney 1987).

CASES CITED

Gideon vs. Wainwright, 372 U.S. 335 (1963)

Manson vs. Brathwaite, 432 U.S. 98 (1977)

United States vs. Lovasco, 431 U.S. 783 (1977)

Wong Sun vs. United States, 371 U.S. 471 (1963)

Probation presentence reports emphasize some offender characteristics more than others do. Rosencrance explains how a stereotyping process is used by probation officers who write these reports, and how their sentence recommendations to judges are determined on the use of a few relatively fixed factors, mainly current offenses and prior criminal history. Presentence reports are produced in order to provide the court with an illusion that each report is based on individual characteristics of the convicted person. Rosencrance questions whether probation agencies can really provide individualized justice, as they claim to do.

MAINTAINING THE MYTH OF INDIVIDUALIZED JUSTICE

Probation Presentence Reports

JOHN ROSECRANCE

The Justice Department estimates that over one million probation presentence reports are submitted annually to criminal courts in the United States (Allen and Simonsen 1986:111). The role of probation officers in the presentence process traditionally has been considered important. After examining criminal courts in the United States, a panel of investigators concluded: "Probation officers are attached to most modern felony courts; presentence reports containing their recommendations are commonly provided and these recommendations are usually followed" (Blumstein, Martin, and Holt 1983). Judges view presentence reports as an integral part of sentencing, calling them "the best guide to intelligent sentencing" (Murrah 1963:67) and "one of the most important developments in criminal law during the 20th century" (Hogarth 1971:246).

Researchers agree that a strong correlation exists between probation recommendations

Reprinted from *Justice Quarterly,* Vol. 5, No. 2, June 1988. Copyright © 1988 Academy of Criminal Justice Sciences. Reprinted by permission.

(contained in presentence reports) and judicial sentencing. In a seminal study of judicial decision making, Carter and Wilkins (1967) found 95 percent agreement between probation recommendation and sentence disposition when the officer recommended probation and 88 percent agreement when the officer opposed probation. Hagan (1975), after controlling for related variables, reported a direct correlation of .72 between probation recommendation and sentencing. Walsh (1985) found a similar correlation of .807.

Although there is no controversy about the correlation between probation recommendation and judicial outcome, scholars disagree as to the actual influence of probation officers in the sentencing process. That is, there is no consensus regarding the importance of the presentence investigator in influencing sentencing outcomes. On the one hand, Myers (1979:538) contends that the "important role played by probation officer recommendation argues for greater theoretical and empirical attention to these officers." Walsh (1985:363) concludes that "judges lean heavily on the professional advice of probation." On the other hand, Kings-north and Rizzo (1979) report that probation recommendations have been supplanted by plea bargaining and that the probation officer is "largely superfluous." Hagan, Hewitt, and Alwin (1979), after reporting a direct correlation between recommendation and sentence, contend that the "influence of the probation officer in the presentence process is subordinate to that of the prosecutor" and that probation involvement is "often ceremonial."

My research builds on the latter perspective, and suggests that probation presentence reports do not influence judicial sentencing significantly but serve to maintain the myth that criminal courts dispense individualized justice. On the basis of an analysis of probation practices in California, I will demonstrate that the presentence report, long considered an instrument for the promotion of individualized sentencing by the court, actually deemphasizes individual characteristics and affirms the primacy of instant offense and prior criminal record as sentencing determinants. The present study was concerned with probation in California; whether its findings can be applied to other jurisdictions is not known. California's probation system is

the nation's largest, however (Petersilia, Turner, Kahan, and Peterson 1985), and the experiences of that system could prove instructive to other jurisdictions.

In many California counties (as in other jurisdictions throughout the United States) crowded court calendars, determinate sentencing guidelines, and increasingly conservative philosophies have made it difficult for judges to consider individual offenders' characteristics thoroughly. Thus judges, working in tandem with district attorneys, emphasize the legal variables of offense and criminal record at sentencing (see, for example, Forer 1980; Lotz and Hewitt 1977; Tinker, Quiring, and Pimentel 1985). Probation officers function as employees of the court; generally they respond to judicial cues and emphasize similar variables in their presentence investigations. The probation officers' relationship to the court is ancillary; their status in relation to judges and other attorneys is subordinate. This does not mean that probation officers are completely passive; individual styles and personal philosophies influence their reports. Idiosyncratic approaches, however, usually are reserved for a few special cases. The vast majority of "normal" (Sudnow 1965) cases are handled in a manner that follows relatively uniform patterns.

Hughes's (1958) work provides a useful perspective for understanding the relationship between probation officers' status and their presentence duties. According to Hughes, occupational duties within institutions often serve to maintain symbiotic status relationships as those in higher-status positions pass on lesser duties to subordinates. Other researchers (Blumberg 1967; Neubauer 1974; Rosecrance 1985) have demonstrated that although judges may give lip service to the significance of presentence investigations, they remain suspicious of the probation officers' lack of legal training and the hearsay nature of the reports. Walker (1985) maintains that in highly visible cases judges tend to disregard the probation reports entirely. Thus the judiciary, by delegating the collection of routine information to probation officers, reaffirms its authority and legitimacy. In this context, the responsibility for compiling presentence reports can be considered a "dirty work" assignment (Hagan 1975) that is devalued by the judiciary. Judges expect probation officers to submit noncontroversial reports that provide a facade of information, accompanied by bottom-line recommendations that do not deviate significantly from a consideration of offense and prior record. The research findings in this paper will show how probation officers work to achieve this goal.

In view of the large number of presentence reports submitted, it is surprising that so little information about the presentence investigation process is available. The factors used in arriving at a sentencing recommendation, the decision to include certain information, and the methods used in collecting data have not been described. The world of presentence investigators has not been explored by social science researchers. We lack research about the officers who prepare presentence reports, and hardly understand how they think and feel about those reports. The organizational dynamics and the status positions that influence presentence investigators have not been identified prominently (see, for example, Shover 1979). In this article I intend to place probation officers' actions within a framework that will increase the existing knowledge of the presentence process. My research is informed by 15 years of experience as a probation officer, during which time I submitted hundreds of presentence reports.

Although numerous studies of probation practices have been conducted, an ethnographic perspective rarely has been included in this body of research, particularly in regard to research dealing with presentence investigations. Although questionnaire techniques (Katz 1982), survey data (Hagan et al. 1979), and decision-making experiments (Carter 1967) have provided some information about presentence reports, qualitative data, which often are available only through an insider's perspective[1], are notably lacking. The subtle strategies and informal practices used routinely in preparing presentence reports often are hidden from outside researchers.

The research findings emphasize the importance of *typing* in the compilation of public documents (presentence reports). In this paper "typing" refers to "the process by which one person (the agent) arrives at a private definition of another (the target)" (Prus 1975:81). A related activity, *designating*, occurs when "the

typing agent reveals his attributions of the target to others" (Prus and Stratten) 1976:48). In the case of presentence investigations, private typings become designations when they are made part of an official court report. I will show that presentence recommendations are developed through a typing process in which individual offenders are subsumed into general dispositional categories. This process is influenced largely by probation officers' perceptions of factors that judicial figures consider appropriate; probation officers are aware that the ultimate purpose of their reports is to please the court. These perceptions are based on prior experience and are reinforced through judicial feedback.

METHODS

The major sources of data used in this study were drawn from interviews with probation officers. Prior experience facilitated my ability to interpret the data. Interviews were conducted in two three-week periods during 1984 and 1985 in two medium-sized California counties. Both jurisdictions were governed by state determinate sentencing policies; in each, the district attorney's office remained active during sentencing and generally offered specific recommendations. I did not conduct a random sample but tried instead to interview all those who compiled adult presentence reports. In the two counties in question, officers who compiled presentence reports did not supervise defendants.[2]

Not all presentence writers agreed to talk with me; they cited busy schedules, lack of interest, or fear that I was a spy for the administration. Even so, I was able to interview 37 presentence investigators, approximately 75 percent of the total number of such employees in the two counties.[3] The officers interviewed included eight women and 29 men with a median age of 38.5 years, whose probation experience ranged from one year to 27 years. Their educational background generally included a bachelor's degree in a liberal arts subject (four had degrees in criminal justice, one in social work). Typically the officers regarded probation work as a "job" rather than a profession. With only a few exceptions, they did not read professional journals or attend probation association conventions.

The respondents generally were supportive of my research, and frequently commented that probation work had never been described adequately. My status as a former probation officer enhanced the interview process greatly. Because I could identify with their experiences, officers were candid, and I was able to collect qualitative data that reflected accurately the participants' perspectives. During the interviews I attempted to discover how probation officers conducted their presentence investigations. I wanted to know when a sentencing recommendation was decided, to ascertain which variables influenced a sentencing recommendation decision, and to learn how probation officers defined their role in the sentencing process.

Although the interviews were informal, I asked each of the probation officers the following questions:

1. What steps do you take in compiling a presentence report?

2. What is the first thing you do upon receiving a referral?

3. What do you learn from interviews with the defendant?

4. Which part of the process (in your opinion) is the most important?

5. Who reads your reports?

6. Which part of the report do the judges feel is most important?

7. How do your reports influence the judge?

8. What feedback do you get from the judge, the district attorney, the defense attorney, the defendant, your supervisor?

In addition to interviewing probation officers, I questioned six probation supervisors and seven judges on their views about how presentence reports were conducted.

The procedure I used to analyze the collected data was similar to the grounded theory method advocated by Glaser and Strauss (1967). This method seeks to develop analyses that are generated from the data themselves (Blumer 1979).

Thus in the beginning of the study I maintained a flexible and unstructured approach. This flexibility was particularly important because I wanted to ensure that my years in the field had not left me with a preconceived conceptual model and that my research was not an attempt to justify conclusions already reached. By facing the issue of possible subjectivity at each stage of the investigation, I let the data lead me rather than the other way around. As the data accumulated and as theories and propositions emerged, they were modified and compared, and in turn formed the groundwork for further data collection. Initially, for example, I attempted to frame the presentence process in the context of factors related to the individual officer (reporting style, experience, or criminal justice philosophy). I could not discern a regular pattern, however, so I analyzed other factors.

FINDINGS

In the great majority of presentence investigations, the variables of present offense and prior criminal record determine the probation officer's final sentencing recommendation. The influence of these variables is so dominant that other considerations have minimal influence on probation recommendations. The chief rationale for this approach is "That's the way the judges want it." There are other styles of investigation; some officers attempt to consider factors in the defendant's social history, to reserve sentencing judgment until their investigation is complete, or to interject personal opinions. Elsewhere (Rosecrance 1987), I have developed a typology of presentence investigators which describes individual styles; these types include self-explanatory categories such as hard-liners, bleeding-heart liberals, and team players as well as mossbacks (those who are merely putting in their time) and mavericks (those who strive continually for independence).

All types of probation officers, however, seek to develop credibility with the court. Such reputation building is similar to that reported by McCleary (1978) in his study of parole officers. In order to develop rapport with the court, probation officers must submit reports that facilitate a smooth work flow. Probation officers assume that in the great majority of cases they can accomplish this goal by emphasizing offense and criminal record. Once the officers have established reputations as "producers," they have "earned" the right to some degree of discretion in their reporting. One investigation officer described this process succinctly: "When you've paid your dues, you're allowed some slack." Such discretion, however, is limited to a minority of cases, and in these "deviant" cases probation officers frequently allow social variables to influence their recommendation. In one report an experienced officer recommended probation for a convicted felon with a long prior record because the defendant's father agreed to pay for an intensive drug treatment program. In another case a probation officer decided that a first-time shoplifter had a "very bad attitude" and therefore recommended a stiff jail sentence rather than probation. Although these variations from normal procedure are interesting and important, they should not detract from our examination of an investigation process that is used in most cases.

On the basis of the research data, I found that the following patterns occur with sufficient regularity to be considered "typical." After considering offense and criminal record, probation officers place defendants into categories that represent the eventual court recommendation. This typing process occurs early in the course of presentence inquiry; the balance of the investigation is used to reaffirm the private typings that later will become official designations. In order to clarify the decision-making processes used by probation officers I will delineate the three stages in a presentence investigation: 1) typing the defendant, 2) gathering further information, and 3) filing the report.

Typing the Defendant

A presentence investigation is initiated when the court orders the probation department to prepare a report on a criminal defendant. Usually the initial court referral contains such information as police reports, charges against the defendant, court proceedings, plea-bargaining agreements (if any), offenses in which the defendant has pleaded or has been found guilty, and the defendant's prior criminal record.

Probation officers regard such information as relatively unambiguous[4] and as part of the "official" record. The comment of a presentence investigator reflects the probation officer's perspective on the court referral:

> I consider the information in the court referral hard data. It tells me what I need to know about a case, without a lot of bullshit. I mean the guy has pled guilty to a certain offense—he can't get out of that. He has such and such a prior record—there's no changing that. So much of the stuff we put in these reports is subjective and open to interpretation. It's good to have some solid information.

Armed with information in the court referral, probation officers begin to type the defendants assigned for presentence investigation. Defendants are classified into general types based on possible sentence recommendations; a probation officer's statement indicates that this process begins early in a presentence investigation.

> Bottom line; it's the sentence recommendation that's important. That's what the judges and everybody wants to see. I start thinking about the recommendation as soon as I pick up the court referral. Why wait? The basic facts aren't going to change. Oh, I know some POs will tell you they weigh all the facts before coming up with a recommendation. But that's propaganda—we all start thinking recommendation right from the get-go.

At this stage in the investigation the factors known to probation officers are mainly legally relevant variables. The defendant's unique characteristics and special circumstances generally are unknown at this time. Although probation officers may know the offender's age, sex, and race, the relationship of these variables to the case is not yet apparent.

These initial typings are private definitions (Prus 1975) based on the officer's experience and knowledge of the court system. On occasion, officers discuss the case informally with their colleagues or supervisors when they are not sure of a particular typing. Until the report is complete, their typing remains a private designation. In most cases the probation officers type defendants by considering the known and relatively irrefutable variables of offense and prior record. Probation officers are convinced that judges and district attorneys are most concerned with that part of their reports. I heard the following comment (or versions thereof) on many occasions: "Judges read the offense section, glance at the prior record, and then flip to the back and see what we recommend." Officers indicated that during informal discussions with judges it was made clear that offense and prior record are the determinants of sentencing in most cases. In some instances judges consider extralegal variables, but the officers indicated that this occurs only in "unusual" cases with "special" circumstances. One such case involved a probation grant for a woman who killed her husband after she had been a victim of spouse battering.

Probation investigators are in regular contact with district attorneys, and frequently discuss their investigations with them. In addition, district attorneys seem to have no compunction about calling the probation administration to complain about what they consider an inappropriate recommendation. Investigators agreed unanimously that district attorneys typically dismiss a defendant's social history as "immaterial" and want probation officers to stick to the legal facts.

Using offense and prior record as criteria, probation officers place defendants into dispositional (based on recommendation) types. In describing these types[5] I have retained the terms used by probation officers themselves in the typing process. The following typology is community (rather than researcher) designated (Emerson 1981; Spradley 1970): (1) deal case, (2) diversion case, (3) joint case, (4) probation case with some jail time, (5) straight probation case. Within each of these dispositional types, probation officers designate the severity of punishment by labeling the case either lightweight or heavy-duty.

A designation of "lightweight" means that the defendant will be accorded some measure of leniency because the offense was minor, because the offender had no prior criminal record, or because the criminal activity (regardless of the penal code violation) was relatively innocuous. Heavy-duty cases receive more severe penalties because the offense, the offender, or the circumstances of the offense are deemed particularly serious. Diversion and straight probation types generally are considered lightweight, while the majority of joint cases are considered

heavy-duty. Cases involving personal violence invariably are designated as heavy-duty. Most misdemeanor cases in which the defendant has no prior criminal record or a relatively minor record are termed lightweight. If the defendant has an extensive criminal record, however, even misdemeanor cases can call for stiff penalties; therefore such cases are considered heavy-duty. Certain felony cases can be regarded as lightweight if there was no violence, if the victim's loss was minimal, or if the defendant had no prior convictions. On occasion, even an offense like armed robbery can be considered lightweight. The following example (taken from an actual report) is one such instance: a first-time offender with a simulated gun held up a Seven-Eleven store and then returned to the scene, gave back the money, and asked the store employees to call the police.

The typings are general recommendations; specifics such as terms and conditions of probation or diversion and length of incarceration are worked out later in the investigation. The following discussion will clarify some of the criteria for arriving at a typing.

Deal cases involve situations in which a plea bargain exists. In California, many plea bargains specify specific sentencing stipulations; probation officers rarely recommend dispositions contrary to those stipulated in plea-bargaining agreements. Although probation officers allegedly are free to recommend a sentence different from that contained in the plea bargain, they have learned that such an action is unrealistic (and often counter-productive to their own interests) because judges inevitably uphold the primary of sentence agreements. The following observation represents the probation officers' view of plea-bargaining deals:

> It's stupid to try and bust a deal. What's the percentage? Who needs the hassle? The judge always honors the deal—after all, he was part of it. Everyone, including the defendant, has already agreed. It's all nice and neat, all wrapped up. We are supposed to rubber-stamp the package—and we do. Everyone is better off that way.

Diversion cases typically involve relatively minor offenses committed by those with no prior record, and are considered "a snap" by probation officers. In most cases, those referred for diversion have been screened already by the district attorney's office; the probation investigator merely agrees that they are eligible and therefore should be granted diversionary relief (and eventual dismissal of charges). In rare instances when there has been an oversight and the defendant is ineligible (because of prior criminal convictions), the probation officer informs the court, and criminal proceedings are resumed. Either situation involves minimal decision making by probation officers about what disposition to recommend. Presentence investigators approach diversion cases in a perfunctory, almost mechanical manner.

The last three typings generally refer to cases in which the sentencing recommendations are ambiguous and some decision making is required of probation officers. These types represent the major consequences of criminal sentencing: incarceration and/or probation. Those categorized as joint (prison) cases are denied probation; instead the investigator recommends an appropriate prison sentence. In certain instances the nature of the offense (e.g., rape, murder, or arson) renders defendants legally ineligible for probation. In other situations, the defendants' prior record (especially felony convictions) makes it impossible to grant probation (see, e.g., Neubauer 1974:240). In many cases the length of prison sentences has been set by legal statute and can be increased or decreased only marginally (depending on the aggravating or mitigating circumstances of the case).

In California, the majority of defendants sentenced to prison receive a middle term (between minimum and maximum); the length of time varies with the offense. Those cases that fall outside the middle term usually do so for reasons related to the offense (e.g., using a weapon) or to the criminal record (prior felony convictions or, conversely, no prior criminal record). Those typed originally as joint cases are treated differently from other probation applicants: concerns with rehabilitation or with the defendant's life situation are no longer relevant, and proper punishment becomes the focal point of inquiry. This perspective was described as follows by a probation officer respondent: "Once I know so-and-so is a heavy-duty joint case I don't think in terms of rehabilitation or social planning. It becomes a matter of how long to salt the sucker away, and that's covered by the code."

For those who are typed as probation cases, the issue for the investigator becomes whether to recommend some time in jail as a condition of probation. This decision is made with reference to whether the case is lightweight or heavy-duty. Straight probation usually is reserved for those convicted of relatively innocuous offenses or for those without a prior criminal record (first-timers). Some probation officers admitted candidly that all things being equal, middle-class defendants are more likely than other social classes to receive straight probation. The split sentence (probation and jail time) has become popular and is a consideration in most misdemeanor and felony cases, especially when the defendant has a prior criminal record. In addition, there is a feeling that drug offenders should receive a jail sentence as part of probation to deter them from future drug use.

Once a probation officer has decided that "some jail time is in order," the ultimate recommendation includes that condition. Although the actual amount of time frequently is determined late in the case, the probation officer's opinion that a jail sentence should be imposed remains constant. The following comment typifies the sentiments of probation officers whom I have observed and also illustrates the imprecision of recommending a period of time in custody:

> It's not hard to figure out who needs some jail. The referral sheet can tell you that. What's hard to know is exactly how much time. Ninety days or six months—who knows what's fair? We put down some number but it is usually an arbitrary figure. No one has come up with a chart that correlates rehabilitation with jail time.

Compiling Further Information

Once an initial typing has been completed, the next investigative stage involves collecting further information about the defendant. During this stage most of the data to be collected consists of extralegal considerations. The defendant is interviewed and his or her social history is delineated. Probation officers frequently contact collateral sources such as school officials, victims, doctors, counselors, and relatives to learn more about the defendant's individual circumstances. This aspect of the presentence investigation involves considerable time and effort on the part of probation officers. Such information is gathered primarily to legitimate earlier probation officer typings or to satisfy judicial requirements; recommendations seldom are changed during this stage. A similar pattern was described by a presentence investigator:

> Interviewing these defendants and working up a social history takes time. In most cases it's really unnecessary since I've already decided what I am going to do. We all know that a recommendation is governed by the offense and prior record. All the rest is just stuffing to fill out the court report, to make the judge look like he's got all the facts.

Presentence interviews with defendants (a required part of the investigation) frequently are routine interactions that were described by a probation officer as "anticlimactic." These interviews invariably are conducted in settings familiar to probation officers, such as jail interviewing rooms or probation department offices. Because the participants lack trust in each other, discussions rarely are candid and open. Probation officers are afraid of being conned or manipulated because they assume that defendants "will say anything to save themselves." Defendants are trying to present themselves in a favorable light and are wary of divulging any information that might be used against them.

It is assumed implicitly in the interview process that probation officers act as interrogators and defendants as respondents. Because presentence investigators select the questions, they control the course of the interview and elicit the kind of responses that serve to substantiate their original defendant typings. A probationer described his presentence interview to me as follows:

> I knew that the P.O. wanted me to say. She had me pegged as a nice middle-class kid who had fallen in with a bad crowd. So that's how I came off. I was contrite, a real boy scout who had learned his lesson. What an acting job! I figured if I didn't act up I'd get probation.

A probation officer related how she conducted presentence interviews:

> I'm always in charge during the interviews. I know what questions to ask in order to fill out my report. The defendants respond just about the way I expect them to. They hardly ever surprise me.

On occasion, prospective probationers refuse to go along with structured presentence interviews. Some offenders either attempt to control the interview or are openly hostile to probation officers. Defendants who try to dominate interviews often can be dissuaded by reminders such as "I don't think you really appreciate the seriousness of your situation" or "I'm the one who asks the questions here." Some defendants, however, show blatant disrespect for the court process by flaunting a disregard for possible sanctions.

Most probation officers have interviewed some defendants who simply don't seem to care what happens to them. A defendant once informed an investigation officer: "I don't give a fuck what you motherfuckers try and do to me. I'm going to do what I fuckin' well please. Take your probation and stick it." Another defendant told her probation officer: "I'm going to shoot up every chance I get. I need my fix more than I need probation." Probation officers categorize belligerent defendants and those unwilling to "play the probation game" as dangerous or irrational (see, e.g., McCleary 1978). Frequently in these situations the investigator's initial typing is no longer valid, and probation either will be denied or will be structured stringently. Most interviews, however, proceed in a predictable manner as probation officers collect information that will be included in the section of the report termed "defendant's statement."

Although some defendants submit written comments, most of their statements actually are formulated by the probation officer. In a sociological sense, the defendant's statement can be considered an "account" (Scott and Lyman 1968). While conducting presentence interviews, probation officers typically attempt to shape the defendant's account to fit their own preconceived typing. Many probation officers believe that the defendant's attitude toward the offense and toward the future prospects for leading a law-abiding life are the most important parts of the statement. In most presentence investigations the probation investigator identifies and interprets the defendant's subjective attitudes and then incorporates them into the report. Using this procedure, probation officers look for and can report attitudes that "logically fit" with their final sentencing recommendation (see, for example, Davis 1983).

Defendants who have been typed as prison cases typically are portrayed as holding socially unacceptable attitudes about their criminal actions and unrealistic or negative attitudes about future prospects for living an upright life. Conversely, those who have been typed as probation material are described as having acceptable attitudes, such as contriteness about the present offense and optimism about their ability to lead a crime-free life. The structuring of accounts about defendant attitudes was described by a presentence investigator in the following manner:

> When POs talk about the defendant's attitude we really mean how that attitude relates to the case. Naturally I'm not going to write about what a wonderful attitude the guy has—how sincere he seems—and then recommend sending him to the joint. That wouldn't make sense. The judges want consistency. If a guy has a shitty attitude but is going to get probation anyway, there's no percentage in playing up his attitude problem.

In most cases the presentence interview is the only contact between the investigating officer and the defendant. The brevity of this contact and the lack of post-report interaction foster a legalistic perspective. Investigators are concerned mainly with "getting the case through court" rather than with special problems related to supervising probationers on a long-term basis. One-time-only interviews rarely allow probation officers to become emotionally involved with their cases; the personal and individual aspects of the defendant's personality generally are not manifested during a half-hour presentence interview. For many probation officers the emotional distance from offenders is one of the benefits of working in presentence units. Such an opinion was expressed by an investigation officer: "I really like the one-shot-only part of this job. I don't have time to get caught up with the clients. I can deal with facts and not worry about individual personalities."

The probation officer has wide discretion in the type of collateral information that is collected from sources other than the defendant or the official record. Although a defendant's social history must be sketched in the presentence report, the supplementation of that history is left to individual investigators. There are few established guidelines for the investigating officer to follow, except that the psychiatric or psychological reports should be submitted when there is compelling evidence that the offender is mentally disturbed. Informal guidelines, however, specify that in misdemeanor cases reports should be shorter and more concise than in felony cases. The officers indicated that reports for municipal court (all misdemeanor cases) should range from four to six pages in length, while superior court reports (felony cases) were expected to be six to nine pages long. In controversial cases (to which only the most experienced officers are assigned) presentence reports are expected to be longer and to include considerable social data. Reports in these cases have been as long as 30 pages.

Although probation officers learn what general types of information to include through experience and feedback from judges and supervisors, they are allowed considerable leeway in deciding exactly what to put in their reports (outside of the offense and prior record sections). Because investigators decide what collateral sources are germane to the case, they tend to include information that will reflect favorably on their sentencing recommendation. In this context the observation of one probation officer is understable: "I pick from the mass of possible sources just which ones to put in the report. Do you think I'm going to pick people who make my recommendation look weak? No way!"

Filing the Report

The final stage in the investigation includes dictating the report, having it approved by a probation supervisor, and appearing in court. All three of these activities serve to reinforce the importance of prior record and offense in sentencing recommendations. At the time of dictation, probation officers determine what to include in the report and how to phrase their remarks. For the first time in the investigation, they receive formal feedback from official sources. Presentence reports are read by three groups important to the probation officers: probation supervisors, district attorneys, and judges. Probation officers recognize that for varying reasons, all these groups emphasize the legally relevant variables of offense and prior criminal record when considering an appropriate sentencing recommendation.[6] Such considerations re-affirm the probation officer's initial private typing.

A probation investigator described this process:

> After I've talked to the defendants I think maybe some of them deserve to get special consideration. But when I remember who's going to look at the reports. My supervisor, the DA, the judge; they don't care about all the personal details. When all is said and done, what's really important to them is the offense and the defendant's prior record. I know that stuff from the start. It makes me wonder why we have to jack ourselves around to do long reports.

Probation officers assume that their credibility as presentence investigators will be enhanced if their sentencing recommendations meet with the approval of probation supervisors, district attorneys, and judges. On the other hand, officers whose recommendations are consistently "out of line" are subject to censure or transfer, or they find themselves engaged in "running battles" (Shover 1974:357) with court officials. During the last stage of the investigation probation officers must consider how to ensure that their reports will go through court without "undue personal hassle." Most investigation officers have learned that presentence recommendations based on a consideration of prior record and offense can achieve that goal.

Although occupational self-interest is an important component in deciding how to conduct a presentence investigation, other factors also are involved. Many probation officers agree with the idea of using legally relevant variables as determinants of recommendations. These officers embrace the retributive value of this concept and see it as an equitable method for framing their investigation. Other officers reported that probation officers' discretion had been

"short-circuited" by determinate sentencing guidelines and that they were reduced to "merely going through the motions" in conducting their investigations. Still other officers view the use of legal variables to structure recommendations as an acceptable bureaucratic shortcut to compensate partially for large case assignments. One probation officer stated, "If the department wants us to keep pumping out presentence reports we can't consider social factors—we just don't have time." Although probation officers are influenced by various dynamics, there seems little doubt that in California, the social history which once was considered the "heart and soul" of presentence probation reports (Reckless 1967:673) has been largely devalued.

SUMMARY AND CONCLUSIONS

In this study I provide a description and an analysis of the processes used by probation investigators in preparing presentence reports. The research findings based on interview data indicate that probation officers tend to de-emphasize individual defendants' characteristics and that their probation recommendations are not influenced directly by factors such as sex, age, race, socioeconomic status, or work record. Instead, probation officers emphasize the variables of instant offense and prior criminal record. The finding that offense and prior record are the main considerations of probation officers with regard to sentence recommendations agrees with a substantial body of research (Bankston 1983; Carter and Wilkens 1967; Dawson 1969; Lotz and Hewitt 1977; Robinson, Carter, and Wahl 1969; Wallace 1974; Walsh 1985).

My particular contribution has been to supply the ethnographic observations and the data that explain this phenomenon. I have identified the process whereby offense and prior record come to occupy the central role in decision making by probation officers. This identification underscores the significance of private typings in determining official designations. An analysis of probation practices suggests that the function of the presentence investigation is more ceremonial than instrumental (Hagan 1985).

I show that early in the investigation probation officers, using offense and prior record as guidelines, classify defendants into types; when the typing process is complete, probation officers essentially have decided on the sentence recommendation that will be recorded later in their official designation. The subsequent course of investigations is determined largely by this initial private typing. Further data collection is influenced by a sentence recommendation that already has been firmly established. This finding answers affirmatively the research question posed by Carter (1967:211):

> Do probation officers, after "deciding" on a recommendation early in the presentence investigation, seek further information which justifies the decision, rather than information which might lead to modification or rejection of that recommendation?

The type of information and observation contained in the final presentence report is generated to support the original recommendation decision. Probation officers do not regard defendant typings as tentative hypotheses to be disproved through inquiry but rather as firm conclusions to be justified in the body of the report.

Although the presentence interview has been considered an important part of the investigation (Spencer 1983), I demonstrate that it does not significantly alter probation officers' perceptions. In most cases probation officers dominate presentence interviews; interaction between the participants is guarded. The nature of interviews between defendants and probation officers is important in itself; further research is needed to identify the dynamics that prevail in these interactions.

Attitudes attributed to defendants often are structured by probation officers to reaffirm the recommendation already formulated. The defendant's social history, long considered an integral part of the presentence report, in reality has little bearing on sentencing considerations. In most cases the presentence is no longer a vehicle for social inquiry but rather a typing process which considers mainly the defendant's prior criminal record and the seriousness of the criminal offense. Private attorneys in growing numbers have become disenchanted with the quality of probation investigations and have commissioned presentence probation reports privately (Rodgers,

Gitchoff, and Paur 1984). At present, however, such a practice is generally available only for wealthy defendants.

The presentence process that I have described is used in the great majority of cases; it is the "normal" procedure. Even so, probation officers are not entirely passive actors in this process. On occasion they will give serious consideration to social variables in arriving at a sentencing recommendation. In special circumstances officers will allow individual defendants' characteristics to influence their report. In addition, probation officers who have developed credibility with the court are allowed some discretion in compiling presentence reports. This discretion is not unlimited, however; it is based on a prior record of producing reports that meet the court's approval, and is contingent on continuing to do so. A presentence writer said, "You can only afford to go to bat for defendants in a few select cases; if you try to do it too much, you get a reputation as being 'out of step.'"

This research raises the issue of probation officers' autonomy. Although I depict presentence investigators as having limited autonomy, other researchers (Hagan 1975; Myers 1979; Walsh 1985) contend that probation officers have considerable leeway in recommendation. This contradictory evidence can be explained in large part by the type of sentencing structure, the professionalism of probation workers, and the role of the district attorney at sentencing. Walsh's study (1985), for example, which views probation officers as important actors in the presentence process, was conducted in a jurisdiction with indeterminate sentencing, where the probation officers demonstrated a high degree of professionalism and the prosecutors "rarely made sentencing recommendation." A very different situation existed in the California counties that I studied: determinate sentencing was enforced, probation officers were not organized professionally, and the district attorneys routinely made specific court recommendations. It seems apparent that probation officers' autonomy must be considered with reference to judicial jurisdiction.

In view of the primacy of offense and prior record in sentencing considerations, the efficacy of current presentence investigation practices is doubtful. It seems ineffective and wasteful to continue to collect a mass of social data of uncertain relevance. Yet an analysis of courtroom culture suggests that the presentence investigation helps maintain judicial mythology as well as probation officer legitimacy. Although judges generally do not have the time or the inclination to consider individual variables thoroughly, the performance of a presentence investigation perpetuates the myth of individualized sentences. Including a presentence report in the court file gives the appearance of individualization without influencing sentencing practices significantly.

Even in a state like California, where determinate sentencing allegedly has replaced individualized justice, the judicial system feels obligated to maintain the appearance of individualization. After observing the court system in California for several years I am convinced that a major reason for maintaining such a practice is to make it easier for criminal defendants to accept their sentences. The presentence report allows defendants to feel that their case at least has received a considered decision. One judge admitted candidly that the "real purpose" of the presentence investigation was to convince defendants that they were not getting "the fast shuffle." He observed further that if defendants were sentenced without such investigations, many would complain and would file "endless appeals" over what seems to them a hasty sentencing decision. Even though judges typically consider only offense and prior record in a sentencing decision, they want defendants to believe that their cases are being judged individually. The presentence investigation allows this assumption to be maintained. In addition, some judges use the probation officer's report as an excuse for a particular type of sentence. In some instances they deny responsibility for the sentence, implying that their "hands were tied" by the recommendation. Thus judges are taken "off the hook" for meting out an unpopular sentence. Further research is needed to substantiate the significance of these latent functions of the presentence investigation.

The presentence report is a major component in the legitimacy of the probation movement; several factors support the probation officers' stake in maintaining their role in these investigations. Historically, probation has been wedded to the concept of individualized treatment. In theory, the presentence report is suited ideally to reporting on defendants' individual circumstances. From a historical perspective (Rothman 1980) this ideal has always been more symbolic than substantive, but if the legitimacy of the presentence report is questioned, so then is the entire purpose of probation.

Regardless of its usefulness (or lack of usefulness), it is doubtful that probation officials would consider the diminution or abolition of presentence reports. The number of probation workers assigned to presentence investigations is substantial, and their numbers represent an obvious source of bureaucratic power. Conducting presentence investigations allows probation officers to remain visible with the court and the public. The media often report on controversial probation cases, and presentence writers generally have more contact and more association with judges than do others in the probation department.

As ancillary court workers, probation officers are assigned the dirty work of collecting largely irrelevant data on offenders (Hagan 1975; Hughes 1958). Investigation officers have learned that emphasizing offense and prior record in their reports will enhance relationships with judges and district attorneys, as well as improving their occupational standing within probation departments. Thus the presentence investigation serves to maintain the court's claim of individualized concern while preserving the probation officer's role, although a subordinate role, in the court system.[7]

The myth of individualization serves various functions, but it also raises serious questions. In an era of severe budget restrictions (Schumacher 1985) should scarce resources be allocated to compiling predictable presentence reports of dubious value? If social variables are considered only in a few cases, should courts continue routinely to require presentence reports in all felony matters (as is the practice in California)? In summary, we should address the issue of whether the criminal justice system can afford the ceremony of a probation presentence investigation.

NOTES

1. For a full discussion of the insider-outsider perspective in criminal justice see Marquart (1986).

2. In a few jurisdictions, officers who prepare investigations also supervise the defendants after probation has been granted, but, this procedure is becoming less prevalent in contemporary probation (Clear and Cole 1986). It is possible that extralegal variables play a significant role in the supervision process, but this paper is concerned specifically with presentence investigations.

3. There was no exact way to determine whether the 25 percent of the officers I was unable to interview conducted their presentence investigations significantly differently from those I interviewed. Personal observation, however, and the comments of the officers I interviewed (with whom I discussed this issue) indicated that those who refused used similar methods in processing their presentence reports.

4. On occasion police reports are written vaguely and are subject to various interpretations; rap sheets are not always clear, especially when some of the final dispositions have not been recorded.

5. I did not include terminal misdemeanor dispositions, in which probation is denied in favor of fines or jail sentences, in this typology. Such dispositions are comparatively rare and relatively insignificant.

6. Although defense attorneys also read the presentence reports, their reactions generally do not affect the probation officers' occupational standing (McHugh 1973; Rosecrance 1985).

7. I did not discuss the role of presentence reports in the prison system. Traditionally, probation reports were part of an inmate's jacket or file and were used as a basis for classification and treatment. The position of probation officers was legitimated further by the fact that prison officials also used the presentence report. I would suggest, however, that the advent of prison overcrowding and the accompanying security concerns have rendered presentence reports relatively meaningless. This contention needs to be substantiated before presentence reports are abandoned completely.

REFERENCES

Allen, Harry E. and Clifford E. Simonsen (1986) Corrections in America. New York: Macmillan.

Bankston, William B. (1983) "Legal and Extralegal Offender Traits and Decision-Making in the Criminal Justice System." Sociological Spectrum 3:1-18.

Blumberg, Abraham (1967) Criminal Justice. Chicago: Quadrangle.

Blumer, Martin (1979) "Concepts in the Analysis of Qualitative Data." Sociological Review 27:651-77.

Blumstein, Alfred J., S. Martin, and N. Holt (1983) Research on Sentencing: The Search for Reform. Washington, DC: National Academy Press.

Carter, Robert M. (1967) "The Presentence Report and The Decision-Making Process." Journal of Research in Crime and Delinquency 4:203-11.

Carter, Robert M. and Leslie T. Wilkins (1967) "Some Factors in Sentencing Policy." Journal of Criminal Law, Criminology, and Police Science 58:503-14.

Clear, Todd and George Cole (1986) American Corrections. Monterey, CA: Brooks/Cole.

Davis, James R. (1983) "Academic and Practical Aspects of Probation: A Comparison." Federal Probation 47:7-10.

Dawson, Robert (1969) Sentencing. Boston: Little, Brown.

Emerson, Robert M. (1981) "Ethnography and Understanding Members' Worlds." In Robert M. Emerson (ed.), Contemporary Field Research. Boston: Little, Brown, pp. 19-35.

Forer, Lois G. (1980) Criminals and Victims. New York: Norton.

Glaser, Barney and Anselm Strauss (1967) The Discovery of Grounded Theory. Chicago: Aldine.

Goldsborough, E. and E. Burbank (1968) "The Probation Officer and His Personality." In Charles L. Newman (ed.), Sourcebook on Probation, Parole, and Pardons. Springfield, IL: Charles C. Thomas, pp. 104-12.

Hagan, John (1975) "The Social and Legal Construction of Criminal Justice: A Study of the Presentence Process." Social Problems 22:620-37.

_____. (1977) "Criminal Justice in Rural and Urban Communities: A Study of the Bureaucratization of Justice." Social Forces 55:597-612.

_____. (1985) Modern Criminology: Crime, Criminal Behavior, and Its Control. New York: McGraw-Hill.

Hagan, John, John Hewitt, and Duane Alwin (1979) "Ceremonial Justice: Crime and Punishment in a Loosely Coupled System." Social Forces 58:506-25.

Hogarth, John (1971) Sentencing As a Human Process. Toronto: University of Toronto Press.

Hughes, Everett C. (1958) Men and Their Work. New York: Free Press.

Katz, Janet (1982) "The Attitudes and Decisions of Probation Officers." Criminal Justice and Behavior 9:455-75.

Kingsnorth, Rodney and Louis Rizzo (1979) "Decision-Making in the Criminal Courts: Continuities and Discontinuities." Criminology 17:3-14.

Lotz, Ray and John Hewitt (1977) "The Influence of Legally Irrelevant Factors on Felony Sentencing." Sociological Inquiry 47:39-48.

Marquart, James W. (1986) "Outsiders as Insiders: Participant Observation in the Role of a Prison Guard." Justice Quarterly 3:15-32.

McCleary, Richard (1978) Dangerous Men. Beverly Hills: Sage.

McCleary, Richard, Barbara Nienstadt, and James Erven (1982) "Uniform Crime Reports as Organizational Outcomes: Three Time Series Experiments." Social Problems 29:361-73.

McHugh, John J. (1973) "Some Comments on Natural Conflict between Counsel and Probation Officer." American Journal of Corrections 3:15-32.

Michalowski, Raymond J. (1985) Order, Law and Crime. New York: Random House.

Murrah, A. (1963) "Prison or Probation?" In B. Kay and C. Vedder (eds.), Probation and Parole. Springfield, IL: Charles C. Thomas, pp. 63-78.

Myers, Martha A. (1979) "Offended Parties and Official Reactions: Victims and the Sentencing of Criminal Defendants." Sociological Quarterly 20:529-46.

Neubauer, David (1974) Criminal Justice in Middle America. Morristown, NJ: General Learning.

Petersilia, Joan, Susan Turner, James Kahan, and Joyce Peterson (1985) "Executive Summary of Rand's Study, Granting Felons Probation." Crime and Delinquency 31:379-92.

Prus, Robert (1975) "Labeling Theory: A Statement on Typing." Sociological Focus 8:79-96.

Prus, Robert and John Stratten (1976) "Factors in the Decision-Making of North Carolina Probation Officers." Federal Probation 40:48-53.

Reckless, Walter C. (1967) The Crime Problem. New York: Appleton.

Robinson, James, Robert Carter, and A. Wahl (1969) The San Francisco Project. Berkeley: University of California School of Criminology.

Rodgers, T.A., G.T. Gitchoff, and I. Paur (1984) "The Privately Commissioned Presentence Report." In Robert M. Carter, Deniel Glaser, and Leslie T. Wilkens (eds.), Probation, Parole and Community Corrections. New York: Wiley, pp. 21-30.

Rosecrance, John (1985) "The Probation Officers' Search for Credibility: Ball Park Recommendations." Crime and Delinquency 31:539-54.

_____. (1987) "A Typology of Presentence Probation Investigators." International Journal of Offender Therapy and Comparative Criminology 31:163-177.

Rothman, David (1980) Conscience and Convenience: The Asylum and Its Alternatives in Progressive America. Boston: Little, Brown.

Schumacher, Michael A. (1985) "Implementation of a Client Classification And Case Management System: A Practitioner's View." Crime and Delinquency 31:445-55.

Scott, Marvin and Stanford Lyman (1968) "Accounts." American Sociological Review 33:46-62.

Shover, Neal (1974) "Experts and Diagnosis in Correctional Agencies." Crime and Delinquency 20:347-58.

_____. (1979) A Sociology of American Corrections. Homewood, IL: Dorsey.

Spencer, Jack W. (1983) "Accounts, Attitudes and Solutions: Probation Officer-Defendant Negotiations of Subjective Orientations." Social Problems 30:570-81.

Spradley, Joseph P. (1970) You Owe Yourself a Drunk: An Ethnography of Urban Normads. Boston: Little, Brown.

Sudnow, David (1965) "Normal Crimes: Sociological Features of the Penal Code." Social Problems 12:255-76.

Tinker, John N., John Quiring, and Yvonne Pimentel (1985) "Ethnic Bias in California Courts: A Case Study of Chicano and Anglo Felony Defendants." Sociological Inquiry 55:83-96.

Walker, Samuel (1985) Sense and Nonsense About Crime. Monterey, CA: Brooks/Cole.

Wallace, John (1974) "Probation Administration." In Daniel Glaser (ed.), Handbook of Criminology. Chicago: Rand-McNally, pp. 940-70.

Walsh, Anthony (1985) "The Role of the Probation Officer in the Sentencing Process." Criminal Justice and Behavior 12:289-303.

IV

CORRECTIONS

It is at the last stages of the criminal justice process that we find the lowest public visibility for organizational practices. Prisons, unlike police and judicial organizations, operate with very little scrutiny until something occurs that comes to the attention of the public. This is why field research is so important in these institutional settings. Although there has historically been numerous studies concerning various aspects of prison life, the enormous growth of prison construction and heterogeneous inmate populations have changed the way those facilities operate.

Qualitative studies through in-depth analyses have attempted to explain the changing prison culture, given a voice to inmates, exposed women prisoners' treatment in single-sex facilities, understand the functioning and populations of both male and female corrections officers, describe the operations of a parole board's decision-making practices.

The seven qualitatively oriented studies selected for this chapter on corrections explore some areas of our criminal justice system that have not received a great deal of attention in recent years. To this end, the exploratory approach utilized by the authors have produced much data that should cause us to rethink our current corrections policies and practices that directly affect the organizational operations of institutional corrections and parole board decision making. If nothing else, we trust that these field studies will enlighten readers to the realities and effects the correctional environment has on both employees and prisoners.

Stojkovic conducted a 12-month study of correctional staff interactions with inmates in a maximum security prison. He used observational techniques to study inmate-correctional officer encounters and ended up interviewing 20 officers at their jobs, in their homes, and in a local bar where they congregated after their work shifts. He also used open-ended question format in order to elicit the officers' perceptions of their relations with prisoners, administrators, and their correctional peers. Stojkovic termed the participants' responses he analyzed as accounts, because they were asked to evaluate many characteristics of their working environment. In short, his interviews focused on bridging the gap between perceived organizational work expectations and the practices that existed. The author's observations of prison life and correctional officer functioning in this custodial world were a necessary component of the qualitative research process. One has to gain insightful understanding for the complexities and functioning of an organizational environment before one can attempt to formulate any type of questioned responses from the study participants.

Of all the examples of qualitative research in this book, the study by Schmid and Jones on prison adaptation strategies used by first-time short-sentenced inmates is the most unique. The problem of gaining unrestricted access to prisoners was largely eliminated because one of the authors was serving a year-long prison sentence in the very correctional facility studied. Jones, the incarcerated author, was permitted to take a graduate school sociology course in field methods. The course developed into a study conducted by Schmid and Jones, and the study evolved into an analysis of novice inmates' experiences as first-time prisoners. Due to Jones's inmate status, the authors were able to examine the correctional socialization process for short-term inmates, both as observer and participant, for 10 months. Schmid largely helped with issues of objectivity for Jones, the researcher-prisoner, as the outside observer who guided the fieldwork project. Jones kept a journal of events and took field notes of his participation in prison activities, observations of prison life, and discussions with other inmates. After Jones was released, both researchers returned to the prison and interviewed 20 novice, short-term inmates to better understand the adaptation process they experienced.

The research process used by Hunt and his colleagues to collect data for the recent changes in prison life involved former prison inmates released to the community and who were now in ex-prisoner organizations, education programs, and participants in a street gang study. Most of their respondents had extensive criminal histories, had been incarcerated often, and were also gang members. The sample consisted of a representation of different ethnic and racial groups. The authors used a structured but open-ended interview format. Aside from eliciting their demographic data and criminal history, the authors focused their questions on knowledge of prison gangs and the perceptions of changes in prison life with the recent proliferation of incarcerated street gang members. This study was an attempt to gain former inmate-gang members' perspectives. Here, the use of a retrospective view by respondents who were released from prison provided them with an opportunity to reflect on their prior prison experiences, which would not be true of study subjects currently involved in prison gang activity. There are real advantages to using a retrospective-reflective qualitative technique in such research, as this study of former prisoners exemplifies.

In interviews with 54 female parolees who were incarcerated at one western state's prison for women, Pogrebin and Dodge examined the retrospective narratives of their prison experiences. Over a 3-month period of time, participants were interviewed and tape-recorded for purposes of qualitative analysis. All participant interviews were conducted in private conference rooms at the time they had appointments to see their parole officers. One distinct methodological advantage in spreading out all the interviews over 3 months was to assure the researchers that they would be including participants who were released from prison at different times. By doing this, they had a stratified population of former inmates who, for the most part, were incarcerated at different times or had their stay in prison overlap. This technique helped to verify much of the information the participants were relating during the interview process. So, female parolees who had been out of prison for over 3 years provided similar information to that of other inmates on parole who were released to the community more recently. By collecting data this way, the veracity of the participants' accounts of prison life was perceived as reliable.

In the next study, Pogrebin and Poole examined the adjustment difficulties and work strategies of female deputies working as corrections officers in four county jails and three local detention centers. These facilities came under the jurisdiction of four sheriffs' departments. A 50% systematic random sample allowed for the selection of 135 female corrections deputies. Of this population, 108 women agreed to participate. The researchers used a semistructured interview format, with each taped session lasting approximately one and one half hours. The interviews were conducted in conference rooms, the library, and visitation rooms. The taped discussions were transcribed for qualitative data analysis, which involved a search for general statements about relationships among categories of observations. That is, the researchers' analysis of the data attempted to discover significant classes of the female corrections deputies' experiences and those properties that characterized them. The researchers then categorized the data into four correctional domains of jail work experiences identified by the deputy study participants.

Based on observations of 236 parole board interviews with male sex offenders, Radelet and

Roberts examined the role that impression management played in parole board members' interpretation of their encounters with inmate candidates for parole release. These observations were conducted in one state over a 14-month period. Each parole hearing lasted approximately 20 minutes and was followed by a short private discussion between board members, which the research team also was permitted to observe. The researchers also conducted in-depth interviews with the board members about the criteria for their decisions and their opinion about the candidates. Field notes were taken based in large part from observations and interviews. The fact that one of the authors of this study was a sitting member of the parole board while the other team member kept notes of the proceedings is a bit unusual. However, having one member of the study as an active participant not only allowed for easy entree to conduct the research, but it resulted in firsthand explanations for the entire board's rationale in their decision-making process, and also how they perceived impression management by prisoners.

Using content analysis as their qualitative methodological approach, West-Smith and her fellow researchers explored prison inmates' perspectives of being denied parole. Data were collected from a nonprofit prisoner advocacy group from letters that were requested (through its quarterly newsletter) from inmates whose parole board hearings had resulted in a denial of parole. Those prisoners who were turned down by the board were asked to send copies of their appeals and the responses they received. One hundred eighty prisoners responded by sending their appeal letters, which ranged from a few paragraphs to several pages in length. Fifty-two letters were eliminated from the study as a result of not addressing the parole candidate's own parole hearing. One hundred twenty-eight letters were analyzed, with a total of 285 complaints identified and categorized using a content analysis method that translates frequency of occurrence and comparisons of content of the discourse. This qualitative technique provided the means to document, classify, and interpret the communication of meaning, allowing for inferential judgments as to the characteristics of the messages that were relayed in the inmates' letters.

Correctional officers' portrayals of problematic aspects of their work worlds are analyzed as accounts that explain perceived gaps between officers' actions and official organizational expectations and procedures. The analysis considers how the officers portrayed their work worlds as filled with problems stemming from the prison system, correctional administrators, and inmates. The officers' accounts of their relationships with inmates is also analyzed, particularly the ways in which the officers explained their accommodative orientation to inmates' "normal" rule violations.

ACCOUNTS OF PRISON WORK

Corrections Officers' Portrayals of Their Work Worlds

STAN STOJKOVIC

Sykes (1958) offers a sociological explanation for correctional officers' tendency to develop unapproved work routines, relationships, and orientations stating that the prison social system involves contradictions and pressures that undermine and, ultimately, "corrupt" correctional officers' authority. Although it is concerned with a variety of

Reprinted with permission from *Perspectives on Social Problems,* Vol. 2, 211–230. Copyright © JAI Press, Inc.

Acknowledgement: The author would like to thank Gale Miller and Jim Holstein for their comments and suggestions about the paper.

human service and social control organizations Lipsky's (1980) analysis of street-level bureaucracies also emphasizes how low level staff in prisons and similar organizations adapt to organizational problem and pressures over which they have little or no control. Lipsky focuses on the ways in which human service and social control professionals cope with such problems by approaching their work in officially disapproved, but functional ways in order to fulfill their professional obligations. He concludes that street level bureaucrats' coping strategies are realistic and necessary because organizational goals are seldom achievable in officially prescribed ways. Unauthorized procedures are often functional for organizational systems and the larger society.

This analysis offers a new way of understanding correctional officers and the work worlds. I consider many of the issues raised in the corrections literature but my focus is on how correctional officers explain and justify their development of officially disapproved work routines, relationships, and orientations Thus, I am not concerned with why correctional officers "really" modify organizational rules and expectations or the function of their actions for the prison system. Rather, I attempt to explicate correctional officers' *accounts* of the actions and relationships. As Scott and Lyman (1968, p. 46) state,

> An account is a linguistic device employed whenever an action is subjected to valuative inquiry. Such devices are a crucial element in the social world since they prevent conflicts from arising by verbally bridging the gap between action and expectation. Moreover, accounts are "situated" according to the statuses of the interactants are standardized within cultures so that certain accounts are terminologically stabilized and routinely expected when activity falls outside the domain of expectations.

By taking accounts as its topic, the paper focuses on the ways that correction officers verbally bridge the gap between their work activities and relationship and official organizational expectations. Accounts are rhetorical; that is, they all expressed as rationales intended to anticipate and counter others' criticisms of persons' actions (Miller and Holstein 1989). Officers use these accounts to make sense of the actions that constitute their everyday work routines. Correctional officers' accounts of their work circumstances and relationships are thus both descriptions of their work world and features of it. The descriptions and rationales are available to, and used by, correctional officers to manage troublesome persons who may criticize them for acting in improper ways.

Setting and Organization of the Study

The study was conducted over a 12-month period in 1982-1983 and involved the observation of correctional staff interactions with prisoners in a maximum-security prison. The prison was built to house prisoners classified as especially dangerous to the public. During the research period, over 75% of the inmates were serving sentences of 20 years or more. Further, most of the inmates had records of violent and disruptive behavior in other prisons in the state. The correctional officer staff consisted of 150 persons, most of whom were new to correctional work. The inexperience of the correctional officer staff was intentional. The warden stated that he wished to put together a correctional officer staff that would bring new ideas, work habits, and attitudes to their work. He stated that hiring correctional officers with little or no experience was important because they would be unfamiliar with the "old ways of doing things," including the corrupt practices that flourish in many prisons.

I observed interactions in all areas of the prison, including its most restrictive segregation unit. Also, 20 correctional officers were interviewed about their work. The interviews were conducted at the officers' homes and/or in a local tavern. The questions asked of correctional officers were open-ended and intended to elicit portrayals of the purposes of the prison, the officers' work in it, and officers' relations with others, particularly inmates, administrators, and other correctional officers. The portrayals may be analyzed as accounts because they were responses to questions which asked the officers to evaluate aspects of their work world and explain disjunctures between officers' depictions of organizational ideals and their behavior. Put differently, the officers' responses are treated as culturally standardized explanations for bridging the gap between organizational expectations and practices.

Most correctional officers portrayed the primary purpose of the prison as maintaining institutional security and control over the prisoners. They expressed little concern for prisoners' rehabilitation. They stated that rehabilitation was not why the prison was built; rather, it was intended to make prisoners more manageable. As one officer stated, "We get all the fuck-ups from the other prisons that nobody else wants." Although correctional officers stated that the security and control of prisoners was the prison's central purpose, they also stated that the accomplishment of this goal was made problematic by the prison's administrative structure and the conflicting demands placed on them by supervisors.

Thus, correctional officers' explanations and justifications of how they maintained a secure prison in an often hostile, uncertain, and contradictory environment is the primary topic of this paper. Officers stated that they maintained order by developing accommodative relationships with prisoners which violated officially prescribed rules and procedures, but which the officers portrayed as realistic and necessary adjustments to their work circumstances. In this way the officers described themselves as acting much as the street-level bureaucrats Lipsky (1980) analyzed. Central to both descriptions is the depiction of low-level organization members as competent and responsible persons trying to cope with difficult work circumstances.

The rest of the paper is organized in three sections. First, I consider how the correctional officers portrayed their work world as filled with problems requiring that they develop officially disapproved work practices and relationships. The officers depicted the practices and relationships as ways of coping with problems over which they had little or no control. Second, I analyze how the officers described their relationships with inmates. They stated that realistic and necessary correctional officer-inmate relationships required that officers' accommodate themselves to inmates' desires and interests by selectively enforcing prison rules. Finally, I conclude by briefly discussing how the officers'

accounts may be analyzed as rhetoric, and noting the research implications of such an approach to the findings.

THE PRISON AS A PROBLEMATIC WORK WORLD

For correctional officers, the prison world was organized in terms of routine activities and relationships. In the abstract, at least, the routines were interrelated ways that correctional officers' achieve the prison's organizational purposes. The officers stated, however, that the meaning of their everyday work activities and relationships was not so simple or clear-cut. They portrayed their work activities and relationships as adaptations to problematic circumstances. Specifically, the correctional officers stated that their work involved three major sources of uncertainty and problems: (1) prison system and correctional officers' place in it, (2) prison administrators' actions and interests, and (3) inmates. According to the officers, each of these aspects of the prison involved different practical problems which they sought to manage. The rest of this section is concerned with the way in which the correctional officers portrayed and oriented to aspects of the prison world as problems.

The Prison System as a Problem

The officers often portrayed themselves as forgotten people in a hostile social system made up of politicians, the public, prison administrators, and inmates. They stated that their problems and low social standing reflected politicians' and the public's negative attitudes toward prisons and correctional officers. The officers stated that members of each of these groups treated them as insignificant, largely incompetent, and expendable parts of the prison organization. Of most immediate importance to the officers, however, were prison administrators' orientations to them. They stated that prison administrators treated correctional officers as scapegoats; that is, administrators protected themselves by passing the blame for system problems from administrators to correctional officers. The officers portrayed prison administrators' and others' attitudes toward correctional officers as counterproductive and self-fulfilling prophecies because correctional officers partly adapt to the prison system by taking on the traits attributed to them by others.

Consider, for example, the following descriptions of the prison world. They are explanations of why correctional officers "have no togetherness" and eventually confirm others' negative evaluations of them. The portrayals center in treating correctional officers' work problems as system problems.

> We are Indians in the correctional system. Everyone shits on us. We have no togetherness in this place. . . . We are the screws no one really cares about. . . . we are shipwrecked in the society and are always labelled as the bad guys . . . they [administration] treat us like assholes and we will eventually become nothing but assholes.
>
> Who gives a fuck about corrections officers? We have to deal with all the assholes in the system and they expect us to like it. . . . It's this kind of attitude we have to live with . . . then they wonder why we are all alcoholics.

The correctional officers further explained that their problems and low standing in the prison were relatively recent developments. According to the officers, the problems were a result of changing prison policies which expanded prisoners' rights and reduced correctional officers' discretion, particularly their right to discipline prisoners as they saw fit. The officers explained that the changes were counterproductive restrictions on their abilities to effectively respond to troublesome prisoners. They stated that the ultimate effect of the changes was a reduction in correctional officers' authority and inmates' respect for officers. Consider, for example, the following discussions of how correctional officers' work circumstances had been adversely affected by changes in prison policies.

> It is not like in the old days when you could beat the shit out of an asshole. I wish they did still have this for some of these guys in this place. Some guys need a good ass kicking, then we wouldn't have that many problems at all in trying to keep them in line.
>
> There is no real punishment in this place. What would have happened in the old days is that the

guy would have gotten his ass beat for about two weeks straight and the other inmates would have known it right away . . . the sad thing is that the inmates know that there is no real punishment and they flaunt it in our faces.

According to the correctional officers, a related problem with the prison system involved officers' inconsistent enforcement of prison rules. They stated that, while every correctional officer was supposed to strictly follow prison rules, they frequently deviated from them. Although the officers' comments might be taken as a call for the strict enforcement of prison rules, they were intended as critiques of the rules which the officers portrayed as unrealistic expectations and standards. Indeed, many officers stated that flexible rule enforcement was needed in the prison because officers could not effectively run their units under a policy of literal enforcement. In this way, the officers cast the enforcement of prison rules and their responsibility to effectively manage prisoners as contradictory aspects of the prison system. As one officer explained,

> If you (inmate) are doing time and you are decent, you will be alright in this place. Rules are meant to be bent in a place like this; you have to be flexible in how you deal with the inmates. If you are not flexible, then you will be in trouble.

However, while the officers portrayed flexible rule enforcement as a necessity, they also stated that it was a major source of work problems because too many officers were too flexible. Officers framed the issue as a practical dilemma. They stated that, on the one hand, the official prison rules to which they were accountable were unrealistic and inadequate because the rules did not take account of the practical contingencies faced by officers in managing inmates. Consequently, correctional officers engaged in selective enforcement to fulfill their larger obligation to maintain order in the prison. On the other hand, the officers stated that, although most of them agreed that they had to be flexible in enforcing prison rules, they did not agree on when and how to do so. According to the officers, the results was inconsistency and uncertainty among officers and inmates about appropriate inmate behavior.

Officers stated that this circumstance had practical consequences because inmates could get by with rule breaking by playing one officer against another much as children negotiate with, and get permission from, their parents by telling one parent that the other approves of their requests. Specifically, inmates responded to correctional officers who tried to strictly enforce prison rules by stating that other officers did not enforce them. The officers stated that such problems were most serious when supervisory officers were more lenient than the officers that they supervised. In this circumstance, officers could actually be punished for enforcing prison rules. Consider, for example, the following correctional officer's complaint about the inmates' practice of taking food from the prison kitchen. He portrays the practice as a practical dilemma and problem which focuses on how officers were sometimes punished for "doing their jobs."

> I am sick and tired of guys bringing all this shit from the kitchen into the housing units. It is something that just has to stop. But the problem is that so many officers allow it to happen and you can't get consistency . . . in rule enforcement. . . . remember one time when two officers stopped a guy with a whole coat full of stuff from the kitchen. The inmate responded that (another) officer allowed it to come to the unit. When they checked it out with the officer, who was their superior, he reprimanded them for enforcing the rules. All they were doing was their jobs. That type of shit is what really pisses me off about this job.

In sum, the correctional officers portrayed the prison system as fraught with problems, contradictions and dilemmas that made it difficult—if not impossible—for them to fulfill their organizational obligations. They further stated that in attempting to cope with the problems of the prison system, correctional officers sometimes produced new problems and injustices, making their work circumstances even more complex and difficult. The officers stated that these problems were exacerbated by problems in the correctional officer-prison administrator relationship. We turn to these problems next.

Prison Administrators as a Problem

The correctional officers portrayed the officer-administrator relationship as filled with tensions and distrust resulting from the prison administrators' lack of respect for correctional officers, over concern for protecting themselves from criticism and negative publicity, and willingness to use correctional officers as scapegoats. In other words, the officers described themselves as *victims* of the policies and practices of prison administrators in order to exonerate themselves from blame for their, and the prison's, failures (Holstein and Miller 1990). Specifically, the officers explained that the tensions and distrust underlying the officer-administrator relationship were based on three factors.

First, correctional officers expressed concern that prison administrators were changing the rules and regulations of the prison so rapidly that officers and inmates did not know what was expected of them. According to the officers, the changes created uncertainty among prisoners about organizational rules and expectations. As one officer stated,

> By fucking with the inmates' minds is where the problems begin. The inmates need to have rules and regulations consistently enforced. But the problem is that the administration always changes the rules of the game for both inmates and staff. Inconsistency pisses off a lot of inmates. Convicts want and need consistent rules. How can we expect them to follow the rules when the rules are always changing?

The officers explained the problem was a result of the prison administrators' unrealistic emphasis on controlling both inmate groups and the correctional officer's union. They stated that maintaining control over such groups was the administrators' highest priority. They further explained that frequent changes in prison policies created uncertainties and divisions between officers and inmates that served the administrators' interests. "All these different rules put inmates against officers and officers against themselves," stated one officer. According to the officers, the major results of the administrators' actions were that correctional officers learned to distrust prison administrators and to rely on their own judgment and methods in controlling inmates. As one correctional officer explained,

> You do what you think is right and you disregard anything the administration says. You are the one who is doing the job, and you do anything that you think will make your job more effective and easy in the long run.

A second issue raised by the officers in explaining their distrust of prison administrators was safety. Specifically, they stated that the administrators were unconcerned with the officers' safety. The officers further stated that the administrators' lack of concern increased the risks associated with their jobs. The officers cited a number of incidents in explaining and justifying their concerns about their personal safety and prison administrators' attitude toward it. One such incident involved an especially violent and disruptive inmate assault on a correctional officer in the cafeteria. The assault was done in the presence of over 30 correctional officers and 100 prisoners. Immediately following the incidents the inmate shouted "What can these assholes do to me anyway? I am serving double-life." The inmate was given segregation and punishment time, yet the officers stated that the assault warranted greater punishment and that the administration should have attempted to transfer the prisoner to another less "luxurious" prison in the state system.

The officers used such incidents to cast the prison as an unsafe place and prison administrators as unconcerned with officers' welfare. They also used the incidents to explain and justify a work orientation that involved avoiding actions that threatened their safety, including allowing inmates to flagrantly violate some prison rules. According to the officers, they had to take care of themselves first because prison administrators were unwilling to protect them. As one officer stated,

> Them administration types don't care about us or our jobs. So, why should I stick my neck out for them? I'll do anything to keep myself safe. . . . If that means letting them [inmates] burn down the place, that's fine with me.

Finally, correctional officers stated that prison administrators were too concerned with inmate lawsuits. According to the officers, the prison administrators' concern resulted in an improper emphasis on pleasing inmates. The effect of the emphasis was to reduce correctional officers' authority and discretion in dealing with inmates. The officers further stated that prison administrators responded to inmate lawsuits by allowing the officers to be blamed for the problems of the prison system. Consider, for example, the following officer's portrayal of the effect of prison administrators' concern for inmate lawsuits. Through his portrayal, the officer casts correctional officers as victims of prison administrators' over emphasis on inmate lawsuits. He also explains and justifies his interest in returning to law enforcement.

> The only reason I became a guard is because I was laid-off from my job as a sheriff. . . . As soon as that picks up, I am getting the fuck out of this place. . . . A lot of these administrators just care for the inmates. That's because inmates file lawsuits and the public thinks we are all assholes. . . . We can't even do our jobs without being thought of as bad by the public.

In sum, the officers stated that many of their problems with inmates were caused by prison administrators' policies. Specifically, prison administrators' policies and actions made it impossible for correctional officers to act as they preferred and/or as required by prison policies. We next consider the officers' descriptions of other sources of tension in the correctional officer-inmate relationship.

Prisoners as a Problem

Although we might expect inmates to resent and resist all rule enforcement by correctional officers, the officers stated that most inmates recognized the importance of prison rules. They stated that, although inmates expected the rules to be enforced in realistic and flexible ways, most inmates recognized that the rules were important to the maintenance of prison order. Officers added that flexibility in rule enforcement was especially important when it involved events which were the most relevant to the prisoners' ability to cope and adapt to the demands and constraints imposed by the prison environment. For example, the officers stated that telephone calls were very important to prisoners because they were the only way in which inmates could regularly interact with friends and relatives on the outside. Thus, for the officers, flexibility in enforcing rules about inmates' use of the telephone was an important way of maintaining stable relations with prisoners. As one officer stated,

> Phone calls are really important for guys in this place . . . you cut off their calls and they get pissed. So what I do is give them a little extra and they are good to me.

While flexibility in rule enforcement was important in interactions between correctional officers and prisoners, the officers stated that they selectively enforced the rules to achieve organizational goals. Put in the officers' language, they enforced the rules to "squeeze" inmates who were severely disruptive to the housing units or posed threats to other inmates. The officers stated that, in doing so, they solved problems for both themselves and inmates, both of whom had an interest in maintaining an orderly prison world. Consider, for example, the following correctional officers' explanations of the usefulness of selectively enforcing prison rules.

> I'll be easy on the rules if the guy is not causing trouble. . . . If he is into all those bullshit games, then I want his ass out of my unit. The problem is that nobody wants him . . . but if you are smart you can get the real troublemakers out of the place.
>
> For the inmate who doesn't force himself on anyone you got to give him a break. . . . I do that by giving him more dayroom [recreation] time and he respects that. . . . You know, you're not always on the guy and inmates admire that in an officer.

A related aspect of the correctional officer-inmate relationship centered in the officers' classification of inmates into those who "knew how to do time" and those who did not. The officers stated that it was the latter group of inmates who were most troublesome because they had no commitment to prison policies and procedures. Specifically, the officers stated that

the younger inmates serving longer sentences had no understanding of what it meant to do time and that their adjustment to prison was, therefore, more difficult. Further, the officers stated that the presence of younger inmates in the prison made their jobs more difficult and problematic. They stated, for example, that although they warned younger inmates about the possible consequences of rule infractions, the warnings had no effect on their behavior.

> It's the bugs [young inmates] that cause all the problems. . . . They are the ones involved in spud juice [alcohol], dope, and sex . . . they don't give a shit about nothing and most have been state raised so they know nothing but prison.

The officers added that their concern for managing troublesome young inmates was shared with the older inmates who had been in prison for a number of years and viewed the prison as their homes. According to the officers, the older inmates also saw the younger inmates as troublemakers who were upsetting the established order developed and perpetuated by themselves and correctional staff.

> It seems to me that the older inmates understand the officer's job and buy into the system of rules and regulations. On the other hand, the younger inmates cause more problems because they don't buy the rules of the enforcers.
>
> Them older guys know what prison life is all about. They know that you're just doing your job and don't want any hassle. . . . You never have any problems with them.

Thus, although the correctional staff were officially obligated to enforce all prison rules all the time, they did not always do so. Rather, they selectively enforced prison rules to control troublesome prisoners and reward cooperative ones, always seeking to manage the practical contingencies associated with their jobs. The officers also used selective enforcement of prison rules to build alliances with inmates who could help them control troublesome inmates. Specifically, the officers depended on and used older inmates to control younger, more troublesome inmates. The older inmates aided the correctional officers by encouraging the younger inmates to cooperate with the officers. They did so by instructing the younger inmates on the practical advantages of cooperation. Thus, although it was not recognized in official prison policies and rules, the correctional officers stated that one way they fulfilled their professional responsibilities was by selectively enforcing rules in order to secure cooperation from older inmates.

The officers stated that it was one of several ways in which they adapted their relationship with inmates to the practical constraints and circumstances of their work. The adaptations were the basis for the accommodative relationships which prevailed in the housing units. We further consider how correctional officers portrayed and justified their relationships with inmates in the next section.

THE SOCIAL ORGANIZATION OF OFFICER-INMATE RELATIONS

Although all of the correctional officers did not agree that capitulation to inmates' desires and needs was appropriate, most of the officers who regularly interacted with inmates were accommodative, particularly those assigned to the housing units. The officers explained that accommodation was necessary because strictly enforcing prison rules did not produce inmate compliance; rather, it destabilized the prison environment and officer-inmate relationships. The officers gave two major reasons for this circumstance. Both reasons involved portraying accommodation with inmates' desires as a practical response to the constraints of correctional officers' work.

First, they stated that the strict enforcement was counterproductive because there was no real punishment attached to many of the violations. They stated that prison punishments were too soft and prison administrators did not support correctional officers in their disputes with inmates. For example, the correctional officers stated that officers who relied on ticket writing as their only way of controlling prisoners were doomed to failure. Ticket writing was the officially approved method of documenting inmates' misbehaviors and, according to the prison administrators, was the first step in taking formal action against troublesome inmates.

The officers stated, however, that tickets were not taken seriously in the prison. As one officer stated,

> Your only formal authority is the tickets you write, but tickets are not written by a lot of officers because they do not really do anything in this place. A lot of tickets are thrown away by superiors anyway.

The officers also stated that writing tickets for many inmate rule violations did not make sense because many of the behaviors were "bullshit"; that is, they are minor offenses that did not warrant official responses. The officers stated that ticketing inmates was only appropriate when nothing else could be done with troublemakers. For example, I observed two prisoners pushing and shoving each other in one of the housing units. An officer broke up the disturbance and sent the inmates on their ways. Later, I asked him why he had not given them tickets for fighting. He replied,

> What for? It only produces trouble between those two guys and myself. If someone got stabbed or seriously hurt, then I would have to write a ticket, but no one did.

Second, the officers stated that, although they could use physical force to gain short-term inmate cooperation, coercion was a last resort response to troublesome inmates because it involved unacceptable long-term costs. They stated that inmates resented such treatment and would respond by withholding future cooperation. Equally important, the officers stated that if they used physical force to manage inmates, it could lead to violent inmate responses, a circumstance that they wished to avoid. Thus, although the correctional officers had official access to resources which presumably allowed them to compel acquiescence from inmates, they did not emphasize them. Rather, they sought to build "noncoercive" relationships with inmates. According to officers, such relationships were realistic and necessary ways of dealing with inmates.

In so explaining and justifying their relationships with inmates, then, correctional officers cast accommodation to inmates' desires and behaviors as a rational response to the practical circumstances of prison life. They further stated that accommodation was good for both officers and inmates. The officers explained that accommodative relationships served the officers' interest in maintaining orderly and stable housing units and inmates' interest in reducing the insecurities of prison life. Although it was less emphasized by the officers, a related reason why accommodative officer-inmate relations prevailed in the housing units was because officers who sought to strictly enforce prison rules seldom remained in the housing units for long. Officers portrayed this approach as unrealistic because it was overly strict. Indeed, inmates referred to "strict" correctional officers as the "police," thereby highlighting their emphasis on rule enforcement.

The officers stated that many strict officers left the housing units and sometimes correctional work because they became frustrated by the selective rule enforcement of other correctional officers. According to the officers, strict officers were caught between their desire to enforce all prison rules and inmates' claims that they should ignore rule violations because other officers did so. In addition to strict officers' requests to leave, their time in the housing units was reduced by the intervention of prison administrators who frequently transferred them to jobs that did not involve regular contact with inmates. The administrators usually did so in response to inmates and/or correctional officers' complaints portraying the strict officers as unreasonable and sources of problems in the housing units. In so responding to officer and inmate complaints, the prison administrators helped maintain and perpetuate accommodative officer-inmate relationships which centered in selected rule enforcement.

According to the officers, then, there were several practical reasons for the prevalence of accommodative officer-inmate relationships in the housing units. The officers further stated that, although the relationships involved violations of formal prison policies and rules, they were realistic, necessary, and served the interests of inmates, prison staff, and the public. The remainder of this section considers correctional officers' accounts of their accommodative orientation to inmates' desires and behaviors and treatment of some inmate rule

violations as deviance. They were explanations and justifications of the correctional officers' routine violation of official prison rules and policies. I discuss the issues in turn.

The Accommodative Orientation

Accommodative relationships between correctional officers and prisoners were rooted in three practices that may be stated as officers' claims:

1. Because correctional officers could not have total control over the inmates, negotiations were central to prisoner control.

2. Once an officer defined or negotiated a set of informal rules with a prisoner or group of prisoners, the rules were to be respected by all parties.

3. Some rule violating behaviors in the prison setting were "normal" and, consequently, did not merit officer attention or sanctioning.

More specifically, the officers stated that proper accommodation to inmates' desires and interests involved "giving respect" to inmates and restricting officers' interactions with inmates. In doing so, correctional officers stated that they sought to effectively control and manage inmates while avoiding troublesome encounters with them.

> The officers stated that giving respect to inmates was a central aspect of building effective relationships with inmates. It involved enforcing only those prison rules that most inmates and correctional officers deemed important and realistic. For the officers, such selective rule enforcement allowed them to maintain an acceptable degree of control in the housing units while enabling inmates to "save face" by providing them with a sense of respect, dignity and self-control. As one officer stated, the importance of giving a man his respect is key to this place. I have found if you give respect you get respect in here. The inmates know it, and for the most part the good guards know it too.

The officers stated that a related and important aspect of giving respect to inmates was that in selectively enforcing prison rules they clearly defined the rules that mattered. That is, both correctional officers and veteran inmates knew and agreed on the types of behavior that called for official action by the officers. The officers stated that their selective enforcement of prison rules resulted in officer-inmate consensus about acceptable inmate behavior and, based on the consensus, a greater sense of predictability and order existed in officer-inmate interactions. The officers further stated that new correctional officers and inmates were partly a problem because they were unfamiliar with the working assumptions and rules of the prison. In learning the practical meaning of giving and getting respect, new officers learned how to properly do their jobs and new inmates learned to do their time.

The second aspect of the correctional officers' accommodative orientation to the officer-inmate relationship involved restricted interaction with inmates. Specifically, correctional officers tried to limit their interactions to those inmates who could help them control other inmates in the housing units. Thus, many inmates had limited and perfunctory dealings with correctional officers, such as fleeting contacts during count times or when inmates were leaving the housing units for jobs, school, or other institutional assignments. The officers explained that they did not interact with most inmates because it was not a necessary part of their jobs. One officer explained his orientation to interactions with inmates in the following way.

> Why should I get involved in something with a prisoner when I don't want to know him? I am not here to love him, only to watch him and make sure the housing unit is secured.

Nonetheless, the correctional officers did regularly interact with some inmates. They did so with inmates who were willing to help the officers fulfill their organizational responsibilities, the most important and cumbersome being the counting of inmates. The counts were conducted at 6:00 a.m. (right before many prisoners went to work), 11:00 a.m. (right before the staggered lunch times for prisoners), 4:00 p.m. (right after the shift changes of officers), and 10:00 p.m. (right before lights out in the prison). Counting inmates was a cumbersome task for the correctional officers because it required that

prisoners be locked in their cells. To ensure this, correctional officers used "trusted" inmates to do their counts for them and help them move prisoners into their assigned cells. In return, the inmates were given privileges that other prisoners did not enjoy, such as extra phone time or dayroom time. They also had greater contact with the correctional officers, although their interactions were focused on the practical problems of counting inmates.

In sum, the correctional officers described their accommodative orientation to prison rules and inmate relationships as a pragmatic adaptation to their work circumstances. They gave respect to inmates because it was an effective way of gaining inmate cooperation and they restricted their interactions with inmates to those who could help them better manage their work problems. Put differently, the officers' portrayals of the accommodative orientation centered in avoiding trouble with inmates. A related way in which they managed inmates and avoided trouble was by treating some inmates' behaviors as normal deviance. The officers described normal deviance as rule violations that were not serious enough to warrant removing prisoners from their housing units or the normal daily activities of the prison. I next consider how the officers explained and justified their treatment of some inmate behaviors as normal deviance.

Avoiding Normal Deviance

According to the correctional officers, the two most important kinds of normal deviance engaged in by inmates were sexual relations and drug use. They were significant to the officers because the behaviors affected the correctional officers' orientation to their work and social control. Specifically, the correctional officers stated that although the behaviors were violations of prison rules, they were ongoing inmate activities which, at best, could only be partly controlled by the strict enforcement of prison rules. For the officers, then, a more realistic and productive orientation to the activities was to treat them as matters of negotiation and accommodation. Officers explained that in treating inmate sexual activities and drug use as negotiable, they were able to maintain a degree of control over them while not engendering the hostility associated with the strict enforcement of prison rules.

The officers stated that sexual relations between inmates was the most problematic kind of normal deviance. It was problematic because, although the correctional officers assumed that it was happening, they did not know when and where to be in the prison in order to avoid discovering it. The officers stated that avoiding the discovery of inmate sexual activities was important because the discovery of inmates having sexual relations was a threat to their safety. The officers explained that an inmate who is confronted by an officer with the fact that he is not a man, but a "sissy," "punk," or "fag" would resort to violence to ensure his respect among other inmates. They stated that no inmate wants to be viewed as being sexually weak, nor does he want other inmates to view him as a "woman" who can be exploited by other prisoners for sexual favors.

Thus, to avoid such confrontations the correctional officers watched for signs of inmate sexual activities and removed themselves from settings where signs of sexual activity were present. The officers explained and justified their actions as a realistic and necessary accommodation to the practical circumstances of prison life. As one officer stated,

> If I see three or four guys crowding around a guy's cell, I know something is going down, either they are getting high or someone is sucking or fucking. If I get in the middle of that shit, I would be crazy because I will either get seriously hurt or killed. I am not going to go down there and write tickets. It would be plain stupid.

This is not to suggest that the correctional officers tolerated all forms of inmate sexual activities. Specifically, they did not tolerate the public display of sexual behavior, inmates "squeezing off" other inmates into the "hole" (a segregation cell for those inmates who were afraid of being sexually assaulted), or coercing sexual relations from weaker inmates. The officers stated that, both they and inmates viewed these forms of sexual relations as intolerable and that they worked to control sexual exploitation. Finally, correctional officers justified their

treatment of inmate sexual activities as normal by portraying the amount of such activity in the prison as less than that found in other prisons in the state. In doing so, they cast inmates' sexual activity as less of a problem than in other settings and, therefore, a tolerable form of rule breaking.

The correctional officers also portrayed their orientation to inmates' drug use as accommodative. They stated that, as in other prisons, narcotics were readily available to inmates in their prison and that they took account of it in their dealings with inmates. The officers further stated that so long as inmates were not causing trouble or exhibiting violent behavior, inmate drug use was a tolerable activity. Indeed, they stated that inmate drug use was a normal and expected part of the inmates' social world. As with inmate sexual activity, the correctional officers avoided confronting inmates about their drug use. The officers tried to anticipate occasions when inmates would being using drugs and avoid situations in which enforcement of prison rules forbidding drug use might be required. They explained that their orientation was realistic because the problems resulting from their enforcement of drug-related rules were more serious than those associated with inmates' drug use. As one correctional officer stated,

> One thing that you don't want to get involved in is the illegal bullshit between inmates. . . . If I know inmates are going to be smoking (marijuana), I'll let it slide if it isn't going to cause any problems. . . . Once you try to step in, then you got problems.

The correctional officers further justified their accommodative orientation to inmate drug use by stating that while drug use was common in the prison, it was not as problematic in this prison as in others in the state. They stated that the most serious danger stemming from inmates' drug use involved new dealers' efforts to move in on the markets of established dealers. According to the correctional officers, however, this problem could be controlled through proper negotiations with dealers, not the strict enforcement of prison rules.

DISCUSSION AND CONCLUSION

Looked at one way, the correctional officers' accounts discussed here are excuses intended to explain away the officers' selective enforcement of prison rules. Viewed this way, they are techniques of neutralization which the officers used to deny responsibility for failing to carry out their officially prescribed responsibilities (Sykes and Matza 1957). The officers partly did so by blaming others (particularly prison administrators) for their actions. In doing so, they cast themselves as victims both of others' actions and, more generally, of the prison system which the officers portrayed as organized to undermine their authority and efforts to fulfill their responsibilities in organizationally approved ways. The officers further described their selective enforcement of prison rules as realistic and necessary adaptations to the prison system.

Implicit in the analysis of the officers' accounts as excuses, however, is an assessment of their accuracy; that is, the accounts are treated as adequate or inadequate explanations of the officers' circumstances, actions, and motives. Further, such an analysis involves taking a side in the officers' disputes with others. By treating the accounts as accurate portrayals of their circumstances, actions and motives, persons align themselves with the officers in their disputes with inmates, prison administrators and others in their social world. On the other hand, emphasizing the inadequacy of the officers' accounts implicitly undermines their claims and the legitimacy of their positions in disputes with others.

There is, however, an alternative orientation to the officers' accounts that treats it as rhetoric—that is, as claims about reality intended to persuade others. Rhetoric is partisan discourse through which persons anticipate and/or counter others' criticisms of their actions and positions on practical issues (Perelman 1979). It is also an interactional procedure for assigning preferred identities to one's self and others. By formulating accounts of their activities that emphasize the practical constraints and injustices making up the prison system, correctional officers anticipated and countered others' criticisms of them as corrupt and uncaring functionaries. They also assigned preferred identities to themselves by portraying their actions as professionally responsible efforts to cope with difficult work circumstances. If we treat officers' accounts as *partisan* and *purposeful*—but not necessarily flawed—versions of reality, we can begin to analyze both how officers experience their work worlds and how they managed and made sense of those worlds through their accounting procedures. A rhetorical analysis can provide insight into how officers *produce* the social organization of their work lives. I conclude by discussing some of the implications of treating the officers' accounts as rhetoric.

First, rhetorical analysis does not involve assessing the truthfulness or accuracy of persons' accounts. Rather, it focuses on the practicalities of account-making; it considers how persons produce accounts to solve practical problems. Such problems include explaining why actions which might be seen as improper are "really" proper, as well as efforts to preserve a preferred image of self while acknowledging that one's actions might be taken as evidence of dispreferred motives. Equally important, rhetorical analysis of the officers' accounts highlights the multiperspectival nature of social relations in the prison. The officers' accounts are expressions and justifications of their orientations to aspects of the prison social world. We should expect that they will differ from prison administrators' and inmates' accounts of prison life.

The difference is not a matter of the truthfulness or accuracy of the officers' and others' accounts; rather it is a matter of orientation. We should expect diverse orientations to everyday prison life and partisan positions on correctional officers' work practices from officers, administrators, and inmates. Members of these groups bring different concerns and interests to their prison experiences, including their experiences with one another. Thus, the accounts of none of the groups are "better" than the accounts of the others, although they involve different reality claims and are used to pursue different practical interests.

A second and related implication of treating the officers' accounts as rhetoric involves the larger social and political context of prison life and relationships. To the extent that they are organized as conflicts of orientation and interest, we would anticipate that correctional officers', inmates', and prison administrators' accounts will involve differing, even opposed, reality claims. Indeed, the data reported here show that correctional officers also differ in their orientations to everyday life in the prison and their professional responsibilities. Although I have emphasized the ways in which the officers justified their accommodative orientation to inmate relationships, all of the correctional officers were not so oriented.

Some officers portrayed their jobs as involving the strict enforcement of prison rules. They justified the orientation by portraying selective rule enforcement as having long-term detrimental consequences for officer-inmate relations and the offices' authority. According to the strict officers, the most serious and detrimental consequence of the accommodative officer-inmate relationship was the encouragement of snitching among inmates. They stated that, although snitches served the short-term interest of correctional officers in maintaining control over the housing units, they created an atmosphere of distrust and increased inmates' sense of uncertainty in their dealings with officers and other inmates. Other officers countered this claim and justified their encouragement of snitching among inmates by stating that it was a necessary part of maintaining control over inmates and had no serious, detrimental consequences for prison life.

Thus, a third implication of analyzing the correctional officers' accounts as rhetoric is that it points to the variety of ways in which members of the same occupational and organizational group may orient to aspects of their work. But rhetoric and account-making are more than simple reflections of persons' orientations to practical issues; they are also interactional procedures for formulating orientations and perspectives. For example, the officers' responses to my interview questions were more than reports on their thoughts and feelings about their work. The questions were occasions for the officers to produce and justify a perspective on their work which they portrayed as based on enduring thoughts and feelings. Further, because the practical circumstances of correctional officers' account-making differ across situations, we should expect that their rhetoric will also vary situationally. For example, their positions on practical issues and justifications of them may differ when dealing with inmates, administrators, and

correctional officers assessed as friendly and supportive versus those assessed as antagonistic.

Future research on correctional officers' rhetoric and account-making, then, might consider how it varies across situations, including how officers' rhetoric changes as the issues and audiences for the officers' rhetoric change. However a rhetorical analysis is developed, this paper points to the usefulness of analyzing correctional officers' accounts of their work circumstances and practices as rhetoric. It displays the interactional and descriptive politics of prison organization and process, and underscores the practical, reality-constructing aspects of the "social problems work" (Miller and Holstein 1989) that constitutes much of the daily activity of prison correctional officers.

REFERENCES

Cullen, F., F. Lutze, B. and N. Wolfe. 1987. "The Correctional Orientation of Prison Guards." Paper presented at the annual meetings of the Academy of Criminal Justice Sciences, St. Louis.

Holstein, J. A. and G. Miller. 1990. "Rethinking Victimization: An Interactional Approach to Victimology." *Symbolic Interaction* 13(1): 101-120.

Jurik, N. 1985. "Individual and Organizational Determinants of correctional Officer Attitudes Toward Inmates." *Criminology* 23: 523-539.

Jurik, N. and R. Winn. 1987. "Describing Correctional-Security Dropouts and Rejects." *Criminal Justice and Behavior* 14: 5-25.

Kauffman, K. 1981. "Prison Officers' Attitudes and Perceptions of Attitudes." *Journal of Research in Crime and Delinquency* 18: 272-294.

Klofas, J. and H. Toch. 1982. "The Guard Subculture Myth." *Journal of Research in Crime and Delinquency* 19: 238-254.

Lipsky, M. 1980. *Street-Level Bureaucracy.* New York: Russell Sage.

Lomardo, L. X. 1981. *Guards Imprisoned.* New York: Elsevier.

Marquart, J. 1986. "Prison Guards and the Use of Physical Coercion as a Mechanism of Prisoner Control." *Criminology* 24: 347-366.

Miller, G. and J. A. Holstein. 1989. "On the Sociology of Social Problems." Pp. 1-16 in *Perspectives on Social Problems,* Vol. 1, edited by J. A. Holstein and G. Miller. Greenwich, CT: JAI Press.

Perelman, C. 1979. *The New Rhetoric and the Humanities.* Dordrectht, Holland: D. Reidel.

Scott, M. B. and S. M. Lyman. 1968. "Accounts." *American Sociological Review* 33: 46-62.

Sykes, G. M. and D. Matza. 1957. "Techniques of Neutralization." *American Sociological Review* 22:664-670.

Sykes, G. M. 1958. *The Society of Captives.* Princeton University Press.

Sykes, G. M. and S. Messinger. 1960. "The Inmate Social System." Pp. 5-19 in *Theoretical Studies in the Social Organization of the Prison,* edited by R. A. Cloward, D.R. Cressey, G.H. Grosser, R. McCleery, L.E. Ohlin, G.M. Sykes and S.L. Messinger. New York: Social Science Research Council.

First-time incarcerated offenders are labeled as prisoners but do not acquire a defining status by merely being part of the prison world. Because this study focused on short-term incarcerated inmates, these prisoners are probably not going to ever acquire a particular prison status. Immersion into the prison social system requires a longer period of incarceration. Short-term prisoners are inhibited in gaining a prison status due to their use of the outside world as a reference group, as compared to the values that characterize the inmate culture for long-term inmates. Schmid and Jones point out that this social situation causes short-term inmates to be socially marginal, which results in an ambivalent status that determines survival strategies within the prison world. This is due in part to their transitional status, which inhibits short-term prisoners from assimilating into the prison culture.

AMBIVALENT ACTIONS

Prison Adaptation Strategies of First-Time, Short-Term Inmates

THOMAS J. SCHMID

RICHARD S. JONES

"Doing time" in a maximum security prison is not simply a matter of being in prison. It is, rather, a creative process through which inmates must invent or learn a repertoire of adaptation tactics that address the varying problems they confront during particular phases of their prison careers.

There is an extensive literature on the informal organization of prison life and the socialization processes through which inmates come to participate in this informal organization. Clemmer (1958) defines prisonization as "the taking on in greater or lesser degree of the folkways, customs, and general culture of the penitentiary"

Reprinted from the *Journal of Contemporary Ethnography*, Vol. 21, January 1993, 439–463. Copyright © Sage Publications, Inc.

Authors' Note: We wish to thank Jim Thomas, Peter and Patricia Adler, and Charles Faupel for their helpful comments on earlier drafts of this article.

(p. 279). Prisonization is thus fundamentally a process of cultural accommodation through which inmates are first initiated into and then made a part of the prison social and cultural system. Neither of the two theoretical models developed to account for inmate adaptations to imprisonment—the "deprivation model" (Goffman 1961; Sykes [1959] 1971; Sykes and Messinger 1960) or the "importation model" (Thomas 1973; Thomas and Peterson 1977)—adequately represent the multiple ambiguities faced by the sociologically distinctive category of inmates who have no prior experience with the prison world and whose imprisonment is relatively brief.[1]

When first-time inmates are sentenced to prison they have already lost their status as free adults but have not yet achieved any meaningful status within the prison world; they are, to older inmates, "fish" (see Cardozo-Freeman 1984; Irwin 1980). They can shed this label through their increasing participation in prison life, but if they are short-term inmates as well as first-timers they are unlikely to ever achieve a significant prison status. Their participation in the prison world will continue to be inhibited by their ties to, and identification with, the outside world. Their social marginality, grounded both in place and in time, is thus parallel to that experienced by immigrants who expect to return to their country of origin within a few years' time (see Morawska 1987; Shokeid 1988) or who otherwise manage to maintain a "sojourner orientation" (Gibson 1988). Immigrant sojourners, however, can typically draw on shared symbols or institutions in their transient adaptations to a new culture. New inmates, in contrast, have little in common with one another except their conventionality (Schmid and Jones 1991) and consequently have fewer collective resources available to resist assimilation into the prison culture.

In this article, we examine how first-time, short-term inmates in a maximum security prison make use of their social marginality, and the sociological ambivalence that results from it, to forge highly delimited adaptation strategies to the prison culture. After describing our methodological approach and fieldwork experiences, we briefly summarize our earlier analysis, which demonstrated that the social marginality of the first-time, short-term inmates we studied shaped their experiential orientations toward the prison world. We then analyze the relationship between ambivalence and inmates' prison strategies and discuss the extended sociological implications of our findings.

METHOD

Ordinarily, one of the most difficult steps in sociological research on prisons is gaining unrestricted access to inmates' day-to-day lives within the prison world. Our study originated with such access, when one of the authors (R. Jones) was serving a year-and-a-day sentence in a maximum security prison for men in the upper midwestern region of the United States. Through negotiations with prison officials, Jones was permitted to enroll in a graduate sociology course in field methods. What began as a directed studies course between professor and former student rapidly evolved, at Jones's suggestion, into a more comprehensive project conducted by co-researchers. At the same time, it evolved from a general observational study of prison life to an analysis of the prison experiences of first-time, short-term inmates.

Jones's prison sentence, our decision to conduct the study together, and our focus on first-time, short-term inmates offered us an unusual strategy for balancing the participant observer's needs for both objective and intimate knowledge about the group or culture being studied (see Davis 1973). This balance can be particularly difficult to achieve in prison research, where suspicions about academic roles often lead researchers to cultivate alternative roles that are more acceptable or better defined (Giallombardo 1966; Jacobs 1977). The circumstances of our study enabled us to examine the prison world for a period of 10 months from the combined viewpoints of both a "complete participant" and a "complete observer" (Gold 1958).

As the "inside observer," Jones had a number of specific advantages. In his interactions with other inmates and with guards, he was not viewed as a sociologist or a student or any other kind of outsider: He was viewed as a prisoner. Moreover, he was not merely assuming the role of a prisoner to learn about the prison world—he *was* a prisoner. He literally shared the experiences of other first-time, short-term inmates, enabling him to contextualize his observations of others with a full measure of sociological introspection (Ellis 1991). Because of his prior training, which included an undergraduate degree in sociology, a university course in participant observation, and a supervised field research project, he was also prepared to document his own experiences and those of his fellow inmates.

Any researcher role closes as well as opens lines of information, and Jones's role had certain limitations as well. As a new inmate, he did not have immediate access to the entire prison world, a limitation that directly influenced our decision to focus on the experiences of first-time inmates. He was also constrained by prison interaction norms, especially those governing relations between members of different racial or ethnic groups. At the prison we studied, these norms were not entirely rigid, but they were sufficiently strong to suggest that Jones's initial observations primarily depicted the experiences of White inmates. (We were able to compensate for this racial selectivity to some extent through a second phase of our fieldwork.) Finally, the most critical question about any "auto-ethnography" (Hayano 1979, 1982) is whether researchers will be able to examine their own social world objectively. Jones expressed concerns about his objectivity early in the directed studies course; it was in response to this problem that we agreed to conduct the research together.

As the "outside" observer for the project, Schmid attempted to guide the direction of the fieldwork by placing Jones's observations in a sociological context—suggesting theoretical concepts that could be useful, additional questions that might be asked, methods that could be used to address these questions, and procedures through which we could test the validity of Jones's initial observations. Schmid also supplemented Jones's field notes with his own observations at the prison, and took a primary role in data analysis.

Our fieldwork essentially began with a journal that Jones started keeping several days before the beginning of his sentence. His early entries were predominantly personal expressions, although they included more traditional ethnographic descriptions as well. Once our research project was formally initiated, Jones restricted his journal entries to personal thoughts and impressions and chronology of his daily experiences. Using a process similar to the "diary-interview" method described by Zimmerman and Wieder (1977), these entries provided a framework for extended conversations between the researchers. Schmid's notes on these conversations were then used to derive new observational strategies and to identify potential analytic themes.

In addition to journal entries, Jones also prepared field notes on his participation in prison activities, his conversations with individual prisoners and groups of inmates, and his general observations of prison life. This procedure meant that the journal and the field notes contained different kinds of information, and it had the additional advantage of keeping the field notes more objective than they otherwise might have been. Although these general observations incorporated the experiences of hundreds of prisoners, most of the field notes were based on his repeated, often daily, contacts with about 50 inmates as well as on personal relationships established with a smaller number of inmates.

We were able to discuss our research progress through letters, occasional telephone calls, and regular meetings arranged with the cooperation of prison officials. Shortly after the beginning of the study, we settled on a communication routine that proved to be quite efficient. Jones prepared one to three field observations each week (averaging 8-10 handwritten pages) and mailed them to Schmid for annotation and suggestions. Every other week Schmid would meet with Jones in an office or testing room provided by the prison's education department. At these meetings, we would review the journal entries and observations, plan our research strategy, and piece together our emerging conceptualization of the prison world.

Following Jones's release from prison, we devoted a year to the analysis of our initial data, and then returned to the prison to conduct focused interviews. Using information provided by prison officials, we were able to identify and interview 20 additional first-time, short-term inmates.[2] The fieldwork we had

Table 1   Orientation and Prison Imagery

	Preprison	*Prison*	*Postprison*
Inmate perspective	Outside looking in	Inside looking in	Inside looking out
Central concerns	Violence/uncertainty	Boredom	Uncertainty
Specific problems	Survival	Endurance	Re-integration
Orientation to space	Prison as separate world	Prison as familiar territory	Prison as separate world
Orientation to time	Sentence as lost time	Killing time/time as measure of success	Sentence as lost time/using time
Supportive others	Family and friends	Partners	"Real" family and friends
Perception of sentence	Justified and unfortunate	Arbitrary and unjust	Arbitrary and unjust (intensified)
Predominant emotion	Fear	Detachment	Apprehension (about outside)

already completed guided our preparation of the interview questions, which addressed inmates' changing prison imagery and adaptation tactics as they progressed through their prison careers. We decided that Jones should do the actual interviewing, on the assumption that inmates would be more willing to talk freely with someone who had only recently completed his own prison sentence. To retain the methodological advantages of having both an "inside" and "outside" observer, Schmid reviewed a tape recording of each interview so that we could continuously refine the interviewing procedures.

Our analysis of the prison experiences of first-time, short-term inmates thus draws on three primary sources of data. Our principal source is the field notes, representing 10 months of participant observation by a "complete participant" in collaboration with a "complete observer." Included in these notes are specific events and interactions, quotations from Jones's fellow inmates, and general observations of the prison world. A second source is Jones's prison journals in which he recorded his own prison experiences. We used these journals throughout our project as a form of research development, and we draw on them to illustrate portions of our analytic model. Our subsequent interviews with other inmates constitute our third source of data; these interviews allowed us to pursue a number of topics in greater depth and provided us with an independent source of data to test our initial findings.

MARGINALITY, PRISON IMAGERY, AND PRISON ADAPTATIONS

Our earlier analysis of experiential orientations to prison (Schmid and Jones 1990) demonstrated that, at the beginning of their sentences, first-time, short-term inmates defined prison from the perspective of an outsider, drawing on the shared public meanings that exist in our society about prison. By the midpoint of their sentences they had not lost their outsiders' perspective completely and still had only a marginal status within the prison world, but they nonetheless defined prison principally in terms of shared subcultural meanings learned from other inmates. This "insider's perspective," however, subsequently gave way to concluding images that again expressed an outsider's point of view. (More precisely, their concluding imagery was a reflection of their marginal involvement in both worlds; it was a synthesis of their anticipatory and midcareer images and hence a synthesis of their outsider's and insider's perspectives). These changes in prison imagery are summarized in Table 1.

Inmates' subjective understandings of the prison world are important because they provide a basis for action (Blumer 1969). Our earlier analysis also demonstrated, in a general way, how inmates' adaptation strategies followed their shifting prison imagery (as summarized in Figure 1). For example, in response to the violence of their initial outsider's imagery, their earliest survival tactics were protective

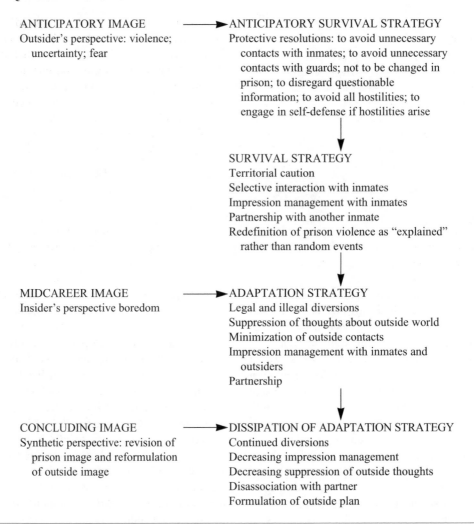

Figure 1   Prison Images and Strategies

and defensive in nature. As cultural outsiders, however, new inmates also recognized their need for more information about the prison world, and virtually all of their early survival tactics served as information seeking as well as protective measures. Thus territorial caution, impression management, and their partnerships (a friendship with another prisoner recognized by other inmates and guards) guided their ventures into the cafeteria, the yard, the gym, and other unexplored areas of the prison.[3] Selective interaction with other inmates, impression management, and their partnerships helped them confront such prison experiences as parole board hearings, cell transfers, legal and illegal recreational activities, and participation

in the prison economy. The barrage of often conflicting information they received through these tactics was the raw material out of which they continuously revised their prison images.[4] Although they continued to view prison with essentially an outsider's perspective, their survival tactics allowed them gradually to acquire an insider's knowledge of the prison and to modify their adaptation tactics accordingly.[5]

A common form of prison adaptation is the creation of a survival "niche" (Seymour 1977) that allows inmates some measure of activity, privacy, safety, emotional feedback, structure, and freedom within the larger, hostile environment of the maximum security prison (Johnson 1987; Toch 1977). Because of their inexperience, first-time inmates were particularly ill-equipped for finding such niches (Johnson 1987, 114), and new short-term inmates were further handicapped by their continuing marginality in the prison world, which restricted their ability to exert personal control (Goodstein, MacKenzie, and Shotland 1984) and inhibited their acceptance by other inmates. But short-term inmates, in contrast to those facing years of imprisonment, needed only to develop a *transient* niche in prison. The problems they faced were similar— understanding the prison status hierarchy and recognizing their place in it, learning whom to trust and whom to avoid, and determining how to evade trouble in a trouble-filled environment— but their solutions did not need to be as enduring. The men we studied were able to achieve such transient "accommodation without assimilation" (Gibson 1988) within a few months' time. To a casual observer, moreover, they soon became indistinguishable from long-term inmates, relying on such adaptive tactics as legal and illegal diversions and conscious efforts to control their thoughts about the outside world. Their relative integration into the prison world was short-lived, however, and their marginality within this world again became evident as they prepared for their departure from prison. Like more experienced inmates, their preparatory concerns included both practical problems, such as finding a job and a place to live, and existential concerns about how the outside world had changed and how the inmates themselves had changed during their time in prison (see Irwin 1970). Faced with these problems, it became increasingly apparent to inmates that most (though not all) of the adaptation tactics associated with their prison orientation were inadequate for dealing with the outside world.

Based on this general pattern, it is tempting to infer that inmates' adaptations strategies change simply because their reference group changes. In this explanation, suggested by Wheeler's (1961) finding of a curvilinear relationship between institutional career phase and conformity to staff expectations, inmates come to abandon the beliefs, values, and norms of the outside world as they acquire more information about and eventually achieve membership in the prison world. In similar fashion, they abandon the beliefs, values, and norms of

the prison world when they are about to regain membership in the outside world. Our earlier analysis (Schmid and Jones 1990) challenged this explanation by focusing on inmates' continuous and active work to *interpret* the prison world. This explanation becomes even more unsatisfactory when we introduce into our analysis the ambivalence that inmates experience throughout their entire prison careers.

AMBIVALENCE AND PRISON STRATEGIES

In its most general sense, ambivalence refers to the experience of being pulled in psychologically different directions; because prison inmates *share* this experience, it becomes sociologically as well as psychologically significant. The ambivalence of first-time, short-term inmates flows directly from their transitional status between the outside social world and the prison's: It is an ambivalence grounded in the marginality of "people who have lived in two or more societies and so have become oriented to differing sets of cultural values . . . [or] of people who accept certain values held by groups of which they are not members" (Merton and Barber 1976, 11-12). Although inmates' ambivalence affects their prison imagery and strategies in various ways, its principal effect is to limit behavioral changes by inhibiting new inmates from becoming fully assimilated into prison culture.

Feelings of ambivalence characterized the thoughts, emotions, and, sometimes, the actions of the inmates throughout their entire prison careers. Their adaptations to prison expressed both the outsider's perspective they preferred and the insider's perspective they provisionally accepted. Because their strategies were guided by their imagery, their outsider's perspective was most apparent in their behavior at the beginning of their sentences, whereas their insider's perspective was most apparent during the middle part of their sentences. Their behavior during the final months of their sentences was a mixture of nonprison forms of interaction and prison adaptive tactics because their concluding imagery was a synthesis of outsider's and insider's perspectives. Yet a closer inspection of inmates' evolving strategies reveals that

Table 2   Experiences of Ambivalence During Prison Career

	Career Experiences	*Reported Ambivalence*
Preprison	Conviction and sentencing Detention in county jail Transportation to prison	Desire to postpone sentence versus desire to proceed with sentenced
Early months of sentence	Holding cell In processing First night in cell Orientation classes (first week) Initial correspondence and visits with outsiders Transfer to another cell Assignment to caseworker First contacts with general inmate population Job or program assignment Cellblock transfer	Desire to insulate self versus desire for sociability Desire to proceed with new experiences versus relief at security of close supervision during first weeks of sentence Desire for greater mobility within prison versus fear of greater contact with inmates
Middle portion of sentence	Work/program participation Legal and illegal diversions Correspondence and visits with outsiders	Desire to discontinue outside contracts and "do your own time" versus desire to maintain outside contacts
Conclusion of sentence	Application for transfer to minimum security Transfer to minimum security Outside passes Home furloughs Transfer to reentry program Release from prison	Desire for greater freedom versus willingness to complete sentence in maximum security Desire to put prison in past and return to free world versus desire to avoid existential concerns about return to free world

the simultaneous influence of the outside and inside worlds was not restricted to the end of their sentences. At every stage of their prison careers, their actions were influenced by the underlying ambivalence that resulted from their marginal position in both the outside and prison social worlds. Table 2 presents the various manifestations of this ambivalence that occurred throughout the prison career.

Preprison and Early Career Experiences

Inmates' ambivalence began before they arrived at prison. Like most outsiders, they viewed prison as a world quite different from their own and had difficulty picturing themselves within that world. In the final days of their freedom, they were faced with conflicting desires: They wanted desperately to avoid their sentences—to escape or be forgotten about—but

they also wanted their sentences to proceed because they knew this was inevitable. They retained an outsider's perspective but knew that they were no longer full members of the outside world.

Their ambivalent feelings continued throughout their sentences, although the form and emphasis of their ambivalence changed as they progressed through their prison careers. But even in their earliest days in prison, the dominant form of their ambivalence emerged: Their desire to insulate themselves from the surrounding prison world was countered by their desire for human sociability (see Glaser 1969, 18-21). Throughout their careers, but especially during the first half of their sentences, both sides of this fundamental conflict between an outsider's detachment and an insider's participation in the prison world influenced their behavior. Of importance here is that inmates began to *act*, albeit cautiously, on their desire for contact with others during the first week of their sentences. Their initial contacts with others were quite limited, and they did not appreciably alter their images or strategies, but these contacts did indicate that their isolation did not need to be as extreme as they had anticipated. A 23-year-old inmate, convicted of narcotics sales, described his earliest encounter with another inmate:

> There was one guy that they brought in with me, and we sort of talked off and on. He was sort of scared too, and it was his first time too. He was talking to a guard; I overheard him talking to a guard. I heard him say that he was just basically scared as hell. The guard was trying to calm him down. We were all together in a group; we eat at the same table and everything, and I got talking to him. So I had somebody to talk to. (Interview)

During their first week in prison, in which they were housed together with other incoming inmates but segregated from the general inmate population, they were able to express their desire for contact with others through limited interaction with both guards and inmates. They learned that not all guards fit their initial stereotypes, and many new inmates encountered one or more fellow inmates with backgrounds similar to their own. They were still intimidated by the prison, particularly by those aspects of prison life that they had not yet experienced, but they began to reduce their isolation and expand their knowledge of the prison world.

The first week thus enabled new inmates, through passive observations and direct interaction, to modify (but not radically transform) both their images and their strategies. Their segregation during this week also led to yet another variant of their ambivalence: They were relieved at the protection of close supervision, but because they knew that they could not avoid facing the general inmate population indefinitely they were anxious to move on to the next phase of their sentences. Similar feelings of ambivalence resurfaced with each new experience. When they learned that they would be transferred to a different cell, and later to another cellblock entirely, they looked forward to the greater mobility these moves offered, but

they feared the increased inmate contact the moves would necessitate:

> After only 2 days they moved me [to another cell]. . . . With this move came more freedom. . . . I could go out in the yard and to the dining hall for meals. I was a little apprehensive about getting out. I had made friends with one guy, so we went into the yard together. We were out for about an hour when we were approached by a black dude. He wanted to get us high. I'm sure that's not all he wanted. . . . It helps to find a friend or two; you feel safer in a crowd. (Field notes)

Their fear mirrored the violence of their prison imagery, whereas their desire to proceed reflected their acceptance that they were now prison inmates.

The evolution of inmates' prison perspectives continued and accelerated through the early months of their sentences. The survival strategies they formulated during these months, like their anticipatory survival strategies, were based on their images of prison. But increasingly their strategies led to modification of these images. This happened because their strategies continued to be influenced by the same motivational factors: (a) their concern for safety but also their recognition that their prison imagery was incomplete and (b) their ambivalence, especially their desire to proceed with new and inevitable prison experiences. The same tactics that gave them new information also reflected the opposing directions of their ambivalence. Their practice of territorial caution and their rudimentary impression management skills expressed their apprehension over contact with other prisoners and their desire for self-insulation, but these tactics also allowed them to initiate or accept limited interaction with others. Their selective interaction with other inmates and their partnership with one other inmate directly expressed their desire for sociability while providing them with a means of maintaining social and emotional distance from the majority of the inmate population.

Midcareer Experiences

Inmates' midcareer adaptation strategies, like their earlier survival strategies, were based on their prison imagery and their ambivalence.

Their adaptation strategies differed from their survival strategies because their images changed and because the form and emphasis of their ambivalence changed. Their survival strategies were intended to insulate them from the violence of their anticipatory images but also to allow them to confront new prison experiences and to provide them with new information about the prison world. By midcareer their imagery was dominated by the theme of boredom rather than violence, and they no longer saw a need for more information. But boredom was only one of the problems associated with "doing time" at midcareer: Their relationships with the outside world presented them with other difficulties. As they approached an insider's perspective on the prison world, they came to share the long-term inmate's belief that preoccupation with the outside world could make their sentences more difficult:

> I was talking with [a long-term inmate] and he was telling me that he doesn't usually hang around short-timers because they are so preoccupied with time. He said it took him a long time to get over counting the days, weeks, and months, and that he doesn't really like to be reminded about it. (Field notes: conversation with middle-aged inmate convicted of murder)

Intimate relationships were likely to be questioned and might even be curtailed (see Cordilia 1983). As expressed by a 37-year-old convicted thief,

> I think it would be almost impossible to carry on a relationship, a real close relationship, being here for 2 years or a year and a half. It's literally impossible. I think that the best thing to do is to just forget about it, and if the relationship can be picked up again once you get out, that's fine. And if it can't, you have to accept that. (Interview)

Similar concerns were raised regarding all outside contacts. A 26-year-old inmate, convicted of the possession and sale of marijuana, told us,

> When they [the inmate's visitors] left I felt depressed. . . . It's a high when they come, and you get depressed when they leave. I was wondering if that's good. Maybe I should just forget that there is an outside world—at times I thought that,

maybe as a survival mechanism to forget that there are good people in the world. (Interview)

Within a few months' time, inmates' adoption of an insider's perspective thus resulted in yet another manifestation of their ambivalence: Their desire to maintain their involvement in the outside world was countered by a temptation to discontinue all outside contacts so that they could do their own time without the infringement of a world to which they no longer actively belonged.

In a matter of months, then, inmates' perspectives underwent a substantial transformation: They were now viewing the outside world from the perspective of the prison world rather than the reverse, and their adaptation strategies, accordingly, were designed to help them cope with their insider's problems of "doing time" rather than their outsider's fears.[6] Their viewpoints were only an *approximation* of an insider's perspective, however, and their insider's tactics were equivocal because they never achieved more than a marginal status within the prison world. During the middle portion of their sentences they may have been tempted to sever all outside contacts to make their time pass more easily, but they did not actually follow through on this temptation. And although the relationships they established in prison, especially their partnerships, might have seemed more important than their outside relationships, they knew that they would not have freely chosen to associate with most of these people on the outside, and they knew that they would not continue most of these relationships once they were released from prison. In this respect, the prison relationships of the men we studied were more cautious than those typically formed by long-term inmates (Cordilia 1983, 13-29; Johnson 1987, 62-63): They acknowledged that they did not fully belong to the prison world in the same sense that long-term or multiple-term inmates do, and they recognized that these other inmates did not fully accept them as members of their world. First-time, short-term inmates, in other words, never completely relinquished their outsider's perspective, even in the middle stage of their prison careers when they were most alienated from the outside world.

Concluding Experiences

Inmates continuing ambivalence was a motivating factor in their decision to apply for a transfer to the minimum security unit in the concluding months of their sentences.[7] Their behavior, once again, embodied both directions of their ambivalence: Their outsider's perspective was apparent in the application itself, which indicated a desire for the greater privileges and outside contacts available in minimum security, whereas their insider's perspective was reflected in their emotional caution about their chances that the transfer would be approved:

> As much as I try to, it is very difficult to keep [minimum security] off my mind. I figure that if I don't think about it, it won't be as agonizing waiting for it to happen. It would be much easier if they would give a date to go, but they won't. (Journal)

If their applications were approved, their ambivalence also influenced their response to the transfer itself:

> I am looking at this transfer a little bit differently from my coming to prison and my transfer to "B" Hall. I don't want to expect too much from [minimum security] because then I won't be disappointed. Also, there is one big difference; if I don't like it out there I can always come back here. (Journal)

They were aware that their transfer marked the final phase of their prison sentences and a first step toward rejoining the outside world, but they were equally aware that they would still be in prison for some time and that they could be returned to maximum security at the whim of prison officials. Consequently, they were reluctant to admit—to themselves or others—that their transfers held great symbolic importance. They armed themselves with an insider's rationalization: If they didn't like minimum security, they could always come back. And if they should be sent back involuntarily, they were now confident of their capabilities to survive the remainder of their sentences in maximum security.

Once inmates were transferred to minimum security, they experienced yet another manifestation of their ambivalence, similar to that reported by long-term inmates after they have been placed in halfway houses (Cordilia 1983, 99-100): They wanted to put their prison experiences behind them and prepare for their return to the free world, but they also wanted to avoid the existential concerns raised by this preparation and to complete their sentences by "doing their own time," just as they did when they were in maximum security:

> Doing time is not as easy as it may sound; actually, it is a rather complicated business. For one thing, you must try to keep yourself busy even though there is very little for you to do. . . . You would like to plan for the future, but it seems so far away that it doesn't really seem like it is worth thinking about. Also, thinking about the future tends to make the time drag. You also don't want to think about the past, because eventually you get around to the dumb mistake that got you in here. So, I guess it must be best to think about the present but that is so boring . . . that it can lead to depression. You don't want to think too much about the outside because it makes you realize all that you are missing, which can be somewhat depressing. But then, you don't really want to just think about the prison, because there isn't anything more depressing at all. (Journal)

In the final months and weeks of their sentences they vacillated between directly confronting questions about their futures and avoiding these questions through their continuing tactics of thought control and diversionary activities.[8]

Each of the manifestations of ambivalence itemized in Table 2 reflects inmates' marginality because each involved a conflict between an outsider's and an insider's point of view. At various stages in their careers, inmates might place more emphasis on one or the other viewpoint but they never fully resolved their feelings of ambivalence. During the middle portion of their sentences, for example, they might believe that thoughts about the outside world made their sentences more difficult (an insider's belief) and hence might consciously suppress these thoughts (an insider's tactic), but they did not generally terminate outside contacts and would be severely disappointed if their visitors or letters had ceased to arrive. Thus, even when inmates placed greatest emphasis on an insider's viewpoint, their perspectives (that is, the interdependent relationship between their images and their strategies) expressed their marginality. Similarly, when they placed most emphasis on an outsider's viewpoint, namely, at the beginning and end of their sentences, closer inspection of their perspective again reveals their marginality. Our analysis thus suggests that inmates' changing imagery and strategies did not represent a total conversion to an insider's point of view and a subsequent reversion to a more conventional point of view, as suggested in Wheeler's (1961) cyclical model of prison socialization. Rather, the inmates we studied experienced a subtler transformation in which their movement toward either an insider's or an outsider's perspective was circumscribed by their ambivalence.

DISCUSSION

Using ambivalence in any explanatory scheme can place social scientists in a precarious position. Psychological ambivalence is such a universal condition, and one that can result from such myriad causes and situations, that its use in sociological analysis inevitably leads to charges of reductionism. Moreover, as Room's (1976) critique of this concept in the alcoholism literature has demonstrated, pervasive ambivalence resulting from ambiguous cultural norms is a seductively easy but not very useful causal explanation for deviant (and other forms of) behavior. And yet the very pervasiveness of ambivalence in social life also suggests that its interactional significance cannot be ignored.

The ambivalence experienced by the inmates we studied was derived from a very specific set of circumstances: involuntary but relatively brief confinement in a total institution that was both entirely unknown and absolutely feared. Similar, if less extreme, feelings of ambivalence can emerge whenever human beings become fully immersed in highly demanding but time-limited social worlds or social situations. For example, we would expect ambivalence to characterize the behavioral adaptations of new mental patients, military recruits, ethnographic researchers, or students entering college or graduate school. The nature and effects of ambivalence will obviously be influenced by a host of other considerations: how the individuals involved define and evaluate the social world in question, whether their participation is voluntary or involuntary, whether participants share a previous culture, the extent to which they desire to maintain that culture, and so on. Although acknowledging the importance of such situational variations, we nonetheless believe that our analysis of inmates' prison adaptations may help interpret the experiences of others whose ambivalence results from social marginality.

In his critique, Room (1976) specifically points to three connotations of the term "ambivalence" that result in theoretical difficulties: that it "draws attention away from the content of norms or values and places the emphasis on the fact of a conflict in values," that it implies a continuous state rather than an occasional condition, and that it suggests "an especially excited and explosive state, where irrational behavior is to be expected" (p. 1053). Although we are using ambivalence in a holistic rather than a causal model (Deising 1971), Room's comments are nonetheless helpful for our specification of how sociological ambivalence operates in the prison world.

First, for a new inmate the conflict of value systems was as important, or more important, than the content. The first-time inmates we studied were socially heterogeneous; one of the few characteristics they had in common was their belief that they were different from other inmates and hence did not "belong" in the prison world (Schmid and Jones 1991). To differing degrees they learned (but did not fully accept) the norms and values of the prison world. The prison strategies of new inmates had to acknowledge and deal with the content of prison norms and values, but it was the conflict between this value system and their outside values that resulted in their marginality.

The second connotation noted by Room (1976)—that ambivalence refers to a pervasive social condition—is a temporal one. But time itself was central to the marginality of the inmates we studied: They knew that they would be in prison for a year or two but they hoped (and later expected) to return to the outside world. Although ambivalence pervaded their entire prison careers, their role in prison, as defined by themselves and other inmates, was primarily determined by their status as short-timers. Their ambivalence was thus situational, imposed by the specific circumstances of their imprisonment.

It is the connotation of an excited, explosive state that makes ambivalence such an attractive variable in causal explanation. Yet this connotation, which derives from the use of ambivalence in the psychotherapeutic literature, is not inherent in the concept itself; citing *Hamlet*, Room (1976) notes that the term has traditionally suggested paralysis more than action (p. 1058). In our analysis, inmates' feelings of ambivalence served sometimes to motivate action (for example, to break through their initial isolation or later to apply for transfer to minimum security) and sometimes to inhibit action (not to break off ties to the outside world during the middle portion of their sentences despite a temptation to do so). At some career points, the inmates' ambivalence offered them no real choice in behavior (after orientation, inmates were transferred to another cellblock regardless of how they felt about it); at other points, they did face choices (decisions about continuing outside contacts). The principal effect of their ambivalence, however, was to circumscribe their behavior, keeping it somewhere between the more extreme perspectives of the prison outsider and the long-term inmate.

The traditional model of prison socialization suggests that inmates enter prison with conventional values, become socialized to the values of an inmate culture, and then subsequently become resocialized to the values of the outside world. Our research suggests an alternative model of the prison experiences of first-time, short-term inmates, in which their social marginality continuously shapes both their subjective understanding of the prison world and their adaptations to it. Specifically, we argue that the ambivalence that results from these inmates' transitional status limits the behavioral adaptations they make in prison and inhibits their assimilation into prison culture.

The importance of ambivalence in the prison experiences of the men we studied extended beyond its effect on their prison behavior: It also affected their identities. As we have shown elsewhere (Schmid and Jones 1991), these inmates drew a distinction between their "true" identities (i.e., their preprison identities) and the artificial "prison identities" they created and presented through impression management. This self-bifurcation was itself an expression of both directions of the inmates' ambivalence. Because their prison interactions were based almost exclusively on their shared prison role, conditions existed for a "role-person merger" (Turner 1978). Actual identity change was moderated, however, by the inmates' marginality within the prison world and their consequent ambivalence toward their temporary prison role. In this respect, ambivalence helped to shape not only inmates' adaptations to the prison world but their subsequent adaptations to the outside world. By extension, if the final measure of cultural assimilation is whether a new cultural identity emerges, understanding cultural ambivalence in specific, time-limited social worlds may have larger theoretical implications as well.

NOTES

1. Sociological research on the prison world relies heavily on information from those who actively participate in this world: inmates who have already served many years in prison. Although long-term prisoners are undoubtedly the best source of information on the inmate social structure, many become so acclimatized to prison life that they have lost their outsider's perspective. First-time inmates, on the other hand, approach their sentences with an understanding of the prison world essentially similar to that of other outsiders, so their experiences offer an ideal vantage point for examining the effects of sudden immersion into the prison world. By further restricting our study to inmates serving relatively brief sentences (by maximum security standards) of 2 years or less, we were able to look at prison through the eyes of men who had generally been convicted of less serious offenses (again, by maximum security standards) and who were in a position to retain a stronger orientation toward the outside world than are inmates who are facing sentences of 5, 10, or an indefinite number of years.

2. Although key prison officials had been aware of our fieldwork activities, the interviews were officially sanctioned on a more formal basis. We were therefore able to collect and validate detailed descriptive data on the interview sample. These inmates ranged in age from 22 to 57 years (mean = 31 years) and had served from 2 to 14 months of their sentences (mean = 7.2 months) at the time of the interviews.

They had been convicted of a variety of Index I crimes: theft (2), narcotics sales (4), fraud (1), burglary (3), aggravated robbery (4), sexual misconduct/assault (4), and terrorism/false imprisonment (2).

3. "Territorial caution" and "selective interaction" are essentially precautionary guidelines that allowed inmates to increase their understanding of the prison world while minimizing danger to themselves. A prison "partnership" is a special friendship bond between two inmates, typically based on common backgrounds and interests (including a shared uncertainty about prison life) and strengthened by the inmates' mutual exploration of a hostile prison world. Such partnerships provided new inmates with a means of interpreting and evaluating information about the prison world, an advocate with officials and other inmates, and the opportunity for interaction with relatively few impression management techniques, which for new inmates consist of all efforts, verbal and nonverbal, to present self-images judged to be appropriate for the prison world (see Goffman 1959; Schlenker 1980). The primary intended audience for new inmates' impression management was other inmates, not prison officials.

4. In keeping with their marginal position in the prison world, their interpretation of this information was partly individual and partly interactive. When alone in their cells they analyzed conflicting information through intermittent self-dialogues that began before their arrival at prison (Schmid and Jones 1991). Their partnerships provided them with an interactive means of interpreting information. Goffman (1961) has observed that "where persons are deprived of knowledge of what is likely to happen to them, and where they are uninformed about how to 'make out' in a situation where making out may mean psychological survival, information itself becomes a crucial good. . . . It is understandable, then, that buddies in all total institutions give mutual aid by 'wising' each other up" (p. 286). Although new prison inmates found information to be cheap, that is to say plentiful but conflicting, their partnerships served a similar "wising" function by allowing them to sort through and interpret this information. Whether alone or with their partners, inmates' refusal to accept fully any single piece of information was the guiding principle of their efforts to understand the prison world.

5. There was another essential process involved in inmates' approximation of an insider's perspective. For inmates to redefine prison as a monotonous world rather than a violent one, their uncertainty and fear about prison had to be reduced. This did in fact occur, though in an erratic manner that was punctuated regularly by such "dramatic events" as assaults, rapes, homicides, or suicides. Each dramatic event represented a setback in the declining uncertainty and fear made possible by inmates' survival tactics. Eventually, dramatic events themselves became subject to definitional change, as they became "explained" as consequences of prison norm violations (see Jones and Schmid 1989; Schmid and Jones 1990).

6. This change in emphasis in the inmates' ambivalence did not result simply from the passage of time, nor was it a simple acceptance of a belief system learned from other prisoners. Rather, it emerged from their interactions with members of both their prison and outside social networks. Beginning with their early, cautious interactions with selected other prisoners, and their gradual development of partnerships with one other inmate, new inmates gradually widened their circle of prison acquaintances. Their estrangement from their outside social network also took place through a gradual process in which inmates and their families and friends, while trying to support or reassure one another, recognized that they were living in separate worlds, mutually withheld certain types of information, and eventually found that their communication was becoming increasingly constrictive.

7. Virtually all of the inmates we studied were eligible for transfer to the minimum security unit. Those inmates who did not apply or were not accepted to the unit experienced similar feelings of ambivalence and were equally cognizant that their sentences were coming to a conclusion. Our data suggest that their careers differed from those of inmates who did transfer primarily in that they were able to postpone (for weeks or months) many of the problems associated with anticipating their return to the free world. To the extent that they confronted these problems while still in prison, of course, they had to do so without benefit of the transition provided by minimum security.

8. The prison careers of first-time, short-term inmates toward the end of their minimum security residence had thus come full circle: They again found themselves about to enter an unfamiliar world and they again found it necessary to construct an image of this world and a plan of action based on their imagery. Like their anticipatory prison images, their reconstructed outside images included their fears and expectations about what lay ahead. Also like their anticipatory images, their outside images (as well as their outside plans) were incomplete and somewhat abstract. Perhaps the most important parallel, however, was that inmates again looked forward to their futures with feelings of ambivalence. Obviously, the emphasis of their ambivalence was different. Their fears about returning to the outside world did not

compare with their earlier fears about entering the prison world. Nonetheless, these inmates' continuing ambivalence at the end of their prison careers was a matter of some consequence because of its implications for their reintegration into the outside world (see Schmid and Jones 1991).

REFERENCES

Blumer, H. 1969. *Symbolic interactionism: Perspective and method.* Englewood Cliffs, NJ: Prentice-Hall.

Cardozo-Freeman, I. 1984. *The joint: Language and culture in a maximum security prison.* Springfield, IL: Charles C Thomas.

Clemmer, D. 1958. *The prison community.* New York: Holt, Rinehart & Winston.

Cordilia, A. 1983. *The making of an inmate: Prison as a way of life.* Cambridge, MA: Schenkman.

Davis, F. 1973. The Martian and the convert: Ontological polarities in social research. *Urban Life* 2:333-43.

Deising, P. 1971. *Patterns of discovery in the social sciences.* Chicago: Aldine-Atherton.

Ellis, C. 1991. Sociological introspection and emotional experience. *Symbolic interaction* 14:23-50.

Giallombardo, R. 1966. *Society of women: A Study of a women's prison.* New York: Wiley.

Gibson, M. A. 1988. *Accommodation without assimilation: Sikh immigrants in an American high school.* Ithaca, NY: Cornell University Press.

Glaser, D. 1969. *The effectiveness of a prison and parole system.* New York: Bobbs-Merrill.

Gold, R. 1958. Roles in sociological field observations. *Social Forces* 36:217-23.

Goffman, E. 1959. *The presentation of self in everyday life.* Garden City, NY: Doubleday.

____. 1961. *Asylums: Essays on the social situation of mental patients and other inmates.* Garden City, NY: Doubleday.

Goodstein, L., D. L. MacKenzie, and R. L. Shotland. 1984. Personal control and inmate adjustment to prison. *Criminology* 22:343-69.

Hayano, D. 1979. Auto-ethnography: Paradigms, problems, and prospects. *Human Organization* 38:99-104.

____. 1982. *Poker faces: The life and work of professional card players.* Berkeley: University of California Press.

Irwin, J. 1970. *The felon.* Englewood Cliffs, NJ: Prentice-Hall.

____. 1980. *Prisons in turmoil.* Boston: Little, Brown.

Jacobs, J. 1977. *Stateville: The penitentiary in mass society.* Chicago: University of Chicago Press.

Johnson, R. 1987. *Hard Time: Understanding and reforming the prison.* Monterey, CA: Brooks/Cole.

Jones, R. S., and T. J. Schmid. 1989. Inmates' conceptions of prison sexual assault *Prison Journal* 69:53-61.

Merton, R. K., and E. Barber. 1976. Sociological ambivalence. In *Sociological ambivalence and other essays,* by R. K. Merton, 3-31. New York: Free Press.

Morawska, E. 1987. Sociological ambivalence: Peasant immigrant workers in America, 1880s-1930s. *Qualitative Sociology* 10:225-50.

Room, R. 1976. Ambivalence as a sociological explanation: The case of cultural explanations of alcohol problems. *American Sociological Review* 41:1047-65.

Schlenker, R. 1980. *Impression management: The self concept, social identity and interpersonal relations.* Belmont, CA: Wadsworth.

Schmid, T. J., and R. S. Jones. 1990. Experiential orientations to the prison experience: The case of first-time, short-term inmates. In *Perspectives on social problems,* edited by G. Miller and J. A. Holstein, vol. 2, 189-210. Greenwich, CT: JAI.

____. 1991. Suspended identity: Identity transformation in a maximum security prison. *Symbolic Interaction* 14:415-32.

Seymour, J. 1977. Niches in prison. In *Living in prison: The ecology of survival,* by H. Toch, 179-205. New York: Free Press.

Shokeid, M. 1988. *Children of circumstances: Israeli emigrants in New York.* Ithaca, NY: Cornell University Press.

Sykes, G. [1959] 1971. *The Society of captives: A study of a maximum security prison.* Reprint. Princeton, NJ: Princeton University Press.

Sykes, G., and S. Messinger, 1960. Inmate social system. In *Theoretical studies in social organization of the prison,* by R. A. Cloward, D. R. Cressey, G. H. Grosser, R. McCleery, L. E. Ohlin, G. M. Sykes, and S. L. Messinger, 5-19. New York: Social Science Research Council.

Thomas, C. C. 1973. Prisonization or resocialization? A study of external factors associated with the impact of imprisonment. *Journal of Research in Crime and Delinquency* 10:13-21.

Thomas, C. C., and D. M. Peterson. 1977. *Prison organization and inmate subcultures* Indianapolis: Bobbs-Merrill.

Toch, H. 1977. *Living in prison: The ecology of survival.* New York: Free Press.

Turner, R. H. 1978. The role and the person. *American Journal of Sociology* 84: 1-23.

Wheeler, S. 1961. Socialization in correctional communities. *American Sociological Review* 26: 697-712.

Zimmerman, D., and D. L. Wieder. 1977. The diary: Diary-interview method. *Urban Life* 5:479-98.

As exemplified in the following article, prison life has changed in recent years from what can be characterized as a once more homogeneous population to a more heterogeneous one. With the substantial increase of younger, more violent prisoners, as well as the growth of racial and ethnic minorities in the population, there has been a steady erosion of the importance of the preexisting inmate code that once governed prisoner behavior. Many of the changes in the inmate culture are a result of the impact prison gangs have had on the daily living environment of inmates. Many of the prison gangs' norms of behavior are due in large part to the importance and impact that street gang values have had on the prison culture. This has resulted in correctional institutions becoming more violent and dangerous than in the past.

CHANGES IN PRISON CULTURE

Prison Gangs and the Case of the "Pepsi Generation"*

GEOFFREY HUNT

STEPHANIE RIEGEL

TOMAS MORALES

DAN WALDORF

Since Clemmer (1958) published the *Prison Community* in 1940, sociologists and criminologists have sought to explain the culture of prisons. A key debate in this literature centers on the extent to which inmate culture is either a product of the prison environment or an extension of external subcultures. Those in the former camp, such as Sykes and

---

*The data for this paper were made possible by funding to the Home Boy Study from the National Institute of Drug Abuse (R01 - DA06487), administered by Mario de la Rosa, Ph.D. The authors are grateful to the anonymous *Social Problems* reviewers of this paper.

Messinger (1977), Cloward (1977), and Goffman (1961), have argued that the inmate social system is formed "as a reaction to various 'pains of imprisonment' and deprivation inmates suffer in captivity" (Leger and Stratton 1977:93). These writers saw the prison as a total institution in which the individual, through a series of "status degradation ceremonies," gradually became socialized into prison life. Analysts such as Irwin and Cressey (1977) challenged this view of prison life, arguing that it tended to underestimate the importance of the culture that convicts brought with them from the outside. They identified two dominant subcultures within the prison—that of the thief and the convict—both of which had their origins in the outside world.

Our interview material did not clearly support one or the other of these opposing views and instead suggested that other dynamics of prison life were key to understanding inmates' experiences. Salient in inmate interviews was a greater degree of turmoil than was common to prison life in the past. The reasons for this turmoil were complex and included newly formed gangs, changes in prison population demographics, and new developments in prison policy, especially in relation to gangs. All these elements coalesced to create an increasingly unpredictable world in which prior loyalties, allegiances, and friendships were disrupted. Even some of the experienced prisoners from the "old school" were at a loss as to how to negotiate this new situation. Existing theories were not helpful in explaining our findings for the current dynamics could not be attributed solely to forces emanating from inside the prison or outside it.

THE SAMPLE

The sample was designed to include offenders who had been released from prison. Respondents lived in the Oakland and San Francisco area and, during 1991 and 1992, were located through contacts with ex-convict organizations, education programs, and respondents in a street gang study. Using a snowball sampling technique (Biernacki and Waldorf 1981), we eventually contacted 39 men, of whom 46 percent

(18) identified themselves as gang members, and 38 percent (6) said they were members of street gangs prior to entering prison. The ethnic backgrounds of respondents were as follows: 16 Chicanos, 14 African-Americans, 5 whites, 2 Native Americans, 1 French Creole, and 1 Chilean. The youngest was 19 and the oldest 60.

The vast majority of respondents had long criminal histories and had served several prison sentences in many different California state prisons. However, within the interviews we concentrated on obtaining information about their last major prison term, which we stipulated had to have lasted for at least one year. Thirty-eight percent (15) of our sample had been convicted for drug related offenses, including selling, distribution, and possession. Robberies (21 percent) were the second major category, followed by burglaries (16 percent), and embezzlement (6 percent). Respondents were sent to a wide range of California prisons including Avenol, Solano, San Quentin, Tracy, Susanville, Folsom, Soledad, Corcoran, Vacaville, and Pelican Bay, and while there, they served a median of 19 months. We used a structured but open-ended interview schedule and in addition to asking questions about ethnicity, age, arrest history, and the different prisons where they served time, the bulk of our interviews concentrated on knowledge of prison gangs and their perceptions of changes in prison life.

Because the sample was relatively small, results can not be considered definitive. Nevertheless, they provide insight not only into contemporary prison life but also into the role of gangs. The available literature on gangs, with a few notable exceptions (see Moore 1978; Jacobs 1974, 1977), takes a correctional and institutional perspective and consequently has made little or no attempt to examine the prisoners' point of view.

THE ESTABLISHED CALIFORNIA PRISON GANGS

According to various accounts (Camp and Camp 1985; Davidson 1974; Irwin 1980; Moore 1978; Porter 1982), the first California prison gang was the Mexican Mafia—a Chicano gang, believed to have originated in 1957 in the Dueul Vocational Institution prison. This Chicano group began to intimidate other Chicanos from the northern part of the state. The non-aligned, predominantly rural Chicanos organized themselves together for protection. They initially called themselves "Blooming Flower," but soon changed their name to La Nuestra Familia. Like the Mexican Mafia, La Nuestra Familia adopted a military style structure, with a general, captains, lieutenants, and soldiers. However, unlike the Mexican Mafia, La Nuestra Familia had a written constitution consisting of rules of discipline and conduct.

The Texas Syndicate, a third Chicano gang, followed the model of the Mexican Mafia and La Nuestra Familia and utilized a paramilitary system with a president at its head. Its members are mainly Mexican-American inmates, originally from Texas, who see themselves in opposition to the other Chicano groups, especially those from Los Angeles, who they perceive as being soft and too "Americanized."

Both black and white prisoners are also organized. The general view on the origins of the Black Guerilla Family (B.G.F.)—the leading black gang—is that it developed as a splinter group of the Black Family, an organization reportedly created by George Jackson. The authorities were particularly wary of this group, both because of its revolutionary language and reports that its members, unlike those of other gangs, regularly assaulted prison guards.

The Aryan Brotherhood—the only white gang identified in California prisons—originated in the late 1960s. It is said to be governed by a 3-man commission and a 9-man council who recruit from white supremacist and outlawed motorcycle groups. According to prison authorities, it is a "Nazi-oriented gang, anti-black [which] adheres to violence to gain prestige and compliance to their creed" (Camp and Camp 1985:105).[1]

The available sociological literature on older prison gangs is divided on the issue of their relationship to street gangs. On the one hand, Moore in discussing Chicano gangs argues that they were started by "state-raised youths and 'psychos'" (1978:114) inside the prisons, while Jacobson sees them as an extension of street gangs. Although Moore sees the

gangs as initially prison inspired, she describes a strong symbiotic relationship between the street and the prison. In fact, she notes that once the gangs were established inside the prisons, they attempted to influence the street scene. "The Mafia attempted to use its prison-based organization to move into the narcotics market in East Los Angeles, and also, reputedly, into some legitimate pinto-serving community agencies" (1978:115).

INSTITUTIONAL ATTEMPTS TO CONTROL THE GANGS

Prison authorities see gangs as highly undesirable and have argued that an increase in extortion, intimidation, violence, and drug trafficking can be directly attributed to their rise. In responding to prison gangs, the California Department of Corrections (CDC) introduced a number of strategies and policies, for example, using "confidential informants," segregating gang members in different buildings and prisons, intercepting gang communications, setting up task forces to monitor and track gang members, locking up gang leaders in high security prisons, and "locking down" entire institutions. These changes were perceived by our respondents who saw the CDC as increasingly tightening its control over the prison system and the gangs.

Prison Guards

In spite of the "official" view that gangs should be eradicated, many prison authorities hold a more pragmatic view and feel that the gangs have "had little negative impact on the regular running of prison operations" (Camp and Camp 1985:xii). Moreover, as Cummins (1991) has noted, there is often a considerable discrepancy between the official stance and what takes place within particular prisons. This point was emphasized by our respondents who portrayed guards' attitudes toward the gangs as complex and devious, and saw the guards as often accepting prison gangs and in some cases even encouraging them. In supporting this view, they gave three reasons why guards would allow gangs to develop or continue.

First, some noted guards' financial incentive to encourage gang behavior. They suggested that guards are keen to create "threats to security" which necessitate increased surveillance and, consequently, lead to overtime work.

> They have a financial interest in getting overtime. . . . Anything that was "security" meant that there were no restrictions in the budget. So if there are gangs, and there are associations, if there is some threat in that focus of security, they make more money (Case 17).

Others went even further and told us that some guards benefited from gangs' illegal activities.

> Well, you know the guards, aren't . . . you'd be surprised who the guard affiliated with. Guards have friends that's in there. They have their friends outside, you know. Guards 'll bring drugs in. Sell 'em. Guards will bring knives in, weapons, food. The guards play a major role (Case 7).

Not only were guards involved in illegal activities, but the practice was often overlooked by other guards. For example, as one respondent philosophically replied in answer to our question: "Were individual guards involved in illegal gang activities?"

> Well, I think you have guards that are human beings that . . . don't really want to do more than they have to. So if they see a guard doing something a little shady, it's easy to turn a blind eye because of the hassle it would take to pursue it (Case 16).

Finally, in addition to these financial incentives, some believed that guards encouraged gang activities and conflict in order to control the prison inmates more effectively and "keep the peace out of prisons" (Case 32).

> They perpetuated the friction because, for instance, what they would do is . . . give false information to different groups. . . . Something to put the fear so that then the Latino would prepare himself for a conflict. . . . And so everybody's on point and the next thing you know a fight would break out and the shit would come down. So it was to their interest to perpetuate division amongst the inmates so that they would be able to better control the institution. Because if you are spending your time fighting each other you have no time . . . to fight the establishment (Case 34).

This divide and rule policy was emphasized by many of our respondents and was seen as a major contributory factor in prisoner conflicts.

Jacketing and the Use of Confidential Informants

According to our respondents, another prison administration tactic was "jacketing"—officially noting in a prisoner's file that he was a suspected gang member. Once identified as a gang member, a prisoner could be transferred to a high security prison or placed in a special housing unit. "Jacketing," which is similar to the "dirty jacket" procedure outlined by Davidson (1974), was seen by our respondents as a particularly arbitrary process and one in which the prisoner had little or no recourse.

> Like I said, if you're a sympathizer you could be easily jacketed as a gang member. You hang around with 'em. You might not do nothing. But hang out with 'em. Drive iron with 'em. Go to lunch with 'em (Case 1).

Many respondents felt the process was particularly unfair because it meant that a prisoner could be identified as gang member and "jacketed" purely on the basis of information from a confidential informant. Confidential informants or "snitches" supplied intelligence information to prison authorities about inmate activities, especially gang-related activities.

> Now let's say you and I are both inmates at San Quentin. And your cellie gets in a fight and gets stabbed. So all of a sudden, the Chicano who is a friend of your cellie says that he'll get the boys and deal with this. They talk about it but nothing happens. All of a sudden one of the snitches or rats, says I think something is cooking, and people are going to make a move to the administration. What will happen is that they [the administration] will gaffel up you and me and whoever else you associate with and put us all on a bus straight to Pelican Bay. They will say we have confidential reliable information that you guys are planning an assault on Billy Bob or his gang. . . . And you're wondering, you've never received a disciplinary

infraction. But by God now, information is in your central file that you are gang affiliated, that you're involved in gang violence (Case 16).

Our respondents distinguished between two types of snitching—dry and hard.

Dry snitching is a guy who will have a conversation with a guard and the guard is just smart enough. He'll say you talk to Joe, don't ya? You say, oh, yeah, Joe's a pretty good ol' boy, I heard he's doing drugs but don't believe it. He might smoke a few joints on the yard, but nothing hard. He just dry snitched. He indirectly dropped a lug on Joe. And then you got the guy who gets himself in a jam and goes out and points out other inmates (Case 16).

Dry snitching could also refer to a prisoner supplying general information to guards without implicating anyone by name. This allowed the prisoner to develop a "juice card" or a form of credit with the guard.

A "juice card" is that you have juice [credit] with a particular guard, a lieutenant, a sergeant or somebody that is part of staff. . . . Let's say that somebody is dry snitching. By dry snitching I mean that they might come up to their juice man that has a "juice card," let's just say it is a sergeant of the yard, and they might go up there and say, "Hey I hear that there is a rumble coming down. I can't tell you more than that but some shit is going to come down tonight." So they alert the sergeant right. The sergeant tells him, "I owe you one." Now the guy might come up to the sergeant and say, "Hey remember you owe me one, hey I got this 115 [infraction] squash it." "Okay I will squash it." That is the "juice card" (Case 34).

Many of our respondents felt there was a growing number of snitches (also see Stojkovic 1986). A key factor promoting this growth was the pressure exerted by the guards—a point denied by the prison authorities in Stojkovic's research.

Pressure could be applied in a number of ways. First, if for example a prisoner was in a high security unit, he often found himself unable to get out unless he "debriefed"; i.e., provided information on other gang members. Many respondents felt that this was an impossible situation because if they didn't snitch their chances of getting out were minimal. As one respondent remarked:

They [the guards] wanted some information on other people. . . . So I was put between a rock and a hard place. So I decided I would rather do extra time, than ending up saying something I would later regret (Case 10).

Second, if the guards knew that a prisoner was an ex-gang member, they might threaten to send him to a particular prison, where he would be attacked by his own ex-gang.

See there is a lot of guys in there that are drop outs from whatever gang they were in, and they are afraid to be sent to a joint where some other tip might be. They even get threatened by staff that if they don't cooperate with them they will be sent to either Tracy, or Soledad and they are liable to get hit by their own ex-gang, so they cooperate (Case 40).

However, it would be inaccurate to suggest respondents accused only the prison authorities, since many also pointed out other developments within the prison system, and especially within the prison population, to explain what they described as deteriorating situation.

PRISON CROWDING, THE NEW GANGS, AND THE "PEPSI GENERATION"

Since 1980, the California prison population has increased dramatically from 24,569 to 97,309 (California Department of Corrections 1991). The net effect of this expansion has been severe overcrowding in the prisons. In 1970, prison institutions and camps were slightly underutilized and the occupancy rate stood at 98 percent. By 1980, they were full, and in 1990, the rate had risen dramatically to 180 percent of capacity. Currently, the inmate population stands at 91,892, while bed capacity is only 51,013. In order to cope with this overcrowding, institutions have been obliged to use all available space, including gymnasiums and dayrooms.

Many respondents graphically described the problems created by this situation and complained about the deterioration in prison services.

However, in talking about prison overcrowding, they tended to concentrate more on the changes in the characteristics of the inmates currently arriving. Specifically, they focused on the growth of new gangs, the immaturity of new inmates, and the problems they caused within the prison. Respondents felt this change in prison population characteristics had a major effect on day-to-day activities, and contributed to the fragmentary nature of prison life.

The New Gangs

According to our respondents, although all five of the older gangs still exist, their importance has diminished. The reasons for this appear to be twofold. First, many of the older gang members have either dropped out, gone undercover, or have been segregated from the rest of the prison population. Second, a new crop of gangs has taken center stage. In other words, prison authorities' efforts to contain the spread of gangs led, unintentionally, to a vacuum within the prison population within which new prison groupings developed.

Information on these new gangs is relatively limited in comparison with information on the older gangs. Thus it is difficult to be precise about their structure and composition. Moreover, a further complication is whether or not these groups fit current definitions of what constitutes a gang. For instance, if we adapt Klein and Maxson's (1989) definition of a street gang—community recognition as a group or collectivity, recognition by the group itself as a distinct group, and activities which consistently result in negative responses from law enforcement—then these new groupings constitute gangs if the prison is considered the community. However, if we compare them with the Mexican Mafia, La Nuestra Familia, or the Black Guerilla Family, which have developed hierarchies or clearly articulated constitutions, they constitute instead territorial alliances which demand loyalties and provide security and protection. Regardless of whether these groups fit traditional definitions, respondents made it clear they had a significant impact on the traditional prison loyalties and allegiances and contributed to conflicts amongst the prisoners.

Chicano and Latino Gangs. Among Chicanos, the Nortenos and the Surenos are the most important groupings or gangs. These two groups are divided regionally between the North and South of California, with Fresno as the dividing line.[2] Although regional loyalties were also important for the Mexican Mafia and La Nuestra Familia, the regional separation between North and South was not as rigid as it is today for Surenos and Nortenos.

In addition to the Nortenos and the Surenos, two other groups were mentioned—the New Structure and the Border Brothers. Our respondents provided differing interpretations of the New Structure. For instance, some noted it was a new Chicano group made up of Nortenos which started in San Francisco, while others implied it was an offshoot of La Nuestra Familia. Opinions differed as to its precise relationship to La Nuestra Familia.

The Border Brothers are surrounded by less controversy. Their members are from Mexico, they speak only Spanish and, consequently, keep to themselves. Most of our respondents agreed this was a large group constantly increasing in size, and that most members had been arrested for trafficking heroin or cocaine.

Although, there was little disagreement as to the Border Brothers' increasing importance, which was partly attributed to their not "claiming territory," there was, nevertheless, some dispute as to their impact on the North/South issue. Some respondents saw the Border Brothers as keeping strictly to themselves.

> The Border Brothers don't want to have anything to do with the Surenos-Nortenos—they keep out of that 'cause it's not our fighting and all of that is stupid. . . . Either you are a Chicano or you're not. There is no sense of being separated (Case 3).

Others predicted that in the future, the Border Brothers will become involved in the conflict and will align themselves with the Surenos against the Nortenos.

> It used to be Border Brothers over there and Sureno and Norteno, stay apart from each other. . . . But now what I see that's coming out is that the Border Brothers are starting to claim Trece now.[3] What I think is going to happen, to

the best of my knowledge, is that the Surenos instead of them knockin' ass with the Nortenos, they're going to have the Border Brothers lock ass with the Nortenos due to the fact that they're South and all that. Maybe in a few years we will see if my prediction is true or not (Case 36).

Black Gangs. The Crips, originally a street gang from South Central Los Angeles, is the largest of the new black gangs. It is basically a neighborhood group.

I. So the Crips is more a neighborhood thing than a racial thing?

R. Oh yeah! That's what it stems from. It stems from a neighborhood thing. There's one thing about the Crips collectively, their neighborhoods are important factors in their gang structures (Case 5).

The Bloods are the traditional rivals of the Crips. Although, like the Crips, they are a neighborhood group, they do not attribute the same importance to the neighborhood.

They're structured geographically in the neighborhood, but it's not as important as it is for the Crips. Only in LA is it that important. Bloods from LA, it's important for them but they don't have as many neighborhoods as the Crips. But anywhere else in Southern California the neighborhoods are not that important. Only in LA (Case 5).

The 415s is a third black prison gang emerging recently. The group is made up of individuals living within the 415 San Francisco Bay area telephone code.[4] Although the group's visibility is high, especially in the Bay area, the organization appears to be loosely structured, so much so that one of our respondents suggested that the 415s were more an affiliation rather than a gang.

All of these gangs are said to be producing a significant impact on prison life. Whereas previously there were four or five major gangs, today there are nine or ten new groupings, each with its own network of alliances and loyalties. These crosscutting and often conflicting allegiances have a significant impact on prison life. They produce a confusing, disruptive situation for many prisoners and can even produce problems for existing friendships. As one Puerto

Rican respondent noted, "When I first started going to the joints . . . it wasn't as bad to associate a guy from the North and the South. It wasn't that big of a deal" (Case 39). But as the fragmentation increased and dividing lines became more rigid, this type of friendship was much less acceptable. According to many of our respondents, another consequence of fragmentation was an increase in intraethnic conflict, especially amongst the black population.

Back then there was no Crips, there was no Bloods, or 415s. It is a lot different now. The blacks hit the blacks. When the blacks at one time were like the B.G.F. where the blacks would stick together, now they are hitting each other, from the Crips, to the Bloods, to the 415, are pretty much all enemies (Case 39).

The picture provided by our respondents is one of an increasing splintering of prison groupings. Allegiances to particular groups, which had previously seemed relatively entrenched, are now questioned. Friendships developed over long prison terms are now disrupted, and where previously prisoners made choices about joining a gang, membership has now become more automatic, especially for Chicanos. Today, what counts is the region of the state where the prisoner comes from; if he comes from South of Fresno, he is automatically a Sureno, if he is from North of Fresno, he becomes a Norteno.

Pepsi Generation

Respondents not only described the conflict arising from the new divisions within the prison population, but also attributed this conflict to new prison inmates. They emphasized that the new generation of prisoners differed from their generation—in their dress, attitudes, and behavior toward other prisoners and the prison authorities. Respondents described themselves as convicts who represented the "old school."

In my point of view there is what is called the old school. . . . And the old school goes back to where there is traditions and customs, there is this whole thing of holding your mud, and there is something you don't violate. For instance you don't snitch, you are a convict in the sense that you go in and you know that you are there to do time. And there is two sides. There is the Department of Corrections and there is you as the convict (Case 34).

A convict, in this sense, was very different from the present day "inmate" who they described as not having

a juvenile record or anything like that, and so that when they come in they have no sense of what it is to do time.... The inmate goes in there and he goes in not realizing that, so that they are doing everybody else's number or expect somebody else to do their number. Which means for instance, that if they can get out of something they will go ahead and give somebody up or they will go against the code. Say for instance, the food is real bad and the convict would say, look we have to do something about this so let's make up a protest about the food and present it to the warden. And the convict will go along with it because it is for the betterment of the convicts. The inmate will go and go against it because he wants to be a good inmate and, therefore, he is thinking about himself and not the whole population (Case 32).

The prisons were full of younger prisoners who were described disparagingly by our respondents as "boys trying to become men," and the "Pepsi Generation," defined as

the young shuck and jive energized generation. The CYA [California Youth Authority] mentality guys in a man's body and muscles can really go out and bang if they want. They are the youngsters that want to prove something—how tough and macho and strong they are. This is their whole attitude. Very extreme power trip and machismo. The youngsters want to prove something. How tough they are. And there is really very little remorse (Case 16).

According to our respondents, the "Pepsi Generation" went around wearing "their pants down below their ass" (Case 40) and showing little or no respect for the older inmates, many of whom had long histories of prison life which normally would have provided them with a high degree of status. Disrespect was exhibited even in such seemingly small things as the way that the younger prisoners approached the older inmates.

They'll come up and ask you where you are from. I had problems with that. They come with total

disrespect. It seems like they send the smallest, youngest punk around and he comes and tries to jam you. You know, you've been around for a long time, you know, you've got your respect already established and you have no business with this bullshit. . . . And here you have some youngster coming in your face, talking about "Hey man, where you from" (Case 2)?

This view was graphically corroborated by a 38 year old Familia member who described the young inmates in the following way:

They're actors. Put it this way, they're gangsters until their fuckin' wheels fall off. . . . I'm a gangster too. But there is a limitation to everything. See I can be a gangster with class and style and finesse and respect. Get respect and get it back. That's my motto, my principle in life. Do unto another as you would like do have done to you. These kids don't have respect for the old timers. They disrespect the old men now (Case 36).

The "younger generation" was not only criticized for its disrespect, but for its general behavior as well. They were seen as needlessly violent and erratic and not "TBYAS"—thinking before you act and speak.

I think they're more violent. They are more spontaneous. I think they are very spontaneous. They certainly don't use TBYAS. I think their motivation is shallower than it was years ago (Case 16).

Their behavior had the effect of making prison life, in general, more unpredictable, a feature many of our respondents disliked.

They have nothing but younger guys in prison now. And ah, it has just changed. I don't even consider it prison now anymore. I think it is just a punishment. It is just a place to go to do time. Which now since there are so many children and kids in prison it is hard to do time now. It is not like it used to be where you can wake up one morning and know what to expect. But now you wake up and you don't know what to expect, anything might happen (Case 12).

INMATE CULTURE REASSESSED

Inmates' picture of prison life is of increasing uncertainty and unpredictability; more traditional groupings and loyalties are called into question as new groups come to the fore. Whereas previously, prisoners believed a clear dividing line existed between convicts and authorities, today they see this simple division disintegrating. This occurs because, in their attempt to control the spread of prison gangs, authorities introduced a series of measures which contained the gangs, but also unexpectedly created a vacuum within the organizational structure of the prison population—a vacuum soon filled by new groups. Group membership was taken from newer inmates, who, according to our respondents, had not been socialized into the convict culture. The dominance of these groups soon led to an environment where the rules and codes of behavior were no longer adhered to and even the more experienced prisoners felt like newcomers. Moreover, the ability of prisoners to remain nonaligned was hampered both by developments amongst the prisoners and by the actions of the authorities. For example, a Norteno arrested in the South and sentenced to a southern prison would find himself in a very difficult and potentially dangerous situation.

> You'll see some poor northern dude land in a southern pen, they ride on [harass] him. Five, six, seven, ten deep. You know, vice versa—some poor southern kid comes to a northern spot and these northern kids will do the same thing. They ride deep on them (Case 2).

Study respondents portrayed prison culture as changing, but the change elements they identified were both inside and outside the institution. The available theoretical approaches, which have tended to dichotomize the source of change, fail to capture the complexity and the interconnectedness of the current situation. Furthermore, the information we received produced no conclusive evidence to prove whether or not the street scene determined the structure of gangs inside the prison or vice versa. For example, in the case of the Crips and the Bloods, at first glance we have a development which supports the approaches of Jacobs (1974) and Irwin and Cressey (1977). The Crips and the Bloods originated in the neighborhoods of Los Angeles and transferred their conflicts into the prison environment. In fact, according to one respondent, once

in prison, they bury their intragang conflicts in order to strengthen their identities as Crips and Bloods.

> Even when they are "out there" they may fight amongst themselves, just over their territory. ... But when they get to prison they are wise enough to know, we gotta join collectively to fend off everyone else (Case 5).

However, although the Crips and Bloods fit neatly into Jacobs' perspective, when we consider the case of the 415s and the Nortenos and the Surenos, we find their origins fit more easily into Cloward's (1977) alternative perspective. According to two accounts, the 415s began in prison as a defense group against the threatening behavior of the Bloods and the Crips.

> It [the 415s] got started back in prison. In prison there is a lot of prison gangs ... and they were put together a lot. They got LA—gangs like the Bloods and the Crips, and they are putting a lot of pressure on the people from the Bay area. And we all got together, we got together and organized our own group (Case G189).

Originally, the Nortenos and Surenos existed neither on the streets nor in the adult prisons but within the California Youth Authority institutions. Gradually this division spread to the adult prisons and soon became powerful enough to disrupt the traditional loyalties of more established gangs. Furthermore, in-prison conflicts soon spread to the outside and, according to information from our San Francisco study, Norteno/Sureno conflicts are beginning to have a significant impact on the streets.

CONCLUSION

As Irwin (1980) noted over ten years ago, prisons today are in a turmoil. From both the Department of Corrections perspective and the interview material, it is clear that the prison system is under immense pressures. As the prison population expands and the Department of Corrections attempts to find more bed space, the problems within the prisons multiply.[5] The impact of this situation on the inmates is clear from the interviews—they complain about the increased fragmentation and disorganization that they now experience. Life in prison is no longer organized but instead is viewed as both capricious and dangerous.

For many, returning to prison after spending time outside means being confronted by a world which they do not understand even though they have been in prison many times before. Where once they experienced an orderly culture, today they find a world which operates around arbitrary and ad hoc events, and decisions seem to arise not merely from the behavior of their fellow prisoners but also from prison authorities' official and unofficial decisions. Where before they understood the dominant prison divisions—prisoners versus guards and black versus white inmates—today they find new clefts and competing allegiances. The Chicanos are split not only between the Mexican Mafia and La Nuestra Familia but also North versus South. A relatively unified black population is divided into different warring camps of Crips, Bloods, and 415s.

The world portrayed by our respondents is an important corrective both to the criminal justice literature, which portrays prison life in very simplistic terms, and to those theoretical approaches which attempt to explain prison culture solely in terms of internal or external influences. Our interviews have shown that the linkages between street activities and prison activities are complex and are the result of developments in both arenas. Therefore, instead of attributing primacy to one set of factors as opposed to the other, it may be more useful and more accurate to see the culture and organization of prison and street life as inextricably intertwined, with lines of influence flowing in both directions.

Notes

1. In addition to these five major groupings, other gangs, including the Vanguards and the Venceremos, are referred to in the literature. Today these groups seem to have disappeared altogether or may in some cases have been incorporated into other gangs. For a further discussion of California gangs, see Castenedo (1981), Conrad (1978), and a report by EMT Associates, Inc. (1985) to the California Department of Corrections. For information on prison gangs in other parts of the United States, see Beaird (1986), Buentello (1984), Crist (1986), Fong (1990, 1991), Jacobs (1977), and Lane (1989).

2. There was some disagreement as to the precise dividing line between North and South. Although Fresno was often cited, others said Bakersfield was the dividing line.

3. The term Trece has a number of meanings especially amongst Chicanos in Los Angeles where it refers to "eme," or "m" the 13th letter in the Spanish alphabet. "Eme" is also used to describe the Mexican Mafia.

4. It should be noted that during 1992, telephone area codes in the Bay area were changed to two codes—415 and 510. The gang's name refers to the period when one code covered the entire Bay area.

5. One can but speculate as to what effect the estimated 5,000 arrests in Los Angeles as a result of recent riots will have on the correctional system.

References

Beaird, Lester H. 1986 "Prison gangs: Texas." Corrections Today 48 July: 12, 18-22.

Biernacki, Patrick, and Dan Waldorf. 1981 "Snowball sampling: Problems and techniques of chain referral sampling." Sociological Methods and Research 10:141-163.

Buentello, Salvator. 1984 "The Texas Syndicate." Texas Department of Corrections. Unpublished report.

California Department of Corrections. 1991 Historical Trends: Institution and Parole Population, 1970-1990. Offender Information Services Branch. Data Analysis Unit. Sacramento.

Camp, George, M., and Camille, G. Camp. 1985 Prison Gangs: Their Extent, Nature and Impact on Prisons. U.S. Department of Justice, Office of Legal Policy, Federal Justice Research program. Washington, D.C.

Castenedo, Esteban P. (compiler). 1981 Prison Gang Influences on Street gangs. Sacramento, Calif.: California Department of Youth Authority.

Clemmer, Donald. 1958 The Prison Community. New York: Rinehart and Co.

Cloward, Richard. 1977 "Social control in the prison." In The Sociology of Corrections, ed. Robert G. Leger and John R. Stratton, 110-132. New York: John Wiley and Sons.

Conrad, John. 1978 "Who's in charge? Control of gang violence in California Prisons." In Report on Colloquium on Correctional Facilities, 1977, ed. Nora Harlow. Sacramento, Calif.: Department of Corrections.

Crist, Roger W. 1986 "Prison gangs: Arizona." Corrections Today 48 July: 13, 25-27.

Cummins, Eric. 1991 "History of gang development in California prisons." Unpublished paper.

Davidson, R. Theodore. 1974 Chicano Prisoners: The Key to San Quentin. Prospect Heights, Ill.: Waveland Press, Inc.

EMT Associates, Inc. 1985 Comparative Assessment of Strategies to Manage Prison Gang Populations and Gang related Violence. Vol. 1-8. Sacramento, Calif.: California Department of Corrections. Unpublished report.

Fong, Robert S. 1990 "The organizational structure of prison gangs: A Texas case study." Federal Probation 54:1.

Fong, Robert, and Salvator Buentello. 1991 "The detection of prison gang development: An empirical assessment." Federal Probation 55:1.

Goffman, Erving. 1961 Asylums. Garden City, N.J.: Anchor.

Irwin, John. 1980 Prisons in Turmoil. Boston: Little, Brown and Company.

Irwin, John, and Donald Cressey. 1977 "Thieves, convicts, and the inmate culture." In The Sociology of Corrections, ed. Robert G. Leger and John R. Stratton, 133-147. New York: John Wiley and Sons.

Jacobs, James. 1974 "Street gangs behind bars." Social Problems 21:395-409.

Jacobs, James. 1977 Stateville: The Penitentiary in Mass Society. Chicago: University of Chicago Press. Klein, Malcolm W., and Cheryl L. Maxson.

Jacobs, James. 1989 "Street gang violence." In Violent Crime, Violent Criminals, ed. Neil Allen Weiner and Marvin E. Wolfgang. Newbury Park, Calif.: Sage.

Lane, Michael P. 1989 "Inmate gangs." Corrections Today July: 98-128.

Leger, Robert G., and John R. Stratton. 1977 The Sociology of Corrections: A Book of Readings. New York: John Wiley and Sons.

Moore, Joan W. 1978 Homeboys: Gangs, Drugs, and Prison in the Barrios of Los Angeles. Philadelphia: Temple University Press.

Porter, Bruce. 1982 "California prison gangs: The price of control." Corrections Magazine 8:6-19.

Stojkovic, Stan. 1986 "Social bases of power and control mechanisms among correctional administrators in a prison organization." Journal of Criminal Justice 14:157-166.

Sykes, Gresham M., and Sheldon L. Messinger. 1977 "The inmate social system." In The Sociology of Corrections, ed. Robert G. Leger and John R. Stratton, 97-109. New York: John Wiley and Sons.

Research on womens' experiences in prison has been a neglected topic until recently. This article examines the subjective experiences of previously imprisoned women. Their retrospective narratives of prison life reveal overt behavioral and underlying structural tensions that create an atmosphere of fear and violence. Furthermore, attitudes of indifference between correctional staff and inmates often contribute to fostering an environment of neglect. Pogrebin and Dodge describe and analyze several aspects of the socialization process for inmates as related to them by former inmates now on parole. The study shows that the "pains of imprisonment" for women are suffered to a greater degree than previously acknowledged. Prison for these women is a social world filled with anxiety and perhaps represents a punishment well beyond what the law intended.

WOMEN'S ACCOUNTS OF THEIR PRISON EXPERIENCES

A Retrospective View of Their Subjective Realities

MARK R. POGREBIN
MARY DODGE

Abstract

This article examines the subjective experiences of previously imprisoned women. Their retrospective narratives of prison life reveal overt behavioral and underlying structural tensions that create an atmosphere of fear and violence. Furthermore, attitudes of indifference between inmates and correctional staff often contribute to fostering an environment of neglect. The study, based on in-depth interviews with fifty-four female subjects, describes and analyzes several aspects of the socialization process for inmates as related by women on parole. The research shows that the "pains of imprisonment" for women are suffered to a greater degree than previously acknowledged. Prison for these women is a social world filled with anxiety and, perhaps, represents a punishment well beyond what the law intended.

Reprinted from the *Journal of Criminal Justice (29)*6, pp. 531-541, "Women's Accounts of their Prison Experience." © 2001 with permission from Elsevier Science.

INTRODUCTION

The number of women in the criminal justice system has spurred a great deal of recent social inquiry, particularly as prison populations continue to soar. Early studies of women in prison focused on pseudo-family and relationship building (Giallombardo, 1966; Larsen & Nelson, 1984; Leger, 1987; Ward & Kassebaum, 1965). Many recent studies have relied on comparisons of female and male prison populations. According to female-male comparative research, women pose less custodial and security risk (Alexander & Humphrey, 1988; Brennan & Austin, 1997; Burke & Adams, 1991; Pollock-Bryne, 1990); women are less likely to riot and assault each other (Hunter, 1984; Rafter, 1990); and women are less apt to commit serious institutional infractions (Austin, Chan, & Elms, 1993). The focus on a gendered dichotomy, however, appears to diminish the fear and violence that delineate the experience of many incarcerated women. This article gives voice to the concerns and hardships as told by formerly incarcerated women.

An Evolving Subculture

The pains of imprisonment and the development of prison subcultures are closely related. In 1958, Gresham Sykes identified the loss of liberty, goods and services, heterosexual relations, autonomy, and personal security as the basic deprivations associated with prison life. Prison subcultures developed as inmates adapted to life in these isolated and stressful environments. Many inmates strive toward normalcy by creating relationships and mores to supplant outside losses. In fact, early research on women inmates focused on the development of social structures based on family and traditional gender roles (Giallombardo, 1966; Ward & Kassebaum, 1965). According to Giallombardo (1966), women alleviated the pains of imprisonment by developing kinship links with other inmates. Similarly, Heffernan (1972) found that adaptation to prison was facilitated by the creation of a pseudo-family. Owen (1998) also notes that the female subculture is based on personal relationships with other women inmates. Others, however, believe that the subculture in women's prisons is undergoing a gradual shift that more closely resembles that of male prisons. Fox (1982) states, for example, that the cooperative caring prisoner community that has embodied characterizations of female prisons has evolved into a more dangerous and competitive climate. Changes in subcultures may be related to the more pronounced deprivations that women inmates experience.

Inmate Experiences and Socialization

Female prisoners generally report that institutional adjustment is more difficult than their male contemporaries for many reasons. Women tend to value privacy more than men (Pollock-Byrne, 1992), and, consequently, experience greater difficulty adjusting to community living and the degrading nature of body searches (Ward & Kassebaum, 1965). Furthermore, women often worry about being abandoned by family and spouses and are concerned with the loneliness they may experience once released (Dobash, Dobash, & Gutteridge, 1986).

Punishment is compounded for many women inmates when they are separated from their children. The majority of incarcerated women are mothers—estimates range from 60 to 80 percent (Bloom & Steinhart, 1993; Henriques, 1996). Most women inmates were living with their children and provided the sole means of family support prior to incarceration (Baunach, 1985; Chesney-Lind, 1997; Datesman & Cales, 1983; Greenfeld & Minor-Harper, 1991; Henriques, 1996). Imprisoned mothers rank estrangement from children as their primary concern (Henriques, 1996; Stanton, 1980). Rasche (2000) notes that the harshest single aspect of being imprisoned may be the separation of mother and child.

Women in prison experience an unparalleled sense of isolation. Added to the pains of imprisonment for women are the frustration, conflict, and guilt of being both separated from and unable to care for their children (Barry, 1987; Bloom & Chesney-Lind, 2000). According to Crawford (1990), as a result of imprisonment, female parents often experience feelings of despair and depression. Crawford further states that these emotions appear to be prevalent, even on the part of women inmates who believe that they were inadequate as parents when they were living with their children at home. Further anxiety arises over fear of losing custody. In some states, authorities use a prison sentence to deprive women of legal custody (Bloom, 1995; Fletcher, Shaver, & Moon, 1993; Pollock-Byrne, 1990).

The loss of adult status and childlike treatment by custodial officers exacerbates the stress that female inmates experience (Fox, 1982). Misbehavior is seldom overlooked. McClellan (1994), who studied rule violations and punishments throughout the Texas Department of Corrections, found from a comparative study of both men and women prisons that women received many more write-ups for minor rule violations than did their male-counterparts. Furthermore, women inmates were more likely to receive the most severe sanctions for their violations. Dobash et al. (1986), for example, found that women consistently were punished more frequently as compared to male prisoners for offenses against prison rules and regulations. They note that the difference is a result of a greater willingness to write-up women for behavior that often is tolerated in male correctional facilities.

Personal autonomy is threatened in numerous ways, but is particularly insidious when women prisoners become the target of sexual abuse, harassment, and sexual misconduct perpetrated by correctional officers. Reporting incidents of mistreatment often proves to be a futile action. The amount of sexual misconduct by staff toward inmates is difficult to determine. Moss (1999) offers numerous reasons for this situation. First, data or investigations are determined in general categories such as assault rather than sexual assault. Second, women fear reprisal or fear they will not be believed by administrators. Third, sexual relations between staff and inmates are seen as beneficial to both parties involved (e.g., trading sex for goods). Fourth, sexual misconduct is difficult to investigate and corroboration of another party is necessary to substantiate a female prisoner's claim. Fifth, prison culture adheres to the code of silence, both for staff and inmates, particularly if both inmates and staff lack confidence that those who report sexual misconduct will be safe from any type of retaliation. Finally, in prison settings staff who report sexual misconduct with female prisoners may be ostracized by other correctional officers.

The factors discussed thus far are illustrative of some of the conditions experienced by women who are serving time. Although current literature offers profiles of the type of women in prison, there is little data that informs us of just how these women, once released, reflect on their years of incarceration. The research presented here sought to explore the varied dimensions of women's imprisonment and to better understand the significance of their experiences. The major themes that emerged include elements of fear, intimidation, and violence; relationships among inmates; drug-related issues; health and medical concerns; and custodial care problems.

METHODS

Data were collected from fifty-four female parolees who were incarcerated at a correctional facility in a western state. With the exception of one former inmate, all the women had served their time at one institution. The facility was constructed in 1968 and had a mixed classification of inmates. The population at the time of this study was approximately 300 women with sixty-one correctional officers, thirty-seven female and twenty-four male. The ethnic and racial composition of the prison population was comprised of the following: 45.6 percent Anglo, 31.5 percent Black, 18.4 percent Hispanic, 1.7 percent Native American, 0.4 percent Asian, and 2.4 percent unknown.

Women on parole were contacted at the time they had appointments to see their parole officers. Each person was told the purpose of the study, volunteered to participate, and gave informed consent. A total of fifty-four women agreed to participate and were interviewed over a three-month period. Their ages ranged from twenty-three to fifty-five (median = 36) and their length of incarceration ranged from one to twelve years (median = 4.8) for all classes of offense.

Interviews were conducted at the parole offices in private conference rooms. Each interview lasted approximately sixty minutes and was tape-recorded with the subject's consent. A semistructured interview format was used, which relied on sequential probes to pursue leads provided by subjects. This approach allowed the women parolees to identify and elaborate on important domains they perceived to characterize their prison experiences retrospectively, rather than the researchers eliciting responses to structured questions.

The interview tapes were transcribed for qualitative data analysis, which involved a search for general relationships among categories of observations employing grounded theory techniques similar to those suggested by Glaser and Strauss (1967). The data were categorized into conceptual domains of the experiences of imprisonment as identified by the subjects. The experiences of these women might not be reflective of all women who have served time, but their narratives add voice and depth to the issues they faced while imprisoned (Ragin, 1994; Seidman, 1998).

All women parolees were guaranteed confidentiality and were told that they could chose not to tape the interview. Three women requested not to be taped and notes were taken during those interview sessions. All of the former inmates were cooperative and seemed willing to discuss their prior prison life. The women appeared to be open and frank in relating their personal experiences, although at times it was an emotionally painful process. Though, according to Linn (1997), relating their stories may have allowed the women to better understand their feelings.

FINDINGS

Initial Impressions

When discussing their initial experiences upon entering prison, most of the women interviewed realized genuine fears in being in such an environment for the first time. One respondent explained:

> I was scared to death. When I went to [the facility], I saw women who looked like men, bigger than me. And they were looking at me and I was like: "Oh No."

When discussing her first few days in the facility, a woman related her feelings about the way correctional officers treated her. This experience was like nothing she had ever encountered before in her life. She stated:

> I try and forget what it was like in prison most of the time. When I just got there they stripped me down and this guard did a full body search. I was shocked, I never had anyone touch me like that, especially with other guards just standing there watching me. Then they threw me these clothes and took me to a cell. While we were walking, some girls were yelling names at me. It was the most scary thing I had ever seen.

Inmates who were new to the system, who did not have extensive histories of serving time in county jail or prison, found being incarcerated quite traumatic. According to one novice inmate:

> Prison was nothing you would believe. I came from a good home. I wasn't prepared. Here I was a middle-class, White female with a drug problem and I was locked up with murderers and gang members and it was bad. You think prison would just be a place where you are locked up, but more stuff goes on there, drugs, sex, and violence. Some of the women knew I was scared and they would harass me. The worst part is the noise.
>
> It is never quiet in there. All night long people are talking from cell to cell, screaming, fighting, and the doors opened continually when guards are doing checks.

For many prisoners adjusting to living in a total institution (Goffman, 1961) for the first time is something no one can prepare for. According to the women in this study, new prisoners, who have had limited criminal backgrounds and had no friends already in prison, had the most difficult time adjusting to this environment. The women had to go through a socialization process for a period of time to survive. The respondents noted that weakness was not a valued attribute among inmates and those who displayed fear and remained nonconfrontational when picked on by more aggressive inmates had to adjust for the sake of survival.

Weaknesses and Harassment

The respondents agreed that women who were threatened by other inmates and did not use aggressive tactics to defend themselves were seen as weak and presented no threat of retaliation. For these respondents, their reputation as weak defined who they were in the eyes of other prisoners. Their passivity to more aggressive women often led to constantly being taken advantage of. One women put this situation in perspective:

> It doesn't matter how tough you might think you are, cause it's all a mind game. But people will be nice to you and I know I was lonely and so like "yeah this isn't so bad," but things happen and then taking it all in and you end up getting shit on. There is a lot of that in there and once you get into a situation like that it is hard to get out and everyone knows they can treat you like that.

An extreme case of an inmate's inability to cope with existing in the prison environment resulted in an attempted suicide. Prisoners who were unable or unwilling to act aggressively and stand up for themselves in circumstances where they were constantly harassed by others might find such an ongoing situation unbearable, and believed that ending their life was the only means of escape. One woman related the following story:

> I saw a girl; she was a real mess. We all knew she wouldn't make it cause she was weak. She cut her wrists real bad and she was lying in her cell and there was blood everywhere. She was real young and she ended up moving somewhere else, but she was a mess and that was hard cause that place ruined her and I know she wouldn't make it cause she was already dead inside.

Instilling fear and intimidation were two strategies that were used by more domineering inmates toward those who showed consistent signs of weakness. That is, there was a utilitarian purpose in instilling fear in weaker prisoners. This is not merely done for reasons of power, but appeared more so for tangible gain. Several former inmates faced this predicament. One subject explained how she resolved her problem with being harassed by other women:

> Other inmates would harass me by trying to intimidate me. Pushing me around, knocking my food over, telling me if I didn't do what they said, they would kill me. I was scared and alone.

Finding herself in an alien world-like prison, this novice inmate turned to a more experienced prisoner, who offered to listen to her problems and befriend her, all for future utilitarian purposes. What occurred because of this so-called empathic relationship happened all too often to those people who had yet to be socialized into the prisonization game. She explained how this friendly relationship turned into one best characterized as exploitative in nature:

> I made the mistake of letting this one girl help me. She had been in for a while and she had a reputation for being tougher. I was new and didn't know much about her. I thought she was just being nice. She told me to stick by her and she would protect me. I was relieved. I couldn't take care of myself, at least I thought I couldn't. Anyway, it started out great, we would take walks together and I would cry about losing my daughter and being locked up. She would just listen and it felt good having someone who seemed to care. After a while she started having me do little things for her, and I didn't mind, we were friends. Then it got bigger and she knew my family had a little money and got me to give [money] to her. It got out of hand and she would be mean if I didn't give it to her and I was kind of scared.

The exploitation of this novice prisoner by the more powerful and experienced inmate lasted for over two years, until the exploiter was transferred to another facility. After she was gone, other prisoners began to demand money from the inmate and her family, but she refused and suffered the consequence for not acquiescing to these demands. The former inmate said:

> Another girl came up to me and threatened me if I didn't give her money, but I wasn't getting into that again and I told her no. She bashed my head one day, I had to get six stitches.

Another respondent reported her experiences of incarceration in a different state prison. It is obvious from her narrative that her time served there was based on fear for her safety. She related her feelings:

> I was in prison in Arizona. It was horrible. I was bullied a lot by other women that were involved in gangs. I was terrified to walk outside my cell, that's how bad it was.

In those instances in which new prisoners were being harassed and threatened by more experienced, aggressive inmates there often was another prisoner willing to intercede on her behalf. One interviewee chose not to play the passive weak role on advice from an older inmate, although she was extremely scared to stand up for herself. She described her experience:

> It was hard cause I was scared, but she came at me one day and I fought back. She beat the crap out of me, but I took it. The guards broke it up and we both [were] sent to isolation for seventy-two hours. After that it got better, she still made smart-ass remarks, but she never really bothered me. I guess Shelly [her friend] was right, well I know she was, no matter how bad it is you need to stand up for yourself, cause if you don't everyone will be coming after you and you won't have a chance.

In this instance, her willingness to engage in physical aggression seemed to pay off. The fact that she was beaten-up appeared to be part of the price for gaining a reputation among prisoners that being taken advantage of would not be tolerated. Exploitation, unfortunately, was part of the prisonization process that both male and female prisoners face in a correctional environment.

An important part of becoming socialized to the prison subculture was not using correctional staff to help solve interpersonal conflicts. In short, "snitching" was taboo, although prison administrators encourage and use the information from inmate informants to maintain social control in the institution (Cloward, 1977). The following incident best illustrates the consequences of an inmate snitching to correctional staff about another inmate's threatening behavior:

You don't really want the guards involved in protecting you because you'll become known as a snitch or an ass-kisser. If someone wants to get you, they will find a way to do it and the guards can't do anything about it even if they know. There was this one chick who was young and scared and this other chick was after her, so she went to one of the guards and they told her they would look into it. It was too late and the girl ended up beating the shit out of her. She was in the hospital a long time.

For those novice inmates the above incident became an integral part of the social process of becoming a prisoner. The fact that one had to quickly learn to handle interpersonal conflicts by not going to the authorities could be an extremely frightening occurrence. Yet, becoming acclimated to such prisonization norms of behavior seems to be a vital part of prison survival skills that all incarcerated persons must follow to avoid as much conflict as possible.

An Atmosphere of Bedlam

Violence and noise were two factors that made institutional living in correctional facilities a difficult adjustment. According to Pollock-Byrne (1992), older women prisoners complain most about the constant noise and violent behavior of younger women. This complaint was heard from the majority of the respondents who claimed that not just older women, but inmates of all ages felt this was a problem. Another former prisoner related a similar experience having been housed with women who were prone to settle disputes in a violent manner:

> Fights happened all the time—yelling and screaming about someone stealing your shit at least once a day. A lot of girls used weapons that they made from eating utensils, anything they could use to hurt someone. It would get bad sometimes and the guards leave to take someone to get stitches. One time this girl hit this other girl's head on a bar and ended up crushing her skull. It happens a lot, a couple girls have been killed, one while I was there.

Two subjects explained what it was like living in prison for the first time. It is obvious from their descriptions that the noise and sporadic violence were new to them and they had to learn to deal with it over time. One woman said:

> There is violence all the time. The first time I saw a fight and the guards came in, I was shocked. After a while you get use to hearing and seeing it, then you just kind of ignore it, or walk away. There is a lot of screaming and fighting. I guess it's just part of the atmosphere.

Another woman described her impressions and feelings:

It's always loud, with a bunch of girls screaming and yelling and fighting. It's hell. There isn't any privacy. I was so lonely and I cried, I just wanted out. I never felt so bad in my life.

Often fights were due to circumstances that were beyond the inmates' control. For example, when an inmate received bad news, there was little a prisoner could do about it, and this frustration could turn into physical acting out. According to one respondent:

Some of the girls in there have been in for a long time and when they find out they've been denied parole or they don't hear from their family or their boyfriend cheats on them they get pissed. Then, once you realize there is nothing you can do about it cause you're locked up, it makes it even worse.

The reality of prison life as portrayed by these former prisoners was one that posed a constant threat of danger. According to the narratives in this research, some women were better at avoiding trouble than others. For those prisoners who find the adjustment to prison life extremely difficult, their existence was best described as fearful and distrustful of both fellow inmates and correctional staff. One respondent described the difficulty of living with women inmates who often act out violently:

Some of them were just plain crazy, they would fly off the handle and go nuts. I tried to stay out of their way. There was one chick who gave me a hard time. She would push me around and give me all kinds of crap. It was getting out of hand. I needed to stand up to her.

Inmate Relationships

This section discusses the relationships among inmates: a subject that has been researched in past studies of women's correctional institutions. Homosexual behavior did exist in the prison where these interview subjects served time and all of those who claimed to have participated in such a relationship were candid and forthcoming in relating their accounts.

Homosexuality in women's correctional facilities tends to be consensual with most of participants engaging in these relationships for purposes of emotional fulfillment (Pollock-Byrne, 1990).

Toch (1975) points out that women in prison have a great need for emotional support and this is a high priority for them. The emotional fulfillment for a supportive relationship was an important factor for one former inmate:

You are locked up with all these girls and you get close with some of them. I had been treated like shit by guys all my life and with women it's just different, it's more of a friendship thing. You get lonely and sad in prison and it is just nice having someone around who understands and cares and knows what you are going through.

According to Bowker (1981), homosexual behavior in women's prison is more in the context of a loving relationship based on interpersonal desire for love as opposed to just sexual activity. One woman related her experiences:

It's funny how we became friends, cause at first we didn't get along and she's a dyke and I just wasn't into that, but then we started talking and got close. It was like we were really good friends and the fooling around part comes second. For us it was much more, we loved and respected each other and we were just really close.

Pearson (1998) claims that female inmates have a desire to be romantically linked to another inmate for reasons of personal security. Many of the respondents explained that they entered into homosexual relationships, but this activity had little to do with lesbianism as a sexual preference once they return to the community. One woman said:

Almost everyone is involved with someone so long as nobody is getting hurt. I was not involved with women before I came to prison and it's difficult when you get out. I didn't think I am a lesbian, but when you are locked up you do anything to pass the time, and I had someone I really cared about. But now that I'm out there I don't think I would be with anyone like that now.

There also were respondents who discussed close friendships with other females, but denied that there was anything sexual about the relationship. They claimed that having a close female friend to share their problems with played an important role in meeting their emotional needs.

A former inmate described the difficulty of leaving a friend inside the prison:

> I am not a lesbian, but I had a few friends. I mean you need people to talk to or you will go crazy. It's hard to know who to trust, but there was one girl who worked in the library with me. She helped me out a lot. She was real smart and she had been in before and when I would get mad she would calm me down. We would talk and we cried together a lot, but it was cool, we helped each other out. You need someone to be your friend to help you just to make it together.

Another woman related similar feelings on the need to have friends while incarcerated:

> I had a few really good friends I met in prison and the funny thing is these girls would do anything for you. I never had anyone like that when I was out. I probably made the best friends I ever had in prison.

Drug Involvement

Much female crime can be attributed to the use of illegal substances (Chesney-Lind, 1991; Chesney-Lind & Pollock, 1995; Snell & Morton, 1994). Crimes such as forgery, shoplifting, drug sales, prostitution, and a host of other property crimes are directly related to drug use. One former inmate related her perception of the drug problems that many women had before coming to prison. She explained:

> A majority of the people in there had a drug problem. Most of us start using at a young age and we just never got the help we needed to get over it. So you start using pot or something and then you go into bigger stuff and use more and more and you get more addicted. So when you go into a prison, there isn't a lot of help and you keep using there and when you get out.

When addressing the issue of drug availability and use of illegal substances while incarcerated the respondents consistently reported the following type of statement:

> A lot of people use drugs, mostly like acid and pot and things like that. Pot is tricky cause of the stench, so you have to be careful not to get caught, but yeah, there are a lot of drugs. A lot of

women used them, that's what most of us were in for anyway, it just kind of continues.

This research can neither attest to the veracity of how many drugs were available in the prison, nor can it show how extensive drug use was among the general population. The vast majority of women, however, did report that drugs were available.

Most women participants claimed that drug treatment services were not available, or if they were, they could not get into a program due to their sentences being in the later stages and this disqualified them from being accepted. Furthermore, there were some drug abusers who were not motivated to enter into any type of substance abuse rehabilitation program. In short, although most of the participants admittedly had some type of substance abuse problem before entering prison, very few were involved in any rehabilitation program during their time inside.

One long-term prisoner disputed the perceptions of most others when she discussed the provision of drug treatment programs. This former inmate served over fifteen years in prison and offered a comparison between the existence of programs in the past and now:

> Things were different fifteen years ago. They didn't have all the treatment programs they have now. They didn't have anyone to help you with drugs or anything.
>
> Now it's different, about the last eight years I was in it got better, there were a lot more things to get involved in, like drug programs, and stuff about sexual and physical abuse. It isn't great, but it's getting better.

Medical Services

The provision of health services in female correctional facilities has long been an issue and is still considered a major problem (Fletcher et al., 1993). The majority of lawsuits involving women inmates deal with problems in attaining professional medical care (Aylward & Thomas, 1984). Furthermore, Dobash et al. (1986) claim that receiving medical services is different for women prisoners and that correctional staff often minimize their need to see a doctor. This dilemma was best illustrated by one woman who related her medical problems while imprisoned and the trouble she had in convincing the staff the urgency of her need for medical attention. According to this former inmate:

> They don't listen and they just don't care. I needed to see a doctor cause I was having a lot of weird vaginal bleeding and I was in pain and I kept telling them this. It took a few weeks for them to let me see a nurse. When she saw me she didn't really check me out too good, and about a week later I passed out and was bleeding real bad so they finally paid attention and took me to a hospital. I was there for about two weeks. I had a prolapsed uterus or something like that. They ended up doing a hysterectomy. They said if they caught it earlier they wouldn't have had to do it, but now I can't have kids cause nobody would listen to me.

After her hysterectomy, the respondent was being transferred from a community hospital back to prison by two correctional officers who apparently were insensitive to her medical condition.

> Those guards are assholes. When I was leaving the hospital, they did a full body search to make sure I wasn't trying to bring anything back with me. The guard rammed her hand up me. I still had stitches and everything hurt like hell. But, that's how it is, none of them care, they just treat us like shit.

The following description of a seriously ill woman points to the inadequate screening of inmate medical complaints by nurses. In one instance, a nurse either misdiagnosed a serious illness or was medically negligent. The respondent relayed the following account:

> They think you're making stuff up when you complain about being sick. But, there are some that really do have something wrong and they have to suffer. My cellmate had a bad cough, it would keep her up at night and it was going on for weeks, they told her it was a cold. One night she was bad, she was throwing up blood and she was burning up. She ended up having pneumonia or something. She never fully recovered and was still in when I left. She was always real weak and looked bad. I felt awful for her.

The attitude on the part of many correctional staff toward prisoners who complain of ill health can best be characterized as one of suspicion. After years of hearing inmate complaints about needing medical attention, when ulterior motives may very likely be involved, can lead to a cynical view of medical complaints (Mitchell, 1988). This attitude on the part of medical and custodial staff might lead to negligent behavior when health services need to be provided. Prevailing cynical attitudes toward inmate health needs, coupled with the lack of adequate health care providers, often meant a delay before women received needed medical attention. A former inmate explained:

> It was like everything else, they were so shorthanded it took forever to see anyone. I got sick a few times and I had a lump in my breast. My mom died of breast cancer so I was scared. It took about a month for me to see the nurse and she kind of felt it and said it was nothing. I had been doing a lot of reading about mammograms and I knew it could be something so I kept on them. Finally, a few months later I saw a doctor and they did a bunch of tests. They ended up doing a biopsy and everything turned out all right, but it was a hassle getting anyone to listen to me.

Relationship Issues with Correctional Officers

The supervision of members of one sex by another often leads to issues related to privacy for inmates. Currently, there are an increasing number of male officers working in women's correctional facilities because of Title VII of the Civil Rights Act of 1964 (Moss, 1999). Cross-gender supervision presents a unique set of problems regarding issues of privacy, sexual harassment, or just sexual accusations against male staff. Most of the respondents claimed that male officers sexually harassed them and that this behavior took many different forms.

The issue of privacy invariably was raised by the former inmates. Almost all of the women had some exposure with male officers seeing them in some stage of undress. A respondent commented:

> Those of us who were minorities were treated bad. They didn't care how they treated us. They would watch us when we were in the showers. I know that they were getting off watching us.

Another former inmate discussed treatment by custodial officers and noted that both female and male custody staff often acted disrespectfully toward inmates in their interpersonal encounters. Inappropriate sexual behavior was included in her discussion:

I had to have six stitches in my forehead because a guard pushed me into a wall and I fell down. Also, the guards were always watching us while we were taking showers. There was a lot of abuse in prison. Most of the abuse was either sexual abuse or emotional abuse.

The most serious allegation against male correctional officers was that of coercing female inmates into having sexual encounters with them. That is, officers using their position of authority who threaten punishment for those women who refuse to cooperate. Even in those circumstances where reciprocity appeared to exist between a male officer and a female inmate, no consent could exist due to the differential power relationship. Often the officer who initiated the proposition for sex with a woman played on her vulnerability. One prisoner who was sexually involved with a guard related this circumstance:

I got caught up in this ring that one of the guards had going. At first, I had no idea what it was about. Then, one day this guard asked if I would like to earn some extra cigarettes. He knew that I smoked and that was his way of getting me in. He told me that I was going to have to give oral sex to one of the guards. At first, I objected, but then I figured that if I didn't do it I would get in trouble or get beat. So I gave the guard oral sex. Before I knew it I was doing other things too. After a while it wasn't a big deal. I learned to block out the experience.

Those former prisoners who were involved in sexual activities with male officers always pointed to being coerced and then bribed with goods to take part. There was a genuine fear of retaliation by those harassing officers if they did not participate. One woman explained:

I used to do thing for guards all the time to get extra things. I would get cigarettes, extra phone time, magazines. I used to get all that stuff. I also

saw women who refused to do things for them begin to get write-ups or would be treated badly. I saw that happen all the time.

Another woman claimed that "guards were always pressuring women to have sex with them." A respondent discussed her experience with a male guard:

They are jerks, they are just doing this job. They just do it badly. They really harass you. I had a lot of trouble with this one guy, he used to follow me around and he made a few threats. I took it for a long time, but it was getting old. I complained a few times, but they just laughed at me. I told my caseworker about it and a formal complaint was written. I guess some other girls had complained in the past, but it was just our words against him and nobody believes a convict. After that it was real bad cause he knew I told on him. I would come back to my cell and stuff would be everywhere and missing and I wouldn't get my mail for a long time. After a while he was transferred and it got a little better, but I did not meet one guard the whole time I was there who really cared or treated us any good.

The low rate of reported sexual misconduct by women is understandable. Apparently, even when inmates report incidents to administrators, the onus of proof is placed upon them. The dilemma for women inmates is really a no-win situation. When they report sexual harassment they are not believed and in those situations where they do make accusations, they suffer from retaliatory acts by the very officers they complained about.

Family Separation

For female inmates in this study, being separated from their children provoked considerable stress, along with threats to their self-esteem. The most difficult aspect of being in prison was voiced by one respondent who seemed to portray a representative opinion for the women who left their children behind. She commented:

It was so long. I missed my kids. I missed my freedom. I went to bed every night and woke up in a tiny cell. I just wish it was all a bad dream and I would wake up and I would still be there.

Often inmates with children begin to perceive themselves as bad people, as expressed by one parent whose child was growing up not knowing her:

> Being away from my daughter affected me a lot. She is only six, so that means that I have been in the system almost her entire life. I haven't been there for her. I feel like a horrible person because of this.

Another great concern for women inmate-parents in this study was the dependability of the father of their children to be responsible for them during their incarceration. There were some cases in which the husband did take responsibility for their children, but left his imprisoned spouse for another woman. Obviously, these circumstances caused great distress for incarcerated women. Feelings of abandonment become very real. One woman stated:

> My husband chose to go to another woman. He cheated on me. It's so much to go through. You lose your husband, you lose your kids, your kid's gonna always love you, but someone else takes care of your kids, another woman, it's so much to go through. It's tragic.

Mothers who were in prison often saw their children living in foster homes when there were no relatives who would assume responsibility. If multiple children are involved, they frequently were placed in different homes and separated, making it difficult for incarcerated mothers to find out where all the children are living. Not being able to see your children for long periods of time was a reality for many inmate parents. One respondent explained:

> My children, there isn't much to say, I had three boys and I lost them when I went in. I haven't seen them since I violated my probation; it's been about five years. I get letters from a social worker telling me how they are doing, but I can't see them or talk to them or anything. I talked to someone from social services about it, but I will never get them back. I really miss them.

Most of the women told of extreme difficulties in their attempts to regain custody of their children. A female parent on parole must show that she has sustained employment, can financially support her children, has a permanent and appropriate residence, and is no longer involved in any criminal activity. Obviously, these criteria presented insurmountable obstacles for some women who wished to regain custodial rights.

DISCUSSION

The women in this study raised a variety of issues that related to the pains of imprisonment and the need to provide safer facilities that could meet their needs. The low inmate population in most states limits the number of options available to prison administrators when dealing with female prisoners. Improvements in prison classification systems, rehabilitation, and medical care represent areas that have been long neglected and may go a long way in diminishing the stress that female inmates experience.

The lack of classification was perhaps the most problematic area. Although classification of inmates certainly cannot prevent all violence, such a system could go a long way in providing the separation of inmates by security and psychological needs. Most women's correctional facilities house inmates under one roof and space is unavailable to segregate the more aggressive prisoners from those women who are less prone to initiate violent means for conflict resolution (Pollock, 1995).

Those inmates who have severe psychological problems often are not segregated from the rest of the population (Clear & Cole, 1997; Farr, 2000). Again, this was usually a consequence of housing inmates together without regard for the needs of those who needed treatment and separation from the rest of the offender population. Often, female inmates claim that their fellow prisoners who suffer from serious psychological problems engage in abnormal and dangerous behavior (Pollock-Byrne, 1992). In addition, there is a serious problem with women inmates who attempt suicide and engage in self-mutilation (Pollock-Byrne, 1990). Obviously, these inmates should be classified and placed in separate parts of the correctional facility with programs that provide mental health services.

Adequate rehabilitation and medical services are crucial to improving the conditions of most prisons. Women prisoners who are substance abusers have distinct treatment needs that should be provided during their period of imprisonment (Prendergast, Wellisen, & Falkin, 1995). These treatment services are related to mental and physical health, vocational training, and issues involving family. Additionally, most women come to prison with more of a need for medical services than male inmates. According to Lord (1995), they are sicker, have more recent injuries, and lack previous health care. Women in prison are in need of pre- and postnatal care, yet gynecological and obstetrical services are rare in most institutions (Belknap, 1996; Lord, 1995).

Sexual misconduct by male correctional staff is a serious problem that threatens the autonomy and self esteem of many female prisoners. According to Human Rights Watch (1996), the grievance or investigatory procedures for threatened and abused women often are ineffectual. Furthermore, correctional employees engage in abuse because they believe that they rarely will be held accountable. Female inmates may not report sexual misconduct by staff because they are afraid of reprisals or fear that they will not be believed, or because sexual activities with staff often offer reciprocity in the way of goods and services (Moss, 1999).

It appeared that being a female imprisoned parent came with a high price. The costs included not seeing your children or, if visits were allowed, having limited contact. In some cases, an inmate parent might suffer the consequences of having the state intercede. The loss of outside personal relationships with husbands or children represented one of the most difficult aspects of imprisonment and was seen by many women as the most painful part of prison life.

This research showed that an important element of prison life for many women was dealing with the fear and violence. While the experiences related by the former inmates in this study might not be representative of all imprisoned women, the overriding focus on the hostility they endured points to the need for a better understanding of their experiences. The narratives suggested that violence in women's prisons was common and that female-male comparisons might depreciate the volatile situations and process of socialization that female inmates undergo.

REFERENCES

Alexander, J., & Humphrey, E. (1988). *Initial security classification guidelines for females.* New York: State Department of Corrections.

Austin, J., Chan, L., & Elms, W. (1993). *Women classification study—Indiana department of corrections.* San Francisco, CA: National Council on Crime and Delinquency.

Aylward, A., & Thomas, J. (1984). Quiescence in women's prison litigation. *Justice Quarterly, 1,* 253-276.

Barry, E. (1987). Imprisoned mothers face extra hardships. *National Prison Journal, 14,* 1-4.

Baunach, P.J. (1985). *Mothers in prison.* New Brunswick, NJ: Transaction Books.

Belknap, J. (1996). *The invisible woman: gender, crime, and justice.* Belmont, CA: Wadsworth Publishing.

Bloom, B. (1995). Public policy and the children of incarcerated parents. In: K. Gabel, & D. Johnston (Eds.), *Children of incarcerated parents* (pp. 271-284). New York: Lexington Books.

Bloom, B., & Chesney-Lind, M. (2000). Women in prison: vengeful equity. In: R. Muraskin (Ed.), *It's a crime: women and justice* (pp. 183-204). Upper Saddle River, NJ: Prentice Hall.

Bloom, B., & Steinhart, D. (1993). *Why punish the children? A reappraisal of the children of incarcerated mothers in America.* San Francisco, CA: National Council on Crime and Delinquency.

Bowker, L. H. (1981). Gender differences in prisoner subcultures. In: L. H. Bowker (Ed.), *Women and crime in America* (pp. 409-419). New York: Macmillan.

Brennan, T., & Austin, J. (1997). *Women in jail: classification issues.* Washington, DC: National Institute of Corrections, Department of Justice.

Burke, P., & Adams, L. (1991). *Classification of women offenders in state correctional facilities: a handbook for practitioners.* Washington, DC: National Institute of Corrections, Department of Justice.

Chesney-Lind, M. (1991). Patriarchy, prisons and jails: a critical look at trends in women's incarceration. *Prison Journal, 71,* 51-67.

Chesney-Lind, M. (1997). *The female offender: girls, women and crime.* Thousand Oaks, CA: Sage Publications.

Chesney-Lind, M., & Pollock, J. M. (1995). Women's prisons: equality with a vengeance. In: J. M. Pollock-Byrne, & A. V. Merlo (Eds.), *Women, law and social control* (pp. 155-175). Boston: Allyn and Bacon.

Clear, T., & Cole, G. (1997). *American corrections* (4th ed.). Belmont, CA: Wadsworth.

Cloward, R. A. (1977). Social control in the prison. In: R. G. Leger, & J. R. Stratton (Eds.), *The sociology of corrections* (pp. 110-132). New York: Wiley.

Crawford, J. (1990). *The female offender: what does the future hold?* Washington, DC: American Correction Association.

Datesman, S., & Cales, G. (1983). I'm still the same mommy. *Prison Journal, 63,* 142-154.

Dobash, R. P., Dobash, R. E., & Gutteridge, S. (1986). *The imprisonment of women.* New York: Basil Blackwell.

Farr, K. A. (2000). Classification for female inmates: moving forward. *Crime and Delinquency, 46,* 3-17.

Fletcher, B., Shaver, L., & Moon, D. (1993). *Women prisoners: a forgotten population.* Westport, CT: Praeger.

Fox, J. G. (1982). Women in prison: a case study in the social reality of stress. In: R. Johnson, & H. Toch (Eds.), *The pains of imprisonment* (pp. 205-220). Prospect Heights, IL: Waveland Press.

Giallombardo, R. (1966). *Society of women: a study of a women's prison.* New York: Wiley.

Glaser, B. G., & Strauss, A. L. (1967). *The discovery of grounded theory: strategies for qualitative research.* London: Weidenfeld and Nicholson.

Goffman, E. (1961). *Asylums.* Garden City, NY: Anchor.

Greenfeld, L. A., & Minor-Harper, S. (1991). *Women in prison* (Bureau of Justice statistics, special report). Washington, DC: US Department of Justice.

Hefferman, E. (1972). *Making it in prison: the square, the cool, and the life.* New York: Wiley.

Henriques, Z. W. (1996). Imprisoned mothers and their children: separation—reunion syndrome dual impact. *Women and Criminal Justice, 8,* 77-95.

Human Rights Watch (1996). *All too familiar: sexual abuse of women in U.S. state prisons.* New York: HRW.

Hunter, S. M. (1984). Issues and challenges facing women's prisons in the 1980s. *Prison Journal, 64,* 129-135.

Larsen, J., & Nelson, J. (1984). Women, friendship, and adaptation to prison. *Journal of Criminal Justice, 12,* 601-615.

Leger, R. (1987). Lesbianism among women prisoners: participants and non-participants. *Criminal Justice and Behavior, 14,* 463-479.

Linn, R. (1997). Soldier's narratives of selective moral resistance. In: Lieblich, & R. Josselson (Eds.), *The narrative study of lives* (pp. 95-112). Thousand Oaks, CA: Sage.

Lord, E. (1995). A prison superintendent's perspective on women in prison. *Prison Journal, 75,* 257-269.

McClellan, D. (1994). Disparity in the discipline of male and female inmates in Texas prisons. *Women and Criminal Justice, 5,* 71-97.

Mitchell, J. (1988). Women, AIDS and public policy. *Law and Public Policy Journal, 3,* 50-51.

Moss, A. (1999). Sexual misconduct among staff and inmates. In: P. Carlson, & J. Garrett (Eds.), *Prison and jail administration* (pp. 189-196). Gaithersburg, MD: Aspen Publishers.

Owen, B. (1998). *In the mix: struggle and survival in a women's prison.* Albany, NY: State University of New York Press.

Pearson, P. (1998). *When she was bad.* New York: Penguin Books.

Pollock, J. M. (1995). Women in corrections: custody and the caring ethic. In: A. V. Merlo, & J. M. Pollock (Eds.), *Women, law, and social control* (pp. 97-116). Boston: Allyn and Bacon.

Pollock-Byrne, J. M. (1990). *Women, prison, and crime.* Pacific Grove, CA: Brooks/Cole.

Pollock-Byrne, J. M. (1992). Women in prison: why are their numbers increasing? In: P. J. Benekes, & A. V. Merlo (Eds.), *Corrections: dilemmas and directions* (pp. 79-95). Cincinnati, OH: Anderson Publishing.

Prendergast, M., Wellisen, J., & Falkin, G. (1995). Assessment of and services for substance-abusing women offenders in community and correctional settings. *Prison Journal, 75,* 240-256.

Rafter, N. H. (1990). *Partial justice: women in state prisons, 1800-1935.* Boston, MA: Northeastern University Press.

Ragin, C. C. (1994). *Constructing social research.* Thousand Oaks, CA: Pine Forge Press.

Rasche, C. (2000). The dislike of female offenders among correctional officers. In: R. Muraskin (Ed.), *It's a crime: women and justice* (pp. 237-252). Upper Saddle, NJ: Prentice Hall.

Seidman, T. E. (1998). *Interviewing as qualitative research: a guide for researchers in education and the social sciences.* New York: Teachers College Press.

Snell, T., & Morton, D. (1994). *Survey of state inmates: women in prison.* Washington, DC: Bureau of Justice Statistics.

Stanton, A. (1980). *When mothers go to jail.* Lexington, MA: Appleton Crafts.

Sykes, G. M. (1958). *The society of captives: a study of a maximum security prison.* Princeton, NJ: Princeton University Press.

Toch, H. (1975). *Men in crisis.* Chicago: Aldine-Atherton.

Ward, D., & Kassebaum, G. (1965). Women's prison: sex and social structure. Chicago: Aldine-Atherton.

This study examines the adjustment problems and work strategies of female deputy sheriffs working in four county jails and three local detention centers. The authors discuss the issues of integration in employment, sex-role stereotyping, gender-based work strategies, and differential treatment within the organization. Pogrebin and Poole found that, in women's roles as jail officers, they experience integration difficulties predominantly imposed on them by their male co-workers. These difficulties include gender stereotyping, role conflict, and differential performance expectations. The authors further analyze the impact of the responses of women deputy jailers to these work-related problems.

WOMEN DEPUTIES AND JAIL WORK

MARK R. POGREBIN

ERIC D. POOLE

During the past 20 years, there has been a dramatic increase in the number of female correctional officers working in the nation's jails. According to a recent study by Zupan (1990, p. 6), women now comprise fully one fifth of the correctional officers employed in the 107 largest jail systems. The primary stimulus for the increased employment and use

Reprinted from *Journal of Contemporary Criminal Justice*, Vol. 14, No. 2, May 1998, 117–134. Copyright © 1998 Sage Publications, Inc.

The authors extend their appreciation to the administrators and staff of the jails and detention facilities for their cooperation and assistance in this study. Special thanks go to those 108 female jail deputies who shared their work experiences with us, as well as to our team of graduate research assistants who devoted their energies to ensuring the project's success.

of female officers has been the need to comply with federal guidelines on hiring (Equal Opportunity Act of 1972 amending Title VII of the Civil Rights Act of 1964), as well as with various court orders to implement hiring quotas to increase female representation or to rewrite entrance exams and requirements to encourage the employment of women (see Morton, 1991). Although the initial stimulus for increased hiring of women was prompted by legislative and judicial mandates, several administrative factors have also driven the need for more female employees. First, jails must house both male and female inmates, and women are needed to supervise the female residents. Second, female officers are needed to conduct searches of female visitors. Third, a rapid expansion of the jail workforce has increased demand and opened job opportunities for qualified female applicants.

The employment gains women have realized in local corrections are even more dramatic when compared with female employment in other areas of the criminal justice system. Women currently comprise a larger percentage of uniformed officers working in jails (21.5%) than in either state (16.7%) or federal (11.2%) adult correctional facilities (Maguire & Pastore, 1994, p. 96; Zupan, 1990, p. 6). Among full-time sworn law enforcement personnel, women make up 15.4% of the deputies in sheriff's departments (the law enforcement agencies typically operating local jails); yet, only 8.1% and 4.6% of officers in local police departments and state police agencies, respectively, are female (Maguire & Pastore, 1994, pp. 51, 52).

Despite women's increased nationwide presence in corrections work, working as a female jail officer is unique in terms of nontraditional work for women; it is qualitatively different from other work in that violence is prevalent in the work environment and it is perceived to be a highly sex-typed male job requiring qualities of dominance, authoritativeness, and aggressiveness. In terms of preferred job characteristics, female qualities of nurturing, sensitivity, and understanding are thought by some to be not merely unnecessary but potentially detrimental to job performance. Because the work of female officers is expected to conform to masculine sex-typed norms, it is likely that the problems faced by women entering this occupation are exaggerated

and therefore more readily identifiable. However, there has been comparatively little written on the integration difficulties of female officers working in local jails.

Based on studies of women working as guards in male prisons, several issues of workforce integration appear particularly problematic: gender stereotyping, role conflict, and differential performance expectations. (Farnworth, 1992; Jurik, 1985; Zimmer, 1986). What is lacking almost entirely from the research literature is a focus on the impact of these problems on the women officers themselves. How do women perceive and experience these problems at work? How do the implied negative consequences of these organizational problems affect women on and off the job? Are there identifiable coping or adaptive work strategies that women adopt in handling these problems? The research presented here seeks to identify the nature of integration difficulties of women working in local jails and understand how these officers respond to their unique work experiences.

METHOD

The data for this study were obtained from semistructured interviews with sworn officers working in four county jails and three adult detention centers located in the Denver metropolitan area. These facilities were managed and staffed by personnel from four sheriffs' departments. Using personnel rosters of deputy sheriffs provided by the respective facilities, we selected a 50% systematic random sample ($n = 135$) of all female officers from each institution. We contacted sampled officers individually to describe the purpose of the study, request their participation, and obtain informed consent. A total of 119 women agreed to participate, and interview times were then scheduled. Because of conflicts related to vacation, sick leave, work assignment, transfer, and so on, interviews with 11 women could not be conducted. Thus, the present study is based on interview data from 108 women deputies. Their ages range from 24 to 51 (*Mdn* = 37), and their length of experience at their present facility ranges from 1 to 15 years (*Mdn* = 5).

Table 1   Inmate and Officer Distributions by Sex for Each Facility

Facility	Inmates		Officers		50% Sample of Female Officers	Female Study Participants
	Male	Female	Male	Female		
Jail 1	279	18	38	21	11	10
Jail 2	391	34	158	26	13	10
Jail 3	656	67	146	29	15	13
Jail 4	1739	172	285	81	41	30
Detention 1	218	27	105	45	23	18
Detention 2	475	53	159	27	14	12
Detention 3	541	35	92	36	18	15

Interviews were conducted at the respective facilities in private conference rooms, library carrels, or visitation rooms during off hours. Each interview lasted approximately 1 1/2 hours, and we tape-recorded the interviews with the subjects' consent. A semistructured interview format was used, which relied on sequential probes to pursue leads provided by subjects. This allowed the deputies to identify and elaborate on important domains they perceived to characterize their experiences in jail work, rather than the researchers eliciting responses to structured questions.

The interview tapes were transcribed for qualitative data analysis. Qualitative data analysis involves a search for general statements about relationships among categories of observations. As Schatzman and Strauss (1973) note, "the most fundamental operation in the analysis of qualitative data is that of discovering significant *classes* of things, persons and events and the *properties* which characterize them" (p. 110). Employing grounded theory techniques advanced by Glaser and Strauss (1967), we categorized the data into four conceptual domains of jail work experiences as identified by the female deputies. The conceptual domains were tokenism, sex role stereotyping, gender-based work strategies, and differential treatment.

It must be noted that in all seven facilities of the present study, women officers were assigned to supervise both male and female inmates. The duties of jail deputies were the same for both male and female officers. This is an important occupational issue because many jails in this nation do not permit female officers to work in male inmate housing units, which results in unequal opportunities for women to advance within the organizations.

RESULTS

Tokenism

Historically, the criminal justice system has been viewed as a male-dominated field of employment. It has been only since the implementation of equal opportunity statutes and development of affirmative action plants that affect public agencies' hiring practices that women have been employed in greater numbers as correctional officers in our nation's jails. Although much progress has been made to recruit and retain women in the corrections field, women remain a numeric minority in all jails nationwide (Zupan, 1990). Because female deputies are relatively few in number, they tend to stand out in the jail environment. This results in their job performance being more closely observed and scrutinized than that of their male peers (Farnworth, 1992). Quite often, female deputies express the feeling that they are judged as members of a gender class, instead of as individuals, as illustrated by the following comments:

There are many men working here and a small number of us, so it is really easy to put us all into one type.

The men still don't see us as equals. When I came here many years ago I heard them say, "Those damn broads don't belong here." And that's how many still see us—as women wearing uniforms, not as fellow officers doing the same job.

Zimmer (1986) notes that differences between token female employees and the dominant male group tend to be exaggerated, whereas similarities between them are often ignored. The female officers frequently claim that their small number results in unfair performance evaluations by their male counterparts.

> We are all judged by what one woman does. If one woman can't cut it, we all are seen as not being able to cut it.
>
> I get pissed off when the male officers complain about something a female officer did or didn't do. Somehow I'm guilty by association. . . . But if a guy fucks up, we don't blame the other male officers because they're men.

Sex Role Stereotyping

Two models of job performance have been applied to methods that men and women use in their work (see Belknap, 1991; Zimmer, 1986; Zupan, 1986). The *gender model* is concerned with what women bring to the job in terms of attitudes, prior experiences, and modes of interaction, and how these factors affect women's occupational experience. The *job model* suggests that gender differences on the job are driven by the nature of the occupation and the structure of the work organization. Our findings on female deputies' work behavior tend to conform with the gender model. First, we find that several problems women officers experience are related to how they deal with sex role expectations at work. The following women officers express difficulties reconciling their gender role socialization with job demands:

> I think most women are raised to be more submissive and more compliant than men, and that's different when you work in jail because you have to be an authority and learn to be appropriately assertive. . . . Women are less likely to be comfortable being assertive and confrontational.
>
> Women must deal with a different set of emotions than men. We feel things differently and react to things differently. . . . Some things are more likely to upset us than men, and although we try not to let it show, it still is going to bother us.

Other gender socialization experiences may present obstacles to competing with male officers. Here a 15-year veteran officer expresses her thoughts on how feminine role values have affected her work:

> I finally realized after years on the job that I've been playing gin rummy and the men have been playing poker. . . . We are socialized to be a team player and sacrifice for the good of the group. . . . Men are like sharks. Play on a team with sharks, they'll eat you alive.

According to Belknap (1991), one may expect that women who pursue job opportunities in a highly stereotyped male occupation would embrace feminist values directly challenging traditional male dominance and authoritarianism. Research on police and corrections officers, however, have found this not to be the case; women officers have tended to espouse traditional sex role attitudes (Martin, 1992; Zimmer, 1986). Nevertheless, our women respondents emphasized the distinction between their roles at home and at work.

> When I'm at home, my husband's the boss of the family. . . . I feel that's good for a marriage. I also feel it is important for me as a female. I have got to have that time to be a woman.
>
> I'm basically an old-fashioned gal, and I have my opinion where females belong, but I don't think that applies to the workplace. In the workplace, we should be equals.

Jurik (1988) observes that female correctional officers may attempt to defuse gender stereotypes by calling attention to job performance. Such a strategy consists of emphasizing professional standards, developing effective interpersonal management skills, emphasizing teamwork, using humor to develop friendships with their male counterparts, and developing mentors to enhance their acceptability. A related issue concerns the consequences of women trying to meet job expectations that require a modification of their traditional sex role appearance and behavior. Baunach and Rafter (1982) note that research on women who are employed as line staff in police and corrections work often have their femininity questioned by those males with whom they work. There is also speculation concerning their sexual preferences (Petersen, 1982). Having a hair style that is not traditionally what male deputies think is the norm will bring derogatory sexual insinuations.

> I get comments about my hair being cut short. The male officers thought I became butch. Petty crap like that happens often.
>
> I don't look good in long hair. I've got kind of a pea head, so I've always worn my hair cropped pretty short. The guys at work were quick to label me a "dyke." I get all sorts of comments about sex acts with other women . . . and they tell me their fantasy is to make me a real woman.

These female staff members also receive comments about their appearance and sexual identify from the male inmates. Quite often this is a strategy that prisoners use to manipulate and intimidate the women deputies. It is another way of testing females officers, one which looks for weaknesses to exploit.

> You learn that inmates will try to find out something about you that they can use against you sometime. Name calling is an obvious one when you're female working with male inmates. . . . Calling me "butch" is pretty tame. You should hear some of the comments.

Gender-Based Work Strategies

Van Voorhis, Cullen, Link, and Wolfe (1991) observe that female correctional officers import different orientations and statuses that condition work perceptions and experiences. Female correctional staff perform their tasks differently than their male peers. For example, female officers tend to employ human resource management strategies, whereas male officers tend to adopt authoritarian control techniques (Crouch, 1985). The former facilitative approach to managing inmates is viewed by female officers as an advantage they possess in a male-dominated work setting.

Jurik (1985) observes that female officers perceive themselves as more sensitive to the needs of inmates and are more able to incorporate a rehabilitative-service approach in their work relations with inmates. As a result, Pollock (1986) notes that both male and female corrections officers believe that women are more responsive to inmates' problems and express more empathy than male coworkers. Female officers note that inmates respond better to this "softer" approach:

> Female officers have a little bit more compassion and more concern about possibly getting somebody rehabilitated. We have more of a sense for feelings that don't get expressed and [are] more likely to sense when something's wrong or bothering an inmate.
>
> Men have a tough time getting in touch with their true feelings. They're afraid to express them because men are going to think they're wimps or weak or something. The inmates seem to open up to us one-on-one.

Many female officers also describe effective inmate management techniques as analogous to good parenting skills. The deputy explains how the socialization of women to be nurturing facilitates working with male inmates in the following:

> I think there is also a time you do need a motherly approach to a situation. . . . It doesn't mean we are a soft touch. Believe me, nobody pulls much over on us. But there are times when you can see that somebody's got a genuine problem. We approach prisoners with problems.

A related gender-based skill that is seen to work well is the ability to listen to inmates and discern the nature of their problems.

> So you're listening to what is not being said, just like you would your child. Your child's telling you he hurt himself and you are using your ability to look at him to judge, to check, to see where he is hurt, to understand what's going on, and I think that's a big advantage in here.
>
> My style as a woman clearly is a plus here. . . . I think that's because women listen better than men. Sometimes inmates just need to talk to someone who will listen. And when you listen, it shows that you are concerned and care about their problems.
>
> A lot of times male officers don't listen as well as we do. They don't take the time to understand what's going on. So we have more of a sense of control over the situation, where the men really don't have a clue.

Another gender socialization skill that female deputies stress is forming judgments or basing decisions on how situations feel (i.e., intuition).

I think women are more on top of things than male officers because we are more intuitive. The guys only see what's in front of them, and they don't see the whole picture as much as we do.

Men take things one at a time and we can handle many things all at the same time. . . . I think it's because women think different than men. It's feminine intuition. Men don't have it. They can't think that way.

One of the most pervasive themes expressed by nearly every female officer in each of the jails studied was the perception that female staff members possess more effective communication skills than do the male staff. Because they tend not to possess the same physical strength as the male officers, the female officers rely on and hone their verbal skills.

I find that my physical strength is not equal to that of male officers. My reasoning and patience are better. I can de-escalate an argument by talking with them.

I'm not big enough to give verbal threats and say that I'm going to do this or that to you, when I can't do it. . . . Women have better communication skills than the male officers. This would be our strength.

Male officers are more confrontational with inmates than are female officers. Men are quicker to use threats to counter inmate disobedience and to resort to force as an immediate solution in effecting inmate compliance to their orders. In short, men working in jails are more willing than women officers to employ threats, intimidation, and physical coercion in order-maintenance tasks. According to the female officers, such aggressive compliance techniques simply exacerbate inmate control problems.

Male officers can make things worse by acting like a man. Their manhood is at stake. . . . But there is that male pride against male pride that does escalate the situation.

I feel sorry for the male officers who go around [acting] tough because I know they're scared. Inmates know this too and know how to get to these officers. It's a . . . test of manhood, like they have to prove something.

The facility of their communication skills has proven to be advantageous for female officers in maintaining social control. Verbal skills are recognized as especially critical in diffusing threatening situations with aggressive inmates, thus avoiding an escalation of violence and the potential for physical injuries (Farnworth, 1992; Simon & Simon, 1993).

Zimmer (1987) reports that female guards are more likely than male guards to develop friendly relationships with inmates to get inmates to follow the rules. One method to facilitate work relationships and gain inmate compliance is through the strategic use of humor (Pogrebin & Poole, 1988). An encounter with an inmate who was acting out was managed by a female officer with a simple, humorous remark:

We had one guy who was an exhibitionist. Every time I would go by his cell on night shift, he'd be in there with no clothes on jerking off. He'd only do it to the female officers. He'd do it for a reaction. I wouldn't give him one. Even last week we had this guy saying, "Is this big enough for you?" To diffuse the incident, I have this little pocket knife that has tweezers on it and I said, "Do you need these?" He gets embarrassed and just walks away.

Male inmates often make sexually explicit overtures to women staff. They say it loudly enough so other inmates can hear; these incidents of insolence threaten to undermine the authority of the officer. One officer describes how she handles such incidents through humor:

The male inmates make a lot of comments [lewd remarks and sexual propositions] about female officers. . . . My way of dealing with these situations is to say, "You haven't been in here that long to be that desperate." They laugh, I laugh, and it would be all be over.

According to Fine (1983), humor fosters "a sense of social control for the participants on how to deal with these threatening or embarrassing topics" (p. 175). For female officers, who are consciously aware of their physical limitations, humor represents an effective means of inmate control for situations in which they are subjected to verbal assaults.

Developing and maintaining good officer-inmate relations in turn serves as an insurance policy in protecting officers against inmate attacks. Following, several women officers point out the importance of inmate backing:

> There are inmates that test you at every occasion, just to see your reaction. But there are limits they won't cross because other inmates won't let them. The other inmates can exert a lot of power and keep things under control.
>
> We share power with inmates. You have to know who's on your side. . . . Inmate peer pressure in the module will keep me from getting attacked.
>
> You have inmates you've helped or taken a personal interest in and you've earned their respect. I can count on their help if I really need it.

Another operational tact that appears to be closely associated with gender-based learning is being organized. More than half of the female officers in this study were single parents. Due to the necessity of playing a traditional family role and working full-time as a jail officer, women must maintain a well-organized lifestyle.

> Sometimes I feel I'm more organized than some of the male deputies. It's simply because all through life I've had to learn to juggle the job, the kids, laundry, groceries, making dinner, planning meals, doing all this stuff. So I've had to learn to organize my time at home and at work.

Women officers feel they are more efficient on the job than the men and attribute their work-performance edge to their having to manage the responsibilities of both the household and full-time employment.

Finally, Worden (1993) reports that female police officers emphasize rules and regulations more and exercise discretion less frequently than do their male counterparts. This is because the standard operating procedures define roles and evaluation criteria, establishing a level playing field with the men. Women jail officers similarly perceive going by the book as a safer method of operation, thus avoiding risky discretionary decision making that may lead to criticism.

> I've learned it's best to know the rules and stick to them in everything you do in here. Someone's always waiting for you to mess up . . . so it's better to have rules you can rely on to do your job. . . . Because if a female officer messes up

because she wasn't following the rules, then it's made 10 times worse.

Most women in our sample also believe that adhering to rules and regulations is a function of their gender socialization.

> Women pay more attention to detail, more strict abidance to the rules. I mean, the rules are the rules, that's the way we've been socialized. We follow the rules or we lose our turn. And we follow the rules well. Even if some rules don't make sense, if it's a rule, we still follow it.

Gender-related behavioral traits provide female officers with nontraditional but effective ways of performing in the male-dominated jail setting; yet, it is not often that such work techniques are appreciated by the male officers and supervisors. Although male and female corrections officers may carry out their job tasks differently, Belknap (1991) argues that women should be judged by their job effectiveness, not by how well they adopt techniques employed by male officers.

Differential Treatment

Kissel and Katsampes (1980) report that the overwhelming majority of female deputies working in the jail they studied were satisfied with their performance and believed they did as good a job as their male peers. Although we also found the women in our sample to express such sentiments, their concern did not lie in self-assessment or appraisals but in their differential treatment by male staff. Equal treatment in collegial relations, equal treatment in performance evaluations, and equal opportunities in work assignments were emphasized as their most persistent employment issues. The women officers were confident in their abilities to do the job and wanted to be treated as equals with the men.

> I am not a women's libber. I don't believe every female can do every male's job, or what's traditionally been a male job. I feel that if a woman is going to do a job, then she better be able to do the whole job. If she can't, she doesn't deserve to have the job. . . . I want people to know that I'm a good officer, not a good female officer.

To be judged as an individual officer based on adequacy of performance was deemed critical in addressing the issue of equal treatment. The women also objected to the application of traditional sex role stereotypes by male officers. Such stereotypes were deemed both inappropriate and demeaning, as well as seen as perpetuating myths that women are inferior to men in performing jail work.

> Some men have a hard time accepting women working in jail that they do everything they can to put us down and keep us down. . . . They make crude remarks and sick jokes about women and sex that make you feel uncomfortable and disgusted.

One area of job performance where the differential treatment women experience is most crucial involves reactions to mistakes an officer makes at work. According to women officers, their mistakes are subject to heightened scrutiny. More attention is paid to their errors and more concern is expressed. The consequences of this differential perception and response are manifested in poorer work evaluations and fewer opportunities for promotion.

> When a female screws up, it is exaggerated by . . . male officers. They may kid you about it more or you may hear about it a little longer; whereas if a male officer makes the same mistake, it's forgotten very quickly.

The women cited the added pressure and stress they were under because their work was more closely monitored. Also, they were concerned that they constantly had to validate themselves as women and as officers.

> [Women deputies] have to prove ourselves in two ways. We have to prove ourselves as being feminine . . . [as] still having those qualities. We also have to prove ourselves as being able to handle stuff on our own, and always be willing to back up our fellow deputies. . . . If we lose the slightest bit of respect . . . you have to prove yourself all over again.

Perhaps the most demoralizing realization for women employed in jails is that their opportunities for advancement up the ranks are limited.

Chapman, Minor, Rieker, Mills, and Bottum (1983) report that female corrections officers perceive unequal opportunities and unequal treatment in promotion. Poole and Pogrebin (1988) uncover a similar perception among female police officers; specifically, after only 3 years on the job, policewomen view their chances of ever being promoted greatly diminished. A veteran officer who had many years working in the patrol side of the sheriff's department tells of her disappointment in not having an opportunity for advancement: "I came off the street as a road deputy after 12 years on the front lines. I really did think I had the skills to come here and make some rank and do well, but that will never happen."

Women in corrections routinely experience exclusion, discrimination, and hostility from male supervisors and coworkers. Their attitudes toward job commitment and aspirations to advance in the profession are adversely affected by such treatment (Flynn, 1982), as illustrated in the following observation: "I can really motivate people. I can get amazing things done by saying 'Please' and 'Thank you.' They [male supervisors] don't see that. It's just a different skill level, but they don't recognize it." Jurik (1985) claims that supervisors who are biased against women working as corrections officers use performance evaluations to discourage them and keep them in subordinate positions. Because performance history is a critical criterion in advancement to supervisory ranks, women officers are viewed as less promotable. One deputy notes the nature of the inequality:

> There is one woman who really is an exceptional deputy and I like her a lot. She is really strong and stern and she knows her job very well. If she were a man, they would think she is the best deputy in the world, but because she is female, they think she is a bitch. But if a male deputy would act like her, they would promote him real fast.

In those rare instances when a female officer receives a choice assignment or a promotion, she is perceived by male staff as not having earned it. For example, women are often teased about trading sexual favors for advancement.

> There are men on this job that think anytime a woman gets ahead, the first thing out of their

mouth is: "Oh, I wonder who she's sleeping with?" If I'd slept with as many men as they say, my butt would be the size of Texas. . . . That's their way of dealing with women who're better than them.

Lourich and Stohr (1993) argue that managers and supervisors in corrections need to work toward transforming the work environment into one where women officers can feel appreciated as valuable resources and feel they are working in an organization that is intolerant of sexual and gender harassment from the men with whom they work. Finally, Kerle (1985) and Zimmer (1989) note that jail administrators must adopt a strong advocacy role in ensuring equal opportunities for career advancement for female officers. Such support will increase the women's security in their positions and their exhibition of leadership behaviors.

DISCUSSION

Gutek and Morasch (1982, p. 59) have argued that gender-based expectations for women's behavior in the workplace is a function of male coworkers perceiving female coworkers as women first and workers second. They offer three interrelated explanations for this perception. First, gender identity is more closely tied to a basic cognitive perspective than to a specific work role; consequently, an individual is initially characterized as a male or female, then as an occupational type. Our research reveals that there was a pervasive expectation that jail guards should act in a manner consistent with the sex role expectations of the traditional male employee. Although female officers may use different means to achieve the same outcome as male officers, their job performance was more likely to be evaluated negatively in comparison with that of their male counterparts. These different work styles and techniques especially challenged traditional organizational norms of maintaining institutional security and control, especially when it comes to one-on-one handling of potentially violent situations involving hostile and threatening inmates.

Second, women may find greater comfort levels associated with adopting stereotypical female roles because they find male coworkers more accepting of them and less threatened by them, which in turn facilitate both social and organizational support. Yet, in jail work, we found that female officers who played to their feminine strengths (e.g., verbal skills, nurturance, empathy) reported that their efforts were not fully understood or appreciated by male officers and supervisors. For example, adopting friendly interaction styles with inmates may be seen as fraternizing and compromising institutional security.

Third, because men are more likely to interact with women in other-than-work roles—which are typically segregated both organizationally and socially—they tend to rely on traditional sex role stereotypes in dealing with female coworkers. Gutek and Morasch (1982) report that "men are more likely than women to project sexuality into ambiguous behavior between sexes at work, and to feel that such sexuality is appropriate in the work environment" (p. 59). The women deputies in our study reported this sexualization of the workplace, ranging from derogatory remarks about their appearance and sexual preference to denigration of work performance because of their femininity.

In sum, the conflict between gender role norms and occupational role norms in jail work poses unique obstacles for female officers. The traditional male attitude about the inherent masculine nature of the job of jail guard makes the prospect of a female coworker particularly offensive to some male officers. The presence of uniformed women deputies in the cell blocks is viewed by these individuals not only as an uncomfortable reality but also as patently unwise. Both the male and female officer become caught up in a double bind, with the men demanding toughness, assertiveness, and physical strength demonstrated by their coworkers; yet, stereotypically, women are not supposed to be tough, aggressive, and physically strong. Ironically, for the female officer to be judged as effective and competent, she must behave less like a woman and more like a man, which may threaten the male officer's sense of masculinity. If the female officer uses feminine skills, she runs the risk of being perceived as unfit for jail work.

The catch-22 situation that confronts female officers has some potentially dangerous implications for both the health of the jail organization and that of the individual jail deputy. For example, research in law enforcement agencies has shown that women and minority officers are especially vulnerable to the psychological and physiological disorders associated with sustained exposure to job-related stress. For example, Wexler and Logan's (1983) study of the sources of stress among female officers in a large metropolitan police department indicated that women's greatest obstacle was in demonstrating that they could be effective officers without compromising their femininity:

> The most significant stressors seem to be ones in which others were denying them as officers, as women, or both. It is psychologically a very threatening and uncomfortable situation when one's self-perception is substantially different from the perception of others. This is particularly the case when such fundamental identities are at stake as one's gender and profession. (p. 53)

Individuals who feel or know they are deemed marginal employees experience anxiety and are more sensitive about their job performance, often assuming a defensive posture, attempting to overcompensate to prove others wrong in their attitudes, or otherwise reacting in ways that may be perceived as inappropriate or undesirable.

The job stress experienced by women working in jails is further exacerbated by their lack of access to the peer-group support structure of fellow male deputies. The informal work subculture often functions to reduce stress, providing individual officers a forum within which they can vent safely. The lack of acceptance of female deputies in this traditional male fraternity thus denies women a critical organizational coping mechanism to mitigate the impact of work-related stress. As noted earlier, female jail deputies, because of their minority or token status, stand out in the work setting and are subject to heightened scrutiny and more critical evaluation. Yet Wexler and Quinn (1985) report that this does not happen to women in fully integrated work groups, suggesting that the number of women present in an organization is more important than their socialization or gender per se. This finding would seem to encourage more aggressive recruitment and retention of women officers, who, by their sheer numbers, may promote the development of an androgynous work culture where an individual officer's success is predicated on ability rather than sexual physiology.

In conclusion, the presence of women in what has long been an exclusively male occupation poses a multitude of individual and organizational conflicts. A generally accepted principle in organizational theory is that the workplace functions as a complex occupational and organizational entity that shapes workers' perceptions of self and others. The relationship between gender and organizational status suggests that those work roles assigned to women are seen as appropriate extensions of their more diffuse social role of nurturance. These arrangements can act to reflect, magnify, or distort gender differences, which then confirm prevailing stereotypes and organizational norms. This has culminated in male coworkers' and supervisors' limited and often inaccurate appraisal of female officers' true potential and capabilities.

To persist in this state of affairs is an untenable situation because consistently evaluating female officers on the basis of male sex-typed norms distracts the organization's attention from competence-based standards and reduces its ability to identify and analyze work problems or formulate and implement solutions. The jail must demonstrate a philosophical commitment to the thorough integration of women within the formal and informal organizational structure. To the extent that women are denied access to informal channels of information gathering and conflict resolution, the more they are compelled to respond formally (e.g., official disciplinary actions, formal grievances and complaints, legal action), with its associated implications of contested control and power. Jail deputies, whether male or female, are less likely to perform effectively if they are not perceived as exercising legitimate authority under conditions of equality.

The nature and scope of jail work continue to increase in complexity, presenting new job expectations and challenges for male and female officers alike. Given the need to adjust and respond to changing organizational demands, it becomes more critical that officers have the opportunity to hone their unique talents and use their special skills with greater latitude.

Developing alternative or multiple work strategies would thus permit officers to maximize their effectiveness and accomplish tasks otherwise beyond their capacity. An important first step in realizing such change in organizational culture is to flatten the hierarchical control mechanisms and eliminate the administrative pressures for worker uniformity that have served to reinforce and maintain traditional job stereotypes in the jail setting.

References

Baunach, P. J., & Rafter, N. H. (1982). Sex-role operations: Strategies for women working in the criminal justice system. In N. H. Rafter & E. A. Stanko (Eds.), *Judge, lawyer, victim, thief: Women, gender roles, and criminal justice* (pp. 341-358). Boston: Northeastern University Press.

Belknap, J. (1991). Women in conflict: An analysis of women correctional officers. *Women & Criminal Justice, 2*, 89-115.

Chapman, J. R., Minor, E. K., Rieker, P., Mills, T. L., & Bottum, M. (1983). *Women employed in corrections*. Washington, DC: Government Printing Office, U.S. Department of Justice, National Institute of Justice.

Crouch, B. (1985). Pandora's box: Women guards in men's prisons. *Journal of Criminal Justice, 13*, 535-548.

Farnworth, L. (1992). Women doing a man's job: Female prison officers working in a male prison. *Australian and New Zealand Journal of Criminology, 25*, 278-296.

Fine, G. A. (1983). Sociological approaches to the study of humor. In P. E. McGhee & J. H. Goldstein (Eds.), *Handbook of humor research—Vol. 1* (pp. 159-181). New York: Springer-Verlag.

Flynn, E. E. (1982). Women as criminal justice professionals: A challenge to tradition. In N. H. Rafter & E. A. Stanko (eds.), *Judge, lawyer, victim, thief: Women, gender roles, and criminal justice* (pp. 308-339). Boston: Northeastern University Press.

Glaser, B. G., & Strauss, A. L. (1967). *The discovery of grounded theory: Strategies for qualitative research*. Chicago: Aldine.

Gutek, B., & Morasch, B. (1982). Sex ratios, sex role spillover, and sexual harassment of women at work. *Journal of Social Issues, 38*, 55-74.

Jurik, N. C. (1985). An officer and a lady: Organizational barriers to women working as correctional officers in men's prisons. *Social Problems, 32*, 375-388.

Jurik, N. C. (1988). Striking a balance: Female correctional officers, gender role stereotypes, and male prisoners. *Sociological Inquiry, 58*, 291-304.

Kerle, K. E. (1985). The American woman county jail officer. In I. L. Moyer (Ed.), *The changing roles of women in the criminal justice system* (pp. 301-317). Prospect Heights, IL: Waveland Press.

Kissel, P. J., & Katsampes, P. L. (1980). The impact of women corrections officers on the functioning of institutions housing male inmates. *Journal of Offender Counseling, Services, and Rehabilitation, 4*, 213-231.

Lourich, N., & Stohr, M. (1993). Gender and jail work: Correctional policy implications of perceptual diversity in the work force. *Policy Studies Review, 12*, 66-84.

Maguire, K., & Pastore, A. L. (1994). *Sourcebook of criminal justice statistics 1993*. Washington, DC: Government Printing Office, U.S. Department of Justice, Bureau of Justice Statistics.

Martin, S. E. (1992). The changing status of women officers: Gender and power in police work. In I. L. Moyer (Ed.), *The changing roles of women in the criminal justice system* (pp. 281-305). Prospect Heights, IL: Waveland Press.

Morton, J. B. (1991). *Change, challenge, and choices: Women's role in modern corrections*. Laurel, MD: American Correctional Association.

Petersen, C. B. (1982). Doing time with the boys: An analysis of women correctional officers in all-male facilities. In B. R. Price & N. Sokoloff (Eds.), *The criminal justice system and women: Women offenders, victims, and workers* (pp. 437-460). New York: Clark Boardman.

Pogrebin, M. R., & Poole, E. D. (1988). Humor in the briefing room: A study of the strategic uses of humor among police. *Journal of Contemporary Ethnography, 17*, 183-210.

Pollock, J. M. (1986). *Sex and supervision: Guarding male and female inmates*. New York: Greenwood.

Poole, E. D., & Pogrebin, M. R. (1988). Factors affecting the decision to remain in policing: A study of women officers. *Journal of Police Science and Administration, 16*, 49-55.

Schatzman, L., & Strauss, A. L. (1973). *Field research: Strategies for a natural sociology*. Englewood Cliffs, NJ: Prentice Hall.

Simon, R. J., & Simon, J. D. (1993). Female guards in male prisons. In R. Muraskin & T. Alleman (Eds.), *It's a crime: Women and justice* (pp. 276-300). Englewood Cliffs, NJ: Regents/Prentice Hall.

Van Voorhis, P., Cullen, F. T., Link, B. G., & Wolfe, N. T. (1991). The impact of race and gender on correctional officers' orientation to the integrated environment. *Journal of Research in Crime & Delinquency, 28,* 472-500.

Wexler, J. G., & Logan, D. D. (1983). Sources of stress among women peace officers. *Journal of Police Science and Administration, 11,* 46-53.

Wexler, J. G., & Quinn, V. (1985). Considerations in the training and development of women sergeants. *Journal of Police Science and Administration, 13,* 98-105.

Worden, A. (1993). The attitudes of women and men in policing: Testing conventional and contemporary wisdom. *Criminology, 31,* 203-237.

Zimmer, L. E. (1986). *Women guarding men.* Chicago: University of Chicago Press.

Zimmer, L. E. (1987). How women reshape the prison guard role. *Gender and Society, 1,* 415-431.

Zimmer, L. E. (1989). Solving women's employment problems in corrections: Shifting the burden to administrators. *Women & Criminal Justice, 1,* 55-80.

Zupan, L. L. (1986). Gender-related differences in correctional officers' perceptions and attitudes. *Journal of Criminal Justice, 14,* 349-361.

Zupan, L. L. (1990). *The employment of women in local jails.* Paper presented at the annual meeting of the Academy of Criminal Justice Sciences, Denver, Colorado.

This research investigates the role of impression management in interviews with perspective parole candidates and how parole board members interpret these managed impressions. The findings indicate that although the paroling authority knows that impression management occurs in the vast majority of board-inmate encounters, the board is not overly concerned about the veracity of the prisoners' presentation about themselves. Instead, board members are mainly interested in whether the candidates' self-conception corresponds with the parole board's perception of the prospective parolee's true self. Board members further believe that what is important is the ability of the candidates to develop and incorporate truthful and convincing impression manage-ment skills for their successful future adjustment in the community.

PAROLE INTERVIEWS
OF SEX OFFENDERS

The Role of Impression Management

MICHAEL L. RADELET

LEIGH M. ROBERTS

T he centrality of parole to the processes of offender rehabilitation and indeterminant sentencing necessitates that parole boards attempt to discover valid information about inmates to use in making their release recommendations. Yet little research has been done that sheds light on the attribution of identities by parole boards (Garber and Maslach, 1979).

Awareness of how parole boards construct impressions is particularly crucial if the offender's release involves a possible serious risk to the community. For those inmates who believe the parole interview is an important determinant of their chances for release, the concept of impression management is useful in referring to their attempts to "play the game,"

Reprinted from *Urban Life*, Vol. 12, No. 2, July 1983, 140–161. Copyright © 1983 Sage Publications, Inc.

Authors' Note: This research was supported in part by Grant MH 14641 from the National Institute of Mental Health. We would like to thank Pamela Richards, Jim Thomas, John M. Johnson, and two anonymous reviewers for their helpful comments on earlier drafts.

construct plausible accounts for their deviance, and otherwise attempt to influence the parole board's assessment of their character and dangerousness. In this article attention is directed to the question of how impression management is viewed by parole board members in interviews with convicted sex offenders who have been mandated by the court to participate in inpatient treatment programs for indefinite periods of time. The focus is not on the identification of factors that might affect release decisions (see Abadinsky, 1977; Carter and Wilkins, 1976; Gottfredson et al., 1978; Smith and Berlin, 1979), but rather on how offenders' efforts at impression management during parole interviews are interpreted by the parole board.

Following Goffman (1959), we define impression management as the selective disclosure of oneself through social behavior and communication. It includes:

> the way in which the individual in ordinary work situations presents himself and his activity to others, the ways in which he guides and controls the impression they form of him, and the kinds of things he may or may not do while sustaining his impression before them [Goffman, 1959: xi].

Impression management is accomplished through a strategic combination of enhancement, embellishment, suppression, ostentation, or misrepresentation of information concerning the self. It may occur with or without the conscious awareness or volitional intent of the actor, but in either case it assumes that the interaction in which impression management is used is at least partially instrumental. Impression management can therefore be seen as a strategy used by an actor to maximize chances for goal attainment (Gove et al., 1980).

Theoretically, two distinct interpretations of impression management are possible. According to one perspective, offenders use impression management as a strategic tactic in a confidence game in a conscious and calculated effort to deceive parole board members. For example, Braginsky et al. (1969) view impression management by mental patients as a subversive counter-power to the hospital staff's authority and as "positive" evidence that patients are capable of assessing others and rationally

adjusting their behavior to maximize interactional outcomes (see also Price, 1973). This viewpoint postulates the existence of an "objective" or "core" self that is camouflaged by impression management but that must be uncovered before valid understanding of the offender and his or her parole prospects can be attained. Alternatively, impression management can be interpreted as evidence of efforts to achieve self-awareness and development. For example, Voysey (1972) describes how impression management can be used by parents of disabled children as a positive and adaptive strategy. She argues that over time the managed impressions can become internalized aspects of the user's identity, inseparable from other aspects of the self and functional in managing problematic situations created by the child's disability. Thus, whereas the former perspective views impression management as deceptive and obstructive, the latter sees it as functional and constructive. An analysis of when and under what circumstances each perspective best explains how a parole board views impression management would therefore contribute to our understanding of the relationship between self-presentation and attributions made about the self by those whose decisions an actor is trying to influence.

With this general background, the initial question raised in this study concerns how often parole board members believe impression management occurs in their interviews with candidates. Is it a strategy they see as used only by a few offenders who want to "con" their way out of the institution, or is it a strategy found in differential degrees in all interviews? A second research issue concerns *how* the presented selves are interpreted in the board's assessment of the candidate's personality. When and under what circumstances is the presented self interpreted as a reliable indicator of the candidate's "true" self? Finally, in predicting the candidate's probability of successfully adjusting to the outside community if released, do parole board members ever see the ability to manage impressions as a positive asset? After initial observations indicated an affirmative answer to this question, the identification of circumstances under which impression management was viewed as a positive or negative asset became the third goal of this study.

SETTING AND METHOD

The analysis reported in this article is drawn from data gathered by systematic observation of parole interviews conducted by Wisconsin's Special Review Board (SRB) over a fourteen-month period. The SRB is a three-member panel mandated to provide parole recommendations for convicted sex offenders (Halleck and Pacht, 1960; Roberts and Pacht, 1965; Schmidt, 1973). The offenders have been sentenced by the court to participate in specialized inpatient treatment programs for stipulated, though extendable, time periods, with no minimum period of institutionalization required for parole eligibility. The SRB is composed of a full-time member of the State Parole Board, a forensic psychiatrist, and a lawyer. The latter two both hold full-time university appointments. The SRB convenes once monthly, seeing an average of fifteen parole candidates per meeting and each participant in the treatment programs at least once annually. Each interview lasts about twenty minutes and is followed by a ten-minute private deliberation period during which the case is discussed. Parole interviews conclude with each candidate either being recommended for parole or deferred for up to (and usually) eleven months. Parole is recommended when the board believes the candidate "is capable of making an acceptable adjustment in society" (Roberts and Pacht, 1965: 864).

Data were obtained from systematic observations of 166 sex offenders, all male, in 236 separate interviews. Observations were also made during the board's private deliberation periods. Of these interviews, 16 were conducted inside the state's maximum security prison and 220 at the maximum security state mental hospital. Offenders seen at the latter site either reside there or were transported there for their interviews from other correctional facilities or the state's two other mental institutions. Of the 236 interviews, 42 resulted in release decisions (17.8%). In addition to the interview, the board also reviews a packet of written materials about the candidate in preparing its decision, including descriptions of his criminal, court, and institutional history, and a report from the hospital or prison staff concerning his therapeutic activities and prognosis (see Kingsnorth, 1969;

McCleary, 1977). These packets were reviewed as part of the research. Extensive interviews with the three SRB members were also conducted, and detailed field notes were taken from the observations and interviews.[1]

THE PERCEPTION OF IMPRESSION MANAGEMENT

The existence of specialized treatment programs for convicted sex offenders suggests that the manifest goal of their institutional commitment is rehabilitation (Halleck, 1978). Reflecting the primacy of rehabilitative objectives, the modal category of questions raised by the SRB in parole interviews concerns personality assessment. According to board members, what is being evaluated is not simply the candidate's past criminality, institutional behavior, or remorse, but also, in the context of predicting future behavior, his total "self-identity." How the self is presented is one factor, but never the sole factor, considered in making this evaluation. While similar attributions of identity are a common ingredient in most social interactions (Telles, 1980), there are few comparable situations in which individuals are judged as explicitly or comprehensively, or in which the stakes (for some) are so high. This background sets the stage for each candidate to enter the interview with strong interests in its outcome, and, for most, a prepared notion of self that he hopes to convey. With this context, impression management in parole interviews can be seen as a structurally pre-disposed interactive strategy.

For a variety of reasons, candidates may wish to present particular images of themselves to the board. The importance of the parole interview in determining the decision to release varies considerably, and the candidates' perceptions of what is at stake will influence what are seen as the rules of the game. In the usual case, the observations indicate that the candidate wants the board to appraise him as appropriate for parole. In other cases, particularly for those whose official records indicate that they enter the interview with little or no chance for release, the candidate might (correctly) see the parole decision as preestablished and nonnegotiable, regardless of his self-account.[2] While such interviews might be seen by candidates as perfunctory meetings meant only to satisfy legal requirements, board members view them as opportunities to check candidates' progress, get to know them better, counsel them, and give them opportunities to hear the board's concerns (Stanley, 1981). In such cases the board might use excerpts from the interviews in their written accounts for the negative parole decision but readily admit that these excerpts are more a justification than a basis for their evaluations. Thus, for these candidates who realize their interviews will not influence their immediate chances of obtaining release recommendations, their presentations are oriented more toward securing evaluations of progress and affecting the board members' expectations in future parole interviews. In general, members felt that impression management was most prominent in interviews in which candidates aspired to have the board respond in a particular way and perceived that the desired response could be obtained best by actively cultivating it.

Realizing the structural predisposition for impression management, the board typically begins each interview by implicitly asking the candidate what type of impression he would like to convey. This is accomplished by asking a very general, open-ended question that permits the candidate to chart the initial direction of the interview:

(1) SRB Member: "What kinds of things would you like to share with us today"

(2) SRB Member: "Well, Mr.____, during the last eleven months, what's been accomplished in regards to your treatment needs?"

In response, it is not uncommon for the candidates to acknowledge the difficulties of presenting themselves as they would like:

Candidate 114: "I know what I'd like to tell you, but I'm not sure how best to put it" [Interview 125].

Were the board not interested in how the candidate presented himself, their questioning would be confined to the clarification of specific issues raised in the written materials. Thus the form of the initial questions asked by the board suggests that they are interested not only in how the candidate sees himself, but also in the manner and style in which this self is presented to them.

Parole board members, therefore, do not view the question of the existence of impression management as at all controversial insofar as impression management is defined as an attempt to influence their characterization of the candidate. Their formal questions to candidates, informal discussions among themselves, and private responses to inquiries by the observer all indicate that they expect, realize, and, as will be elaborated below, might even encourage both verbal and nonverbal persuasive attempts by candidates. The critical issue in the eyes of board members concerns not the existence of impression management, but rather the degree to which the presented self is congruent with what they believe to be the candidate's "true" self. This construction of an image of the candidate's true self represents a second indicator of the candidate's identity, overlapping with the presented self, with the perceived congruence between the presented self and the true self forming the foundation for the interpretation of the presented self.

The board's notion of the candidate's true self is continually being constructed.[3] While this concept of "real" or "true" self is amorphous, what *is* real is the board's response to and labeling of candidates based on its attributions of self (Turner, 1976; Warren, 1982). The "true" self is thus a theory and an attribution. It is composed of a number of personality hunches the board uses to make sense out of the candidate's deviance (Tedeschi and Lindskold, 1976: 157). Before the interview begins, the board members implicitly begin to construct a vague and tentative theory about the candidate and what may have led to his sexual deviance (see Hawkins, 1982; Turner, 1976; Pfohl, 1979). In psychiatric terms, this emergent theory of true self includes the patient's diagnosis, the problem's severity and prognosis, and implications for therapeutic intervention (MacNamara, 1977). Its treatment component consists of vague or general ideas about what is necessary for the candidate to change or establish before he could be seen as a satisfactory parole risk. The theory utilizes information contained in the candidate's written file, which is delivered to board members and read before the day of the interview, information collected in any of his previous appearances before the board, and board members' knowledge of other individuals who have had similar histories of deviance:

(1) SRB Member (referring to social worker's written report): "You've read the staff report, and it looks to me like they say you're not really attempting to deal with your problems" [Interview 230].

(2) SRB Member (during private deliberation period): "This is the first time we've seen him when it appears he's attempting to make some progress" [Interview 174].

(3) SRB Member (during private deliberation period): "He is way above the average risk for an incest case" [Interview 174].

The board's theory of the candidate's true self continues to develop during the parole interview and the board's subsequent private deliberation, thereby encompassing the presented self within it. Because the board's image of the candidate and his probability of future dangerousness is modified or solidified by his appearance, conveying an acceptable impression can be seen as a necessary, though not a sufficient, determinant of a release recommendation.

How the board interprets the conveyed impression is therefore dependent on a context of expectations and attributions deduced from a more comprehensive personality theory that begins to develop prior to the actual parole interview. There are two general ways in which the conveyed impressions are interpreted, distinguishable by the degree to which the presented self is judged as congruent with the board's theory of the candidate's true self. The first type of impression management is imputed when the candidate's self-presentation is viewed as an accurate reflection of the board's personality theory. Here, the candidate's presentation confirms or is congruent with the board's expectation. For example, the written reports from the institution and the candidate's interview might lead him to be labeled as both recalcitrant and still potentially dangerous.

SRB Member (referring to written report that says candidate is uninvolved in therapy): "Do you intend to get involved in any programs?"

Candidate 165 (with no eye contact, clenching teeth): "No, I don't feel they have anything to offer me. I'm therapy burned out."

SRB Member: "Well, we would encourage you to be involved in the treatment program."

Candidate 165: "No way" [Interview 229].

Similarly, the written materials and a congruent presentation both might be compatible with the board's criteria for an acceptable risk, thus leading to a parole recommendation. This occurs when the candidate presents a self that demonstrates awareness of what the board feels might have led to his deviance, but that has changed while he was in the institution to a degree that suggests he is now a relatively low risk:

SRB Member: "What do you suppose caused your crimes?"

Candidate 104: "Basically, I felt my family didn't love me. I'm now learning to accept my problems and deal with them" [Interview 214].

SRB Member (during private deliberation): "The staff seems to think he's ready. If he gets involved in outpatient therapy, I think he can make it" [Interview 214].

Because this claim is supported by additional information (particularly the social worker's report), it is interpreted as an indicator that the candidate has accepted the institution's assessment of his problems, and has begun to deal with them to an extent that indicates improvement can be sustained outside the institution. Thus the presented self is interpreted by the board on the basis of their perception of the presented self's validity as an indicator of the candidate's true self, and similar presentations by two candidates will be interpreted differently as they vary in their correspondence with perceptions of the true self. That theory of the true self, as refined by the candidate's presentation, becomes the basis of the board's release recommendations. The reciprocal interaction between the board's prior expectations and the actual self-presentations therefore prohibits attribution of the release decision solely to the interview without reference to the contextual expectations of the audience.

The second major way in which the conveyed impressions are interpreted occurs when the presented self is judged as incongruent with the candidate's true self. Here, the candidate's claims to a particular identity are not granted. However, as in the cases of congruent presentations above, the board views the presented self as primarily an indicator of the candidate's self-conception. Therefore, any inconsistencies between the presented self and what the board theorizes as constituting the true self are attributed to poor self-understanding or what board members label "insufficient insight." Because it is realized that self-conceptions vary in their correspondence with "true" selves, the issue of the veracity of the candidate in presenting himself rarely arises. Even blatant inconsistencies between the board's conception of the candidate's true self and his presented self are most often attributed to poor insight, and are rarely seen solely as a conscious effort by the candidate to "con" the board. For example, consider the following two interviews with parole violators:

(1) SRB Member: "When we released you a couple of years ago, I was under the impression that you had been treated."

Candidate 163: "So was I. But I guess I had some problems that I wasn't aware of" [Interview 205].

(2) Candidate 133: "I guess I wasn't ready, but I didn't know that before I got out" [Interview 191].

The board's private discussions following these two interviews, as well as their responses to the researchers' questions, indicate a belief in the possibility of a candidate presenting an impression that honestly reflects his self-conception, but that is grounded in superficial insight into his "true" personality. The possible deception in the interview when these men were released is here interpreted as self-deception, rather than blatant lying. And, given the absence of an independent standard with which to evaluate the candidate's self-conception, the board rarely concerns itself with judging whether or not the candidate's self-presentation is a true or sincere reflection of his self-conception. Thus, in cases with inconsistent presentations, what Goffman (1959: 17) calls

"belief in the part one is playing" becomes nearly irrelevant. Instead, "insufficient insight" into what is seen by the board as the offender's true personality was the reason given by the board for their decisions in the majority of cases in which parole was not recommended.

THE UTILITY OF IMPRESSION MANAGEMENT

Preparation and rehearsal of a desired impression by a candidate before his interview are not necessarily seen by the board as barriers to assessing the candidate's chances for successfully adjusting to the community. In fact, for many candidates the ability and inclination to construct and sustain a favorable impression are seen by the board as positive assets. In the following two interviews, the candidates failed to sustain the impression that they had been attempting to develop their self-understanding:

(1) SRB Member: "What treatment programs are you in now?"

Candidate 92: "Well, um, none. Except something like 'social skills' training" [Interview 204].

(2) SRB Member: "What do you suppose caused the incident with the little girl?"

Candidate 154: "I have no idea" [Interview 170].

Here the questions indicate that the board is looking for some awareness by the candidate of what is believed to be the nature and severity of his sexual problems, or at least some evidence that he is actively trying to develop his awareness through treatment programs. In both cases, the board's reaction to the presentations was that they were unprepared and nonreflective, thus indicating insufficient progress in the treatment programs. Alternatively, the attempts of other candidates to "play the game" are often met with praise. For example:

SRB Member (during private deliberation): "He is active in treatment programs and seems sincere. His remarks are not too insightful, but obviously he has been trying to understand" [Interview 194].

While this candidate was seen as making progress, neither of the first two candidates demonstrated awareness of the board's concerns by anticipating their questions and preparing responses that might have lent support to their claimed (parolable) identities. More thorough preparation of an impression through anticipation of the board's preinterview personality theory would have been helpful.

From the board's perspective, a candidate's demonstration of an ability and willingness to articulate an insightful reflection on his criminal behavior, even if staged, is at least a positive first step. This is particularly true for candidates who, when first entering the treatment programs, are perceived to be withdrawn or reticent, to have relatively lower intelligence, or to have difficulties with interactive social skills. The board does not demand a highly polished presentation of self or fully developed insight before these candidates are recommended for parole, as such criteria might lead to indefinite "warehousing" (see Tippett v. Maryland, in Brooks, 1974: 493-497). As one board member commented:

SRB Member (during private deliberation): "His insight still isn't terrific, but he's probably done about all he can do [in the hospital]" [Interview 97].

Instead of a polished performance or developed insight, in such cases external controls might be required before release would be recommended, such as medication, continued counseling, or structured living arrangements. The board views attempts to manage impressions by this group as potentially helpful, since doing so requires some self-reflection, knowledge of how one's behavior is interpreted by others, and some awareness of the board preinterview assessment of a candidate's problems. The board also views impression management skills among this group as potentially useful in adjusting to the outside community, as "playing the game," and the expertise and inclination to adjust public self-presentations routinely in accordance with others' assumptions about the actor might avoid some potential conflicts when he is released. "If he can't adjust at [the hospital]," commented one SRB member,

"he'll have a terrible time on the streets" (Interview 209).

Nevertheless, not all candidates are encouraged to develop their impression management skills. In interviews with candidates who are perceived to be relatively skillful at self-presentation, the board becomes more cautious and less tolerant of what they see as superficial rationalizations, unreflective "textbook" insight, a focus on secondary or marginal problems, evasiveness, distortion, or exaggeration. Superficial, intellectual awareness is distinguished from reflective insight motivated by a strong inner desire for change. This is particularly true for candidates with relatively higher educational or occupational status, those with more developed intellectual or communicative skills, those who tend to exaggerate reliable information, and those who have failed in a previous parole opportunity. For example, the following case involved a well-dressed college graduate, in his first appearance before the board, who had been convicted of sexual activities with disabled children in an institution where he had been employed in a client-care capacity:

Candidate 163: "The job was my life. The kids were my family. They asked for me."

SRB Member #1: "Would you do that with your family?"

Candidate (reticently): "No."

SRB Member #2: "What kind of explanation is that for kids with limited intelligence?"

Candidate: "It's hard to explain."

SRB Member #2: "And to understand" [Interview 212].

Or, during the deliberation period in a case involving an articulate man who appeared especially eager for parole, board members commented:

SRB Member #1: "He does everything but speak to the treatment issue."

SRB Member #2: "Yes. His insight is negative zero" [Interview 76].

Were these explanations presented by men who the board perceived as more limited in their mental or communicative abilities, the questioning would not have been as confrontal. "A person with his abilities should have known better," commented one board member after the first case above. Therefore, the board's reaction to the candidate's self-presentation is a function not only of its objective content, but also of their evaluation of the candidate's capacities to understand and express himself. Because the above candidates were perceived to be relatively articulate and intelligent, their explanations were interpreted as denials, rationalizations, and deceptions. As with those perceived as having poor interactive skills, the board encourages those in this group to develop their self-understanding by reflecting and developing new insights into their behavior patterns (see Madden, 1977). The observations indicate that similar self-presentations by other, less intelligent or socially skilled candidates might be interpreted as reflecting the most insightful self-understanding of which they were capable. Thus the board recognizes different levels of impression management skills, and in effect encourages all candidates to modify their skills in the direction of the group's collective median.

CONCLUSIONS

Two major conclusions can be drawn from this study. First, the board members believe that impression management, in different degrees, occurs in all parole interviews. The crucial question they address is therefore not *if* managed impressions are presented, but rather *how* the presented impressions should be interpreted. They attempt to answer this question by developing a theory about the candidate's "true" personality, using the correspondence between this theory and the presented impression as an indicator of the candidate's self-understanding. This suggests that our initial conceptualization of impression management can be refined by distinguishing whether or not the presented self is interpreted as consistent with what the audience perceives to be the actor's true self. The interpretation of presented selves, as magnified in parole interviews, utilizes structural and historical information as a context for evaluating the interaction in which the presented self is

situated. Thus the prediction of a candidate's chances for making an acceptable adjustment to the outside community is based on an assessment of self that is only partially constructed during the face-to-face interaction.

Consequently, any inconsistencies between the image of the candidate's true self and his self-presentation are usually attributed to a poor level of self-understanding by the candidate rather than to lying. Exceptions to this pattern of attribution are rare because of the absence of an independent standard to evaluate the candidate's self-understanding. Thus, contrary to the notion that many parole candidates are seen by parole boards as attempting to present fraudulent impressions, this board attributes most inconsistencies to the candidates' "poor levels of self-insight." In other words, the board views the possibility of any conscious attempt by the candidate to deceive or manipulate them as secondary to the broader issue of the correspondence between the presented self and their theory of the candidate's true self. Whether any lack of correspondence results from intentional deception or unreflective insight is viewed as a secondary and frequently unresolvable issue that rarely attracts the board's attention.

A second conclusion from this study is that the development and use of impression management skills is not always discouraged by the board or seen as a barrier to knowing the candidate. Instead, the development of such skills among certain categories of candidates is seen by the board as constructive. This occurs when the board perceives that learning its criteria for a satisfactory parole risk, including its general theory of why the candidate deviated from sexual norms, might stimulate the candidate to develop a greater level of self-understanding (and hence self-control), and change his personality to meet the standards of an acceptable parole risk. Thus Voysey's (1972) conclusion from her research on parents with disabled children that impression management can be useful and constructive is partially supported. On the other hand, the argument by Braginsky et al. (1969) that impression management is a manipulative strategy that can obstruct valid understanding of mental patients is also partially supported. This evaluation is most often applied to candidates who are relatively educated and articulate, but whose presentation of self is interpreted as "superficial and intellectualized." However, whereas Braginsky et al. view impression management as a potential obstruction to the hospital staff's understanding of patients (specifically the patient's desire to remain in the hospital), the SRB most often views perceived superficial rationalizations as primarily a reflection of a poor level of self-understanding by the candidate. Board members' discussion of the candidates and their responses to direct questions indicate that they frequently believe they know more about the candidates' deviant sexuality than do the candidates themselves.

Because the observations were limited to a single three-person board that dealt only with a very specific category of offenders, any generalizations to other parole boards must be made with caution. Other boards, especially those composed of members with careers in corrections, might be more prone to label disagreeable candidates as rationalizers or psychopathic manipulators. This parole board, however, supports Halleck's (1967: 308) contentions that "offenders are hardly more manipulative than any other group of people" and "too much concern (with dishonesty) is unrewarding and unnecessary" (p. 301). The board sees a central problem of sex offenders as an insufficient level of self-understanding, and functions to encourage the candidates to develop a more insightful understanding of themselves and the impact of their behavior on others in the community. Board members view self-understanding, as reflected in self-presentations, as a central key to self-control. While their predictions of future behavior are not always correct, they do support the notion that the existence of impression management is not necessarily seen as a technique that is intentionally used by offenders to deceive, manipulate, or "con" parole boards.

NOTES

1. The second author (a psychiatrist) has been one of the three SRB members for the last twenty years. He arranged for the first author to observe the interviews upon which this report is based. The first author thus sat unobtrusively in the room compiling field notes while the second author participated in the actual interviews. All quotations contained in this article are verbatim.

2. In three cases the offender refused to meet with the board.

3. Since the board made unanimous decisions about whether or not to parole candidates in 98% of the observed interviews, its evaluations will be treated as unitary and consensual. For an outstanding discussion of how consensus is developed among treatment staff in predicting dangerousness, see Pfohl (1977, 1979).

REFERENCES

Abadinsky, H. (1977) Probation and Parole: Theory and Practice. Englewood Cliffs, NJ: Prentice-Hall.

Braginsky, B. N., D. D. Braginsky, and K. Ring (1969) Methods of Madness. New York: Holt, Rinehart & Winston.

Brooks, A. D. (1974) Law, Psychiatry, and the Mental Health System. Boston: Little, Brown.

Carter, R. M. and L. T. Wilkins (1976) Probation, Parole, and Community Corrections. New York: John Wiley.

Garber, R. M. and C. Maslach (1979) "The parole hearing: decision or justification?" pp. 445-465 in S. Messinger and E. Bittner (eds.) Criminology Review Yearbook, Vol. 1. Beverly Hills, CA: Sage.

Goffman, E. (1959) The Presentation of Self in Everyday Life. Garden City, NY: Doubleday.

Gottfredson, D. M., L. T. Wilkins, and P. B. Hoffman (1978) Guidelines for Parole and Sentencing. Lexington, MA: D. C. Heath.

Gove, W. R., M. Hughes, and M. R. Geerken (1980) "Playing Dumb: a form of impression management with undesirable side effects." Social Psychology Q. 43: 89-102.

Halleck, S. L. (1978) "Violence: treatment versus correction," pp. 377-393 in I. Kutash et al. (eds.) Violence: Perspectives on Murder and Aggression. San Francisco: Jossey-Bass.

_____ (1967) Psychiatry and the Dilemmas of Crime Berkeley: Univ. of California Press.

_____ and A. PACHT (1960) "The current status of the Wisconsin state sex crime law." Wisconsin Bar Bull. 33: 17-26.

Hawkins, K. (1982) "The interpretation of evil in criminal settings." Centre for Socio-Legal Studies, Oxford University. (unpublished)

Kingsnorth, R. (1969) "Decision making in a parole bureaucracy." J. of Research in Crime and Delinquency 6: 210-218.

McCleary, R. (1977) "How parole officers use records." Social Problems 24: 576-589.

MacNamara, D. E. J. (1977) "The medical model in corrections." Criminology 14: 439-447.

Madden, D. J. (1977) "Voluntary and involuntary treatment of aggressive patients." Amer. J. of Psychiatry 134: 553-555.

Pfohl, S. (1979) "From whom will we be protected? Comparative approaches to the assessment of dangerousness." Int. J. of Law and Psychiatry 2: 55-78.

_____(1977) Predicting Dangerousness: The Social Construction of Psychiatric Reality. Lexington, MA: D. C. Heath.

Price, R. (1973) "The case for impression management in schizophrenia: another look," pp. 262-275 in R. H. Price and B. Denner (eds.) The Making of a Mental Patient. New York: Holt, Rinehart & Winston.

Roberts, L. M. and A. R. Pacht (1965) "Termination of inpatient treatment for sex deviates: psychiatric, social, and legal factors." Amer. J. of Psychiatry 121 (March): 873-880.

Schmidt, P. W. (1973) "The Special Review Board." Wisconsin Law Rev. 172: 172-209.

Smith, A. B. and L. Berlin (1979) Introduction to Probation and Parole. New York: West.

Stanley, D. T. (1981) "The parole board hearing." Pp. 231-243 in R. G. Culbertson and M. R. Tezak (eds.) Order Under Law. Prospect Heights, IL: Waveland.

Tedeschi, J. T. and S. Lindskold (1976) Social Psychology. New York: John Wiley.

Telles, J. L. (1980) "The social nature of demeanor." Soc. Q. 21: 321-334.

Turner, R. H. (1976) "The real self: from institution to impulse." Amer. J. of Sociology 81: 989-1016.

Voysey, M. (1972) "Impression management by parents with disabled children." J. of Health and Social Behavior 13: 80-89.

Warren, C. (1982) The Court of Last Resort: Mental Illness and the Law. Chicago: Univ. of Chicago Press.

The bulk of parole decision making focuses almost exclusively on the discretion exercised by parole board members and the factors that affect their decision to grant or deny parole. This study seeks to advance the work on parole decision making by considering the inmates' perspective, specifically, the viewpoint of inmates whose release has been denied. In this research, the authors explore the nature of the problems inmates experienced.

DENIAL OF PAROLE

An Inmate Perspective

MARY WEST-SMITH

MARK R. POGREBIN

ERIC D. POOLE

L ike many other discretionary decisions made about inmates (e.g., classification, housing, treatment, discipline, etc.), those involving parole are rather complex. Parole board members typically review an extensive array of information sources in arriving at their decisions, and empirical research has shown a wide variation in the decision-making process. The bulk of research on parole decision-making dates from the mid 1960s to the mid 1980s (e.g., Gottfredson & Ballard, 1966; Rogers & Hayner, 1968; Hoffman, 1972; Wilkins & Gottfredson, 1973; Scott, 1974; Carroll & Mondrick, 1976; Heinz et al., 1976;

Reprinted with permission from *Federal Probation*, 2000, Vol. 64, 3–10.

Talarico, 1976; Garber & Maslach, 1977; Sacks, 1977; Carroll et al., 1982; Conley & Zimmerman, 1982; Lombardi, 1984). Virtually all of this research focuses on the discretion exercised by parole board members and the factors that affect their decisions to grant or deny parole. Surprisingly, only one study, conducted over 20 years ago, has examined the inmate's perspective on the parole decision-making process (Cole & Logan, 1977). The present study seeks to advance the work on parole decision-making from the point of view of those inmates who have had their release on parole denied.

Inmates denied parole have often been dissatisfied with what they consider arbitrary and inequitable features of the parole hearing process. While those denied parole are naturally likely to disagree with that decision, much of the lack of acceptance for parole decisions may well relate to lack of understanding. Even inmates who have an opportunity to present their case through a personal interview are sent out of the room while discussions of the case take place (being recalled only to hear the ultimate decision and a summary of the reasons for it). This common practice protects the confidentiality of individual board members' actions; however, it precludes the inmate from hearing the discussions of the case, evaluations of strengths and weaknesses, or prognosis for success or failure. More importantly, this practice fails to provide guidance in terms of how to improve subsequent chances for successful parole consideration. A common criticism of parole hearings has been that they produce little information relevant to an inmate's parole readiness (Morris, 1974; Fogel, 1975; Cole & Logan, 1977); thus, it is unlikely that those denied parole understand the basis for the decision or attach a sense of justice to it.

PAROLE BOARDS

The 1973 Supreme Court decision in *Scarpa v. United States Board of Parole* established the foundation for parole as an "act of grace." Parole is legally considered a privilege rather than a right; therefore, the decision to grant or deny it is "almost unreviewable" (Hier, 1973, p. 435). In fact, when federal courts have been petitioned to intervene and challenge parole board actions, the decisions of parole boards have prevailed (see *Menechino v. Oswald*, 1970; *Tarlton v. Clark*, 1971). While subsequent Court rulings have established minimal due process rights in prison disciplinary proceedings (*Wolff v. McDonnell*, 1974) and in parole revocation hearings (*Morrissey v. Brewer*, 1972), the parole hearing itself is still exempt from due process rights. Yet in *Greenholtz v. Nebraska* (1979) and *Board of Pardons v. Allen* (1987), the Supreme Court held that, although there is no constitutional right to parole, state statutes may create a protected liberty interest where a state's parole system entitles inmates to parole if they meet certain conditions. Under such circumstances, the state has created a presumption that inmates who meet specific requirements will be granted parole. Although the existence of a parole system does not by itself give rise to an expectation of parole, states may create that expectation or presumption by the wording of their statutes. For example, in both *Greenholtz* and *Allen*, the Supreme Court emphasized that the statutory language—the use of the word "shall" rather than "may"—creates the presumption that parole will be granted if certain conditions are met. However, if the statute is general, giving broad discretion to the parole board, no liberty interest is created and due process is not required. In Colorado, as in most other states with parole systems, the decision to grant parole before the inmate's mandatory release date is vested entirely within the discretion of the parole board. The legislatively-set broad guidelines for parole decision-making allow maximum exercise of discretion with minimal oversight.

In Colorado, the structure of parole board hearings depends on the seriousness of the inmate's offense. A full board review is required for all cases involving a violent crime or for inmates with a history of violence. A quorum for a full board review is defined as four of the seven parole board members and a decision to grant parole requires four affirmative votes. However, two parole board members conduct the initial hearing and submit their recommendation to a full board review. Single board members hear nonviolent cases. The board member considers the inmate's parole application, interviews the inmate, makes the release decision, and decides the conditions of parole. The personal interview may be face-to-face or by telephone. If the decision is to grant parole, an additional board member's signature is required. Given the variety of backgrounds and experiences board members bring to the job, individual interpretation and application of the broad statutory guidelines can make parole decision-making appear idiosyncratic.

In their 1986 study of parole decision-making in Colorado, Pogrebin and his colleagues (1986) concluded from their observations that the "overriding factor in parole decisions was not the relative merits of the inmate's case, but the structure of the board itself" (p. 153). At the time of their study, at least two board members rather than the current single board member made the majority of decisions. One may speculate that with only one decision-maker the decision to grant or deny parole is now even more dependent on the individual board member's background and philosophy.

Normalization and Routinization

Sudnow's (1965) classic study of the processes of normalization and routinization in the public defender's office offers insights into the decision-making processes in parole board hearings. Like Sudnow's public defender, who works as an employee of the court system with the judge and prosecutor and whose interests include the smooth functioning of the court system, the parole board member in Colorado works with the prison administration, caseworkers, and other prison personnel. Public defenders must represent all defendants assigned to them and attempt to give the defendants the impression they are receiving individualized representation. However, public defenders often determine the plea bargain acceptable to the prosecutor and judge, based on the defendant's prior and current criminal activities, prior to the first meeting with the defendant (Sudnow, 1965).

The parole board theoretically offers individual consideration of the inmate's rehabilitation and the likelihood of future offending when deciding whether or not to release an inmate. However, the parole board, like the public defender, places a great deal of emphasis on the inmate's prior and current criminal record. The

tremendous volume of cases handled by the public defender necessitates the establishment of "normal crime" categories, defined by type and location of crime and characteristics of the defendant and victim, which permit the public defender to quickly and easily determine an appropriate and acceptable sentence. Such normalization and routinization facilitate the rapid flow of cases and the smooth functioning of the court system. Similarly, a two-year study of 5,000 parole decisions in Colorado in the early 1980s demonstrated that the parole board heard far too many cases to allow for individualized judgments (Pogrebin et al., 1986, p. 149).

Observations of parole hearings illustrate the rapid flow of cases and collaboration with other prison personnel. Typically, the case manager, in a brief meeting with the parole board member, discusses the inmate, his prior criminal history, current offense, institutional behavior, compliance with treatment programs, progress and current attitude, and makes a release or deferral recommendation to the parole board member prior to the inmate interview. The inmate and family members, if present, are then brought into the hearing room. The parole board member asks the inmate to describe his prior and current crimes, his motivation for those crimes, and the circumstances that led to the current offense. Typical inmate responses are that he was "stupid," "drunk," or "not thinking right." Inquiries by the parole board about the programs the inmate has completed are not the norm; however, the inmate is often asked how he thinks the victim would view his release. The inmate typically tries to bring up the progress he has made by explaining how much he has learned while institutionalized and talks about the programs he completed and what he learned from them. A final statement by the inmate allows him to express remorse for the pain he has caused others and to vow he will not get into another situation where he will be tempted to commit crimes. Family members are then given time to make a statement, after which the inmate and family leave the hearing room. A brief discussion between the parole board member and the case manager is followed by the recommendation to grant or defer parole. A common reason given for a deferral is "not enough time served." If parole is granted, the parole board member sets the conditions for parole.

"Normal" cases are disposed of very quickly. The time from the case manager's initial presentation of the case to the start of the next case is typically ten to fifteen minutes. Atypical cases require a longer discussion with the case manager before and after the inmate interview. Atypical cases also can involve input from other prison personnel (e.g., a therapist), rather than just the case manager. Those inmates who do not fit the norm, either through their background or the nature of their crime, are given special attention. The parole board member does not need to question the inmate to discover if the case is atypical since the case manager will inform him if there is anything unusual about the inmate or his situation.

During the hearing, the board member asks first about the prior and current crimes and what the inmate thinks were the causal factors that led to the commission of the crimes. Based on his observations of public defenders, Sudnow (1965) concludes, "It is not the particular offenses for which he is charged that are crucial, but the constellation of prior offenses and the sequential pattern they take" (p. 264). Like the public defender who attempts to classify the case into a familiar type of crime by looking at the circumstances of prior and current offenses, the parole board member also considers the criminal offense history and concentrates on causal factors that led the inmate to commit the crimes. It is also important for the board member that the inmate recognize the patterns of his behavior, state the reasons why he committed his prior and current crimes, and accept responsibility for them. The inmate, in contrast, generally wants to describe what he has learned while incarcerated and talk about the classes and programs he has completed. The interview exchange thus reveals two divergent perceptions of what factors should be emphasized in the decision-making process. In Sudnow's (1965) description of a jury trial involving a public defender, "the onlooker comes away with the sense of having witnessed not a trial at all, but a set of motions, a perfunctorily carried off event" (p. 274). In a similar manner, the observer at a parole board hearing has the impression of having witnessed a scripted, staged performance.

As a result of their journey through the criminal justice system, individual inmates in a prison have been typed and classified by a series of criminal justice professionals. The compilation of prior decisions forms the parole board member's framework for his or her perception of the inmate. The parole board member, with the help of previous decision-makers and through normalization and routinization, "knows" what type of person the inmate is. As Heinz et al. (1976) point out, "a system premised on the individualization of justice unavoidably conflicts with a caseload that demands simple decision rules. . . . To process their caseloads, parole boards find it necessary to develop a routine, to look for one or two or a few factors that will decide their cases for them" (p. 18). With or without the aid of parole prediction tools to help in their decision, parole board members feel confident they understand the inmate and his situation; therefore, their decisions are more often based on personal intuition than structured guidelines.

THEORETICAL FRAMEWORK

Based on a combination of both formal and informal sources of information they acquire while in prison, inmates believe that satisfactory institutional behavior and completion of required treatment and educational programs, when combined with adequate time served, will result in their release on parole. They also believe that passing their parole eligibility date denotes sufficient institutional time. Denial of parole, when the stated prerequisites for parole have been met, leads to inmate anger and frustration. As stories of parole denials spread throughout the DOC population, inmates are convinced that the parole board is abusing its discretion to continue confinement when it is no longer mandated.

Control of Institutional Behavior

The majority of inmates appearing before the parole board have a fairly good record of institutional behavior (Dawson, 1978). Inmates are led to believe that reduction in sentence length is possible through good behavior (Emshoff & Davidson, 1987). Adjustment to prison rules and regulations is not sufficient reason for release on parole; however, it comprises a minimum requirement for parole and poor adjustment is a reason to deny parole (Dawson, 1978). Preparation for a parole hearing would be a waste of both the prisoner's and the case manager's time and effort if the inmate's behavior were not adequate to justify release.

Research suggests that good behavior while incarcerated does not necessarily mean that an inmate will successfully adapt to the community and be law-abiding following a favorable early-release decision (Haesler, 1992; Metchik, 1992). In addition, Emshoff and Davidson (1987) note that good time credit is not an effective deterrent for disruptive behavior. Inmates who are most immature may be those most successful at adjusting to the abnormal environment of prison; inmates who resist conformity to rules may be those best suited for survival on the outside (Talarico, 1976). However, institutional control of inmate behavior is a crucial factor for the maintenance of order and security among large and diverse prison populations, and the use of good time credit has traditionally been viewed as an effective behavioral control mechanism (Dawson, 1978). Inmates are led to believe that good institutional behavior is an important criterion for release, but it is secondary to the background characteristics of the inmate. Rather than good behavior being a major consideration for release, as inmates are told, only misbehavior is taken into account and serves as a reason to deny parole.

Inmates are also told by their case manager and other prison personnel that they must complete certain programs to be paroled. Colorado's statutory parole guidelines list an inmate's progress in self-improvement and treatment programs as a component to be assessed in the release decision (Colorado Department of Public Safety, 1994). However, the completion of educational or treatment programs by the inmate is more often considered a factor in judging the inmate's institutional adjustment, i.e., his ability to conform to program rules and regimen. Requiring inmates to participate in prison programs may be more important for institutional control than for the rehabilitation of the inmate. Observations of federal parole hearings suggest that the inmate's institutional behavior and program

participation are given little importance in release decisions (Heinz et al., 1976). Non-compliance with required treatment programs or poor institutional behavior may be reasons to deny parole, but completion of treatment programs and good institutional behavior are not sufficient reasons to grant parole.

Release Decision Variables

Parole board members and inmates use contrasting sets of variables each group considers fundamental to the release decision. Inmates believe that completion of treatment requirements and good institutional behavior are primary criteria the parole board considers when making a release decision. Inmates also feel strongly that an adequate parole plan and demonstration that their families need their financial and emotional support should contribute to a decision to release on parole.

In contrast, the parole board first considers the inmate's current and prior offenses and incarcerations. Parole board members also determine if the inmate's time served is commensurate with what they perceive as adequate punishment. If it is not, the inmate's institutional behavior, progress in treatment, family circumstances and parole plan will not outweigh the perceived need for punishment. Inmates, believing they understand how the system works, become angry and frustrated when parole is denied after they have met all the stated conditions for release.

Unwritten norms and individualized discretion govern parole board decision-making; thus, the resulting decisions become predictable only in retrospect as patterns in granting or denying parole emerge over time. For example, one of the difficulties Pogrebin et al. (1986) encountered in their study of parole board hearings in Colorado was developing a written policy based on previous case decisions:

> This method requires that a parole board be convinced that there exists a hidden policy in its individual decisions. . . . [M]ost parole board members initially will deny that they use any parole policy as such . . . [and] will claim that each case is treated on its own merits. . . . [However] parole decisions begin to fit a pattern in which

decisions are based on what has been decided previously in similar situations (p. 149).

METHOD

In October of 1997, Colorado-CURE (Citizens United for Rehabilitation of Errants), a Colorado non-profit prisoner advocacy group, solicited information through its quarterly newsletter from inmates (who were members of the organization) regarding parole board hearings that resulted in a "setback," i.e., parole deferral. Inmates were asked to send copies of their appeals and the response they received from the parole board to Colorado-CURE. One hundred and eighty inmates responded to the request for information with letters ranging in length from very brief one- or two-paragraph descriptions of parole board hearings to multiple page diatribes listing not only parole board issues, but complaints about prison conditions, prison staff, and the criminal justice system in general. Fifty-two letters were eliminated from the study because they did not directly address the individual inmate's own parole hearing. One hundred and twenty-eight inmate letters were analyzed; one hundred and twenty-five from male and three from female inmates. Some letters contained one specific complaint about the parole board, but most inmates listed at least two complaints. Several appeals also contained letters written to the parole board by family members on the inmate's behalf. Two hundred and eighty-five complaints were identified and classified into thirteen categories utilizing content analysis, which "translates frequency of occurrence of certain symbols into summary judgments and comparisons of content of the discourse" (Starosta, 1984, p. 185). Content analytical techniques provide the means to document, classify, and interpret the communication of meaning, allowing for inferential judgments from objective identification of the characteristics of messages (Holsti, 1969). In addition, parole board hearings, including the preliminary presentation by the case manager and the discussion after the inmate interview, were observed over a three-month period in 1998. These observations were made to provide a context for understanding the nature of the hearing process

from the inmate's perspective and to document the substantive matter of parole deliberations.

The purpose of the present study is not to explore the method the parole board uses to reach its release decisions; rather, our interest is to examine the content of the written complaints of inmates in response to their being denied parole.

FINDINGS

Table 1 presents the frequency of complaints regarding parole denial and the percentage of inmates having each complaint. Those complaints relating to parole hearings following a return to prison for a parole violation and those complaints regarding sex offender laws will not be addressed in the following discussion. Parole revocation hearings are governed by different administrative rules and are subject to more rigorous due process requirements and are thus beyond the scope of the current study. In addition, sex offender sentencing laws in Colorado have evolved through dramatic changes in legislation over the past several years and a great deal of confusion exists regarding which inmates are eligible for parole, when they are eligible, and what conditions can be imposed when inmates are paroled. Future analysis of sex offender laws is necessary to clarify this complex situation. We now turn to an examination of the remaining categories of inmate complaints concerning parole denial.

Inadequate Time Served

Forty-eight percent of the inmates reported "inadequate time served" as a reason given for parole deferment. Their attempt to understand the "time served" component in the board's decision is exemplified by the following accounts:

> . . . if you don't meet their [the parole board's] time criteria you are "not" eligible. Their time criteria is way more severe than statute. . . . [The risk assessment] also says, if you meet their time amounts and score 14 or less on the assessment you "shall" receive parole. This does not happen. The board is an entity with entirely too much power. . . .

* * *

Table 1   Frequency of Complaints and Percentage of Inmates Having Complaint

Nature of Complaint	Frequency of complaints	Percentage of inmates with complaint
1. Inadequate time served, yet beyond P.E.D.	61	48%
2. Completed required programs	45	35%
3. Denied despite parole plan	35	27%
4. Board composition and behavior	27	21%
5. Longer setbacks after parole violation	26	20%
6. Family need for inmate support ignored	22	17%
7. Case manager not helpful	17	13%
8. New sex offender laws applied retroactively	16	12%
9. Required class not available	11	9%
10. Few inmates paroled on same day	7	5%
11. Appeals not considered on individual basis	6	4%
12. Miscellaneous	12	9%

I don't understand how your P.E.D. [parole eligibility date] can come up and they can say you don't have enough time in.

* * *

If the court wanted me to have more time, it could have aggravated my case with as much as eight years. Now the parole board is making itself a court!

* * *

. . . I [was] set back again for six months with the reason being, not enough time spent in prison. I've done 5 calendar years, I'm two years past my PED, this is my first and only felony of my life, I've never been to prison, it's a non-violent offense, it's not a crime of recidivism, I do not earn a livelihood from this crime or any criminal activity. So what is their problem?

* * *

[Enclosed] is a copy of my recent deferral for parole, citing the infamous "Not enough time served" excuse. This is the third time they've used this reason to set me back, lacking a viable one.

These responses of the inmates to the "inadequate time served" reason for parole deferral demonstrate that they believe the parole board uses a different set of criteria than the official ones for release decisions. Inmates do not understand that the "time served" justification for parole deferment relates directly to the perception by the parole board member of what is an acceptable punishment for their crime.

They believe the parole board is looking for a reason to deny parole and uses "time served" when no other legitimate reason can be found.

Completed Required Programs

Thirty-five percent of the inmates complained that their parole was deferred despite completing all required treatment and educational programs. Related complaints, expressed by 9 percent of the inmates, were the lack of mandatory classes and the long waiting lists for required classes. The following excerpts from inmate letters reflect this complaint:

When I first met with them [the parole board] I received a 10 month setback to complete the classes I was taking (at my own request). But was told once I completed it and again met the board I was assured of a release. . . . Upon finishing these classes I met the board again [a year later]. . . . I noticed that none of my 7 certificates to date were in the file and only a partial section of the court file was in view. I tried to speak up that I was only the 5th or 6th person to complete the 64 week class and tell about the fact that I carry a 4.0 in work plus have never had a COPD conviction or a write-up. He silenced me and said that meant nothing. . . . I later was told I had been given another one year setback!!!

* * *

They gave me a six month setback because they want me to take another A.R.P. class. . . . [I]t was my first time down [first parole hearing], and I have taken A.R.P. already twice. . . . I have also taken . . . Independent Living Skills, Job Search, Alternatives to Violence, workshops and training in nonviolence, Advanced Training for Alternatives to Violence Project, mental health classes conducted by addiction recovery programs. I also chair the camp's A.A. meetings every week and just received my two year coin. I have also completed cognitive behavioral core curriculum. . . .

* * *

I'm one of the Colorado inmates that's been shipped to Minnesota. . . . I went before the parole board [in Colorado] . . . and they set me back a year, claiming that I needed to complete the mental health classes. . . . Then Colorado sends me to Minnesota where they don't even offer the mental classes that the board stated I needed to complete.

Inmates view completion of required programs as proof that they have made an effort to rehabilitate themselves and express frustration when the parole board does not recognize their efforts. The completion of classes was usually listed with other criteria the inmates viewed as important for their release on parole.

Parole Denied Despite Parole Plan

Deferral of parole even though a parole plan had been submitted was a complaint listed by 27 percent of inmates. It is interesting to note that this complaint never appeared as a solo concern, but was always linked to other issues. These inmates seem to believe that a strong parole plan alone will not be sufficient to gain release and that the parole plan must be combined with good institutional behavior and the completion of required classes. Even when all required criteria are met, parole was often deferred. The frustration of accomplishing all of the requirements yet still being deferred is expressed in the following excerpts:

. . . I was denied for the third time by the D.O.C. parole board even though I have completed all recommended classes (Alcohol Ed. I and II, Relapse Prevention, Cognitive Skills and Basic Mental Health). I have a place to parole to [mother's house], a good job and a very strong support group consisting of family and friends. . . . To the present date I have served 75% of my 3-year sentence.

* * *

I had everything I needed to make parole, i.e. an approved plan, job, adequate time served. . . . [The parole board member] listed "release" on my paperwork, but "release denied" on my MRD (mandatory release data).

* * *

[After having problems with a previous address for the parole plan] . . . my parents and family . . . were assured . . . that all I needed to do is put together an alternative address. I managed to qualify for and arrange to lease a new low-income apartment at a new complex. . . . My family was helping with this. I also saw to it that I was preapproved at [a shelter in Denver], a parole office approved address, so that I could go there for a night or two if needed while I rented and had my own apartment approved by the parole office. My family expected me home, and I had hoped to be home and assisting them, too. I arranged employment from here, and looked forward to again being a supportive father and son. . . . I received a one-year setback! I was devastated, and my family is too. We are still trying to understand all of this. . . . I am . . . angry at seeing so many sources of support, employment, and other opportunities that I worked so hard at putting together now be lost.

Preparing an adequate parole plan requires effort on the part of both the inmate and the case manager. When a parole plan is coupled with completion of all required treatment and educational programs and good institutional behavior, the inmate is at a loss to understand how the parole board can deny parole. Inmates often expressed frustration that the plans they made for parole might not be available the next time they are eligible for parole. "Inadequate time served" is often the stated reason for parole deferment in these cases and does not indicate to the inmate changes he needs to make in order to be paroled in the future.

Parole Board Composition and Behavior

Twenty-one percent of the inmates complained about the composition of the parole board or about the attitude parole board members displayed toward the inmate and his or her family. Several inmates expressed concern that at the majority of hearings, only one parole board member is present and the outcome of an inmate's case might depend on the background of the parole board member hearing the case:

> The man [parole board member] usually comes alone, and he talks to the women worse than any verbal abuser I have ever heard. He says horrible things to them about how bad they are and usually reduces them to tears. Then he says they are "too emotionally unstable to be paroled!" If they stand up for themselves, they have "an attitude that he can't parole." If they refuse to react to his cruel proddings, they are "too cold and unfeeling." No way to win!! Why in the *world* do we have ex-policemen on the parole board?? Cops always want to throw away the key on all criminals, no matter what. Surely that could be argued . . . as conflict of interest!

* * *

> As I was sitting in the parole hearing for me I was asked some pretty weird questions. Like while I was assaulting my victim was I having sex with my wife also. My answer was yes. Then this man [the parole board member] says, "Sounds like you had the best of both worlds, huh?" I was taken back by this comment and wonder why in the world this guy would think that this was the best of any world.

* * *

> My hearing was more of an inquisition than a hearing for parole. All of the questions asked of me were asked with the intent to set me back and not the intent of finding reasons to parole me. It was my belief that when a person became parole eligible the purpose was to put them out, if possible. My hearing officer did nothing but look for reasons to set me back.

Inmates often expressed the view that the parole board members conducting their hearings did not want to listen to their stories. However, if parole board members have generally reached a decision prior to interviewing the inmate, as indicated by the routinization of the hearing process, it is logical that the board member would attempt to limit the inmate's presentation. In addition, if board members have already determined that parole will be deferred, one would expect the questions to focus on reasons to deny parole. One inmate stated, "I believe

that the parole board member that held my hearing abused his discretion. I had the distinct feeling that he had already decided to set me back before I even stepped into the room."

Family's Need for Inmate's Support

Many inmates criticized the parole board for failing to take into account their families' financial, physical, and emotional needs. Seventeen percent of the inmates expressed this concern, and several included copies of letters written by family members asking the board to grant parole. The primary concerns were support for elderly parents and dependent young children:

> My mom has Lou Gehrig's disease. . . . [S]he can't walk and it has spread to her arms and shoulders. . . . [No] one will be there during the day to care for her. The disease is fast moving. . . . My mom is trying to get me home to care for her. . . . I am a non-violent first time offender. I have served 8 years on a 15. I have been before the parole board 5 times and denied each time. . . . (I got 6, 6, 9, 6, 12 month setbacks in that order). Why I'm being denied I'm unsure. I've asked the board and wasn't told much. I've completed all my programs, college, have a job out there, therapy all set up, and a good parole plan.

* * *

> I have everything going for me in the community. I have a full-time job. I have a 2 year-old son that needs me. I have a mother that is elderly and needs my help. This is all over an ounce of marijuana from [1994] and a walk-away from my own house. I have over 18 months in on an 18 month sentence.

* * *

> [My 85-year-old mother] has no one. Her doctor also wrote [to the chair of the parole board] as well as other family members, including my son. All begging for my release. She *needs* me!! I wish you could [see] . . . how hard I have worked since I have been in prison. . . . Being good and trying hard does not count for much in here. . . . This is my 5th year on an 8 year sentence.

The parole board does not consider a dependant family as a primary reason to release an inmate on parole; however, inmates regard their families' needs as very important and are upset that such highly personal and emotionally charged circumstances are given short shrift during their parole hearing. And if they believe they have met the conditions established for release, inmates do not understand why the parole board would not allow them to return home to help support a family.

Case Manager Not Helpful

Thirteen percent of the inmates expressed frustration with their case manager, with a few accusing the case manager of actually hurting their chances to make parole. Although the inmate was not present during the case manager's presentation to the board member, many inmates declared satisfaction with their case manager and felt that the board did not listen to the case manager's recommendation. Since the present study focuses on inmate complaints, the following excerpts document the nature of the dissatisfaction inmates expressed concerning their case managers:

[The case manager] has a habit of ordering inmates to waive their parole hearings. Many inmates are angry and do not know where to turn because they feel it is their right to attend their parole hearings. . . . [He] forces most all of his caseload to waive their parole hearing. That is not right! . . . How and why is this man allowed to do this? I would not like my name mentioned because I fear the consequences I will pay. . . . [T]his man is my case manager and I have not seen the parole board yet.

* * *

I have not had any writeups whatsoever and I have been taking some drug and alcohol classes since I have been back [parole revoked for a dirty U.A.]. I had a real strong parole plan that I thought that my case manager submitted but he never bothered to. I was planning on going to live with my father who I never asked for anything in my life and he was willing to help me with a good job and a good place to live. My father had also wrote to [the chair of the parole board] and asked if I could be paroled to him so he can help me change my life around.

* * *

[Some] case managers are not trained properly and do not know what they are doing. Paperwork

is seldom done properly or on time. Others are downright mean and work *against* the very people they are to help. Our liberty depends on these people, and we have no one else to turn to when they turn against us.

Inmates realize they must at least have a favorable recommendation by the case manager if they are to have any chance for parole. Yet they generally view the case manager as a "marginal advocate," often going through the motions of representing their interests but not really supporting or believing in them. Case managers after all are employees of the Department of Corrections, and their primary loyalties are seen by inmates to attach to their employer and "the system."

Few Inmates Paroled the Same Day

Five percent of the inmates related in their letters that very few inmates were paroled on a given hearing day, leading them to suspect that the parole board typically denies release to the vast majority of inmates who come up for a hearing.

I just received a letter . . . and she told me that 2 out of 24 made parole from [a Colorado women's facility]. . . . [Also] out of 27 guys on the ISP non-res program from [a community corrections facility] only 4 made parole!! . . . What is going on here?!! These guys [on ISP] are already on parole for all intents and purposes.

* * *

Went [before parole board] in June '97. 89 went. 2 made it (mandatory).

* * *

I realize they're not letting very many people go on parole or to community. It's not politically correct to parole anyone. Now that Walsenburg is opening, I'm sure they will parole even less people. I have talked to 14 people that seen the Board this week. 2 setbacks. . . .

Inmates circulate such stories and cite them as evidence that the parole board is only interested in keeping prisoners locked up. Many inmates express their belief that the parole board is trying to guarantee that all the prisons are filled to capacity.

Appeals Not Considered
on an Individual Basis

Although Colorado-CURE asked inmates to send copies of their appeal and the response to the appeal, the majority of inmates mailed copies of their appeal before they received the response. Thus, it is not surprising that only four percent of the inmates discussed the apparent uniformity of appeal decisions. The standard form letter from the chair of the parole board, included by those who stated this complaint, reads as follows:

> I have reviewed your letter . . . , along with your file, and find the Board acted within its statutory discretion. Consequently, the decision of the Board stands.

Word of the appeals circulates among the general prison population and between prisons via letters to other inmates. Inmates suggest that the form letters are evidence that the parole board is not willing to review cases and reconsider decisions made by individual board members.

> I finally got their response. They are basically sending everyone the same form letter. I was told by someone else that it [is] what they were doing and sure enough that is what they are doing.

* * *

> After receiving the denial of my appeal, I spoke with a fellow convict about his dilemma, which prompted him to show me a copy of his girlfriend's denial of her appeal. . . . It seems that [she] was given an unethical three (3) year setback, even though she has now completed 3/4 of her sentence. And she too received a carbon copy response from the [chair of the parole board's] office. It should be crystal clear that these files are *not* being reviewed as is stated in [the] responses, because if they had been, these decisions would surely seem questionable at best.

Conclusion

The nature of the written complaints reflects the belief among many inmates that the parole board in Colorado is using criteria for release decisions that are hidden from inmates and their families. A parole board decision, made without

public scrutiny by members who have no personal knowledge of the inmate, depends on the evaluation of the likelihood of recidivism by others in the criminal justice system. While guidelines and assessment tools have been developed to help with the decision-making process in Colorado, it is unclear the extent to which they are used. Release decisions by the parole board appear to be largely subjective and to follow latent norms that emerge over time. The emphasis on past and current crimes indicates that inmates—regardless of their institutional adjustment or progress in treatment, vocational, or educational programs—will continue to be denied parole until they have been sufficiently punished for their crimes. As one inmate lamented in his letter of complaint,

> When the inmate has an approved parole plan, a job waiting and high expectations for the future and then is set back a year . . . , he begins to die a slow death. They *very often* use the reason: *Not enough time served* to set people back. If I don't have enough time served, why am I seeing the parole board? Or they will say: *Needs Continued Correctional Treatment.* If I have maintained a perfect disciplinary record and conformed to the rules, what more correctional treatment do I need. . . . I had a parole plan and a job in May when I seen the Board. I was set back one year. I will see them in March. . . . I will have no job and nowhere to live. . . . The Colorado Dept. of Corrections does not rehabilitate inmates. That is solely up to the inmate. What they do is cause hate and bitterness and discontent.

Findings of this study indicate that the factors inmates believe affect release decisions are different from the factors the parole board considers and thus suggest why inmates fail to understand why their parole is deferred despite compliance with the prerequisites imposed upon them. As evidenced by the above examples, inmates are not only confused and angry when they believe parole should be granted, they begin to question whether or not it is worth the effort if they are only going to "kill their numbers" (i.e., serve the full sentence). The prison grapevine and the flow of information among the entire Department of Corrections inmate population allow such stories and theories to spread. Prison officials should be concerned that if inmates feel compliance with prison rules and regulations is pointless, they will be less likely to conform to the administration's requirements for institutional control. Currently, inmates who are turned down for parole see themselves as victims, unfairly denied what they perceive they have earned and deserve. Each parole eligible case that is deferred or set back becomes another story, duly embellished, that makes its rounds throughout the prison population, fueling suspicion, resentment, and fear of an unbridled discretionary system of power, control, and punishment.

Inmates denied parole are entitled to a subsequent hearing usually within one calendar year. But the uncertainty of never knowing precisely when one will be released can create considerable tension and frustration in prison. While discretionary release leaves them in limbo, it is the unpredictability of release decisions that is demoralizing. As we have found, this process has resulted in bitter complaints from inmates. Perhaps the late Justice Hugo Black of the U.S. Supreme Court best summarized the view of many inmates toward the parole board:

In the course of my reading—by no means confined to law—I have reviewed many of the world's religions. The tenets of many faiths hold the deity to be a trinity. Seemingly, the parole boards by whatever names designated in the various states have in too many instances sought to enlarge this to include themselves as members (Quoted in Mitford, 1973, p. 216).

REFERENCES

Board of Pardons v. Allen, 482 U.S. 369 (1987).

Carroll, J.S., Wiener, R.L., Coates, D., Galegher, J., & Alirio, J.J. (1982). Evaluation, diagnosis, and prediction in parole decision making. *Law and Society Review, 17,* 199-228.

Carroll, L., & Mondrick, M.E. (1976). Racial bias in the decision to grant parole. *Law and Society Review, 11,* 93-107.

Cole, G.F., & Logan, C.H. (1977). Parole: The consumer's perspective. *Criminal Justice Review, 2,* 71-80.

Colorado Department of Public Safety (1994). *Parole guidelines handbook.* Denver, CO: Division of Criminal Justice.

Conley, J.A., & Zimmerman, S.E. (1982). Decision making by a part-time parole board: An Observational and empirical study. *Criminal Justice and Behavior, 9,* 396-431.

Dawson, R. (1978). The decision to grant or deny parole. In B. Atkins and M. Pogrebin (Eds.), *The invisible justice system: Discretion and the law* (pp. 360-389). Cincinnati: Anderson.

Emshoff, J.G., & Davidson, W.S. (1987). The effect of "good time" credit on inmate behavior: A quasi-experiment. *Criminal Justice and Behavior, 14,* 335-351.

Fogel, D. (1975). *. . . We are the living proof: The justice model for corrections.* Cincinnati: Anderson.

Garber, R.M., & Maslach, C. (1977). The parole hearing: Decision or justification? *Law and Human Behavior, 1,* 261-281.

Gottfredson, D.M., & Ballard, K.B. (1966). Differences in parole decisions associated with decision-makers. *Journal of Research in Crime and Delinquency, 3,* 112-119.

Greenholtz v. Nebraska Penal Inmates, 442 U.S. 1 (1979).

Haesler, W.T. (1992). The released prisoner and his difficulties to be accepted again as a "normal" citizen. *Euro-Criminology, 4,* 61-68.

Heinz, A.M., Heinz, J.P., Senderowitz, S.J., & Vance, M.A. (1976). Sentencing by parole board: An evaluation. *Journal of Criminal Law and Criminology, 67,* 1-31.

Hier, A.P. (1973). Curbing abuse in the decision to grant or deny parole. *Harvard Civil Rights-Civil Rights Law Review, 8,* 419-468.

Hoffman, P.B. (1972). Parole policy. *Journal of Research in Crime and Delinquency, 9,* 112-133.

Holsti, O.R. (1969). *Content analysis for the social sciences and humanities.* Reading, MA: Addison-Wesley.

Lombardi, J.H. (1984). The impact of correctional education on length of incarceration: Non-support for new paroling policy motivation. *Journal of Correctional Education, 35,* 54-57.

Menechino v. Oswald, 430 F.2d 402 (2nd Cir. 1970).

Metchik, E. (1992). Judicial views of parole decision processes: A social science perspective. *Journal of Offender Rehabilitation, 18,* 35-157.

Mitford, J. (1973). *Kind and unusual punishment: The prison business.* New York: Knopf.

Morris, N. (1974). *The future of imprisonment.* Chicago: University of Chicago Press.

Morrissey V. Brewer, 408 U.S. 471 (1972).

Pogrebin, M.R., Poole, E.D., & Regoli, R.M. (1986). Parole decision making in Colorado. *Journal of Criminal Justice, 14,* 147-155.

Rogers, J., & Hayner, N.S. (1968). Optimism and accuracy in perceptions of selected parole prediction items. *Social Forces, 46,* 388-400.

Sacks, H.R. (1977). Promises, performance, and principles: An empirical study of parole decision making in Connecticut. *Connecticut Law Review, 9,* 347-423.

Scarpa v. U.S. Board of Parole, 414 U.S. 934 (1973).

Scott, J.E. (1974). The use of discretion in determining the severity of punishment for incarcerated offenders. *Journal of Criminal Law and Criminology, 65,* 214-224.

Starosta, W.J. (1984). Qualitative content analysis: A Burkean perspective. In W. Gudykunst & Y.Y. Kim (Eds.), *Methods for intercultural communication research* (pp. 185-194). Beverly Hills, CA: Sage.

Sudnow, D. (1965). Normal crimes: Sociological features of the penal code in a public defender's office. *Social Problems, 12,* 255-276.

Talarico, S.M. (1976). The dilemma of parole decision making. In G.F. Cole (Ed.), *Criminal justice: Law and politics,* 2nd edition (pp. 447-456). North Scituate, MA: Duxbury.

Tarlton v. Clark, 441 F.2d 384 (5th Cir. 1971), *cert. denied,* 403 U.S. 934 (1971).

Wilkins, L.T., & Gottfredson, D.M. (1973). *Information selection and use in parole decision-making: Supplemental report V. Davis,* CA: National Council on Crime and Delinquency.

Wolff v. McDonnell, 418 U.S. 539 (1974).

V

FIELDWORK EXPERIENCES IN CRIMINAL JUSTICE

Ethical Dilemmas

The advantages and disadvantages of full participation as a researcher are discussed by two authors, and a third analyzes gender as a factor in affecting her involvement in a fieldwork project. In discussing their first-hand research accounts, the authors reflectively analyze the methodological, ethical, and problematic issues that confronted them. Reflective accounts of researchers' experiences conducting fieldwork offer a unique perspective of the conflicting dilemmas that readers rarely are privy to. That is, such attempts at retrospective self-evaluation of one's past research experiences allow for a self-critique of the researcher's activities and methods.

It could perhaps be said that all field researchers encounter ethical dilemmas at one time or another during their time in the field. How each of us deals with often conflicting loyalties is a study in itself. There just are no easy solutions that can guide one's behavior in situations that are often ambiguous at best. As our three authors explain in the following articles, there is no one best way to resolve the conflicting, sometimes ethical, dilemmas that qualitative fieldworkers encounter while practicing their trade. Because life is unpredictable at times, so are the situations all researchers have to face during their stay in the field. It is in these unpredictable moments that

each person has to make decisions that will affect the research product one way or another. Each article in this section directly addresses these problematic situations.

For Van Maanen, it was being served with two subpoenas ordering him to appear at two different depositions and to provide certain field notes, tapes, and other materials he had produced during this fieldwork study on police. These formal legal requests involved two different cases and point to the moral issues Van Maanen faced as a result of his participant observation research with a police department.

Gender influence became a real issue for Gurney when she was conducting a long-term field research project in a male-dominated county prosecutor's office. She provides advice for women who will be conducting field studies in such gender-biased settings and suggests that they be aware that sexism and harassment exist. She suggests that women researchers develop a strategy on ways to respond to such situations before they occur. Gurney believes that preparing strategies ahead of time should make it less difficult to arrive at solutions for these problems, should they occur.

In Marquart's case, full immersion into the prison guard role led to his being involved in physical confrontations with inmates. By necessity, he had to accept using legitimate force when called for. He also developed a good relationship with inmate informants who provided him with information of their activities, which violated prison rules, but Marquart kept them confidential in order to preserve the reciprocal, trusting relationship that developed between them. Finally, role conflict was the most difficult problem to reconcile. That is, being a researcher on one hand and a prison guard on the other can lead to a blurring of these two roles, which Marquart discusses in terms of perceiving guards as the good guys in describing their actions. Through the process of extensive note taking, he was able to maintain a conscious effort to balance the role conflict he experienced.

As you read these three articles that describe moral and ethical dilemmas that these researchers faced, ask yourself what you would do if you were confronted with the types of situations and circumstances these authors found themselves in. Only by attempting to place yourself in their role can you have an empathetic understanding of what these three fieldworkers faced. As you may conclude, there are no clear-cut guidelines that provide a correct path to follow conducting research in the field, which is fraught with obstacles and ethical dilemmas that one has to react to as they arise. Being involved in the practice of qualitative research can often prove to be a lonely business, one in which ethical conflicts often arise.

*   *   *

Immersing oneself into the everyday world of a city police department is what Van Maanen did in conducting his participant observation field research. In this retrospective account, the author points out that when the fieldworker establishes an intimate and trusting relationship with those being studied, unexpected and harmful side effects often can occur if the researcher fails to perform in ways that those being studied had expected from their understanding of the reciprocal commitment to the researcher. The moral choices that often confront field researchers in various situations are conflicting and have no easy solutions. In his case, Van Maanen, who was perceived by the police he studied as an insider, and furthermore, was counted on to not go against the interests and culture of the organization, found himself facing a moral dilemma.

THE MORAL FIX

On the Ethics of Fieldwork

JOHN VAN MAANEN

BACKGROUND

While a graduate student at the University of California, Irvine, in September, 1969, I began contacting police officials across the country seeking permission to conduct a one-man field study inside a large, metropolitan law-enforcement agency. I wished to study the kinds of cultural understandings necessary to operate in the occupational world of patrolmen by witnessing at firsthand the way in which young men went about learning the ropes of city policing. Although I encountered some initial difficulties in locating a department willing to tolerate my planned foray into its organizational spheres, eventually I managed to gain access to one police

Reprinted with permission from *Social Science Methods, Vol. I: Qualitative Social Research*, 115–139. Copyright © 1982, Ballinger Publishing Company.

Many people have helped me with this paper. Conceptually, Peter K. Manning provided a most illuminating critique of an earlier draft, a critique that forced me to attempt to spell out many more of the assumptions that governed my actions in the field than would otherwise have been the case. Operationally the conclusion of the story presented here might well have been different were it not for the aid and comfort provided me by James D. Carroll, the director of an important study conducted at Syracuse University on the "Confidentiality of Research Sources and Data" (Russell Sage Foundation, 1976). Professor Carroll provided some knowledgeable assistance to the attorneys struggling to build some sort of case to defend the stance I had taken in the legal matters discussed in this paper. Finally, my faculty colleagues as well as the administration at M.I.T. never backed away from my case and supported my position both financially and, with few exceptions, morally.

organization largely through the sponsorship of a man I met almost by happenstance, a university professor who had several rather close and well-placed friends in the police department. After a short, almost *pro forma* period of negotiations with the ranking officials in this agency (herein referred to under the pseudonym Union City Police Department), I entered a regular recruit training class in April 1970 with a reserve police commission. I had tentative approval for a period of observation in the patrol division (subject to my graduation from the police academy) and, perhaps most importantly, something of an administrative commitment from the Chief of Police to see my research carried out.[1]

Throughout the study I worked in the fashion of a traditional ethnographer or participant observer, made no attempt to disguise my scholarly aims or identity, and met with little overt hostility from the men whose everyday affairs were the explicit subject of my investigation. In most respects I felt my mode of inquiry approximated both the substance and spirit of Evans-Pritchard's classic formulation of the ethnographic technique: "to get to know well the persons involved and to see and hear what they do and say" (quoted in Barnes, 1967:202). To this end I completed the thirteen-week police academy course in Union City and then spent a little over five months as an observer riding patrol with both rookie and veteran police officers in several selected districts of the city — in particular, the skid row district. After an absence of over two years I returned to Union City for several months in early 1973 and again spent considerable time viewing police actions from the vantage point of patrol cars. Since that period I have been back to Union City on several occasions both to renew friendships and to check out certain findings.

The writings that have emerged from this lengthy but interrupted period of fieldwork have focused primarily upon patrolmen and their work. Specifically, I have been concerned with such topics as police socialization (Van Maanen, 1973, 1975), work rules (Van Maanen, 1974), and police labeling practices (Van Maanen, 1978a). More general publications have also relied substantially, although less exclusively, upon my police experiences (Van Maanen, 1977; Van Maanen and Schein, 1977). In all of these writings, I have made much use of the field notes I compiled during and following my various stays in Union City. These notes selectively detail the diverse sights and sounds, facts and fictions, conversations and actions, thoughts and feelings that I experienced while embedded within, and preoccupied with, the police scene.

Critically, my methodological goal during the study was to become an accepted part of the Union City policeman's day-to-day work world. That is to say, I wanted my presence in the training class, in the patrol car, on the street, in the courtroom, in the city jail, in a saloon, or wherever certain policemen might be at a given time to be taken as more or less natural. From the outset of the study I wanted to work (some may say worm) my way into a research position wherein my presence would not alarm or otherwise disturb those policemen with whom I was to share a portion of my life. While I was not welcomed with obvious glee, I believe that over time I was able by and large to approach this position, a position somewhat akin to a state of grace. But there was both a personal and social price to be paid for such a success. It is to certain troublesome and altogether chilling implications of this success that the remainder of my remarks in this paper are directed.

A Case in Point

In October of 1974, while teaching in Cambridge, Massachusetts, many miles from Union City, I was served with two subpoenas ordering me to appear at a deposition hearing to give oral testimony and to surrender certain research materials concerned with matters stemming from a libel action brought by several Union City police officers against a major Union City newspaper. One subpoena read in part: "You are further required to bring with you all your notes and other file materials covering the periods commencing July, 1970 and ending March, 1973." The other subpoena was somewhat more specific, asking for "notes, tapes, and other file materials made pertaining to the arrest of Chester A. Blazier" (all names used here are, of course, disguised). The deposition hearing and the occurrences that led up to it and followed it provide a convenient and concrete frame of reference through which some inescapable and perhaps insoluble ethical dilemmas of fieldwork can be examined. The story itself is complicated, but it illustrates several crucial moral issues at stake when one undertakes first-hand observation.[2] I will first tell the story and then attempt to draw out several rather vexing ethical problems that penetrate to the very core of the tale.

Chester Blazier was arrested on a slow Sunday night in February, 1973. He was also beaten severely that night in the back of a patrol car summoned to transport him to the city jail. He wound up lying in the intensive-care unit of a Union City hospital with three broken ribs, a punctured lung, lacerations to the head and body, temporarily blinded in one eye. He was charged with several criminal offenses, all resulting from actions that took place after he had been arrested on "suspicion of public drunkenness." The events leading up to this exercise in what I have elsewhere called "street justice" (Van Maanen, 1974) can best be recounted by the field notes I wrote some five or fix hours after the incident itself (and only several weeks after I had returned to Union City following a long absence). This excerpted (and slightly edited) account begins about an hour into the 7 P.M.-3 A.M. shift I was working with Officers Barns and McGee.[3]

> . . . While parked under the elevated highway drinking coffee and chatting, a slow moving freight train rumbles by and both men play idly with the squad car spotlights trying to see if any tramps are free-loading on the flatbeds or rails. As always, McGee is quiet, almost taciturn, and Barns, ever talkative, seems to run the show. Over the radio comes a familiar call to investigate a disturbance complaint lodged by the owner of a tavern well known to the skid row cops as a "fag joint."
>
> . . . arriving at the Tavern, the owner tells us simply that this middle aged black man sitting calmly at the end of the bar is "causing a commotion and refuses to leave." The Tavern at that moment has three other patrons sitting in a booth quietly sipping their drinks and watching us. Barns then walks briskly over to the man and asks for some identification. McGee, following Barns, jerks a half-full bottle of whiskey from the man's back pocket and hands it to me. The man pulls out his wallet, removes his driver's license from its plastic container (indicating to the officers

that perhaps they are dealing with a "cop wise" character who has had previous dealings with the police), hands it to Barns, who, after looking at the license, then pulls the wallet from the man's hands and rummages through its contents revealing among other things, an unemployment check, a naval shipyard identification badge, and a soiled picture of a woman and two children. "This your wife?" asks Barns. "Yeah," says the man now believed to be Chester A. Blazier. McGee chimes in with the remark, "You know this is a fag joint, don't you? You like gay people?" Blazier, to his undoing, replies smartly, "Yeah, don't you?" The following exchange then took place:

McGee: "Get the fuck outta here now."

Blazier: "Come on man, I ain't doing no harm, just minding my own business."

McGee: "Listen you cocksucker, this lady here called and said you threatened her and are causing a disturbance in this 'fine' establishment. Now get going."

Blazier: "Sure, sure, I'm going. Gimme back my stuff. . . . You got my check."

Barns: "Here you are, 'sir.' Now shag your black ass down that road 'cause if we see you around here again tonight, you're going in. Got it?"

We walk the "troublemaker" out to the street. McGee takes the man's whiskey bottle from me and smashes it against the curb, gives Blazier a light shove to get moving, and we walk back to the patrol car parked across the street. Both men comment on what a "jerkoff" Blazier was and how they have to deal with "his kind" all the time. They also wonder whether or not they've seen him before in their district. They can't decide. We then drive around the block and return to the vicinity of the bar. Rounding the corner, Barns notes that Blazier has changed his direction from the time we last saw him and now appears to be heading back toward the Tavern. Enraged, Barns flips on the lights and siren, says, "That's it, let's take him, the sonofabitch." McGee calls the station asking for the "wagon" (the police van used to take prisoners to the city jail). Blazier, having noticed the sudden police reappearance, quickly picks up his pace and walks right past the tavern. Both Barns and McGee yell at him to stop: "Hold it, asshole, you're going in." Blazier halts in his tracks and the two officers, jumping from the prowl car, grab him, perform a hasty but rough body search, set him down on the curb and then stand a few feet away to await the arrival of the wagon.

. . . When the wagon arrives, Blazier is readied for his short ride to the city jail, there to be booked as a "stand-up drunk" (suspicion of public drunkenness). As they attempt to push him into the wagon, Blazier balks by stretching both arms across the backdoor entrance to the van. It was as if a signal had been provided to both Barns and McGee, for all hell breaks loose. McGee kicks Blazier at the knees and Blazier falls to the ground and begins to rather half-heartedly kick back (a serious mistake). Barns and McGee, both kicking and swinging, finally succeed in getting Blazier into the wagon. Both of them now follow Blazier into the van and Barns has his personal "nigger-knocker" [nightstick] out. From outside the wagon I can hear the very distinct smack of wood meeting flesh and bone. After perhaps a half a minute or so, Blazier, thoroughly dazed and maybe unconscious, is pulled from the wagon, bounced to the pavement, handcuffed and tossed back into the van.

McGee then told the reserve officer driving the police van to take Blazier to the emergency room at Hillside Hospital. The reservist, however, did not know how to get there, so Barns led a two vehicle procession to Hillside. On the drive over, Barns remarked: "What a place to try and put somebody out. It's so fucking cramped and dark in that van you don't know what's going on. I kept hitting something with my stick but didn't know what it was until I heard that creep's glasses shatter. Then I kept hitting that same spot until I felt it get kind of squishy."

When we reached the hospital, Barns called the squad sergeant on the phone, explained briefly what had happened, and asked him to come over to the hospital. The reserve officers went back to the street and Barns, McGee, and I went to the employee's cafeteria at the hospital to begin doing some of the paperwork associated with the arrest. Barns suggested a number of possible charges to be brought against Blazier: resisting arrest, assaulting a policeman, disturbing the peace, disorderly conduct, carrying a concealed weapon (a "church key"—sharp-edged bottle opener), using abusive language, and so forth. . . . The initial draft of the major arrest report was, however, received by the squad sergeant in the following manner: "I don't like the way it sounds. You've gotta remember that IID (the Internal Investigation Division of the Union City Police Department) won't talk to you

first, they'll just read this report and ask themselves why didn't you guys just shove him in the wagon and forget it."

. . . returning to the station house, Barns filled out the many reports associated in the incident and passed each of them to the sergeant for approval. The sergeant carefully read each report and then returned the "paper" to Barns saying that he better claim he was kicked in the face *before* he entered the patrol wagon or Barns would get a heavy brutality complaint for sure. He also told Barns . . . heavier charges (against Blazier) were necessary to protect Barns from IID. Finally, after some discussion and two rewrites, Barns finished a report which the sergeant said "covered their asses." (February, 1973)

The sergeant was apparently wise to the ways in which such affairs unfold, for the next day Blazier filed a formal complaint charging the arresting officers with the use of unnecessary force. Two Internal Investigation Division (IID) officers were assigned to investigate the affair, an investigation that resulted in five interviews—Blazier, the four officers on the scene of the arrest (Barns, McGee and the two reserve officers handling the wagon), and myself. Two days after the arrest occurred, I gave my account to IID in testimony that was both under oath and tape recorded. In that testimony I recounted the incident as accurately as I could from memory (not including the report-writing encounter with the squad sergeant). I did not bring my notes of the incident to the IID interview nor did I make reference to their existence. Almost five weeks later the officers were exonerated by IID, and the complaint itself was ruled "unfounded." Blazier, then out of the hospital and out on bail, threatened through his attorney to file a civil suit against the city, charging economic and physical impairment as a result of the police beating. Several days before his scheduled trial on the felony counts, the district attorney's office agreed to drop all charges against Blazier if he in turn would sign a waiver absolving the city from all responsibility in the matter. He signed.

The story, which is a common one in police circles, would have ended there had it not been for a relationship I developed with a police reporter in Union City. I had been introduced to this reporter by, oddly enough, Officer Barns at a squad party several weeks after the Blazier arrest, and we became rather good friends over the course of the following year. We visited with one another, exchanged many letters, and in general talked a good deal about police work. We had both spent considerable time in the skid row district of Union City and had observed the particularly active and aggressive patrol tactics used in that part of town. Since we both knew Barns rather well, the Blazier incident arose in a few of our conversations. Indeed, while I was still in Union City, the reporter, Barns, and I had once talked rather candidly and argumentatively about the events (and our various interpretations of them) that surrounded the beating of Chester Blazier.

In early 1974, almost a year after we had met, my reporter friend wrote a series of articles on "Skid Row Cops." Each article was constructed as something of a profile on the working style of a particular patrolman. The articles all dealt with patrolmen I had known well, although I had nothing directly or knowingly to do with the production of the articles themselves. Appended to the profile on Officer Barns was a story about the Blazier incident entitled "A Citizen Fights for His Rights—Was He Wrong?" In this story, the reporter recounted interviews he had held with Blazier, Barns, and McGee sometime well after the incident had been disposed of by the courts; he also quoted from the arrest report filed the night Blazier was arrested. No mention was made in any of the articles of my presence on the scene in Union City, nor could I detect the use of any private information I conceivably might have slipped to this reporter about the Blazier incident during our numerous conversations. Moreover, I felt then (and now) that taken as a whole the stories were, if anything, biased toward the police view of the world, romantic in their depiction of the "harsh, bitter, and dangerous tasks performed by the men in blue," and downright evasive when it came to describing the circumstances through which Blazier almost lost his life.

Nonetheless, the patrolmen who were featured in the stories—in particular, Barns—were agitated and angered by what they took to be a rude violation of their privacy and with what they also took to be the antipolice stance taken by the paper. Within a month after the articles appeared, two separate civil suits were filed by the Union City Patrolmen's Association on behalf of two of the profiled officers (including Barns), charging the newspaper with libel and slander.[4] The newspaper then subpoenaed my testimony and records, apparently on the reporter's request, in order to support what they must have felt to be the essential truthfulness of the stories.

I was in a moral fix. I could obey the subpoena, turn over my notes, and perhaps assist in making the newspaper's case. Or I could refuse to comply, risk possible sanction, but in the process protect what I took to be the best interests of the patrolmen I had known in Union City. I chose the latter on multiple grounds. First, the terms of the subpoenas were so broad and inclusive that many other officers (across the ranks) would unavoidably be made vulnerable to departmental or legal sanction for actions having nothing whatsoever to do with the Blazier incident. Buried within my notes were numerous raw details about questionable, irregular, and illegal police actions with the names of those involved (or said to be involved) necessarily attached. For instance, I had materials bearing on possible police burglaries, drug dealings, payoffs, planting of evidence, and so on. Many of these incidents were, to be sure, merely conjecture on my part or unverified (and perhaps unverifiable) stories I had heard told by patrolmen in Union City (usually about other patrolmen). But a few of these tales had been confirmed by my own observations.

Needless to say, however, I wished to keep information gathered in confidence confidential, and although I had no doubt betrayed this principle through some of my all-too-casual conversations with the police reporter, I was not about to compound this error with another patently more serious and extensive betrayal. Second, I had previously given sworn testimony on the Blazier incident, and a tape of my interview was presumably available from the police department. This tape was eventually turned over to the newspaper, although it took a court order to pry it out of a most reluctant department. Finally, the attorney representing the newspaper in the case had also been a key public figure, a special federal prosecutor in a police scandal that had erupted in Union City several years before, and hence would have probably been a poor choice indeed to handle sensitive materials. At the deposition hearing itself I appeared and brought with me the subpoenaed materials but refused to turn them over to either the court or the newspaper. On the advice of my lawyers I based my claims for privilege on the elegant, prestigious, but thoroughly nonexistent grounds of "research confidentiality."

The legal staff representing the newspaper then began preparing a case for a district court in Massachusetts in which they would ask the court to find me in criminal contempt for not having complied with the terms of the subpoena. They would argue that the public's right to know (in this case, the newspaper's right to know) clearly outweighed my ambiguous claims for research confidentiality. Before I went to trial, however, a Union City judge in a preliminary hearing on one of the police libel and slander suits dismissed the case on the grounds that the officers had failed to show damage as a result of the newspaper articles. The other suit was soon dropped by the Patrolmen's Association, and my case then became moot. This was most fortunate, for I had been advised by a number of attorneys and scholars that I had a very poor case and would most likely lose in the district court. Hypothetically, at least, I was at the time prepared to go to jail if necessary, believing it unlikely (but untested) that I would be kept there for more than a few days. Yet in cases of this variety there are precious few precedents to go by.[5]

FIELDWORK ETHICS

It would be easy to oversimplify the ethical issues raised by this case. My dilemma was not simply deciding post hoc whether or not to turn over what I took to be confidential materials to the court or the newspaper. Rather, as the case partially illustrates, I was making ethical choices (some good, some not so good) every day during the study. Merely my presence among the skid row squad of patrolmen may have served symbolically as a signal to the press that perhaps something unusual or interesting was occurring there, something that had potential for "good copy." Nor was my dilemma confined simply to deciding post hoc what material

to publish. Very clearly, moral choices are made day in and day out in the field when deciding what data to go after, how to get them, who to talk to, how and where to record and store data, and so forth.[6] Too often, discussions of ethical materials in the social sciences turn only on either the decisions concerning the disclosure of research intent to those who are studied, or on the problems posed by the publication of sensitive materials, so that the privacy, reputation, and good will of the studied are protected. These are important matters, of course, but they fail to touch directly on the sorts of immediate, personal, and excruciating decisions made by a researcher working out practical solutions to the multitude of problems faced in the field.[7]

From this standpoint virtually every aspect of my study in Union City represents the personal resolution of various ethical dilemmas. There are no easy or a priori moral stances to be taken by the researcher in fieldwork situations. Certainly, fieldworkers cannot know what they are "getting into" until they "get into" it. As Becker (1964) has observed, there may be some very broad guidelines available, such as not violating confidences or bringing harm to subjects, but in practice these guidelines are elusive and mean different things to different people. Seldom has there been even a modest attempt to provide a detailed interpretation of the behavioral or contextual implications of guidelines as protecting one's informants. Indeed, there is something of a general consensus—at least among sociologists—that rejects the idea of producing concrete, specified rules for the "ethical conduct" of field research.[8] Some reject the idea primarily as inadvisable and impractical, since such rules would likely preclude the gathering of certain kinds of data (Douglas, 1976; Roth, 1962). Others reject it as reprehensible, if not repugnant, since such rules would in effect place the fieldworker in a debatable but morally superior position vis-à-vis others, including those who are studied (Klockars, 1974; Rainwater and Pittman, 1967). Still others reject it as theoretically impossible, given the inherently incomplete and evolutionary character of all rules (Mehan and Wood, 1975; Becker and Friedson, 1964). Nonetheless, ethical decisions do get made and accounted for by fieldworkers. Below I will briefly review what I consider to be the most ethically troublesome areas raised by the in situ observation of the police. I hasten to add, however, the following discussion merely illustrates rather than resolves the moral fix a fieldworker may encounter when working in law-enforcement settings. In short, there is no suitable solution that will fit the peculiar and always particular issues that are raised in field studies. Ultimately, the choice about when and where to draw a moral and ethical line must rest on an individual, not a collective, conscience.

PARTICIPATION

How far does a participant observer go in assisting the police with their daily tasks? Had Blazier actually been fighting the officers, for instance, I have few doubts that I would have entered the fray on the side of the police. This is a sort of "member test" for ethical decision making. If one joins with the police in order to study them, one is under considerable obligation to help them when needed. The height of moral duplicity would be for an observer to pose as a friend and supporter of the police (and there is unlikely to be any way around this if one is to develop a sustained and intimate research relationship with them) and then refuse to abide by this pose when aid is required. I know from my own experience that on occasion patrolmen entered certain situations without additional police support solely because of the additional safety they felt my presence provided them. Of course, this does not imply that the researcher need go along on all matters that do not endanger the safety of the observed, nor does it necessarily mean that one go along blindly on all matters that do. But the fieldworker does have the obligation to inform those who are studied just where the line will be drawn or perhaps just when that line is being approached. As I have suggested elsewhere, I drew few lines (Van Maanen, 1978b).

It is important to note also that many if not most of the agreements between the researcher and researched in field situations are tacit. That is, research understandings about who will do what, when, and where arise recursively over time as a result of, for example, previous silences maintained by the researcher about potentially incriminating and embarrassing matters. These understandings may also come about as a consequence of specific cooperative or collusive arrangements that emerge from particular incidents. I once was privy to a conversation in which a veteran police officer constructed a cover story with the able assistance of several other officers concerning the sloughing off of a knife on an unwary suspect arrested for a relatively minor offense (Van Maanen, 1973). Shortly thereafter, since I had not reported the incident, I too was embraced in the verbal conspiracy that surrounded the affair and was therefore as vulnerable to sanction as were all the officers involved in developing the story line. I suspect any researcher who spends more than a superficial amount of time with the police is party to much information of a discrediting (and probably illegal) nature. Thus, those who remain are likely to have entered, however inadvertently, into a silent bond of mutual protection—a bond supported by what Westley (1970) called the "no-rat rule." Yet, if one wishes to be where the action takes place in police organizations, a certain moral relativism is required. As Buckner (1967) suggests, first-hand observation may well require the suspension of single-minded (perhaps simple-minded) standards for judging the behavior of others. At least in police organizations, fieldwork demands of the researcher an ability to allow to pass without accusatory comment certain actions that may well be viewed as morally repugnant. The hope, of course, is that in the end the truth, when it is depicted fully, will help us all out.

Nonetheless, the observer in police settings is subject normally to the same restrictions, both legal and departmental, that presumably regulate the conduct of those who live everyday in the setting. The fieldworker is not beyond the law in this respect. The Blazier affair makes this point quite well. I felt I was under an obligation to report what I had witnessed to IID when ordered to do so. And, if called upon, I would have been willing to testify in court upon this matter, but *only* upon this particular matter. I was under no illusions that the cloak of science could or should protect me from legal complications. In refusing to testify to broader matters, I exercised a moral freedom, not a legal one. The point here is simply what I see to be the ethical necessity facing researchers to share the same risks as those they observe. This is the "dirty hands test." The researcher whose hands are dirty must run the same risks as anyone else in the situation. Fieldworkers may refuse to give information on a specific incident, but they cannot expect special compensation for so doing simply because they were also doing something called research. It is not a cost/benefit ratio that will decide the just and proper ethics of the fieldworker's response to a certain situation. Indeed, there is no way the vague program called "advancing knowledge" can ever be balanced on the same scale against legal and human considerations.

Being forced into the fire, as it were, makes immediate and practical the ethical choices made by researchers in police situations. They may choose to observe illegal acts, but they do so with the knowledge that they are as culpable as those performing such acts. Of course, researchers may voice their objections to what they observe, thus forcing the police to contend with yet another influence on their actions, but these choices will be made in context, not on the basis of decree. The real dilemma for persons doing police studies comes after some illegal activity has been observed. Then the researcher must decide what shall be done, if anything, with or about such observations.[9]

Guilty Knowledge and the Protection of Individuals

As the documentary films of Frederick Wiseman graphically demonstrate, people will engage in sometimes incredibly stark and incriminating actions while in front of klieg lights and cameras. Those who have studied the police firsthand report much the same thing (e.g., Skolnick, 1966; Reiss, 1971; Rubinstein, 1973; Manning, 1977). Perhaps police departments, like all organizations, are characterized as much by patterned evasion of some norms as they are by strict adherence to other norms. If one wishes to observe these evasions repeatedly, it is obvious that the only tool available is a verbal and behavioral commitment to protect the confidentiality of sources who reveal and sometimes demonstrate such evasions. This means in effect that the researcher must violate the law in order to understand something of its

implementations. There is no way around this; if fieldworkers were to reveal their personal sources of information (as the law technically demands), it would not be long before they had no personal sources of information left.

Maintaining the confidentiality of individual informants is then intended not only to protect the individual from harm, but also to protect the research enterprise itself. Fieldwork proceeds more or less successfully depending upon the degree to which those with the data trust those who want the data to protect them from personal, social, or organizational injury. Thus, there are expedient, self-serving, and moral reasons for guarding the trust of informants. Perhaps with information gathered covertly some moral strings are cut, but even here the researcher must place considerable reliance on the data resulting from human ties the covert observer has established within the organization—ties that *would not exist* were it not for the fact that research is being done. Only the "unobserved observer," who works entirely but surreptitiously with data gathered unobtrusively from public, archival, or other indirect sources, would seem to be free of this moral constraint binding researchers to those whom they observe. In studies where any disclosure of purpose is made, the rule of thumb would appear to be that the closer one is to an informant and the more explicit the promise of confidentiality, the greater the researcher's obligation becomes to protect the informant.

This rule of thumb is hardly absolute, however. How far would I have gone to protect my police acquaintances had Blazier been killed by the police that January evening? There must always be the possibility that the researcher's personal morality will force him to violate implicit or explicit research agreements or perhaps even to abandon the study itself. To suggest the contrary would be to make a machine of the researcher and to dehumanize fieldwork.

Who Is to Be Harmed?

Becker (1967) has argued with considerable justification that the principal ethical problem in publishing the results of field studies lies in deciding who is to be harmed, not whether or not harm will result. Paraphrasing Becker, any study that is done well will no doubt please some people and anger others. Thus, the choice boils down to who will be angered. This problem arises precisely because the social scientist, of necessity, often reports on matters that some would prefer to keep quiet. When fieldworkers write up a research report, they will inevitably betray the trust and confidence some informants have placed in them. To wit, throughout my study I attempted continually to convey the impression to police administrators that my work was harmless to them. Eventually, however, I knew I was bound to violate whatever misplaced trust I might have created, since the tone and thrust of what I wrote would undoubtedly indicate that things were not as the administrators said they were and, furthermore, that little or nothing was being done about it.

For the general readership individuals are relatively easy to disguise in field reports. Particular administrations and organizations are less easy to disguise, although it is common practice to try. This latter problem I find less morally bothersome than the former, since administrations and organizations have far greater resources to defend themselves or to strike back than do individuals, particularly those at the lower levels, who are relatively helpless. Yet, even in disguise damage may result to those inside an organization, where it may be reasonably easy to determine who's who in the fieldworker's report. For example, I have little doubt that several of the individuals involved in certain anecdotes I have published are, at best, thinly disguised and hence recognizable to intimates within the Union City Police Department. The problem, of course, lies in forecasting the likely consequences of any given report, a near impossible task.

To take the Blazier case again as an illustration, when I appeared at the deposition hearing, the attorney representing the Union City newspaper read for the record a section of one of my published papers that dealt with the incident in detail and used the fictive names of Barns and McGee to identify the officers involved. I was then asked the true identities of not only Barns and McGee but of the sergeant, the reserve officers, and other policemen on or around the scene that night. I refused to answer publicly, again on the feeble grounds of "research confidentiality."

Privately I refused to answer because of the general research bargain that had unfolded between myself and the police in Union City, because of my close personal ties with the particular officers, and because of the potential complications that my answering one question might have on the other more general questions that were being asked. Further, the Blazier case was over, I could do nothing to erase what had already happened nor was I at all interested in seeing the officers reprimanded for an act all too familiar to police observers (Chevigny, 1968, 1972; Reiss, 1971; Westley, 1970). To disclose my notes and memories of the incident beyond that which I had done for the IID investigators would very clearly have injured the officers involved. Yet, there was also a related factor in this decision, a factor I now discuss with some trepidation.

Overrapport

Before beginning my studies, I felt, in the abstract, that if and when I penetrated the patrol division in Union City, I could carve out a rather non-participatory research role. For a vast number of reasons discussed elsewhere this did not turn out to be the case (Van Maanen, 1978b). Indeed, after the police academy I wished to be treated as any other rookie might be treated and wanted to see the "real" nature of police work. By and large this occurred, but I also believe that I created the conditions under which a rather tragic charade was acted out for my benefit partially as a result of my initial and rather full acceptance into the police world.

I had just returned to Union City after an absence of over two years when Chester Blazier was arrested. The men I spoke with during my return stay were apparently quite happy to see me again and, of critical importance here, were seemingly very willing to display what they had learned occupationally since we had parted. This prideful situation was not obvious to me at the time, but it was some six weeks later. I began to develop an inkling about what might be occurring as I watched my former classmates work rather hard—in comparison to what I had observed to be the routines several years before—at certain aspects of their job. Indeed, several men remarked that they wanted to show me what it was like now that they "really knew" what they were doing on the street. On patrol we always ate in the better restaurants at a reduced or nonexistent price. This so-called policeman's discount or freebie was on several occasions enforced openly and argumentatively by my police hosts on patrol. I watched some of my former colleagues as they sought out, pushed around, and goaded several of their informants apparently only to demonstrate to me the fact that they now had their own intelligence networks—though to a man they thought their informants to be "scum." I once witnessed a bizarre encounter in which a boy, perhaps ten or eleven years old, was verbally assaulted and then thrown to the pavement because he had aimed a ceremonially upright third finger in the direction of the patrol unit as it passed by — a gesture from a child that would have been routinely ignored (or returned) in my previous experiences. These and other similar events forced me eventually to reckon with the possibility that perhaps my police friends were literally showing off for my benefit. They were occasionally taking action on my account as a part of documenting their acquired competence. In short, they were demonstrating for my benefit (though perhaps for their own as well) that they had learned the police game thoroughly. They were now in command and therefore, as many said in both word and deed, "did not have to take any shit on the street." I cannot unequivocally prove that the Blazier incident was a direct result of my presence on the scene, though I believe this to be the case.[10]

Skolnick (1966:36) has remarked ". . . if an observer's presence does alter police behavior, I believe it can be assumed that it does so only in one direction. I can see no reason why police would, for example, behave more harshly to a prisoner in the presence of an observer than in his absence." I think perhaps I have stumbled sadly upon one such reason. The police, like all of us, take considerable pride in some of the work they do. And when the occasion presents itself, they will exhibit the special skills they believe they possess, particularly for what they take to be an appreciative audience. The participant observer who has gained their trust and who seems therefore to exhibit a good deal of existential concern for their welfare is no doubt representative of an unusually appreciative audience. After all, the observer claims to guarantee anonymity, often provides assistance on mundane and not-so-mundane matters, is empathic to an extreme, is nonevaluative in the field, and in general acts out the part of a knowledgeable "police buff." The paradox is that this is the way I believe the researcher must behave if he is to penetrate the rings of individual and collective secrecy enclosing police actions.[11]

Miller (1952:98) coined the apt but bulky term *overrapport* to express "the idea that the researcher may be so closely related to the observed that his investigations are impeded." He used this term to refer to those field situations in which the researcher cannot question closely the basic attitudes of the observed because such questioning might destroy the "all-accepting friendships" that have been carved out in the setting. He also used the term to refer to those situations in which the observer becomes so closely attached to the feelings and sentiments of the studied group that the detachment necessary to carry out the ethnographic craft is lost (i.e., "to go native"). To these very real dangers of fieldwork I would add a third: Overrapport can be said to exist in those situations where the observed consistently behave in a fashion designed to increase or maximize their status and worth in the eyes of a peculiar kind of intimate, the fieldworker. I choose these words carefully for I am talking of matters that go well beyond the conventional experimenter effects described in the behavioral science literature (Rosenthal, 1976). Indeed, as the term itself implies, I am referring only to those situations in which a warm and trusting relationship has already been created and the researcher is known by the researched to have some knowledge of the everyday activities that take place in the setting. It is therefore not so much merely a Goffmanesque matter of impression management per se as it is a matter of the particular impression that is to be managed. The phenomenon I am describing is something akin to youngsters considering whether or not to dive from the highest springboard at the public plunge. They will spend their courage, as it were, only during those periods when their familiar and respected acquaintances are both present and watching. Overrapport, in the sense that I append to it here, implied that it is the close personal regard between the observer and the observed that is crucial to the matter, not the simple presence of the observer. . . .

Given that there is likely to be no "best" way to conduct field studies and that each study depends upon the situational and biographical particulars of who is observing whom for what purpose, what strategic options does the fieldworker have available to choose from in order to counter the potential trap of overrapport? Taking the so-called neutral stance is perhaps one tactical option. Yet, at least in the police world neutrality is unlikely to get the researcher very far. Indeed, the game of work played by most policemen pits various teams, cliques, cabals, or other vertically and horizontally partitioned players within the organization against one another (Manning, 1976a; Rubinstein, 1973; Van Maanen, 1973). Hence, an observer who wants to gain any appreciable knowledge about the players on any given team must at least appear to stand with them at least for a while. Furthermore, patrolmen in general must be assured that the fieldworker understands their orientation and position on certain matters. Yet, to demonstrate such an understanding implies an ability to take the side of the observed by using their language, demonstrating a concern for their problems, and displaying the ability to evaluate their actions as they do. Over many occasions such a stance is unlikely to be interpreted as neutral. The bromide of "neutrality" is therefore both unstable and replete with the possibility of entrapment for the researcher. . . .

In the final analysis establishing the proper amount of rapport with the observed is something of an intangible creation, and even if it can be achieved, it is certain to decay. It represents at best a passing or transitional stage in the long-range temporal history of a research relationship. Whether or not such a relationship will eventually move toward under- or overrapport is a matter over which the fieldworker has some control, though probably less control than desired (or perhaps believed).

I do not think overrapport is common in police studies. In my case it arose out of a lengthy and intense period of participation during the observed's initiation period into the occupation. In this period camaraderie and identification with

one another were both natural and unavoidable. Furthermore, many of my most difficult moral problems arose primarily because of a long absence in which a warm welcome back should have been (but was not) expected. The overly aggressive patrol tactics I witnessed upon my return more or less disappeared once I had reestablished a routine observational post in the patrol division. Indeed, the convincing bit of evidence I draw on in this regard comes from those officers with whom I spent three or more shifts upon my return. By the third shift together things had begun to settle down into a rather normal tour of patrol duty. Such tours again began to be filled by long breaks, much conversation about non-police matters, and a working style governed by the calls dispatched from headquarters over the police radio. Yet even here there was a certain pretense about the police activities I observed that told me that at least some patrolmen were apparently trying harder to be "good cops" than they normally would. A few in private said as much. Consider the following, in part congratulatory, yet nonetheless chilling remark made to me by a young patrolman I had once worked closely with on the street:

> You know John, I miss you a lot out there. You really got me to thinking about some shit I don't usually think about. . . . It was fun working with you 'cause you're not like most of the other bulls around here who don't really want to do very much at all. *When you were along, we always seemed to find some real police work to do.*

The choice of what the researcher should do under these circumstances still remains unanswered. And, as I have tried to show in this paper, this choice will always be difficult for there are no magical formulas to offer which can alleviate the very real moral dilemmas of fieldwork and yet allow the work to proceed unchanged. In my own case, I have continued my work in Union City, avoiding whenever and wherever possible those officers whom I felt were most likely to become carried away with their police performance as a result of my presence on the scene.[12] However, it is certainly the case that other fieldworkers might have left the scene entirely. Others might have become far more actively engaged in the social drama than I. Unfortunately, even with the luxury of considerable hindsight, I can not conclusively or with total conviction say that the moral choice I made was a good one. To be sure, I can defend it but it is up to others to decide whether or not to accept my defense.

NOTES

1. My method and the problems I encountered in carrying it out are detailed elsewhere (Van Maanen, 1978b). . . . Several reviews of the field methods employed in studying the police are available; see Manning (1972, 1976b), McCall (1978: chapter 3), and Fox and Lundman (1974). The best description I have read on the use of observational techniques to study the police is located in the appendix of Buckner's (1967) unpublished doctoral dissertation.

2. In general, discussions concerned solely with the ethical and moral issues involved in fieldwork (or for that matter in all social research) are few and far between. There are some notable exceptions, however. See in particular Myrdal (1944: Appendix 2) and Sjoberg (ed.) (1967).

3. All quotes appearing here are only as accurate as my memory and ear allow. During the observational sequences of the Union City study I did not employ a recording device and took very few notes while on the street with my police informants. However, excluding those instances when weariness got the better of me, I typed out as extensively as I could my recollections of the "day's" events, talks, hunches, and so forth immediately upon returning to the relative sanctuary of my home.

4. To be more complete, I should note that in the background of the two police suits against the newspaper stand several other pertinent details. Among most of the policemen I knew in Union City ran some intense and hostile feelings toward the paper. It was seen as "a liberal rag," "out to get the police," "distorting the news," and more generally quite unsympathetic to the men of the police department. Furthermore the paper had also kept a recent police scandal in the daily headlines, whereas the other major paper in the community appeared to play down the story, relegating the emerging specifics of the corruption disclosures to the inside pages. Needless to say most policemen did not take kindly to the one paper's screaming display of embarrassing matters. Finally, the Patrolman's Benevolent Association (the organization sponsoring the libel actions) also had an ax to grind since its president was at times mocked and treated quite unseriously on the editorial pages of the paper. All of these factors probably played a part in the officers' decision to sue the paper. More details were no doubt also pertinent, but, since I was some distance from Union City during the time of legal maneuvering, the face-to-face social relations necessary to learn some of these details were unavailable to me. I should note too that because of this distance my own anxieties in the matter were heightened, since I could not really understand what exactly was going on beneath the public surface in Union City at that time. Only later did I learn some of the factors that apparently prompted the police suit, factors which I have summarized in a most incomplete and dross fashion here. See Harris (1973:50-52) for a similar view of how the police view the press.

5. Despite some claims to the contrary I must emphasize the point that *there is absolutely no legal protection guaranteed to the social scientist on the grounds of research confidentiality*. Perhaps the leading legal works on the confidentiality of sources and data in social research are Ruebhausen and Brim (1965) and Nejelski and Lerman (1971). However, both of these articles were written before the U.S. Supreme Court's decision in the Branzburg v. Hayes (33L. Ed. 2d 626) case, in which the court ruled that the First Amendment does not provide a newsman (and perhaps, by implication, a researcher) any constitutional testimonial privileges against answering court-directed questions as to either the identity of particular research subjects or information received in confidence. However, the only occasion I know of in which a social scientist was actually jailed for refusing to divulge information was the Samuel Popkin case in Massachusetts. In 1972 Popkin served seven days for refusing to provide a grand jury certain information regarding the activities of Daniel Ellsberg at the Rand Corporation. Popkin was interviewing Rand personnel (including Ellsberg) during the period in which the Pentagon Papers were released, and the grand jury was interested in what he might know about the circumstances under which the secret papers were made public (see Carroll, 1973, for a full discussion of this case). For a broader perspective on some of these legal issues see Yablonski (1965, 1968); Vidich, Bensman, and Stein (eds.) (1964); and a special issue of *Social Problems*, 14, 2, 1967.

6. Further complications in these matters have been introduced of late with the advent of university committees and rules on what is often called the "experimental use of human subjects." If this trend continues, it may make certain kinds of research increasingly difficult to pursue, since, to receive approval for a particular project, the researcher may have to produce some stringent documentation as to the "importance" of the planned study as well as the "care" that has been taken beforehand to protect the subjects of the investigation from potential harm or embarrassment.

7. Aside from the writing around the issue of a fieldworker's use of either open or disguised observational techniques, little is available in the literature that bears upon the everyday decision making engaged in by the researcher while in the field. The implication is consequently that the fieldworker need not worry much about ethical matters until deciding what material to publish and how to present it ("do whatever you want in the field, but be careful when writing it up"). Perhaps the problem lies in the relatively few detailed descriptions of what it is that fieldworkers do.

8. Take for example Rule 5 of the American Sociological Association's Code of Ethics, which reads in part: "Confidential information provided by a research subject must be treated as such by a sociologist. Even though research information is not a privileged communication under the law, the sociologist must *as far as possible* protect subjects and informants. *Any promises* made to such persons must be honored . . ." (italics mine). On the basis of this professional edict certain questions can be raised not only about the meaning of the phrase "as far as possible," but also about the meaning of "promises." Since subjects may deceive themselves as to what the research is about, interpreting what constitutes a "promise" may well be difficult. As I have suggested elsewhere, the research bargains that are struck in the field always have a fluid character (Van Maanen, 1978b).

9. Ironically, the best discussions on these matters are to be found in the literature on observing criminals. Polsky (1967:109-143) is both succinct and blunt when he argues: "If one is effectively to study adult criminals in their natural settings, he must make the moral decision that in some ways he will break the law himself. He need not be a 'participant' observer and commit the criminal acts under study, yet he has to witness such acts or be taken into confidence about them and not blow the whistle" (133). See also Becker (1970b:30-45).

10. Obviously, other interpretations are also possible. Perhaps the patrolmen I knew had really learned to be *continually* brutish, nasty, and downright vicious on the street. Perhaps too the fact that the night was slow or that Blazier had "mouthed off" to the officers had much to do with the incident. Maybe the trigger for the beating was Blazier's race, social status as a "welfare case," or apparent sexual preference. Whatever alternatives exist, they are all beyond my reach to thoroughly overrule, though personally I find these reasons unconvincing in light of my own experiences in the police world. It is probable that all of the above accounts provide something of the necessary or enabling conditions for the event's occurrence; however, I believe that it was my presence that represented the sufficient or clinching condition.

11. I must note that these "tactics" were hardly conscious or sharply motivated ploys I developed to further the study itself. At the time, unfortunate as it may be, I thought about them little more than I thought about when to draw a breath. In retrospect, the tendency is to make my methods appear considerably more rational and sly than in fact they were. I wished only to get as close to the "action" as I could, and I felt the best way to do so would be to develop personal friendships in the field. Once these friendships were struck, however, they took on a momentum of their own. Furthermore, both the Blazier affair and the concrete fear of being jailed forced me to consider far more closely my methods than perhaps I would have done otherwise. Although my field notes do allow me to trace many of the specific details of what at the time seemed to be a most inchoate set of complex and shifting beliefs about my emerging fieldwork methodology, I am in agreement with Burke (1961:446) that "the situation remembers, not the man."

12. Unlike the issues of participation, privacy, and who is to be harmed, the fieldworker has few moral or strategic options available to him other than avoidance when it becomes clear that certain others are continually reacting more to his affable presence on the scene than to the more ordinary matters at hand. In such situations, he has become a part of what he originally wished to understand and has ruptured the necessary link between sustained observation and minimal disruption of social world under investigation. The researcher may not have "gone native" in the sense of adopting the ways and perspectives of the observed, but his observations are likely to be as misleading, if not more so, than if he had. Based upon my own experience, I suspect such troubling situations are far more common in police field studies than one would gather from reading the carefully assembled research reports that have appeared. Indeed, it is often difficult simply to detect the presence of the person who stands behind the research report. See van Maanen (1978b) for a further discussion of this issue.

Barnes, J.A. (1967). "Some ethical problems in modern field work." In D.C. Jongmans & Gutkind, P. (Eds.), Anthropologists in the Field (pp. 193-213). Assen, The Netherlands: Van Gorcum.

References

Becker, Howard S. (1964). Problems in the publication of field studies. In Arthur J. Vidich, J. Bensman, & M.R. Stein (Eds.), Reflections on Community Studies (pp. 267-284). New York: Wiley.

Becker, Howard S. (1967). Whose side are we on? Social Problems, 14, 239-248.

Becker, Howard S., & Eliot Freidson (1964). Against the code of ethics. American Sociological Review, 29, 409-410.

Buckner, H. Taylor (1967). The police: the culture of social control agency. Unpublished Ph.D. Dissertation. University of California, Berkeley.

Chevigny, Paul (1968). Police power: police abuses in New York City. New York: Pantheon.

Chevigny, Paul (1972). Cops and rebels. New York: Pantheon.

Douglas, Jack D. (1976). Investigative social research: individual and team field research. Beverly Hills: Sage.

Klockers, Carl B. (1974). The professional fence. New York: Free Press.

Manning, Peter K. (1976a). Rules, colleagues and situationally justified actions. In R.A. Blankenship (Ed.), Colleagues in Organization. New York: Wiley.

Manning, Peter K. (1977). Police work. Cambridge, MA: M.I.T. Press.

Mehan, Hugh, & Houston Wood (1975). The reality of ethnomethodology. New York: Wiley.

Miller, S.M. (1952). The participant observer and 'over-rapport'. American Sociological Review, 17, 97-99.

Rainwater, Lee, & David J. Pittman (1967). Ethical problems in studying a politically sensitive and deviant community. Social Problems, 14, 357-366.

Reiss, Albert J., Jr. (1971). The police and the public. New Haven: Yale University Press.

Rosenthal, Robert (1976). Experimenter effects in behavioral research. New York: Irvington.

Roth, Julius A. (1966). Hired hand research. American Sociologist, 1, 190-196.

Rubinstein, Jonathan (1973). City police. New York: Farrar, Straus & Giroux.

Skolnick, Jerome H. (1966). Justice without trial: law enforcement in democratic society. New York: Wiley.

Van Maanen, John (1973). Observations on the making of policemen. Human Organization, 32, 407-418.

Van Maanen, John (1974). Working the streets: a developmental view of police behavior. In Herbert Jacobs (Ed.), Reality and Reform: The Criminal Justice System. Beverly Hills: Sage.

Van Maanen, John (1975). Police socialization. Administrative Science Quarterly, 20, 207-228.

Van Maanen, John (1977). Organizational careers: some new perspectives. New York: Wiley.

Van Maanen, John (1978a). The asshole. In Peter K. Manning & John Van Maanen (Eds.), Policing: A View From the Streets. Pacific Palisades, CA: Goodyear.

Van Maanen, John (1978b). Watching the watchers. In Peter K. Manning and John Van Maanen (Eds.), Policing. Pacific Palisades, CA: Goodyear.

Westley, William A. (1970). Violence and the police: a sociological study of law, custom, and morality. Cambridge, MA: M.I.T. Press.

* * *

The influence of the researchers' gender and its effect on the conduct of the study are very much dependent on the length of time they are actually in the field. Gurney distinguishes the difference between long- and short-term lengths of fieldwork and found that her being a female in conducting short-term research had minimal disadvantages, and that being a woman could possibly be an advantage in gaining access to those being studied. On the other hand, her long-term fieldwork experiences in a predominantly male-dominated agency proved to be more difficult. She discusses and analyzes how this affected her relationship in a prosecutor's office, where she spent a lengthy period of time.

FEMALE RESEARCHERS IN MALE-DOMINATED SETTINGS

Implications for Short-Term Versus Long-Term Research

JOAN NEFF GURNEY

Much has been written about the process of entering and becoming established within a field-research setting. Gaining entrée to the research site is, quite obviously, an essential part of every field-research endeavor; if the researcher cannot get into the setting, then he or she is not going to do very much research. Once inside, the researcher faces the dual problems of trying to maintain rapport, which involves adjusting and accommodating to the demands and predilections of his or her hosts while at the same time trying to collect the best possible data for the study. Oftentimes, actions that might be in the best interests of data collection (probing, prodding, and prying, for example) may run counter to actions required to maintain a good working relationship with one's host. When the fieldworker is faced with decisions that pit data collection against rapport, it is critical to the continuation of the study and to the validity of the research that the correct decisions be made. Yet as any experienced field researcher knows, one is never really in a position of knowing exactly what the correct decisions are until after the fact, and then it may be too late to salvage either the data or the rapport (or perhaps both).

Although efforts to get in and establish rapport are crucial for all researchers, they may be especially tricky for researchers whose personal characteristics are in some way at odds with those of the group they are studying. Anthropologists are quite likely to experience this problem because they often study cultures with which they have had no prior experience and interact with people who are quite different from them with respect to race and social class, as well as norms, values, and beliefs. However, even field-workers who remain within their own cultural settings may encounter unanticipated difficulties with respect to entrée and rapport because they differ in significant ways from those whom they wish to observe and interview. One way in which the researcher may differ from his or her hosts is with respect to gender. Although many types of field research settings today are "coed," there are still some arenas that are dominated by one gender or the other. A field researcher who becomes interested in a setting in which participants are predominantly members of the opposite sex may experience some awkward moments as he or she attempts to gain the respect, trust, and cooperation of those participants.

Elsewhere (Gurney, 1985b) I have observed that most of the instructional literature on fieldwork assumes that the researcher is "Anyman," and tends to ignore the possible influences of gender on the conduct of field research. In thinking about the impact of gender upon my own research over the past 15 years, I have come to the conclusion that its effect has been very different depending upon the length of time I spent in any particular field setting. In large part this is attributable to differences in the nature of the relationship that a researcher is able to establish with his or her hosts depending upon whether the research is short-term or long-term. Thus in discussing the ways in which gender has influenced my research I will begin with a brief analysis of the differences between short-term and long-term fieldwork. Then I will describe the nature of my experiences in both types of fieldwork as they relate to the issue of gender and its impact on gaining entrée and

maintaining rapport. Most of my discussion will focus on the dilemmas faced by a female researcher attempting to conduct research in a setting dominated by males.

SHORT-TERM VERSUS LONG-TERM FIELDWORK

Short-term field research may last anywhere from a few minutes to several days. Long-term fieldwork, on the other hand, involves staying in the field for a protracted period, such as weeks, months, or even years.

Obviously, the nature of the relationship a field-worker forms with his or her hosts is affected by the length of time spent with them. In short-term research the researcher enters and exits the setting relatively quickly. The field-worker-host relationship tends to remain primarily at the formal or secondary level because the time spent together is focused almost exclusively on the business at hand, precisely as a result of the short duration of the contact. There is relatively little time for the relationship to change or evolve. The field-worker and host barely have time to scratch the surface of one another's personalities. In contrast, long-term research involves a greater commitment, not only of time but also of self on the part of both field-worker and host. In addition, the potential for their relationship to change over time is a much more significant factor for both parties. Initial suspicions and anxieties on both sides can become either alleviated or exacerbated as field-worker and host move beyond surface formalities and niceties.

I have experienced the types of pitfalls and dilemmas unique to both short- and long-term field research. My short-term fieldwork experiences have included studies of community responses to various types of disasters (e.g., floods, hurricanes, tornadoes, and plane crashes) and studies of how local communities attempt to divert juveniles away from the formal justice system. My major long-term research effort involved an examination of a specialized unit within a county prosecutor's office. In both types of research, I have confronted issues of gaining entrée, establishing rapport, and maintaining appropriate relationships with hosts for the duration of the study. In my experience the impact of gender on these aspects of fieldwork has been quite different depending upon whether the duration of the research was short- or long-term.

THE IMPACT OF GENDER ON SHORT-TERM FIELD RESEARCH

Gaining entrée to a research setting can be just as problematic in short-term research as it is in long-term research, although the nature of the problem is somewhat different. In short-term research, the intrusion into the hosts' setting is relatively brief; therefore, they may be less reluctant to participate because it will not involve a significant time commitment on their part. On the other hand, respondents may not be very trusting of a stranger who arrives on their doorstep one day to conduct research and then leaves after only a few hours, never to be seen or heard from again. In such situations the presence of a female researcher may be a definite asset, especially in a male-dominated setting, because females generally are perceived as warmer and less threatening than males (Weitz, 1976). Of course, the other side of this coin is that women may not be taken as seriously as men, which poses a threat to the validity of the information a female field-worker obtains in doing short-term research. Thus being a female field-worker in a male-dominated setting is something of a double-edged sword. It may make getting in easier, but it may jeopardize the ultimate research goal of obtaining valid and reliable data.

Fortunately, there are ways of overcoming the potential disadvantages of being a female in conducting short-term research. The problem of not being taken seriously can be dealt with in a variety of ways, primarily by emphasizing appearance and credentials. For example, my short-term field experiences have been largely in occupational fields dominated by professionals of one kind or another (e.g., judges, psychologists, and hospital administrators). I have always dressed as professionally as possible when attempting to gain entrée into these settings. I wear my best clothes; a suit, if possible. (Of course, it was not easy to "dress for success" on a graduate student's stipend.) Carrying some type of legitimizing credentials can also bolster the status of the female field-worker. Such credentials may take the form of an ID card, business cards, and/or a letter of introduction from someone whom the hosts already know or whom they are likely to respect or accept as an authority. As a graduate student conducting research on disasters, I carried a black vinyl-covered folder that bore a prominent gold emblem bearing the seal of the university that housed the research center I represented. I also carried a formal letter of introduction from the directors of the center. I rarely needed to produce the letter; the vast majority of hosts accepted my word that I was indeed a legitimate representative of the center.

At the time I was conducting the disaster research (mid-1970s) I was aware of the issue of sexism and considered myself a feminist. However, I was not as sensitive as I am now to the subtle ways in which sexist attitudes and beliefs affect daily interactions and reinforce institutionally based gender discrimination. In the context of conducting several hundred intensive interviews with a wide variety of male respondents, I never seriously considered that my gender might have had an impact upon the way in which I established rapport with my respondents or upon the nature of the data I was collecting. Although I was unmarried and in my early twenties at the time, I do not recall ever having had any problems with male respondents that I could attribute to my being female. Of course, some male respondents were more friendly, hospitable, or cooperative than others, but I never considered that their behavior toward me in the research setting might have been influenced significantly by my gender. In fact the only truly difficult, or rather impossible, interview situation I encountered involved a female respondent who was the administrator of a sizable Roman Catholic hospital that had treated a large number of casualties during a disaster I was assigned to study. No matter what I did or said, this individual was not going to grant me permission to interview other members of her staff. I finally left the research site without having obtained that portion of the data, much to the dismay of my superiors.

My other experiences with short-term field research have involved intensive interviewing of juvenile court personnel, including judges, probation officers, and other court employees. The research was conducted in various localities, both urban and rural, throughout a southeastern state during the mid-1980s. Thus I was about 10 years older, and I was married, wearing a rather wide wedding band on my left hand. I had been through a long-term fieldwork experience (to be discussed below) in which I felt that my gender may have affected the conduct of the research. I was, therefore, more attuned to the possible intrusions of this factor upon my juvenile court interviewing. Nevertheless, I once again did not have any indications that my gender was a prominent issue during the course of this study. A number of my respondents were female, but a sizable percentage, including all of the judges, were male. I never perceived any overt sexism in the manner in which I was treated by my male respondents, nor was I the target of any sexual overtures from males. Ironically, however, the only difficult interview situation once again involved a female respondent.

In summary, it has been my experience that gender is a relatively unimportant variable in short-term research. A female researcher who establishes herself as a professional at the outset is likely to experience little difficulty with respondents on account of her gender. The brief duration of the relationship tends to mitigate against some of the more serious problems encountered by female researchers in other settings (such as sexism, hustling, and harassment). Perhaps in short-term research the field-worker does occupy the status of "Anyman."

THE IMPACT OF GENDER ON LONG-TERM FIELD RESEARCH

During the late 1970s I decided to study the prosecution of white-collar crime by engaging in a case study of an economic crime unit within a county prosecutor's office in a midwestern state (Gurney, 1982, 1985a, 1985b). This was my first experience with long-term field research. Although I felt quite well prepared to conduct the study at the time, in retrospect I realize that I was unprepared to cope with or respond to some of the challenges that

a female researcher in a male-dominated setting encounters over a longer period.

Gaining initial entrée to the prosecutor's office was not highly problematic. Another graduate student had conducted some research on a major case of corporate fraud in which the economic crime unit had been involved. Her dissertation advisor offered to contact the unit to see whether they would be receptive to having yet another graduate student spend some time in their office collecting data. They were quite receptive to the idea and after an initial meeting to outline the nature of the research, I was granted access.

The economic crime unit (ECU) was a small subunit of the prosecutor's office. It was staffed by three full-time attorneys, one full-time investigator, one part-time legal intern, and a full-time secretary. The secretary was the only female member of the unit. I was able to establish fairly good rapport with most of the ECU staff. Once again, interestingly, the most difficult person I encountered in terms of initially establishing rapport was the female secretary. I perceived here, at first, as being rather cold, aloof, and unfriendly. I attributed her negative attitude to the fact that I had to go through her in order to gain access to some of the closed case files I wished to examine. Her days were fairly busy, and I represented one more added burden to her total list of responsibilities. After several weeks of my presence, she began to warm up a bit. She eventually accepted me, and we even established a friendly relationship.

For the most part, my fieldwork at the ECU went relatively smoothly. I was given access to all the case files I asked to see and I was permitted to watch the prosecutors as they went about their work when it involved something that was observable, such as meetings, trials, interviews, and so forth. I also was treated courteously and cordially; no one was ever hostile toward me or acted overtly as if they did not want me around. But as I review my field notes 10 years later (yes, I still have them), I can still conjure up all of the doubts, hesitancies, and uncertainties I experienced at the time, just as if they were happening today.[1]

Most of my discomfort and anxiety occurred during the early stages of my work and centered on the issue of establishing rapport with my hosts. Some concerns were more persistent, however, and remained sources of tension through the entire experience. Some of these difficulties were directly related to my status as a female in a male-dominated setting. One clear-cut example of a problem related to my gender was an instance of sexual hustling on the part of one of the prosecutors. He tried, on several different occasions, to get me to come over to his apartment on the pretense of having me use his computer. One of his strategies was to offer to let me use his computer to analyze some of the data I was collecting. When that failed, he asked me if I knew anyone who might be willing to come to his apartment to help him program his computer to analyze bank accounts in embezzlement cases. I said I did not know anyone, but offered to post an advertisement for him at the university. He rejected that idea and never raised the issue again. It is, of course, entirely possible that these were not subtle forms of sexual hustling. This prosecutor might very well have approached a male researcher in exactly the same way. Nevertheless, as a female I necessarily considered such overtures as potential instances of hustling and tried to respond to them in a manner that was simultaneously polite and self-protective.

Another example of a gender-oriented difficulty was the uttering of sexual remarks, innuendos, and jokes in my presence. On most of the occasions when this occurred, I was the only female in the room. I could not help but feel that the remarks or jokes were directed toward me or at least were meant to have some effect on me. Such remarks were not a daily occurrence, but were embarrassing to me when they did occur. However, I chose to ignore them or to respond in an offhand manner without letting the perpetrators know that I was disturbed by them. I felt it was better to respond passively or mildly to such things rather than to make a major issue of them. I wanted to avoid, at almost any cost, doing anything that might damage my rapport with my hosts.[2] In addition, I felt a sense of gratitude toward my hosts for allowing me to observe their files and their endeavors, and I did not want to appear ungrateful by giving them stern lectures on their sexist behavior.

An additional concern during my research on the ECU centered on the problem of "invisibility." As Warren (1988) has observed, females often are relegated to positions of invisibility within organizations in general and male-dominated ones in particular. Women traditionally have occupied low-status positions such as file clerk, secretary, and receptionist. As such, they generally go about their work quietly and unobtrusively, but they have access to all types of information and to all parts of the organization.

Although being invisible certainly has the merits that Warren describes, it also has drawbacks. It is possible to be so invisible that one is ignored or forgotten about, and thereby misses out on important events. I found this to be something of a problem in my study of the ECU. I frequently was given advance notice of important meetings concerning ongoing cases only to discover, after waiting a considerable length of time to be called to the meeting, that the prosecutors had forgotten about me and I had missed the meeting. I therefore developed a procedure of taking casual walks through the hallway by the open doors of the prosecutors' offices when I knew that an important meeting was coming up, hoping that seeing my face would trigger their memories to call me when the event was about to take place. After I began this procedure, I was called more often and missed fewer of these important opportunities for observation.

My invisibility was part of a larger concern that a male researcher might have been able to learn things or obtain access to areas that I was unable to see. At the first internal staff meeting I was permitted to attend, the ECU director told the group that it was all right for me to be present because they were not going to discuss anything sensitive. As time went on, I was permitted to attend a wider variety of meetings; however, I was barred from meetings concerning a case of political corruption involving a state official. The ECU director said later that the case had been too politically sensitive to allow me to observe any closed-door meetings while it was an open, ongoing case. I have always wondered whether a male researcher would have been similarly excluded from that case. In my musings I have envisioned a male researcher who would have been accepted more fully as part of the group; who would have gone to the prosecutor's apartment to see his computer; and who would have "gone out with the guys" for drinks after work.

It is, of course, possible to spend a great deal of unproductive time speculating about how things would have turned out differently if only one had been male rather than female. I have not spent an inordinate amount of time pondering that question; nevertheless, speculation about such issues is important if for no other reason than it allows one to become more self-conscious about how gender does affect one's fieldwork.

CONCLUSION

In closing, if I were to address a group of young female field researchers who were about to make their first foray into a long-term field-research setting dominated by males, I would probably offer them several pieces of advice.

First, I would urge them to consider carefully how their appearances might affect their interactions with respondents. If the research is to take place in a professional setting, they should try to conform as closely as possible to whatever dress code appears operative for the professional women in the setting. Second, female researchers should be as knowledgeable as possible about the nature of the setting and the roles occupied by males and females within the setting before attempting to gain entrée. Such prior knowledge increases one's sensitivity to the types of difficulties or obstacles women may routinely face in that environment. Third, when female researchers encounter instances of sexism or sexual hustling, they should consider addressing these issues, at first, in a sensitive and diplomatic fashion with the responsible party. It is best to deal with the issue in a private setting if at all possible. (Obviously, such a strategy should only be used when there is no apparent threat to the researcher's physical safety.) Publicly chastising or criticizing one's hosts will probably only serve to raise their defenses and may make the situation more difficult to resolve amicably. If a private communication does not seem appropriate or does not seem to have the desired effect, it may be possible to approach another member of the setting with whom reasonably good rapport has been established and ask that individual how best to handle the situation.

Finally, female researchers need to recognize that instances of sexism, sexual hustling, and sexual harassment do occur in the field. Some consideration should be given to how best to respond to hypothetical instances of these behaviors before the fieldwork begins. Having some notion of how these situations might be dealt with ahead of time may make it easier to respond to them when they do occur.

NOTES

1. I don't know whether other field-workers experience similar "flashbacks" upon reviewing their old field notes years later, but I would like to hear from anyone else who does.

2. Since then I have wondered whether one truly has rapport with respondents who utter insensitive remarks in one's presence.

REFERENCES

Gurney, J.N. (1985a). Factors Influencing the Decision to Prosecute Economic Crime. *Criminology*, 23, 609-628.

Gurney, J.N. (1985). Not One of the Guys: The Female Researcher in a Male-Dominated Setting. *Qualitative Sociology*, 8, 42-62.

Gurney, J.N. (1982). Implementing a National Crime Control Program: The Case of an Economic Crime Unit. In M. Morash (Ed.), *The Implementation of Key Criminal Justice Policies*. Beverly Hills, CA: Sage.

Warren, C.A.B. (1988). Gender Issues in Field Research. Newbury Park, CA: Sage.

Weitz, S. (1976). Sex Differences in Nonverbal Communication. *Sex Roles*, 2, 175-184.

* * *

This article addresses the dilemmas for the participant observer conducting field research when actually joining the occupation being studied. The participant role allowed the author to become an insider in a job-related world that permitted him to collect data on behavior that would not have been available to other researchers. Becoming a prison guard and researching others in that role can prove to be problematic, and Marquart discusses the ethical dilemmas he encountered as a full participant in a prison setting.

DOING RESEARCH IN PRISON

The Strengths and Weaknesses of Full Participation as a Guard

JAMES W. MARQUART

The dominant mode of prison guard research is survey methodology, and in the past decade guards have been polled on such numerous topics as role stress (Poole and Regoli 1980), turnover (Jacobs and Grear 1977), role conflict (Hepburn and Albonetti 1980), occupational socialization (Crouch and Alper 1982), and race relations and the guard culture (Jacobs and Kraft 1978). These inquiries have contributed greatly to the literature on guards and their role within prison organizations. Questionnaire data, however, are collected from a "distance" and fail to penetrate the inner or backstage prison behavioral settings. On the other hand, some investigators (e.g., Sykes 1958; Carroll 1974; Jacobs and Retsky 1975) have collected qualitative data on guards, but they entered the setting in the

Reprinted from *Justice Quarterly*, Vol. 3, No. 1, March 1986. Copyright © 1986 and reprinted with permission of the Academy of Criminal Justice Sciences.

This is a substantially revised version of a paper presented at the 1984 Southern Sociological Society meetings. I am indebted to Julian B. Roebuck, David Demo, Frank Cullen, Sheldon Ekland-Olson, and Geoff Alpert for their critical readings of earlier drafts of this paper and to Ben. M. Crouch for his support and counsel throughout the project.

This research was supported by the Law and Social Science Program, NSF (SES-8410925).

All names in this paper are pseudonyms.

typical observer role as nonparticipants or "outsiders-as-researchers." These prison methodologies offer only a restricted or limited view of guards and their organizational role. Specifically prison researchers, unlike those who have become police officers to study police work (see Van Maanen 1973), have avoided full participation as a means to study guards and prisons.

In the spring of 1981, I became a prison guard to examine the official and unofficial methods of prisoner control and discipline in a large maximum security penitentiary within the Texas prison system. I worked as a researcher-guard for nineteen months (June 1981 through January 1983) and collected ethnographic materials while working, participating, and observing in a variety of locations and activities (e.g., cell blocks, dormitories, visitation areas, recreation periods, dining halls, shower rooms, solitary confinement, disciplinary hearings, and hospital). I eventually obtained unlimited access to the unwritten and more sensitive aspects of guard work, prisoner control, and the guard culture.

The activities of entering the prison, negotiating a research role, establishing field relations, studying social control and order, and exiting the field were not the clear and orderly processes so often described in ethnographic reports. Instead, immersion in the prison scene placed some unusual demands on me as an observer (and person) not generally experienced by other more "traditional" qualitative researchers (see also Styles 1979; Van Maanen 1982). Complete participation is a viable research role, yet there are some pitfalls. This paper addresses the strengths, weaknesses, and ethical implications of the researcher-guard role and full participation as a prison methodology.

BECOMING AN OUTSIDE-INSIDER

My first experience with Texas prisons was in the summer of 1979 when I participated in a project evaluating guard training, supervision, and turnover throughout the Texas prison system. During the research, I met a warden who in turn made arrangements for me to visit the Eastham Unit—a maximum security facility housing 3200 prisoners over the age of twenty-five who had been incarcerated more than three times. My first visit was spent touring the institution with the warden, meeting various ranking guards, observing disciplinary court, and driving around the prison's 14,000-acre agricultural operation. The warden informed me at the end of the tour that I was welcome to visit Eastham.

For the next year and a half I went to Eastham almost every other month, with each trip lasting five to eight hours. I had complete freedom to walk unescorted throughout the compound and converse with guards at work and with inmates while they ate, worked, spent recreation time in the gym, or lounged in their cells. I often followed an officer for several hours to observe his work routine. During these trips, I met several "old time" convicts who described in detail the rich folklore surrounding Texas prisons. Moreover, each time I visited Eastham, my guard and inmate contacts pressed me to work as a guard to see the "real" penitentiary. I avoided their suggestions, explaining that I wanted to remain impartial, free to roam the prison. Actually, my real reason was outright fear of the prisoners. Yet I knew they were correct and after assessing my research goals, I realized full participation would foster the necessary inside perspective to examine prisoner control. In April 1981, the warden arranged for me to begin work in June 1981.

I entered Eastham without a clearly-defined role (c.f., Jacobs 1977). Although the warden, a few guards, and several inmates knew I was a graduate student in sociology, they did not know the exact details of my research plans. The Texas prison system was at this time embroiled in the bitterly contested prison reform case of *Ruiz v. Estelle* (1980).[1] This suit alleged, among other things, that guard brutality was rampant and that the building tender system (using dominant/aggressive inmates to control other inmates) was abusive. Eastham was a target unit in the case. One of my research goals was to observe and analyze the building tender system (see Marquart and Crouch 1984).[2] I felt, however, that if I revealed my aims to the security staff they would not allow me to work as a guard or even conduct research. Therefore, I kept the specifics of the project vague and told the warden of my interest in guards, guard work, and the ways in which various court orders have affected the staff's ability to maintain control and order. Moreover, my presence as a researcher-guard was not officially announced to the prison community. I had no official letter from the director of the prison system or the warden identifying me as a researcher. I was to be treated as any other employee, which was reflected in my first shift assignment—the third shift (9:45 p.m.-5:45 a.m.).

I never at any time misrepresented my identity. I "passed" as a sociology doctoral student who was tired of the books and sought real prison experience. If asked about my personal or educational background, I gave true information in order to prevent suspicion and rumor. But this strategy was not enough of an explanation and precipitated several rumors. The prison grapevine had it that I was an F.B.I. agent or an official from the Department of Justice "placed" at Eastham to investigate and report on prison operations. Some inmates thought I was a writer and followed me for hours detailing their life of crime and violence, hoping I would write their life histories. I was also tagged as Mr. Estelle's (then, the director of the prison system) son, a rumor that lasted throughout the research. I also foolishly contributed to these rumors when I was seen photographing the prison compound. Like most prison field observers (Giallombardo 1966; Carroll 1974; Jacobs 1974), I had to prove constantly that I was not a spy or government agent.

I relied on two contacts, both of whom eventually became trusted informants and friends, to facilitate my acceptance and quell rumors. One was PP, a high ranking guard and Ph.d. student at a nearby university. We had met during an earlier visit and shared our research interests. He was well-respected by the guards and prisoners and introduced me to the two most politically powerful inmates at Eastham. I told them of my background and interest in Texas prisons. They agreed to be interviewed only because they said "PP told us to." In addition, I met MM, an older politically powerful prisoner who introduced me to other important prisoners. These latter contacts in turn introduced me to others and soon I developed (through snowball sampling) an extensive network of inmate informants. As for the guards, I befriended several workmates who became allies and informants.

PP's and MM's assistance enhanced my status tremendously; however, their endorsement did not ensure immediate acceptance or totally eliminate doubt about "what I was really up to." Many guards and inmates respected my willingness to work as a guard, but they did not regard me as reputable. In their eyes, I was an untested novice who had to earn their favor before being accepted, respected, and able to collect data.

CHARACTER DEVELOPMENT AND DATA COLLECTION

Maximum security prisons are rife with fear, conflict, paranoia, racial animosities, and intense factionalism. Building rapport and establishing trust in the context of a research role is difficult and time-consuming. Prison researchers are on center stage and their behavior is constantly scrutinized by officers and inmates who look for clues (or cues) that reveal the observer's character and intentions. I followed a careful strategy in establishing field relations.

Three Factors Leading to Acceptance

First, I kept a low profile and concentrated on working hard to establish a reputation as a reliable employee. In this institution, following orders without hesitation was an important value within the guard subculture. I accepted without complaint difficult and boring work assignments, broke up inmate fights, and wrote disciplinary reports on several inmates. My eagerness so impressed my supervisors that I was promoted to Hall "Boss" (inmates referred to the guards as "boss" or "bossman"). Hall bosses were regarded by the guards and prisoners alike as the cream of the non-ranking officers. Obtaining one of these positions was also viewed as a promotion by the officers, his peers, supervisors, and prisoners. Moreover, all line staff sought to become one of these officers because they were free from cell block duty and worked closely with ranking guards which aided in rank-obtaining promotions. Among the three shifts, there were around 25 hall officers, the majority of whom were white. With this advancement, I became quickly and deeply involved in the guard world and I was an ally of the building tenders, who taught me the official and unofficial means of prisoner control.

Second, I began weightlifting and boxing in the prison gym with several prisoners. One inmate, WW, was my "teacher" and we worked out daily, played basketball, jogged, as well as trained on the "heavy bag." Others loaned me their body-building magazines and books, and gave assorted advice on how to weight train. These inmates were weightlifting experts and I used their suggestions. I soon won their trust because I listened and never questioned their knowledge, but instead let them tell me what to do—a reversal of their normally subordinate status. By deferring to them, I demonstrated my acceptance of their expertise and this fostered a bond that established a high degree of rapport. While we exercised, they described how the guards recruited snitches, used unofficial force to punish and control inmates, and told me which officers were respected and why. Moreover, weightlifting and boxing (especially in prison) were prized masculine activities and my eagerness to learn enhanced my status among the prisoners. In fact, many prisoners based their respect for other inmates and officers on their ability to exhibit superior strength (mental and physical) or compulsive masculinity (see Toby 1966).

The third and most important factor which established my credibility, and earned the guards' and prisoners' respect was an occurrence on December 15, 1981. This event and my subsequent behavior solidified my reputation as a "good" officer (i.e., not afraid of the inmates, firm but fair) and a "true" insider. At approximately 11:25 p.m., another hall officer and I went to 1-block (a solitary confinement area) to help several other hall officers search inmate Friar's property which was in a large canvas sack. He had been placed in solitary confinement earlier that day for assaulting an officer. Friar, who weighed nearly 300 pounds, stood in the Hall (central corridor in the prison) waiting for us to inventory his property. I ordered him to take his property out of the sack. He remained motionless. I then said, "unsack it." He lifted the bag and spilled the contents on the floor, threw the sack in the air, and then punched me in the forehead nearly knocking me unconscious. I was forced to defend myself. With the help of two other hall

officers, Friar was finally subdued and quartered in solitary confinement. I required medical attention for a large knot on my forehead.

Early the next morning, I was standing near the Commissary (prison store) when Supervisor L approached me and said:

> L: "Hey, there's the raging bull. Tell us what happened. What happened?"

I then retold the story to his delight. The following morning another ranking guard pointed at me and yelled "Hey, there's Bruiser." Then he came over and started shadow boxing with me. That evening two second shift hall officers, who had previously avoided me, also asked me about the incident. After finishing the story, these officers stated they would help me with anything they could.

The fact that I had been assaulted and had defended myself in front of several officers and building tenders raised my esteem and established my reputation. The willingness to fight inmates was an important trait rewarded by the ranking guards (see Marquart and Roebuck 1984). Due to this "fortunate" event, I earned the necessary credibility to establish rapport with the prison participants and allay their previous suspicions of me. I passed the ultimate test—fighting an inmate even though in self-defense—and was now a trustworthy member of the guard subculture. I had character, or the "balls" or "nuts," to stand up for and defend myself. The significance of this fight is underscored in the following conversation, which occurred months later with LC, a politically powerful black prisoner:

> LC: "Well, I didn't trust you until that deal you had down there on 1-block with Friar. I heard you got hit and defended yourself and took care of business. After that I was more willing to talk to you than before. I trust you now, otherwise, I wouldn't talk to you."

I entered Eastham as a guard to discover "how things really operated," but this was not a ticket to obtaining good data. As an outsider-insider, I had to prove myself through hard work and by standing up to the inmates. More important, I had to share and actually experience the traumas, risks, violence, and dangers of the prison environment. My presence and acceptance depended on how well I negotiated these daily realities. Although the Friar incident ultimately secured my acceptance, I continually had to demonstrate loyalty to the guards and building tenders. Few research roles are ever finalized (complete acceptance) and this situation heightens the fieldworker's awareness of the necessity to constantly guard against overconfidence in matters of acceptance (Lofland 1971). Consequently, when the situation rose, I broke up fights, hauled bleeding self-mutilators or attempted suicides to the prison hospital, and utilized legitimate force in subduing inmates (e.g., in dining halls, shower rooms, cells). I even wrestled with and took a knife away from an inmate who slashed open his own stomach out of despair.

Insider Status and Data Collection

Hard work, often involving "dirty work," and the willingness to use official force enabled me to recruit informants among the guards and inmates, particularly the building tenders. I quickly made friends with several officers, told them my research interests, and they willingly agreed to work as surrogate observers, describing events or incidents on the other shifts (see Scott 1965). I also interviewed officers in their homes, in bars, or on the job. From these interviews and countless conversations, data was obtained on, for example, morale, the staff's recruitment of snitches, and when and where the guards used unofficial force (beatings) to subdue, control, and terrorize "unruly" inmates. These home interviews were tape-recorded while those on the job were written down and reconstructed later.

From my inmate informants, I collected data on how the guards officially recruited and coopted the most dominant and aggressive inmates to become building tenders. Because of my guard role, I closely associated with these inmate elites and nearly a dozen were key informants. They showed me how they made liquor or "pruno," stole food from the prison kitchen, made knives, and sold tattoo patterns and machines. These latter activities were clearly illegal but I kept their trafficking confidential; this too demonstrated my trustworthiness. The ability to "keep one's mouth shut" was a highly

prized asset and I quickly internalized this important value. I also made sure that all interviewees were told that their conversations were confidential and off the record. The gathering of information, however, was not one-sided and I reciprocated when and wherever possible (see Wax 1971). I often helped inmates obtain job or cell changes, new uniforms or shoes, or hospital appointments. I also periodically bought my key inmate informants sodas, cigars, candy, or coffee. After exiting the field, I wrote letters of recommendation to the parole board for five prisoners, all of whom are now free citizens.

Building rapport and earning trust in the prison community was initially difficult but my actions eventually secured my acceptance. Like Jacobs (1974), once I was regarded as an insider, I had little trouble making the necessary contacts to obtain information. However, with my ability to establish trust came the problem of deep involvement in the guard subculture. I tried to balance my roles, to be both a sociologist studying prisoner control and a legitimate member of the prisoner control apparatus. The participative or outside-inside role is emotionally and physically taxing because the researcher, in any scene or setting, must in essence wear "two hats." One persistent problem, to be discussed below, was that the guard role often superceded my sociological interests.

PROBLEMS OF THE
PARTICIPATIVE RESEARCH ROLE

As a researcher-guard or outside-insider, I was able to collect data on activities concealed from most other prison researchers (e.g., beatings, verbal intimidation, the use of snitches). I was a member of good standing in the setting and I used this position to my advantage, especially in actually experiencing the daily feelings, mood shifts, and emotions of the prison participants. The participative research role was not problem-free and three major difficulties were encountered throughout the fieldwork.

Occupational Pressures

One of the most pervasive problems, stemming from my work role, was remaining a uniformed sociologist (or outsider). I spent my first three months working cell blocks and this assignment severely restricted my ability to make contacts or ask questions. In the fourth month, I was promoted to hall "boss," which afforded the needed mobility to traverse the prison compound. Yet at certain times of the day my work duties (e.g., counting, searching cells, monitoring inmate traffic to and from meals, showers, and work) tied me down for several hours. Prison is a structured world and the work role demanded that I do the same things each day at the same time. To manage this role conflict, I scheduled my "free" time to interview, gather records, and review ideas or data with informants. This does not mean that I did not collect data while actually working. On the contrary, I observed, interviewed, listened to, and conversed with inmates and guards wherever and whenever I could. But as a guard, it was necessary to be security conscious first and a researcher second—a problem inherent in the participative prison research role. This strain would also pose problems for investigators who become police officers or hospital orderlies—the official work role in these cases must supercede, when the situation arises, research interests.

I also collected data off-duty while exercising with several inmates in the prison gym. Once rapport was established, they eventually became key informants and I used these recreation periods to interview, reformulate ideas, or simply discuss our personal lives. I was extremely close to these inmates, who provided a rich data source. As for the officers, we sometimes spent after-hours playing football, swimming, target shooting, drinking beer and shooting pool, eating pizza, and relaxing. I listened to and participated in their conversations about guard work, fights they had with inmates (or other officers), their supervisors, other guards, troublesome inmates, or the Texas prison system. I made mental notes of their comments and reconstructed these conversations later. I even had several key officer informants tape record their thoughts about work, prisoner control, careers, or other prison-related subjects. Not only did these off-duty sessions provide data, but they enabled me to form lasting and meaningful friendships.

Clearly, the most difficult problem in being an outside-insider was role conflict. During the first few months on the "job," I had little difficulty remaining a uniformed sociologist. However, I slowly adopted the guard perspective due to my participation and deep involvement in the guard world. I laughed while guards teased and taunted inmate homosexuals, nodded approvingly when others described how they ripped apart an inmate's cell during a search, and kept a straight face when supervisors threatened to kill inmates. I also remained silent when observing guards and building tenders beat and physically injure inmates. Where and when possible, I defended the system and guards to naive outsiders. I explained to them that guards were the "good guys" and that prisons were necessary to isolate social predators. In many respects I was an apologist for the guards (see Manning 1972).

I was a guard forced to confront the enormous pressures of occupational socialization; this is the major drawback of full participation. I was expected to think, act, and talk like a guard. It was a personal battle to refrain from "going native," especially after the promotion to sergeant in November, 1982. Three factors helped me to adjust and maintain some role stability and distance. First, I left the prison on my designated days off. I worked seven days and then was off three days, which were spent debriefing in my dissertation advisor's office, with friends, and with other faculty members. Maintaining non-guard associations were critical in remaining objective. Second, I never insulted or fought inmates for fun. Many new guards displayed bravado ("John Wayne syndrome"), acting and talking tough to the inmates. I completely avoided this fronting behavior because I knew prison was too dangerous a place to act tough. Some guards paid the price both physically and mentally when an inmate called their bluff. Finally, I made extensive field notes about this role conflict and kept myself aware of how "deeply" I was moving into the guard subculture. In short, I was extremely sensitive to this problem and forced myself not to lose all objectivity.

Reactivity

The concept of reactivity specifies the proclivity of the research subjects to alter their behavior as a consequence of the researcher's presence (Vidich 1970). Because of his or her presence, a researcher does not observe the subjects' true behavior—a problem endemic to participant observation. Did the guards and prisoners alter their behavior in my presence? I entered Eastham with the full knowledge and approval of several high ranking prison officials. Even though I was known to some of the subjects beforehand, the majority had no idea who I was and treated me as another guard. However, some of the prison participants regarded me as a possible undercover agent investigating Eastham for the Department of Justice. Rumors were also spread about my "intentions" and several guards avoided me.

To negate these suspicions, I embarked on a strategy of earning the guards' trust to combat their false impressions of me and to minimize reactivity. I made it a point to work hard and share the emotional highs and lows of institutional life. In addition, it took nearly eight months of careful interaction, laying low, and "passing" various character tests to prove I was trustworthy. Most fieldworkers do not have this amount of time to invest in character development. After eight months, I was considered to be a "good" officer and this reputation facilitated data collection.

I also observed a great deal of backstage behavior. For example, I witnessed fifty incidents in which guards beat inmates (some were severely injured)—and all of these guards were well aware of my identity as a researcher. Had ranking staff members been afraid or leery of my presence, they would have assigned me to isolated duty posts. Instead, they viewed me as a loyal member of the subculture. To them, I was an employee and they did not have time to alter their behavior in my presence when breaking up brawls, fighting inmates in cells, disciplining inmates, searching cells or inmates, rushing attempted suicides or self-mutilators to the prison hospital, or stopping knife fights among inmates. These behaviors were spontaneous and occurred in similar fashion with or without my presence. Other researchers have noted that once respondents have accepted you (in whatever role) they tend to act as if you were one of them or as if you were not on the scene (see Skolnick 1966).

The vast majority of the inmates considered me to be "just another guard." Some initially told me that they, like some guards, were hesitant to talk with me. The support of third parties allayed some of their apprehensions but my reputation as a fair officer won their confidence, enabling me to secure key informants. Most of my inmate allies were building tenders who occupied positions of power and status within the prisoner society. They candidly answered questions and trusted me because I expressed a true interest in their welfare. Most importantly, I kept everything they said strictly confidential.

Although I cultivated the friendship of a number of inmate elites, I had great difficulty interviewing the "run of the mill" inmates. My uniform was a barrier that limited access to these prisoners and I never completely resolved this problem. I was able to get close to only ten "ordinary" inmate informants who described, from their perspective, snitching, homosexuality, staff use of force, rules and regulations, and verbal threats from the guards. To obtain this information, I often interviewed them in their cells, shower rooms, or on their way to and from meals. The insider role "slotted" me in the prison social structure and almost completely curtailed any contact with Hispanic inmates (c.f., Davidson 1974). For cultural reasons and because of their minority status, these inmates generally stayed away from other inmates and avoided almost all contact (e.g., saying hello, talking about sports, asking questions about various rules) with the staff. For many Hispanic inmates, voluntary interaction with guards was viewed as "ratting" and something to be avoided. Therefore, my contacts with these and most other ordinary inmates were primarily official.

Coping with Violence

Maximum security prisons are conflict-ridden societies where violence or the threat of it is a daily reality. As an outside-insider, I saw, took part in, and was personally affected by the inescapable presence of violence. Full participation brought me face-to-face with actual fear and terror, emotions most field observers never encounter (c.f., Van Maanen 1982). It is difficult for me to describe how I felt when I saw officers punch, kick, and knock inmates senseless with riot clubs as they screamed and begged for mercy. On several occasions I assisted guards in restraining inmates while medics sutured their wounds without any anesthetic. These incidents were shocking experiences. I also observed building tenders throw inmates head first into the bars and "blackjack" others who failed to report for work, remained too long in the dining hall, or cheered for the Houston Oilers instead of the Dallas Cowboys. One brawl involving four building tenders and one inmate so unnerved me that I almost quit. This event was so disturbing that I could not even write about it until several weeks later.

I knew prisons were violent, but only through the writings and experiences of other people. I learned to cope with the ever-present violence and tension by accepting it as an element of this milieu. Violence in prison is banal and everyone must learn to cope with it or else retreat from the situation. For officers, retreat often resulted in quitting and for inmates, in isolation. My particular coping strategy was indifference, the route of most prison participants. If people got hurt, especially inmates, I maintained a cold detachment. However, inwardly I was hurt because human suffering appalled me. In the end, I coped and survived as well as I could (see Jacobs 1974).

MORAL AND ETHICAL
DILEMMAS OF FULL PARTICIPATION

All fieldworkers run the risk, due to their presence, of obtaining "guilty knowledge" (see Van Maanen 1982). Because of my insider status, I was privy and party to discrediting information about the nature of guard work and prisoner control. I was firmly entrenched in the prison world—and this may raise some complaints from other researchers. There are ethical dilemmas surrounding this methodology which stem primarily from the observation of numerous violations, not only civil but legal as well. I observed the following incident but had a guard participant tape record his own description.

"I was sitting at the Searcher's desk and Rick (convict) and I were talking and here comes Joe (convict) from 8-block. Joe thinks he knows kung-fu, hell he got his ass beat about four months ago. He comes down the Hall and he had on a tank top, his pants were tied up with a shoe lace, gym shoes

on, and he had all his property in a large sack. As he neared us, Rick said 'Well, Joe's fixing to go crazy again today.' He came up to us and Rick asked him what was going on and Joe said they (staff) were fucking with him by not letting him have a recreation card. I told him 'Well take your stuff and go over there to the Major's office' and there he went. Officer A went over and stood in front of Joe, so did Officer B who was beside Joe, Officer C was in back of A, and two convicts stood next to Officer A. Inmate James, an inmate who we "tuned up" in the hospital several days before, stood about ten feet away. All of a sudden Joe took a swing at Officer A. A and B tackled Joe. I ran over there and grabbed Joe's left leg while a convict had his right leg and we began kicking his legs and genitals. Hell, I tried to break his leg. At the same time B was using his security keys, four large bronze keys, like a knife. The security keys have these points on their ends where they fit into the locks. Well, B was jamming these keys into Joe's head. Joe was bleeding all over the place. Then all of a sudden another brawl broke out right next to us. Inmate James threw a punch at Officer D as he came out of the Major's office to see what was going on. James saw Joe getting beat and he decided to help Joe out. I left Joe to help Officer D. By the time I got there (about two seconds), Officer D and about six convicts (building tenders) were beating the shit out of James. Officer D was beating James with a blackjack. Man, you could hear that crunch noise every time he hit him. At the same time a convict was hitting him in the stomach and chest and face. These other inmates were kicking him and stomping him at the same time. It was a wild melee, just like being in war. I got in there and grabbed James by the hair and Officer D began hitting him, no love taps. He was trying to beat his brains out and yelling 'you mother fucker, you think you're bad, you ain't bad, you mother fucker, son of a bitch, you hit me and I'll bust your fucking skull'. I think we beat on him alone for ten minutes. I punched him in the face and head. Then Officer D yelled 'take him (James) to the hospital'. Plus we punched and stomped him at the same time. At the hospital, Officer D began punching James in the face. I held his head so D could hit him. Then D worked James over again with a blackjack. We then stripped James and threw him on a bed. D yelled at James 'I'm going to kill you by the time you get off this unit'. Then D began hitting him in the shins and genitals with a night stick. Finally we stopped and let the medics take over. James had to leave via the ambulance. Joe required some stitches and was subsequently put in solitary."

This brutal episode was frightening and certainly went beyond any departmental regulation concerning the proper use of force to subdue an inmate. No civil suits were ever filed against the officers and the incident was "closed." My field notes contain the identities of all the actors. Like Van Maanen (1982) in his police fieldwork, I witnessed many illegalities at Johnson but "did not see them." To block or neutralize the moral predicament of seeing "too much," I kept quiet and simply observed. In fact, I could not "tell all" because this would have violated the implicit research bargain assumed by the officials when I entered the situation—an agreement not to use information to injure the subjects. I could not stop the violence and perhaps no one ever will. During the project, the Texas prison system came under a sweeping court order (*Ruiz v. Estelle*) to end guard and building tender brutality. I was contacted by an attorney in the Special Master's Office, who knew of my background, to testify against the Texas Department of Corrections. I told the lawyer that I had nothing to say. I believed my materials were confidential and even envisioned going to jail for contempt of court. Fortunately, this never happened.

I rationalized the violence as being a part of prison life and as something a full participant would in all likelihood have to face. Complete involvement or immersion means just that, and like it or not the insider must sometimes come to grips with various difficult and trying situations (see Styles 1979). Direct observation is unpredictable and the researcher has little control over the strange and unusual events in the setting. There are no formal standards for doing this research and therein lies the problem of full participation. In some cases, getting too close to the data might force the observer to compromise his or her values and morals in order to remain a trusted member. In the end, ethics are purely situational and no research method is completely safe for the researcher and the subjects (Humphreys 1970).

A REVERSAL OF RESEARCH ROLES: IS IT POSSIBLE?

I returned to Eastham in September 1984 under the sponsorship of the National Science Foundation to collect data on the impact of the *Ruiz v. Estelle* decision on prisoner control, order maintenance, and violence, among other things. For nearly four months, I was granted complete access to the prison. Prior to my arrival, the warden circulated a document among the guard staff clearly identifying my research role. I also wrote several inmates to alert them of my arrival date and full research aims. In this research, I entered the prison in the traditional fieldwork role of outsider, not as an insider or prison guard. Further, I openly carried a tape-recorder, notepads, and sometimes a camera, symbols to legitimize my presence and research role within the institution.

Given this new set of circumstances, I was curious about how I would be treated by the prisoners and guards and how it would affect my ability to collect data. My first week was spent re-establishing ties and reminiscing with friends (guards and inmates) as well as further clarifying my role and research purposes. To my good fortune, many of my previous informants were still at the prison and all agreed to assist in the research. Their cooperation was primarily due to the reputation that I had established while working as a guard. This time I was able to develop contacts among the general inmate population, including Hispanic inmates. The majority of the prisoners knew of my previous official role and many asked whether or not I was a guard. I responded truthfully to all queries about my background and only one inmate (a prison gang chieftain) denied to be interviewed. In addition, I had countless inmates (and officers too) stop and ask me when they were going to be interviewed.

My previous research role as a guard in no way hampered the research process. More to the point, my involvement as a guard actually enhanced my position as a participant observer. My reputation as a fair and trustworthy officer was the critical factor in the relative ease in reaffirming contacts and rapport. I was not subjected to the character tests or loyalty checks that I had experienced as a researcher-guard. I had been a credible person in the past and this was sufficient proof for the subjects. In the new research, the participative research role proved to be an asset that paved the way for data collection. Researchers who favor full participation must develop good working relations with their subjects because, if future research is planned in any research role, the problems associated with access, rapport, and data collection will be greatly reduced.

CONCLUSIONS

The research process is filled with our own biases and preconceptions which influence the groups or settings that we study and how we study them (Styles 1979). The question "to participate or not?" presents the investigator with a profound moral decision. Indeed, there are strengths and weaknesses associated with both the outside and inside research roles. I am not arguing that one way is superior to another; this is a value judgment that depends on what one wants to study (Becker 1978). Both are important methodologies that should be carefully evaluated before entering the field. I chose to study the prison setting in the participative role. By studying prisoner control as a guard, I collected some unique data but observed much wrongdoing. Yet this is the necessary risk in full participative field research; I took this risk when I made the decision to become a guard. In a positive light, involvement enabled me to experience face-to-face the totality of prison life. In addition, the insider role promotes a firsthand view of the institution and whether or not policies are being complied with or circumvented. Prison reform and prisoner control have historically been intense political and social issues. For this reason, an insider's knowledge can be extremely useful to officials or administrators.

When a researcher decides to participate as a prison guard, several issues must be weighed beforehand. First, the participative role restricts access to some events and can lead to biased sampling. That is, the participant-researcher cannot continuously be on the scene. Further, the fact that he or she is "slotted" in an official role hinders the researcher's ability to make contacts with some prisoner groups. Second, full participation is extremely time-consuming due to the special problems of building rapport and earning respect. I "had" to suffer a physical attack before I was regarded as "alright." Third, this methodology can create complex ethical issues for the researcher. The problem of personal commitments versus social issues can become overwhelming and affect the research process. Finally, full participation breeds questions about reactivity. The direct observer must document how and in what ways, if any, his or her presence affects the scene and validity of the data.

As in any form of research, there are a variety of costs and benefits. By studying prisons from the inside, we can learn how desperately we need new theories and techniques to understand these institutions adequately. If we can obtain this information, then we can provide informed input into new policies and procedures, thus making a genuine contribution to reform.

NOTES

1. This prison reform case, the most sweeping in penal history, was a massive class action suit filed against the Texas Department of Corrections. A federal judge ruled that many TDC operations were unconstitutional and that wholesale organizational changes (e.g., health care, inmate housing) be instituted to remedy the situation.

2. Building tenders (BTs) were the physically and mentally superior inmates officially recruited and coopted (given special privileges) by the guard staff to control the inmates in the living areas. BTs had a pro-staff orientation and work hand-in-hand with the guards to control the other prisoners.

REFERENCES

Abbott, J.H. (1981), *In the Belly of the Beast*. New York: Random House.

Becker, H.S. (1978), "Practitioners of Vice and Crime." In N.K. Denzin (editor) *Sociological Methods: A Sourcebook*. New York: McGraw-Hill.

Bettelheim, B. (1943), "Individuals and Mass Behavior in Extreme Situations." *Journal of Abnormal and Social Psychology* 38:417-452.

Bulmer, M. (1982), "When is Disguise Justified? Alternatives to Covert Participant Observation." *Qualitative Sociology* 4:251-264.

Carroll, L. (1974), *Hacks, Blacks and Cons: Race Relations in a Maximum Security Prison*. Lexington MA: Lexington Books.

Charriere, H. (1970), *Papillion*. New York: Basic Books.

Clemmer, D.C. (1940), *The Prison Community*. New York: Holt, Rinehart and Winston.

Crouch, B.M. and G. Alpert (1982), "Sex and Occupational Socialization Among Prison Guards: A Longitudinal Study." *Criminal Justice & Behavior* 9(2):159-176.

Davidson, R.T. (1974), *Chicano Prisoners: Key to San Quentin*. New York: Holt, Rinehart, and Winston.

Giallombardo, R. (1966), *Society of Women: A Study of Women's Prison*. New York: John Wiley.

Hepburn, J.R. and C. Albonetti (1980), "Role Conflict in Correctional Institutions." *Criminology* 17(4):445-459.

Humphreys, L. (1970), *Tearoom Trade*. Chicago: Aldine.

Irwin, J. (1970), *The Felon*. Englewood Cliffs, NJ: Prentice-Hall.

Jacobs, J. (1974), "Participant Observation in Prison." *Urban Life and Culture* 3(2):221-240.

____ (1977), *Stateville: The Penitentiary in Mass Society*. Chicago: University of Chicago Press.

Jacobs, J. and M. Grear (1977), "Drop-outs and Rejects: An Analysis of the Prison Guard's Revolving Door." *Criminal Justice Review* 2(2):57-70.

Jacobs, J. and L. Kraft (1978), "Race Relations and the Guard Subculture." *Social Problems* 25(3): 304-318.

Jacobs, J. and H. Retsky (1975), "Prison Guard." *Urban Life* 4(1):5-29.

Lofland, J.A. (1971), *Analyzing Social Settings*. Belmont, CA: Wadsworth.

Manning, P.K. (1972), "Observing the Police: Deviants, Respectables, and the Law." In J. Douglas (editor) *Research on Deviance*. New York: Random House.

Marquart, J.W. and B.M. Crouch (1983), "Coopting the Kept: Using Inmates for Social Control in a Southern Prison." Paper presented at the American Society of Criminologists annual meetings, Toronto.

Marquart, J.W. and J.B. Roebuck (1984), "The Use of Physical Force by Prison Guards: Individuals, Situations, and Organizations." Paper to be presented at American Sociological Assoc. Meetings in San Antonio (August).

Poole, E. and R. Regoli (1980), "Role Stress, Custody Orientation and Disciplinary Actions." *Criminology* 18:215-227.

Roebuck, J. (1965), *Criminal Typology*. Springfield, IL: Charles C. Thomas. *Ruiz v. Estelle*, 503 F. Supp. 1265 (S.D. Texas) 1980.

Scott, W.R. (1965), "Field Methods in the Study of Organizations." In J.G. March (editor) *Handbook of Organizations*. Chicago: Rand McNally Co.

Schutz, A. (1944), "The Stranger: An Essay in Social Psychology." *American Journal of Sociology* 49:499-507.

Simmel, G. (1908), *Sociology*. Leipzig: Dunker and Humblot.

Skolnick, J.H. (1966), *Justice Without Trial: Law Enforcement in Democratic Society*.

Solzhenitsyn, A.I. (1973), *The Gulag Archipelago*. New York: Harper and Row.

____ (1975), *The Gulag Archipelago II*, New York: Harper and Row.

Styles, J. (1979), "Outsider/Insider: Researching Gay Baths." *Urban Life* 8:135-152.

Sykes, G. (1958), *The Society of Captives*. Princeton, N.J.: Princeton University Press.

Thomas, J. (1979), "Some Aspects of Negotiated Order, Loose Coupling and Mesostructure in Maximum Security Prisons." *Symbolic Interaction* 4:213-231.

Toby, J. (1966), "Violence and the Masculine Ideal: Some Qualitative Data." *ANNALS* 364 (March): 19-27.

Van Maanen, J. (1973), "Observations on the Making of Policemen." *Human Organization* 32:407-418.

____ (1982), "Fieldwork on the Beat." In J. Van Maanen et al. (editors) *Varieties of Qualitative Research*. Beverly Hills: Sage Publications.

Vidich, A. (1970), "Participation Observation and the Collection and Interpretation of Data." In W.J. Filstead (editor) *Qualitative Methodology: Firsthand Involvement With the Social World*. Chicago: Markham.

Wax, R.H. (1971), *Doing Fieldwork: Warnings and Advice*. Chicago: University of Chicago Press.

Webb and Morris (1978), Prison Guards: The Culture and Perspective of an Occupational Group. Coker Books.

INDEX

About the Editor

Mark R. Pogrebin is a professor and Director of Criminal Justice in the Graduate School of Public Affairs at the University of Colorado at Denver. He has conducted numerous field studies in the areas of police undercover work, tragic events, African American policewomen, emotion management, women jailers, psychotherapists' deviant behavior with clients, women in prison and on parole, and the strategic uses of humor among police. He has published three books and numerous journal articles and has had over 20 of his publications reprinted in anthologies.

CONTRIBUTOR AFFILIATIONS

Mary Dodge, Assistant Professor of Criminal Justice, Graduate School of Public Affairs, University of Colorado at Denver.

Robert M. Emerson, Professor of Sociology, University of California, Los Angeles.

Debra S. Emmelman, Associate Professor of Sociology, Southern Connecticut State University.

David N. Falcone, Associate Professor of Criminal Justice, Illinois State University.

Roy B. Flemming, Professor of Political Science, Wayne State University.

Lisa Frohmann, Associate Professor of Department of Criminal Justice, University of Illinois, Chicago Circle Campus.

Joan Neff Gurney, Professor of Sociology, University of Richmond.

Milton Heumann, Professor and Chair of Political Science, Rutgers University.

Geoffrey Hunt, Institute for Scientific Analysis, San Francisco.

Jennifer Hunt, New York City. Formerly with Montclair State College.

Richard S. Jones, Associate Professor of Sociology, Marquette University.

Danny L. Jorgensen, Professor of Sociology with the Center for Interdisciplinary Studies in Culture and Society at the University of South Florida.

Sherryl Kleinman, Professor of Sociology, University of North Carolina.

Peter K. Manning, Professor of Criminal Justice, Northeastern University.

James W. Marquart, Professor of Criminal Justice, Sam Houston State University.

Mike McConville, Professor, University of Warwick Law Clinic.

Chester Mirsky, Professor of Law, New York University.

Tomas Morales, Institute for Scientific Analysis, San Francisco.

Melvin Pollner, Professor of Sociology, University of California, Los Angeles.

Eric D. Poole, Professor of Criminal Justice, Graduate School of Public Affairs, University of Colorado at Denver.

Michael D. Radelet, Professor of Sociology, University of Colorado in Boulder.

Stephanie Riegel, Institute for Scientific Analysis, San Francisco

Leigh M. Roberts, Professor of Psychiatry, University of Wisconsin.

John Rosecrance, Professor of Criminal Justice, University of Nevada-Reno; deceased.

Thomas J. Schmid, Professor of Sociology, Mankato State University.

William B. Shaffir, Professor of Sociology, McMaster University.

James Spradley, Professor of Anthropology, Manchester College; deceased.

Robert A. Stebbins, Professor of Sociology, University of Calgary.

Barbara Stenross, Assistant Dean in the General College, University of North Carolina-Chapel Hill.

Stan Stojkovic, Professor of Criminal Justice and Associate Dean of the School of Social Welfare, University of Wisconsin – Milwaukee.

John Van Maanen, Erwin Schell Professor of Organizational Studies in the Sloan School of Management at Massachusetts Institute of Technology.

William B. Waegel, Professor of Sociology, Villanova University.

Don Waldorf, Institute for Scientific Analysis, San Francisco.

Ralph A. Weisheit, Professor of Criminal Justice, Illinois State University.

L. Edward Wells, Associate Professor of Criminal Justice, Illinois State University.

Mary West-Smith, Graduate Student, Graduate School of Public Affairs, University of Colorado at Denver.